Heightening Competition in the Postal and Delivery Sector

ADVANCES IN REGULATORY ECONOMICS

Series Editors: Michael A. Crew, *CRRI Professor of Regulatory Economics and Director, Center for Research in Regulated Industries (CRRI), Rutgers, The State University of New Jersey, Newark, USA and* Paul R. Kleindorfer, *Anheuser-Busch Professor Emeritus of Management Science, The Wharton School, University of Pennsylvania, USA and Paul Dubrule Professor of Sustainable Development, INSEAD, Fontainebleau, France*

Edited by Michael A. Crew and Paul R. Kleindorfer, this series aims to advance research in theory, practice and policy in the area of regulatory economics. While regulation is all-pervasive in the modern economy and touches almost every aspect of economic life, this series focuses on microeconomic issues in regulation rather than macro policies. Topics of interest include contributions in the following areas: network industries, environmental, health and safety, risk and insurance, and financial services. Regulatory economics deals with both direct instruments affecting profits and prices in these industries and governance structures in regulated industries, including self-regulation. Contributions may address specific instruments across industries as well as in-depth sector-specific studies.

Titles in the series include:

Liberalization of the Postal and Delivery Sector
Edited by Michael A. Crew and Paul R. Kleindorfer

Competition and Regulation in the Postal and Delivery Sector
Edited by Michael A. Crew and Paul R. Kleindorfer

Handbook of Worldwide Postal Reform
Edited by Michael A. Crew, Paul R. Kleindorfer and James I. Campbell Jr.

Progress in the Competitive Agenda in the Postal and Delivery Sector
Edited by Michael A. Crew and Paul R. Kleindorfer

Heightening Competition in the Postal and Delivery Sector
Edited by Michael A. Crew and Paul R. Kleindorfer

Heightening Competition in the Postal and Delivery Sector

Edited by

Michael A. Crew

Rutgers, The State University of New Jersey, Newark, USA

and

Paul R. Kleindorfer

University of Pennsylvania, USA and INSEAD, France

ADVANCES IN REGULATORY ECONOMICS

Edward Elgar

Cheltenham, UK • Northampton, MA, USA

Published by
Edward Elgar Publishing Limited
The Lypiatts
15 Lansdown Road
Cheltenham
Glos GL50 2JA
UK

Edward Elgar Publishing, Inc.
William Pratt House
9 Dewey Court
Northampton
Massachusetts 01060
USA

A catalogue record for this book
is available from the British Library

Library of Congress Control Number: 2009937923

Mixed Sources
Product group from well-managed
forests and other controlled sources
www.fsc.org Cert no. SA-COC-1565
© 1996 Forest Stewardship Council
FSC

ISBN 978 1 84844 698 4

Printed and bound by MPG Books Group, UK

Contents

Contributors

António Manuel Amaral, Head of Strategic Studies, CTT Correios de Portugal S.A.

Stéphane Bernard, Head, Department of Economic Modelling, La Poste.

François Boldron, Economist, European and National Regulation Division, La Poste.

Claire Borsenberger, Economist, European and National Regulation Division, La Poste.

Bénédicte Bouin, Senior Analyst, Tariffs and Accounting Unit, Postal Regulation Division, ARCEP.

Michael D. Bradley, Professor of Economics, George Washington University, Washington, DC.

Lawrence G. Buc, President, SLS Consulting, Inc.

Joan Calzada, Associate Professor, Universitat de Barcelona.

James I. Campbell Jr., Attorney and Consultant.

Catherine Cazals, Professor, IDEI, Université des Sciences Sociales.

Margaret Cigno, Assistant Director of Auditing and Costing, United States Postal Regulatory Commission.

Robert Cohen, George Mason University, Fairfax, VA.

Jeff L. Colvin, Manager, Finance, United States Postal Service.

Adolfo Consiglio, Head of Economic Analysis, Poste Italiane.

Helmuth Cremer, Professor, Toulouse School of Economics (GREMAQ, IDEI and IUF).

Michael A. Crew, CRRI Professor of Regulatory Economics and Director – CRRI, Rutgers Business School, Rutgers University, New York, NJ.

João Cristovão, Economist, Strategic Studies, CTT Correios de Portugal S.A.

Nicolas Curien, Commissioner, ARCEP and Professor of Economics at Conservatoire National des Arts et Métiers (CNAM).

Philippe De Donder, Professor, Toulouse School of Economics (GREMAQ-CNRS and IDEI).

Paul Dudley, Head of Regulatory Economic Analysis, Royal Mail Group.

Richard Eccles, Partner, Bird & Bird LLP.

Frédérique Fève, Researcher, IDEI, Université des Sciences Sociales.

Massimo Filippini, Professor, University of Lugano and ETH Zurich.

Jean-Pierre Florens, Professor, IDEI, Toulouse School of Economics, University of Toulouse.

Alessandra Fratini, Partner, Fratini Vergano – European Lawyers.

Damien Geradin, Partner, HOWREY LLP, and Professor of Competition Law and Economics at Tilburg University Netherlands.

Sander S. Glick, Vice President, SLS Consulting, Inc.

Caroline Gomez, La Poste.

Stefano Gori, Head of International Business Strategy, Poste Italiane and PhD student, Bristol Business School, University of West of England.

Greg Harman, Managing Director, LECG.

David Henry, Attorney, Howrey LLP.

Christian Jaag, Managing Partner, Swiss Economics, and Lecturer of Economics, University of St. Gallen.

Denis Joram, Chief Economist, European and National Regulation Division, La Poste.

Leeni Kiikkilä, Development Manager, Itella Corporation, Finland.

Paul R. Kleindorfer, Paul Dubrule Professor of Sustainable Development, INSEAD, and Professor Emeritus, University of Pennsylvania.

Wim Koevoets, Managing Consultant, LECG.

Martin Koller, Economist, Swiss Post and ETH Zurich.

Guillaume Lacroix, Director of the Postal Regulation Division, ARCEP.

Sébastien Lécou, Economist, La Poste.

Paulo Louro, Economist, Strategic Studies, CTT Correios de Portugal S.A.

Clément Magre, Regulatory Accounting Expert, European and National Regulation Division, La Poste.

Charles McBride, George Mason University, Fairfax, VA.

Lise Martin, La Poste.

Diane Monaco, Economist, US Postal Regulatory Commission.

Carla Mota, Economist, Strategic Studies, CTT Correios de Portugal S.A.

Norma B. Nieto, Managing Consultant, IBM Global Business Services.

Andrei Obrea, Senior Fellow, Pitney Bowes, Inc.

John C. Panzar, Professor of Economics, University of Auckland.

Edward S. Pearsall, Consultant.

Emiliano Piccinin, CEO staff, Poste Italiane.

Maria Rita Pierleoni, IPI and University of Rome 'Tor Vergata'.

Leon A. Pintsov, Chief Scientist and Vice President, Pitney Bowes, Inc.

Alejandro Requejo, Director, LECG.

Frank Rodriguez, Royal Mail Group.

Bernard Roy, Director, European and National Regulation Division, La Poste.

Paul C. Smith, Special Counsel, UPS.

Soterios Soteri, Head of Economic Forecasting, Royal Mail Group.

Peter A. Soyka, President, Soyka & Company, LLC.

Daniel J. Tobias, Senior Consultant, IBM Global Business Services.

Joëlle Toledano, Commissioner, ARCEP and Professor of Economics, Supelec.

Urs Trinkner, Managing Partner, Swiss Economics, and Senior Research Associate, University of Zurich.

Erik van der Merwe, Senior Consultant, LECG.

Joost Vantomme, Executive Director, Strategic & Regulatory Affairs, La Poste/De Post Belgium.

Vincenzo Visco Comandini, Professor in Institutional Economics, University of Rome 'Tor Vergata'.

Paul E. Vogel, Director, Deloitte Consulting.

Navin Waghe, Senior Managing Consultant, LECG.

Sponsors

La Poste
Royal Mail
Deutsche Post World Net
Pitney Bowes
La Poste/De Post
Österreichische Post AG
R.R. Donnelley & Sons
UPS
ANACOM
CTT Correios de Portugal S.A.
Postal Services Commission
Siemens AG
Bank of America
Posten AB
Itella Corporation
ARCEP
LECG
Swiss Post
Poste Italiane
Canada Post Corporation
Communication Workers Union
Federal Express
FTI
NERA Economic Consulting
TNT Post
International Post Corporation
Canadian Union of Postal Workers
IBM Global Services
Oxera
Venable LLP
Bird & Bird LLP
Commission for Communications Regulation
Fratini Vergano – European Lawyers
Frontier Economics
Posten Norge AS
SLS Consulting, Inc.
George Mason University School of Public Policy
An Post
Association of Postal Commerce
Global Envelope Alliance
London Economics
Jimenez Consulting
K&L Gates LLP
National Association of Letter Carriers
New Zealand Post Limited
US Postal Regulatory Commission
Parcel Shippers Association

Foreword: Enduring questions and some lessons from practice

Joëlle Toledano

My first CRRI (Centre for Research in Regulated Industries) conference was the one held in Stockholm in 1994. Much has changed since then, but there are also a few constants. This conference certainly underlines both the changes we have seen as well as some persistent themes. In my remarks, I would like to touch on both. After a few words about the French regulator ARCEP and its main postal tasks, I would like to share with you two issues.

The first one is a practitioner's issue: what are the consequences of information asymmetry on the behavior of operators and regulators and their strategies?

As it compares the present to the past, the second issue is not especially one that a woman usually likes to address . . . but I shall endeavor to do so; for the past 15 years – and I hate to confess I have been there since those early times – why have so many questions remained the same? Why do so many topics still seem to be unsolved?

Let us start with the French Telecommunications and Posts Regulatory Authority, ARCEP (Autorité de Régulation des Communications Électroniques et des Postes). In 2005, the law gave the former Telecommunications Regulatory Authority (ART) the additional responsibility of the postal sector. Seven commissioners – I am one of them – are appointed for six years and their terms are not renewable. The President of the Republic appoints three of them, including the chairman. The President of the National Assembly appoints two other members as also does the President of the Senate. The seven commissioners together are in charge of Telecommunications and Posts. There is no specialization. A total of 160 people work in ARCEP, 11 on postal issues and 80 on telecommunications issues, with the rest of the staff supporting the Economic, Legal, International, Communication and General Administration Departments and working for both sectors.

Like other postal regulatory authorities and like almost all of us at this conference, ARCEP is mainly focused on its Universal Service Obligation (USO) and market organization. We monitor the USO, ensuring its funding while protecting consumers. This implies studying prices and setting price caps, cost accounting, monitoring quality of service, and assessing the cost of the USO. The role of ARCEP is to check that La Poste carries out its universal service missions properly, especially in terms of quality of service, and to supervise the funding of these missions. In this capacity, we regulate La Poste's universal service tariffs, especially through designing the incumbent operator's price cap.[1] In addition, ARCEP sets the accounting rules and establishes accounting system specifications, that is, the reporting format for regulated accounts. Last but not least, we are in charge of monitoring the conditions under which universal service is financed. In particular, the Postal Law charges ARCEP with recommending to the government all measures necessary for guaranteeing the provision of universal service. The possibility of a compensation fund is also foreseen in the Law.

The second main scope of ARCEP's postal regulation, besides the USO, is postal market organization and the introduction of competition. This implies delivery of market authorizations, upstream regulation and statistical information. However, the day-to-day regulatory activity may also include very technical matters, such as access to mailboxes in apartment buildings or rulings on multiple postmarks on mail items. Opening up the postal market reveals unanticipated switching costs that are not always easy to reduce.

During the last CRRI Conference, in Albufeira, ARCEP presented the market situation in France.[2] Broadly, with regard to letter mail, only some 10 local operators are registered for domestic delivery. End-to-end competition is not significant at a macro level, but the upstream market is developed and it is quite open. Some 200 enterprises are active in the upstream market. It is estimated that mailing houses process 85 percent of advertising items. As for international mail, almost all incumbents of neighboring countries are present in the French market.

With regard to informational problems, it is well known that information is critical for regulation and information asymmetry can be a strategic issue. However, in my view, we should be more careful about it than we have been so far, and in a more practical way. It is a common element of theoretical models of economic regulation that the incumbent tends to keep secret as much information as possible in order to preserve its information rents. However, as a practitioner (on both sides) of the asymmetry dilemma, I have progressively acquired the strong intuition that cooperation with the regulator may also be a good strategic choice for an incumbent. I shall try here to reconcile these two opposing statements.

Let me begin by noting the robust theoretical finding from game theory that repeated games tend to promote cooperation and efficiency. The same is true in regulation. For example, theoretical contributions have shown how repetition tends to reduce the incentives incorporated in a price-cap mechanism. Indeed, if the financial results at the end of the first period show undue rents, the regulator will modify the price cap for the second period, making it difficult to preserve rents. Price caps are, of course, not the only 'repeated game'.

Indeed, the relationship between an incumbent and a regulator is a durable one. Since, not all topics are examined all the time, and some are subject to regulatory scrutiny only under exceptional conditions, it could be a winning strategy not to disclose some data. But many issues are examined on a continuing basis, such as accounting, quality of service, rates, and so on. In this process, no regulator likes discovering that requested information was hidden or distorted. According to my own experience, it is one of the more sensitive subjects: information is the regulator's raw material, as fuel is for an engine.

Fearing detection, an operator involved in a regulatory relationship may come to understand that 'reasonable' cooperation may also be a long-term profitable good practice – even if a part of its information rent seems to be more specifically at risk in the short run. However, the question remains: how can the regulator discover that information is false or hidden? We have learned from the economic history of monopoly regulation how difficult this is.

The quality of information available to the regulator should depend not only on the incumbent's good will and good faith. The incentives for cooperative practice are greater when the regulator can rely on alternative sources, with the evident risk for a non-cooperating company of ultimate discovery of distorted information. There are at least four alternative sources.

The first source is trivial: *competition*, which enhances the quality of information except in the case of collusion. Indeed, markets yield information on prices and costs. This is duly observed in the case of the telecommunications sector, where competitors are also very helpful to the regulator as they provide valuable contributions in the process of public consultations. But, in the postal sector, competition is somewhat low. Moreover, the main competitors are incumbents in foreign countries. Although they are able to take part in the regulatory process and contribute to public consultation, they are reluctant to disclose information that could harm their interests in their own country. As for smaller competitors, it would cost them too much to participate efficiently as they lack the skills and the resources.

The second external source of information is *benchmarking*. Comparing European operators provides a remedy to deal with information asymmetry. Benchmarking functions like yardstick competition, highlighting the worst performers in a sample group and requiring them, implicitly or explicitly, to move closer to the best-practice frontier. In the telecommunications case, rules and procedures of the European regulatory framework are highly harmonized. Since regulators' tools and practices are very similar, benchmarks are useful and efficient tools. Unfortunately, things are not so easy in the postal sector, where only principles are harmonized in the postal European regulatory framework. Even the definition of the mail market may differ from one country to another! So it is more difficult to interpret discrepancies across European operators.

The third source is to be found in reports about operators' stock market rating (if listed), earnings and financial reports provided by *market information sources*. This could be new for academic and/or postal economists. When I learned about telecommunications regulation at ARCEP, I was actually surprised by the important role played by financial analysts. As the regulatory process is technical and time consuming, financial analysts appear to be almost the only observers who understand debates and decisions precisely. In order to understand the companies involved in the postal sector, they use benchmarks such as stock market information. It may also be the case that operators pay more attention to stock rating and investor relations than to regulation! That is why financial analysts of the telecommunications sector can be so well informed and useful. In contrast, very few postal companies, even privatized ones, are listed on stock markets. So, postal analyses are much less well informed than their telecommunications counterparts.

With competition, *innovation* is another dynamic driver of information revelation. Innovation and other disruptive changes create uncertainty for both operators and regulators. The present financial crisis and the drop in mail traffic may also be seen as a powerful incentive to share information. When preparing the Universal Postal Union's 'High Level Conference' in April 2009, operators, although usually reluctant to disclose data, decided to participate in a consolidated report devoted to the 'Impact of the economic crisis on postal activities'. Although no data on specific operators are available in the report, the report reveals that the situation is similar in all countries and is similar to the express industry.

To sum up, competition, international benchmarking, financial analyses, innovation and drastic contextual changes provide additional incentives to convince incumbents that it would be useful to share more, if not all, information with the regulator. Since regulation is a durable relationship, it could be more costly for incumbents to conceal information, especially if such a practice is discovered. However, information asymmetry is probably much more critical for post than for other markets, such as telecommunications. Certainly, information asymmetry does exist in the latter. But if one compares the information available in the two sectors, respectively, and if one investigates how that information can be checked, it becomes very clear that the postal regulator does not enjoy the same opportunities for getting information as does the telecommunications regulator.

It is difficult to conclude without any reference to the harsh realities of the current period. As in many other markets, the mail market is falling. The trends observed before the financial crisis were already disquieting. On average and since the beginning of the 1990s, traffic growth in industrialized countries has been less than the economic growth rate. Even worse, in most of these countries, traffic has been stagnating since the beginning of the decade. What is worrying in the more recent data is the drop in direct marketing mail. Until the current crisis, that market segment was seen as a growth driver balancing the decline in transactional mail. It remains to be seen whether the recent severe decline in volume will recover after the current economic crisis has passed. Alternatively, it may be that the concurrent impact of the financial crisis and the structural impact of Internet-based electronic substitution will give rise to a permanent and irreversible decline in volume.

Although most problematic, the decline in mail volume is not completely unexpected. More surprising is the invariance that appears between the postal debates of the early 1990s and those of today. Some issues that were at the center of the policy debate, such as quality of international service or terminal dues, are less prominent now. But very central issues, such as USO, the counters network, and their financing, are still open, and not just in Europe. They are at the core of the Postal US Regulatory Commission report and of the 2009 conference program. In the same spirit, the British Hooper report published at the end of 2008 provides an excellent summary of the current regulatory challenges in the UK postal market,[3] but it looks just like a younger brother of the British Green Paper published in 1994.

In most other regulated sectors, whether regulation is considered in a positive or negative light, it seems that questions have changed. Why is this not the case in the postal sector? Is it because our answers, as economists, have not been adequate? Or is it because we have not asked the right questions? One thing is clear, however: the level of analysis has improved significantly, fostered by these conferences and the books arising out of them.

NOTES

1. See Bouin, Curien and Lacroix, ch. 6 in this volume for a discussion of the history and structure of the French price cap, which is unique in its approach to adjusting for unanticipated changes in demand or cost, while attempting to maintain strong incentives for efficiency.
2. See Catherine Gallet-Rybak, Cécile Moreno, Daniel Nadal and Joëlle Toledano. 'The French postal market in the wake of the postal law of 2005', in Michael A. Crew, Paul R. Kleindorfer and James I. Campbell Jr. (eds), *Handbook of Worldwide Postal Reform*, Cheltenham, UK and Northampton, MA, USA: Edward Elgar Publishers, 2008
3. Ricard Hopper, 'Modernise or decline: policies to Maintain the universal postal service in the United Kingdom', an independent review of the UK postal services sector, December 2008.

Preface and acknowledgements

This book is a result of the Center for Research in Regulated Industries (CRRI) 17th Conference on Postal and Delivery Economics which was held from May 27 to May 30, 2009 in Bordeaux, France. This conference and this book follow earlier conferences and workshops. In 1990, the first Conference on Postal and Delivery Economics was held at Coton House, Rugby, England, July 22–25, 1990, in honor of the 150th anniversary of the Penny Post and the contributions of Sir Rowland Hill. To date there have been 17 conferences, 3 workshops and now 16 edited volumes as part of CRRI's program on Postal and Delivery Economics.

The 2009 Conference was made possible by the support of its generous sponsors. We would like to thank the sponsors not only for financial support, but also for their advice and encouragement, and for serving on the organizing committee. In particular, we would like to thank Nabil Allaf, José Amado da Silva, John Baldwin, Maynard Benjamin, Jody Berenblatt, Kristin Bergum, Robert Bernau, Geoff Bickerton, Dan Blair, Lawrence Buc, Bernhard Bukovc, Philip Burns, Eduardo Cardadeiro, João Castro, Jeff Colvin, Julien Coulier, Robert Curry, Bernard Damiens, Gene Del Polito, Paul Dudley, Richard Eccles, Charles Fattore, Stephen Ferguson, Alessandra Fratini, Lee Fritschler, Stephen Gibson, Stefano Gori, Greg Harman, John Hearn, Jan Bart Henry, Richard Hern, Stuart Holder, George Houpis, Christian Jaag, Luis Jimenez, Denis Joram, David M. Levy, Walter Maschke, Leonardo Mautino, James Pierce Myers, Heikki Nikali, Louis O'Brien, Chris Osborne, Wolfgang Pickave, Alberto Pimenta, Leon Pintsov, Gerard Power, Bernard Roy, Jim Sauber, Michael Scanlon, Gennaro Scarfiglieri, Michael Shinay, Paul C. Smith, Nancy Sparks, Gregory Swinand, Joëlle Toledano, Urs Trinkner, Mark van der Horst, Joost Vantomme, Ian Volner, Sture Wallander, John Waller, Tim Walsh and David Williams.

The host country plays an important role in these conferences. This year's conference, the 17th Conference on Postal and Delivery Economics, benefited greatly from the efforts of our host La Poste. Bernard Roy, who has had a long and fruitful association with the conference, was a gracious host. He and his colleagues, including Denis Joram, provided both advice and assistance on numerous occasions and contributed greatly to the success of the event.

We would like to thank our distinguished dinner speakers, Joëlle Toledano of ARCEP, Jean-Paul Bailly of Groupe La Poste, and Robert Campbell of Mount Allison University. These speeches addressed current issues of regulation and postal reform against the background of the ongoing financial crisis, maintaining the conference tradition of stimulating presentations by distinguished leaders in the industry.

We benefited from the contributions of Karen Walters. Karen, Assistant Director of CRRI, provided assistance in support of the conference and this book. We would like to thank all authors and participants of the conference, without whom the conference and this book would not have been possible. The usual disclaimers are applicable. In particular, the views expressed reflect the views of the authors and are not necessarily those of the sponsors.

Michael A. Crew and Paul R. Kleindorfer

1. Access and the USO under full market opening*

Michael A. Crew and Paul R. Kleindorfer

1 INTRODUCTION

There has been considerable interest in the topic of access in regulated industries, following the widespread movement to open up markets to competition. In the postal sector, early forms of market opening took the form of worksharing, which is usually understood to mean the provision of upstream services, for example, presorting, by major mailers and competitors. Indeed, on the matter of upstream access and worksharing where end-to-end (E2E) bypass is not allowed, the current situation in most countries, some consensus has emerged in the literature and among regulators on the benefits and the structure of efficient pricing for worksharing (Crew and Kleindorfer, 2008b). However, there has not been the same level of progress for the problem of access under bypass. How to address the access problem with bypass is now of considerable importance as the EU prepares for full market opening (FMO) in 2011/13.

In some countries, the issue of access under bypass is of immediate importance. For example, markets in the UK were fully opened to competition in 2006, with extensive downstream access going far beyond traditional worksharing (Dudley et al., 2009).[1] Competitors have been quick to take advantage of the business opportunity provided by this development, with access volumes growing from 1.2 to 4.1 billion over a three-year period ending 2007–08 (Dudley et al., 2009). Similar interest and activities in downstream access are evident in Germany where the market was fully opened at the beginning of 2008. Indeed, the issue of access under bypass is of general interest in the postal sector as it is likely to be faced by all national postal operators (POs) where markets are fully opened to competition. This chapter is motivated by the unresolved problems remaining in the approach to access under bypass.

The chapter proceeds as follows. Section 2 is concerned with background and motivation of the problem of developing policies toward access under FMO. Section 3 develops a model of access under bypass. The focus will be on downstream access only.[2] Section 4 examines some of the implications of the model and provides a summary and conclusion. Appendix 1A contains proofs and derivations of the main results.

2 THE ACCESS PROBLEM UNDER BYPASS

Providing access to its facilities by competitors occurs in a particular class of industries. For example, a brewer or a baker does not provide access to its facilities to competitors to brew beer or bake bread. Access is provided primarily in network industries where natural monopoly exists with unique or essential facilities. Telecommunications companies (TELCOs) have since the early days seen the benefits of interconnection. In such cases access was provided on a reciprocal basis. Similarly, national post offices, known henceforth as universal service providers (USPs), have had a long relationship, administered by the Universal Postal Union (UPU), of reciprocal delivery of each other's mail. More recently access in telecommunications has taken a different form from interconnection between two monopolists. TELCOs have been required to provide access to their facilities to rivals including some competitors, who provided E2E service. There is an extensive literature on access and bypass in telecommunications, for example, Mandy (2009). Similarly, in the postal sector access has, with few exceptions, been provided only to upstream facilities. A consensus has emerged on the approach to upstream access in the postal sector. However, a similar consensus on the issue of downstream access with bypass or E2E competition has yet to emerge. Neither the literature on TELCO access with E2E competition nor upstream postal access throws much light on the problem of access under E2E competition in the postal sector.

The experience in TELCOs is of little benefit to solving the problem of access in the postal sector for several reasons. TELCOs have sunk or essential facilities, that is, facilities that cannot be readily duplicated. Not surprisingly, duplication of facilities, the local telephone network, is not common. So, head-to-head competition, so-called 'facilities competition', does not occur often, but intermodal and therefore differentiated competition is becoming increasingly widespread. Cable (CATV) and wireless telephone compete with traditional TELCOs.

By contrast in the postal sector there are minimal sunk and effectively no essential facilities but there is potential for considerable head-to-head competition. Until the emergence of FMO in Europe, however, there has been minimal competition in the postal sector. Traditionally, entry was prohibited to enable the funding of the Universal Service Obligation (USO), the obligation to provide ubiquitous service at a uniform price. Under FMO, the USO still remains a fundamental obligation of the USP. Thus, the interactions of access pricing and bypass and their relationship to the USO under FMO are central issues in the analysis that follows.[3]

The impact of intermodal competition has been significant even with the presence of sunk or essential facilities as in the case of TELCOs. The impact on long distance has been dramatic in the US. The unlimited calling or flat rate service that traditionally applied to local service has now become available on a widespread basis. TELCOs continue to lose landlines at rapid clip as consumers switch to CATV and wireless. USPs, like TELCOs, face intermodal competition. In fact, the same type of technology that made telecommunications more competitive is putting pressure on the postal sector, namely computers, information technology, fiber optics, broadband service and the Internet. For telecommunications this has meant cost reduction, greater product variety and intermodal competition. CATV, TELCOs and wireless can now compete because of the existence of voice over Internet protocol (VOIP). Along with the ability for intermodal competition has come a considerable increase in demand as a result of the availability of new services, for example, email, information, data and video. These new technologies also result in intermodal competition in the postal sector, but unfortunately they do not simultaneously provide an increase in demand but rather a serious reduction in demand. The mail survived or even thrived under the telephone and it outlived the fax, which has been mostly displaced by email. However, the Internet and email are different. They pose a threat unlike any ever faced by the mails in the past. Advertising and transactions mail have been and will continue to be eroded by competition from the Internet and email.[4] The new information technologies using barcoding provide lower-cost mail processing and enhanced services. However, there is less and less demand. In short, the cross-elasticities between new electronic technologies and mail have been seriously underestimated, perhaps because the nature and extent of the structural change in the market was not foreseen. Electronic technologies provide a serious threat to volumes but have provided few of the benefits for POs in terms of cost reduction and product enhancement they provide in TELCOs.[5]

Thus, the discussion of this chapter on developing policies for access under direct competition implied by FMO must be seen within the context of perhaps an even greater revolution, namely, the intermodal competition from the Internet. The model developed in the next section is a static one focused only on competition among POs. The model does take into account the nature of entry in the postal sector and other critical characteristics of the business – low entry barriers and the USO – but it does not consider 'the elephant in the room', namely, intermodal competition from the Internet, which may be of much greater consequence.

The model employs a 'microstructure' approach in that it focuses on the decisions of individual access customers/competitors. The model has a number of features that are novel relative to earlier contributions. In particular, it addresses the issue of minimum discounts. The key regulatory decision variables in the model are the single-piece price and the minimum discount from the single-piece price. It differs in other respects from the earlier literature. In the traditional postal world, the access problem has often been modeled by separating demand into low-cost and high-cost areas and between upstream and downstream operations required for E2E service. Under worksharing forms of access, the focus has been on the worksharing discount for various levels of mail preparation activity. Common forms of this have been the Efficient Component Pricing Rule (ECPR) and various adjustments to it (see De Donder (2006) and Crew and Kleindorfer (2008b) for a review of these). Viewing the access problem through the lens of worksharing, however, gives rise to serious problems under bypass. The reason is that the worksharing approach to access pricing is based on discounts from underlying single-piece prices (for example, First or Second Class letters), typically based on upstream cost avoided through worksharing. However, as shown in, for example, Crew and Kleindorfer (2006a) this 'retail-minus' approach is not efficient in the presence of bypass and exacerbates the problems of the USP charged with covering the costs of the USO.

Others have recognized this problem, notably, Bloch and Gautier (2008), and Billette de Villemeur et al. (2007). The latter provide a model of access under bypass that departs from retail-minus approaches like ECPR.[6] The model here is similar to that of Billette de Villemeur et al., in that it assumes that households are not served by entrants. However, it has a more general cost structure for entrants and allows costs to vary by multiple zones and not just two zones, urban and rural, which is the case of Billette de Villemeur et al. In addition, they assume that the entrant only delivers in urban areas while the model here represents zones on a continuum from low- to high-cost zones.

3 A MODEL OF THE USO WITH ACCESS AND ENTRY

The model is an extension of the zonal pricing model of Crew and Kleindorfer (2006a) to include alternative access policies and heterogeneous customers. In an attempt to reduce complexity and to concentrate on downstream access the model does not consider traditional upstream worksharing. It considers only two products, E2E and access. There are two types of customers, households and small business mailers (consumers of single-piece letter mail, henceforth referred to as 'households'), and business customers (users of business services, henceforth referred to as 'businesses'). Households can buy only E2E from the USP, that is, single-piece mail. Bulk mail/wholesale customers can buy both E2E service and access from the USP.

The USP, assumed to be the incumbent PO, faces four constraints: (i) a uniform price for all delivery zones for single-piece mail; (ii) a specific access regime governing the structure of access prices; (iii) a USO, which is assumed to imply fixed costs to establish and maintain; and (iv) a financial viability constraint, taken here to be a zero-profit constraint on prices of all products provided by the USP. The USO is assumed to require, *inter alia*, that a single-piece service be offered at a uniform price and with ubiquitous coverage.

Let the set of delivery zones be represented by the interval $[0, T]$, with these zones ordered by delivery cost from low to high. The USP provides all services to households/single-piece mailers, which are priced at a uniform price P_I.[7] Bulk mail services for business customers are provided at zonal prices $P(t)$, which are assumed to be non-decreasing in t, with other restrictions imposed below. All mail has constant marginal upstream cost of $C_{UI,}$ and constant marginal delivery cost of $C_{DI}(t)$ for $t \in [0, T]$.

Entrants compete with the USP for business customers. It is assumed that some entrants with E2E service capability have already achieved sufficient minimum volumes that a competitive E2E service is available, and that this service costs less in the low-cost (urban) areas than that of the USP and costs more in the high-cost (rural) areas. The unit delivery cost of entrants is given by $C_{DE}(t)$, and for the incumbent by $C_{DI}(t)$, both of which are assumed continuous and strictly increasing on $[0, T]$. It is assumed that $C_{DE}(0) < C_{DI}(0)$, so that entrants enjoy a cost advantage in some of the low-cost areas.

Upstream unit preparation cost for entrants $C_{UE}(k)$ is assumed to vary across entrants, where 'k' denotes an entrant's type. Figure 1.1 illustrates the situation of entrants of type k. To simplify notation in what follows, entrant type is identified with upstream costs, that is, $C_{UE}(k) = k$.[8] Entrants' type k is assumed to belong to the interval $[0, \bar{k}]$. $F(k)$ denotes the number of entrants with unit upstream cost $\leq k$. Quantity demanded in zone $t \in [0, T]$ is denoted by $D_H(t)$ for households and by $D_B(t, k)$ for business customers of type k. $D_H(t)$ and $D_B(t, k)$ do not depend on price, implying that customers will be willing to pay between zero and their reservation price for the given quantity in zone t.

There is assumed to be no reserved area for the incumbent with Bertrand competition between the USP and entrants/consolidators, who are assumed sufficiently numerous and homogeneous that they can be treated as a competitive fringe. This implies that the entrants' prices are driven down to those of the least-cost provider. The model does not distinguish between entrants, consolidators and large customers who may provide mail preparation, access or E2E services. Indeed, E2E service might be provided by a large customer itself, perhaps in cooperation with a mail preparation company, and possibly

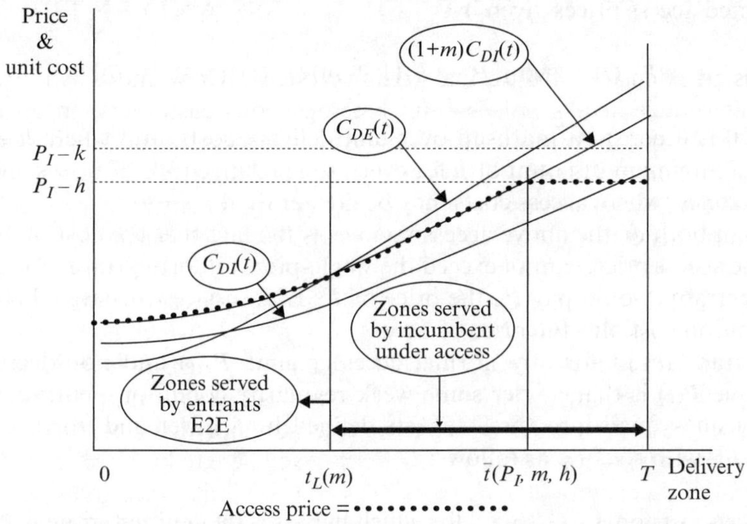

Figure 1.1 Illustrating zonal access pricing and zones served for an entrant of type 'k' *when the incumbent's minimum discount is* h > 0 *and entrant's upstream cost is* k ≤ h

by a separate delivery service provider, or any combination of these types of organization. The model is concerned only with identifying services provided by the USP and by non-USP market participants.[9]

Access regimes are defined in terms of the price for delivery service $P_A(t)$ in each zone $t \in [0, T]$. An access regime is called 'normal' if it is non-decreasing in price for $t \in [0, T]$ and $P_A(0) > C_{DI}(0)$ (so that the access price covers the incumbent's unit delivery costs for at least the lowest-cost zones). Common access regimes that are normal include retail minus and zonal access pricing, as defined below.

Retail-minus access prices discount the basic E2E single-piece service by a constant 'w':

$$P_{A_r}(t) = P_{A_r} = P_I - w, \ t \in [0, T]. \tag{1.1}$$

A particular form of retail minus pricing in widespread use is the ECPR, in which $w = C_{UI}$, so that, for ECPR, $P_{Ar}(t) = P_I - C_{UI}$ uniformly for all $t \in [0, T]$. The retail-minus approach to access is not efficient in the postal context, as uniform prices across all delivery zones do not reflect costs (Crew and Kleindorfer, 2008b). Such prices would be vulnerable to cream-skimming when bypass is possible.[10]

A more efficient alternative is zonal access pricing by the USP, which will be the focus of the analysis. For the same reason that uniform access prices are not efficient, it is clear that uniform E2E prices are not efficient. Thus, zonal access prices begin with E2E bulk mail services for zone t that are geared to cost. The form of such zonal prices analyzed here assumes that E2E bulk prices are given by:

$$P(t) = \text{Min}[P_I, h + (1 + m) C_{DI}(t)], \ t \in [0, T], \tag{1.2}$$

with associated access prices given by:

$$P_{Az}(t) = \text{Min}[P_I - h, (1 + m)C_{DI}(t)], \ t \in [0, T] \tag{1.3}$$

where $m \geq 0$ is a constant mark-up over unit delivery costs, and where $h \geq 0$ assures entrants of a minimum discount of h for every zone relative to E2E prices, including the most costly zones (where access costs may be greater than $P_I - h$).

Reflected in both of the above access regimes is the fact that the cost of E2E service, including the access price, cannot exceed the single-piece uniform price P_I for any delivery zone since entrants would pay P_I, the price of I's E2E service whenever this is less than their preparation cost plus the price of access.

An important result for any normal access regime $P_A(t)$ and non-decreasing E2E pricing regime $P(t)$ is that, under some weak regularity conditions, entrants will partition their business mail into three subsets defined by a lower and upper cut-off zone $t_L, t_U \in [0, T]$, with $t_L \leq t_U$, as follows:

1. the lowest-cost zones $t \in [0, t_L]$ for which bypass is the optimal strategy (that is, E2E service provided by the entrant);
2. a set of mid-range zones $t \in [t_L, t_U]$ in which access is optimal (the entrant does the upstream work and the USP provides delivery service); and
3. a set of high-cost zones $t \in [t_U, T]$ in which the entrant will use the E2E service of the USP at price P_I.

The cut-off zones t_L and t_U used to characterize the three subsets above depend on the cost/type k of the entrant and are defined as follows:

$$C_{DE}(t_L) = \text{Min}[P_A(t_L), P(t_L) - k] \tag{1.4}$$

$$P(t_U) - k = \text{Min}[P_A(t_U), C_{DE}(t_U)]. \tag{1.5}$$

In the event that there are multiple solutions to (1.4), t_L is defined as the minimum such solution. In the event that there are multiple solutions to (1.5), t_U is defined as the maximum such solution. Finally, in the event than no solution exists to (1.5) in $[0, T]$, $t_U = T$.[11]

Equations (1.4)–(1.5) can be interpreted as follows. Since the minimum of two quantities is $\leq$ either of them, adding k to both sides of (1.4) implies both $k + C_{DE}(t_L) \leq k + P_A(t_L)$ and $k + C_{DE}(t_L) \leq P(t_L)$. Using the monotonicity of $C_{DE}(t)$ and $P_A(t)$, and the fact that t_L is the first zone in $[0, T]$ at which equality occurs in (1.4), these same two inequalities must hold for all $t \leq t_L$. The first of these implies that bypass is lower cost than access and the second of these implies that bypass is lower cost than E2E service provided by I. In summary, for $t \leq t_L$ bypass is optimal for any entrant of type k. A similar argument holds for (1.5) in the sense that for $t > t_U$, E2E service provided by I dominates either bypass or access.

Note that it is possible that for some entrants $t_L = t_U$ (namely, when the minimum on the RHS of (1.4) is achieved at $P(t_L) - k$). In this case, the access region $[t_L, t_U]$ is the null set (implying that only bypass or E2E service by the USP could be optimal for entrants of this type). To avoid numerous special cases, the following two conditions are assumed to hold:

(SCA) The *single-crossing condition* holds such that there is a unique $t \in [0, T]$ for which $C_{DE}(t) = P_A(t)$. (In Figure 1.1 this occurs at $t_L(m)$.)

(BDA) The *bounded* k condition holds if $C_{DE}(0) \leq P_I - \bar{k}$. This implies for all k that $C_{DE}(0) \leq P_I - k$, so that for every entrant there is at least one delivery zone (namely $t = 0$) for which the single-piece price P_I would be at least as large as $\bar{k} + C_{DE}(t)$, the E2E cost of entrant $\bar{k}$.

The assumption BDA can be made without loss of generality, since any entrant k that did not satisfy this condition would always use the USP's E2E service (rather than either bypass or access). Such entrants can therefore be assumed to be among the single-piece mailers (the households in our model).

For the rest of the chapter, SCA and BDA hold and with the focus on the zonal access regime with a minimum discount constraint defined in (1.3). To avoid uninformative notational complexities, one final assumption for this access regime is used. Namely, for every $k \in [0, \bar{k}]$, the intersection of $C_{DE}(t)$ and $(1 + m)C_{DI}(t)$ occurs at a lower-cost zone than that at which the intersection of $(1 + m)C_{DI}(t)$ and $P_I - k$ occurs. (This implies the same for $P_I - h$, with the result that attention can be confined to $h \in [0, \bar{k}]$.) This assumption is a strengthening of the BDA condition, which states that upstream costs of either entrants or the USP are not so high as to cause access/bypass decisions in the low-cost zones to be driven by these upstream costs. Given this assumption, together with SCA and DBA, the values of t_L and t_U for the zonal access regime with minimum discount constraint are characterized as follows:

$$\begin{aligned} C_{DE}(t_L) &= (1 + m)\, C_{DI}(t_L), && \text{if } k < h \\ k + C_{DE}(t_L) &= h + (1 + m)\, C_{DI}(t_L), && \text{if } k \geq h \end{aligned} \tag{1.6}$$

$$\begin{aligned} t_U &= T, && \text{if } k < h \\ t_U &= t_L, && \text{if } k \geq h. \end{aligned} \tag{1.7}$$

In Figure 1.1, $k < h$ entrants of type k purchase access for the delivery zones $t_L(m)$ to T as their own (opportunity) costs exceed the incumbent's access prices of $(1 + m)C_{DI}(t_L)$ or $P_I - h$.

Given the minimum discount constraint, zonal access prices are capped at $P_{Az}(t) \leq P_I - h$. Define the crossover zone $\bar{t} = \bar{t}(m, h)$ as the zone at which access price is just equal to the E2E single-piece price:

$$P_I - h = (1 + m)\, C_{DI}(\bar{t}), \tag{1.8}$$

where it is assumed that there is a solution to (1.8) satisfying $\bar{t} \leq T$.

The characterizing equations (1.6)–(1.7) imply that whenever $k < h$, entrants bypass for all zones $t < t_L$ and they use access for all zones $t \geq t_L$, that is, they never use E2E. Similarly, if $k \geq h$ then entrants bypass all zones $t < t_L$ and use I's E2E service for $t \geq t_L$. For example, $k > h$ implies that $h + (1 + m)C_{DI}(t)$ is lower than $k + (1 + m)C_{DI}(t)$ (and, for zones $t > \bar{t}$, $P_I - k$ is lower than $P_I - h$) resulting in a loss for the entrant of $k - h$ if the entrant uses access relative to using I's E2E service.

Denote by $G(P_I, m, h, k)$ the incumbent's gross profits derived from business customers of type k. There are two cases, depending on whether $k < h$ or $k \geq$ h. From (1.4)–(1.8), for $k < h$ (where $t_U = T$):

$$G(P_I, m, h, k) = \int_{t_L(m,h,k)}^{\bar{t}(P_I,m,h)} [m C_{DI}(t) D_B(t,k)] dt + \int_{\bar{t}(P_I,m,h)}^{T} \{[P_I - h - C_{DI}(t)] D_B(t,k)\} dt. \quad (1.9)$$

This captures the fact that, for $k < h$, entrants of type k will use bypass for $t \in [0, t_L]$, and they will use access provided by I for $t \in [t_L, T]$. In the interval $t \in [t_L, \bar{t}]$, I's gross profit per unit is given by the margin m on each unit of access provided. Once the upper limit on access prices of $P_I - h$ is reached at $\bar{t}$, this gross profit per unit is reduced to $P_I - h - C_{DI}(t)$.

From (1.4)–(1.8), for $k \geq h$ (where $t_U = t_L$):

$$G(P_I, m, h, k) = \int_{t_L(m,h,k)}^{\bar{t}(P_I,m,h)} \{[h + m C_{DI}(t)] D_B(t,k)\} dt + \int_{\bar{t}(P_I,m,h)}^{T} \{[P_I - C_{DI}(t)] D_B(t,k)\} dt - \int_{t_L(m,h,k)}^{T} C_{UI} D_B(t,k) dt, \quad (1.10)$$

which captures the fact that, for $k \geq h$, entrants will use bypass for $t \in [0, t_L]$ and they will use the USP's E2E service for $t \in [t_L, T]$.

Total profits for the USP are the sum of profits across over all business customers and the household sector, net of USO costs. From (1.8)–(1.10):

$$\Pi(P_I, m, h) = \int_0^{\bar{k}} G(P_I, m, h, k) dF(k) + \int_0^T [P_I - C_{UI} - C_{DI}(t)] D_H(t) dt - F_U, \quad (1.11)$$

where F_U are the fixed costs of the USO.[12]

The welfare associated with a given access regime can be expressed as the weighted sum of consumer and producer surpluses:

$$W(P_I, m, h) = \alpha S_H(P_I) + S_B(P_I, m, h) + \Pi(P_I, m, h), \quad (1.12)$$

where S_H and S_B are the respective consumer surplus measures for sectors H and B, Π is the profit function for the USP in (1.11), and $\alpha \geq 1$ is the weight associated with household surplus relative to that of business customers and the USP (the welfare weights for the USP and business customers are assumed equal).

Assume the reservation price/value per letter in sector j is v_j for $j \in \{H, B\}$. From the above definitions:

$$S_H(P_I) = (v_H - P_I) \int_0^T D_H(t)\, dt. \tag{1.13}$$

Surplus for the business sector must be separately computed for customers of type $k < h$ and $k \geq h$. For $k < h$ (where $t_U = T$):

$$\begin{aligned} S_B(P_I, m, h, k) = v_B \int_0^T D_B(t,k)\, dt &- \int_0^{t_L(m,h,k)} [k + C_{DE}(t)] D_B(t,k)\, dt \\ &- \int_{t_L(m,h,k)}^{\bar{t}(P_I,m,h)} [k + (1+m) C_{DI}(t)] D_B(t,k)\, dt \\ &- \int_{\bar{t}(P_I,m,h)}^{T} (k + P_I - h) D_B(t,k)\, dt. \end{aligned} \tag{1.14}$$

For $k \geq h$ (where $t_U = t_L$):

$$\begin{aligned} S_B(P_I, m, h, k) = v_B \int_0^T D_B(t,k)\, dt &- \int_0^{t_L(m,h,k)} [k + C_{DE}(t)] D_B(t,k)\, dt \\ - \int_{t_L(m,h,k)}^{\bar{t}(P_I,m,h)} [h + (1+m) C_{DI}(t)] D_B(t,k)\, dt &- \int_{\bar{t}(P_I,m,h)}^{T} P_I D_B(t,k)\, dt. \end{aligned} \tag{1.15}$$

Finally, S_B in (1.12) is computed as:

$$S_B(P_I, m, h) = \int_0^k S_B(P_I, m, h, k)\, dF(k). \tag{1.16}$$

Consider now the solution $\langle P_I^*, m^*, h^* \rangle$ to the Ramsey problem of maximizing (1.12) over non-negative prices P, m, h, and subject to the viability constraint that $\Pi(P_I, m, h) \geq 0$:

$$\text{Maximize}\langle W(P_I, m, h) \mid \Pi(P_I, m, h) \geq 0; P_I \geq 0; m \geq 0; h \geq 0 \rangle.$$

The solution to maximizing welfare (ignoring the profit constraint) is the following (see Appendix 1A for the derivation).

Welfare Optimal Solution

$$P_I^*;\ m^* = 0;\ h^* = C_{UI}, \tag{1.17}$$

where P_I^* is the lowest price that does not distort the efficient bypass and access choices of entrants. As noted below, this is the price corresponding to $t_L^* = t_L(m^*, h^*, h^*) = t_L(0, C_{UI}, C_{UI})$, characterized by:

$$P_I^* = C_{UI} + C_{DE}(t_L^*) = C_{UI} + C_{DI}(t_L^*). \tag{1.18}$$

The central feature of the welfare optimal solution is to assure that the least-cost provider provides the service. Breakeven constraints are not applicable here. Indeed, it is clear that the USP will not break even at the welfare optimal since only the direct costs of upstream and delivery operations are covered for business customers in this solution and, from (1.18), the single-piece delivery costs are not fully covered for household customers for zones $t > t_L^*$.

The assumption that the welfare weight on single-piece, household customers is no less than that on business customers and profits (that is, $\alpha \geq 1$) drives price at the welfare optimal solution to the lowest level compatible with least-cost service provision.[13] The lower bound on prices that do not disrupt least-cost service provision is the price P_I^* in (1.18). Any price above P_I^* (and less than the reservation price levels of consumers) will still have entrants providing E2E service (that is, bypass) precisely when they can provide this service at lower cost than the USP. Recall from (1.6) that for zones $t \in [t_L^*, T]$ all entrants of type $k < C_{UI}$ will use access and entrants of type $k \geq C_{UI}$ will use I's E2E service, which corresponds to the least-cost provision for each respective element of the postal value chain. Note from (1.6) that entrants of type $k \geq C_{UI}$ will actually start using I's E2E service in some zones $t \leq t_L^*$. Such entrants of type $k \geq C_{UI}$ will start using I's E2E service at the zone $t_L(0, C_{UI}, k) \leq t_L(0, C_{UI}, C_{UI})$ at which I's E2E service is cheaper than entrant k's E2E service.

Ramsey Optimal Solution

The conditions characterizing the Ramsey optimal solution are derived in Appendix 1A. In contrast to the intuitive simplicity of the welfare optimum, these conditions are more difficult to interpret. The basic tradeoff embodied in determining the optimal mark-up (m) and discount (h) is clear: achieving breakeven operations with a minimum distortion of least-cost provision of services. What makes this tradeoff complicated is the fact that increases in the mark-up and minimum discount will affect the zones that are served by bypass, by access and by the incumbent's E2E service. Balancing the distortions in least-cost provision associated with these changes against the resulting changes in profit is the key tradeoff captured in the Ramsey solution.

Consider Figure 1.1 which shows the outcomes for an entrant of type $k < h$. In the figure, if m is reduced, then the intersection of $C_{DE}(t)$ and $(1 + m)C_{DI}(t)$ clearly decreases, so that $t_L(m)$ is lower and entrants of type $k < h$ will supply a lower quantity of E2E service and buy more access. For this type of entrant, increasing the minimum discount h would not change the amount of access purchased but would decrease the zone $\bar{t}$ at which the minimum discount constraint becomes binding. More generally, the comparative statics developed in the Appendix 1A establish that t_L is increasing in m and non-decreasing in h (strictly increasing for $k \geq h$). This means for the USP *ceteris paribus* that its E2E and access volumes both decrease if m is higher, or if h is lower. In contrast, if h is increased, the USP's access volumes increase and its E2E volumes decrease.[14]

Increasing h and increasing m to achieve a given profit level (or to cover a fixed level of USO costs) can increase profits. Increasing h until it equals C_{UI} also increases welfare. As shown in the appendix, increases in h beyond C_{UI} definitely decrease welfare, for any solution (not just the welfare optimal solution). However, the same is not true generally of profits. Sufficient conditions below for $h^* \leq C_{UI}$ to be true are analyzed in the appendix.

Condition 1: The total volume of single-piece mail from the household sector exceeds the volume of business mail customers using the incumbent's E2E service and the profit constraint is not too stringent.

Condition 2: The total volume of business mail customers with mail preparation costs $k > C_{UI}$ is negligible.

Concerning Condition 1, what this means is that (if the volume constraint is satisfied) the trajectory of Ramsey solutions that begins at the welfare optimal solution and ends at the profit-maximizing solution begins in a southeasterly direction from the welfare optimum ($m^* = 0$ and $h^* = C_{UI}$), with m increasing and h decreasing as the profit constraint becomes more binding. Concerning Condition 2, this condition implies that increasing h beyond C_{UI} has no benefits in terms of capturing additional access volumes from business customers, but it will decrease E2E volumes and will increase the number of high-cost zones in which the minimum discount constraint is active (those zones for which $t > \bar{t}$ as defined in (1.8)). Given this, a better approach for increasing profit without distorting least-cost service provision is to increase m rather than h.

Setting $h = C_{UI}$ and with I competing on m would send the efficient signals to entrants and customers in choosing between I's access services and its E2E services. It would also limit the subsidy on access and E2E services in the highest-cost zones, which could have a significant impact on the ability of the USP to finance its USO. The Ramsey optimal mark-up under the condition that $h = C_{UI}$ is obtained from the general Ramsey results in the appendix and is given as follows:

$$\hat{m} = r\left[\frac{\int_0^{\bar{k}}\int_{t_L}^{\bar{t}} C_{DI}(t)\,D_B(t,k)\,dt\,dF(k)}{\int_0^{\bar{k}} C_{DI}(t_L)\,D_B(t_L,k)\dfrac{dt_L}{dm}dF(k)}\right], \tag{1.19}$$

where $r \in [0, 1]$ is the Ramsey number (which increases from the welfare optimal level $r = 0$ to the profit-maximizing level $r = 1$). The numerator in (1.19) is the total delivery cost for all business customers in the zones served by I's access or E2E services, which represents the marginal revenues resulting from a change in the mark-up m on the cost of these services. The denominator represents the marginal loss in revenues lost to bypass through increases in m. If $h = C_{UI}$ is imposed, then there are no revenue implications in the zones $t > \bar{t}$ (where both E2E price and access price are determined by P_I and h, and not m), with the result that the Ramsey optimal mark-up is set to balance the two competing factors in the numerator and denominator of (1.19).

4 DISCUSSION AND IMPLICATIONS

The nature of regulation of access is of major concern. Experience in other industries, namely telecommunications, would seem to imply continued and significant regulation of the terms and pricing of access. However, in the postal sector, sunk costs and transactions-specific investments are of considerably less importance than in telecommunications. Entry is much easier. In addition, mail faces electronic competition that may be more threatening than competition from entrants. Not only does electronic competition reduce the demand for transactional products but it also reduces the demand for access products. Such reasons provide the basis for arguing that access should be completely unregulated, for example, de Bijl et al. (2006).

Despite the case for deregulation of access, the PO's facilities might not be freed from regulation. A number of arguments will be put forward by competitors and regulators against deregulation including the dominant position of the PO, the PO's scope economies and significant scale economies in delivery. While these are supporting arguments for regulation, they are likely to be overblown in the presence of the two powerful forces of FMO and electronic competition.

This chapter has revealed some of the complexities of the problem of regulating access. The analysis of the previous three sections has provided insights on Ramsey and profit-maximizing solutions to the problem, but has not addressed explicitly the issue of the regulatory regime for implementing these. Following the arguments of Crew and Kleindorfer (2008a), and in line with current regulatory practice, regulation could be implemented by means of a combination of a regulated single-piece price as part of the USO and additional pricing constraints on a subset of access products as part of a global price cap. In view of the complexities involved with access under FMO and a continued USO, it is going to be very difficult for any regulator to set the minimum discount, let alone Ramsey mark-ups that result in breakeven, at an efficient level. Thus, considerable discretion in setting these should be left to the USP. For example, if the regulator sets h too high, inefficiencies will occur to the extent that even entrants with delivery costs that are more expensive in every zone than the incumbent's could find it profitable to enter. Although this case is excluded in the model above because of the single-crossing assumption, it illustrates a problem that is likely to occur in practice. Take the case of an entrant with $k \geq h$ and $C_{DE}(t)$ everywhere greater than $(1 + m)C_{DI}(t)$. Increasing the discount h such that $h > k$ would mean that this entrant instead of producing zero E2E service and buying no access now becomes a purchaser of access. The only reason such an entrant would purchase access was that the entrant was being subsidized by the excessive amount of the discount h.

A further complexity that is central to the analysis and an important backdrop to access under bypass is the interaction between the pricing of corresponding E2E products and the pricing of related access products. This raises important issues for regulation regarding uniform pricing constraints on E2E products. The argument for minimal regulation not only applies to setting the minimum discount h but also suggests that the regulator should reduce the extent of the uniform E2E pricing constraints on E2E products linked to access products for business mail. This would allow greater flexibility to the incumbent to manage the increasing market risks of electronic substitutes. Similarly, to facilitate the theoretical analysis, the model here assumed that access prices reflect a constant mark-up across zones. However, as long as access prices are non-discriminatory and 'normal', there is no reason to impose such a uniformity constraint on mark-ups in practice.

Some of the general principles that have been applied to access absent bypass continue to be relevant if regulation were to continue under bypass, namely, avoid a rigid regulatory structure and micromanagement. A global price cap provides one step towards a less rigid structure. However, as argued in Crew and Kleindorfer (2008a), a global price cap by itself does not preclude regulatory rigidity as there are many levels of intervention and product definition possible for including access products in a global price cap.

Besides price-stability and price-level restrictions embodied in price caps, 'structural' constraints might be imposed on access products by regulators. Such constraints (and incentives to meet them) would include quality regulation, not just in the context of the administration of the USO but also in connection with concerns that access conditions may have the effect of raising rivals' costs.[15] Similarly, discriminatory treatment of entrants and customers of the incumbent might be a concern of regulators and is prohibited in any case by the Postal Directive. Further structural approaches could include the imposition of constant mark-ups. However, in view of the complexities of access pricing and in view of strong and growing intermodal competition, regulation of profit levels and margins should be designed with sufficient flexibility left to the USP to finance the USO and to price its products competitively.

This chapter, by providing an in-depth analysis of the access problem, has thrown additional light on the extent and nature of competition in the postal sector. A major conclusion of this analysis is that the complexities of access pricing are so significant that the ability and the benefits of regulators of intervening constructively in this process under competition are highly limited. Viewed against the increasing threat of the elephant in the room of intermodal competition, these considerations lead to the general conclusion that if ever there was a time and place for minimal regulation it is in the case of postal access policies under FMO.[16] The complexity of access pricing under FMO and, more importantly, the threat of intermodal competition, cast doubts on the viability not just of access regulation, but of the USO and the postal sector itself. The mix of FMO and excessive access regulation ignores not only the nature of competition in the postal sector, but also the critical threat posed by electronic substitution.

NOTES

* Prepared for presentation at the 17th Conference Postal and Delivery Economics, Bordeaux, May 27–30, 2009. The authors acknowledge the support of Royal Mail Group in the preparation of this chapter. The views expressed are solely those of the authors and do not necessarily reflect those of Royal Mail Group. The authors thank their discussants Michael MacClancy and Gonzales d'Alcantara for helpful comments.

1. Interestingly, the United States Postal Service (USPS) has provided downstream access for several years, even though it is not subject to or likely to be subject to FMO. The issues arising in this case have been discussed extensively in Crew and Kleindorfer (2008b).

2. Traditional upstream worksharing is only relevant for the model to the extent that presorting and other bulk mail preparation activities are subsumed in the technical conditions for the USP to accept mail for downstream access.
3. In telecommunications in the US, the USO is addressed by means of an explicit subsidy. All subscribers pay a universal service fee, which is redistributed to rural TELCOs. Such USO funds have also been discussed for the postal sector, and some funds have been set up in the form of direct transfers from the government (for example, the USO subsidy in France), but such funding is subject to increased scrutiny to monitor cross-subsidies between universal services and other products.
4. Students of the industry have been concerned with the issue of electronic substitution, notably Nikali (2008), who sees the potential for considerable losses in mail volume especially in the B2C market. Jimenez et al. (2008), examining primarily demographic factors, consider some less pessimistic scenarios.
5. E-commerce may offer a potential for growth in the parcel business but this is relatively small compared to mail and competitors are very much ahead of USPs in their application of the new technologies. O'Brien et al. (2008) indicate some of the potential that new technologies might have in the design and costing of innovative postal products.
6. Armstrong (2008) also addresses the issue of bypass in the postal sector. However, while he recognizes the problem of using ECPR, his solution involves an explicit subsidy using a universal service fund, which is ruled out here.
7. The assumption here is that the single-piece price serves as a backstop service for business mail. The analysis that follows would not be materially affected if there were distinct single-piece E2E prices for households and business mailers, where the latter might receive lower E2E prices in return for upstream preparation and worksharing activities. The essential ingredient for the analysis that follows is that some underlying E2E service is provided to business mailers at a uniform price, unaffected by the ultimate delivery zone for the mail. This is a consequence of the USO.
8. Note that entrant upstream costs are assumed to be independent of the ultimate downstream entry point to which mail is delivered. More generally, C_{UE} might be expected to depend on t, with $C_{UE} = C_{UE}(k, t)$ increasing in t to reflect the added transportation costs of serving downstream delivery to outlying zones. With the extensive use of remote printing and the dominance of local versus long-distance transportation costs, however, these distance-related costs are likely to be minimal and are neglected here.
9. In particular, market segmentation and service design issues are not considered here. As analyzed in Crew and Kleindorfer (2001), the actual process of market share loss by the USP is likely to be at the customer level, and segment-specific strategies relating to pricing and access policies are therefore central elements of USP strategy under market liberalization that need to be explored in future research. Only the impact of access pricing in the face of heterogeneous upstream mail preparation costs (k) is considered here.
10. Aside from the pricing uniformity issue of importance in the postal sector, ECPR may not be efficient in other contexts either, as it preserves the monopoly rents when applied to a bottleneck controlled by a monopolist.
11. For any normal access regime, it can be shown that t_L, t_U exist, are unique and that $t_L \leq t_U$ as long as the SCA and BDA conditions given below hold.
12. See Crew and Kleindorfer (2006b) for an extended discussion of the welfare tradeoffs associated with the scope of the USO.
13. When $\alpha = 1$, a range of single-piece prices P_I achieve the first-best outcome, the lowest of which is P_I^* in (1.18).
14. Single-piece volumes are not affected by m or h (or P_I as long as it is below the reservation level). Similarly, for bulk mail, in the present model P_I does not affect either access or E2E volumes (assuming that reservation levels are not exceeded). This is just a consequence of the assumption of completely inelastic demand. As noted earlier, the conclusions of this analysis would not be affected if E2E price for the underlying single-piece service were different for households and businesses. The key ingredient of the analysis here is that there be a uniform price E2E backstop service against which the minimum discount constraint is defined.
15. Crew and Kleindorfer (2009) examine the issue of quality in a model with varying zonal costs.
16. Crew and Kleindorfer (2008a,b) argue that a negotiated process, subject to global price caps and non-discriminatory treatment, is likely to be a more efficient approach.

REFERENCES

Armstrong, Mark (2008), 'Access pricing, bypass and universal service in post', *Review of Network Economics*, 7(2), June, 172–87.

Billette de Villemeur, Etienne, Helmuth Cremer, Bernard Roy and Joëlle Toledano (2007),

'Worksharing, access and bypass: the structure of prices in the postal sector', *Journal of Regulatory Economics*, **32**(1), 67–85.
Bloch, Francis and Axel Gautier (2008), 'Access, bypass and productivity gains in competitive postal markets', in M.A. Crew and P.R. Kleindorfer (eds), *Competition and Regulation in the Postal and Delivery Sector*, Cheltenham, UK and Northampton, MA, USA: Edward Elgar, pp. 125–35.
Crew, Michael A. and Paul R. Kleindorfer (2001), 'Whither the USO under entry: a microstructure approach', in M.A. Crew and P.R. Kleindorfer (eds), *Future Directions in Postal Reform*, Boston, MA: Kluwer Academic Publishers, pp. 117–40.
Crew, Michael A. and Paul R. Kleindorfer (2006a), 'The welfare effects of entry and strategies for maintaining the USO in the postal sector', in M.A. Crew and P.R. Kleindorfer (eds), *Progress toward Liberalization of the Postal and Delivery Sector*, New York: Springer Science+Business Media, Inc, pp. 3–22.
Crew, Michael A. and Paul R. Kleindorfer (2006b), 'Approaches to the USO under entry', in M.A. Crew and P.R. Kleindorfer (eds), *Liberalization of the Postal and Delivery Sector*, Cheltenham, UK and Northampton, MA, USA: Edward Elgar, pp. 1–18.
Crew, Michael A. and Paul R. Kleindorfer (2008a), 'Regulation and the USO under entry', in M.A. Crew and P.R. Kleindorfer (eds), *Competition and Regulation in the Postal and Delivery Sector*, Cheltenham, UK and Northampton, MA, USA: Edward Elgar, pp. 3–22.
Crew, Michael A. and Paul R. Kleindorfer (2008b), 'Pricing for postal access and worksharing', in M.A. Crew, P.R. Kleindorfer and J.I. Campbell Jr. (eds), *Handbook of Worldwide Postal Reform*, Cheltenham, UK and Northampton, MA, USA: Edward Elgar, pp. 32–66.
Crew, Michael A. and Paul R. Kleindorfer (2009), 'Service quality, price caps and the USO under entry,' in M.A. Crew and P.R. Kleindorfer (eds), *Progress in the Competitive Agenda in the Postal and Delivery Sector,* Cheltenham, UK and Northampton, USA: Edward Elgar, pp. 1–22.
de Bijl, Paul W.J., Eric van Damme and Pierre Larouche (2006), 'Regulating access to stimulate competition in postal markets?', in M.A. Crew and P.R. Kleindorfer (eds), *Progress toward Liberalization of the Postal and Delivery Sector*, New York: Springer Science+Business Media, Inc., pp. 153–72.
De Donder, Philippe, Helmuth Cremer, Paul Dudley and Frank Rodriguez (2006), 'A welfare analysis of price controls with end-to-end and access services', in M.A. Crew and P.R. Kleindorfer (eds), *Liberalization of the Postal and Delivery Sectors*, Cheltenham, UK and Northampton, MA, USA: Edward Elgar, pp. 53–72.
Dudley, Paul, Stephen Agar, Leonardo Mautino and Felipe Flórez Duncan (2009), 'Competition through downstream access in the UK postal sector: the first four years', in M.A. Crew and P.R. Kleindorfer (eds), *Progress in the Competitive Agenda in the Postal and Delivery Sector*, Cheltenham, UK and Northampton, MA, USA: Edward Elgar, pp. 52–66.
Jimenez, Luis, Matthew C. Harding and Michael Lintell (2008), 'The impact of economic and demographic dispersion on aggregate mail volumes', in M.A. Crew and P.R. Kleindorfer (eds), *Competition and Regulation in the Postal and Delivery Sector*, Cheltenham, UK and Northampton, MA, USA: Edward Elgar, pp. 74–88.
Mandy, David M. (2009), 'Pricing inputs to induce efficient make-or-buy decisions', *Journal of Regulatory Economics*, **36**(1), August, 29–43.
Nikali, Heikki (2008), 'Substitution of letter mail for different sender–receiver segments', in M.A. Crew and P.R. Kleindorfer (eds), *Competition and Regulation in the Postal and Delivery Sector*, Cheltenham, UK and Northampton, MA, USA: Edward Elgar, pp. 89–106.
O'Brien, Louis F., Leon A. Pintsov and Andrei Obrea (2008), 'Cost analysis and pricing of innovative products', in M.A. Crew and P.R. Kleindorfer (eds), *Competition and Regulation in the Postal and Delivery Sector*, Cheltenham, UK and Northampton, MA, USA: Edward Elgar, pp. 128–44.

APPENDIX 1A

The first-order conditions for the Ramsey results are provided along with some of the consequences of these FOCs reported in the text. From the definitions of S_H, S_B and Π in (1.16), (1.13) and (1.11), and the definitions of t_L, t_U and $\bar{t}$ in (1.6)–(1.8), are computed:

$$\frac{\partial S_H}{\partial P_I} = -\int_0^T D_H(t)\,dt$$

$$\frac{\partial S_B}{\partial P_I} = -\int_0^{\bar{k}}\int_{\bar{t}}^T D_B(t,k)\,dt\,dF(k)$$

$$\frac{\partial \Pi}{\partial P_I} = \int_0^T D_H(t)\,dt + \int_0^{\bar{k}}\int_{\bar{t}}^T D_B(t,k)\,dt\,dF(k)$$

$$\frac{\partial S_H}{\partial m} = 0$$

$$\frac{\partial S_B}{\partial m} = -\int_0^{\bar{k}}\int_{t_L}^{\bar{t}} C_{DI}(t)\,D_B(t,k)\,dt\,dF(k)$$

$$\frac{\partial \Pi}{\partial m} = \int_0^{\bar{k}}\left[-m\,C_{DI}(t_L)\,D_B(t_L,k)\frac{\partial t_L}{\partial m} + \int_{t_L}^{\bar{t}} C_{DI}(t)\,D_B(t,k)\,dT\right]dF(k)$$
$$+ \int_h^{\bar{k}}\left[(C_{UI} - h)\,D_B(t_L,k)\frac{\partial t_L}{\partial m}\right]dF(k)$$

$$\frac{\partial S_H}{\partial h} = 0$$

$$\frac{\partial S_B}{\partial h} = \int_0^h\int_{\bar{t}}^T D_B(t,k)\,dt\,dF(k) - \int_h^{\bar{k}}\int_{t_L}^{\bar{t}} D_B(t,k)\,dt\,dF(k)$$

$$\frac{\partial \Pi}{\partial h} = (C_{UI} - h)\left[\int_{t_L(m,h,h)}^T D_B(t,h)\,dtf(h) + \int_h^{\bar{k}} D_B(t_L,k)\frac{\partial t_L}{\partial h}dF(k)\right]$$
$$- \int_0^h\int_{\bar{t}}^T D_B(t,k)\,dt\,dF(k) + \int_h^{\bar{k}}\int_{t_L}^{\bar{t}} D_B(t,k)\,dt\,dF(k)$$
$$- m\int_h^{\bar{k}} C_{DI}(t_L)\,D_B(t_L,k)\frac{\partial t_L}{\partial h}dF(k),$$

where $f(k)$ is the marginal distribution of $F(k)$ and where t_L is evaluated at $t_L(m, h, k)$ unless otherwise noted (for example, in the first term of the above expression). Form the Lagrangean for the Ramsey-constrained welfare maximization of interest as:

$$\begin{aligned} L(P_I, m, h, \lambda) &= W(P_I, m, h) + \lambda \Pi(P_I, m, h) \\ &= \alpha S_H(P_I) + S_B(P_I, m, h) + (1 + \lambda)\Pi(P_I, m, h). \end{aligned}$$

Using the above derivatives yields the Ramsey results. Regarding FOCs for P_I, since demand is inelastic, increasing price (below the reservation levels for H and B) will lead to increases in profit and decreases in consumer surplus. Ramsey optimality requires P_I be set to achieve zero profits. In addition to the condition $\Pi(P_I, m, h) = 0$, the following FOC for P_I applies:

$$\begin{aligned} \frac{\partial L}{\partial P_I} &= \alpha \frac{\partial S_H}{\partial P_I} + \frac{\partial S_B}{\partial P_I} + (1 + \lambda)\frac{\partial \Pi}{\partial P_I} \\ &= (1 + \lambda - \alpha) \int_0^T D_H(t)\, dt + \lambda \int_0^k \int_{\bar{t}}^T D_B(t, k)\, dt\, dF(k). \end{aligned}$$

This solution only holds, if $1 + \lambda < \alpha$. When $1 + \lambda \geq \alpha$, then the profit constraint is sufficiently binding that P_I is driven to its upper limit of min $[v_H, v_B]$. Assuming an interior solution, setting this expression to 0 yields the second necessary condition between λ, P_I, m, h (recalling from (1.8) that $\bar{t} = \bar{t}(P_I, m, h)$). Similarly, the FOC for m is:

$$\begin{aligned} \frac{\partial L}{\partial m} &= \alpha \frac{\partial S_H}{\partial m} + \frac{\partial S_B}{\partial m} + (1 + \lambda)\frac{\partial \Pi}{\partial m} \\ &= \lambda \int_0^{\bar{k}} \left[\int_{t_L}^{\bar{t}} C_{DI}(t) D_B(t, k)\, dT \right] dF(k) \\ &\quad - (1 + \lambda) \int_0^{\bar{k}} \left[m C_{DI}(t_L) D_B(t_L, k) \frac{\partial t_L}{\partial m} \right] dF(k) \\ &\quad + (1 + \lambda) \int_h^{\bar{k}} \left[(C_{UI} - h) D_B(t_L, k) \frac{\partial t_L}{\partial m} \right] dF(k). \end{aligned}$$

Setting this to zero yields the characterizing condition for m^*.

$$m^* = \left(\frac{\frac{\lambda}{1 + \lambda} \int_0^{\bar{k}} \int_{t_L}^{\bar{t}} C_{DI}(t) D_B(t, k)\, dt\, dF(k)}{\int_0^{\bar{k}} C_{DI}(t_L) D_B(t_L, k) \frac{dt_L}{dm} dF(k)} \right)$$

$$+\frac{+(C_{UI}-h)\int_0^{\bar{k}} D_B(t_L,k)\dfrac{\partial t_L}{\partial m}dF(k)}{\int_0^{\bar{k}} C_{DI}(t_L)\,D_B(t_L,k)\dfrac{dt_L}{dm}dF(k)}.$$

In similar fashion, the FOC for h^* is:

$$\frac{\partial L}{\partial h} = \alpha\frac{\partial S_H}{\partial h} + \frac{\partial S_B}{\partial h} + (1+\lambda)\frac{\partial \Pi}{\partial h}$$

$$= \lambda \int_h^{\bar{k}} \left[\int_{t_L}^{\bar{t}} D_B(t,k)\,dT\right] dF(k) - \lambda \int_0^{h} \left[\int_{\bar{t}}^{T} D_B(t,k)\,dT\right] dF(k)$$

$$-(1+\lambda)\int_h^{\bar{k}} \left[m\,C_{DI}(t_L)\,D_B(t_L,k)\frac{\partial t_L}{\partial h}\right] dF(k)$$

$$+(1+\lambda)\,(C_{UI}-h)\left\{\int_h^{\bar{k}} \left[D_B(t_L,k)\frac{\partial t_L}{\partial h}\right] dF(k) + \int_{t_L(m,h,h)}^{T} D_B(t,h)\,dtf(h)\right\}.$$

Setting $\lambda = 0$ in the above FOCs for m and h, the necessary conditions for the welfare optimal solution are obtained. The reader can note by inspection that $m = 0$ and $h = C_{UI}$ solves these FOCs, that is, when $\lambda = 0$, setting $m = 0$ and $h = C_{UI}$ leads directly to $\partial L/\partial m = 0$ and $\partial L/\partial h = 0$. It can be shown that, except in knife-edge cases, this is the only solution satisfying these necessary conditions. Since the objective function is continuous and the relevant decision space for (P_I, m, h) is nonempty and compact (namely P_I, m, h can all be assumed to be no greater than the reservation level v_B of business customers), there is an optimal solution. Thus, $m = 0$ and $h = C_{UI}$ is the welfare-maximizing solution, where the welfare-maximizing solution for P_I can be any value in the interval $[\hat{P}_I, \mathrm{Min}\{v_H, v_B\}]$, where $\hat{P}_I$ is the value of C_{DE} corresponding to $t_L = t_L(0, C_{UI}, \bar{k})$, which from (1.6) is given by:

$$\hat{P}_I = C_{DE}(t_L) = C_{DI}(t_L).$$

The amount of access and E2E service provided by the incumbent are now analyzed. The details are given by the following expressions, where AV = total access volumes served by I (where upstream work is done by entrants) and EV = total E2E volumes served by I (where all work is done by the incumbent).

$$AV = \int_0^{h}\int_{t_L}^{T} D_B(t,k)\,dt\,dF(k)$$

$$EV = \int_0^{T} D_H(t)\,dt + \int_h^{\bar{k}}\int_{t_L}^{T} D_B(t,k)\,dt\,dF(k).$$

Comparative statics (using the fact that $\partial t_L/\partial h = 0$ for $k < h$ (see (1.6)) are as follows:

$$\frac{\partial AV}{\partial m} = -\int_0^h D_B(t_L,k)\frac{\partial t_L}{\partial m}dF(k) < 0$$

$$\frac{\partial EV}{\partial m} = -\int_h^{\bar{k}} D_B(t_L,k)\frac{\partial t_L}{\partial m}dF(k) < 0$$

$$\frac{\partial AV}{\partial h} = \int_{t_L}^T D_B(t,h)\,dt > 0$$

$$\frac{\partial EV}{\partial h} = -\int_h^{\bar{k}} D_B(t_L,k)\frac{\partial t_L}{\partial h}dF(k) - \int_{t_L}^T D_B(t,h)\,dtf(h) < 0,$$

where the lower limits in the integrals in the last two equations are evaluated at $t_L = t_L(m, h, h)$. Thus, increases in m decrease both access and E2E volumes. However, increases in h increase access volumes and decrease E2E volumes.

Now let us examine the Ramsey solution in more detail. The key issue here is whether the Ramsey solution lies to the northeast or southeast of the welfare optimal solution. Intuitively the Ramsey solution is expected to lie to the southeast of the welfare solution. Some sufficient conditions for this are provided below. First, the following easily established fact is noted:

$$\left.\frac{\partial W}{\partial h}\right|_{h>C_{UI}} < 0; \quad \left.\frac{\partial W}{\partial m}\right|_{h>C_{UI}} < 0.$$

This fact follows from $\partial t_L/\partial m > 0; \forall k$; $\partial t_L/\partial h > 0$ for $k > h$. For example, the first inequality results as follows:

$$\frac{\partial W}{\partial h} = -m\int_0^{\bar{k}} \left[C_{DI}(t_L)D_B(t_L,k)\frac{\partial t_L}{\partial h}\right]dF(k)$$

$$+ (C_{UI} - h)\left\{\int_h^{\bar{k}} \left[D_B(t_L,k)\frac{\partial t_L}{\partial h}\right]dF(k) + \int_{t_L(m,h,h)}^T D_B(t,h)\,dtf(h)\right\}$$

$$-m\int_0^{\bar{k}} \left[C_{DI}(t_L)D_B(t_L,k)\frac{\partial t_L}{\partial h}\right]dF(k) \leq 0.$$

Thus, the iso-welfare contours are cigar-shaped and tilted from southeast to northwest in (m, h) space whenever $h > C_{UI}$.

Proving that all Ramsey solutions are to the southeast of the welfare optimal solution in (m, h) space has been elusive. However, sufficient conditions for this to be the case are readily established. Assume $h > 0$ at the Ramsey optimal, so that an interior solution obtains for the FOCs. Given this, and assuming a binding profit constraint so that $\lambda > 0$, it can be verified by inspection of the expression $\partial L/\partial h$ that a sufficient condition that $C_{UI} \geq h$ is that the first term in this expression be positive. This follows by setting $\partial L/\partial h = 0$ and solving for $(C_{UI} - h)$, yielding:

$$(C_{UI} - h) = \frac{\frac{\lambda}{1+\lambda}\{\int_0^h [\int_{\bar{t}}^T D_B(t,k)\,dT]\,dF(k) - \int_h^{\bar{k}} [\int_{t_L}^{\bar{t}} D_B(t,k)\,dT]\,dF(k)\}}{\left\{\int_h^{\bar{k}}\left[D_B(t_L,k)\frac{\partial t_L}{\partial h}\right]dF(k) + \int_{t_L(m,h,h)}^T D_B(t,h)dtf(h)\right\}}$$

$$+ \frac{\int_h^{\bar{k}}\left[m\,C_{DI}(t_L)D_B(t_L,k)\frac{\partial t_L}{\partial h}\right]dF(k)}{\left\{\int_h^{\bar{k}}\left[D_B(t_L,k)\frac{\partial t_L}{\partial h}\right]dF(k) + \int_{t_L(m,h,h)}^T D_B(t,h)dtf(h)\right\}}.$$

Since the second term in this expression is clearly positive, a sufficient condition for $h^* \leq C_{UI}$ is that the numerator in the first term be positive, that is, that the Ramsey optimal solution $\{P_I^*, m^*, h^*\}$ satisfies:

$$\Gamma(P^*_I, m^*, h^*) = \int_0^{h^*}\left[\int_{\bar{t}}^{T} D_B(t,k)\,dT\right]dF(k) - \int_{h^*}^{\bar{k}}\left[\int_{t_L}^{\bar{t}} D_B(t,k)\,dT\right]dF(k) \geq 0,$$

with t_L evaluated at (m^*, h^*, k). Since $\Gamma(P_I^*, m^*, h)$ can be shown to be increasing in h, it suffices, in fact, to show that $\Gamma(P_I^*, m^*, C_{UI}) \geq 0$. If this is so, then whatever h^* is, $\Gamma(P_I^*, m^*, h)$ will be positive for $h > C_{UI}$, and it must be the case therefore that $h^* \leq C_{UI}$. If the quantity

$$\Psi(P_I^*, m^*, h^*) = \int_{h^*}^{\bar{k}}\left[\int_{\bar{t}}^{T} D_B(t,k)\,dT\right]dF(k)$$

is added and subtracted in the expression for $\Gamma(P_I^*, m^*, h)$, $\Gamma(P_I^*, m^*, h)$ can be rewritten to obtain the following equivalent sufficient condition:

$$\Gamma(P_I^*, m^*, h^*) = \int_0^{\bar{k}}\left[\int_{\bar{t}}^{T} D_B(t,k)\,dT\right]dF(k) - \int_{h^*}^{\bar{k}}\left[\int_{t_L}^{T} D_B(t,k)\,dT\right]dF(k) \geq 0.$$

Now note from FOC $\partial L/\partial P_I = 0$ that:

$$\int_0^{\bar{k}}\int_{\bar{t}}^{T} D_B(t,k)\,dt\,dF(k) = \left(\frac{\alpha - 1 - \lambda}{\lambda}\right)\int_0^T D_H(t)\,dt.$$

Thus, if $\lambda < (\alpha - 1)/2$, then $(\alpha - 1 - \lambda)/\lambda \leq 1$. Setting $h^* = C_{UI}$, from these last two expressions it follows that $\Gamma(P_I^*, m^*, C_{UI}) \geq 0$ whenever λ is sufficiently small and

$$\int_0^T D_H(t)\,dt \geq \int_{C_{UI}}^{\bar{k}}\left[\int_{t_L}^{T} D_B(t,k)\,dT\right]dF(k). \tag{1A.1}$$

In plain English, $h^* < C_{UI}$ whenever the profit constraint is not too stringent and when single-piece mail volumes (the LHS of the above expression) are no less than the volumes served by the USP E2E for high-cost business customers (those with type k larger than C_{UI}). In particular, if (1A.1) holds, then the Ramsey optimal path connecting the welfare optimal solution to the profit-maximizing solution in (m, h) space starts at $(0, C_{UI})$ and goes southeast for at least a while (namely for low values of λ).

An alternative, and easier sufficient condition for $h^* < C_{UI}$ is that the demand of customers of type $k > C_{UI}$ be negligible. In this case, inspection of the above shows that $\Gamma(P_I, m, C_{UI}) > 0$ holds for every $m > 0$ (since the second term in this expression is negligible under the noted condition).

Generally, one might expect the result $h^* \leq C_{UI}$ to hold for any Ramsey solution under fairly general assumptions. As it turns out, there are counterexamples to this conjecture in general, but it seems that rather unusual conditions have to hold for this condition to be violated. The reader should also keep in mind that the model here assumes a constant mark-up m across all zones. Relaxing this constraint would reinforce the presumption that $h^* \leq C_{UI}$ since (as shown above) there are clear welfare losses from setting $h^* \geq C_{UI}$, as well as profit losses (assuming that uniformity constraints do not interfere with the preferred alternative for increasing profits by increasing mark-ups for selected delivery zones).

2. Access to infrastructure and service elements in the postal sector*

Alessandra Fratini, Bernard Roy and Joost Vantomme

1 INTRODUCTION

Access obligations are generally imposed *ex post* by competition authorities or courts in the context of antitrust cases as a remedy to the benefit of entrants, who cannot effectively compete without having access to essential facilities. In network industries, involving former de jure monopolies or natural monopolies, access is dealt with through regulation. The definition of regulatory access obligations requires *ex ante* in-depth analysis and remains a last resort solution. The postal sector does not escape from this scrutiny. The opening of the markets in 2011/13 puts the issue of access regulation high on the agenda. The Third Postal Directive has explicitly broadened the scope of the access from traditional essential facilities to particular information or services historically controlled by the incumbent, referred to as infrastructure or service elements, such as information on change of address and postcodes, post office (PO) box delivery, redirection and return to sender services. As the case that the last mile is an essential facility is weak, regulatory intervention is based on promoting upstream competition.

Far from being a peculiarity of the postal sector, exclusive control over network elements or facilities, which are crucial gateways for market access or are 'essential' for competing downstream, is a key issue in the regulation of network industries undergoing liberalization. From a legal point of view, third-party access to such elements or facilities may be addressed under general (*ex post*) competition law and (*ex ante*) sector-specific regulation. Under EC competition law, outright refusals to supply an essential facility (as well as the establishment of access terms and conditions that amount to refusal to supply) can lead to the incumbent being required to grant access to that facility to one or more competitors.[1] However, in sectors with enduring market failures and economic bottlenecks, where 'structural competition problems persist',[2] *ex post* competition law alone is rarely sufficient and *ex ante* access regulation is necessary to allow market entry and create competition. This is the case for the EC access regimes established in the electronic communications, energy and railways markets, where *ex ante* intervention is focused on areas where it is actually required and targets only those markets and those situations where it is strictly needed.

Section 2 discusses the motivation behind the provision in the Postal Directives dealing with access to infrastructure or service elements. Section 3 evaluates why and how access should be granted in the postal sector. Section 4 provides concluding comments.

2 ACCESS REGULATION IN THE POSTAL DIRECTIVE

The First Postal Directive:[3] Access to Universal Services

The first Postal Directive of December 1997 stipulates that the basic aim of universal services is to offer all users easy access to the postal network, particularly through the provision of a sufficient number of access points and by ensuring satisfactory conditions with regard to the frequency of collection and delivery. Moreover, should this prove necessary, measures shall be adopted with a view to ensuring the transparency and non-discriminatory nature of conditions governing access to the public postal network in member states. This basic access principle is formulated as follows: 'The European Parliament and the Council, acting on a proposal from the Commission . . . shall adopt such harmonisation measures as are necessary to ensure that users and the universal service provider(s) have access to the public postal network under conditions which are transparent and non-discriminatory'. The 1998 Notice on competition rules[4] confirms these basic principles and introduces the concept of 'downstream access': 'all postal operators allow some kind of downstream access to their postal network, for instance by allowing or even demanding (sorted) mail to be deposited at an expediting or sorting centre. This permits in many cases a higher reliability (quality of service) by bypassing any sources of failure in the postal network upstream'.

The Third Postal Directive:[5] Access to Elements of Infrastructure or Services

While the notion of non-discriminatory and transparent access to the public postal network was left unchanged in Article 11 of the Directive, the concept of access to elements of postal infrastructure or services was explicitly introduced. Article 11*bis* reads: Whenever necessary to protect

> the interest of users and/or to promote effective competition, and in the light of national conditions and national legislation, Member States shall ensure that transparent, non-discriminatory access conditions are available to elements of postal infrastructure or services provided within the scope of the universal service, such as postcode system, address database, post office boxes, delivery boxes, information on change of address, re-direction service and return to sender service. This provision shall be without prejudice to the right of Member States to adopt measures to ensure access to the postal network under transparent, proportional and non-discriminatory conditions.

The European Commission's approach[6] to this new concept has to be seen in the context of a multi-operator environment where several postal undertakings provide services within the universal service area. In conformity with the subsidiarity principle, it is for the member states to assess whether some elements of the postal infrastructure or certain services, generally supplied by universal service providers (USPs), should be made accessible to other operators providing similar services. The aim should be to promote effective competition and/or to protect all users by ensuring the overall quality of the postal service. The Directive further stipulates[7] that

> where several universal service providers with regional postal networks exist, Member States should also assess and, where necessary, ensure their interoperability in order to prevent

impediments to the prompt transport of postal items. As the legal and market situation of these elements or services is different among the Member States it is appropriate to only require Member States to adopt an informed decision on the need, extent and choice of the regulatory instrument, including where appropriate on cost sharing.

Access to postal networks can take place at various levels, usually referred to in the literature as 'upstream' (worksharing) or 'downstream'. In contrast with regulation in network industries such as railways, electricity and natural gas, the postal 'network' discussion is usually seen from a perspective of 'last mile' delivery. In this respect, the downstream elements may show some bottleneck features. Traditionally, competition law provides for remedies in order to tackle discriminatory behavior, especially by vertically integrated undertakings. In most situations, if not all, postal services can be duplicated in an 'end-to-end competition' market situation without the need to access the incumbent's infrastructure or other elements of its postal system. As stated by the European Commission[8] in the preparatory work for the Third Postal Directive, regulatory intervention for downstream access can be deemed appropriate for a number of reasons, particularly to address possible anticompetitive behavior by the incumbent in setting prices and access conditions. Other reasons can be the preference for concentrating on the promotion of competition and universal service coverage outside the last mile of delivery or the willingness to address the scale and unit cost challenge faced by entrants who may find it difficult to replicate nationwide delivery networks at a competitive price.

The Third Postal Directive contains a non-exhaustive list of elements of the postal infrastructure: postcode system, address database, post office boxes, delivery boxes, information on change of address, redirection service and return to sender service. It can be argued that these infrastructure elements are not 'essential facilities'[9] or actual bottlenecks but there may be common ground to assert that the competitive development of the market may be hindered if access to some of the mentioned elements is refused. According to Plaut Economics (2007, p. 16):

> Regulation of these infrastructure and service elements may not be driven by the need to enhance competitiveness. Some of the mentioned elements such as PO boxes and change of address, call for co-ordination regulation that was not necessary in the past. Monopolistic bottlenecks constitute assets of market players that can be characterised by well-defined economic criteria. The postcode system, address databases, PO boxes, collection and delivery boxes, information on change of address, re-direction service, return to sender service etc. are not monopolistic bottlenecks in the sense of stable entry barriers. These services can rather be understood as technical functions of co-ordination and must be differentiated from postal services in the strict sense.

As a result of policy developments, competition has flourished up to now in various forms, ranging from upstream competition with downstream network re-injection to end-to-end networks bypassing the incumbent's network. Some member states have conferred to the national regulatory authorities (NRAs) the power to regulate downstream access such as in the United Kingdom, Germany, Denmark, France, Hungary, Poland and Sweden. The NRAs in the United Kingdom, Germany, Denmark and Portugal have made use of their regulatory powers.

3 NEW FORMS OF REGULATORY INTERVENTION FOR POSTAL INFRASTRUCTURE

After a brief survey on the emergence of the access regulation, the six types of access to the elements of postal infrastructure referred to in the Third Postal Directive will be screened, in order to analyze why, how, and at what price these elements could be made available to competitors. The aim of this section is to provide a toolkit for understanding the rationale of unbundling infrastructure, information or services in the postal sector, and to examine practical examples in some member states.

The First Steps of a Blossoming Regulation

The Swedish case on postal infrastructure regulation may be instrumental for some member states seeking to install competition neutrality: between 1993 (introduction of full competition) and 1999, the Swedish government hesitated to regulate the postal infrastructure. The Postal Services Act did not contain special rules and voluntary agreements between operators were an underlying regulatory assumption. Disputes started to arise concerning pricing, access conditions and unannounced changes to postcodes. The revision of the Postal Act in 1999 introduced access regulation to selected postal infrastructures. It was aimed at implementing conditions for a more competition-neutral use of the incumbent's postal infrastructure, which was made necessary by ongoing operational conflicts between CityMail and later local operators and the postal incumbent.

Mainly the postal code system and access to PO boxes were disputed. Andersson (2006) phrased it as follows:

> Sweden Post receives this mail with a price corresponding to its own cost savings. . . . Partly the Competition Act handles access conditions because dominant firms must provide access on equal and non-discriminatory terms. However, competition law has turned out to be weak and slow because abuses are usually not decided upon in the highest Court of Instance until several years later when a new entrant can already have been forced to exit. Sector specific regulation has stronger power. Thus, the Government Commission in 2005 proposed that access regulation be introduced in the Postal Act in a similar way, as is already the case for telephone services.

The French postal act of May 2005 is probably unique in the area of postal legislation, as it covers a global type of access regulation to infrastructure elements: the act identifies four elements (PO boxes, postcode directory/link between the code and the geographical address information, change of address and redirection, and access to letterboxes) to which access has to be guaranteed but no *ex ante* decision powers are granted to the NRA, whose intervention is limited to the settlement of disputes, if any.

In the member states that are currently discussing the transposition of the Third Postal Directive, the issue of mandatory access to infrastructure elements is often embedded in the new draft legislation (Belgium, Poland) or in the yet adopted new legislation (Netherlands). For instance, the recent Dutch postal act[10] contains an obligation for all operators to provide access to the various infrastructure elements (postcodes, address database, PO boxes, delivery boxes, change of address, redirection and return to sender service). The universal service provider (at present TNT) is obliged to deliver these services for all postal operators under non-discriminatory conditions. The NRA can issue determinations if the negotiations are not working out. The focus is put on the non-discriminatory treatment rather than on the access obligation *per se*. The NRA is to issue a report to the ministry on the effectiveness of the access obligation no later than one year after the implementation of the new act.

In the United Kingdom, the current Postal Services Act and Royal Mail's license provide for the incumbent's obligation to maintain a Postcode Address File (PAF), accompanied by an advisory board of PAF users, and to make it available to all persons on reasonable terms and conditions. Postcomm imposes a Code of Practice on 'Common Operational Procedures' on licensed operators to handle multi-operator interconnections on misdirected letters and return to sender services. Following the Hooper review in 2008, the UK government Department for Business Enterprise and Regulatory Reform (BERR) authored a new set-up of postal services legislation. On 26 February 2009, the government published a draft Postal Services Bill aimed at ensuring the maintenance of a universal postal service and securing the future of a healthy publicly owned Royal Mail. The draft bill confers power on Ofcom (the successor of Postcomm) to impose general access conditions on postal operators, only if it appears to Ofcom that those conditions are necessary for either or both of the following purposes: (i) protecting the interests of the users of postal services; (ii) promoting effective competition.

Access to PO Boxes

Delivery to PO boxes is an alternative to home delivery. Clients sign a contract with the operator, specifying that mail will no longer be delivered at home, but to a postbox physically located elsewhere (generally in the USP's building). For this service, the rental of the box is charged to the client-recipient. Clients choose delivery in PO boxes either because they want to have their mail delivered in the morning earlier than at the regular postman's visit, or because they do not want it delivered at home for whatever reason. In this case, the address on the envelope specifies the name of the addressee and the number of the box, as well as the postcode to identify the delivery unit of destination. In most cases, the street address is no longer necessary.

The rationale of access to PO boxes

PO boxes are generally located inside the delivery office, or in remote offices, belonging to the incumbent. As opposed to a traditional private letter box, PO boxes do not have a slot. They are filled by the postmen from the rear, in the restricted area of the office, to which only the incumbent's staff have access. The addressee enters the office through a public entrance and opens the box with a key. An alternative end-to-end delivery network faces an operational problem when confronted by PO box delivery (that is, the address on the envelope includes the PO box number and location): how to deposit it in the recipient's box, who will do it, and at what price? This is why some form of cooperation is needed between the incumbent and its competitor. It is worth noting that this access should be reciprocal. Competitors could build PO box facilities, but the problem would then be for the incumbent to pass over mail to its competitors for final delivery.

Practical access and pricing a PO box delivery

For obvious reasons, it is inconceivable to allow a competitor into a delivery unit, where all mail and parcels are handled by the incumbent. Moreover, it is not possible to load a box from outside (no slot).

During the transposition process of the First Postal Directive in France, leading to the 2005 law, political advisors expressed the idea of building a private corridor behind the PO boxes locked with a key, which would be made available to all licensees as well as to the incumbent. This would however require important transformations to the building, and prohibitive costs. Therefore, the most practical solution is handing over the mail to the incumbent for loading the PO boxes. The problem consists in finding the best (and cheapest) way to enter the incumbent's network with PO box mail. Obviously, the competitor cannot inject its mail anywhere in the entrance of the delivery unit ('hand to hand'): this would imply problems regarding billing, contracting and transfer of responsibility (disruption of the logistic chain). In order to avoid extra costs, the competitor must 'plug in' at the stage where collection of mail is already provided. In France, competitors choose to hand over mail as closely as possible to the location of PO boxes in order to inject it during their delivery route. In order to be able to control the pass-over (responsibility, billing, identity of who is passing over the mail), the collection is made where small business customers deposit their mail, or at the sorting center where business mail is deposited.

Pricing on a 'retail-minus' basis is possible (as in the Efficient Component Pricing Rule (ECPR) for instance), but is not really realistic when such a large part of the process is avoided. Considering the specificity of this service, where a lot of the process can be bypassed by the competitor if the mail is given to the incumbent close to the location of the PO boxes, pricing based on cost plus reasonable profit seems to be more appropriate. In Sweden, the pricing principles are driven by competition law: prices must cover costs and avoid squeezing effects. Alternative operators may open PO boxes in their own plants and pricing principles are symmetric. In 2000, the price for delivering in a PO box in Sweden was 0.75 SEK per item (about 8 eurocents). In France, the price comprises two parts, one fixed and one variable, very much inspired by the German case (RegTP decision of 30 June 2004). The fixed part represents the cost of acceptance and billing, and the variable part represents the costs for conveying the mail from the place of acceptance to the delivery unit (if relevant) and depositing the mail in the PO boxes. A specific pricing of PO box mail, tailored on costs for one competitor only, leads to an analysis of the sustainability of uniform pricing between 'home delivered mail' and PO box mail. If PO box mail represents a large quantity of mail, competitors could use their license to access this offer, and undercut the price function of the incumbent in order to offer a special price to clients for this mail, leading to usual questions of possible inefficient entries. The price would then need to be 'de-averaged' by the incumbent, in order to cope with this new form of competition. John Panzar (2008) develops a frame for pricing PO box access, by taking into account the two-sided characteristics of the PO box market: the users pay a fee for PO box rental and the incumbent receives the access charge from competitors when handling their mail. Spillover effects between these markets should be taken into account to price in the most economical way.

Postcode Database

A postcode is historically a geographic area covered by one delivery unit. It partitions the territory of a postal organization. Therefore, the basic discounts start when clients accept having their mail sorted by postcode, allowing the incumbent to avoid sorting, and to convey bundles of presorted mail directly to the right delivery office.

The rationale of accessing a postcode database

Access to information on postcodes was first put in place in Sweden, in the mid-1990s, when CityMail chose to build an alternative delivery network on part of the territory only, the densest areas corresponding exactly to some postcodes in Stockholm. It was a strategy motivated by the fact that the largest clients, already sorting their mail for Sweden Post, could simply handle the bundles corresponding to the coverage of CityMail at no extra cost. For this type of selective entry, it is clear that, had Sweden Post changed the postcode system without informing CityMail, the latter would have had to deal with problems in its delivery process, as its geographic coverage areas would no longer correspond to the way clients would naturally presort their mail.

Access to postcodes is not identified by most NRAs as a bottleneck issue calling for regulatory intervention. However, the Irish case is worth mentioning since in Ireland there is no national postal code system. Attempts to introduce the principle of postcodes have not resulted in a concrete new structure, methodology or algorithm. Competing postal operators may consider the historical knowledge and delivery processes of the incumbent as a first-mover advantage of the latter where the need for regulatory intervention can be voiced.

Discerning whether access to a postcode database is essential for delivering mail is not so obvious. Thanks to new technological means, the use of GPS coordinates coding each address is probably a smarter way to proceed, and large clients could sort according to the delivery areas of the competitors or incumbent, in a more efficient way than through the traditional postal means. However, there are also 'non-geographical' postcodes that correspond to special types of delivery (such as PO boxes, for instance, or direct deliveries to some companies). In this case, the physical address is sometimes not mentioned on the envelope, and the actual delivery is a match between the postcode and the location of delivery (see Dieke and Schölermann, 2008). This is why mandatory access to postcodes could be imposed in order to allow competitors to correctly deliver. The matter is still sensitive in Sweden. The postcode system continues to be managed by Posten AB but decisions about changes are handled by a 'Postcode Council' with representatives of Posten AB, CityMail/the confederation of private postal operators and government agencies. Posten AB is obliged to allot private operators postcodes for PO box facilities. The regulator (Swedish Post and Telecom Agency – PTS) can put changes to the system on hold. It can also act as a mediator or issue statements but it has no right to enforce changes.

Practical access and pricing a postcode database

The question of pricing, or the technical design of the unbundling, is less relevant here. Making the postcode database available to a competitor is as simple as doing it for clients, and the price may be considered as quite affordable for everyone, as the costs are low and shared by many. Squeeze problems, inefficient entry via cream-skimming, or the need for 'de-averaging' prices for the incumbent are not relevant issues in this type of access. The actual questions concern possible changes of the internal organization of the incumbent operator, for instance when suppressing or adding delivery units, leading to a redesign of the areas covered by postcodes. The fact of making the information available may not be enough as the changes may also affect the competitor's organization.

Information on Change of Address

Access to the change of address database is without doubt a more important issue than access to the postcode database for delivering mail. The question was very important in Sweden in the liberalization process. When someone changes his/her address, the information is given to the incumbent, to make sure that mail will be correctly redirected. Some other organizations, such as banks, telecom operators or energy providers, also have the information of the address changes of their clients, but the information is spread among different competing networks. However, the postal incumbent has the most reliable and up-to-date database, because it delivers to every recipient in a country. It is not really conceivable that a client changing his/her address should be obliged to give the information to all licensees (and even so, it would not solve the problem of the newest entrants). This is why sharing the information on address changes could be required by law.

The rationale of accessing address change information

Without the information on change of address, competitors may face extra work or deliver to the old (wrong) address. While the largest senders are generally quickly informed about the change of address of their clients, and although they keep their database 'clean', direct mailing is more vulnerable to the change of address problem, as clients usually do not inform advertisers of the change. The original information is collected manually every day throughout the territory, when the information is made available by recipients. In France, the information is then centralized in a database that traces the old and the new addresses. Delivery offices periodically receive the address change of the recipients they covered initially, through a secured wire line.

Practical access and pricing the change of address information

Access to the change of address database is a kind of 'information unbundling'. It is linked with redirection of mail to the new address, and/or informing the sender of the change of address of the recipient. In France, a specific issue arises because of the confidentiality of the information. An authority created in the late 1970s (CNIL)[11] protects citizens' personal information, to prevent any general cross-filing of the population. A file containing both the old and new addresses is considered to be potentially misused; as such, it falls under CNIL's protection and cannot be released or sold. It is still possible though to inform that one has changed address (without giving the new one), or to 'clean up' a file replacing the old address by the new one. New entrants in France have a CNIL authorization, on the same terms as La Poste, to maintain a file like the one described above, provided that security rules are complied with.

The pricing of making the database available to competitors poses real conceptual difficulties. Regularly collecting information and keeping the database updated are important (and very costly) tasks, and could be shared by competitors. On the other hand, the incremental costs for making the information available to competitors are low. Alternatively, it could be noted that addresses have a 'market price': for marketing reasons, direct mailers sell address databases to one another. In France, imposing the market price to competitors for delivery purpose would have been considered disproportionate. Prices for addresses are therefore lower, covering incremental costs plus reasonable profit, but the use of these prices implies the interdiction to re-sell the information or to use it for marketing purposes. In Sweden, the database is held by a company, called Svenska Adressändring AB (SvA AB), owned by Posten AB (85 percent) and CityMail (15 percent). Clients deal directly with SvA AB when they change their address. Information is transmitted twice a day to the large operators, twice a week to small operators, and once a day to the state (tax recovery department).

Redirection of Mail

Redirection of mail is a service used almost automatically by citizens when they move from one address to another. It consists in giving the new address to the postal operator and having mail redirected to the new address for a certain period of time, allowing the client to inform all his/her correspondents of the new address. This involves extra processes for the postal operator. Generally, the price of the stamp covers the extra process. It could also be possible that the receiver pays a fee that covers the cost of this extra conveyance but, to our knowledge, this situation has never been observed. In most countries, the 'Rowland Hill principle' (the sender pays it all) is strictly followed. The client who changes address pays a fee for administrative costs, but the price does not cover the costs of handling the mail from the old address to the new one. In the US, the administrative cost is not even charged to the client; all mail is redirected for free for a one-year period.

The need for accessing a redirection of mail service

Possessing the new address of a recipient does not mean that a competitor can deliver to the new address. If the competitor has only partial coverage, it can be confronted with a new address outside the area of delivery. In Germany, redirection is allowed only if the licensee does not cover the geographic area where mail must be redirected, and only for mail initially addressed within the area of the license. In France, it is possible to use the redirection facility even if mail is redirected within the area of the licensee. Indeed, in practice, some competitors declare a large area in their license, but need time to really cover each address in the area. For this reason, La Poste has so far redirected all mail, even within the area of the licensee.

Practical access and pricing redirection of mail

For the incumbent, the traditional process for mail redirection is to convey the mail to the delivery unit of the old address, as the information is revealed only during the in-office process. Each postman has the information of the redirection order locally. He/she puts the mail aside, and prints and sticks the new address on the envelope, or alternatively uses a large envelope for redirection, containing several items for the same addressee. The mail is then sent through the network, and processed as a single-piece mail. New sorting center technology makes it possible for the machines to read all the information on the envelope, recognize the old address by a test to a remote database, automatically apply the new address and process it from there. Non-automated mail still retains the old processes. When accepting redirected mail from a competitor, the incumbent must unbundle a service previously tied up for its clients. However, on what basis is it relevant to price this service? While always possible, a cost-based approach requires an extensive cost accounting system. Redirecting mail involves the use of almost all parts of the process. The service is very similar to that for the conveyance of single-piece mail, and this is why a retail-minus approach seems more appropriate.

In France, contracts for redirection have been signed, and the service is carried out provided that licensees stick the correct (new) address on the envelope. Whether a cost-based or retail-minus approach is sustained, the price level must not encourage inefficient behavior, for example, for a competitor to use the redirection facility in its own area of delivery. Moreover, if the price is too low, competitors could strategically minimize their area coverage, and use redirection for remailing instead of having the incentive to develop their own network. In practice, as the price is 'close' to the single-piece price, because of a very similar process, and mail initially originates from bulk mail lots (the preferred competitors' market), paying the redirection fee annuls the margins of the competitor on the corresponding flows. This is why competitors try to avoid using redirection of all mail, especially when it is not strictly necessary with regard to 'the purpose' of the mail. For direct mail, in order to avoid extra costs, competitors inform their clients of the change of address but do not use redirection.

Return to Sender

The Third Directive has added the possibility of enforcing access to a 'return to sender' service. The 'return to sender' case occurs when delivery is made impossible. Change of address (when no address to redirect mail exists, or after the redirect contract has expired), death of the addressee, wrong address, and absence of a mailbox are some of the reasons why it may be impossible to deliver mail. When delivery is impossible, mail is sent back to the sender, provided that a return address is printed on the envelope. If not, mail is opened in a special plant in order to identify the sender. When it proves to be impossible to identify the sender, the mail is kept for one year and destroyed if no one claims it.

The rationale of access

The obligation for the incumbent to provide access to a return to sender service reflects the idea that an entrant covering part of the territory may need to deliver mail outside its area (if delivery is impossible), depending on where the sender is located. The entrant would thus need to use the incumbent's network for returning undeliverable mail. The case is not straightforward. For bulk mail, the sender is a company depositing mail in dedicated mail platforms. It is hard to understand why the entrant would need the incumbent to return mail to its client, even if the latter does not 'live' in the entrant's area of coverage. Depositing bulk mail requires a physical contact between the provider and the client, and it could be the occasion to return undelivered mail. As to single-piece mail items that originate from the area of delivery covered by the competitor, there is no reason why a return to sender service should be needed from the incumbent. This would certainly be the general case as collection is usually part of the delivery process (mail is collected during the delivery routes). Again in this case, mandatory access to a return to sender service is meaningless.

In theory, access for a return to sender service provided by the incumbent would be rational only in very few and unusual cases: for example, single-piece flows, where the sender sends mail in an area covered by a competitor, but does not live in that area, which still leaves open the question of how or where mail was handed over by the sender to the operator. In practice, another case must be examined: the competitor *does not know* that mail is not correctly delivered, either because it made a mistake during delivery (wrong box), or because there is no indication that the addressee has left. Mail falls into the letterbox of the wrong person, who places it back in the first street box he/she finds. This is how mail falls back into the network of the incumbent.

In Sweden, as in France more recently, the following case happens frequently: although the envelopes correctly mention the operator who delivered the mail, addressees use the incumbent's network, more adapted for single-piece acceptance, to throw mail back into the postal pipeline. The issue is more 'how to deal with found items', than introducing obligations on the incumbent to provide the return to sender service.

Practical access and pricing the return to sender service

In Sweden, an elegant and simple solution has been put in place. The total cost of the return to sender service has been estimated, and shared by all operators. In France, providing access to a return to sender service for competitors is not mandatory. Nevertheless, flows found in the street boxes of La Poste must be dealt with. The competitors happen to focus their activity on bulk mail, and there is no competition yet on single piece. Therefore, the only case where mail needs to be treated is mail incorrectly delivered by competitors. Entrants have expressed a preference to retrieve mail and handle it themselves with their clients (the senders), instead of having La Poste send it back. In this case, La Poste transports the 'found items' to its plants (sorting centers in general), and informs its competitors that they can pick it up. So far, no fee has been charged for this service.

Access to Letterboxes

It is straightforward to consider that the ability to access letterboxes of the recipients is a basic condition for the emergence of end-to-end competition. Nevertheless, sometimes public intervention may be necessary to ensure that this access is granted. The most obvious case is when the letterbox belongs to the incumbent, or, more generally, when access is restricted by law to the incumbent (USA, Austria). One can consider that duplicating mailboxes makes no sense, and sharing this bit of property is common sense. The access charge, if any, could reflect the investments made by the incumbent. If the letterbox is a bottleneck, the access charge could also include a fee for financing the universal service obligation (USO).

An interesting case can occur, as in France for instance, where some letterboxes are placed in the lobby of the buildings (as in the case of urban-dense areas). The private property starts at the door, outside the lobby, which means that any operator who wants access to the lobby needs an authorization. These buildings are sometimes protected by more or less sophisticated security systems (pin-codes, keys, magnetic systems). In France, an access right to buildings is given by law to licensed postal operators,[12] including competitors of La Poste. Without this right, a conflict could occur between the property right, allowing each inhabitant to prevent access to his/her private property, and the possibility of competition, which relies on access to letterboxes. The problem can easily become quite complex as postal delivery involves more products than just letter mail, especially in the post bag of a new entrant. Items of correspondence are often embedded with historical competitive products, such as unaddressed mail, parcels or newspapers, to benefit from scope economies. The right to access letterboxes can create distorting effects on these historically competitive markets, which do not benefit from this right when provided solely.[13] On the other hand, one may question why a special regulation for accessing letterboxes should be put in place, as the delivery of parcels, newspapers or unaddressed items has successfully developed without any *ad hoc* regulatory intervention.

Access to the private mailbox has been subject to discussion, regulation and litigation in the following member states: Austria,[14] France, Poland, Hungary, Slovakia and Germany (albeit for a relatively small number of addresses). In most cases, the keys or codes of the entrance slots held by the incumbent are not shared with competitive operators for reasons of safety, privacy, exclusive property and liability. ECORYS (2008) considers these practices as an important barrier to competition requiring attention at EC and/or national level.

4 REGULATORY POLICIES: CONCLUSIONS

In the e-communications, energy and railways sectors, the rationale for *ex ante* regulatory intervention is that efficient competition in downstream markets would be impeded in the absence of mandated access to the incumbent's network and facilities at appropriate prices, terms and conditions. The basic mechanism by which access issues are addressed in network industries is negotiations between the parties, under specific requirements of transparency, non-discrimination and regulatory scrutiny. There is generally an obligation to negotiate and refusals have to be justified under the specific grounds provided for by the applicable directives. The scope of regulatory intervention changes from sector to sector and the balance between *ex ante* regulation and *ex post* competition enforcement also depends upon the nature and the competitive structure of each market. While *ex ante* intervention is required where entry barriers are high and enduring economic bottlenecks – such as non-replicable legacy facilities – exist, general competition rules are better suited to prevent incumbents from excluding other operators from the market where competition is freely attainable and sustainable.[15] In the words of Advocate General Francis Jacobs: 'The mere fact that by retaining a facility for its own use a dominant undertaking retains an advantage over a competitor cannot justify requiring access to it'.[16]

The discussion on whether regulatory intervention needs to take place in the area of infrastructure or service elements in the postal sector is probably essentially based on the need for technical coordination among postal operators in a multi-operator interoperability environment.

The Postal Directive leaves the window for regulation open to member states, and some NRAs have actually used their powers in this respect. While most member states are still in the process of transposing the new Directive, the following regulatory policies on access to the mentioned elements can be identified: (i) *ex ante* access obligations for the incumbent with conditions imposed by law or by the NRA, (ii) mandatory negotiation of access terms and conditions in agreements with the other market players and NRA's intervention where no agreement can be reached and (iii) no *ex ante* obligations. In practice, defining *ex ante* access conditions in the postal sector will deter incentives to replicate the elements of infrastructure or services subject to access. A clear example is the UK situation, where, instead of encouraging end-to-end competition, the market organization by the NRA resulted in the absence of real alternative delivery service offerings. Should there be reasons to believe that some elements of infrastructure, information or services held by the incumbent would be made available to entrants in order to let competition emerge, the applicable *ex ante* specifications would imply such a quantity of information to make it impossible for the NRA or the lawmaker to define access conditions in the most appropriate way.

NRAs and member states could tackle the need for regulation along the following think-path: are there structural, legal or de facto practical barriers for development of competition in a multi-operator environment? Does the lack of mandatory access underpin the quality of service or will it have an effect on the trust and confidence of users in the mail as communication medium? Should the NRA be entrusted with *ex ante* or *ex post* intervention powers and remedies? What is the role of the competition authority in this area? A regulatory model with mandatory access and discretionary intervention powers for the NRA to set terms and conditions will easily be judged as unproportioned over-regulation. Arguments such as transparency, legal certainty and facilitation of entry are to be properly counterbalanced with the de facto market environment and the negotiation freedom of the parties involved. The direct and indirect costs for the incumbent of such a regulatory scheme should also be evaluated against the principle of creating a level playing field by free negotiations.

The issue is not necessarily *ex ante* regulation versus *ex post* competition law at the general level.[17] There will and should be a combination of general competition rules and sector-specific regulations according to the different market situations prevailing. The examples in the postal sector show that '*ex ante* soft' regulation, where the NRA intervenes only in the case of disputes, seems to be the emerging model. Parties can best define among themselves the most appropriate way to ensure interoperability.

NOTES

* This chapter only reflects the views of the authors and does not necessarily represent the views of La Poste (Belgium) or La Poste (France).

1. See *Commercial Solvent v. Commission*, Case 7/73, [1974] ECR 223; *United Brands v. Commission*, Case 27/76, [1978] ECR 207; *Telemarketing v. CLT*, Case 311/84, [1985] ECR 3261; *Radio Telefis Eiremann and Independent Television Publications Limited v. Commission*, (Magill), [1995] ECR I-743; *IMS Health GmbH & Co. OHG v. NDC Health GmbH & Co. KG, 2004*, Case C-418/01, [2004] ECR I-5039.
2. Neelie Kroes, European Commissioner for Competition Policy (Kroes, 2009).
3. Article 11 of Directive 97/67/EC.
4. Notice from the Commission on the application of the competition rules to the postal sector and on the assessment of certain State measures relating to postal services, point 2.5.
5. Directive 2008/6/EC.
6. Recital 34 of the Third Postal Directive.
7. *Ibid.*

8. European Commission, Staff working document, accompanying the proposal for the Third Postal Directive, Impact assessment, p. 17.
9. The notion of 'essential facilities' is used to describe a facility or infrastructure which is essential for providing services to the market and which cannot be replicated by any reasonable means. The 'essential facility doctrine' finds its roots in American antitrust law; in EC competition law, it does not constitute a distinct rule under Article 82 EC.
10. *Wet van 25 maart 2009, houdende regels inzake de volledige liberalisering van de postmarkt en de garantie van de universele postdienstverlening.*
11. Commission Nationale de l'Informatique et des Libertés.
12. Law of 20 May 2005 transposing the 1997 Postal Directive. Competitors must be licensed in France to deliver mail.
13. In France, this complexity has been amplified by the existence in some buildings of a special security system, so-called 'Vigik', managed by La Poste. In 2007, pressured by competitors, ARCEP launched a public consultation. A solution has been found whereby all licensees can benefit from the Vigik code ensuring the safety of security dispositions.
14. The problem was addressed in the legislation but the relevant provision in the law has been annulled by judgment of the Constitutional Court on 25 April 2006. A new legislative initiative is expected.
15. Detailed access-based policies may lead to negative effects. While enhancing consumer welfare in the short term, they could compromise dynamic efficiency because they reduce investment returns and so the incentives to invest. New entrants, in fact, may delay investing in infrastructure and focus on obtaining services at attractive wholesale prices and reselling them to customers, rather than designing innovative products/services giving customers greater choice.
16. *Oscar Bronner GmbH & Co. KG v. Mediaprint Zeitungs und Zeitschriftenverlag GmbH & Co. KG*, Case C-7/97, [1998] ECR1-7791. In the US, Circuit Judge Richard Posner said: 'As the emphasis of antitrust policy shifted from the protection of competition as a process of rivalry to the protection of competition as a means of promoting economic efficiency . . . it became recognized that the lawful monopoly power should be free to compete like everyone else; otherwise the antitrust laws would be holding an umbrella over inefficient competitors . . . Today, it is clear that a firm with a lawful monopoly power has no general duty to help its competitors, whether by holding a price umbrella over their heads or by otherwise pulling its competitive punches' (*Olympia Equipment Leasing Co., Alfco Telecommunications Co., and Paula Jeanne Feldman, v. Western Union Telegraph Co.* – United States Court of Appeals for the Seventh Circuit, October 6, 1986, 55 USLW 2081; 797 F.2d 370).
17. In any case, existence of (and compliance with) *ex ante* regulation does not prevent the application of general competition law.

REFERENCES

Andersson, P. (2006), 'The liberalisation of postal services in Sweden – goals, results and lessons for other countries', working paper, Department of Management and Economics, Linköping University, Sweden.

ARCEP (2007), 'Consultation publique relative à l'accès aux boîtes aux lettres installées dans des immeubles équipés d'un système de contrôle d'accès', l'Autorité de Régulation des Communications Électroniques et des Postes, November.

Cave, M. (2007), 'The regulation of access in the telecommunications: a European perspective', Barcelona Graduate School of Economics, Master in Competition and Market Regulation, Regulation and Competition Seminar Series.

de Bijl, P., E. van Damme and P. Larouche (2005), 'Light is right, competition and access regulation in an open postal sector', Report for TNT and Deutsche Post, Tilburg Law and Economics Center, June, pp. 11–38.

Dieke, A. and S. Schölermann (2008), 'Postcodes in competitive postal markets: is there a case for regulation?', in M.A. Crew and P.R. Kleindorfer (eds), *Competition and Regulation in the Postal and Delivery Sector*, Cheltenham, UK and Northampton, MA, USA: Edward Elgar, pp. 189–98.

Directive 91/440/EEC of the Council on the development of the Community's railways, as amended by Directive 2001/12/EC of the European Parliament and of the Council of 26 February 2001, OJ 2001/L 75/1, by Directive 2004/51/EC of the European Parliament and of the Council of 29

April 2004, OJ 2004/L 164/164 and by Directive 2007/58/EC of the European Parliament and of the Council of 23 October 2007, OJ 2007/L 315/44.
Directive 95/18/EC of the Council on the licensing of railway undertakings as amended by Directive 2001/13 of the European Parliament and of the Council of 26 February 2001, OJ L2001, 75/26.
Directive 96/92/EC of the European Parliament and of the Council of 19 December 1996 concerning common rules for the internal market in electricity, OJ 1997/L 27/20.
Directive 97/67/EC of the European Parliament and of the Council of 15 December 1997 on common rules for the development of the internal market of Community postal services and the improvement of quality of service, OJ L 15, 21.1.1998.
Directive 98/30/EC of the European Parliament and of the Council of 22 June 1998 concerning common rules for the internal market in natural gas, OJ 1998/L 204/1.
Directive 2001/14/EC of the European Parliament and of the Council on the allocation of railway infrastructure capacity and the levying of charges for the use of railway infrastructure and safety certification, OJ 2004/L 164/44.
Directive 2002/19/EC on access to, and interconnection of, electronic communications networks and services, OJ 2002/L 108/7.
Directive 2002/21/EC on a common regulatory framework for electronic communications networks and services, OJ 2002/L 108/33.
Directive 2003/54/EC of the European Parliament and of the Council of 26 June 2003 concerning common rules for the internal market in electricity and repealing Directive 96/92/EC, OJ 2003, L176/37.
Directive 2003/55/EC of the European Parliament and of the Council of 26 June 2003 concerning common rules for the internal market in natural gas and repealing Directive 98/30/EC, OJ 2003, L 176/57.
Directive 2008/6/EC of the European Parliament and of the Council of 20 February 2008 amending Directive 97/67/EC with regard to the full accomplishment of the internal market of Community postal services, OJ L 52, 27.2.2008.
Dziadykiewicz, E. (2007), 'Refusal to grant third-party access by an electricity transmission system operator: Overview of competition law issues', *Journal of Energy and Natural Resources Law*, **25**(2), 114–49.
ECORYS (2008), 'Main developments in the postal sector (2006–2008), report for the EC', September.
Eisenkopf, A. (2006), 'The liberalization of rail transport in the EU', *Intereconomics*, **41**(6), 293–313.
European Commission, Notice on the application of the competition rules to the postal sector and on the assessment of certain State measures relating to postal services, OJ, 98/C 39/02.
European Commission, Report from the Commission to the European Parliament and the Council on the implementation of the first railways package, COM(2006) 189 final, May 2006
European Commission, Staff working document, accompanying the proposal for the Third Postal Directive, Impact assessment, COM (2006), 594 final, October 2006.
European Commission, Recommendation 2003/311/EC of 11 February 2003, OJ 2003/C 114/45, replaced by Recommendation 2007/879/EC on relevant product and service markets within the electronic communications sector susceptible to *ex ante* regulation of 17 December 2007, OJ 2007/L 344/65.
European Commission, Report from the Commission to the Council and the European Parliament on the application of the Postal Directive (Directive 97/67/EC as amended by Directive 2002/39/EC), COM(2008) 884 final, December 2008.
European Commission, Communication from the Commission – Community guidelines on State aid for railway undertakings, OJ, C 184/13, 22 July 2008.
European Regulators' Group (2004), Common Position on the approach to appropriate remedies in the new regulatory framework, § 1.2.1, ERG (03) 30rev1.
Frontier Economics (2005), 'Process and costs of misdirected mail – a report prepared for Postcomm', April.
Hatzopoulos, V. (2006), 'The EU Essential Facilities Doctrine', Research Papers in Law, 6, College of Europe, Brugge and Natolin.

Helberger, N. (2007), 'Some critical reflections about access obligations under the European Community Framework', *Communication and Strategies*, **58**, 2nd quarter, pp. 1–100.
Hooper, R., D. Hutton and I. Smith (2008), 'Modernise or decline. Policies to maintain the universal postal service in the United Kingdom', An independent review of the UK postal services sector, 16 December.
ICT Regulation Toolkit (2009), Joint production of infoDev and the International Telecommunication Union.
Jones, Chr. (2006), *EU Energy Law: The Internal Energy Market*, Monograph, Belgium: Claeys & Casteels.
Koumpli, V. (2007), 'Competition rules or sector-specific regulation for the liberalization of the European electricity markets? With reference to the English, Greek and German third-party access regimes', *Journal of Energy and Natural Resources Law*, **25**(2), 168–85.
Kroes, N. (2009), 'The interface between regulation and competition law', paper presented at the Bundeskartellamt conference on 'Dominant Companies – The Thin Line between Regulation and Competition Law', Hamburg, 28 April available at: http://europa.eu/rapid/pressReleasesAction.do?reference = SPEECH/09/202&format = HTML&aged = 0&language = EN&guiLanguage=en.
Moriarty, R. and P. Smith (2005), 'Barriers to entry in post and regulatory responses', in M.A. Crew and P.R. Kleindorfer (eds), *Regulatory and Economic Challenges in the Postal and Delivery Sector*, Boston, MA: Kluwer Academic, pp. 101–200.
Nikolinakos, N. (2006), *EU Competition Law and Regulation in the Converging Telecommunications Media and IT Sectors*, Monograph, Kluwer Law International – International Competition Law Series.
OECD Round Tables (2007), 'Energy Security and Competition Policy', DAF/COMP(2007)35.
Panzar, John C. (2008), 'Interaction between regulatory and antitrust policies in a liberalized postal sector', in M.A. Crew, P.R. Kleindorfer and J.I. Campbell (eds), *Handbook of Worldwide Postal Reform*, Cheltenham, UK and Northampton, MA, USA: Edward Elgar, pp. 20–27.
Plaut Economics (2007), 'Opening postal markets in Switzerland. Monopolistic bottlenecks, technical co-ordination and social regulations', Olten, January.
Postcomm (2005), 'Postal Code of Practice for Common Operational Procedures – a decision document', August.
Postcomm (2006), 'Sharing redirection data', Postcomm's proposals to facilitate a multi-operator redirection service, August.
PricewaterhouseCoopers (PWC) (2006), 'The Impact on Universal Service of the Full Market Accomplishment of the Postal Internal Market in 2009', Final Report, Study commissioned by the European Commission, Brussels.

3. National regulation of postal services under the 2008 EU Postal Services Directive

Richard Eccles

1 INTRODUCTION

The EU Postal Services Directive 2008 (Directive 2008/6, 'the 2008 Directive')[1] marks the coming of age of European postal legislation. Not only, as is well known, does the 2008 Directive require full liberalization by Member States, but it also for the first time introduces important counterbalancing measures to support the universal service provider (USP) with regard to pricing and compensation. This is essential in order to safeguard the continuing primary objective of the EU Postal Services Directive as originally introduced in 1997[2] and amended in 2002 (by Directive 2002/39,[3] 'the 2002 Directive') – the permanent provision of the universal service. The 1997 Directive as amended by the 2002 and 2008 Directives, will now be referred to as 'the Directive'.

The 2008 Directive emphasizes that, in a liberalized environment, USPs must as far as possible be allowed to set prices in accordance with normal commercial conditions, and must be allowed pricing flexibility in line with the general principle of cost-orientation. The scope of the uniform tariff obligation is now to be limited to, essentially, single-piece tariff items (stamps and metered mail) under the 2008 Directive. The pricing flexibility for USPs in respect of the provision of downstream access is also increased and the 2008 Directive allows us to see competition law as the main source of pricing control in this area going forward. The Directive requires the introduction at national level of mechanisms to compensate the USP for any unfair financial burden of the net costs of providing the universal service, either by means of a compensation fund or a cost-sharing mechanism as between postal operators. Moreover, the 2008 Directive introduces a restructured and fuller set of provisions regarding the extent to which universal service obligations, obligations of similar effect, and other quality or standards obligations respectively, can be imposed on USPs and other operators. The 2008 Directive thus imposes much clearer obligations on national postal regulatory authorities that must be taken into account in the exercise of regulatory powers at national level.

A key question which continues under the 2008 Directive, which dates back to the original 1997 Directive, is the question of the scope of the universal service obligation (USO) under the Directive, and the extent to which national authorities could or should define the universal service broadly or narrowly at national level in the light of the services and requirements of the EU Directive. The reforms that are introduced by the 2008 Directive bring this question into sharper focus.

The Directive is and should be seen as the over-riding source of postal regulation in all of the EU Member States. Its primary purpose continues to be to safeguard the permanent provision of the universal postal service to specified levels in all of the Member States. Liberalization, as distinct from the promotion of competition is an additional objective. Moreover, the principles of the EU law as established in the jurisprudence of the European Court of Justice (ECJ) demonstrate that actions or measures adopted by national regulatory authorities which are inconsistent with the EU Directive are open to challenge in national courts by a USP or any other affected postal operator. This could be by means of defense to enforcement action taken by the regulator or by means of direct challenge on appeal or through judicial review action to an exercise of the regulator's powers.

Section 2 below assesses the provisions of the Directive, especially the 2008 Directive, concerning price controls on USPs, with regard to affordability, cost orientation and uniform tariffs, respectively. Section 3 reviews the position concerning downstream access, Section 4 covers the scope of the USO and quality of service obligations, and Section 5 explains the position regarding compensation for any unfair financial burden of the USO, under the Directive and in particular the 2008 Directive. Section 6 reviews the significance of EU case law concerning the direct effect of provisions of EU directives, in relation to the Directive, and Section 7 sets out the overall conclusions.

2 INCREASED PRICING FLEXIBILITY FOR USPs

The 2008 Directive has clarified the requirements on Member States in a liberalized environment to ensure that the universal service is provided in conditions of financial equilibrium.[4] It is well established under EU law that services of general interest should be allowed to be provided in conditions of economic equilibrium.[5] This term is not defined in ECJ judgments, but is understood to mean self-financing of the full actual costs of providing the relevant service.

Under the 2008 Directive, universal service prices must be affordable and must be cost oriented (replacing the previous 'geared to costs' requirement). Any uniform tariff obligation must be restricted to single-piece items.[6] USPs are to be allowed pricing flexibility, in line with the requirement of cost orientation, as regards the provision of services for businesses or bulk mailers and consolidators of mail from different users.[7]

Affordability

The primary obligation in the Directive concerning universal service pricing, is a requirement of affordability of USO prices. The Directive sets out no definition of affordability, nor does it prescribe how affordability should be measured or determined. Moreover, affordability will often be represented by a range of prices rather than a single price level. A regulator should not conclude that a price level is outside the range of affordability without taking a fully informed and reasoned decision taking into account all relevant socioeconomic factors. Indeed, one could argue that price controls imposed by a national regulator would be incompatible with the Directive if and insofar as they could not be shown to be based on an objective assessment of both affordability (in the economic and social context) and cost orientation.

Affordability is linked to cost orientation, but cost orientation of prices will not automatically constitute affordable prices, depending on the efficiency levels of the USP. The Member States take various different approaches to price regulation to achieve the affordability objective, ranging from controls linked to the rate of inflation as measured by a retail or consumer price index, price caps and cost-related controls, based on past or future costs. This is shown in two studies prepared for the European Commission by WIK-Consult in 2006[8] and by ECORYS in 2008.[9] Where Member States use controls based on a price index, they are in effect treating recent price levels as a starting point in determining affordability, on the basis of past readiness of consumers to purchase postal services. Such an application of the affordability criteria is then a matter of limiting increases in prices rather than imposing absolute price levels. However, this approach can be called into question, in an environment of declining postal volumes, especially if this is combined with an increasing need for modernization on the part of the USP, resulting in increased costs to be recovered from lower levels of consumption.

USPs can clearly argue that they have a legal right to ensure that their prices for USO services must be allowed to cover the full cost of the service provision, whether or not those costs represent fully achievable efficiency. The Directive does not require prices to be oriented to the costs of an efficient operator, but only the actual costs of the USP.

On this basis, USO prices which reflect the actual full costs of service provision should at least not be disallowed on grounds of affordability, in the absence of full enquiry and a reasoned decision on the part of the regulator to the effect that the resulting prices are not affordable.

The Geared to Costs or Cost-orientation Requirement

There is considerable ECJ case law on the meaning of 'cost-oriented' pricing under EU directives, derived in particular from the telecommunications sector. The leading authority on this issue is the judgment of the ECJ in the *Arcor* case[10] which specifically concerned the interpretation of the regulatory requirement for cost orientation of tariffs for unbundled access to the local loop under EC Regulation 2887/2000 (Article 3(3)). The ECJ ruled that in determining cost-oriented prices, national regulatory authorities have to take account of actual costs, namely costs already paid by the incumbent and also forward-looking costs based, where relevant, on an estimation of the costs of replacing the network or certain parts of it.[11] In setting the tariffs, account must be taken of the incumbent operator's costs and investments in putting its infrastructures in place and also the interest on capital invested and depreciation of fixed assets deployed for the initial implementation of the local loop infrastructure.[12] Further, the tariffs must enable a reasonable return to the incumbent in order to ensure the long-term development and upgrade of existing infrastructures.[13] A similar approach was taken by the ECJ in the *Mobistar* case[14] which concerned the setting of cost-oriented prices for the implementation of number portability. Cost-oriented pricing therefore refers to the full costs rather than the variable or incremental costs only. There is an exception where pricing by reference to full costs would result in an unjust benefit in the form of an excessive offset of the original costs to the incumbent, as shown by the *KPN Telecom* case.[15] However, the national regulator must set prices on the basis of actual costs in setting cost-oriented prices, reflecting the full investment in and depreciation of the relevant infrastructure, including a reasonable return to the incumbent.

The ECJ stated the more general requirement, in the *Arcor* case, that in applying the requirement of cost orientation 'account must be taken not only of the wording of that principle but also of its context and the objectives pursued by the legislation laying down that principle'.[16] As a basic premise, any universal service will not be viable in the medium to long term (the Directive requires the permanent provision of a universal service) if the revenue from such services does not cover the full costs attributable to the provision of those services, including the costs of investments in maintaining and modernizing the infrastructure used in providing the universal service. This applies whether or not the regulator provides incentives for increased efficiency over that timeframe. The universal postal service could not be provided in the medium to long term, and could not be provided permanently as required by the Directive, if the universal service revenue did not cover the fully distributed costs or full costs however defined of setting up, providing and renewing the required infrastructure.

The purpose of assessing the full cost of service provision is quite different here from the purpose of measuring the existence of a cross-subsidy in relation to a competitive service. In this regard the incremental costs (long-run incremental costs) may be relevant to determine whether the pricing for the competitive service is viable on a standalone basis (that is, without cross-subsidy from a protected or monopoly service).[17]

As against fully distributed costing, economists may argue that it is unreliable, that it involves a formulaic attribution of common costs which is inefficient, and that it requires comprehensive accounting data to be implemented. Despite these difficulties, the Directive maintains a set of requirements on cost accounting for USPs which are based on principles of fully allocated costing and which form a platform for assessing the cost orientation of USO pricing under the Directive and also for assessing the existence of any cross-subsidization under competition law. Under these requirements and Article 14, USPs are required to operate internal accounting systems on the basis of consistently applied and objectively justifiable cost accounting principles.[18] These accounting systems must allocate costs in accordance with specified principles (in Article 14(2)) as follows:

1. Under the 2002 Directive, USPs must keep separate accounts within their internal accounting systems at least for each of the services within the reserved sector on the one hand and for the non-reserved services on the other; second, such accounts kept by universal services providers for non-reserved services must distinguish between services which are part of the universal service and other services.
2. Under the 2008 Directive, following the abolition of the reservable area, the above requirements for separate accounting in relation to reserved area and non-reserved area activities are replaced by a single requirement on USPs to keep separate accounts distinguishing between services which are part of the universal service and those which are not.

Article 14(3) requires allocation (for accounting purposes) not only of direct costs but also of all common costs, either on the basis of direct analysis of the origin of the costs, use of an indirect linkage to a cost category or group of costs categories, or where no other such method is possible, using a pro rata allocation basis.

The practical position is that the requirement for fully distributed costing under the Directive is generally not fulfilled. The two studies for the European Commission, by

WIK-Consult in 2006[19] and by ECORYS in 2008[20] drew attention to the fact that the regulatory system envisaged in the Directive depends upon the USP maintaining separate accounts for each relevant service within the universal service. Both studies confirmed that this approach has not been fully implemented and that it is at best questionable whether national regulatory authorities have sufficient data to apply the requirements of orienting prices to costs for *each* service within the universal service as required by Article 12 and Article 14(2) of the Directive.

In any event, there is solid support for the principle that the costs of the universal service for the purposes of the 'geared to costs' and cost-orientation requirements (under the 2002 and 2008 Directives, respectively) are the fully distributed costs. A study carried out by the economists CTcon for the European Commission (DG Markt) of July 2001, 'on the cost accounting systems of providers of the universal postal service', observed that 13 of the then 15 USPs in the EU were using fully distributed costing for the universal service (p. 42).

The CTcon study concluded firmly that fully distributed costing is appropriate for price regulation of postal businesses. The paper stated the following:

> Regulating according to the Directive means that prices should be 'geared to costs'. Costs should be understood as fully distributed costs because prices shall cover total costs. Partly distributed costing methods like direct costing or allocating efficient costs would allow the universal service provider to set prices due to his subjective decision. Therefore, partly distributed costing methods are not useful for price regulations. (p. 60)

CTcon recommended that 'geared to costs' under Article 12 of the Directive should be defined as 'geared to fully distributed costs', where Article 14(3) sets allocation rules. The margin for profit may be different for different services but shall be equal for customers using the same services.

CTcon further concluded that the long-run incremental costs (LRIC) test is not a useful basis for price regulation. Although the LRIC test is referred to as an appropriate test for identifying adverse cross-subsidy (p. 53), for purposes of price regulation it is stated that fully distributed costs have to be taken into account and that LRIC is not an appropriate test (p. 54): 'For setting prices the long run incremental costs are a floor which should not be undercut, at least not for a long period of time. However, a price floor is not a price'. CTcon stated in summary: 'All objectives of managing the postal business . . . can be covered very well by an application of activity-based fully distributed costing', with total costs being split between direct and common costs, and common costs being split between variable and fixed costs.[21]

Other regulators have previously concluded in favor of fully distributed costing as a basis for USO price controls. The Swedish National Post and Telecom Agency previously stated[22] that the fully distributed costs method has the advantage of enabling calculated costs to be verified against the annual accounts, despite the arbitrariness of the allocation of overheads and other common costs, as well as the historical nature of the costs considered. The Irish regulator, the Office of the Director of Telecommunications Regulation (now ComReg) issued a consultation paper in November 2002[23] which stated that the 'geared to costs' principle would be monitored on the basis of the USP's fully distributed costs, including depreciation, until such time as a (different) consensus had emerged throughout Europe on how these principles should be defined. The same paper also stated that one purpose of the 'geared to costs' principle is to ensure that services are not priced 'below cost' (so as to keep potential competitors out of the market or to risk doing so).[24]

Taking all these factors into account, a USP has a strong argument for asserting, especially in the liberalized environment introduced by the 2008 Directive, that its prices should not be limited by the national regulatory authority unless it can be shown that prices demonstrably do not reflect the fully allocated cost of service provision using the specific formula laid down in Article 14 of the EU Postal Directive and taking into account the best accounting information available to the regulator, or that the prices are *not affordable* by reference to an objective and reasoned socioeconomic assessment of relative price levels. Moreover, the USP has an especially strong argument that its USO prices must not be limited at a level below the fully distributed costs (calculated as far as possible in accordance with the method set out in Article 14 of the Directive) in the absence of such a reasoned and objective assessment by the regulator concluding that such prices would be outside the range of affordability.

The Limitation of the Uniform Tariff Obligation under the 2008 Directive

The maintenance of a uniform tariff obligation clearly results in a loss of pricing flexibility and removes the ability of a USP to reflect the differential costs required to deliver in different areas, for example urban versus rural areas. A uniform tariff obligation therefore introduces a deviation from the normal principle of cost-reflective pricing, with the potential for market distortion. Indeed, the Directive requirement that prices be 'geared to costs' ('cost-oriented' under the 2008 Directive) can only be achieved by reference to a nationwide assessment while a uniform tariff obligation remains in force.

The 2008 Directive requires that any uniform tariff obligation be limited to (basically) single-piece tariff mail (that is, mainly stamps and franked mail).[25] As a result, while a uniform tariff obligation can be imposed on stamps and metered mail, it cannot in future be maintained in respect of bulk mail. Even with this reduced scope of uniform tariff obligation, however, there is a residual level of distortion of the price–cost relationship on a geographic basis, by comparison with competing postal operators which have complete freedom to adjust their prices on a route-by-route basis.

The reduction in permitted scope of the uniform tariff obligation is directly related to full liberalization, that is, the prohibition and abolition of the reserved area. On this basis, it might be argued that the national authorities of those Member States which have already achieved full liberalization should already interpret their national law and regulation concerning the uniform tariff in a manner that conforms with the 2008 Directive, that is, so as to limit the scope of the uniform tariff to single-piece items (and to books and newspapers) in accordance with the Directive. This is by way of exception to the general EU law obligation on Member States to implement EU directives and to interpret national legislation in accordance with any EU directives only as from the required implementation date under the directive. In the present context full liberalization at any stage (as already achieved in Finland, Germany, Sweden and the UK) constitutes implementation of the Directive, but moreover incomplete implementation, if the uniform tariff obligation is not reduced in scope at national level in accordance with the 2008 Directive.

3 DOWNSTREAM ACCESS TO THE USP POSTAL NETWORKS

The relevant provisions of the Postal Services Directive concerning downstream access to the postal network are set out in Article 12 (fifth indent) and recital 39 of the 2008 Directive. The Postal Services Directive (as amended by the 2002 Directive) requires the following: 'Whenever universal service providers apply special tariffs, for example, services for businesses, bulk mailers or consolidators of mail from different customers, they shall apply the principles of transparency and non-discrimination with regard both to the tariffs and to the associated conditions'.[26] This provision also requires that the tariffs 'shall apply equally both as between different third parties and as between third parties and the universal service providers supplying equivalent services'.

It can be seen from this provision that the Directive does not require the provision of downstream access. Rather, where a universal service provider elects to provide special terms or discounts based on work-sharing, for downstream access, a USP is required to abide by a comprehensive non-discrimination requirement ensuring equivalence as between, first, direct access (bulk mail) customers, second, consolidators or competing operators, and third, the USP's own equivalent (upstream) services. This ensures a degree of equivalence as between the incumbent's own services and those of competitors and also direct access customers.

Article 12 of the Directive as amended by the 2002 Directive required that where access to the USP's postal network is granted under special terms in this way, the tariffs must 'take account of the avoided costs, as compared to the standard service covering a complete range of features offered for the clearance, transport, sorting and delivery of individual postal items'. The 2008 Directive has moved this provision from Article 12 to recital 39 (of the 2008 Directive). There, the requirement to take account of the *avoided costs* is set out in the context of a statement within recital 39, as follows: 'For the provision of services for all users including businesses, bulk mailers and consolidators of mail from different users, universal service providers *may enjoy more price flexibility* in line with the cost-orientation principles' (emphasis added).

Recital 39 of the 2008 Directive sets out the principle, which is relevant under the general requirements of purposive interpretation of the EU Directives, that regulators take into account the avoided cost (as compared with the full standard postal service) when setting any price controls for downstream access services. This does not mandate a retail-minus approach to price setting, but should prevent a different approach being used without at least taking into account the avoided costs approach. Moreover, the report by ECORYS for the European Commission[27] observed that in EU Member States where downstream access is mandated, generally the avoided cost approach to access pricing is followed, and that the UK is the only Member State where it was not followed. The ECORYS study stated (p. 69):

> Most countries with mandatory access adopted the principle that access prices should be based on the retail prices minus the avoided cost of the NPO [national postal operator]. It seems that only Postcomm in the UK is in favour of linking the access prices to the cost of downstream delivery. The difference between the two methods is that in the latter no compensation for the fixed costs upstream at the point of injecting the access mail is included.

Having regard to the pricing flexibility required under the 2008 Directive for USPs, including for the provision of downstream access, it can be expected that the EU competition rules on margin squeeze (pursuant to Article 82 EC on abuse of dominant position) will be the main basis for controlling downstream access prices. In the UK, the current approach taken to controlling downstream access prices has been regulation based, through the maintenance of a 'headroom margin' under Royal Mail's operating license[28] under the Postal Services Act 2002. This approach to regulation has not been based, or has certainly not been directly based on cost-orientation principles but rather on the maintenance of a historical differential between the retail price of each regulated service of Royal Mail and the price for the corresponding access service, respectively.

The key features for the competition law test to identify a margin squeeze or price squeeze are as follows: first, two distinct markets must be in existence (an upstream market and a downstream market); second, a vertically integrated undertaking must be dominant in the upstream market and active (whether or not also dominant) in the downstream market; third, operators on the downstream market must have a *need* for access to an input from the upstream market in order to operate in that downstream market; fourth, the essence of the margin squeeze is the existence of a relationship between the dominant company's upstream and downstream prices which excludes the ability of an 'equally efficient competitor' to compete downstream, by reference to the long-run incremental cost of the dominant operator. (This is by reference to the judgment of the European Court of First Instance in the *Deutsche Telekom*[29] case and the decision of the European Commission in *Telefónica*).[30] As stated by the European Commission in *Telefónica*,[31] the test is one of 'whether a competitor having the same cost function as the downstream arm of the vertically integrated company is able to be profitable in the downstream market given the wholesale and retail prices levied by the vertically integrated company'.

One of the ingredients of margin squeeze is the dependence of competitors on access to an upstream input from the vertically integrated operator. On this basis, it could be argued that once a competitor establishes a competitive bypass end-to-end system on a viable basis, a competition law margin squeeze cannot occur because the actions of the bypass competitor demonstrate that it is possible to establish an alternative downstream delivery network rather than relying on the USP's. One of the required components of the margin squeeze test would then not be fulfilled. However, caution needs to be exercised. In its *Telefónica* decision, the European Commission rejected the significance of an alternative means of delivering broadband services for the following reasons: Telefónica had a regulatory duty to supply the upstream inputs (network access), which resulted from a balancing by the public authorities of the incentives of Telefónica and its competitors to invest and innovate, and because the need to promote downstream competition in the longer term by imposing access to Telefónica's upstream inputs exceeded the need to preserve Telefónica's *ex ante* incentives to invest in its upstream infrastructures.[32]

Despite these considerations, the assessment of whether there could be a margin squeeze in relation to postal network access pricing, could be decided differently, in a situation where a competitor had in fact already replicated the downstream elements of the overall end-to-end postal service. The stronger and more widespread that bypass competition might become, the stronger this argument could be. However it is likely that bypass competition will become established in the foreseeable future only in respect of certain types of routes, for example urban to urban routes. This could then leave open the question of whether the margin squeeze test should be applied only in relation to routes or types of routes not covered by the bypass network, such as urban to rural or rural to rural routes, because for these types of routes access to the USP's network would still be a necessary input for competing operators.

In any event, the competition law margin squeeze test requires full account to be taken of the relevant costs of the incumbent. To this extent it is consistent with the cost-orientation principle of the Directive. Also, the use of competition law rather than specific regulatory conditions is more consistent with the pricing flexibility that is to be allowed for a USP in a liberalized environment, which is a clear objective of the 2008 Directive.

4 THE SCOPE OF THE USO AND QUALITY OF SERVICE OBLIGATIONS

The definition of the scope of the USO is, under the 2008 Directive, more central than ever to the regulation of postal services. This definition determines the following: first, the extent to which the affordability requirement and cost-oriented price controls can be imposed on the USP; second, the extent to which other operators could be considered to be providing services 'within the scope' of the universal service so as to be subject to the imposition of quality and performance obligations under Article 9(2); third, the scope of activities which should be taken into account in assessing any net cost to and any unfair financial burden on the USP which could be made the subject of any compensation fund or cost-sharing mechanism; and fourth, the scope of any services provided by other operators which could be considered to be 'within the scope of' the USO so as to give rise to a possible financial obligation under such a cost-sharing mechanism.

The Directive, while not specifying the precise scope of the USO, requires only that Member States ensure that the activities described in Article 3 of the Directive are performed by the designated USP(s). It is entirely consistent with this approach and with the need to ensure a sustainable universal postal service in a liberalized environment that the scope of the USO be limited to sufficient products to fulfill the requirement of Article 3 of the Directive while allowing other products which comprise similar activities of the USP to remain outside the USO and therefore to be provided free of the USO constraints on standards and pricing. This would achieve the basic Directive objective of ensuring that all users enjoy a specified level of universal service in accordance with Article 3(1) of the Directive.

In many Member States, a broad approach has been taken to the definition of the USO so as to include all or most specific services which correspond to the general requirements of Article 3 of the Directive. This tends to maximize the national regulator's powers of regulation. However, in a fully liberalized environment in which the USP is faced with competition from other operators which are free of the constraints of USO regulation, it is logical for the national regulator to consider reducing the scope of the USO to the extent necessary to ensure that private consumers and small businesses receive the essential basic postal services they require, on a regulated basis, without extending such USO regulation to all of the USP's products and services which fall within the broad range described by Article 3 of the Directive. The broader the scope of the USO, the more at risk the USP could be in a liberalized environment of being unable to fulfill the USO in conditions of financial equilibrium, depending on the extent of price and performance controls imposed by the national regulator.

Article 3 of the Directive requires Member States to ensure that the USP provides a minimum level of universal service, in particular the provision of, every working day and not less than five days a week (amended to read 'not less than five working days a week' in the 2008 Directive), one clearance and one delivery to the home or premises of every natural legal person, in respect of postal items of up to 2kg, postal packages up to 10kg (or 20kg at the option of the national regulatory authorities) and services for registered items and insured items.[33] USPs must also ensure that the universal service complies with the *essential requirements* (confidentiality of correspondence, security of the network and, where justified, data protection, environmental protection and regional planning), offers an identical service to users under comparable conditions, is made available without any discrimination, is uninterrupted, and evolves in response to technical, economic and social environments and to the needs of users.[34]

The imposition of specific USOs on other licensed operators is allowed under the Directive as amended by the 2002 Directive, but this is excluded under the 2008 Directive. In this respect, the 2008 Directive imposes two clear limitations. First, Article 9(2) is amended to provide that 'universal service obligations' and the minimum obligations comprising the universal service as defined in Article 3 can only be imposed on a designated USP. Second, recital 23 makes it clear that where Member States designate more than one USP, they may only do so in order for the two or more designated operators to provide different elements of the universal service or to cover different parts of the national territory, but may not allow the USOs of different operators to overlap. Thus the 2008 Directive prevents Member States from imposing USOs (as referred to in Articles 3 or 9(2)) on more than one operator for the same part of the territory (or for the same service elements).

However, Article 9(2) (as amended by the 2008 Directive) does allow for the imposition of quality and performance obligations on operators other than the USP in respect of services which 'fall within the scope of the universal service', in order to guarantee compliance with the essential requirements and to ensure the provision of the universal service. This in turn raises the question of which service providers are operating within the scope of the universal service. Recital 27 states that Member States should assess

> whether the services provided by such undertakings may from a user's perspective be regarded as services falling within the scope of the universal service, as they display inter-changeability to a sufficient degree with the universal service, taking into account the characteristics of the services, including added value features, such as the intended use and the pricing. These services do not necessarily have to cover all the features of the universal service such as daily delivery or complete national coverage.

Quality or performance obligations on operators within the scope of the universal service could include a daily delivery obligation. Clearly another operator providing services within the scope of the universal service would gain a distinct competitive advantage if it were allowed to make deliveries only two or three days per week instead of five or six days per week, in terms of operational cost savings resulting from such a reduced level of service. While the imposition of quality or performance obligations on a postal operator other than the USP under Article 9(2) would need to be sufficiently differentiated from universal service obligations, there appears to be a good argument that a daily delivery obligation (that is, an obligation to deliver at least five working days per week) would be a valid quality or performance obligation imposed on service providers operating within the scope of the universal service, provided that the delivery obligation is not expressed to extend to the premises of every natural or legal person in the country (as would be required for a USP under Article 3(3)).

It would also need to be demonstrated that the imposition of such quality and performance obligations is proportionate to the need to ensure the provision of the universal service (or compliance with the essential requirements). If such obligations were merely a disguised means of protecting the USP against the effects of liberalization, their validity under the Directive could be called into question. Also, before imposing such quality or performance obligations, the national authorities would need to be able to demonstrate that the USO could not be adequately safeguarded by alternative, less intrusive means such as relaxation or removal of universal service price controls or the uniform tariff obligation.

The provisions of the 2008 Directive combine to demonstrate a clear need for Member States to define the appropriate scope of the USO within a liberalized environment and to make a proper assessment of the impact of liberalization on the ability of the USP to ensure the permanent provision of the universal service.

5 COMPENSATION FOR ANY UNFAIR FINANCIAL BURDEN OF THE USO

National regulatory authorities may make any authorization to providers of services falling within the scope of the universal service, under Article 9(2), subject to an obligation to make a financial contribution to a cost-sharing fund. For this purpose, the national authorities must determine that the USO entails a net cost which represents an unfair financial burden on the USP. They may then introduce a compensation mechanism benefiting the USP from public funds, or a mechanism for sharing such net cost as between other service providers and/or users. Thus Article 9(2) of the 2008 Directive gives Member States considerable options to ensure a level playing field to protect the performance of the USO, by imposing quality and performance obligations on operators providing services within the scope of the universal service, or by requiring such operators to contribute to a cost-sharing mechanism to compensate the USP for any unfair financial burden of the costs of the USO. However, Recital 33 of the 2008 Directive makes clear that Member States may not require such operators both to contribute financially to the costs of the universal service and also to meet quality obligations that are intended to have the same purpose as universal service obligations. Thus national regulatory authorities can require operators providing services within the scope of the universal service to 'pay' or 'play' in respect of the universal service, but not both, when exercising their powers under Article 9(2) of the 2008 Directive.

The conditions for a Member State and its regulatory authorities to provide a compensation fund or cost-sharing mechanism to benefit the USP (and thus provide protection from the loss of the reserved sector) are set out in Article 7 and Annex I of the 2008 Directive.

The calculation of the net cost of the USO, for the purpose of determining whether the USO poses an unfair financial burden on the USP, is a far from straightforward matter for a national regulatory authority under the 2008 Directive. The criteria for calculating the net costs of the USO (set out in Annex I) focus on the difference between the net cost of the USP operating with the USO and the same postal service provider operating without the USO. The calculation must take into account all other relevant elements including any intangible and market benefits which accrue to a service provider designated as USP, plus the entitlement of a reasonable profit and incentives for cost efficiency. Due attention is to be given to correctly assessing the costs that any designated USP would have chosen to avoid had there been no USO. The net cost calculation must assess the benefits, including intangible benefits, to the USP. This calculation is far more than an accounting exercise, involving as it does assessment of the counterfactual, that is, if the position of the USP were not required to fulfill the USO, and intangible benefits of being a USP.

All Member States and their regulatory authorities have a primary obligation under the Directive to ensure the permanent provision of the universal service, which must mean the provision of the USO in conditions of long-term financial equilibrium.

Therefore if regulatory conditions are maintained in a manner too onerous for the USP to be able to fulfill the USO on a permanent, long-term basis, the national authorities of a Member State must find a means of making this possible, by relaxing price controls and other regulatory controls to allow the USP sufficient flexibility to react to competition and to fulfill its USO obligations in conditions of financial equilibrium. Alternatively or in addition, the national authorities should impose performance obligations on other operators providing services within the scope of the universal service, and/or determine the net cost and any resulting unfair financial burden to the USP, and implement a compensation fund or cost-sharing mechanism accordingly. In any event, national regulatory authorities need to limit their intervention against the USP, in accordance with the Directive, by ensuring that the regulatory regime, together with any compensation fund or cost-sharing mechanism, allows a level playing field between the USP and other operators.

6 THE DIRECT EFFECT OF THE EU POSTAL SERVICES DIRECTIVE AT NATIONAL LEVEL

A national postal regulator's discretion in setting and applying license conditions is constrained by the obligations on Member States in the Postal Services Directive. Supremacy of EU law requires national regulators to apply the Directive.

EU directives are generally addressed to Member States and do not at the outset create obligations which are enforceable by individuals, companies or undertakings. However, Member States and all national authorities have an EU law duty to implement the provisions of a directive into national law by the date specified by the Directive. Where the Member State has failed properly to implement such provisions by the required date, those provisions of a directive which are *unconditional* and *sufficiently precise* are capable of direct effect and direct enforcement against the relevant Member State authorities by individuals, companies and undertakings. This is well established in the case law of the ECJ.[35] A postal operator, including a USP or a new entrant postal operator, could take action (in appropriate cases) to enforce relevant provisions of the Directive which are unconditional and sufficiently precise against the relevant Member State authority, including a national postal authority.

The logic of allowing direct effect of appropriate provisions of directives which have not been implemented by the Member States on time is that the Member State and national authorities should not be allowed to benefit from the state's failure to fulfill its EU obligations of transposing the directive into national law. EU directives are addressed to Member States, not to individuals or other legal persons.

In addition, national courts and authorities are under an EU law duty to interpret national laws and regulations in a manner which is as far as possible consistent with a relevant EU directive, based on the *Von Colson*[36] and *Marleasing*[37] judgments of the ECJ. On this basis, national postal legislation and regulatory measures in the postal sector must be interpreted as far as possible consistently with the Directive.

Any postal operator, including a USP, which is affected by actions by a national postal regulator which are in breach of the requirements of the Directive, can invoke EU law in its defense to any enforcement action taken at national level by the regulator. Failure to respect the requirements of the Directive could constitute grounds for appeal by the affected postal operator against an enforcement decision, to the courts. The courts also have the power to refer a question of interpretation of EU law, such as an issue of interpretation of a relevant EU directive, to the ECJ for a ruling on the point of EU law under Article 234 EC, where this is necessary to enable judgment to be given. The ECJ ruling would then have to be applied to the national court to the facts of the case.

Insofar as the relevant provisions of the Directive are sufficiently precise and unconditional, a national postal regulator is required under EU law, as a state authority, to give effect to those provisions in the adoption and enforcement of regulatory conditions. In exercising delegated powers under postal legislation, it is required to comply with the directly effective provisions of the Directive, and would be acting contrary to EU law insofar as it adopts or enforces conditions which are incompatible with such directly effective provisions.

Based on *Marleasing*, national postal regulators have a duty to interpret license conditions, or other regulatory conditions applying to postal operators, in accordance with the provisions of the Directive, where the deadline for national implementation has passed or where the provisions in question have been implemented into national law in advance. Moreover national regulators must also on the same basis interpret and apply the relevant enabling provisions of the applicable national legislation in accordance with the Directive. National legislation should be presumed to have been intended to implement the directive in question. Therefore, powers conferred on a national postal regulator to adopt and apply regulatory conditions should be regarded as being subject at national level to the obligation on Member States to comply with the EU law obligations contained in the Directive.

7 CONCLUSIONS

A national postal regulator would be acting outside its powers if and insofar as it adopts or enforces regulatory conditions which are incompatible with the Directive. Insofar as the provisions of the Directive can be shown to have direct effect (that is, those provisions which are sufficiently precise and unconditional), the regulator will be directly in breach of EU law. Insofar as the provisions in question cannot be given direct effect, where possible the national enabling legislation should be interpreted in accordance with the Directive so that, at national level, a regulator is required to exercise his powers in accordance with the Directive.

The 2008 Directive contains a structure of inter-related provisions all of which need to be taken into account by a regulator in determining, in accordance with national conditions, how best to regulate the USP so as to ensure that the permanent provision of the universal service is safeguarded while at the same time respecting the liberalization objective of the Directive. Now that USPs will no longer be able to rely upon a reserved sector to ensure protected revenue to finance the financial service, there is a greater onus on regulators to take decisions which allow sufficient flexibility to the USP to respond to competition and ensure the continued, economically stable provision of the universal service.

The regulator needs first to define its position on the scope of the universal service, in particular on the question of which services fulfilling the requirements of Article 3 of the Directive should be regulated as being part of the USO, and which services falling within the range of Article 3 activities can be left out of the USO for regulatory purposes, provided that the designated universal services cover all of the requirements of Article 3 of the Directive. This in turn will determine the extent of the affordability, cost orientation, non-discrimination and quality and performance obligations that can be imposed on a USP. Also, within the scope of the USO, the regulator will need to ensure that the USP is allowed to set cost-reflective (cost-oriented) prices in accordance with the Directive, notwithstanding the reduction in overall mail volumes, and the possible further reduction in volumes carried by the USP in the face of competition.

Any price controls based on the affordability requirements must be founded on a full assessment of socioeconomic factors by the regulator, especially if the regulator were to seek to impose price controls below the full cost of service provision, irrespective of considerations of efficiency of the USP. There is also now a greater onus on the regulator to consider imposing quality and performance obligations on other postal operators in order to ensure a sufficiently level playing field. Where the combination of obligations and controls imposed by the regulator and the market conditions together result in the universal service being loss-making, then the regulator can implement a compensation fund or cost-sharing mechanism to protect the USP under Article 7 and Annex I of the Directive. However, the calculation of net cost and unfair financial burden to the USP under Annex I requires consideration of counterfactual and intangible issues and therefore is not straightforward.

In any event EU case law, in particular the judgments of the ECJ, show that the application of the principle of cost orientation as set out in the 2008 Directive means that universal service prices should cover the full costs, meaning the costs of service provision and of investment in the infrastructure needed to provide the services, including the costs of depreciation, maintenance and renewal. Therefore, in order to ensure the permanent provision of the universal service based on cost-oriented tariffs as required by the Directive, national regulators must allow the USP to set universal service prices that cover these full costs.

A national postal regulator could be in breach of the requirements of the Directive not only by disregarding a specific provision of the Directive, but also by failing to carry out an assessment or process that is expressly or implicitly required by the Directive for the resulting regulatory controls to be justified. It is an underlying purpose of the 2008 Directive that national regulators limit their regulatory interventions in a liberalized market to the extent necessary to ensure that the universal service is safeguarded, but at the same time the 2008 Directive imposes more decision-making requirements on regulators than previously. Also, the opportunities for national regulators to be challenged under EU law will not be reduced, but could be increased, as a result of the 2008 Directive.

NOTES

1. OJ (2008) L52/3.
2. Directive 97/67, OJ (1998) L15/14.
3. OJ (2002) L176/21.
4. See Recital 38.
5. See, for example, the judgment of the ECJ in *Case C-320/91, Corbeau [1993] ECR I-2533* at paragraph 19.
6. By reference to Recital 38, the uniform tariff can also be maintained in respect of other postal items, in particular newspapers and books, where it is necessary to protect the general public interest and democratic values such as the freedom of the press.
7. Recital 39.
8. 'Main developments in the postal sector (2004–2006)', May 2006, p. 79.
9. 'Main developments in the postal sector (2006–2008)', 11 September 2008, Appendix 1.
10. *Case C-55/06, Arcor KG & Co. KG v. Bundesrepublik Deutschland, Deutsche Telekom AG* intervening judgment of 24 April 2008.
11. Paragraph 119.
12. Paragraphs 65, 72 and 84.
13. Paragraph 69.
14. *Case C-438/04, Mobistar SA v Institut belge des services postaux et des còmmunicatiòns (IBPT), Belgacom Mobile SA and Base SA* intervening judgment of 13 July 2006.
15. *Case C-109/03, KPN Telecom BV v OPTA in the presence of Denda Multimedia BV and Denda Directory Services BV*, judgment of 25 November 2004.
16. Paragraph 57.
17. *Case COMP/35.141 – Deutsche Post AG*, Commission Decision of 20 March 2001, OJ (2001) L125/27.
18. Article 14(3).
19. 'Main developments in the postal sector (2004–2006)', May 2006.
20. 'Main developments in the postal sector (2006–2008)', 11 September 2008.
21. The paper further states that prices should be based on actual total costs, not the costs of an efficient operator (p. 49).
22. *Uniform Tariffs and Prices Geared to Costs?*, 1 July 2000.
23. Regulation of Postal Services – Universal Service Obligation, Tariff Principles and miscellaneous issues, Document No. ODTR02/95, 6 November 2002.
24. See sections 5.3 on p. 24, and 5.3.2 on p. 25
25. Article 12, second indent, and recital 38; Member States may also maintain uniform tariffs for some other mail items to protect general public interests, for example, newspapers and books.
26. Article 12, fifth indent.
27. 'Main developments in the postal sector (2006–2008)', 11 September 2008.
28. Condition 21(5).
29. Case T-271/03.
30. *Case COMP/38.784 Wanadoo España vs Telefónica*, Commission Decision of 4 July 2007.
31. Paragraph 315.
32. Paragraphs 303 and 304.
33. Article 3(3) – (5).
34. Article 5(1).
35. See, for example, *Case 8/81 Becker v Finanzamt Munster Innenstadt (1982) (ECR 53)* and *Case 152/84 Marshall v Southampton & South West Hampshire Area Health Authority [1986] ECR 723*.
36. Case 14/83, (1984) ECR 1891.
37. Case C-106/89, (1990) ECR 4135.

4. Abuse of dominance in the postal sector: the contribution of the Guidance Paper on Article 82 EC

Damien Geradin and David Henry

1 INTRODUCTION

On 15 December 2005, the European Commission ('Commission') released a controversial Discussion Paper on Article 82 EC,[1] the provision of the EC Treaty dealing with abuses of a dominant position. This policy document triggered a long and protracted debate not only among competition law experts but also within the Commission itself. The Commission's plan to distance itself from a 'form-based' approach to the enforcement of Article 82 EC, which sits uneasily with modern economic principles, towards an 'effects-based' approach more in line with such principles was welcomed. Some aspects of the Discussion Paper were criticized nonetheless as being unclear, impracticable, or still overly restrictive. Following the Discussion Paper and the ensuing academic debate on Article 82 EC, the Commission published (on 3 December 2008) its somewhat shorter and more wieldy 'Guidance on the Commission's Enforcement Priorities in Applying Article 82 EC Treaty to Abusive Exclusionary Conduct by Dominant Undertakings' ('Guidance Paper'),[2] which essentially sets out the Commission's enforcement priorities with respect to exclusionary abuses.

In line with the approach already taken in the fields of Article 81 EC and merger control,[3] the Commission, through its Guidance Paper, has vowed to take a more effects-based approach to exclusionary abuses by dominant undertakings. This is illustrated by the admissibility of familiar economic concepts such as the efficiency defense and the introduction of the 'equally efficient competitor' test. The core premise of Commission intervention now rests on a finding that a dominant undertaking has engaged in conduct that is likely to lead to anticompetitive foreclosure, that is, exclusionary conduct that is liable to cause consumer harm.

Although there is much merit in the Commission's new approach to exclusionary conduct, it is open to debate whether it goes far enough. One of the limitations of the Guidance Paper is that it fails to provide for 'safe harbors'. For instance, pricing schemes that do not exclude equally efficient competitors because the price set by the dominant firm is above its costs may nevertheless be considered abusive in some circumstances.[4] Hence, (postal) operators whose prices are above their costs cannot be sure that their pricing is not incompatible with Article 82 EC. The Guidance Paper also contains some lacunae as it does not address, for instance, exploitative behavior or price discrimination that are particularly contentious issues under EC competition law. Finally, the nature of the Guidance Paper is ambiguous. The Guidance Paper is not intended to be a statement or interpretation of the law, but instead sets out the Commission's 'enforcement priorities' with respect to Article 82 EC. This raises the issue whether the Commission is bound to apply the principles developed in the Guidance Paper or whether it can apply the more restrictive and formalistic principles contained in the Community courts' case law.

In the context of the postal sector the advent of the Guidance Paper is particularly propitious in light of the crucial changes that are taking place. The recently promulgated Third Postal Directive ('Postal Directive') provides the legal basis for the full market opening of the postal sector,[5] which is to be accomplished by 31 December 2010. A corollary of the abolition of any remaining, exclusive or special rights is that new possibilities for increased competition in the postal sector will be created. At the same time, however, the removal of the reserved sector is likely to increase the frequency of claims by entrants that incumbent postal operators are engaging in abusive behavior to maintain their market power in liberalized markets. With this in mind, the Guidance Paper provides dominant (postal) undertakings with a set of parameters within which they can assess conduct addressed in it, that is, exclusive dealing, tying and bundling, predatory practices, and refusal to supply.

The Chapter is structured as follows. Section 2 reviews the approach taken by the Guidance Paper with respect to the assessment of dominance. Section 3 examines the test that the Guidance Paper intends to apply to determine whether a given practice amounts to anticompetitive foreclosure. Section 4 explores the approaches proposed by the Guidance Paper when addressing the various categories of abuse that may be committed by dominant firms, particularly postal operators. Finally, a short conclusion is provided in Section 5.

2 DOMINANCE

Article 82 EC is applicable where one undertaking has a dominant position or where two or more undertakings hold a collective dominant position[6] on a relevant market.[7] The definition of the relevant market plays a fundamental role in the application of Article 82 EC. The object of defining the relevant market, from both a product and geographic dimension, is to identify those products and services that can be characterized as substitutes for one another and therefore act as a competitive constraint on the behavior of the operators that supply the given product or services in question. As will be seen below, dominance analysis presents several challenges.

In view of the fact that some Member States continue to maintain a reserved sector for the benefit of the incumbent postal operator these operators are inherently in a dominant position.[8] With the recent promulgation of the Postal Directive, defining a dominant position on a relevant postal market will be necessary not only in those parts of the postal sector that are already open to competition (for example, international express delivery) but also in those that are currently, but will soon no longer be, reserved to the incumbent postal operator.

In the Guidance Paper, the concept of dominance is described as a situation whereby the relevant company enjoys substantial market power over a period of time.[9] In line with the 2005 Discussion Paper, the Guidance Paper takes a broad view of dominance analysis in that it indicates that the Commission will review a variety of factors other than market shares to determine whether a firm is dominant on one or several markets. In its assessment of substantial market power, which translates into the ability to charge supra-competitive prices, the Commission relies on three fundamental criteria, namely (i) the market position of the dominant undertaking and its competitors, (ii) the ease with which actual or potential competitors can enter the market, and (iii) countervailing buyer power.[10] These three criteria are in turn briefly discussed in the light of their relevance to the postal sector.

Market Position of the Dominant Undertaking and Its Competitors

Market share is often used as a first screen to determine the presence of a dominant firm in the relevant market. Economics teaches, however, that market share alone represents a blunt surrogate for establishing dominance. The Guidance Paper thus takes the right approach when it states that '[m]arket shares provide a useful first indication for the Commission of the market structure and of the relative importance of the various undertakings active on the market' but that it 'will interpret market shares in the light of the relevant market conditions, and in particular of the dynamics of the market and of the extent to which products are differentiated'.[11]

The Commission considers that low market shares are generally a good proxy for the absence of substantial market power. It considers that a position of dominance is unlikely to be found where an undertaking holds a market share of less than 40 percent in the relevant market.[12] Market shares below 40 percent do not, however, represent an absolute safe harbor as the Commission considers that 'there may be specific cases below this threshold where competitors are not in a position to constrain effectively the conduct of a dominant undertaking'.[13] At the opposite end of the spectrum, the Commission considers that the higher the market share and the longer the period of time during which it is held, the 'more likely it is that it constitutes an important preliminary indication of the existence of a dominant position'.[14] This may be a problem for incumbent postal operators on the markets that will be liberalized as a result of the Third Postal Directive as these operators will most likely retain high market shares in the years following liberalization.

However, the Commission indicates that, as a general rule, it will not take a decision on the opportunity to investigate a case without examining the various factors which may constrain the behavior of the undertaking in question.[15] In this respect, an issue of growing importance is the extent to which competition from electronic mail services affects market definition and dominance analysis. This of course depends on the degree of substitution between electronic mail and traditional mail, as well as the extent to which electronic mail places a constraint on postal incumbents.

Expansion or Entry

In recognition of the fact that competition is a dynamic process, the Guidance Paper accords importance to the potential impact of expansion by actual competitors or entry by potential competitors, including the threat of such expansion or entry. According to the Commission, an undertaking can be deterred from increasing prices if expansion or entry is likely,[16] timely[17] and sufficient.[18]

It follows that an important element of the analysis of market power is the consideration of any barriers to expansion or entry. In the postal sector, even in the absence of the reserved sector, legal or regulatory barriers may continue to exist, although the possibility for Member States to maintain a reserved sector will end in December 2010. Barriers to entry or expansion may also take the form of advantages specifically enjoyed by the dominant undertaking, such as economies of scale and scope, privileged access to essential inputs and so on.

Such barriers to entry, however, appear to be low in the postal sector, at least compared to the barriers that may exist in other network industries (or some other segments of these industries). Network effects faced by customers in switching to a new supplier seem to be limited, sunk costs are lower (or even negligible for the most part) (de Bijl et al., 2005) in the postal sector than in other network industries, such as for instance, electricity or rail transport where heavy irrecoverable investments have to be made by network operators. In the light of a high percentage of variable costs, entry is easily possible at different scales (Heitzler, 2008). In addition, entrants on postal markets can compete successfully even with relatively low market shares.

Despite these arguments, there is still considerable debate as to whether the basic mail service is contestable considering that the 'last mile' of the postal network is responsible for the majority of mail delivery costs and it may not necessarily be possible to duplicate it (although the developments made in the preceding paragraph suggest that the last mile is duplicable). Some member states have, however, addressed this issue by imposing obligations of access, hence suggesting that incumbent postal operators have market power on a (putative) market for the delivery of mail.

Countervailing Buyer Power

The market position of buyers may also act as a competitive restraint on the behavior of a supplier. The Guidance Paper recognizes that an undertaking with a high market share may not be in a position to act to an appreciable extent independently of customers with sufficient bargaining strength.[19] Such is the case when a firm faces a small number of customers whose buyer power effectively constrains its ability to charge supra-competitive prices.

Given the large number of customers of incumbent postal operators (that is, the lack of concentration of demand for postal services), the postal sector does not seem to be characterized by countervailing buyer power, although some large customers (banks, administrations and so on) may be able to negotiate attractive deals with postal operators. The fact that a subset of users may be able to extract advantageous terms from the incumbent may not, however, be sufficient to prevent a finding of dominance if 'it only ensures that a particular or limited segment of customers is shielded from the market power of the dominant undertaking'.[20]

In light of the above, dominance analysis in the postal sector will have to be carried out on a case-by-case basis relying on the various factors referred to by the Commission in the Guidance Paper.

3 ANTICOMPETITIVE FORECLOSURE

The Guidance Paper expresses an intention to move away from the formalistic approach that the Commission has traditionally taken in Article 82 EC cases,[21] in favor of a new approach based on balancing each case on its economic merits.

The Foreclosure Test

The Guidance Paper states that the objective of the Commission's enforcement efforts with respect to exclusionary conduct is 'to ensure that dominant undertakings do not impair effective competition by foreclosing their rivals in an anticompetitive way and thus having an adverse impact on consumer welfare'.[22] The term 'anticompetitive foreclosure' is then defined as 'a situation where effective access of actual or potential competitors to supplies or markets is hampered or eliminated as a result of the conduct of the dominant undertaking whereby the dominant undertaking is likely to be in a position to profitably increase prices to the detriment of consumers'.[23]

This suggests that in order to establish an exclusionary abuse in contravention of Article 82 EC the Commission must demonstrate two elements. First, it must show foreclosure, namely: 'effective access of actual or potential competitors to supplies or markets is hampered or eliminated' due to the dominant firm's conduct. Second, it must establish 'consumer harm' in that, due to the foreclosure effects of its conduct, the dominant firm is 'likely to be in a position to profitably increase prices to the detriment of consumers'. This combined reference to the presence of foreclosure and consumer harm is critical. It suggests that, in order to demonstrate that the alleged anticompetitive conduct violates Article 82 EC, it is not sufficient for the Commission to show that, as it has done in some past cases, the dominant firm's competitors are at a competitive disadvantage (Petit, 2009). While competition may harm competitors, it will be good for consumers.

The Guidance Paper also states that the Commission will rely on a number of factors to assess the foreclosure effects of a dominant firm's conduct, including the position of the dominant undertaking, the conditions on the relevant market and the position of the dominant undertaking's competitors and so on.[24] The Commission's assessment will also be carried out by comparing 'the actual or likely future situation in the relevant market (with the dominant undertaking's conduct in place) with an appropriate counterfactual, such as the simple absence of the conduct in question or with another realistic alternative scenario, having regard to established business practices'.[25]

Overall, the Commission's proposed approach to the determination of anticompetitive foreclosure should be welcomed by dominant postal operators as it is based on economic grounds rather than on a narrow legal approach that has been taken by the Commission in past cases, some of which will be discussed below. Given the uncertain legal nature of the Guidance Paper, however, it is unclear whether the Commission will always apply an effects-based approach in Article 82 EC cases. With respect to a number of practices (for example, rebates, tying and so on), the case law of the Community courts is particularly favorable to the Commission as it does not have to show the effects of the conduct in question to establish a violation of Article 82 EC. As will be seen below, this is particularly the case with regard to loyalty rebates to which the Community courts apply a quasi *per se* test. While the Guidance Paper provides that the Commission will follow an effects-based approach, there is always the danger when the effects of a dominant firm's conduct are difficult to demonstrate that the Commission will revert to its traditional approach as supported by the Community courts' case law.

The Efficient Competitor Test

In relation to price conduct, the Commission will normally only intervene where the conduct under scrutiny forecloses rivals that are 'as efficient' as the dominant firm. According to this standard, as long as a dominant firm sells its products at a price that is above a certain measure of its costs, the price in question should be legal even if it has the effect of eliminating weaker competitors. The implication of this test will be made clear in our discussion of the Guidance Paper's approach to rebates, a practice that is not uncommon in the postal sector. Tests which rely on competitors' costs or any other benchmark exceeding the dominant firm's own costs would protect less efficient competitors and ultimately deprive consumers of the beneficial effects of price competition.

However, the Guidance Paper shows the Commission's willingness to deviate from the 'as efficient' standard in order to protect less efficient competitors when it states that it:

> recognises that in certain circumstances a less efficient competitor may also exert a constraint which should be taken into account when considering whether a particular price-based conduct leads to anticompetitive foreclosure. The Commission will take a dynamic view of this constraint, given that in the absence of an abusive practice such a competitor may benefit from demand-related advantages, such as network and learning effects, which will tend to enhance its efficiency.[26]

This approach is regrettable since it leaves dominant (postal) firms in a situation of uncertainty as a result of which they may, for instance, decide not to grant some forms of pro-competitive rebates owing to the fact that they are concerned by the possible antitrust implications.[27] Even if there are settings where above cost-pricing could arguably lead to foreclosure, such settings seem rare. More generally, the benefits of preventing dominant firms from cutting their prices on the ground that this may eliminate competitors that may later force them to provide even lower prices are speculative (Hovenkamp, 2006).

Two cost benchmarks are to be employed when assessing whether an equally efficient competitor would be foreclosed, namely the long-run average incremental cost (LRAIC) and average avoidable cost (AAC). Failure to cover AAC indicates that the dominant undertaking is sacrificing profits in the short term and that an as efficient competitor cannot serve the targeted customers without incurring a loss.[28] Failure to cover LRAIC indicates that the dominant undertaking is not recovering all the product-specific fixed costs and that an as efficient competitor could be foreclosed from the market. Pricing between LRAIC and AAC would seem to be in a gray zone and require a more searching enquiry into the price-based conduct in question.

Efficiencies

The Commission considers that a dominant (postal) undertaking may justify conduct leading to foreclosure of competitors on the ground of efficiencies that are sufficient to guarantee that no harm to consumers is likely to arise. In a manner redolent of Article

81(3) EC, the dominant undertaking will be expected to demonstrate, with a sufficient degree of probability, and on the basis of verifiable evidence, that the following cumulative conditions are fulfilled: (i) 'the efficiencies have been, or are likely to be, realised as a result of the conduct'; (ii) 'the conduct is indispensable to the realisation of these efficiencies'; (iii) 'the likely efficiencies brought about by the conduct concerned outweigh any likely negative effects on competition and consumer welfare in the affected markets'; (iv) 'the conduct does not eliminate effective competition, by removing all or most existing sources of actual or potential competition'.[29]

It would seem, however, that a dominant (postal) undertaking may find it difficult to satisfy the restrictive set of cumulative conditions set out above (Geradin, 2009) Furthermore, against the fact that the rationale of the Guidance Paper is to provide guidance, it is to be lamented that only few examples are given of situations where the efficiency defense may actually apply.[30]

4 APPLICATION OF THE GUIDANCE PAPER TO EXCLUSIONARY PRACTICES IN THE POSTAL SECTOR

This section reviews the implications of the Guidance Paper's analytical framework on exclusionary abuses for operators active in the postal sector. This review is undertaken in light both of the postal sector's characteristics and the Commission's recent decisional practice and of the Community courts' case law in the postal sector.

Predatory Pricing

Predatory pricing is a deliberate strategy by a dominant firm of setting very low prices to drive its competitors out of the market. After existing competitors have been eliminated and entry deterred it can raise prices and earn higher profits.

In *AKZO*, the European Court of Justice applied the following test to determine whether the prices set by a dominant firm are predatory:[31] if the dominant firm's prices are set below its average variable cost (AVC), unlawful predation is presumed as pricing below AVC has no economic rationale other than the elimination of competitors, since every unit sold represents a net financial loss. In contrast, if the dominant firm's prices are set above its AVC but below its average total cost (ATC), unlawful predation can only be established on the basis of additional evidence. Firms may, in certain circumstances, rationally price above AVC and below ATC, as it still allows the recovery of a share of their fixed costs. As predation is not the sole economic rationale for such a pricing policy, competition authorities are required to produce additional elements of proof: prices below ATC 'will be regarded abusive if they are determined as part of a plan for eliminating a competitor'.[32]

In the postal sector, the Commission had moved away from its traditional approach to predatory pricing towards an approach better suited to multi-product firms such as incumbent postal operators. In its 2001 *Deutsche Post* Decision, the Commission laid down the test for establishing predatory pricing when there is cross-subsidization between the reserved sector and the sector open to competition.[33] The test relied upon by the Commission stipulated that a multi-service undertaking, in order to avoid predatory pricing, 'must earn revenue on [the specific service open to competition] which at least covers the costs attributable to or incremental to producing that particular service'. Applying the incremental costs test to the case, the Commission found that in the period between 1990 and 1995, Deutsche Post's revenue from mail order parcels was below the incremental costs of providing this specific service. This meant that during the period in question, every sale by Deutsche Post in the mail order parcel services business represented a loss, which comprised all the capacity maintenance costs and at least part of the additional costs of providing the service. In such circumstances, every additional unit sold not only failed to recover at least part of these additional costs, but also made no contribution towards the carrier's capacity maintenance costs. As a result the market was foreclosed to more efficient competitors.

The Guidance Paper does not specifically address the standard to be applied to predatory pricing cases involving multi-product firms. The circumstances at play in the *Deutsche Post* case, whereby an incumbent postal operator was engaged in activities that were open to competition and activities not open to competition as part of the reserved sector, have however become less frequent due to the growing liberalization of the postal sector, and will even completely disappear on 31 December 2010 when the postal sector will be completely open to competition. This does not mean, however, that predation strategies will disappear, but they will lose the specificity of the *Deutsche Post* case. The generic predation test suggested by the Commission is thus of direct relevance to postal operators.

The Guidance Paper states that the Commission will generally intervene against a dominant operator where there is evidence showing that it is engaging in predatory conduct by deliberately incurring losses or forgoing profits in the short term so as to foreclose or be likely to foreclose one or more of its actual or potential competitors with a view to strengthening or maintaining its market power, thereby causing consumer harm. In relation to predatory pricing, the Guidance Paper draws an analytical distinction between 'sacrifice' and 'foreclosure':

1. *Sacrifice* Sacrifice is defined as a situation where a dominant undertaking's conduct leads to avoidable losses through the charging of low prices or an increase of output of a particular product over a specified period of time.[34] The relevant cost benchmark when assessing sacrifice is the AAC.[35] Sacrifice may thus be deemed to exist where the dominant undertaking's prices are below AAC.[36] In that respect, the test put forward by the Guidance Paper is not very different from the *AKZO* test, but for the fact that it relies on AAC rather than ATC as the relevant cost benchmark.

   The Commission seems, however, to go beyond the case law when it states that the concept of sacrifice includes not only pricing below AAC, but also situations where the alleged predatory conduct 'led in the short term to net revenues lower than could have been expected from a reasonably alternative conduct, i.e. whether the dominant undertaking incurred a loss that could have been avoided'.[37] This additional test is open ended. One could argue that an alternative conduct would have been more profitable than the one that was undertaken by the dominant firm and it is not clear that competition officials are well placed to make those kinds of call. In addition to the relevant cost benchmarks in establishing predation, the Commission states that it will rely on direct evidence, such as documentation, that shows clearly a predatory strategy.

2. *Anticompetitive foreclosure* If sufficient data is available, the Commission will apply its 'as efficient competitor' test in order to determine whether the relevant conduct constitutes anticompetitive foreclosure.[38] Only pricing below LRAIC is capable of foreclosing as efficient competitors from the market. In this regard, the Commission will investigate whether and how the suspected conduct reduced the likelihood that rivals will compete.[39] The Commission does not, however, consider it necessary to show that competitors have exited the market in order to show that there has been anticompetitive foreclosure.[40]

   Moreover, the Commission asserts that consumers are likely to be harmed if the dominant undertaking can reasonably expect its market power after the predatory conduct comes to an end to be greater than it would have been had the firm not engaged in that conduct in the first place, that is, if an undertaking is likely to be in a position to benefit from the sacrifice.[41] In this regard, the Commission will not only intervene if the dominant firm would be likely to be able to increase its prices above the level persisting in the market before the conduct. It is sufficient, for instance, that the conduct would be likely to prevent or delay a decline in prices that would otherwise have occurred.[42]

The complete liberalization of the postal sector is likely to stimulate price competition among postal operators, hence increasing the risk for dominant operators of being targeted by undertakings claiming predation. The Guidance Paper does not fundamentally change the *AKZO* test although it alters the cost benchmarks that will apply to its foreclosure test. In this respect, the safest approach for downstream postal operators is to ensure that their prices remain above LRAIC.

Refusal to Supply and Margin Squeeze

With regard to refusal to supply, the Commission starts from the position that any undertaking, whether dominant or not, should have the right to choose its trading partners and to dispose of its property freely. It is recognized that the imposition of an obligation on a dominant firm to supply may undermine its incentive to invest and innovate and, thereby, possibly harm consumers. Such recognition is important considering that the Commission has traditionally given greater importance to the benefits of mandatory supply or access as a tool to open markets than to the potentially negative effects of mandatory access/supply on dominant firms' incentives to invest (Geradin, 2004).

The Guidance Paper indicates that competition issues will typically arise when the dominant undertaking competes on a 'downstream market' with the firm to which it refuses to supply.[43] In the postal sector, this situation arises when a postal operator that owns 'essential infrastructure' (for example, the last mile of the postal distribution network – although whether this last mile is essential is keenly disputed) would refuse to grant access to it to another operator with which it competes at the services level. In this case, the competition claims would be that the postal operator would use its control of the infrastructure to prevent market entry. The Commission does not consider it necessary for the refused product to have been already traded as it is 'sufficient that there is demand from potential purchasers and that a potential market for the input at stake be identified'.[44] It is also unnecessary that there be actual refusal on the part of a dominant (postal) undertaking; constructive refusal is sufficient. In the postal sector, a *Deutsche Post* case is instructive in this regard.[45]

All cases of refusal to supply a (potential) competitor on a downstream market will be considered an enforcement priority where three cumulative conditions are present.[46] First, the refusal relates to a product or service that is objectively necessary (that is, indispensable) to be able to compete effectively on a downstream market.[47] Second, the refusal is likely to lead to the elimination of effective competition on the downstream market.[48] Third, the refusal is likely to lead to consumer harm.[49]

Of particular importance for postal operators is the fact that the Commission considers it does not need to assess whether the three cumulative conditions are present to show anticompetitive foreclosure in two sets of circumstances: (i) when a regulatory authority has already imposed an obligation to supply on the dominant firm and/or (ii) the upstream market position of the dominant undertaking has been developed by virtue of special or exclusive rights or has been financed by state resources. The Guidance Paper asserts that in such cases imposing an obligation to supply is not capable of having negative effects on the input owner's and/or other operators' incentives to invest and innovate upstream.[50] Dominant undertakings in the postal sector may fall within this category when the upstream market (that is, the postal infrastructure) has been developed under the protection of special or exclusive rights (although this scenario appears less likely in the postal sector than in industries where the infrastructure has been clearly built with the revenues of the protected monopoly prior to liberalization) or by virtue of Member State legislation providing for access obligations.

A margin squeeze involves situations in which a vertically integrated dominant firm hampers downstream rivals' competitiveness in (i) raising the wholesale price of its essential input and/or (ii) reducing the retail price of the product or service. In fact, margin squeeze cases are refusal to provide access cases in disguise. Rather than refusing access to an essential infrastructure, a vertically integrated firm reduces the margin of the access seeker at an unsustainably low level. Margin squeeze scenarios are particularly likely to arise in markets that are liberalized and where the incumbent operator is vertically integrated and forced to give access to elements of infrastructure to downstream competitors. As far as the postal sector is concerned, margin squeeze is thus likely to be observed in liberalized markets when the incumbent's downstream competitors (entrants on the postal services' markets) rely on its network infrastructure (for example, the last mile) to provide their services.

In this regard, the Guidance Paper, in a move away from the formalistic approach taken by the Community courts in the area of margin squeezes,[51] states that a dominant undertaking may charge a price for the product on the upstream market which, compared to the price it charges on the downstream market, does not allow even an as efficient competitor to trade profitably in the downstream market on a long-lasting basis. In margin squeeze cases the benchmark on which the Commission will generally rely to determine the costs of an as efficient competitor is the LRAIC of the downstream division of the integrated dominant firm (Eccles and Kuipers, forthcoming).[52]

Rebates

The granting of rebates is a commercial practice that both dominant and non-dominant (postal) firms rely upon to increase their sales with resulting efficiencies, such as the realization of economies of scale, the faster recovery of fixed costs and so on (Ridyard, 2002).

Rebates may, however, be used by dominant firms to foreclose competitors. The Commission and the European courts have usually taken a strict stance towards the assessment of rebates.[53] An illustration of the Commission's formalistic approach to rebates can be found in the Commission's *Deutsche Post* decision in 2001 where Deutsche Post's rebate policy was summarily condemned.[54] The Commission's investigation revealed that between 1974 and 2000, Deutsche Post infringed Article 82 EC by granting a special price to customers for mail-order services only in exchange for requiring the customer to send via Deutsche Post its entire requirements (or a high percentage thereof) of non-bulky parcels up to 20 kg or 31.5 kg or of catalogues weighing over 1 kg. According to the Commission, the fidelity rebate scheme prevented private competitors from gaining the critical mass (estimated at an annual volume of 100 million parcels) necessary to enter the German mail-order delivery market. Rather than engage in an economic analysis of the rebates along the lines proposed by the Guidance Paper, the Commission summarily condemned Deutsche Post's rebates on the ground that they were 'loyalty rebates' rather than 'quantity rebates'.

Such case law, which established a quasi *per se* illegality rule for rebates having loyalty-enhancing effects, was harshly criticized by many legal and economic scholars as sitting uneasily with economic theory, and hence prohibiting rebates which may be pro-competitive and a source of efficiencies. In reaction to these criticisms, the Discussion Paper proposed a move away from this approach towards an assessment of a dominant firm's rebates through proper economic reasoning. Indeed, the Commission abandoned the reference to the notion of loyalty rebates, preferring to draw a distinction between conditional[55] and unconditional[56] rebates.

The price–cost test proposed by the Discussion Paper for the assessment of *unconditional* rebates borrows from the standard applied in the assessment of predatory pricing practices (except that the cost standard on which it relies is unnecessarily strict as will be seen in the discussion below).[57] According to such test, the effective price P_e (standard price P minus a rebate R),[58] will be presumed predatory when $P_e < AAC$, whereas $P_e > ATC$ will be presumed non-predatory.[59] When $P_e > AAC$ and $P_e < ATC$, unlawful predation can only be established on the basis of additional evidence of predatory intent.[60]

Regarding *conditional* rebates, the Discussion Paper draws a further distinction between incremental rebates and retroactive rebates. While incremental rebates are subject to a predation test similar to the one applicable to unconditional rebates,[61] retroactive rebates are subject to a much more problematic 'suction effect' test which for reasons that will be made clear below should rather be described as a 'leveraging test'.[62] The suction effect test is a price–cost test designed to assess whether a rebate scheme can exclude efficient rivals from the 'contestable' part of a customer's demand. It can be explained as follows.

Let us assume that a dominant supplier sells to a particular company. The supplier has an assured base of sales to that customer because, for a portion of the customer's demand, there are no proper substitutes.[63] These sales represent the non-contestable share of that company's demand. However, the portion of the customer's demand for which substitutes are available is the contestable share of that customer's demand.[64] The dominant supplier offers the company a retroactive rebate. This gives the customer a rebate over all the quantities sourced if it purchases more than the rebate threshold level within the reference period.[65]

The competition concern is that when the non-contestable part (*NC*) of the customer demand in question is large compared to the contestable part (*C*), that is, when $NC > C$, the retroactive rebate may allow the dominant supplier to leverage its position of strength in the non-contestable to the contestable part of a customer's sales.[66] Indeed, while the dominant supplier can recoup the rebate on its overall sales including both contestable and non-contestable parts (that is, the dominant firm does not incur losses on the whole range of sales), competing suppliers will have to recoup the rebate over a smaller base represented by the contestable part.[67] This retroactive rebate scheme could thus have the effect of excluding equally efficient rivals from that part of the customer's sales that would otherwise be contestable. According to the Discussion Paper, this would happen if the rebate scheme leads to the dominant supplier selling units in the contestable part of demand at an effective price P_e that does not cover the *ATC* of supplying them.[68]

In the Guidance Paper, the Commission proposes a variation of that test involving three different scenarios. First, the Commission states that as long as P_e remains consistently above the *LRAIC* of the dominant undertaking, this normally allows an equally efficient competitor to compete profitably notwithstanding the rebate. The rebate is normally not capable of foreclosing.[69] Second, where $P_e < AAC$, as a general rule the rebate scheme is capable of foreclosing even as efficient competitors.[70] Third, where $AAC < P_e < LRAIC$, the Commission states it will investigate whether other factors point to the conclusion that entry or expansion even by as efficient competitors is likely to be affected. The Commission will in particular investigate whether and to what extent rivals have realistic and effective counterstrategies at their disposal. Where competitors do not have such counterstrategies at their disposal, the Commission will consider that the rebate scheme is capable of foreclosing equally efficient competitors.[71]

This test is apparently more flexible than the test suggested in the Discussion Paper as $P_e < LRAIC$ does not automatically mean that the rebate in question will be considered as capable of having a foreclosure effect. According to the Commission, this depends on whether and the extent to which the dominant firm's rivals have countervailing strategies at their disposal. However, the example of countervailing strategy provided by the Commission, that is, the rivals' capacity to also use a 'non-contestable' portion of their buyer's demand as leverage to decrease the price for the relevant range, is not completely clear.[72]

The main difficulty with this suction effect analysis of retroactive rebates is its complexity. It is difficult to distinguish the respective scope of the contestable and non-contestable share of a given customer demand and there is thus a risk that competition authorities take mistaken – or worse, arbitrary – decisions on this point. In this respect, an easier approach would be to apply to retroactive rebates the same predation test as the Commission intends to apply to incremental rebates. While incremental and retroactive rebates are pricing strategies frequently used by suppliers of goods such as tires, computer chips and so on it is not clear whether they are used by postal operators. As will be seen in the next subsection, because of their multi-product nature, postal operators are more likely to rely on tying and bundled rebates as exclusionary strategies.

Tying and Bundling

Tying usually refers to a practice whereby customers that purchase one product (the tying product) are additionally required to purchase another product from the dominant undertaking (the tied product). Tying can take place on a technical or contractual basis.[73] Bundling, which is closely related to the concept of tying, usually refers to the way products are offered and priced by the dominant undertaking. A further distinction can be drawn between pure bundling and mixed bundling (also known as a multi-product rebate). In the case of pure bundling, the products are only sold jointly in fixed proportions. With mixed bundling the products are also made available separately, but the sum of the prices when sold separately is higher than the bundled price.

Tying and bundling are not uncommon practices by both dominant and non-dominant postal undertakings since, as in the case of rebates, they can be the source of efficiencies. Similarly, mixed bundling may allow consumers to save significant amounts of money on products, as well as to try new products at a fraction of the cost they would have to pay if they were purchased on a stand-alone basis.

The competition problem is that tying and bundling may in some circumstances be used by dominant (postal) firms to exclude their competitors, hence the need for competition authorities and courts to devise legal tests to separate pro-competitive tying and bundling practices from anticompetitive ones. One could imagine a scenario whereby a postal operator that is dominant on postal service A would require its customers to buy its postal service B in order to obtain service A. This strategy may be more difficult to carry out in the postal sector as some postal services must be provided as part of universal service, although alternative strategies may be used to achieve the same result as illustrated by the Commission's decision in *De Post–La Poste* where it was held that De Post–La Poste had abused its dominant position by making a preferential tariff in the general letter mail service subject to the acceptance of a supplementary contract covering a new (B2B) mail service.[74]

The Commission will normally take action under Article 82 EC against a dominant undertaking when two conditions are present: (i) the tying and tied products are distinct products and (ii) the tying practice is likely to lead to anticompetitive foreclosure. With regard to distinct products, two products are distinct if, in the absence of tying or bundling, a substantial number of customers would purchase or would have purchased the tying product without also buying the tied product from the same supplier, thereby allowing stand-alone production for both the tying and the tied product. The Guidance Paper briefly alludes to a number of ways in which tying and bundling could anticompetitively foreclose competition. In particular, the assertion is made that the risk of anticompetitive foreclosure is expected to be greater where the dominant undertaking engages in technical tying.

With regard to multi-product rebates, such a rebate may be anticompetitive on the tied or the tying market if it is so large that as efficient competitors offering only some of the components cannot compete against the discounted bundle.[75] In its analysis of the foreclosure effects of multi-product rebates, the Commission states that if the incremental price that customers pay for each of the dominant undertaking's products in the bundle remains above the LRAIC of the dominant firm from including that product in the bundle, it will normally not intervene. Enforcement action may, however, be warranted if the incremental price is below the LRAIC because in such a case even an equally efficient competitor may be prevented from expanding or entering.[76]

5 CONCLUSION

Article 82 EC has played a pivotal role in the liberalization of network industries, including the postal sector. Until recently, the Commission, supported by the case law of the Community courts, took a legalistic and interventionist approach to the assessment of a dominant firm's conduct. In reaction to criticisms of such approach, the Commission displayed in its Discussion Paper and its Guidance Paper an intention to take an effects-based approach to the enforcement of Article 82 EC. This new direction is to be welcomed, although it remains to be seen whether the Commission will apply this approach in all its cases or revert to its former formalistic approach when the effects of alleged exclusionary conduct are difficult to prove. Against the hope that the Commission will move away from its former formalistic stance, the Guidance Paper provides dominant (postal) operators with a reasonably lucid exposition of the principles that the Commission will apply in its future assessments of allegedly anticompetitive conduct.

NOTES

1. DG Competition Discussion Paper on the application of Article 82 of the Treaty to exclusionary abuses, December 2005 ('Discussion Paper').
2. COM(2008).
3. See for example, Commission Guidelines on Vertical Restraints (1999) O.J. C 291/1 and Commission Guidelines on the assessment of non-horizontal mergers under the Council Regulation on the control of concentrations between undertakings (2008) O.J. C 265/6.
4. Guidance Paper para. 23.
5. Directive 2008/6/EC of the European Parliament and of the Council of 20 February 2008 amending Directive 97/67/EC with regard to the full accomplishment of the internal market of Community postal services (2008) O.J. L 52/3.
6. The Guidance Paper only relates to abuses committed by undertakings holding single dominance.
7. See Commission Notice on the definition of the relevant market for the purposes of Community competition law (1997) O.J. C-372 and the Notice from the Commission on the application of the competition rules to the postal sector and on the assessment of certain State measures relating to postal services (1998) C-39/2 which provides guidance on market definition in the postal sector.
8. See Commission Decision of 5 December 2001, *De Post–La Poste* (2002) O.J. L 61/32: 'La Poste holds the postal monopoly . . . . It thus has a dominant position on the Belgian market for the general letter post service for items weighing less than 350 grams'.
9. Guidance Paper para. 10. In relation to the holding of substantial market power a period of two years is normally deemed to be sufficient.
10. Guidance Paper para. 12.
11. Id. at 13.
12. Id. at 14.
13. Id.
14. Id. at 15.
15. Id.
16. For the Commission to consider expansion or entry likely it must be sufficiently profitable for the competitor or entrant, taking into account factors such as barriers to expansion or entry and the likely reactions of the allegedly dominant undertaking and other competitors, see Guidance Paper para. 16.
17. For expansion or entry to be considered timely, it must be sufficiently swift to deter or defeat the exercise of substantial market power, see id. at 16.
18. For expansion or entry to be sufficient, it must be of such a magnitude as to be able to deter any attempt to increase prices by the putatively dominant undertaking in the market.
19. See Guidance Paper para. 18.
20. Id.
21. See in particular Judgment of the European Court of First Instance of 30 September 2003, Case T-203/1, *Michelin v. Commission* [2003] ECR II-4071.

22. Guidance Paper para. 19.
23. Id.
24. Id. at para. 20.
25. Id.
26. Id. at 23.
27. Moreover, if they decide to go ahead with a rebate regime which prima facie appears in line with EC competition law (and which they need to grant to realize pro-competitive efficiencies or meet competition), but is *in fine* challenged by the European Commission, the resulting investigation will result in significant legal costs, damage to the brand, possible fines and follow-on private litigation.
28. Guidance Paper para. 25.
29. Id. at 29.
30. In relation to tying, the Commission may consider whether such practices reduce transaction costs for customers, who otherwise would be forced to buy the components separately.
31. Case C-62/86, *AKZO Chemie v. Commission* [1991] E.C.R. 1-3359.
32. Id.
33. See Commission Decision of 20 March 2001, *Deutsche Post AG* (2001) O.J. L 125/27.
34. See Guidance Paper paras 63 to 65.
35. The Commission recognizes that in most cases the AVC and the AAC will be the same, as often only variable costs can be avoided. According to the Commission, however, in circumstances where AVC and AAC differ, the latter better reflects possible sacrifice: for example, if the dominant firm had to expand capacity in order to be able to predate, then the sunk costs of this extra capacity should be taken into account in looking at the dominant undertaking's losses. These costs would be reflected in the AAC, but not the AVC.
36. Pricing below AAC will in most cases be viewed as a clear indication of sacrifice, see para. 63.
37. The Commission makes it clear that undertakings should be allowed to put forward a defense in this regard. Undertakings should not be penalized for incurring *ex post* losses where the *ex ante* decision to engage in the conduct was taken in good faith, that is, if they can provide conclusive evidence that they could reasonably expect that the activity would be profitable.
38. Guidance Paper para. 66.
39. Id. at para. 67.
40. Id. at para. 68.
41. Id. at para. 69.
42. The Guidance Paper has not insisted on recoupment of losses which is in line with the ECJ judgment in *Wanadoo*, see Judgment of the European Court of Justice, Case C-202/07 P.
43. Guidance Paper para. 75.
44. Id. at para. 78
45. See Commission Decision of 25 July 2001, *Deutsche Post AG – Interception of Cross-Border Mail* (2001) O.J. L 331/40.
46. Guidance Paper para. 78.
47. Objective necessity is shown by demonstrating that rivals cannot effectively duplicate the input produced by the dominant undertaking in the foreseeable future, see Guidance Paper para. 82.
48. Elimination of effective competition can be shown by demonstrating high market shares on the part of the dominant firm in the downstream market, see Guidance Paper para. 84.
49. Consumer harm may, for instance, arise where the competitors that the dominant undertaking forecloses are, as a result of the refusal, prevented from bringing to market innovative goods or services and/or where follow-on innovation is likely to be stifled. This may be particularly the case if the undertaking which requests supply does not intend to limit itself essentially to duplicating the goods or services already offered by the dominant undertaking on the downstream market, but intends to produce new or improved goods or services for which there is potential consumer demand or is likely to contribute to technical development, id. at para. 87.
50. See Id. at 81.
51. See Judgment of the European Court of Justice, Case T-271/03, *Deutsche Telekom v. Commission*, not yet reported at para. 237 where it is stated '[A] margin squeeze between the applicant's wholesale and retail charges will *in principle* hinder the growth of competition in the downstream markets' (emphasis added).
52. In light of the specific obligations that are to be imposed by Member States pursuant to the Postal Directive, it is questionable whether an incumbent postal operator should ever be accused of margin squeezing as far as network access is concerned provided that it complies with the requirement to offer the same discounts to upstream competitors as it does to direct customers, see Eccles and Kuipers (forthcoming).
53. Witness Case T-203/01, *Manufacture française des pneumatiques Michelin v. Commission* (Michelin II), [2003] ECR II-4071; Case T-219/99, *British Airways plc v Commission*, [2003] ECR II-5917 and Case C-95/04 P, *British Airways plc v Commission*, [2007] ECR I-2331.
54. See supra note 33.

55. 'Conditional rebates are granted to customers to reward a certain (purchasing) behaviour of these customers'. See the Discussion Paper at para. 137.
56. 'Unconditional rebates, while granted to certain customers and not to others, are granted for every purchase of these particular customers, independently of their purchasing behaviour'. Id. at para. 137.
57. The Guidance Paper does not specifically address unconditional rebates. The test proposed in the Discussion Paper is no doubt still valid but for the fact that the Commission has replaced its *ATC* cost standard by *LRAIC*.
58. In other words, the rebated price.
59. See supra note 1 at para. 171.
60. Id.
61. Id. at paras 168–9.
62. Id. at paras 152 *et seq*. While the Discussion Paper uses the term 'suction effect' test (since, retroactive rebates may in certain circumstances have the effect that units above the threshold are inevitably 'sucked up' by the dominant firm), it is a leveraging test.
63. See supra note 1 at para. 143.
64. Id. at para. 156.
65. Id. at para. 152.
66. Note, however, that 'to induce such an effect it is necessary that the dominant supplier sets the threshold above the level that the buyer would purchase from the dominant company in the absence of any conditional enhancing obligation or rebate . . . If the threshold is only set at the level that would anyhow be purchased by the buyer from the dominant company, the rebate will not have a conditional enhancing effect. If the threshold is set above the amount that would otherwise be purchased, the rebate may induce the buyer to purchase more than it would otherwise do, in particular by diverting purchases from other suppliers to the dominant company, in order to be able to benefit from the rebate on all its purchases and thus effectively lower the price for all its purchases'. Id. at para. 152.
67. The Discussion Paper notes that 'the suction effect in principle is strongest on the last purchased unit of the product before the threshold is exceeded' for which the price will often be negative. However, it correctly observes that 'what is relevant for an assessment of the conditional enhancing effect is not competition to provide an individual unit, but the foreclosing effect of the rebate system on commercially viable amounts supplied by (potential) competitors of the dominant supplier'. Id. at para. 154.
68. Id.
69. Guidance Paper para. 42.
70. Id. at para. 43.
71. Id.
72. This example seems to refer to a situation where both the dominant firm and its rivals enjoy an *NC* share of the buyer in question's demand (an ambiguity is, however, generated by the fact that the Guidance Paper refers to 'their' buyer demand). Assuming that this is the correct interpretation, the circumstances in which this countervailing strategy will be available appear to be limited. Unless the rebates granted by the dominant firm are particularly high, the fact that $P_e < LRAIC$ suggests that the *NC* of the dominant firm *vis-à-vis* the buyer in question is likely to be high and that therefore the *NC* of the rivals is likely to be small, hence limiting their ability to counter-leverage the dominant firm's prices in the contestable share.
73. Technical tying alludes to the impossibility of taking one product without the other, that is, where the tied product is physically integrated into the tying product. Contractual tying occurs when the customer who purchases the tying product undertakes also to purchase the tied product (and not the alternatives offered by competitors).
74. See supra note 8.
75. Guidance Paper para. 58.
76. Id. at para. 59.

REFERENCES

de Bijl, P., E. van Damme and P. Larouche (2005), '"Light is right": competition and access regulation in an open postal sector', Law and Economics Center, Tilburg, The Netherlands, June.

Eccles, R. and P. Kuipers (forthcoming), 'The proper scope of the rules on abuse of dominant position in a liberalised postal services market', not yet published.

Heitzler, S. (2008), 'Traditional regulatory approaches and the postal service market', DIW Berlin and TU Berlin available at http://www.ipc.be/index.php?option=com_news&task=view&id=1183&Itemid=208, accessed 12 October 2009.

Hovenkamp, H. (2006), 'Discounts and exclusions', *Utah Law Review*, **3**, 841–61.

Geradin, D. (2009), 'A proposed test for separating pro-competitive conditional rebates from anti-competitive ones', *World Competition*, **32**(1).

Geradin, D. (2004), 'Limiting the scope of Article 82 of the EC Treaty: what can the EU learn from the US Supreme Court's judgment in *Trinko* in the wake of Microsoft, IMS, and Deutsche Telekom', *Common Market Law Review*, **41**(1519).

Petit, N. (2009), 'From formalism to effects? The Commission's communication on enforcement priorities in applying Article 82 EC', *World Competition*, **32**(481).

Ridyard, D. (2002), 'Exclusionary pricing and price discrimination abuses under Article 82 – an economic analysis', *European Competition Law Review*, **6**(286).

5. The *Altmark* ruling and approaches to measuring efficiency of postal operators

Vincenzo Visco Comandini, Adolfo Consiglio, Stefano Gori, Emiliano Piccinin and Maria Rita Pierleoni

1 INTRODUCTION

This chapter addresses one of the most striking differences between Europe and the US in antitrust law: state aid regulation. It focuses on the postal sector, where state aid legislation is becoming increasingly important in the light of the liberalization of the European market. Post Office network reorganization, including investments in next generation network (NGN) broadband optical fiber technologies and Universal Service Obligations (USOs) are measures that may require finance through public subsidies. However, subsidies are illegal if they distort competition by favoring the recipient over its competitors. The cornerstone in this issue is the European Court of Justice's *Altmark* decision, which defined four conditions so that compensation for public services is not considered to be state aid, described in Section 2. The chapter addresses specifically the fourth condition, which applies if the beneficiary undertaking is not selected by a public procurement procedure.

Since the aim of the decision is to guarantee an efficient use of the public subsidy, basic requirements for a public service to be efficiently provided are highlighted in Section 3, where the conceptual framework proposed by Le Grand (2007) is used. This section discusses the economic reasons for choosing a public tender as a market-simulating efficient outcome, with particular reference to the peculiar public good characteristics of USOs. Williamson (1985) and Sappington and Stiglitz (1987) clearly explain the stringent circumstances under which this may occur, making public procurement an ineffective tool for postal USO assignment.

If the fourth *Altmark* condition fully applies, an efficiency assessment of the subsidized firm is then requested. As we argue, developing efficiency estimates presents problems in the postal sector. Section 2 describes state aid regulation in the EU, while Section 3 explains why the usual bidding scheme is unlikely to be suitable for postal USO assignments. Section 4 provides an empirical method that may be viewed as a means of complying with the fourth *Altmark* requirement if applied to the European postal sector. By using appropriate econometric techniques this method enables postal administrations to be ranked by cost efficiency while taking account of exogenous variables (for example, those out of the control of the provider). In the postal industry, scale production levels, geographic and social characteristics of the service provision and wage levels are generally recognized as the main variables affecting costs. Their inclusion in the econometric model, estimated with OLS (ordinary least squares) and GLS (generalized least squares) translog total cost function as well as a DEA (data envelopment analysis) non-parametric statistical method, allows us to assess whether a postal undertaking beneficiary of public subsidies in fulfilling its obligations operates at an efficient level or not. This exercise is a first step toward the development of a comprehensive method, able to be empirically applied not only by economists, but also by law scholars such as national regulatory authorities, the European Commission, or courts.

2 STATE AID IN THE EU AND *ALTMARK* RULING

Among the differences between the US and the EU in antitrust policies, the most remarkable is state aid, virtually non-existent in the former while explicit policy in the latter. While in Europe it became an important issue in the light of the building of a single European market, it has not been a key issue for US antitrust basically because of historical reasons. In the US the legislation was implemented following the creation of a single country and integrated market which aimed to dismantle cartels, since government-owned firms are less relevant than in Europe (Gori and Visco Comandini, 2009). In contrast, services of general economic interest (SGEI) do play a fundamental role in the shared values of the EU. These SGEI are industries of national interest (such as public transport, telecommunications, postal services and local government services) which have a special obligation to fulfill public tasks not performed by the usual market mechanisms. Although expected to promote social and territorial cohesion, SGEI are fully subject to antitrust law. The incumbent companies were previously in monopoly situations and often have enjoyed the legacy of a universal service provision. Furthermore, they were often involved in delivering a mix of commercial and public services. In such circumstances they can receive financial support to perform public services where they are also active in commercial markets for which they do not receive support. The focus of the EU antitrust on state aid arises when there is a risk that the compensation that such undertakings, either directly or indirectly owned by the state, receive for delivering public services could leak into their commercial markets and distort competition, especially harming companies from other European member states (Boyd and Teal, 2004).

In Europe, SGEI regulation is expected to harmonize antitrust law with public/universal service obligations, as stated in the Communication from the Commission on Services of general interest in Europe (European Commission, 2000). In 2003, the European Court of Justice (ECJ) through the '*Altmark* ruling'[1] defined the four conditions so that compensation for public services is not considered state aid. The ECJ decision applies directly to urban transport public undertakings, but quickly became a milestone for evaluating whether giving public subsidies complies with competition rules on state aid. *Altmark* has 'decentralized' the law regarding the USO (Travers, 2003). Provided that the four conditions identified in the judgment are met, USO payments can be considered to fall outside Article 87(1) of the European Treaty, that is, they do not constitute illegal state aid. If they do not constitute state aid then they do not have to be notified to the European Commission acting as the European Antitrust Authority. This allows local/national decision makers some discretion over whether or not notification is necessary, rather than forcing central decision taking by the European Commission. The conditions are the following:

1. The recipient undertaking must actually have public service obligations (USOs) to discharge and those obligations must be clearly defined.
2. The parameters on the basis of which the compensation is calculated must be established both in advance and in an objective and transparent manner.
3. The compensation cannot exceed what is necessary to cover all or part of the costs incurred in the discharge of the public service obligations (USOs), taking into account the relevant receipts and a reasonable profit.
4. Where the undertaking is not chosen in a public procurement procedure (Franchise bid), the level of compensation must be determined by a comparison with an analysis of the costs that a typical undertaking well run and adequately provided would have incurred, taking into account the relevant receipts and a reasonable profit from discharging the obligations.

The first condition places a greater emphasis on the need to clearly identify the obligations. *Altmark* suggests that this would be derived from national legislation and/or licenses.

The second condition ensures that there is no economic advantage which may favor the recipient's undertaking over competing undertakings: 'Payment by a Member State of compensation for the loss incurred by an undertaking without the parameters of such compensation having been established beforehand . . . therefore constitutes a financial measure which falls within the concept of State aid within the meaning of Article [87(1)10] of the Treaty'. The key word is 'parameters'. A parameter can be 'a measurable or quantifiable characteristic of a system' and also 'a limit or boundary which defines the scope of a particular process or activity'. It is not, in this context, equivalent to an algorithm. It is unclear how much flexibility there might be in any particular case. To what extent can a public authority incorporate mechanisms to adjust the public contribution as necessary (Boyd and Teal, 2004)?

The third condition is clearly linked to the second. Without a well-defined mechanism for assessing the 'true' cost of the USO, the risk of overcompensation may be high. The issue of what constitutes a 'reasonable profit' has been considered in the case law relating to the market economy investor principle.[2]

The fourth condition raises a certain number of questions when the USO is auctioned. To what extent can USOs be effectively tendered through a public procurement procedure in order to guarantee their least-cost provision? If they cannot, what is an average, well-managed company providing public services to use as a benchmark? If the beneficiary is a nationwide market postal administration, can the benchmarking exercise be used against companies in other EU member states?

3 BIDDING USOs

Theoretical arguments for the advantages of private ownership of the means of production are synthesized in the fundamental privatization theorem (Sappington and Stiglitz, 1987), which provides conditions under which government objectives can be obtained by an appropriately designed auction of the rights to produce a given product or service. It is a general theorem which shows under which conditions privatization is optimal and government involvement cannot improve upon the performance of the private market. The ideal setting is an auction system whereby potential producers bid for the right to provide the good. This result requires three crucial assumptions: (i) the number of bidding firms must be large enough to avoid collusion; (ii) firms must be risk neutral, and (iii) firms must share information on least-cost production technology. These ideal conditions are rather strict, hence in practice we are dealing with 'privatization failures' symmetric to market failures (Bös, 1991). The assignment of the universal service task through competitive bid seems to be inappropriate when, as in postal services, the number of potential bidders is de facto very low (Santamato and Pesaresi, 2004). Moreover, franchise bidding may be a policy full of hurdles in its implementation. This regulatory failure depends not only on the low number of bidders (in the best scenario, the incumbent and perhaps one competitor), but also on the 'mixed' nature of the good/service that is being bid upon – specifically the USO burden. A bundle of public, private and merit good characteristics[3] is in fact difficult to tender effectively. While the private good component of USO can generally be auctioned, the public merit[4] good component cannot: the competitive bid is very likely to turn on a market failure, risking either being under- or overpriced (compensated) because of the public good component. The public good component of postal USO exhibits both non-rivalry in consumption (the consumption of an additional output does not harm other consumers) and non-excludability (its supply is de jure generalized to all citizens with a known address). This implies that it is not possible, in a competitive bid, *ex post* to observe fully if the winner is fulfilling all of its obligations defined in the contract. Take the example of minimum quality requirements, for example, the specific postal USO to deliver mail to all national addressees in a predefined time window (one or three days). In this case, opportunistic behavior (Williamson, 1985) is like to arise in a competitive bid because the obligations are difficult and costly to monitor, since final letter recipients are generally unable to check the true quality of delivery.[5] This is the reason why, information asymmetries being relevant, the usual market mechanism fails, and a regulator is usually asked to perform this task.

Sappington and Stiglitz argue that the main difference between public and private ownership involves the residual rights of intervention. Under public enterprise, the government retains some authority to intervene directly in the production arrangements and implement major policy changes when it is deemed necessary to do so. Under private ownership, rights of intervention exist for creditors (in the event of bankruptcy) and major financial interests, who can gather the resources necessary to finance a takeover of the private firm.

Le Grand (2007) has recently summarized the basic attributes a public service is expected to hold, rather similar to a government's objectives in choosing among alternative forms of production: the service should be (i) of high quality, (ii) efficiently produced and operated, (iii) responsive to the needs and wants of users, (iv) accountable to taxpayers, and (v) delivered equitably. Quality has several possible dimensions, ranging from measurement of inputs and outputs, to process or outcomes, and is a central feature of any public provision. Efficiency and effectiveness are also important, because stakeholders (users, citizens, taxpayers, voters) require the maximum quality-adjusted output at least cost. Their measurement, however, may be problematic in several cases, since the real price of a service is not the money that was spent on providing it, but the cost of the other services that could have been provided had the money not been spent in that way. If an alternative (for example, a service able to at least partly substitute for it) does not exist, the opportunity cost of its provision cannot be adopted as a benchmarking criterion.

4 USING ECONOMETRICS TO APPLY *ALTMARK* TO THE POSTAL SECTOR

The application of the fourth Altmark condition raises several practical issues for industries, like postal services, where under certain circumstances state subsidies may be the only feasible tool for USO financing (Fratini and Filpo, 2006). In the light of *Altmark*, a direct public subsidy to the USO provider may become incompatible with the European Treaty if both the government and the recipient are unable to prove to the European Commission that the grant covers only efficient costs faced for USO provision (Koenig and Haratsch, 2003). The fulfillment of this condition is not easy, for at least three reasons.

The first is that efficient costs of a legal or de facto monopoly are by definition the observed costs if no other firms operating under similar conditions can be taken as a benchmark. The second reason is that if there are only a few potential providers for a certain service, a survey of typical costs would not prove useful. The third reason relates to the technology. The postal industry charged with USO exhibits significant economies of scale, mainly if not exclusively in delivery (Cohen et al, 2002, 2004; PWC, 2006; Campbell et al., 2008; Cohen and McBride, 2008).[6] Postal operators (POs) operating at a low scale (low per capita volumes) therefore face higher unit costs than those with high volumes.

Moreover, postal services are more labor intensive than other regulated industries such as water, telecommunications, energy or transportation. POs face low fixed capital costs but high recurrent fixed labor costs. In the postal sector, USO requirements, which include maximum allowable time for delivery or minimum opening hours for existing post offices, have the effect of converting at least part of what a private firm would consider a variable cost into a fixed one. These legal obligations require the postal administration to hold a fixed delivery network, designed for fulfilling assigned standards, regardless of postal volumes treated: trucks or planes shall leave mail exchange hubs on time independently of their saturation level (Lettieri and Visco Comandini, 2001). In addition to these fundamental issues, this sector has not experienced a dramatic change in technology and growth in consumption as have telecommunications and energy. Indeed, due to the gradual shift of messages from paper-based to digital (e-substitution), postal volumes in industrialized countries have stagnated in the past few years, and a further decrease is expected in the future.

Thus, a simple comparison of the efficiency of a specific PO with averaged values of other POs – a naive interpretation of the *Altmark* ruling – is very likely to be biased toward those operators enjoying large economies of scale or other favorable exogenous factors. Therefore, a correct benchmarking of POs requires specific efficiency estimation.

Several studies have investigated, often with an econometric approach, the efficiency of a PO, but the focus has mainly been concentrated on its internal efficiency in specific operations such as delivery (Roy, 1999; Horncastle et al., 2006; Moriarty et al., 2006) or processing (Fenster et al., 2008). Other studies highlight the impact of environmental variables such as route characteristics on the costs of POs facing competition because of market liberalization (d'Alcantara and Amerlynck, 2006). Most of these findings show that delivery costs (that is, the largest cost component of a PO) are strongly affected by several characteristics, acting as exogenous variables on the efficiency measurement.

In the next section, we present some econometric results of a cross-country benchmarking model, designed with the specific purpose of creating a first step toward both a methodological framework and an empirical tool to fulfill the fourth *Altmark* requirement. We are aware that a full investigation of POs' efficiency would require the availability of detailed data on environmental variables, which are very difficult to collect mainly because of the reluctance of POs to disclose sensitive information in an already competitive environment. Nevertheless our exercise, using only publicly available data such as urbanization rate or number of households – a pale proxy of the full gamut of exogenous variables likely to affect postal costs – seems to be promising.

Its aim is to provide results generated by alternative methods of measuring and ranking efficiency levels for some European POs. We use OLS, GLS and DEA efficiency measurement estimates, benchmarked against simple average unit cost. Each statistical method has its own pros and cons, but the availability of different estimates may underpin rather than complicate the test. In fact the goal of the fourth *Altmark* requirement is to ascertain whether a European PO receiving public subsidies operates at the average efficiency level, for example, the empirical test only excludes the presence of substantial inefficiencies. This is a simplified task compared to usual benchmarking exercises, where each position in the ranking (either at the top or at bottom of an array of observations) always matters. A PO receiving subsidies will presumably pass this test if across the different techniques it is ranked at least at an average position, controlling for relevant exogenous factors. Any better rank reinforces the result, but does not matter *per se*. Similarly, if all techniques indicate significantly below-average efficiency, the test is unambiguously not passed. Some evaluation problems may arise if a particular firm turns out to be efficient according to some techniques but inefficient according to others. In this case a deeper investigation is required.

5 THE MODEL

Our model is based on two key points: (i) the use as a starting database of only publicly available data, and (ii) accounting for economies of scale and other exogenous factors. The basic approach is to extend and refine the total cost function analysis of European postal services estimated by NERA (2004) and, with some additional statistical adjustments, by Gori et al. (2005). For both OLS and GLS the translog total cost function,[7] which allows for variable returns to scale, has been deliberately chosen to comply with the results of the general postal cost function estimated by Cohen et al. (2002; 2004) and Campbell et al. (2008). This assumption is crucial, because it shows that, all other things being equal, the national postal market width (measured as annual per capita postal items) is the key unit cost driver. The use of the translog total cost function (which does not require a priori restrictions like CES (constant elasticity of substitution) or Cobb–Douglas on either the substitution possibilities among the factors of production or on scale economies) allows us to rank POs by efficiency. Thus, POs' efficiency is benchmarked for a similar scale of operations (for example, per capita volume), wages and environmental variables, all presumed exogenous.

The generic form of the estimated equation for OLS and GLS is:

$$\begin{aligned} \text{Log}C = \ & \alpha_0 + \alpha_1 \text{*Log(Volumes)} + \alpha_{11} \text{*Log(Volumes)*Log(Volumes)} \\ & + \beta_1 \text{*Log(Wage)} + \beta_{11} \text{*Log(Wage)*Log(Wage)} \\ & + \gamma_{11} \text{*Log(Volumes)*Log(Wage)} + \delta_1 \text{*Log(Households)} \\ & + \delta_2 \text{*(Urbanization Rate)} + u_i. \end{aligned}$$

Residuals u_i were used to calculate the relative efficiency of each postal administration for each year.

However, both OLS and GLS as efficiency estimators have the ability to confound inefficiency measurement with observation error. If inefficiency typically measured by residuals u cannot be distinguished from observation noises, a bias may emerge in the identification of the average behavior, in our case very relevant since it works as the dividing line between administrations passing the fourth *Altmark* test and those not. In fact, we cannot exclude the possibility that most postal administrations are inefficient, because neither OLS nor GLS would capture this phenomenon. To overcome this problem we have estimated a third efficiency rank across postal administrations by using DEA. DEA is a non-parametric method, based on a pure input–output relation, unable to include environmental/exogenous variables directly. Therefore we have used a two-stage approach, proposed by Laureti (2008), where efficiency results generated by the DEA procedure are regressed with environmental variables. The estimated efficiency values will then include the effect due to exogenous variables:

$$\text{Log(volumes)} = \text{DEA [Log (Total Costs), Log (wage)]}$$

$$\text{EFFDEA} = \alpha_1 \text{*Log(Households)} + \alpha_2 \text{*(Urbanization Rate)} + u_i,$$

where EFFDEA = efficiency values estimated by DEA.

The model is therefore improved by the availability of potentially different rankings obtained by three econometric techniques. As a result, the risk of systematic and non-observable biases in efficiency measurement is minimized.

Data

Data presented a number of problems, which we attempted to address. The starting database, the only one that is publicly available, is that created by NERA for the European Commission (2004), improved by Gori et al. (2005)[8] and updated to year 2007. Data were not available for each variable, in each country for every year, so when necessary and possible we have substituted some missing observations by data generated through a Monte Carlo simulation. The result is a 102-observations database for 13 European member states, ranging from 1997 to 2007. Data collection involved the following variables: mail operating cost, postal volumes, unit labor cost, number of households and percentage of population living in urban areas.

As described by Gori et al. (2005) data collection involved the following activities:

1. *Mail operating cost*: data were collected when available from various annual reports, websites and operators' answers to our questions; otherwise we estimated mail costs consistently with respect to mail volume. In countries where we had no information on the split of total costs between letters, parcels, express and financial services we had to make broader assumptions, based on the division of mail revenues. When mail volumes or operating costs included parcels, we used Universal Postal Union data on parcel volumes and calculated the implicit letter mail volumes or parcel operating cost.
2. *Mail volumes* were collected from annual reports and websites.
3. *Unit labor cost* data, defined as staff costs (including social security payments and pension costs) divided by the number of full-time equivalent postal workers were taken from NERA (2004, Table 5.5, p. 69).
4. *Number of households*: as in the NERA study we used the variable 'dwelling stock' which includes only the conventional (permanent) dwelling, whether occupied or not (source: database model of the Statistical Division, United Nations Economic Commission for Europe UNECE/STAT). For some countries we did not have the values for the whole period. In these cases we collected data from the national statistical institute of each country.
5. *Percentage of population* living in urban areas: UNECE website, integrated with data available on the Eurostat and World Urbanization Prospect websites.

Results

The plotted observations of unit costs with respect to per capita volumes in Figure 5.1 suggest that the shape of the cost curve is very steep for low volumes but tends to be flat for high volumes. This is very similar to the general cost curve estimated by Cohen et al. (2002, 2004), and reinforces the hypothesis that the translog function form of the estimated equation is the most appropriate when volumes strongly affect unit costs, and cost elasticities are increasing with volumes.

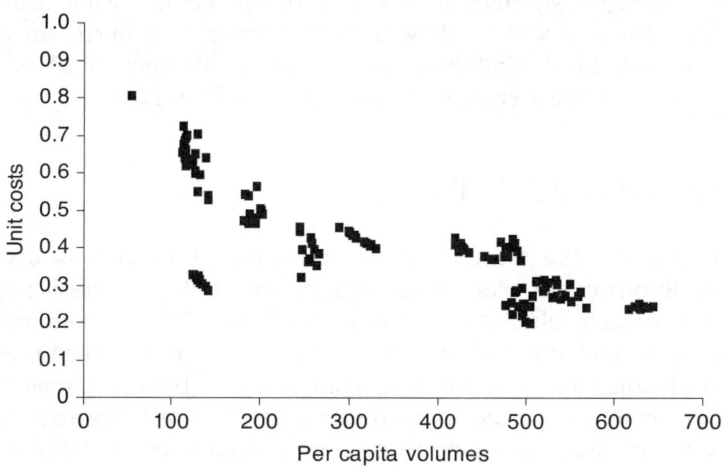

Figure 5.1 Unit costs versus per capita volumes

Tables 5.1 and 2 show the results for OLS and GLS estimates.

As our dataset consists of pooled cross-section and time-series data, the assumption of non-constant variance in residuals/errors u_i may be violated. In order to verify the possible presence of heteroskedasticity, we run a test for equality of variances between series using three methods (Bartlett, Levene and Brown-Forsythe) (Table 5.3).

Probability values (< 0.05) for all tests show that the null hypothesis can be accepted,[9] so OLS estimates are not biased by heteroskedasticity for this dataset. Nonetheless, both OLS and GLS estimates are reported here for completeness.[10]

Table 5.4 shows the results of regressing the two exogenous variables (households and urban population) on the efficiency values directly generated by DEA. By using the estimated (and highly significant) coefficients we get the final DEA efficiency values which include their effect.[11]

Main results of the model are shown in Table 5.5.

The first column of Table 5.5 shows the efficiency differentials for each postal administration with respect to the mean value measured for observed unit costs. The most efficient firm is E, followed by H, I and A, while K, C and M are the least efficient. Not surprisingly, both OLS and GLS results exhibit a lower variance (for example, lower differences in efficiency), suggesting that the impossibility of selecting error noises from true efficiency may be a problem if only OLS and GLS are used. The variance goes up in column 4, where results are generated by the DEA procedure without environmental variables, but are also high in column 5 where exogenous variables are included as controls.

If we analyze the results horizontally country by country and we set the minimum reasonable efficiency threshold to ≥ -1.0 percent, firm A dramatically changes its rank, switching from highly efficient in column 1 to average efficiency in columns 2 and 3, but it improves its score and rank in column 5. Firm B is slightly above average in columns 1–3 but is the most efficient of the whole sample according to DEA estimates. Firm C is highly inefficient according to both the observed average unit cost and DEA without external variables, but it goes beyond the minimum efficiency threshold in all other measurements. Firm D passes the test unambiguously, while I shows conflicting results. Firms G and H are unambiguously efficient regardless of the method, while firm K is always highly inefficient. Firms J and M show a similar trend: very inefficient according to observed unit cost and DEA, slightly above the average efficiency threshold in OLS and GLS. L is slightly below the average for all measurements but DEA.

6 CONCLUDING REMARKS

The cornerstone in the state aid issue in Europe is the ECJ's *Altmark* decision, which defined the conditions under which compensation for public services is not considered to be state aid. Especially relevant is the fourth condition of the *Altmark* decision which applies whenever the undertaking is not chosen in a public procurement procedure compensation and identifies the need for a benchmarking of the operations of the public service provider against market-determined standards. This task has many hurdles when applied to sectors in countries where there is no company operating in a comparable market and it becomes difficult to identify 'a well-run operator' (Hansen et al., 2003). The postal sector fits into this category because in all European countries there is an

Table 5.1 Pooled OLS estimates (cross-section translog)

Dependent variable: log total costs
Sample: 1997–2007
Included observations: 13
Total panel (unbalanced) observations 102

Variable	Coefficient	Std error	*t*-statistic	Prob.
Constant	−18.81122	7.46192	−2.52096	0.01330
Log volumes	1.64746	0.58532	2.81465	0.00590
Square log volumes	−0.06935	0.02188	−3.16877	0.00200
Log wages	8.46123	3.15063	2.68557	0.00850
Square log wages	−1.87574	0.66564	−2.81795	0.00580
Log wages * log volumes	−0.125478	0.13724	−0.91428	0.36280
Log households	0.40069	0.02969	13.49479	0.00000
% urban population	−0.31858	0.16597	−1.91957	0.05780
Weighted statistics				
R-squared	0.98952	Mean dependent var.		7.76625
Adjusted *R*-squared	0.98879	S.D. dependent var.		1.07185
S.E. of regression	0.11	Sum squared resid.		1.28827
F-statistic	1,348.872	Durbin–Watson stat.		0.93960
Prob (*F*-statistic)	0.00000			

Table 5.2 GLS estimates (cross-section weights translog)

Dependent variable: log total cost
Sample: 1997–2007
Included observations: 13
Total panel (unbalanced) observations 102

Variable	Coefficient	Std error	*t*-statistic	Prob.
Constant	−23.20894	4.33933	−5.34851	0.00000
Log volumes	1.82428	0.25663	7.10854	0.00000
Square log volumes	−0.06747	0.00963	−7.00402	0.00000
Log wages	10.54764	2.01113	5.24464	0.00000
Square log wages	−2.35948	0.46292	−5.09699	0.00000
Log wages * log volumes	−0.17382	0.06844	−2.53976	0.01260
Log households	0.39226	0.01551	25.29762	0.00000
% urban population	−0.34442	0.09833	−3.50271	0.00070
Weighted statistics				
R-squared	0.99933	Mean dependent var.		9.83069
Adjusted *R*-squared	0.999280	S.D. dependent var.		3.86139
S.E. of regression	0.10361	Sum squared resid.		1.07353
F-statistic	21,216.08	Durbin-Watson stat.		1.39624
Prob (*F*-statistic)	0.00000			

Table 5.3 Test for equality of variances between series

Sample: 1997–2007
Included observations: 12

Method*	Df degree of freedom	Value	Probability
Bartlett	11	25.21488	0.008479
Levene	(11, 95)	2.959757	0.002058
Brown–Forsythe	(11, 95)	2.315470	0.014524

Category Statistics

Variable*	Count	Std dev.	Mean diff.	Median diff.
res A	11	0.086997	0.066450	0.065800
res B	11	0.104558	0.084138	0.082048
res C	11	0.046137	0.035232	0.034919
res D	11	0.063661	0.051838	0.050843
res E	11	0.090957	0.071230	0.070693
res F	11	0.028494	0.021810	0.021251
res G	11	0.093055	0.076535	0.076049
res H	3	0.045515	0.034192	0.028956
res I	2	0.068168	0.048202	0.048202
res J	3	0.042445	0.032604	0.025380
res L	11	0.049528	0.039837	0.039066
res M	11	0.107744	0.092150	0.089078
All	107	0.110164	0.058208	0.056884

Notes: Bartlett weighted standard deviation: 0.077952.
* One country is missing because the test cannot be run with only one observation.

Table 5.4 GLS estimates (cross-section weights)

Dependent variable: DEA efficiency results
Sample: 1997–2007
Included observations: 13
Total panel (unbalanced) observations 143

Variable	Coefficient	Std error	*t*-statistic	Prob.
Log households	0.005335	0.000439	12.15493	0.00000
% urban population	0.912011	0.015776	57.81070	0.00000
Weighted statistics				
R-squared	0.937856	Mean dependent var.		1.1641
Adjusted *R*-squared	0.937416	S.D. dependent var.		0.805462
S.E. of regression	0.201501	Sum squared resid.		5.72499
F-statistic	2,127.94	Durbin–Watson stat.		0.399267
Prob (*F*-statistic)	0.00000			

Table 5.5 Relative efficiency results (average values 1997–2007)

Country	1 Δ % with respect to observed averaged European unit cost	2 Δ % with respect to OLS efficient threshold with exogenous variables	3 Δ % with respect to GLS efficient threshold with exogenous variables	4 Δ % with respect to DEA efficient threshold without exogenous variables	5 Δ % with respect to DEA efficient threshold with exogenous variables
A	7.3%	−0.1%	0.3%	2.3%	6.9%
B	0.4%	1.7%	2.1%	27.7%	30.8%
C	−13.9%	−0.7%	−0.3%	−31.5%	0.0%
D	0.5%	−0.8%	−0.4%	0.6%	13.3%
E	14.5%	−0.2%	−0.2%	29.8%	−22.0%
F	−0.4%	−0.5%	0.0%	31.5%	14.3%
G	6.6%	0.2%	0.2%	26.9%	6.0%
H	13.4%	6.1%	6.9%	31.5%	6.7%
I	10.1%	5.1%	6.0%	15.6%	−16.1%
J	−6.2%	2.1%	2.6%	−39.3%	−25.4%
K*	−19.1%	−10.5%	−10.2%	−64.7%	−21.8%
L	−1.7%	−1.0%	−0.4%	19.4%	28.2%
M	−11.3%	0.2%	0.5%	−49.5%	−20.9%
Variance	0.010	0.001	0.002	0.109	0.035

Note: *Country K has only one observation year.

incumbent, which operates throughout the country and guarantees a universal service while private providers cover only certain geographical areas or products (mainly for business users), often for a limited number of days per week.

In this chapter we have attempted to provide a first step toward developing a national benchmark by means of an econometric benchmarking exercise across 13 EU countries. We had to take into account that the postal sector is one of the European network industries with the widest variance in per capita physical consumption (for example, letters) between member states (ranging from 30 items per capita in the country with the lowest consumption to 650 items per capita in the country with the highest consumption). We used the only publicly available database on the cost structure of POs, that created by NERA for the European Commission (2004), improved by Gori et al. (2005) and updated the data using the Monte Carlo simulation method to fill in for the missing years.

We have obtained two main results: (i) the scale factor is very significant, and (ii) the availability of several econometric results may help in some cases to identify whether or not a PO can be said to operate at an average efficiency level. In our study of 13 European POs, six are unambiguously more efficient than the average, two are unambiguously inefficient, and one is inefficient if exogenous variables are not considered but of average efficiency if they are taken into account. The availability of better data may strengthen the results of this evaluation method. Future improvements of this project may include the collection of better and more precise data on exogenous variables, as well as enlarging the set of statistical techniques by including stochastic frontier analysis.

The policy implications of the results are: (i) in the absence of a company operating in a comparable market, an econometric approach based on both a clear-cut causal nexus of relations between the variable affecting costs, and an appropriate functional form (such as the translog), can in most cases effectively identify a 'well-run operator'; and (ii) national characteristics (for example, national wages, per capita consumption, and social and geographical factors such as the number of dwellings or the urbanization rate) need to be encompassed – in a typical *ceteris paribus* approach – in the efficiency analysis.

NOTES

1. Case C-280/00 *Altmark Trans GmbH and Regierungspräsidium Magdeburg v Nahverkehrsgesellschaft Altmark GmbH*, judgment of 24 July 2003.
2. The approach taken is the following: the court is asked to consider whether the investment is state aid or not. The alleged beneficiary needs to show that the state invested on the same basis as a private investor would, that is, that the state expects to earn an economic return on its investment in the same way as a private investor would.
3. The private good component is the technical output supplied, while the public good is the obligation *per se*, similar to a legal rule.
4. The merit good component is the political decision to provide a service with USO, a clear government meta-preference. Even if well grounded from the economic standpoint, it is still a command imposition over the customer's demand (Gori et al., 2002).
5. The multisided market nature of ordinary postal services (Dietl et al., 2008; Jaag and Trinkner, 2008; Boldron et al., 2009; Visco Comandini et al., 2009) may explain differences in demand, benefits and costs between senders and addressees.
6. The United States Postal Service (USPS) is the only relevant PO in the world charged by the legislation to fully disclose all its data on costs; it has recently provided a Report on Universal Postal Service and the Postal Monopoly (USPS, 2008).
7. Horncastle et al. (2006) show the superiority of translog compared to other functional forms in estimating efficiency levels of postal delivery offices in the UK.
8. For the detailed procedure used for creating the dataset, see Gori et al. (2005).
9. One possible weakness of the result is that the dataset, as described above, has been enlarged by a Monte Carlo simulation, generating missing data under the hypothesis of constant variance in distribution (see Visco Comandini et al., 2009, footnote 23).
10. Tests shown in Table 5.3 indicate that heteroskedasticity is not a problem for our dataset, so OLS estimates could be used for these data. Nonetheless, GLS estimates are potentially useful in that the variance (and, thus, standard errors) of the coefficients tend to be underestimated by OLS even in the presence of mild heteroskedasticity, inflating *t*-scores and sometimes making insignificant variables appear to be statistically significant.
11. Since the DEAFrontier program used does not allow for missing values, output data of the country with only one observation have been inflated (for this purpose only) by copying the same value for all years.

REFERENCES

Boldron, F., H. Cremer, P. De Donder, D. Joram and B. Roy (2009), 'Network externalities and the USO: a two-sided market approach', in M. Crew and P. Kleindorfer (eds), *Progress in the Competitive Agenda in the Postal and Delivery Sector*, Cheltenham, UK and Northampton, MA, USA: Edward Elgar, pp. 184–95.

Bös, D. (1991), *Privatization: A Theoretical Treatment*, Oxford: Oxford University Press.

Boyd, A. and Teal J. (2004), 'Interpreting the *Altmark* decision – the challenges from a private practitioner's perspective', McGrigors.com, 31 May.

Campbell J.I., R. Cohen, A. Dieke, A. Fritschler, R. John, J. Panzar, C. Pommering and F. Wolak (2008), 'Study on Universal Postal Service and the Postal Monopoly', George Mason University School of Public Policy, November.

Cohen, R. and C. McBride (2008), 'Estimates of the Current Costs of the PSO in the U.S., Study on Universal Postal Service and the Postal Monopoly', Appendix F, Section 3, George Mason University.

Cohen, R., C. Pace, M. Robinson, G. Scarfiglieri, R. Scocchera, V. Visco Comandini, J. Waller and S. Xenakis (2002), 'A comparison of the burden of universal service in Italy and the United States', in M. Crew and P. Kleindorfer (eds), *Postal and Delivery Services: Pricing, Productivity, Regulation and Strategy*, Boston, MA: Kluwer Academic, pp. 87–101.

Cohen, R., M. Robinson, G. Scarfiglieri, R. Sheehy, V. Visco Comandini, J. Waller and S. Xenakis (2004), 'The role of scale economies in the cost behavior of Posts', Wissenschaftliches Institut für Kommunikationsdienste (WIK), 8th Königswinter Seminar on 'Regulating Postal Markets – Harmonised Versus Country Specific Approaches', February, 16–18.

D'Alcantara, G. and B. Amerlynck (2006), 'Profitability of the universal service postal provider under entry with economies of scale in collection and delivery', in M. Crew and P. Kleindorfer (eds), *Progress toward Liberalization of the Postal and Delivery Sector*, New York: Springer Science+Business Media, Inc., pp. 39–58.

Dietl, H., A. Grütter and M. Lutzenberger (2008), 'Defensive strategies in two-sided markets: the example of the European mail industry', Working Paper, Third Global Postal Research and Education Network Conference, Lausanne, April 28.

European Commission (2000), Communication from the Commission on Services of General Interest in Europe (COM/2000/0580 final).

Fenster, L., D. Monaco, E. Pearsall and S. Xenakis (2008), 'Are there economies of scale in mail processing? Getting the answers from a large-but-dirty sample', in M. Crew and P. Kleindorfer (eds), *Competition and Regulation in the Postal and Delivery Sector*, Cheltenham, UK and Northampton, MS, USA: Edward Elgar, pp. 315–37.

Fratini, A. and F. Filpo (2006), 'PSO public financing at the cross road between the Monti package and the forthcoming reform of the postal directive', in M. Crew and P. Kleindorfer (eds), *Liberalization of the Postal and Delivery Sector*, Cheltenham, UK and Northampton, MS, USA: Edward Elgar, pp. 277–92.

Gori, S., C. Lettieri, M. Marè and V. Visco Comandini (2002), 'The myth of the uniform price', paper presented at the International Conference on Public Finance, Helsinki, August 29–31.

Gori, S., E. Piccinin, S. Romit and G. Scarfiglieri (2005), 'On the use of cost functions in the assessment of the impact of liberalization on the postal universal service burden: restricted versus flexible specifications', in M. Crew and P. Kleindorfer (eds), *Progress toward Liberalization of the Postal and Delivery Sector*, New York: Springer Science+Business Media, pp. 59–69.

Gori, S. and V. Visco Comandini (2009). 'Antitrust law and public services performances with reference to the postal industry: a discussion paper', Institute of Governmental Studies Working Paper, University of California, Berkeley.

Hansen, M., S. Zuehlke and A. Van Ysendyck (2003), *Altmark Trans*: European Court of Justice outlines conditions for public service compensation', Practical Law Company, 7 August, available at http://www.lw.com/upload/pubcontent/_pdf/pub892_1.pdf accessed 14 September 2009.

Horncastle, A., D. Jevons, P. Dudley and E. Thanassoulis (2006), 'Efficiency analysis of delivery offices in the postal sector using stochastic frontier and data envelopment analysis', in M. Crew and P. Kleindorfer (eds), *Liberalization of the Postal and Delivery Sector*, Cheltenham, UK and Northampton, MS, USA: Edward Elgar, 149–64.

Jaag, C. and U. Trinkner (2008), 'Pricing in competitive two-sided markets', in M. Crew and P. Kleindorfer (eds), *Competition and Regulation in the Postal and Delivery Sector*, Cheltenham, UK and Northampton, MS, USA: Edward Elgar, pp. p. 136–49.

Koenig, C. and A. Haratsch (2003), 'The licence fee based financing of public service broadcasting in Germany after the *Altmark Trans* Judgment', *European State Aid Law Quarterly*, **4**, 569–77.

Laureti, T. (2008), 'Modelling exogenous variables in human capital formation through a heteroscedastic stochastic frontier', *International Advances in Economic Research*, **14**, 76–89
Le Grand, J. (2007), *The Other Invisible Hand*, Princeton, NJ: Princeton University Press.
Lettieri, C. and V. Visco Comandini (2001), 'Comparing postal and telecommunication networks: similarities and differences', *Journal of Network Industries*, **2** (2), 163–206.
Moriarty, R., S. Yorke, G. Harman, J. Cubbin, M. Meschi and P. Smith (2006), 'Economic analysis of the efficiency of royal mail units and the implication for regulatory policy', in M. Crew and P. Kleindorfer (eds), *Liberalization of the Postal and Delivery Sector*, Cheltenham, UK and Northampton, MS, USA: Edward Elgar, pp. 165–82.
NERA Economic Consulting (2004), 'Economics of Postal Services: Final Report', a report to the European Commission, July, available at: http://ec.europa.eu/internal_market/post/doc/studies/2004-nerafinal-postal-report_en.pdf, accessed 14 September 2009.
PricewaterhouseCoopers (PWC) (2006), 'The Impact on Universal Service of the Full Market Accomplishment of the Postal Internal Market in 2009', Final Report, available at: http://ec.europa.eu/internal_market/post/doc/studies/2006-impact-report_en.pdf, accessed 14 September 2009.
Roy, B. (1999), 'Technico-economic analysis of the costs of outside work in postal delivery', in M. Crew and P. Kleindorfer (eds), *Emerging Competition in Postal and Delivery Services*, Boston, MA: Kluwer Academic, pp. 101–22.
Santamato, S. and N. Pesaresi (2004) 'Compensation for services of general economic interest: some thoughts on the *Altmark* ruling', *Competition Policy Newsletter*, No. 1, Spring, 17.
Sappington, D. and J. Stiglitz (1987), 'Privatization, information and incentives', NBER Working Paper 2196, National Bureau of Economic Research, Cambridge, MA.
Travers, N. (2003), 'Public service obligations and state aid: is all really clear after *Altmark*?', *European State Aid Law Quarterly*, **3**, 387–90.
USPS (2008), 'Report on Universal Postal Service and the Postal Monopoly', US Postal Service, October.
Visco Comandini, V., S. Gori, M. Lintell, M. Pierleoni and B. Tisdahl (2009), 'Postal price elasticities and intermedia competition: a multisided market approach', in M. Crew and P. Kleindorfer (eds), *Progress in the Competitive Agenda in the Postal and Delivery Sector*, Cheltenham, UK and Northampton, MA, USA: Edward Elgar, pp. 163–83.
Williamson, O.E. (1985), *The Economic Institutions of Capitalism*, New York: Free Press.

6. Price cap postal regulation: the French experience

Bénédicte Bouin, Nicolas Curien and Guillaume Lacroix

1 INTRODUCTION

The law of May 20, 2005 concerning the regulation of the postal sector charged ARCEP (l'Autorité de Régulation des Communications Electroniques et des Postes) with the responsibility of overseeing the opening and effective functioning of the French postal market. This responsibility is focused on licensing of postal activities, monitoring quality of service and regulating tariffs of universal service. Tariff regulation in France includes: oversight and approval by ARCEP of the multi-year price cap governing universal service offerings, and approval of tariffs for services in the reserved sector.[1]

This chapter describes the implementation of price regulation in France through a price-cap regime started in 2006. The previous period was characterized by a negotiated regulatory contract between the government and La Poste. Such an administrative contract suffered from the weakness of setting multiple and somewhat vague objectives and recommendations.[2] A report of the Administrative Court[3] noted that postal tariffs had risen less than the consumer price index (CPI) until 2003: the stamp price for a mail item of less than 20 grams remained stable at €0.46 from 1996 to 2003 prior to two sharp increases, one in 2003 which took the price to €0.50 and the other in 2005 setting it at €0.53. Such a price trajectory, characterized by tariff adjustments after a long period of stability, was difficult for La Poste to manage and also led to increased uncertainty on the demand side. From this experience emerged the necessity of implementing a tariff framework that would allow La Poste, and its customers, to enjoy medium- and long-term transparency on the evolution of postal tariffs and pricing policies.

This chapter describes the main features of the approach undertaken by ARCEP to price-cap regulation. In Section 2, we present the 'consumer price index minus X' structure of the price cap, with a special focus on the process used for determining the 'efficiency factor' X as well as on the adjustment mechanism year to year. Two three-year price-cap contracts have already been set up: the first was established for the period from 2006 to 2008. Thereafter, the framework was reviewed and a new price cap was implemented for the 2009–11 period. In Section 3, we provide a preliminary assessment of the first price-cap period and we discuss the changes in the contractual setting which were adopted for the second period (2009–11). Section 4 concludes.

2 SETTING THE REGULATORY FRAMEWORK

Price Regulation: Alternatives and Issues

The first question of interest of course is: what form of price regulation should be adopted? ARCEP decided to implement price-cap regulation (PCR), in line with the current practice of other European postal regulators (for example, the UK, Italy, Sweden, Belgium and Portugal).

In the economic literature, PCR is presented as having better incentives for efficiency than, for instance, rate-of-return (ROR) regulation. PCR, first introduced by Littlechild (1983), provides the operator with strong incentives to reduce cost and to increase productivity. These incentives are made effective by allowing the operator to keep a share of the benefits achieved by productivity improvements, for the duration of the price-cap contract period (Crew and Kleindorfer, 1996).

Incentives for cost reduction are more effective the longer the contractual period. On the other hand, the contract has to remain viable in response to changing circumstances through a transparent adjustment process specified in advance (Vogelsang, 2002). If adjustment proves unnecessary, then the contract is unrevised, this stability being the very foundation of incentives under price caps.

In the French context, a time horizon of three years was set for the PCR regime: on the one hand, the 2005 postal law[4] imposes a minimum of two years for tariff regulation; on the other hand, a period longer than three years was considered difficult to legitimate due to uncertainties about the major driving parameters of the price cap. The three-year PCR horizon provided appropriate visibility, allowing the postal operator (PO) to plan its tariffs in compliance with the price-cap constraints as well as with tariff principles applying to universal service offerings.

Since the incentive is focused on cost reduction, PCR could have the effect of degrading service quality. To avoid this, it is possible to introduce adjustments for quality into the price-cap constraint in order to penalize (or reward) the PO for under- (or over-) achievement of its quality targets (Crew and Kleindorfer, 2009). Such quality adjustments were not incorporated into the French PCR regime. Instead, ARCEP preferred to require La Poste to monitor quality and to publicize the results of ongoing measurements, a stimulus to improve quality whenever the levels attained were unsatisfactory. In particular, transparent reporting of quality allows customers to compare La Poste with competitors, as well as to react on the basis of publicized statistics. Quality and reliability targets for universal service are set by the minister in charge of the postal sector, with implementation and monitoring under the responsibility of ARCEP.

A crucial issue in the implementation of any price-cap regime is the determination of the efficiency factor X. This is complicated by the asymmetry of information between the regulator and the regulated firm, where the latter has better information on the potential productivity gains that might be achieved. In this context, it may be helpful to find a mechanism that provides incentives to the regulated firm to reveal information that is central to setting the X factor. Crew and Kleindorfer (1996) suggested an approach that sets a floor level of X acceptable for the regulator, with built-in incentives for the PO to choose a value of X greater than this floor, based on sharing increasing benefits with the PO if larger values of X are chosen. In the French context, such a mechanism of prenegotiation of X with the PO was not implemented and X was determined rather by the regulator on the basis of a thorough auditing of postal accounts and with the objective of preserving the profitability ratio (operating margin over revenue); any extra productivity gain above X that is achieved during the contractual period is retained by the PO, which then enjoys a greater profit margin.

Structure of the Price Cap

The regulatory framework should lead the PO to maintain an acceptable level of profitability, subject to market conditions, and subject to the request that the PO achieves productivity gains at least as great as those foreseen at the initialization of the price, these gains being shared appropriately with customers. In addition, the framework should take account of the risks on the demand side, thus allowing a sharing of volume-driven risks between the PO and customers. Finally, the structure should provide cost-reduction incentives, allowing the PO to appropriate gains beyond the norm set by the contract.

Structure of the price cap and determination of X

The price cap is defined as a contract between the regulator and the PO, with the objective of managing the price trajectory of the PO for products in the scope of universal service (whether those products belong to the reserved area or already face competition). In a given sectoral and macroeconomic exogenous context, characterized by the trend of postal traffic and the rate of inflation, the contract should allow the PO to maintain an agreed profitability ratio (operating margin over revenue) for a contract period of three years, and even to increase that ratio by improving productivity above the minimum level required by the regulator. Maintaining a constant profitability ratio amounts to aligning the respective rates of change in the PO's costs and revenues across the portfolio of USO products.

Let us now enter into the formalized derivation of the price-cap mechanism.

First, the annual rate of change of revenue, denoted $\dot{R} = \Delta R/R = (R_{n+1} - R_n)/R_n$ for year n, depends on the combined evolution of volumes and prices. The price elasticity of demand, $e < 0$, naturally moderates the purely mechanical effects of price changes, so that (using '·' to denote rate of change over time):

$$\dot{R} = \dot{P} + \dot{Q}^* + e(\dot{P} - I^*) = I^* + \dot{Q}^* + (1 + e)(\dot{P} - I^*),$$

where :

I^* is the CPI (rate of inflation);
$\dot{P}$ is the rate of change of the postal price index, in nominal terms;
$\dot{Q}^*$ is the base rate of annual volume changes for universal service under the assumption of constant prices in real terms ($\dot{P} = I^*$); and
e is the price elasticity of demand for universal service products.

Second, costs follow a base rate which is affected at the margin by potential efforts to improve productivity (an endogenous factor) and by possible changes in the base level of demand (an exogenous factor). The annual rate of change in costs can be written:

$$\dot{C} = \dot{c}^* + I^* + a(\dot{Q} - \dot{Q}^*) - (X - X^*),$$

where:

$\dot{c}^*$ is the base rate of change of costs in real terms;
$\dot{Q} - \dot{Q}^*$ is a possible 'shock' affecting the natural trend of traffic $\dot{Q}^*$;
a ($0 < a < 1$) measures the cost impact of a change in the volume of activity, given some degree of rigidity when adjusting costs downward in reaction to declining volumes ($a = 0$ means infinite rigidity and $a = 1$ means no rigidity); and
X^* is the required level of productivity improvement and X is the level of such improvement effectively realized.

Third, at the date of initial implementation of the price cap, it is necessary to project the average annual rate of inflation $I = I^*$ during the following three years, as well as the base annual trend in volumes $\dot{Q} = \dot{Q}^*$. Assume that the level of productivity effort achieved is the lower limit of acceptable effort (so $X = X^*$). Under these conditions, if the price cap is to be constructed so that the profitability ratio (which can be written $r = 1 - C/R$) is maintained at a constant level, then variations in charges should be mirrored exactly in equal variations in revenue:

$$\dot{R}^* = \dot{C}^* \Rightarrow \dot{Q}^* + (1 + e)(\dot{P} - I^*) = \dot{c}^*,$$

from which we derive the price-cap formula:

$$\dot{P}^* = I^* - X^* \text{ with } X^* = \frac{\dot{Q}^* - \dot{c}^*}{1 + e}.$$

It is important to underline the incentives embodied in this formulation of the price cap. If the productivity efforts realized by the PO are above the minimum required (so that $X > X^*$), then the profitability ratio r will be above the guaranteed level r^* and the benefits thereof will be appropriated by the PO. The key variable in this contract is therefore clearly the X factor. Formally:

$$r - r^* = (C^* - C)/R^* = -(1 - r^*)(C - C^*)/C^* = (1 - r^*)(X - X^*) > 0.$$

Scope of the price cap
The price-cap regime applies to products included in the postal universal service. For a particular year n, the annual change in prices of universal service offerings is calculated as the change in the average price at year n with respect to year $n - 1$, based on volumes for year $n - 2$:

$$\dot{P}_n = \Sigma\,[(P_n - P_{n-1}) \cdot Q_{n-2}] \,/\, \Sigma\,[P_{n-1} \cdot Q_{n-2}].$$

The basket over which the sum in this formula is defined includes: first and second class letters, direct mail, registered letters and insured items, outgoing international letters, universal service parcels, readdressed and relocation mail services.

Thus, the price cap extends over all elementary products of the universal service with the exception of incoming international mail and that of newspapers and magazines which are subject to a specific price regulation under the Code for Postal and Electronic Communications,[5] with the goal of promoting pluralism in social and political expression.

Adjustment Mechanisms

Once the price cap is initialized, the value of I^* is fixed at the predicted annual rate of increase of the consumer price index. X^* it is fixed through the above formula $\dot{X}^* = (\dot{Q}^* - \dot{c}^*)/(1 + e)$, on the basis of an econometric estimate of price elasticity (e) and of anticipated average annual variations of volumes ($\dot{Q}^*$) and charges ($\dot{c}^*$) over the period of the contract. This value of X^* is kept constant over the three-year period of the price-cap regime.

Now, adjustments may modify the contract during its period of execution. This occurs in the case of a discrepancy between anticipated and realized values for the rate of inflation and for the traffic trend.

First, to the extent that observed inflation, one year and then two years after initialization of the price-cap contract, is significantly different from initial expectation, revised expectations are used to correct the price cap. The value of inflation for the second year of the price cap and its value for the third year (starting January 1) are determined by the projections published in the Finance Bill in autumn of the preceding year, thus providing La Poste with sufficient time to plan its pricing changes for the coming year; such changes may intervene at any time during the year provided that they do not exceed the price-cap constraint.

Second, if the trend of traffic volume (estimated as a moving average of a volume index over the previous three years), when assessed after one year, and then after two years of contracting, is significantly lower (greater) than the initially projected trend, the same minimal level of productivity growth being requested, the price-cap constraint must be loosened (or tightened). Thus, the price-cap framework foresees that in the case of a loss in volumes in excess of the baseline estimations, the price-cap constraint has to be relaxed. On the other hand, if the observed outcomes of postal traffic are more favorable than projected, the framework enforces a tightening of the price-cap constraint with resulting benefits flowing to the consumer.

Third, formally, in case of a shock $\Delta\dot{Q}^* = \dot{Q} - \dot{Q}^*$ affecting the natural trend of postal traffic, the associated shock for the rate of cost evolution (in real terms) can be written $\Delta\dot{c}^* = a\Delta\dot{Q}^*$. Differentiating the price-cap formula $\dot{P}^* = I^* - X^*$ then yields the adjustment to the price cap in the case of a shock $\Delta I^* = I - I^*$ for the inflation rate and a shock $\Delta\dot{Q}^* = \dot{Q} - \dot{Q}^*$ for the trend in traffic:

$$\Delta\dot{P}^* = \Delta I^* - \Delta X^* = \Delta I^* - \frac{\Delta\dot{Q}^* - \Delta\dot{c}^*}{1 + e} = \Delta I^* - \frac{1 - a}{1 + e}\Delta\dot{Q}^*.$$

Setting $b = (1 - a)/(1 + e)$, we finally have:

$$\Delta\dot{P}^* = \Delta I^* - b\Delta\dot{Q}^*,$$

from which we derive the formulae for contract adjustment:

$$\text{1st year (year } n\text{): } \dot{P}_n = I^* - X^*$$

$$\text{2nd year (year } n+1\text{): } \dot{P}_{n+1} = \dot{P}_n + (I_1^* - I^*) + b(\dot{Q}_1^* - \dot{Q}^*)$$

$$\text{3rd year (year } n+2\text{): } \dot{P}_{n+2} = \dot{P}_n + (I_2^* - I^*) + b(\dot{Q}_2^* - \dot{Q}^*).$$

In these expressions I_k^* and $\dot{Q}_k^*$ denote the revised values for the inflation rate and trend of traffic at date $n + k$ ($k = 1, 2$).

In the absence of an accurate estimate, the cost inertia coefficient, a, was set at its median value within the interval [0, 1], that is, $a = 0.5$; then using an econometric estimate of traffic price elasticity ($e = -0.28$),[6] coefficient b can be computed as $b = 0.70$. This value amounts to a 70–30 percent sharing of the risk between the consumer and the PO, in the case of an unexpected shock affecting postal activity.

3 IMPLEMENTING THE FRAMEWORK

The implementation of PCR has taken place during a period of transition of the postal market towards a more competitive structure, with full liberalization having been initially fixed for 2009. This period is also characterized by increased investments of La Poste, arising from its initiatives to modernize its mail processing operations. Since 2003 La Poste has undertaken initiatives to improve productivity and quality that should bring a level of performance comparable to that of other major POs in Europe. Indeed, in 2005, the 3.9 percent operating margin of 'Group La Poste' was lower than that of other major European POs for the same period, many of these POs having rationalized their operations earlier.

In such a context, the pricing regulatory scheme implemented by ARCEP was designed to permit La Poste to conduct the necessary reorganization and allow it to realize the productivity and quality improvements expected by its customers.

The First Price-cap Regime, 2006–2008

In this subsection we first present the determination of the first price-cap formula and then assess the results that were achieved under that control.

Initial values for price-cap parameters

The growth in the CPI was set at $I^* = 1.8$ percent per annum, according to the projection of inflation provided by the Ministry of Finance for 2006 and used in the state budget.[7]

In order to set the initial value X^* of X, one needs to agree on a baseline projection of postal volumes and a baseline evolution of costs over the period considered. The evolution of volumes was approximated by that of letter mail, for which the best data were available and which exhibits strong correlations with volumes of other products. La Poste anticipated a decline in letter mail volumes of −0.65 percent per annum because of the effects of electronic substitutes for mail as well as rationalization of mail campaigns by large mailers. ARCEP imposed an alternative and more optimistic scenario of a loss of

$\dot{Q}^* = -0.35$ percent per annum over the three years of the price-cap regime; this estimate was based on the average annual change in volumes of universal service products as observed from 2003 to 2005.

Total costs for universal service products were projected to grow at a rate of 1.65 percent per annum in nominal terms, that is, $\dot{c}^* = -0.15$ percent in real terms, during the period of the price cap.

Given the estimated price elasticity $e = -0.28$, the value of X^* is computed from the formal model presented above:

$$X^* = \frac{\dot{Q}^* - \dot{c}^*}{1 + e} = \frac{-0.35 + 0.15}{1 - 0.28} = -0.3\%.$$

The negative value of X implies allowed price increases in real terms. This still implies that the PO is expected to undertake significant productivity improvement efforts through modernizing its infrastructure and managerial organization ($\dot{c}^* < 0$). In addition, it implies that this productivity improvement is expected to be more than offset by a decline in the volume of demand which is not expected to lead to immediate cost reductions, because of short-run cost rigidity ($\dot{Q}^* - \dot{c}^* < 0$).

The financial situation faced by La Poste at the start of the price-cap period was characterized by a low operating margin in comparison to other major European POs. Maintaining its historical levels of productivity growth would, under the price-cap mechanism described, only provide the tariff flexibility to maintain the current margin, whereas increasing this margin was necessary. La Poste therefore had a natural incentive to increase its productivity in order to improve its profitability and this natural incentive was further reinforced under the PCR approach.

Assessment of the 2006–2008 PCR regime

Two questions arise. (i) How well did the initial projections made in setting up the PCR regime hold up over the three-year period of the price cap? (ii) What was the behavior of La Poste in terms of costs, quality and prices in response to the PCR scheme implemented?

Accuracy of initial projections of key PCR parameters

- *Inflation* The initial value of 1.8 percent is close to the average value (1.7 percent) of the three projections provided by the Ministry of Finance over the period. However, this average value was a mild underestimate of actual inflation during the period (as measured by the CPI), arising from the atypical inflation of 2008 due to the surge in oil price and the increase in the price of raw materials. The 2008 update of the initial estimate of inflation (1.6 percent instead of 1.8 percent) led to a tightening of 0.2 percent in the price cap for its last year of execution (Table 6.1).
- *Volume* The projected trend was set at −0.35 percent at the beginning of the PCR regime. Volume reductions were, however, stronger than predicted: letter mail volumes[8] experienced a 1.4 percent decrease in 2006 and a 1.0 percent decrease in 2007. The total letter mail volumes for the Groupe La Poste decreased by 1.0 percent in 2006 and 2007 and by 3.0 percent in 2008; an even greater decline is

Table 6.1 Comparison between projected inflation and actual inflation during the period 2006–08

	2006	2007	2008	Average annual rate
Projected inflation (%)	1.8 %	1.8 %	1.6 %	1.7 %
CPI (%)	1.6 %	1.5 %	2.8 %	2.0 %

Sources: Projected inflation: Initial Finance Bills for 2006, 2007 and 2008. CPI: INSEE.

expected for 2008 across the portfolio of universal service products. In total, these differences between actual and predicted volumes gave rise to an upward revision of the price cap amounting to 0.24 percent over the three-year period.

- *Operating expenses of La Poste*[9] A preliminary analysis based on La Poste's accounts exhibited controlled operating expenses (+0.5 percent per annum) during the 2005–07 period with a decrease of the personnel expenses (−1.2 percent per annum). However this trend includes the effect of a general reduction of social contributions applied to the lower end of the wage scale for the personnel employed under contract (application of the so-called Fillon Act) and a decrease in pension expenses due to the implementation of the new system for financing pensions for civil servants. Neutralizing these exogenous shocks, the personnel expenses increased (+1.6 percent per annum).
- *Service quality* As indicated above, in contrast to the PCR framework developed for example in Portugal (Castro and Franco, 2009), the French PCR regime does not include any adjustment related to service quality. This is nonetheless an area of great interest for ARCEP and postal customers, and results were monitored and published regularly. Following the implementation of PCR in 2006, service quality for universal service improved in all categories, as illustrated in Table 6.2 for the reliability of delivery for Priority letters and USO parcels.

These data show that service quality for priority letters experienced a progressive improvement of 5 percent between 2005 and 2008 in terms of $D+1$ reliability. Similar improvements were observed for USO parcels, despite a small reversal in $D+2$ reliability in 2008. These results are considered encouraging by ARCEP, although they are still somewhat below levels achieved by other major European POs, which typically reach rates of delivery reliability in excess of 90 percent. Some distinctive aspects of the French market, notably geographic characteristics, explain these differences in part. The modernization plan undertaken by La Poste[10] is expected to further improve service quality, but it has not yet been fully deployed. Of course, ARCEP will continue its role of monitoring quality of universal service.

Response of La Poste to the price cap and resulting evolution of tariffs Over the three years of the first PCR regime, the price cap authorized La Poste to raise its tariffs in nominal terms a total of 6.34 percent, which can be decomposed as follows in relation to the structure of the price-cap formula:

Table 6.2 Service quality indicators (percent of products for La Poste delivered within the specified timeframe)

		2005	2006	2007	2008
Priority letters	*D*+1	79.1	81.2	82.5	83.9
	> *D*+2	4.6	3.8	3.7	3.2
USO parcels	*D*+2	83.8	84.1	85.8	85.0
	D+3	92.2	95.5	95.9	96.3
	D+4		98.5	98.6	98.7

Note: For complete results, see: http://www.laposte.fr/IMG/pdf/Les_resultats_de_la_qualite_du_service_universel_postal_pour_l_annee_2008.pdf?espace=groupe.

Baseline allowance in the PCR mechanism: 2.10% × 3 = +6.30%

Additional volume-based adjustments: +0.24%

Adjustments based on the actual evolution of inflation: –0.20%

Over the same period, the actual price increases implemented by La Poste for the regulated basket of universal service products amounted to a total of 5.30 percent: 1.38 percent in 2006, 2.41 percent in 2007 and 1.42 percent in 2008, the annual average increase being 1.74 percent.

The stronger price evolution registered in 2006 reflects, on the one hand, increases of the priority and non-priority letter tariffs in 2005 (respectively, 6.5 percent and 7.3 percent), which had a carryover impact on 2006, and, on the other hand, increases in the prices of the following products: parcels (+3.5 percent in March 2006), single-piece domestic (+3.3 percent for letters and +4.2 percent for non-priority mail in October 2006), semi-bulk mail (+4.6 percent in October) and international mail (+2 percent in October).

In 2007, bulk mail prices were increased by 2.6 percent and parcel prices by 2.0 percent. The overall change in the basket of universal service prices of 2.41 percent is due to these increases as well as to a partial carryover to 2007 of 2006 price increases noted above. It is interesting to note that in 2006 and 2007, the price increases for the universal service basket were of the same magnitude as price increases for products in the competitive sector.

In 2008, increases in the price index for the universal service basket resulted from increases in single-piece products (+2.1 percent for priority letters and +2.5 percent for non-priority mail) and parcels (+2.8 percent).

Finally, over the three-year period, the base stamp price for letters of less than 20 grams was increased from €0.53 in 2005 to €0.55 in 2008.

Altogether, La Poste did not exhaust the total flexibility for price increases it was allowed under its price cap. The effective starting of the contract in June 2006 rather than January 1 is one reason La Poste notes for this; however, ARCEP would have accepted a price increase during the first semester of 2006, later regularized within the price cap. A more relevant reason is that, due to an economic environment less favorable than predicted, market constraints did not permit La Poste to exhaust the maximum possibilities it was granted. This situation benefited consumers who experienced lower increases than had been projected, with universal service prices increasing at an average annual rate of 1.74 percent, roughly equal to the annual rate of inflation over the period.

The Second Price-cap Regime, 2009–2011

The second PCR regime, put in place by ARCEP for the 2009–11 period, maintains several characteristics of the first price cap. The general principle in the design of the second regime has remained the maintenance of profitability ratio over the period. The scope of products falling under the price cap also remains the same, namely universal service products. However, one additional constraint was added that recognized the increasing role of competition in regulating prices of some products in the universal service basket.

Recognizing the role of competition

In implementing PCR, ARCEP was concerned (i) to protect captive customers of La Poste from excessive margins and price increases, and (ii) to not unduly constrain pricing in market segments where market forces would suffice to establish an efficient equilibrium between the PO and market participants.

In order to design a new PCR, ARCEP examined pricing strategies of La Poste and the structure of margins for the entire portfolio of universal service product offerings. Several segmentations may be used (individuals versus professional users, small versus large mailers and so on) to evaluate which product segments might be left more to the discipline of the market than being constrained by the price cap. The relevant criterion in this regard is market power. ARCEP conducted a study on this issue, which led to the following conclusions:

1. The target market for competition is bulk advertising mail (Direct Mail). Consequently, regulatory oversight would naturally be focused on the possibility of prices below attributable costs for this segment. If, in addition, one considers the financial situation of mailers in this segment, La Poste enjoys little maneuvering room for significant price increases in this market segment.
2. A further consideration is that mailers in the banking and utility sector represent a captive customer base. However, those customers are concentrated and therefore enjoy significant negotiating power in respect of La Poste.
3. Finally, one can split the segment of effectively captive customers, to which ARCEP gives priority, into two types of mailers: individuals and small and medium-sized enterprises (SMEs). Mail originating from individuals is typically stamped mail, while mail from SMEs is usually posted using an automated franking machine. Those two subsegments exhibit different margins resulting from identical prices but different costs. In practice, La Poste typically increases simultaneously, and according to a fairly uniform structure, the prices of the entire ensemble of priority and non-priority letter products, and registered letters, whether or not these are posted using stamps or franking machines. Thus, measures directed at reducing the deficit in stamped letter mail have an ancillary effect of increasing the prices and margins of

other single-piece products for all mailers using these products, notwithstanding the potential cost differences across these products and serving these mailers.

ARCEP sought solutions that would solve this problem within the general scope of the renewal of the PCR regime for 2009–2011. Two main options were examined:

> *Option 1: focus on captive users.* Under this option only services for 'captive users' would be regulated, namely services destined for use by individuals and SMEs, capping those at the rate of inflation. La Poste could then adjust its margins where these are negative and simultaneously limit increases to products used by SMEs. Tariff adjustments for other segments would be uncapped, being constrained by market forces.
>
> *Option 2: focus on stamped mail, USO parcels and registered mail.* Under this option, the formula of the preceding price cap would be maintained, thereby allowing La Poste the flexibility to adjust prices for products with negative margins, while adding the specific requirement that the price of single-piece machine-franked products, primarily purchased by SMEs and presently showing very significant positive margins, should not increase more than the rate of inflation.

Option 2 was chosen, with the intention of moving La Poste to rationalize its pricing structure by differentiating the tariffs for priority and non-priority letters depending on the method of franking.

Structure of the price cap

The new price cap is composed of a basic tariff framework similar to the PCR of the first regime, together with a supplementary constraint. Average annual increases for the global price index of universal service products are required to be no greater than $\dot{P}^* = I^* - X^*$, where I^* is the base annual rate of inflation for the period and X^* is the efficiency factor. To this overall constraint applied to the full basket of universal service products is added a specific constraint applying to the portfolio of single-piece products that are machine franked. For these products, the average annual rate of price increases is required to be no greater than the rate of inflation, that is, $\dot{P}'^* = I^*$.

The volume-related adjustment is identical to that in the first PCR period (see above), while the adjustment for inflation is slightly modified, a correction being added to take into account a possible significant discrepancy between the projected value and the realized value. This adjustment arose from the following considerations. At the time (third quarter of 2008) ARCEP started discussing with La Poste the implementation of the new framework, there was a particular concern arising from the surge in oil and raw material prices. The gap between the forecast of the Ministry of Finance and the CPI for 2008, together with the projected continuation of high oil prices, led to an integration of an adjustment for the value of the rate of inflation in the case of important departures from forecast values. Nonetheless, to overcome any reversal in projected trends, additional flexibility was introduced by having the inflation adjustment triggered only upon the explicit request of either ARCEP or La Poste. The same holds with regard to adjustment for the trend of volumes.

To be precise, accounting for annual inflation begins by taking the forecast value I_n^*

published by the Ministry of Finance in October of year $n-1$ for year n. A correction is applied in year n if and only if the actual rate of inflation $\hat{I}_{n-1}$ for year $n-1$ (as known at the beginning of year n) differs from I^*_{n-1} by more than 25 percent. I_n being the value of inflation in the price cap constrained and denoting $\Delta I_{n-1} = \hat{I}_{n-1} - I^*_{n-1}$, the adjustment procedure proceeds as follows:

$n = 1$	$I_1 = I^*_1$	
$n = 2$ or 3	$I_n = I^*_n$	if $\lvert\Delta I_{n-1} / I^*_{n-1}\rvert \leq 25\%$
	$I_n = I^*_n + \Delta I_{n-1}/2$	if $\lvert\Delta I_{n-1} / I^*_{n-1}\rvert > 25\%$.

The inflation adjustment is implemented for both the entire basket of universal service as well as the sub-basket of single-piece products that are machine franked. The adjustment for volumes applies only to the global basket.

Calibration of the contract

In the third quarter of 2008, when ARCEP and La Poste undertook a study to support the revised PCR framework, a decrease in volumes was confirmed for the French postal markets. The three-year period encompassed by the revised PCR will be characterized by this decrease, accentuated further by the economic slowdown. La Poste is still engaged in a period of important investments, with its project Cap Qualité Courrier for industrial modernization ongoing until 2010. Added to this is perhaps the most central event in decades in postal history, the full opening of the postal market to competition on January 1, 2011. It is within this context of demanding change that ARCEP has had to decide on the values for parameters for the new price-cap regime:

1. The growth in the CPI has been estimated at $I^* = 2$ percent per annum, from the published forecast by the Ministry of Finance for the year 2009.
2. On the basis of the average rate of decline from 2006 to 2008, volumes are anticipated to decline at a rate of $\dot{Q}^* = -1.3$ percent per annum during the price-cap period.
3. Total costs in the universal service scope have been estimated to grow by 0.9 percent per annum in nominal terms ($\dot{c}^* = -1.1$ percent in real terms).

Using these data yields the value of X^* factor, unchanged as compared to the first price cap:

$$X^* = \frac{\dot{Q}^* - \dot{c}^*}{1 + e} = \frac{-1.3 + 1.1}{1 - 0.28} = -0.3\%.$$

With the parameters of the 2009–2011 PCR regime, La Poste will have the possibility of increasing its prices across the basket of universal services at a rate of some 2.3 percent per annum ($I^* - X^* = 2 + 0.3$), but with the additional constraint of rebalancing tariffs across single-piece products, single-piece letters posted by franking machines facing price increases no greater than 2 percent (the projected rate of inflation for the period).

Response of La Poste to the new price cap

For the first year of operation of the second PCR regime, price increases announced by La Poste in the major products show that the PO is pursuing a rebalancing of its margins across universal service products – however, subject to significant demand-side pressures. Indeed, increases have been lower than those observed in the first PCR regime for bulk mail, where current price increases have been limited to 1 percent (around c€0.5). Increases for single-piece mail products have been similar to previous changes for the weakest weight bands (the base stamp price for a 20-gramme letter has been increased by one eurocent to €0.56) but price increases have been smaller for the superior weight bands.

Caught between the need to preserve its revenues and its concern not to disrupt demand with too drastic changes in tariff structures, the operator seems to have adopted a conservative approach. The future will show if this course of action will later lead to painful revisions.

4 CONCLUSION

Perhaps the most important property of a good price-cap regime is that it provides incentives for efficiency while promoting the public interest, in particular protecting captive customers. It should, in addition, give the regulated firm sufficient visibility to allow it to predict the pricing constraints it will face going forward and, in the perspective of full opening of the market to competition, give flexibility to restructure tariffs. Finally, it is important to emphasize that these theoretical principles can only be specified concretely for a given economic environment, characterized by the specifics of the market, the sector and the operator.

Concerning the price-cap regime instituted in France, the structure and calibration of the price cap reflected the realities of the French postal market for the 2006–09 period, characterized as it was by the end of growth in volumes and the significant restructuring of the operations of La Poste. The PCR regime also clearly did provide improved predictability of future revenues for the operator when compared with the previous system of pre-approval of tariffs, which created uncertainties that made the elaboration of the annual budget more difficult. However, two limitations to the efficiency of the PCR should be mentioned.

First, the economic context did not allow La Poste to fully use the flexibility given by the price cap in order to rebalance its tariff structure, namely to lower the tariffs of bulk mail and to increase those of single-piece mail: indeed the operator did not increase the tariffs addressed to single-piece mailers (households and SMEs) as much as would have been appropriate (as it feared a negative reaction of demand) and had recourse to increasing bulk mail tariffs to preserve its revenues. In the same vein, within the single-piece submarket, the operator seems to have delayed uncoupling the pricing of stamped mail from that of franked mail, which was one of the explicit incentival elements incorporated in the second PCR regime (2009–11).

Second, the price cap is not the most appropriate instrument to protect consumers in the case of an increase in tariffs for low-revenue product categories, with limited financial consequences and thus with negligible impact on the universal service price index, but nonetheless of interest for the consumer segments affected. A clear instance of this surfaced when La Poste prohibited sending small merchandise items under the letter mail tariff, requiring instead that these mail items be posted as parcels, at an increased price.

To deal with such cases, the price-cap regulation must be complemented by appropriate regulatory decisions.

NOTES

1. In accordance with the Third Postal Directive, complete opening of the French postal market to competition is required by January 1, 2011. Until this date, the sector reserved for La Poste includes mail items weighing less than 50 grams and whose tariffs are less than 2.5 times the basic tariff. With regard to service offerings in the competitive sector, in accordance with the Decree of January 5, 2007 setting the characteristics of universal service, the universal service provider (USP) is required to inform ARCEP of tariffs changes at least a month in advance of posting new prices, to allow ARCEP to issue and publish a notice on those proposed changes.
2. Summary Report of the 'Cour des Comptes', October 3, 2003.
3. Report of the 'Cour des Comptes' on postal accounts for 1991–2002.
4. See Article I.5-2 of the Post and Electronic Communications Code.
5. See the second section of Article L.4 of the Post and Electronic Communications Code.
6. See Florens et al. (2004).
7. This forecast can be found in the 2006 Initial Finance Bill.
8. Those figures are obtained as the difference between sales changes and price movements in the scope of the universal service.
9. The regulatory accounts are not public. That is why this chapter presents expense movements in the larger scope of La Poste's accounts: 2006 and 2007 Financial Report.
10. Named 'Cap Qualité Courrier'.

REFERENCES

Castro, J. and A. Franco (2009), 'Price and quality of service regulation in Portugal', in Michael Crew and Paul Kleindorfer (eds), *Progress in the Competitive Agenda in the Postal and Delivery Sector*, Cheltenham, UK and Northampton, MA, USA: Edward Elgar, pp. 34–51.

Crew, M. and P. Kleindorfer (1996), 'Incentives regulation in the United Kingdom and the United States: some lessons,' *Journal of Regulatory Economics*, **9**(3), May, 211–26.

Crew, M. and P. Kleindorfer (2009), 'Service quality, price caps and the USO under entry', in Michael Crew and Paul Kleindorfer (eds), *Progress in the Competitive Agenda in the Postal and Delivery Sector*, Cheltenham, UK and Northampton, MA, USA: Edward Elgar, pp. 1–22.

Florens, J.-P., S. Marcy and J. Toledano (2004), 'La demande de courrier à court et long terme', in J. Toledano (ed.), *Économie postale, Les fondements*, Paris: Economica, pp. 50–71.

Littlechild, Stephen C. (1983), 'Regulation of British Telecommunications Profitability', London: Department of Trade and Industry.

Vogelsang (2002), 'Incentive regulation and competition in public utility markets: a 20-year perspective', *Journal of Regulatory Economics*, **22**(1), 5–27.

7. Some dynamic models for mail demand: the French case*

François Boldron, Catherine Cazals, Jean-Pierre Florens and Sébastien Lécou

1 INTRODUCTION

The objective of this chapter is to empirically analyze the mail demand for postal services[1] provided by La Poste for the 1996–2007 period, notably by identifying links between mail volumes and some economic variables. A further aim is to estimate price elasticities. The last results on the French market can be found in Florens et al. (2002), which used annual data from the 1969–99 period. In particular, they identify a positive link between GDP and mail volume, show the impact of strikes on mail volumes and derive a price elasticity for mail of −0.28.

In addition to three major evolutions of tariffs, two major events took place during the 1999–2007 period that could have an impact on mail demand. First, the regulatory environment has changed with the transposition of the 2002 European Directive. In France, as in many countries in Europe, the reserved area has been reduced progressively to letters below 100 grams in 2003 and below 50 grams in 2006. The introduction of competition usually leads to significant changes in demand due to the greater choice of products for consumers, a new tariff structure, or innovation on product portfolios offered by firms.

Second, this period has been characterized by a deeper penetration of information technology in business processes and a large diffusion of broadband Internet access for residential customers (Figure 7.1).

These two simultaneous trends impact on the 'business-to-customer' (B2C) activities, especially those related to customer relation management and the corresponding marketing strategies, since postal products used to be an efficient input for these processes.

Since there is a new legal and regulatory environment and because of the development of electronic substitutes, it is useful to update the results and to address some new issues for the postal sector. In particular, price elasticities are useful for regulatory decisions or competition case law as they could be used to define relevant markets or to determine market power. As a consequence, we have started a research program to investigate demand, and this chapter will present preliminary work.

To identify the impact of the changing environment on mail demand, we have built a dynamic model which we estimate using aggregated quarterly data for the 1996–2007 period. Generally, a demand model for a given good is estimated in order to obtain an assessment of the effect of the various factors that have an influence on the demand level.

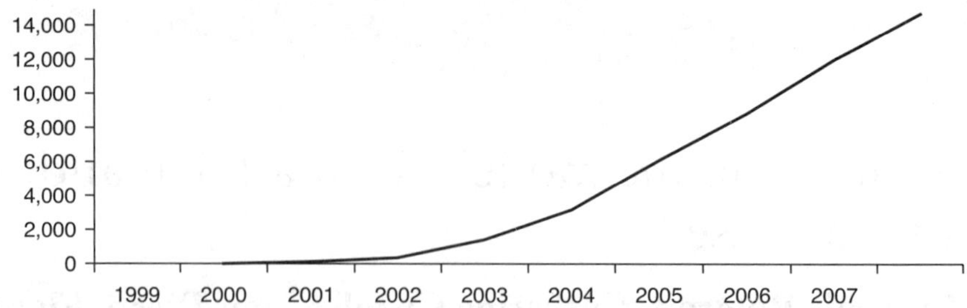

Source: ARCEP.

Figure 7.1 Number of households (thousands) with broadband ADSL access

It is very important to estimate own- or cross-price elasticities. Of course other factors are often introduced in the demand model to assess their impact, such as major economic indices which reflect the economic environment.

After a brief description of the data and a review of trends in French mail traffic in Section 2, Section 3 examines the methodology used for the demand model. In Section 4, the estimates are presented for the total traffic (First Class, Second Class and direct mail), but also for transaction mail: First plus Second Class. Long-run own- and cross-price elasticities for transaction mail and links between mail volumes and, for instance, GDP or quality of service are presented and analyzed. Section 5 explain why our database needs improvement. In particular, we shall focus on the case of electronic substitution. Section 6 concludes that there is a need to complement these types of study with more dedicated analyses so as to understand better the major trends for postal traffic in the future.

2 DATA AND TRENDS IN FRENCH MAIL TRAFFIC

The data used to estimate a demand model are quarterly time-series data about mail volumes, prices, quality of service, and various macroeconomic indicators for the 1996–2006 period. The macroeconomic indicators are provided by INSEE, the French national institute of statistics. The postal data (volume, turnover, transit times) are provided by La Poste.

Mail Traffic

The information that is provided is about volumes and revenues for three categories of mail: First Class (1C) mail (letter), Second Class (2C) mail and direct mail. Figure 7.2 shows the evolution of the total traffic during the period.

The figure underlines an increasing global trend and is the sum of heterogeneous variations. Before 2005, there were only two years of decreasing traffic (1997 and 2002). Since 2005, total traffic is continuously decreasing which might indicate a change in the trend. Furthermore, the traffic of 1C mail has decreased during the period whereas the traffic of direct and 2C mail has increased, as shown in Figure 7.3.

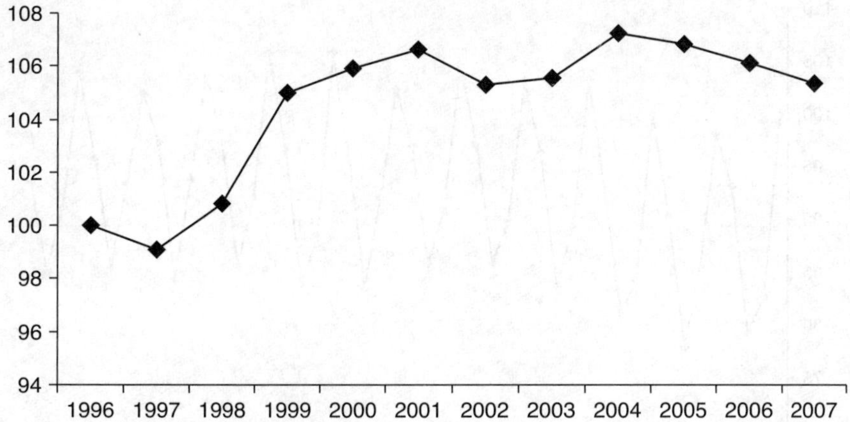

Figure 7.2 Total traffic index, 1996–2007, yearly (base 100 in 1996)

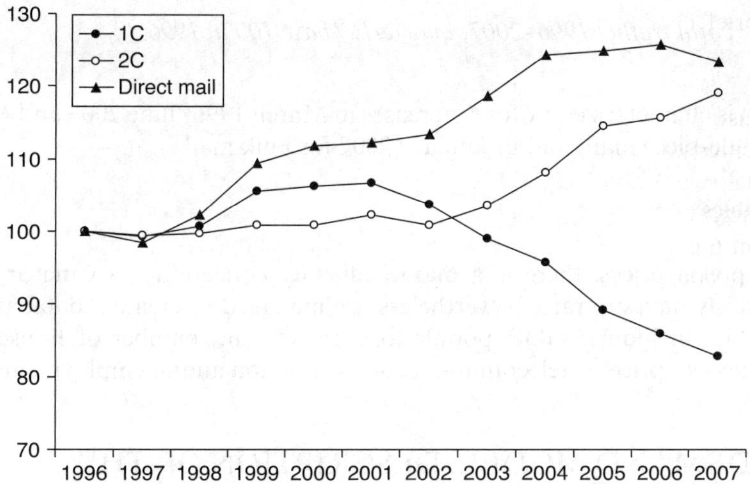

Figure 7.3 Traffic index (base 100 in 1996)

Finally, such quarterly data highlight an important seasonality effect. There are major differences of mail volume during the year, as Figure 7.4 illustrates.

We can observe the seasonal movement with the greatest values for the first quarter and lowest values for the third quarter. Those seasonal movements will not be analyzed in depth in this chapter but raise important issues in terms of tariffs or capacity constraints.

Postal Prices

The prices are defined here as the unit revenue for each type of mail (that is, the total sales revenue divided by the volume). They do not take into account the structure of postal rates according to the size and the weight of the item. Nevertheless, the period

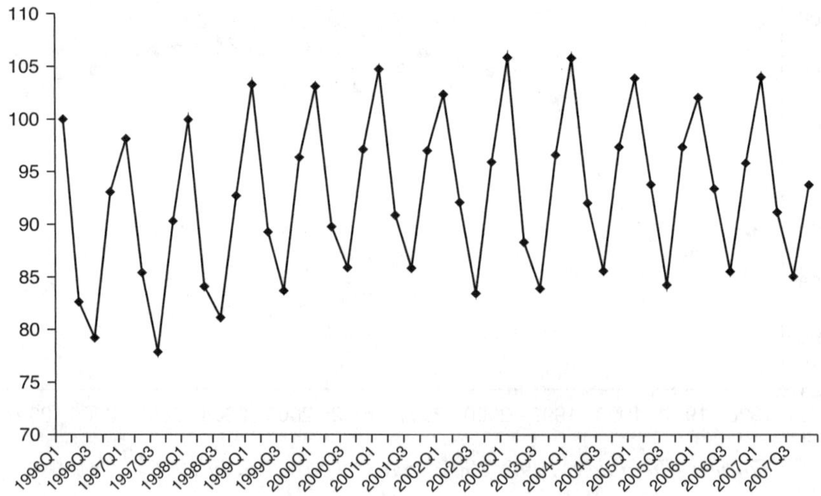

Figure 7.4 Total traffic, 1996–2007, quarterly (base 100 in 1996:1)

(1996–2007) is characterized by four increases in March 1996, June 2003 and March 2005 (only for single-piece mail) and in January 2007 for bulk mail.[2]

Other Variables

Except for postal prices, there is a major difficulty concerning explanatory variables: public quarterly data are rare. Nevertheless, we managed to create a database with different variables including: GDP, population, transit time, number of households with broadband access, price of telecommunications, inflation and unemployment rate.

3 THE DEMAND MODEL: DESCRIPTION OF THE METHODOLOGY

Usually the purpose of the estimation of a demand model for a given good is the evaluation of the impact of various factors on the level of demand. One of the more useful derived results for a policy maker with the estimation of a demand function rests with the price elasticities.

In order to estimate a demand equation for a particular good using aggregated time series, the simplest way to specify the model consists in a demand equation in the shape of a log-linear regression model. In this type of model, also called 'constant elasticity specification', we express the demand as a linear function of prices, revenues, economic and demographic variables and a time variable, where the variables are transformed logarithmically. A simple example of such a model, when T observations are available for all used variables, is as follows:

$$\text{Ln}Q_t = a + b\text{Ln}P_t + c\text{Ln}R_t + d\text{Ln}X_t + u_t, t = 1,\cdots,T, \tag{7.1}$$

where Q_t is the volume of demand at time t, P_t is a vector of prices (price of the studied good and eventual prices for substitute goods), R_t is an indicator for the revenue at time t (more often the GDP), X_t represents a vector of other pertinent variables and u_t is the standard random error term. In this model the regression coefficients can be directly interpreted as long-run elasticities of the demand with respect to the corresponding variable.

In the case of postal demand, this type of model has been applied for example for the US Postal Services (USPS) in Thress (2006). The author estimates demand equations with a functional form very close to equation (7.1) for 28 different categories of mail using quarterly data from 1971 to 2005. Apart from prices (of studied goods and competing goods), he introduces macroeconomic indicators (retail sales, mail-order retail sales, employment and investment), some variables describing the Internet environment (consumption expenditures on Internet service providers, number of broadband subscribers and Internet advertising expenditures), seasonal variables and time trends. Moreover for some types of mail he takes into account lagged values (up to four quarters) of prices in the demand equation.[3] Nikali (1997) also applies this methodology to estimate demand models for letter mail and its substitutes for the Finland case.

However, this type of specification for a demand model with an estimation using time series can be proved insufficient. Indeed we are unaware that the time series can be nonstationary and we do not take into account the possible existence of a long-run relation between some variables. Then the main drawback when doing a regression of a nonstationary series on other nonstationary series is the possibility of *spurious* regression, that is the standard significance tests are usually misleading (see, for example, Granger and Newbold, 1974). Yet many aggregated time series exhibit nonstationary behavior.

More precisely, a time series is stationary when its mean and autocovariances are independent of time.[4] A time series y_t is said to be integrated of order 1 (denoted I(1)) if when taking the first difference, $y_t - y_{t-1}$ (denoted Δy_t) produces a stationary time series.[5]

When we consider many variables simultaneously which are integrated with the same order (say I(1), for example), these variables are cointegrated if there is a linear combination of the variables that is stationary. This linear relation is called a 'cointegration equation' and is interpreted as a long-run equilibrium relationship between these variables.

The appropriate model frequently used to deal with cointegrated variables is the 'error correction model'. This specification restricts the long-run behavior of the endogenous variables to converging toward their equilibrium relation (the cointegration equation) and also describes some dynamic phenomena in the short run.

To give a simplified presentation of this model we consider only two variables, denoted x_t and y_t, which are both integrated of order 1, and a linear combination of these two variables, which is stationary. This linear combination represents a long-run equilibrium relationship that may be written, for example:

$$y_t - \beta x_t - \alpha = 0. \tag{7.2}$$

In the short run a deviation from this equilibrium may appear, and then the relation is rewritten as:

$$y_t - \beta x_t - \alpha = e_t, \tag{7.3}$$

where e_t represents the deviation or error from the long-run equilibrium and is stationary.

A general form for a vector error correction model is:

$$\begin{cases} \Delta x_t = a + \gamma e_{t-1} + \sum_{j=1}^{p} \phi_j \Delta x_{t-p} + \sum_{j=1}^{p} \lambda_j \Delta y_{t-p} + u_t \\ \Delta y_t = a' + \gamma' e_{t-1} + \sum_{j=1}^{p} \phi'_j \Delta x_{t-p} + \sum_{j=1}^{p} \lambda'_j \Delta y_{t-p} + u'_t \end{cases}$$

or

$$\begin{cases} \Delta x_t = a + \gamma (y_{t-1} - \beta x_{t-1} - \alpha) + \sum_{j=1}^{p} \phi_j \Delta x_{t-p} + \sum_{j=1}^{p} \lambda_j \Delta y_{t-p} + u_t \\ \Delta y_t = a' + \gamma' (y_{t-1} - \beta x_{t-1} - \alpha) + \sum_{j=1}^{p} \phi'_j \Delta x_{t-p} + \sum_{j=1}^{p} \lambda'_j \Delta y_{t-p} + u'_t \end{cases} \tag{7.4}$$

In these equations all terms are stationary. This model describes an adjustment process. It contains the first differences of the variables which represent the short-run fluctuations and the levels of the variables (with $e_{t-1} = y_{t-1} - \beta x_{t-1} - \alpha$) which take into account the long-run dynamics. Of course we can generalize this specification by introducing, for example, exogenous variables to the right of the equations.

When the variables y_t and x_t are in logarithmic form, the differences Δy_t and Δx_t represent growth rates of these variables. Thus we express the growth rates of each variable as a function of past growth rates of the two variables and of deviation from the long-run target at the previous period. The coefficients γ and γ' measure the speed of adjustment of variables to the long-run term. This methodology has been applied for the UK postal services in Nankervis et al. (1999 and 2002) and for the Portuguese postal services by Pimenta and Ferreira (1999). We apply this methodology in this chapter to estimate a dynamic mail demand model for the French postal services (La Poste). More precisely we consider three endogenous variables: mail volume (Q_t), price (P_t) and gross domestic product per capita (GDP_t). These variables are shown to be nonstationary and cointegrated, and the error correction specification is then appropriate.[6] The results for the cointegration tests are given in Appendix 7A.

4 ESTIMATION RESULTS

We consider two types of model. First, we estimate a model for the total traffic (that is, 1C 2C mail and direct mail) issued by all types of sender. Second, we distinguish between 1C and 2C mail, and estimate a model for each of these categories, from which we derive own- and cross-price elasticities.

Note that in these two models the price and GDP variables are entered with their real value using the CPI provided by INSEE as a deflator.

Model for Total Traffic from All Senders

We estimate error correction models as specified in equation (7.4), with 1 lag ($p = 1$ in (7.4)) and the variable corresponding to y_t, which represents the dependent variable in the long-run relation, is the total traffic per capita. Moreover we add the following exogenous variables in the model: an indicator of the quality of service represented by an indicator of the transit time measurement (denoted *QoS*), the proportion of households with a broadband subscription, denoted *NBROAD*, the net change in the number of businesses (denoted *NFIRM*), seasonal and time dummies, denoted *S2*, *S3*, *S4* and *DyearQquart*, respectively (for example, D03Q1 is equal to 1 at date 2003q1 and 0 elsewhere) and trend. The model is estimated using the Johansen algorithm (Hamilton, 1994).

Our goal is mainly to obtain an estimate of the magnitude for the price elasticity. We must then find the most appropriate model to explain the trajectory of the mail demand over the observed period, using available information about relevant variables. The criteria we use to assess the performance of various models are the standard criteria: R2, information criteria such as AIC (Akaïke Information Criteria) or Schwartz criteria, and graph of fitted versus actual values.

Given the fundamental role of the value of the price elasticity for the decision maker, it is important to obtain some robust results about estimates. In many cases, the econometrician has available only partial information about the relevant variables to be taken into account in a model. To introduce or to omit some variables in a model may result in relatively large modifications on the parameter of interest (such as in our case the price elasticity) while giving very similar adjustment performances. One of the reasons for this may be, for example, the colinearity between some variables, which is a technical problem with no really satisfactory solution, particularly in an economic model in which economic theory makes it inevitable that some variables are taken into account (for example, prices and revenue in a standard demand model).

In our case, as is often the case with time-series analysis, in order to offset the lack of information about some relevant economic phenomenon, and to improve the performance of the model, we introduce some time dummy variables. In a first step we estimate a model for the total mail demand defined as the sum of transaction and direct mail. The results are shown in Table 7.1.

First, note that there is a good adjustment performance for this model with a value of adjusted R^2 equal to 0.99. The results for the long-run relation show a long-run elasticity of GDP equal to 0.4, which tends to be stable to the specification of the model (in terms of the different variables which are introduced).

The long-run price elasticity is equal to −0.679, which is significantly different from the previous estimate of Florens et al. (2002). Traffic appears to be more sensitive to price. In the short-run relation, there is a significant negative effect of the proportion of households with a broadband subscription and the positive effects of the net number of firms setting up and quality of service, lagged for 1 period.

However, according to the introduction or withdrawal of some dummy variables the range for the price elasticity varies[7] with very similar adjustment performance for the different models. Therefore, this result should be analyzed and interpreted with caution.

In a second step we consider a model where the total traffic is defined only by the transaction mail (we drop the direct mail). The results are shown in the Table 7.2.

First, note that there is a good quality of adjustment of the estimated equations as the value of adjusted R^2 is 0.98.

The long-run elasticity of transaction mail to GDP is equal to 0.738, which is a higher value than in the model for total mail. This value is robust to the specification of the

Table 7.1 Estimated coefficients of error correction equation for total traffic (transaction plus direct mail)

Long-run relation (cointegrating equation)		
Variables	Dependent variable: Ln Q_t	
	Coeff.	*t*-ratio
Ln P_t	−0.679	−3.63
Ln GDP_t	0.416	5.42
Constant	11.428	

Short-run equation		
Variables	Dependent variable: ΔLn Q_t	
	Coeff.	*t*-ratio
e_{t-1}*	−1.0177	−7.45
ΔLn Q_{t-1}	−0.0800	−0.91
ΔLn P_{t-1}	0.2491	2.11
ΔLn GDP_{t-1}	−0.5944	−1.72
Constant	−0.2462	−0.75
S2	−0.1455	−10.00
S3	−0.2503	−12.23
S4	−0.1149	−6.27
NBROAD	−2.9708	−5.22
Ln(QoS_{t-1})	0.1236	3.81
Ln($NFIRM_{t-1}$)	0.0426	1.35
T03	0.0282	4.71
D99	0.0174	3.19
D96Q4	0.0423	4.04
D98Q2	−0.0308	−2.94
D00Q3	0.0289	2.82
D02Q1	−0.0370	−3.55
D03Q2	−0.0486	−4.50
D05Q1	−0.0310	−3.03
D06Q1	−0.0260	−2.51
D07Q4	−0.0432	−3.97
Adj. R^2	0.9929	

Note: *e_{t-1} *represents the cointegrating equation, defined as in equation (7.3)*

model as we obtained a range between 0.7 and 0.8 according to different exogenous variables or dummies introduced into the model.

The long-run price elasticity is equal to −0.539, but this result is not very stable, as was the case with the previous model for total traffic. Indeed, as in the preceding model, according to the introduction or withdrawal of some dummy variables the price elasticity varies with very similar adjustment performance for the different models. We have chosen to show here the results for the model with a minimum number of time dummies.

Table 7.2 Estimated coefficients of error correction equation for transaction mail

Long-run relation (cointegrating equation)		
Variables	Dependent variable: Ln Q_t	
	Coeff.	*t*-ratio
Ln P_t	−0.539	−2.20
Ln GDP_t	0.7386	4.69
T	−0.0034	−3.20
Constant	15.135	
Short-run equation		
Variables	Dependent variable: ΔLn Q_t	
	Coeff.	*t*-ratio
e_{t-1}*	−1.0763	−5.13
ΔLn Q_{t-1}	0.0637	0.46
ΔLn P_{t-1}	0.2336	1.37
ΔLn GDP_{t-1}	−0.1827	−0.35
Constant	−0.7021	−1.58
S2	−0.1397	−6.77
S3	−0.2071	−7.23
S4	−0.1114	−5.21
NBROAD	−1.5085	−2.00
QoS	0.1991	4.71
$NFIRM_{t-1}$	0.0840	1.99
T03	0.0118	1.37
D99	0.0218	2.49
D98Q2	−0.0330	−2.04
D00Q3	0.0363	2.22
Adj. R^2	0.981	

Note: *e_{t-1} *represents the cointegrating equation, defined as in equation (7.3).*

Finally, there is a small but significant decreasing trend. Compared to the results of Florens et al. (2002), sensitivities are higher. Indeed, they obtained a price elasticity of −0.27 and a GDP elasticity of 0.75 with an increasing trend. This might reflect profound changes in the mail demand due to the development of the Internet. In future research it will therefore be necessary to have a variable reflecting the price, the development of alternative media, and telecommunications.

In the short-term relation, note the negative effect of the proportion of households with a broadband subscription and the positive effects of the net number of firms setting up, lagged for 1 period, and of the quality of service.

1C and 2C Mail Models

We have estimated the same type of model using information about the two categories of mail: First and Second Class.

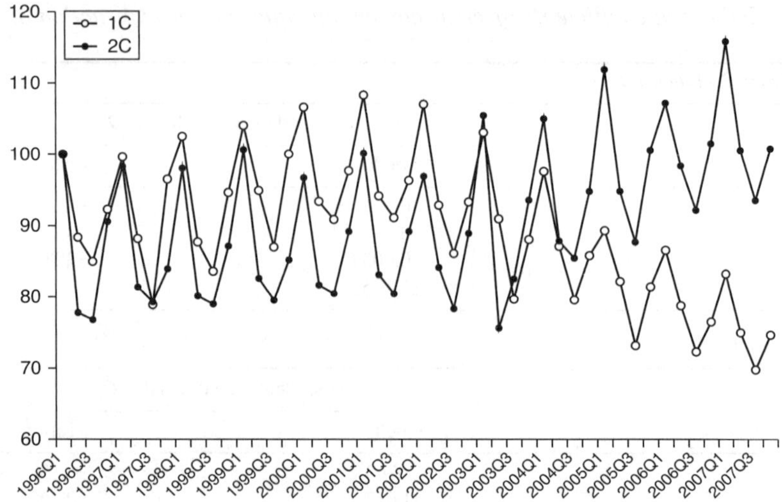

Figure 7.5 1C and 2C mail volumes, 1996–2007 (base 100 in 1996:1)

Figure 7.5 shows the evolution of the volumes of the two categories of mail for firms during the observed period. We observe the same structure of seasonality as for the total traffic, with the greatest values for the first quarter of each year. Note an increasing trend for 2C mail with acceleration after 2002. For 1C mail, we observe an increasing trend until 2001 and a decreasing trend after. Note that 2C mail represents around 44 percent of transaction mail (1C and 2C) until 2004, and increases to 54 percent in the last year.

Table 7.3 gives the results for the error correction model for these two categories.

First, we obtain a good quality of adjustment of the estimated equation as the adjusted R^2 are equal to 0.99 for each equation.

We find the same problem as in the aggregated model. According to the introduction or withdrawal of some dummies or trends, the range for the own-price elasticities is between −0.46 and −0.7 for 1C mail and between −0.7 and −0.9 for 2C mail. For cross-price elasticities these ranges are: between 0.5 and 0.8 for the 1C mail model; and between 0.4 and 0.6 for the 2C mail model; The elasticity of GDP tends to be stable in the two models: between 0.9 and 1 in the 1C mail model and around 0.5 in the 2C mail model.

Note the significant and negative effect of the proportion of households with a broadband subscription and the positive effect of the quality of service in the short-term relations for the 2 models. In addition, for the 2C mail model we have a significant positive effect of the net number of firms setting up, lagged for 1 period.

In addition, we attempted to estimate a model for direct mail, and also to distinguish the type of sender (households and enterprises) for these models, but the results were not consistent.

Table 7.3 Estimated coefficients of error correction equations for 1C and 2C mail

Long-run relation (cointegrating equation)					
First Class mail			Second Class mail		
Variables	Dependent variable: Ln $Q1C_t$		Variables	Dependent variable: Ln $Q2C_t$	
	Coeff.	t-ratio		Coeff.	t-ratio
Ln $P1C_{t-1}$	−0.5498	−2.837	Ln $P1C_{t-1}$	0.422	3.112
Ln $P2C_{t-1}$	0.5243	2.605	Ln $P2C_{t-1}$	−0.730	−3.878
Ln GDP_{t-1}	0.9271	9.042	Ln GDP_{t-1}	0.492	6.007
T	−0.0021	−2.447	T	−0.004	−5.140
Constant	19.2004		Constant	12.999	
Short-run equation					
Variables	Dependent variable: ΔLn $Q1C_t$		Variables	Dependent variable: ΔLn $Q2C_t$	
	Coeff.	t-ratio		Coeff.	t-ratio
e_{t-1}*	−1.124	−11.461	e_{t-1}*	−1.962	−18.544
ΔLn $Q1C_{t-1}$	−0.319	−4.637	ΔLn $Q1C_{t-1}$	0.635	8.815
ΔLn $P1C_{t-1}$	−0.311	−2.216	ΔLn $P1C_{t-1}$	−0.156	−0.839
ΔLn $P2C_{t-1}$	−0.142	−1.149	ΔLn $P2C_{t-1}$	−0.231	−1.438
ΔLn GDP_{t-1}	0.469	1.503	ΔLn GDP_{t-1}	−1.734	−4.568
Constant	0.262	25.483	Constant	−1.734	−5.843
S2	−0.108	−11.801	*S2*	−0.114	−10.328
S3	−0.251	−18.874	*S3*	−0.152	−10.316
S4	−0.189	−14.464	*S4*	−0.186	−16.084
NBROAD	−0.796	−8.032	*NBROAD*	−0.916	−2.042
QoS_{t-1}	0.137	5.208	*QoS*	0.316	11.880
T02	−0.003	−4.764	$NFIRM_{t-1}$	0.178	6.323
D97Q3	−0.097	−11.135	*T03*	0.018	3.160
D97Q2	−0.062	−7.420	*D05*	0.035	5.754
D97Q1	−0.043	−5.064	*D97Q2*	0.044	3.796
D98Q2	−0.084	−9.424	*D97Q4*	−0.033	−3.141
D98Q3	−0.082	−8.991	*D98Q2*	−0.043	−4.105
D99Q4	0.036	4.168	*D00Q1*	−0.031	−2.929
D00Q4	0.033	3.927	*D02Q1*	−0.054	−5.092
D00Q2	−0.055	−5.727	*D02Q3*	−0.054	−4.708
D01Q2	−0.038	−4.535	*D06Q1*	−0.066	−6.516
D02Q3	−0.035	−3.985	*D07Q4*	−0.064	−5.904
D02Q2	−0.027	−3.220			
D05Q1	−0.064	−7.972			
Adj. R^2	0.995		Adj. R^2	0.995	

Note: *e_{t-1} represents the cointegrating equation, defined as in equation (7.3)

5 A NEED FOR A BETTER DATABASE

As we have seen, some of our results are not stable with respect to the introduction of dummy variables. The elasticities we have estimated are affected by this lack of stability and will thus have to be treated with caution. In addition to the fact that our period of observation is rather short, several other limitations in our data and our model could account for this problem.

First, price changes for postal products are rare, limiting the precision of the estimates of price elasticities. In 10 years, there were only three price changes for single-piece mail. Moreover, the three changes all occurred in the same direction (price increases) making it impossible to study elasticities associated with price drops. Another drawback is that we do not study elasticities relating to real prices but rather to average revenues, and therefore we do not take into account the modifications in the structure of rates (according to weight or size).

Finally, an issue that will grow in importance is the need to take into account the effects of competition on volumes. Competition in the mail market will certainly have to be taken into account after 2011, but it is not likely to affect our present results. However, other forms of competition, that is, intermodal competition, already exist. One form of competition not taken into account in the model is the competition between the different advertising channels. Demand for direct mail is likely to be affected by the price of advertising on close substitutes (or complements as we shall see) such as television, radio or the press. More generally, further work remains to be done in order to fully incorporate the effects of electronic substitution in the model.

We have found a negative effect on mail volume of the proportion of households with a broadband subscription. This result could be interpreted as a sign of electronic substitution. However, electronic substitution is a complex matter, and our approach which consists in capturing this effect by using only one variable is certainly too limited. A proper analysis of this issue should be able to take into account the facts that there is a strong phenomenon of electronic substitution, that this substitution is concomitant with a similar process of complementarity and finally, that these different processes are explained by different variables.

First it is well documented that electronic substitution is indeed a cause of the decrease in certain categories of mail. Email is certainly the most straightforward issue when one is thinking about electronic substitution. With regards to transactional mail, this form of substitution can be, for instance, illustrated in France by the rise in income declarations using electronic means. The number of these electronic declarations rose from 119,000 in 2002 to 7.5 million in 2007. An additional example concerns the Mail Order Business sector: people use mail less often to order goods as Figure 7.6 shows.

With regard to direct mail, it seems that non-solicited advertising is more easily accepted in the area of traditional mail than in electronic mail. However, it does not mean that direct mail is not also affected by substitution. There is a rise in advertising budgets directed toward the Internet that could lead to a decrease in the budgets affected by direct mail campaigns. Soteri et al. (2009) find an important substitution effect between Internet advertising and direct mail: an increase of 1 percent in Internet advertising budgets would lead to a 4 percent drop in direct mail expenses. However, different advertising channels can also be complementary. In traditional media, there are signs of complementarity

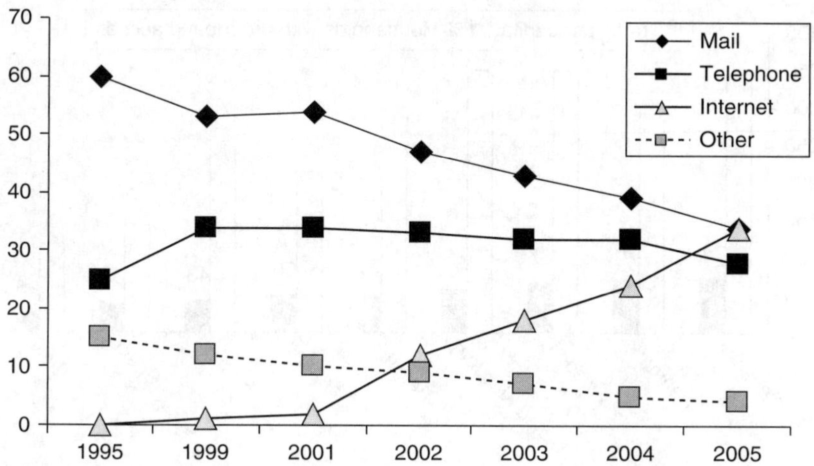

Source: MINEFI (2007).

Figure 7.6 Method of payment (France, %)

between television and direct mail campaigns. The existence of a similar effect with the Internet remains to be studied in France.

This leads us to a second important issue, that is, the possible existence of complementarity between mail and electronic communications. Our approach in this chapter is too aggregated to isolate such a phenomenon that could coexist alongside electronic substitution. However, such an effect also seems to be well documented and should be considered in future research.

Figure 7.7 shows a correlation between mail traffic per capita and the percentage of households with broadband access. Of course, this does not mean that there is a causal link between the two variables. However, it certainly shows that the development of an electronic society does not automatically lead to the collapse of the mail market. In contrast, there are many examples showing that electronic communication can lead to an increase in mail volume. The more obvious case for electronic complementarity in the postal market concerns parcels associated with online commerce. Nevertheless, the growth of e-commerce is also, to a lesser extent, susceptible to generating mail traffic such as billing or direct mail. For example, in 2008 more than 50 million train tickets (27 percent of the total) were bought on the Internet site of the SNCF (the French national railway company), which is proposing to send out the tickets by mail; such a possibility did not exist before. Moreover, in its report on the development of new technology, the Ministry of the Economy, Finances and Employment (Ministère de l'Économie, des Finances et de l'Industrie: MINEFI, 2007) underlines the fact that 20 percent of households buying on the Internet choose to pay by sending a check in a letter. In comparison, 84 percent say that they sometimes pay by credit card.

The global impact of electronic competition on mail volume is not yet clear, despite some attempts to quantify the different complementarity and substitution effects. For example, Robinson (2006) shows that the estimations of elasticities in the US between 1997 and 2004 presented no major changes, despite a drastic rise in Internet penetration.

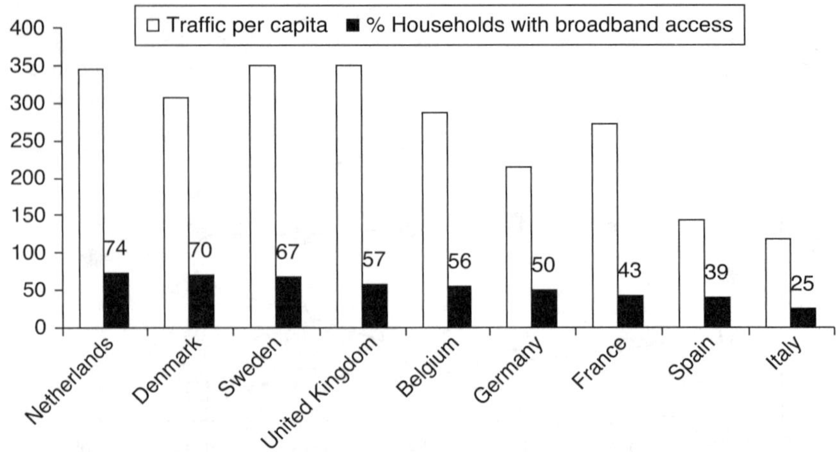

Source: MINEFI (2007).

Figure 7.7 Mail traffic per capita and percentage of households with broadband ADSL access

Visco Comandini et al. (2009) even find that elasticities could be decreasing with time. In contrast, Nikali (2008) finds evidences of electronic substitution for business-to-business (B2B) and (Customer-to-Business/customer) (C2B/C) mail. Hong and Wolak (2008) also find that the adoption of a personal computer during the 1994–2000 period reduced postage consumption of households by 23 percent. This percentage decreases after 2000, showing the possible growth of online transactions associated with delivery services.

Thus, we see that there is no unique trend of substitution, but several phenomena of substitution and several phenomena of complementarity. It is likely that each phenomenon is explained by different variables (not completely correlated, for example the rise of online commerce occurred after the rise in emails), making it impossible to study the impact of electronic communications thanks to a single variable. Moreover, in order to have a precise understanding of this issue and its heterogeneity according to the identity of the senders, it would certainly prove useful to conduct an econometric study at a more microeconomic level as in Hong and Wolak (2008), in particular by using panel data.

6 CONCLUSION

The econometric analysis of postal demand during the 1996–2007 period has highlighted several tendencies that should be validated by further research. First, there is a small but significant decreasing trend for mail volume. Second, price sensitivities are larger than they were before 1996. Third, quality of service has a positive impact on mail volume. Fourth, the proportion of households with a broadband subscription has a negative impact on mail volume. Note that these results have to be regarded some with caution, since our model has some limitations. First, there are not enough variables in order to take into account fully the phenomenon of electronic substitution. This can be a major problem in an environment where electronic substitution tends to be seen as one of the main drivers of volume evolution. Furthermore, it must also be highlighted that the postal sector is in a period of major uncertainty. Consumer practices are evolving rapidly and it is not yet clear if demand in 2007 can be explained by the same model as the one used to explain demand in 1996. Moreover, we need to build a model that explains the demand for direct mail, which will probably be possible using micro econometrics.

NOTES

* The views expressed in this chapter are those of the authors and do not necessarily reflect the views of La Poste.

1. Mail demand originating from the 'Banque postale' has been excluded from the data.
2. Note that in January 2002 with the arrival of the euro, postal prices changed slightly and an increase occurred in October 2006.
3. This model belongs to the class of 'distributed lag models'.
4. This definition refers to the concept of weak stationarity. Strong stationarity requires that the distribution of the variable is independent of time.
5. More generally a time series is I(*d*) if after being first differenced *d* times it becomes stationary. However, we shall deal here only with I(1) variables because it is the more frequent situation with economic variables.
6. We use the augmented Dickey–Fuller test to test the presence of unit roots (nonstationarity) and the Johansen test to prove the cointegration.
7. Note that compared to the work done by Florens et al. (2002), we always observe a higher price sensitivity.

REFERENCES

Florens J.P., S. Marcy and J. Toledano (2002), 'Mail demand in the long and short term', in M.A. Crew and P.R. Kleindorfer (eds), *Postal and Delivery Services: Pricing, Productivity, Regulation and Strategy*, Boston, MA: Kluwer Academic, pp. 171–90.

Granger, C.W.J. and P. Newbold (1974), 'Spurious regressions in econometrics', *Journal of Econometrics*, **74**, 226–42

Hamilton J.D. (1994), *Time Series Analysis*, Princeton, NJ: Princeton University Press.

Hong, S.H. and F.A. Wolak (2008), 'Relative prices and electronic substitution: changes in household-level demand for postal delivery services from 1986 to 2004', *Journal of Econometrics*, **145**, 226–42.

MINEFI (2007), *Tableau de bord des TIC et du commerce électronique (entreprises – ménages)*, Ministéere de l'Économie, des Finances at de l'Industrie, Paris.

Nankervis, J., I. Carslake and F. Rodriguez (1999), 'How important have price and quality of service been to mail volume growth?', in M.A. Crew and P.R. Kleindorfer (eds), *Emerging Competition in Postal and Delivery Services*, Boston, MA: Kluwer Academic.

Nankervis, J., S. Richard, S. Soteri and F. Rodriguez (2002), 'Disaggregated Letter Traffic Demand in the UK, in M.A. Crew and P.R. Kleindorfer (eds), *Postal and Delivery Services: Pricing, Productivity, Regulation and Strategy*, Boston, MA: Kluwer Academic, pp. 203–18.

Nikali, H. (1997), 'Demand models for letter mail and its substitutes: results from Finland', in M.A. Crew and P.R. Kleindorfer (eds), *Managing Change in the Postal and Delivery Industries*, Boston, MA: Kluwer Academic, pp. 133–61.

Nikali, H. (2008), 'Substitution of letter mail for different sender–receiver segments', in M.A. Crew and P.R. Kleindorfer (eds), *Competition and Regulation in the Postal and Delivery Sector*, Cheltenham, UK and Northampton, MA, USA: Edward Elgar, pp. 89–106.

Pimenta, A. and P. Ferreira (1999), 'Demand for letters in Portugal', in M.A. Crew and

P.R. Kleindorfer (eds), *Emerging Competition in Postal and Delivery Services*, Boston, MA: Kluwer Academic.
Robinson, A. (2006), 'A review of price elasticity models for postal products', Pitney Bowes background paper 2007-01.
Soteri, S., F. Fève, J.P. Florens and F. Rodriguez (2009), 'Internet advertising and direct mail: trends and analysis for the UK', in M.A. Crew and P.R. Kleindorfer (eds), *Progress in the Competitive Agenda in the Postal and Delivery Sector*, Cheltenham, UK and Northampton, MA, USA: Edward Elgar, pp. 209–22.
Thress, T.E. (2006), 'Direct Testimony of Thomas E. Thress on behalf of the United States Postal Service', Postal Rate Commission, Docket No. R2006-1.
Visco Comandini, V., M. Lintell, S. Gori, M.R. Pierleoni and T.B. Tisdahl (2009), 'Postal price elasticities and intermedia competition: a multisided market approach', in M.A. Crew and P.R. Kleindorfer (eds), *Progress in the Competitive Agenda in the Postal and Delivery Sector*, Cheltenham, UK and Northampton, MA, USA: Edward Elgar, pp. 163–83.

APPENDIX 7A

The following tables show the results for the Johansen cointegration rank tests (trace and maximum eigenvalue) for total traffic, transaction mail (1C + 2C) and 1C mail and 2C mail models. The two tests indicate the rejection of the hypothesis of no cointegration in each model.

Table 7A.1 Total traffic

H0: Max number of cointegrating relations	Trace statistic	Max-Eigen statistic
None	135.1832*	129.4618*
At most 1	5.721346	4.140131
At most 2	1.581216	1.581216

Note: *Denotes rejection of the hypothesis at the 0.05 level.

Table 7A.2 Transaction mail

H0: number of cointegrating relations	Trace statistic	Max-Eigen statistic
None	144.7168*	131.5276*
At most 1	13.18921	8.666215
At most 2	4.522997	4.522997

Note: *Denotes rejection of the hypothesis at the 0.05 level.

Table 7A.3 1C mail

H0: number of cointegrating relations	Trace statistic	Max-Eigen statistic
None	135.4803*	103.6883*
At most 1	31.79197	17.91634
At most 2	13.87563	10.30408
At most 3	3.57155	3.57155

Note: *Denotes rejection of the hypothesis at the 0.05 level.

Table 7A.4 2C mail

H0: number of cointegrating relations	Trace statistic	Max-Eigen statistic
None	132.4192*	102.9497*
At most 1	29.46956	14.60381
At most 2	14.86575	11.45498
At most 3	3.410772	3.410772

Note: *Denotes rejection of the hypothesis at the 0.05 level.

8. Forecasting mail volumes in an evolving market environment*

Frédérique Fève, Jean-Pierre Florens, Frank Rodriguez and Soterios Soteri

1 INTRODUCTION

Postal markets, in common with other markets, adapt and respond to developments in technology and the wider economy. Quantitative estimates of the historic impact of these influences can be obtained using standard econometric modeling techniques.[1] For example, in the USA, the UK and Finland, econometric time-series models are used to generate national postal operator (NPO) forecasts and inform scenario analysis. In an environment where conditions in the postal market going forward in time are similar to those that existed when these models were estimated, model-based projections can be expected to yield broadly unbiased, although potentially highly uncertain, conditional forecasts.

However, if the forecast period contains significant changes in the external environment, related for example to advances in technology or the introduction of competition into a traditional monopoly area, projections for postal volumes based on standard econometric models alone are likely to be biased and subject to wide confidence intervals.[2] By acknowledging the potential for structural breaks to occur in the forecast time period, it is possible to develop non-standard econometric-based models to attempt to allow for such breaks, and improve postal volume projections.

This chapter adopts a theoretical stylized model to explore how changes in the external environment can impact on postal demand and how, via iterative analysis of outcomes compared to projections, it is possible to learn about the nature of such structural changes and reduce the level of uncertainty surrounding NPO volume projections. The theoretical framework underpinning this model is Bayesian in character and generates initial mail market and firm-level projections based on priors informed by traditional econometric techniques and other types of business information. The dynamic and interactive nature of information flows and projection updates are explicitly embodied within the model, such that it allows for the structured updating of projections and model parameters as new outcome information on the evolving environment becomes available over time and new information regarding the future environment also becomes available. The theoretical framework assumes that assumptions are updated in the light of partial observations using a Bayesian version of the Kalman filter approach and results are illustrated via simulation analysis.

In recent years the environment that NPOs are operating within has been affected simultaneously by, among other factors, increasing levels of postal competition, advances in technology, environmental or 'green' concerns and uncertain economic conditions. The continuous and dynamic nature of external shocks means that it is difficult to disentangle individual effects. To construct model-based volume forecasts that directly address structural changes in postal markets, our theoretical stylized model considers just two of these: increasing levels of electronic substitution and the introduction of postal competition within a traditional monopoly market. In reality, postal competition is present and intensifying in many developed postal markets. Furthermore, factors other than technological change, for example economic uncertainty, are also impacting on mail volumes. The approach developed in this chapter can be applied more widely to address these other factors.

Section 2 describes a simple model of the demand for mail in a pre- and post-competitive entry environment. Section 3 provides an analysis of why the theoretical model-based projections are likely to differ from outcome data and how business forecasters can use partial information to update model assumptions to improve future projections. Section 4 uses Monte Carlo simulation techniques to assess the extent to which the incomplete but continuous arrival of new information over time can be used to improve NPO letter volume projections. Furthermore, this section also examines the potential improvement in modeling postal volumes by including off-model business intelligence in the projection process. Section 5 contains a summary and conclusion.

2 THE MODEL

A simple stylized model is adopted for ease of exposition. This model assumes that the market is characterized by a monopoly NPO offering two end-to-end (E2E) goods with volumes $Q1$ and $Q2$ up to and including period T. In the post-competition environment, period $T + 1$ onwards, it is assumed that two types of structural shocks occur. First, competitors enter the postal market and offer to collect mail directly from customers, sort this mail to some pre-specified level and pay the NPO an access charge (PA) to deliver the entrants' mail volume (QE) to its final destination. This can be viewed as being broadly similar to the downstream access form of entry that has taken place in a number of countries. Second, it is assumed that technology-related changes reduce the overall demand for letter mail due to electronic substitution. Therefore in the post-competition period, it is not clear to the NPO whether changes in the demand for goods 1 and 2 are due to the impact of competition, changes in technology, randomness of the pre-competitive entry model, or a mixture of all three.

It is assumed, initially, that the NPO projects the potential impact of technology-related substitution and competition in period T, in advance of competitive entry taking place in period $T + 1$. That is, the NPO generates *prior forecasts* in period T, for periods $T + 1$ onwards using information available up to and including period T. Thereafter, the model assumes that the NPO observes a number of outcome data points in time period $T + 1$ together with any other information that may become available in that period regarding future developments that may affect mail volumes in later periods. The NPO then reviews its prior assumptions in the light of the new information available in period $T + 1$ for later periods, say, to periods $T + q$, and generates updated mail volume projections for periods $T + 2$ onwards. An equivalent process is assumed to occur in each successive future period.

Forecasting the Demand for Mail in the Pre-competition Era

Prior to competitive entry, that is up to and including period T, it is assumed that the NPO models the demand for letter mail through a two-equation model of the following form:[3]

$$q1_t = \alpha_1 + \beta_1 q1_{t-1} + \gamma_1 p1_t + \delta_1 p2_t + \iota_1 t + u_{1t} \quad (8.1)$$

$$q2_t = \alpha_2 + \beta_2 q2_{t-1} + \gamma_2 p1_t + \delta_2 p2_t + \iota_2 t + u_{2t} \quad (8.2)$$

where all lower-case variables denote logarithmic values of upper-case variables in time period subscript t (for example, $q1_t = \ln(Q1_t)$); pi is the price of good i ($i = 1, 2$); t is a time trend variable equal to 1 in the model's first observation period $t = 1$, equal to 2 in the following period $t = 2$, and so on up to $t = T$; α_i, β_i, γ_i, δ_i, ι_i are estimated parameters; economic theory suggests that $\gamma_1 < 0$, $\delta_1 > 0$, $\gamma_2 > 0$, $\delta_2 < 0$, and u_{it} is a random disturbance term for model i.

The total demand for mail, Q, is assumed to be equal to:

$$Q = Q1 + Q2. \quad (8.3)$$

Information Available to the NPO Prior to Competitive Entry

It is assumed that the NPO knows that its monopoly status will expire in advance of the first period of competitive entry in period $T + 1$ and that competition will take place via upstream competition. In period T, the NPO is assumed to have in its possession an econometric model for mail demand, estimated using standard ordinary least squares (OLS) time-series modeling techniques that it developed in the pre-competitive environment (that is, (8.1) and (8.2) above). Furthermore, as competitive entry is assumed to take place via downstream access, the NPO is assumed to know two additional pieces of information for periods $T + 1$ onwards. First, the price the NPO will charge competitors for access to its downstream network, PA. Second, *ex post*, the size of the total mail market (that is, $Q = Q1 + Q2 + QE$) as it delivers all items, either for its own E2E services (that is, $Q1 + Q2$) or for entrants (that is, QE).

However, in period T, and indeed in the post-competition era $T + 1$ onwards, it is assumed that the NPO does not know the price entrants charge customers (PE). The difference between the price entrants charge customers and the access price ($PE - PA$) reflects unknown competitor upstream collection and sorting costs and entrants' margins. In addition, it is assumed that advances in technology are having an impact on the demand for mail in the post-competition period, but the NPO is unable to directly observe or quantify this impact with certainty, even after the event has taken place, for it is just one of a number of factors impacting on the observed volume of mail.

Forecasting the Demand for Mail in a Changing Market Environment

In our model, prior to the introduction of competition in period T, the NPO is assumed to know that the post-competition mail market will consist of three mail goods ($Q1$, $Q2$ and QE) and three prices ($P1$, $P2$, PE). In addition, it is also assumed that the NPO believes that advances in technology are impacting on the demand for mail. However, in the absence of any observable outcome data it is not possible for the NPO to extend its econometric time-series model, to, say, a three-equation system in order to forecast the impact of either competitive entry or changes in technology. While there is no direct observable outcome data on each of these two effects up to and including period T, other less formal information may exist. Such information may include non-econometric-type forecasting models calibrated with business expert information on the potential extent of technology-related substitution, or business opinion and market research on the extent to which customers may switch supplier at different price levels, perhaps informed by contingent valuation market research.

It is therefore possible to postulate a market model for mail in a post-competitive environment affected by technology-related substitution and, also, to populate the model parameters and assumptions using information prior to such changes taking place. Such a model could then be used to project mail volumes in an evolving and changing market environment. While, at least initially, such a model may not be based entirely on fully observed historical data, outcome information will accumulate over time. The model parameters and input assumptions can be reviewed and amended in the light of post-competitive entry outcome data. In particular, regular and rigorous *outcome versus projection* (OVP) investigations can be conducted to assess model parameter and input assumptions. The findings of successive OVP investigations can then be used to recalibrate model parameters and update input assumptions over time. In addition, other external information on future changes to the business or technology environment or customer preferences may also become available in each time period. All such information is relevant potentially for updating forecasts in the next period. In the long run, it would be preferable to estimate a fully specified mail market model using observed outcome data. However, in the absence of directly observable data for some factors or variables, and while the market is evolving towards a stable long-run end state, it is not possible to use standard econometric techniques alone to estimate such a model.

Specifying the Demand for Mail Model in a Changing Market Environment

We consider a postal demand model that contains three submodels. First, a full market model (*MM*) to project mail market volumes, including the impact of technology changes. Second, a switching model (*SM*) to predict the extent to which NPO mail traffic moves to postal entrants. Third, a postal entry model (*EM*) that estimates competitors' price and relative quality offerings in the mail market.

The full market model (*MM*) is assumed to be of the form:

$$q1_t^* = \alpha_{1t} + \beta_1 q1_{t-1}^* + \gamma_1 p1_t^* + \delta_1 p2_t^* + \iota_1 t + \mu_1 t + u_{1t}^* \tag{8.4}$$

$$q2_t^* = \alpha_{2t} + \beta_2 q2_{t-1}^* + \gamma_2 p1_t^* + \delta_2 p2_t^* + \iota_2 t + \mu_2 t + u_{2t}^* \tag{8.5}$$

$$P1_t^* = P1_t(1 - f1_t) + PE_t f1_t \tag{8.6}$$

$$P2_t^* = P2_t(1 - f2_t) + PE_t f2_t \tag{8.7}$$

$$Q1_t = Q1_t^*(1 - f1_t) \tag{8.8}$$

$$Q2_t = Q2^*_t(1 - f2_t) \tag{8.9}$$

$$QE_t = Q1^*_t f1_t + Q2^*_t f2_t \tag{8.10}$$

$$Q_t = Q1^*_t + Q2^*_t = Q1_t + Q2_t + QE_t, \tag{8.11}$$

where qi^*_t is equal to the logarithm of the volume of good i ($i = 1, 2$) mail that the NPO delivers E2E (Qi) plus the volume of good i mail that has switched to a competitor in period t also delivered by the NPO ($Qi^*_t fi$); fi_t refers to the proportion of good i traffic that has switched to an entrant in period t; Pi^*_t is a price index weighted by the proportion of mail sent via the NPO's good i mail and the proportion of good i mail that has switched to sending mail via the entrant's good (QE) in period t; Qi_t is the volume of good i mail that the NPO collects and delivers on an E2E delivery basis in period t; QE_t is the volume of mail handled by entrants in period t; $\alpha_i, \beta_i, \gamma_i, \delta_i, \iota_i, \mu_i$ are parameters; ι_i is a time trend parameter accounting for the impact of technology-related changes on mail demand in the pre-competitive environment; μ_i is a time trend parameter accounting for additional technology-related changes on mail demand taking place in the third period of competitive entry onwards, such that $\mu_i = 0$ for periods up to and including $T + 2$, and thereafter (that is, $T + 3$ onwards) $\mu_i < 0$ and the total impact of technology related changes on the demand for Qi_t is assumed to be $\iota_i + \mu_i$; u^*_{it} is a random disturbance term for the model qi^*_t; and other variables are as defined above. Note that economic theory suggests that $\gamma_1 < 0, \delta_1 > 0, \gamma_2 > 0, \delta_2 < 0$ and that α_{it} is a constant that can differ in the pre- and post-competition periods. In particular, it is generally assumed that α_{it} is higher in period $T + 1$ onwards to reflect increased consumer choice in the market.

The switching model (SM) is assumed to comprise two simple logistic functions for $i =$ 1, 2, which depend on relative price and quality attributes and are of the form:

$$fi_t = v_{it}\frac{A_i}{1 + \exp\left\{B_i\frac{P^E_t}{P_{it}} + C_iS_{it} + \varepsilon_{it}\right\}} \tag{8.12}$$

$$v_{it} = 1 - e^{-v_i(t-T)}, \tag{8.13}$$

where fi is the share of demand for good i switching to entrants; A_i, B_i, C_i and v_i are parameters; and ε_{it} is a random disturbance term.

The entrants' price (PE) and relative quality (Si) are assumed to be set in the entry behavior model (EM) using the following formulae:

$$PE_t = PA_t + a_1(P1_t - P2_t) + \rho_t \tag{8.14}$$

$$S1_t = s_1 + s_3(t - T) + \sigma_{1t} \tag{8.15}$$

$$S2_t = s_2 + s_3(t - T) + \sigma_{2t}, \tag{8.16}$$

where PE_t is assumed to comprise the access price (PA), which is assumed to be a proportion (λ) of the NPO good 2 price and a margin to cover competitors' unknown upstream collection and sorting costs. The latter is assumed to be a fraction (a_1) of the difference between the two NPO good prices plus an element of uncertainty (ρ_t). It is also assumed that $P1 > P2 > PE > PA$. *Si* denotes entrants' product quality of service relative to that offered by the NPO for good *i*; s_i are parameters and σ_{it} are random disturbance terms.

The economic behavior described by the model may be used to generate NPO post-competition projections prior to competition and electronic substitution taking place (that is, undertake projections in period *T*, for periods $T + 1, T + 2, \ldots, T + k$) as follows. First, subject to the NPO setting prices for its two goods ($P1$, $P2$), the entry model equations (*EM* equations (8.14) to (8.16)) can be used to generate predictions for entrants prices (PE_t) and relative quality (Si_t). Second, projections for the proportion of traffic switching from the NPO good 1 and good 2 can be estimated via the switching equations (*SM* equations (8.12) to (8.13)). Third, forecasts for market prices can be deduced from equations (8.6) and (8.7) in the mail market elements of the model (*MM*). Fourth, subject to the above, predictions for total mail demand (Q^*), NPO good 1 and good 2 volumes ($Q1$, $Q2$) and entrants' access traffic volumes (QE) can be generated by the remaining mail market model equations (*MM*, equations (8.4), (8.5) and (8.8) to (8.11)).

In contrast to the two-equation model in the pre-competitive environment, the post-competitive environment requires the NPO to adopt a considerably more complex projection process. In this simple model, projections for the post-competition era involve additional equations that include a large number of parameter estimates. In practice, of course, the problem would be considerably more complex due to the greater number of products, number of factors impacting on demand and the possibility of expectations regarding future changes to key factors such as technology or customer preferences. Note that in the absence of a technology break and no market entry from $T + 1$ onwards then $f1_t = f2_t = 0$ and the post-competition model is equivalent to the pre-competitive entry model.

Populating the Changing Market Model with Informative Priors

Having specified a theoretical model to project mail market volumes in a changing environment, prior to any such changes taking place what information can and should be used to inform the parameter set Θ? Due to a lack of observed historical data (that is, competition and electronic substitution have not taken place yet) standard econometric techniques cannot be employed. However, a Bayesian approach to informing model parameters can be adopted. In particular, hypotheses about the probability distribution of the model parameter set, that is a *prior distribution for* Θ, can be formed in advance of changes in the market environment taking place. As new information becomes available in the post-competition era, this can be used to update the initial prior parameter distribution to form an updated parameter probability distribution, which is technically referred to as the *posterior distribution*. The posterior distribution itself will change and evolve in the light of new information leading to an updating of the prior distribution and projections for subsequent time periods.

Four potential sources of information exist to form prior distributions for the model parameter set Θ. First, statistical studies and parameter estimates using outcome data in the pre-competitive entry environment. Second, market research, and in particular stated preference and contingent valuation studies, into customer switching behavior in a hypothetical competitive mail market environment. Third, business expert opinion and

Table 8.1 Model parameter priors formed in advance of changes to market environment

	Parameters	Prior mean values informed by:	Prior parameter likelihood distribution
Market model: Θ_{MM} (12 parameters)	$\alpha_1, \beta_1, \delta_1, \gamma_1, \iota_1$ $\alpha_2, \beta_2, \delta_2, \gamma_2, \iota_2$	Pre-competition OLS econometric model estimated parameters ((8.1) & (8.2))	Normal distribution informed by estimated variance of OLS estimators
	μ_1, μ_2	Business expert opinion	u_1^*, u_2^*
Switching model: Θ_{SM} (8 parameters)	$\nu_1, A_1, B_1, C_1,$ $\nu_2, A_2, B_2, C_2,$	Business information; business expert opinion; stated preference market research	Normal distribution with variance informed by stated preference research and/or business expert opinion ($\varepsilon_1, \varepsilon_2$)
Entry model: Θ_{EM} (4 parameters)	a_1, s_1, s_2, s_3	Known access prices; estimates for margin, competitors upstream & sorting costs; market research; business opinion	Normal distribution with variance set by business forecaster using business expert information ($\rho_1, \sigma_1, \sigma_2$)

analysis using internal business data. Fourth, information from other relevant markets, including postal markets in other countries.

For example, if the prior distribution for the parameter set Θ was assumed to be normal, then priors formed in the pre-competition era could be used to generate model parameter likelihood distributions as follows. In the case of the market demand model, the prior distribution for the majority of Θ_{MM} parameters could be informed by a mean vector equal to the OLS estimators and variance equal to the estimated variance of the OLS estimation. Where no information on parameter values exists, such as that regarding the potential magnitude of future trend breaks due to technology change (that is μ_i), expert opinion or market research could be used to provide a prior estimate. Table 8.1 provides a summary of how the pre-structural change period priors concerning the value of the model parameters and their likelihood distribution could be formed. In order to simplify the model it was assumed that the two constants α_{1t} and α_{2t} in equations (8.4) and (8.5) were not time dependent.[4]

3 OUTCOMES, PROJECTIONS AND BUSINESS INFORMATION

Forecasting Mail Volumes in a Changing Market Environment

In our framework the pre-competitive environment model projects volumes up to period T for two streams of traffic ($Q1$ and $Q2$). Assuming the estimated model is a good representation of reality and no structural breaks in the demand for mail take place, forecast uncertainty is dependent on the uncertainty surrounding the estimated parameters in equations (8.1) and (8.2) (that is α_i, β_i, γ_i, δ_i, ι_i) and the random disturbance terms u_i. Projections for mail volumes in a changing market environment, undertaken prior to having observed any form of competitive entry and before any additional negative technology impacts have taken place, involve a greater degree of uncertainty for products 1 and 2. In particular, in addition to the uncertainty associated with factors similar to the pre-competitive entry projections, there is also uncertainty associated, among other factors, with the following: the impact of technology-related substitution on the underlying stability of the market model parameters, such that, for example, $\mu \neq 0$ or $\gamma_{1,T+1} < \gamma_{1,T}$ in expression (8.4); the extent to which competition stimulates the market (that is the extent to which α_{iT+1} is greater than α_{iT}); the generation of projections using switching functions (*fi*) based on market research of statements of intent rather than observed behavior; and the price that entrants actually charge customers (*PE*).

With the advance of time, it is possible to assess the pre-market change projections and assumptions via OVP analysis in the post-market change era. Such an analysis could be used to re-assess the pre-market change priors and inform NPO projection updates. However, since not all variables that influence behavior in the post-market change model are observable to the NPO, such OVP analysis could benefit from business intelligence (obtained, for example, from NPO customer exit interviews or customer mailing profile data) to inform future priors.

However, it is not clear how new outcome information should be used to update model-based projections and whether such updates will necessarily reduce future forecast uncertainty. For example, in our simplified model, once the NPO observes the first post-competition era outcome data in period $T + 1$, it can identify the volume of mail it delivers via its E2E product range separately (that is, $Q1_{T+1}$ and $Q2_{T+1}$) and, as it delivers all mail, the total demand for mail (that is, $Q_{T+1} = Q1_{T+1} + Q2_{T+1} + QE_{T+1}$). However, the NPO operator does not observe the proportion of access traffic that has switched from its good 1 or good 2 product range. The magnitude of $Q1^*_{T+1}$, $Q2^*_{T+1}$, $f1_{T+1}$ and $f2_{T+1}$ are all individually unobservable to the NPO operator in period $T + 1$, or indeed any period thereafter. This, in addition to not knowing the price entrants charge customers in period $T + 1$ (PE_{T+1}), means that the NPO reviews model parameter estimates and model input assumptions adopted in period T (that is Θ_T) in the light of incomplete information. For example, if we were to observe that the outcome for $Q1_{T+1}$ was lower than the model projected in period T, there may be several hypotheses, generally not mutually exclusive, that could have contributed to this outcome. These include:

1. an unpredictable and random negative event occurred (that is, the difference between the outcome and projected value is due to u^*_{1T+1});
2. the entrants' price (PE_{T+1}) was lower than assumed by the NPO;
3. the entrants' relative quality ($S1_{T+1}$) was higher than was assumed;
4. more $Q1$ traffic switched to competitors than the NPO expected ($f1_{T+1}$ was underestimated);
5. the effect of competition stimulated the market but was less than expected (α_{1T+1} was overestimated);

6. the demand for mail experienced a negative structural break due to greater levels of technology-related substitution (that is $\iota_{1T+1} < \iota_{1T}$ or equivalently $\mu_i < 0$); and
7. customers became more responsive to price (for example, γ_1 in period $T + 1$ is lower than in period T).

A combination of outcome time-series information from the OVP analysis, business knowledge, market intelligence, opinion and judgment are all required to review and update model priors and set testable hypotheses. Some examples include the following. First, given that in period $T + 1$ the NPO knows that its price for good 2 is $P2_{T+1}$ and that it charges entrants an access price of PA_{T+1}, a reasonable prior to adopt is that PE_{T+1} lies between PA_{T+1} and $P2_{T+1}$. Second, on the basis of engineering cost estimates or information provided in the market, the NPO is likely to assume an expected entry price, $E(PE_{T+1})$, that could lie within a relatively narrow range around the true actual value. If this were assumed to be in the range PA_{T+1} to $PA_{T+1} + x$, then subject to this prior being true, the NPO may decide to recalibrate particular assumptions in its switching function model and hence update parameters contained in Θ_{SM}. Third, if the overall mail market volume projection in period $T + 1$ (Q_{T+1}) were broadly in line with the NPO's outcome total delivered volume, but the model-based volume projections substantially overestimated $Q1_{T+1}$ and simultaneously underestimated $Q2_{T+1}$, it may be reasonable to assert that the switching models be recalibrated, for the given prices $P1_{T+1}$ and $P2_{T+1}$ and the assumed entrants price PE_{T+1}, to yield more $Q1$ and less $Q2$ switching in period $T + 1$. Furthermore, this recalibration exercise could also benefit from business expert estimates of the proportion of observed entrants traffic (QE) that would otherwise have been sent via NPO product $Q1$, NPO product $Q2$ or not sent at all. Fourth, customer surveys examining business and consumer sent/received mail over time, possibly using panel survey methods, could provide quantitative estimates of technology-related substitution or complementary effects.

Repeating the OVP analysis in the light of new business intelligence received in the next period, $T + 2$, will provide the forecast analyst with more information to assess the priors adopted in period $T + 1$. As new information evolves over time the combination of OVP analysis with business information and market intelligence will help to refine forecast judgments. Such a methodology is consistent with a Bayesian approach to updating model-based projections. That is, it is consistent with an approach that explicitly acknowledges that *all information is useful* and that it is statistically and theoretically desirable to update prior assumptions in the light of new information on an ongoing basis.[5]

Augmenting Model Priors with Business Information and Market Research

Our model assumes that in the post-competition environment the NPO is unable to observe all the model variables. In particular it is assumed that the NPO is unable to observe with certainty the following: the impact of technology change on the demand for mail; entrants' prices (PE); the relative quality of the access service offered by entrants to the NPO (Si); the share of the demand for good i switching to entrants (fi); and the total level of demand for good i (Qi^*).

The extent to which NPO mail volume projections could benefit from improving their business intelligence data-gathering processes and their interrogation of such data, are explored in this chapter by augmenting the post-competition OVP analysis with additional information. In particular, it is assumed that business intelligence is able to provide the NPO business forecaster with two additional pieces of information in each time period. First, it is assumed that competitor intelligence experts provide the business forecaster with a prior distribution for the true unobserved mail volumes switching from its product range (that is, $f1$ and $f2$) and the unobserved impact of technology on the demand for mail (that is, μ_1 and μ_2). Second, it is assumed that these experts also provide a forecast distribution for the true rates of switching and generate a forecast distribution of projections of the impact of technology on the demand for mail. The distribution of the historic estimates and future projections of the true unobserved variables are assumed to be based on information (I) available up to the time period in which projections are made. In terms of future projections, this additional information is denoted as follows:

$$fi_{T+k}|I_{T+k-1} = \hat{fi}_{T+k} + \omega_i \tag{8.17}$$

$$\mu_{i,T+k}|I_{T+k-1} = \hat{\mu}_{i,T+k} + \psi_i, \tag{8.18}$$

where fi_{T+k} is the actual but unobserved proportion of traffic switching from the NPO good i ($i = 1, 2$) in period $T + k$; I_{T+k-1} denotes all available information up to the period before the projection is made (that is, information available prior to $T + k$); $\hat{fi}_{T+k}$ is the expected proportion of traffic switching from the NPO good i in period $T + k$ based on information available up to $T + k - 1$ (I_{T+k-1}); ω_i reflects a random normally distributed disturbance term with a mean value of zero and standard deviation that depends on ε_i; $\mu_{i,T+k}$ is the actual but unobserved impact of technology change on the demand for good i in period $T + k$; $\hat{\mu}_{i,T+k}$ is the expected impact of technology change on the demand for good i in period $T + k$ based on information available up to $T + k - 1$ (I_{T+k-1}); and ψ_i reflects a random normally distributed disturbance term with a mean value of zero and standard deviation that depends on u_i.

4 USING MONTE CARLO SIMULATION TECHNIQUES TO PROVIDE INSIGHTS INTO MODELING A CHANGING MARKET ENVIRONMENT

In this section we report the results of a Monte Carlo simulation exercise undertaken to illustrate the properties of the theoretical model described in Section 2. A number of additional assumptions were adopted to simplify the simulations. In particular, it was assumed that the structure of the model is known, contains fixed parameters and that the disturbance term variances are known. These assumptions isolate forecast uncertainty to be solely due to three factors: first, the random disturbance terms; second, the model parameters; and third, the unobservable input assumptions (such as *PE* and *Si*). As the discussion above explained, there are other sources of uncertainty that are important but we focus on these three factors in the simulation part of the chapter. In principle the approach can be extended and applied more generally.

The hypothetical *true* parameter values used to populate the model in the Monte Carlo simulation analysis are reported in Table 8.2. In some cases, these are informed by

Table 8.2 Hypothetical true fixed parameter values for illustrative simulations

Mail market demand parameters (Θ_{MM})			
$\alpha_1 = 1.0$	$\delta_1 = 0.15$	$\alpha_2 = 1.75$	$\delta_2 = -0.40$
$\beta_1 = 0.50$	$\iota_1 = -0.005$	$\beta_2 = 0.25$	$\iota_2 = 0.00005$
$\gamma_1 = -0.35$	std $u_1 = 0.01$	$\gamma_2 = 0.10$	std $u_2 = 0.01$
$\mu_1 = -0.001$	std $\mu_1 = 0.0005$	$\mu_2 = -0.00005$	std $\mu_2 = 0.0003$
Switching function parameters (Θ_{SM})			
$A_1 = 0.40$	$v_1 = 0.20$	$A_2 = 0.8$	$v_2 = 0.20$
$B_1 = 0.05$	std $\varepsilon_1 = 0.03$	$B_2 = 0.2$	std $\varepsilon_2 = 0.03$
$C_1 = -0.10$		$C_2 = -0.3$	
Entry prices and relative quality parameters (Θ_{EM})			
$s_1 = -2.0$	$s_2 = -0.5$	$s_3 = 0.05$	$\lambda = 0.60$
std $\sigma_1 = 0.01$	std $\sigma_2 = 0.01$	$a_1 = 0.20$	std $\rho = 0.01$

Note: std = standard deviation.

publicly available studies.[6] However, it should be noted that the values are stylized and should not be considered to be values applying to any particular NPO.

The properties of the model using these parameter values are summarized in Figure 8.1. In general, it is assumed that the demand for the NPO good 1 ($Q1$) is on a downward trend while the demand for good 2 ($Q2$) remains relatively stable. In general, mail prices are assumed to remain relatively constant over time and entrants' prices in the post-competition era (PE) are lower than NPO prices ($P1$, $P2$). In the case of relative quality, the entrants' offer is initially assumed to be considerably lower than that offered by the NPO. However, as time goes by, entrants' relative quality is assumed to improve and eventually offer a better quality product than the NPO good 2.

Predictions Prior to Changes in the Market Environment Taking Place

Monte Carlo simulations were constructed to generate projections and assess the degree of uncertainty surrounding the impact of changes in the external market environment prior to them taking place. Our model constructed these projections in six steps. Step 1 assumed, for illustrative purposes only, the existence of a set of *true* fixed model parameters that are not known by the NPO, as reported in Table 8.2. Step 2 assumed that the probability distribution of all the disturbance terms and therefore the parameters are known. Step 3 drew repeated samples of parameters and disturbance terms from the probability distribution for periods T to $T + q$ (where $q = 20$ in our example). Step 4 used these values to compute all the exogenous variables (Pi, PA and t) for $T + 1, \ldots, T + q$ using q draws of all the residuals of the model. Step 5 used the exogenous variables generated in step 4 and the parameter values and disturbance terms drawn in step 3, to compute all the endogenous model variables ($q1^*_t$, $q2^*_t$, QE_t, PE_t, $f1_t$, $f2_t$, $S1_t$, $S2_t$) for $t = T + 1, \ldots, T + q$. Step 6, used the results obtained in steps 1 to 5 and repeated the procedure 1000 times to yield 1000 sets of forecasts. These were then used to generate forecast

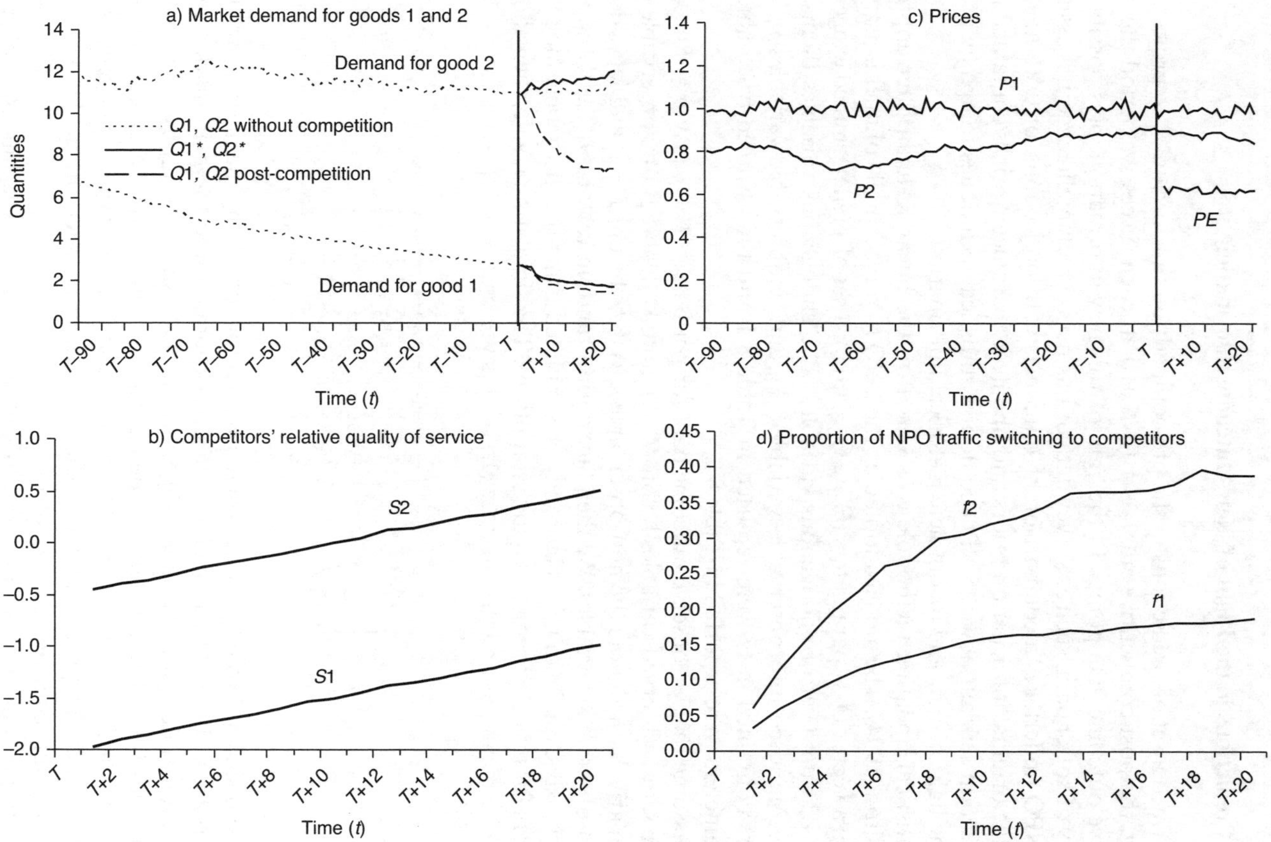

Figure 8.1 Hypothetical stylized model 'true' values

mean and standard deviations for each time period T to $T + q$ and construct forecast confidence intervals for mail volume projections undertaken in period T for periods $T +$ 1 to $T + q$.

Updating Predictions in the Light of New Outcome Information

Having formed a set of predictions in the pre-competition time period T, to project mail volumes in the post competitive era $T + 1$ to $T + q$, at each successive period the NPO will observe outcome data points. In the light of this new information, plus possibly the availability of softer data, such as survey data or business expert intelligence, it is assumed that the NPO undertakes a comparison of outcomes with projections, or OVP analysis, to assess the original information priors and update its parameter priors contained in Θ. This subsection sets out how the NPO could use statistical techniques to update projections in the light of new and incomplete historical information.

The statistical updating methodology is based on the linear Kalman filter approach (see Hamilton, 1994). The model adopted by the NPO to project mail volumes is assumed to contain: a vector Θ of parameters (Θ_{MM}, Θ_{SM}, Θ_{EM}); a set of predetermined exogenous variables, Z_t; and a set of endogenous variables. The endogenous variables themselves may be decomposed into observable variables, Y_t, and unobservable variables η_t.[7] The parameters contained in Θ were reported in Table 8.1 and the assumed true values of these parameters were reported in Table 8.2.

Let us assume that we observe outcome data for period $t = T + p$ (say $p = 5$). Let Y_1 denote the set of observed variables before $T + p$ and Y_2 denote future observable variables. Similarly, let η_1 denote the non-observable variables before $T + p$ and let η_2 denote future non-observable variables. We then face a joint random vector (Θ, Y_1, Y_2, η_1, η_2).

As previously explained, this vector may be simulated using the theoretical model and initial priors for model parameters and assumptions. The simulation results then allow us to deduce the mean (m) and the variance (Σ) of this vector.

$$m = \begin{pmatrix} m_\Theta \\ m_Y \\ m_\eta \end{pmatrix} \quad \Sigma = \begin{pmatrix} \Sigma_{\Theta\Theta} & \Sigma_{\Theta Y_1} & \Sigma_{\Theta Y_2} & \Sigma_{\Theta\eta_1} & \Sigma_{\Theta\eta_2} \\ \Sigma_{Y_1\Theta} & \Sigma_{Y_1Y_1} & \Sigma_{Y_1Y_2} & \Sigma_{Y_1\eta_1} & \Sigma_{Y_1\eta_2} \\ \Sigma_{Y_2\Theta} & \Sigma_{Y_2Y_1} & \Sigma_{Y_2Y_2} & \Sigma_{Y_2\eta_1} & \Sigma_{Y_2\eta_2} \\ \Sigma_{\eta_1\Theta} & \Sigma_{\eta_1Y_1} & \Sigma_{\eta_1Y_2} & \Sigma_{\eta_1\eta_1} & \Sigma_{\eta_1\eta_2} \\ \Sigma_{\eta_2\Theta} & \Sigma_{\eta_2Y_1} & \Sigma_{\eta_2Y_2} & \Sigma_{\eta_2\eta_1} & \Sigma_{\eta_2\eta_2} \end{pmatrix}. \tag{8.19}$$

The left-hand side of expression (8.19) denotes a vector containing the mean of the three sets of variables: the NPO parameter values incorporated into the mail market model (m_Θ); observed endogenous variables (m_Y); and model estimated unobservable endogenous variables (m_η). The right-hand side expression denotes the variance–covariance matrix for the model parameters and the observed and unobservable endogenous variables. For example, $\Sigma_{Y_1\Theta}$ is the matrix of the covariances between the model parameters (Θ) and observable endogenous variables (Y_1).

In our example application with five additional periods of data, the dimension of Θ (dim Θ) is 24, dim $Y_1 = 3 \times 5 = 15$ (3 variables, 5 periods) dim $Y_2 = 3 \times 15 = 45$ (3 variables, 15 periods) dim$\eta_1 = 6 \times 5 = 30$ (6 variables, 5 periods) and dim$\eta_2 = 6 \times 15 = 90$ (6 variables, 15 periods). The dimension of this vector is then 204 and Σ is a 204×204 matrix.

The Kalman filter updating approach requires the NPO to confront three questions. First, how should the model parameters (Θ) be updated? Second, how should values for the unobservable past variables (η_1) be updated? Third, how should forecasts for the observable variables (Y_2) and non-observable variables (η_2) be updated?

First, with respect to updating parameters, the NPO information priors may be assumed to be a function of the state of knowledge on Θ in time period $T + p$. It is the case that the expected value of Θ in time period $T + p$ can be computed as follows:

$$E(\Theta|Y_1) = E(\Theta) + \mathrm{Cov}(\Theta, Y_1)V(Y_1)^{-1}[Y_1 - E(Y_1)]$$
$$= m_\Theta + \sum\nolimits_{\Theta Y_1} \sum\nolimits_{Y_1 Y_1}^{-1} (Y_1 - m_{Y_1}), \tag{8.20}$$

and the distribution that these new values are drawn from can be computed using information from observed outcome data to update the variance of Θ as follows:

$$V(\Theta|Y_1) = V(\Theta) - \mathrm{Cov}(\Theta, Y_1)V(Y_1)^{-1}\mathrm{Cov}(Y_1,\Theta)$$
$$= \sum\nolimits_{\Theta\Theta} - \sum\nolimits_{\Theta Y_1} \sum\nolimits_{Y_1 Y_1}^{-1} \sum\nolimits_{Y_1\Theta}. \tag{8.21}$$

Expression (8.20) is the Kalman filter equivalent of updating model parameters in the light of an OVP investigation. That is, in the light of $T + p$ outcome data for the observable endogenous variables (Y_1), the Kalman filter updates the initial model parameter priors (m_Θ) via a linear function ($\Sigma_{\Theta Y_1}\Sigma_{Y_1 Y_1}^{-1}$) of the difference between the observed values of the endogenous variables and their expected value ($Y_1 - m_{Y_1}$). Similarly, expression (8.21) estimates the amendment of the initial model parameter variances ($\Sigma_{\Theta\Theta}$) via a linear function ($\Sigma_{\Theta Y_1}\Sigma_{Y_1 Y_1}^{-1}$) of the extent to which the model parameters are related to the new observable endogenous variable outcome data ($\Sigma_{Y\Theta}$).

Second, the expected values of the unobservable past variables (η_1) and their variance can be updated in period $T + p$, using observable outcome data (Y_1) as follows:

$$E(\eta_1|Y_1) = m_{\eta_1} + \sum\nolimits_{\eta_1 Y_1} \sum\nolimits_{Y_1 Y_1}^{-1} (Y_1 - m_{Y_1}) \tag{8.22}$$

$$V(\eta_1|Y_1) = \sum\nolimits_{\eta_1\eta_1} - \sum\nolimits_{\eta_1 Y_1} \sum\nolimits_{Y_1 Y_1}^{-1} \sum\nolimits_{Y_1\eta_1}. \tag{8.23}$$

Expressions (8.22) and (8.23) can be interpreted in a similar manner to (8.20) and (8.21) above. That is, expression (8.22) explains how the linear Kalman filter updates the historic values of unobservable variables (η_1) in the light of new information on observable endogenous variables (Y_1) obtained in periods $T + p$. Similarly, expression (8.23) refers to the extent to which the variance for the distribution of the unobservable variables is amended.

Third, forecasts for the expected value and variance of future observable variables (Y_2) and unobservable variables (η_2) can be updated in the light of new information on the observable endogenous variables (Y_1) obtained in periods $T + p$, in the simulation exercise using the following expressions:

$$E(Y_2|Y_1) = m_{Y_2} + \sum\nolimits_{Y_2 Y_1} \sum\nolimits_{Y_1 Y_1}^{-1} (Y_1 - m_{Y_1}) \tag{8.24}$$

$$E(\eta_2|Y_1) = m_{\eta_2} + \Sigma_{\eta_2 Y_1}\Sigma_{Y_1 Y_1}^{-1}(Y_1 - m_{Y_1}) \tag{8.25}$$

$$V(\eta_2|Y_1) = \Sigma_{\eta_2\eta_2} - \Sigma_{\eta_2 Y_1}\Sigma_{Y_1 Y_1}^{-1}\Sigma_{Y_1\eta_2} \tag{8.26}$$

$$V(Y_2|Y_1) = \Sigma_{Y_2 Y_2} - \Sigma_{Y_2 Y_1}\Sigma_{Y_1 Y_1}^{-1}\Sigma_{Y_1 Y_2}. \tag{8.27}$$

Kalman Filter Updating and Illustrative Monte Carlo Simulation Results

The application of the linear Kalman filter updating approach to our stylized model generates projections for both the observed (Z_t and Y_t) and unobserved (η_t) variables contained within the model for each point in time. Figure 8.2 contains a plot of the true values of the NPO and entrants' mail volumes contained within the model; the Monte Carlo simulation's mean and 95 percent confidence interval for projections undertaken in period T; and the mean value of the one-period-ahead and four-period-ahead projections.

The Monte Carlo simulations reported in Figure 8.2 provide two key insights. First, the degree of uncertainty surrounding NPO postal volume projections in a changing market environment is considerable. In particular, the simulations show that projections undertaken in period T, prior to the introduction of competition and the negative impact of additional technology effects, possess extremely wide confidence intervals.[8] A second important insight provided by the zoom lens graphics reported in Figure 8.2 is that the NPO can improve its forecasting performance by undertaking OVP analysis to learn about the structural changes taking place in the mail market. For example, the Monte Carlo simulation results show that by updating its prior assumptions each period, the NPO is able to generate reasonably good short-term one-period-ahead projections. In the case of longer-term forecasts, for example four-period-ahead projections, the Monte Carlo simulation exercise shows that initially the NPO is likely to make considerable forecast errors. However, again, as time goes by and the NPO learns about the behaviors underpinning the evolving nature of competition and technology-related substitution, it can update and recalibrate its mail market model to improve its longer-term forecast performance.

Business Intelligence and Mail Forecasts

The key factor underpinning the forecast improvements in the Kalman filter updating exercise reported in Figure 8.2 is the receipt of new information. In terms of the availability of new information for the observed variables (for example $Q1$, $Q2$, QE) the updating process depends on advances in time. However, for unobserved variables (such as, PE, $S1$ and $S2$) the updating exercise is also dependent on the quality of business intelligence. That is, the Kalman filter routine will in practice depend on a number of factors including the state of internal business data, in particular its quality and scope, and the extent to which market research is used to provide qualitative and quantitative evidence on the wider market and customer behavior.

The impact on mail volume forecasts of improving or extending the scope of business data to provide better quality business intelligence is examined via the use of Monte Carlo simulation analysis. The simulations analyzed in this section examined the relative

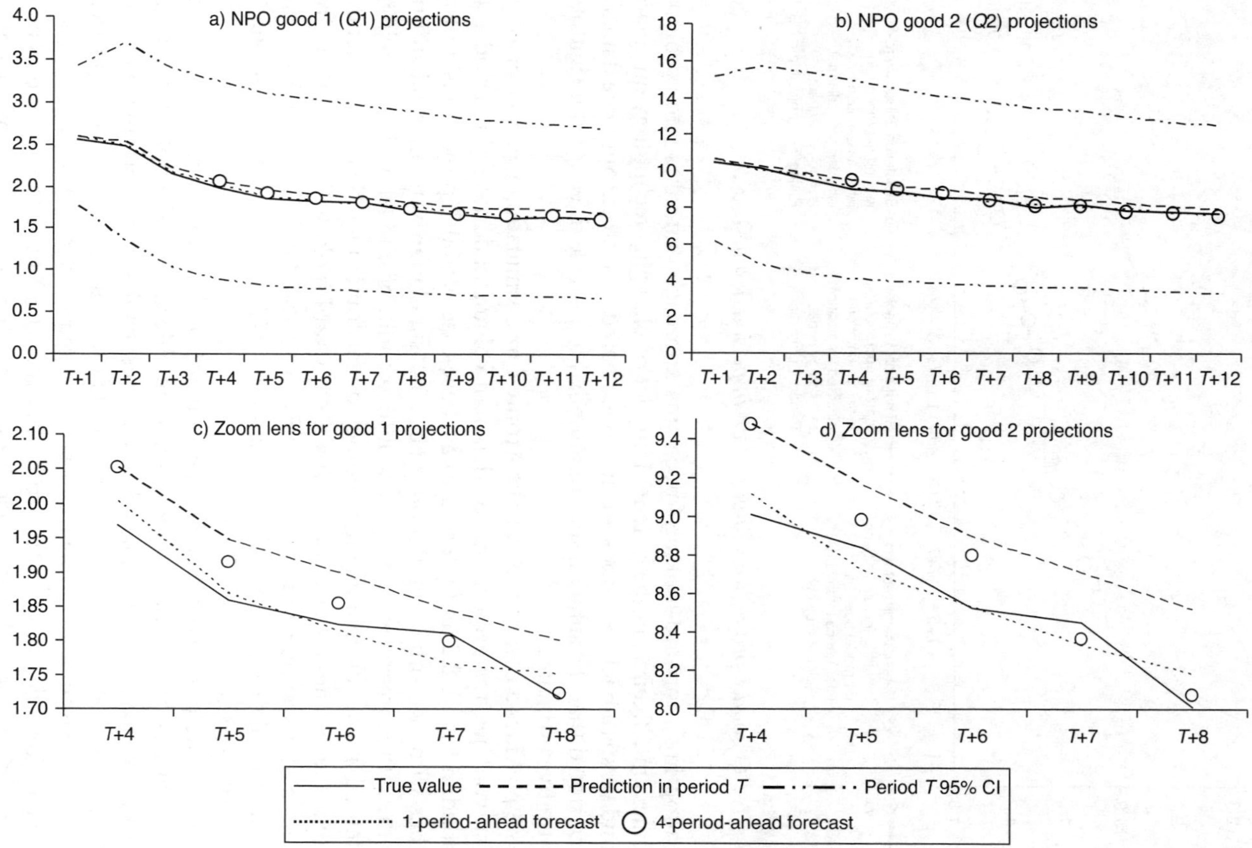

Figure 8.2 Hypothetical stylized model projections and confidence intervals

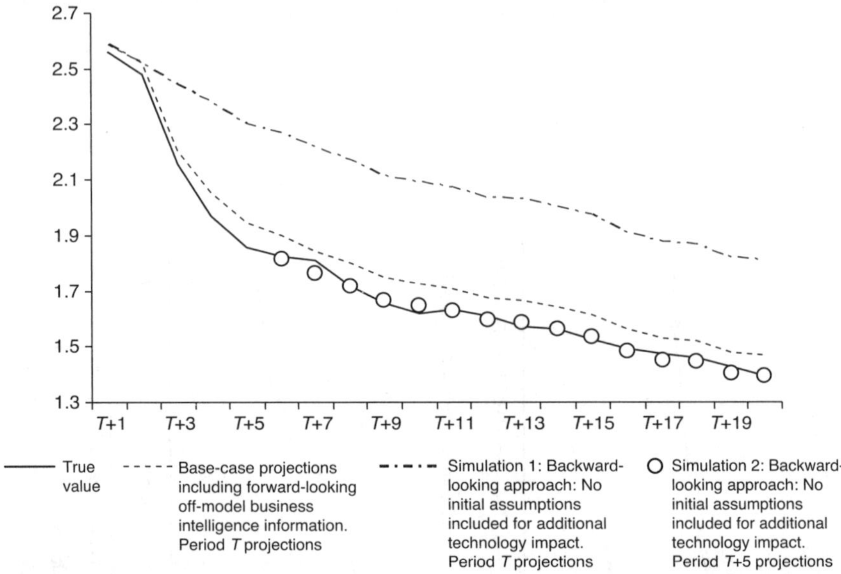

Figure 8.3 NPO good 1 projections undertaken in period T *and* T + *5*

merits of adopting a forward-looking forecasting approach that takes into account off-model business intelligence on the potential impact of changing technology on customer mail demand versus a backward-looking approach based on historic outcome data alone. It should be noted that the simulations are intended to provide directional insight rather than quantitative estimates.

Figure 8.3 provides a comparison of the Monte Carlo simulation true values for NPO good 1 mail volumes, the projections for this mail volume undertaken in period T (that is, as reported in Figure 8.2 and referred to as 'base-case period T projections' in Figure 8.3) together with two other simulations. The first simulation was undertaken on the basis that the NPO forecaster does not take into account off-model business intelligence of the potential impact of changing technology on customer mail demand. Instead, it is assumed that the business forecaster adopts a backward-looking forecasting approach to modeling mail market demand that uses only historical data. The second simulation assumes that after observing four outcome data points (that is, $T + 1$ to $T + 4$) the NPO revises its projections on the same basis.

The results reported in Figure 8.3 provide a number of valuable insights. First, including reliable forward-looking off-model business intelligence on the potential impact of technology in advance of it taking place leads to considerable improvements in projecting mail volumes. In particular, it should be noted that despite the simulation 1 projections comfortably lying within the confidence interval range reported in Figure 8.2, these projections are considerably further away from both the true NPO good 1 volumes and the base-case scenario that included off-model business intelligence estimates of the impact of technology. Second, revising projections and model parameters after a technology effect has taken place can substantially improve future NPO mail volume projections. Third, during the learning stage of the backward-looking approach the model-based projections could be significantly improved by adopting a forward-looking approach that directly incorporates reliable business intelligence.

5 SUMMARY AND CONCLUSIONS

This chapter examined some key issues in modeling and forecasting mail volumes in a changing and evolving market environment. In particular, it focused on an environment where a traditional monopoly market is evolving towards a fully competitive environment and technology is negatively impacting on mail volumes. Prior to structural changes of this kind taking place, or more generally in the early stages of such changes, it is not possible for the NPO to use standard econometric modeling techniques alone to adequately model the demand for mail in the new market environment. This chapter develops instead a modeling approach that can be adopted that is Bayesian in character.

A key conclusion reached is that Bayesian-type models can be constructed by NPOs and used to forecast mail volumes in a changing market environment. Information priors can be used to populate such models, in advance of any outcome data being available, and model parameter and input assumptions can be reviewed and amended in the light of historical information that accumulates over time. For example, while there may be no, or limited, direct outcome data on the impact of competition and technology-related substitution prior to such changes taking place, a number of less formal information sources, including business expert opinion and market research, may exist.

Over time, as outcome data on the evolving market environment and new business intelligence become available, model parameter and input assumptions can be reviewed and amended. In particular, OVP analysis using historical observations and business expert analysis can be used to review and revise model parameters and unobservable input variable assumptions on an ongoing basis. Monte Carlo simulation techniques and a linear Kalman filter statistical updating routine were used to assess the extent to which the partial but continuous arrival of new information over time could be used to improve mail volume projections.

The simulation analysis revealed a number of insights. First, the degree of uncertainty surrounding NPO postal volume projections in a changing market environment is considerable. Second, NPO mail volume uncertainty associated with changes in the market environment can be reduced considerably if observable outcome data and off-model business intelligence are reviewed regularly and used appropriately. By this we mean that such information should be used to update and improve estimates of model parameters, rather than leave unchanged previous estimates and so implicitly assume that differences between outcomes and projections are due solely to random disturbance terms. Third, the regular review and updating of model assumptions and parameters in the light of OVP analysis should be actively encouraged in markets undergoing structural changes. Fourth, it is beneficial to augment historical OVP analysis with good quality business information and market research when reviewing and updating model parameter and input assumptions.

NOTES

* The analysis contained in this chapter reflects the views of the authors and not necessarily those of Royal Mail Group.

1. See Tolley (2001), Nankervis et al. (2002), Thress (2006), Trinkner and Grossmann (2006), Nikali (2008), Soteri et al. (2009).
2. An examination of the effect of a negative and unexpected technology impact on forecasting mail demand using standard econometric models is examined in Cazals et al. (2008).
3. In practice a number of other explanatory variables may be included in modeling the demand for mail (for example, economic activity and quality of service). However, for ease of exposition our simple model is limited to those contained in equations (8.1) and (8.2).
4. It is possible to extend the model to include a shift effect on the constants $\alpha_{it} = \alpha_i + \alpha_i' I(t > T)$ resulting from competition. In this case α_i would have a distribution coming from the OLS estimation but α_i' would have a pure prior distribution.
5. See Robert (1992) and Gelman et al. (1995).
6. For example, the magnitude of the parameter values for the price variables (γ_i and δ_i) and the lagged dependent variable (β_i) have been informed by Nankervis et al. (2002), Cazals et al. (2008) and Soteri et al. (2009).
7. Note that Z_t comprises $P1$, $P2$, t, PA; Y_t comprises $Q1_t$, $Q2_t$, QE_t; η_t comprises PE_t, $S1_t$, $S2_t$, $f1_t$, $f2_t$, $Q1^*_t$. Note also that since $Q_t = Q1^*_t + Q2^*_t$ and it is the case that Q_t is observable to the NPO (since $Q_t = Q1_t + Q2_t + QE_t$) then only one of the Qi_t (where, $i = 1,2$) is unobservable.
8. This finding is similar to conclusions reached by Cazals et al. (2008). However, unlike the model adopted by Cazals et al., our model does not include a full set of explanatory stochastic variables explaining mail demand, such as economic growth and demographic variables. The absence of uncertainty associated with projecting such variables into the future is therefore not included in our model. This is one of the main reasons why the confidence intervals reported in Figure 8.2 remain relatively flat over the forecast time horizon and do not, as in Cazals et al., reflect the more general case where confidence intervals widen over time.

REFERENCES

Cazals, C., J.P. Florens, F. Rodriguez and S. Soteri (2008), 'Forecast uncertainty in dynamic models: an application to the demand for mail', in M.A. Crew and P.R. Kleindorfer (eds), *Competition and Regulation in the Postal and Delivery Sector*, Cheltenham, UK and Northampton, MA, USA: Edward Elgar, pp. 63–73.

Gelman, A., J.B. Carlin, H.S. Stern and D.B. Rubin (1995), *Bayesian Data Analysis*, Texts in Statistical Science, London: Chapman & Hall.

Hamilton, J. (1994), *Time Series Analysis*, Princeton, NJ: Princeton University Press.

Nankervis, J., S. Richard, S. Soteri and F. Rodriguez (2002), 'Disaggregated letter traffic demand in the UK', in M.A. Crew and P.R. Kleindorfer (eds), *Postal and Delivery Services: Pricing, Productivity, Regulation and Strategy*, Boston, MA: Kluwer Academic, pp. 203–18.

Nikali, H. (2008), 'Substitution of letter mail for different sender–receiver segments', in M.A. Crew and P.R. Kleindorfer (eds), *Competition and Regulation in the Postal Delivery Sector*, Cheltenham, UK and Northampton, MA, USA: Edward Elgar, pp. 89–106.

Robert, C. (1992), *The Bayesian Choice: A Decision-Theoretic Motivation*, New York: Springer.

Soteri, S., F. Fève, J.P. Florens and F. Rodriguez (2009), 'Internet advertising and direct mail: trends and analysis for the UK', in M.A. Crew and P.R. Kleindorfer (eds), *Progress in the Competitive Agenda in the Postal and Delivery Sector*, Cheltenham, UK and Northampton, MA, USA: Edward Elgar, pp. 209–22.

Thress, T.E. (2006), 'Direct Testimony of Thomas E. Thress on behalf of the United States Postal Service', Postal Rate and Fee Changes Docket No. R2006-1.

Tolley, G.S. (2001), 'Direct Testimony of George S. Tolley on behalf of the United States Postal Service', Postal Rate and Fee Changes Docket No. R2001-1.

Trinkner, U. and M. Grossmann (2006), 'Forecasting Swiss mail demand', in M.A. Crew and P.R. Kleindorfer (eds), *Progress toward Liberalization of the Postal and Delivery Sector*, New York: Springer Science+Business Media, Inc., pp. 267–80.

9. The effect of falling volumes on traditional efficiency analysis

Greg Harman, Wim Koevoets, Alejandro Requejo, Erik van der Merwe and Navin Waghe*

1 INTRODUCTION

In the context of the liberalization of the European postal market and the continued need to fund a Universal Service Obligation (USO), the Third EC Postal Directive requires that regulators provide incentives for cost efficiency.[1] These incentives can be provided through price regulations. The Directive requires member states to ensure that prices for universal services are affordable, cost oriented, transparent and non-discriminatory. To achieve these objectives *ex ante* price-cap models are often used, where the initial price is rolled forward annually over the period of the price control by a factor of CPI-X, where CPI is a general inflation index (normally the national consumer price index or retail price index) and X is the so-called efficiency factor. The X-factor is meant to reflect, *inter alia*, the expected net gains or losses in productivity over the price control period, or more specifically the difference between possible productivity gains in the regulated entity and the average gains in the economy generally.[2]

Hence, in setting a price control, regulators in the EC need to consider the efficiency factor. Estimating an efficiency factor is particularly difficult for postal operators as there are few comparable operators which can serve as benchmarks for measuring efficiency. The decision about the level of the efficiency factor is, therefore, normally informed by a range of analytical techniques, including bottom-up analysis of company forecasts, total factor productivity analysis, international benchmarking with other postal operators and internal benchmarking of the operators' mail centers (MCs) and delivery offices (DOs).

The operations of universal service providers are generally organized so that the same activities are replicated in each geographic area covered by the USO. For example, the delivery of mail to domestic and business premises generally takes place from an office that covers a particular geographic area. The repetition of functions, such as delivery, across a large number of units within a postal operator provides the opportunity to assess the comparative efficiency of each unit carrying out a particular function. In this chapter, we refer to this analysis as 'internal benchmarking'. Such analysis can provide the management of the postal operator with valuable comparable information about sources of best practice and underperformance.

Internal benchmarking can be based on simple statistics such as mail volume, overall cost performance, labor productivity, overtime cost or absenteeism. The main weaknesses of single performance ratios are that they are susceptible to the bias of the observer and cannot reliably test the interaction of more than one efficiency driver. That is, simple ratio analysis cannot explain performance variations between operational areas due to a combination of factors such as output volume mix, technology differences, building structure and the external labor market. Simple ratio analysis can be extended, however, using advanced quantitative (that is, econometric) techniques.

Econometric analysis involves fitting a mathematical function to data. This function can contain many arguments reflecting the factors just discussed. Different criteria may be adopted to specify what constitutes a good fit to the data, and these form the basis of alternative estimating methods such as deterministic and stochastic frontier analysis (DFA and SFA) and data envelopment analysis (DEA). In the past, single-period econometric models have been used to estimate the X-factor (LECG, 2005) and have generated robust results (Moriarty et al., 2006). A question is whether single-period models still produce robust results given the cost structure of the industry and recent volume trends.

In a recent report, the European Commission indicates that member states with mature postal markets can expect only modest growth or even declines in their mail volumes. Member states like the UK and the Netherlands have already experienced declining addressed mail volumes (European Commission, 2008).[3] Although declining volumes in the postal sector is a relatively recent phenomenon, it may continue with liberalization and the increased use of e-substitutes.

Declining volumes will affect incumbents in mature postal markets for the following reasons. Incumbent operators are subject to the USO that constrains their ability to reduce labor and to close DOs in order to adjust to lower volumes. Additionally, incumbents tend to be public sector bodies where the influence of trade unions and collective agreements is traditionally stronger than in the private sector (Wachter and Perloff, 1991). Therefore, the ability of incumbents to adjust their labor costs is limited when volumes are declining. Consequently, unit costs may increase over time.[4] Increasing unit costs should not be confused with inefficiency. The inability to remove costs is not necessarily due to inefficient management but due to these labor constraints that prevent the removal of costs.

Regulators commonly refer to the impact of volume on costs as 'cost marginality'. Many regulators consider marginality and efficiency separately. Both factors are required to project future costs and hence to set prices over time.

A key question, therefore, is whether traditional methods of calculating efficiency (for example, single-period econometric models) might bias the calculation of actual relative efficiency, when volumes have either increased or decreased during the period. Consequently, prices may be set at the wrong level, misaligning incentives and potentially jeopardizing the provision of the USO.

In this chapter, we focus on issues relating to single-period SFA models, which have been increasingly used by regulators to assess cost efficiency.[5] The issue that we address is whether an SFA using data on DOs for only one period may confuse inefficiency with management's inability to adjust labor and operating inputs when mail volumes are declining. Specifically, we perform efficiency analysis for postal operators that (i) have a limited ability to adjust labor and (ii) experience a decline in mail volumes in their DOs.

Our main finding is that standard SFA models may overestimate cost inefficiency when volumes have been declining. Additionally, calculating the degree to which costs change with volume is a complex issue for all postal operators and there is a risk that this factor may also be miscalculated. The impact of overestimating inefficiency and of miscalculating the ability to change costs when volumes change can have serious consequences for the financial position of a postal operator. The risk is that an insufficient allowance will be given in prices to cover costs.

Consequently, consideration needs to be given as to whether alternative approaches to single-period SFA exist, which provide robust estimates of efficiency as volume changes, and provide a more robust assessment of the degree to which costs change as volumes change. In our conclusion we discuss such alternative approaches.

This chapter is structured as follows. In Section 2, we present the set-up of our analysis. In Section 3, we explain our approach. In Section 4, we present our results. In Section 5, we present our main finding and its implications for postal regulators' assessment of efficiency.

2 IMPLICATIONS OF FALLING VOLUMES FOR COST EFFICIENCY

Falling volumes matter for both future projections of unit costs and the assessment of achievable cost savings. SFA provides a powerful tool to undertake such an assessment because it estimates cost inefficiencies while accounting for the effects of factors driving costs. Recently, SFA has been applied in the UK postal sector using a cross-section of data on DOs and MCs including various cost drivers (LECG, 2005). The use of this type of analysis has been the subject of further debate by stakeholders in the European postal market (Horncastle et al., 2006).

With falling volumes, it is possible in a cross-section SFA to confuse cost inefficiency with unit cost increases because of a limited ability to adjust labor. This holds even if one includes various cost drivers that vary across DOs or MCs in the analysis.

In this section, we show how unit cost increases, arising from a limited ability to adjust labor in response to falling volumes, can be mistaken for cost inefficiency. We first present the basic setting for our analysis and then the consequences of a negative volume shock.

Basic Setting

We focus on a DO, which uses labor only for deliveries. We consider two periods, period 0 and period 1, and assume that wages are equal in both periods. In the first period (period 0), the DO is cost efficient. It optimizes its deliveries by minimizing its labor costs, given a wage and a mail volume.

Between period 0 and period 1, the DO experiences a negative volume shock, which causes a reduction in the volume it needs to deliver. Its labor costs in period 1 depend on its ability to adjust labor following the new lower volume in period 1.

Implications of Being Unable to Adjust Labor to Volume Shocks

We assess the effects of the volume decline on the labor costs of the DO in period 1 by considering three cases: (i) the DO cannot adjust labor ('no adjustment'); (ii) the DO

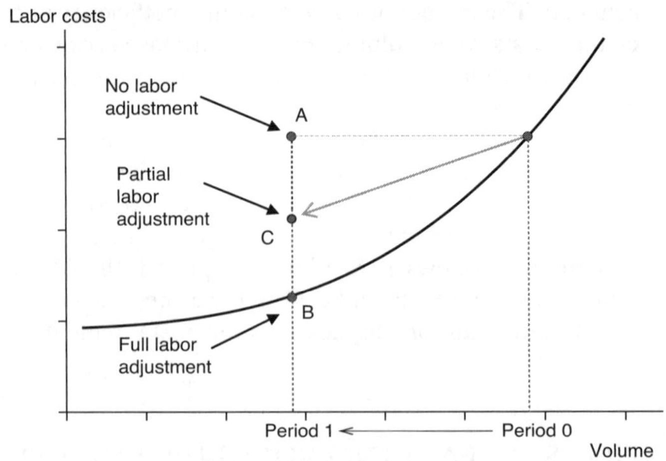

Figure 9.1 Volume shocks and labor adjustment

can adjust all its labor to changes in volume ('full adjustment'); and (iii) the DO can only adjust a fraction of the labor it needs to adjust in order to remain cost efficient ('partial adjustment'). We assume that the DO cannot adjust labor fully to volume declines due to factors outside of management control and not, for example, because there are no incentives for management to adjust labor. Figure 9.1 shows, for each of the three cases, the labor costs in period 1.

For a given wage, the curved line in the figure represents the minimum labor costs required to deliver volumes. In period 0, the DO is cost efficient and its labor costs are on the cost frontier.

After the shock, the DO needs to deliver a lower volume (see the left vertical line in the figure). If the DO cannot adjust its labor, its labor costs are at point A. If the DO can adjust its labor fully, its costs will be on the cost frontier in period 1 (point B). If, however, the DO can only adjust labor partially, then its labor costs are above the cost frontier in period 1 (point C).

This setting provides the basis for our approach. It allows us to construct a data set at the level of DOs and to undertake a standard cost frontier analysis. The aim of this analysis is to assess whether and how an SFA will identify inefficiencies inappropriately where unit costs are impacted by imperfect labor adjustments. In the next section, we explain our approach.

3 APPROACH

Due to the confidential nature of European postal operators' cost and network information, there is no information in the public domain on costs at the level of DOs. Therefore, we simulate data on costs at the level of DOs for a postal operator with 1000 DOs. All DOs are cost efficient until each of them experiences a negative volume shock to which they cannot adjust their labor fully.[6] Our approach involves three steps:

1. For each of the DOs we use a simple model to derive their labor costs following the occurrence of a negative volume shock.[7] This allows us to construct a dataset of 1000 DOs.
2. We construct various datasets containing information on the hourly wage, the mail volume and the labor costs for each DO following a volume shock. The datasets vary according to the size of the volume shocks (for example, small, medium or large) and the degree to which DOs can adjust their labor.
3. For each dataset we undertake an SFA that calculates the cost efficiency of each DO.

Below we explain each of these steps in more detail.

A Simple Model Addressing Volume Shocks

To investigate the impact of declining volumes on efficiency calculations we use a simple model in which a DO minimizes its labor costs by employing just enough labor to deliver a certain mail volume. We assume that a volume y can be produced with n hours of labor and a Cobb–Douglas production technology: $y = n^{\alpha}$. The parameter α indicates economies of scale. It reflects increasing returns to scale if it is larger than one, decreasing returns to scale if it is smaller than one and constant returns to scale if it equals one.

We model the volume shock as follows. If the shock equals –10 percent this means that it causes a volume decline of 10 percent. We assume that for reasons outside of management control a DO may not be able to adjust its labor to the lower volume. We model the ability to adjust labor as the actual change in labor hours relative to the change required to remain cost efficient. We define m as the fraction of labor adjustment needed to be on the cost frontier in period 1.[8] If m equals 0 then there is no change in labor hours after the volume shock, reflecting a DO being unable to adjust its labor. If m equals 100 percent then the DO is able to adjust its labor fully following a change in volume. If m equals 25 percent then the DO is able to adjust only 25 percent of the labor hours needed to remain cost efficient.

Given a volume shock ρ (< 0) and an ability to adjust labor, m, we derive the following labor cost for the DO just after the volume shock (Appendix 9A1 shows the derivation):

$$c = wy^{\frac{1}{\alpha}}\left[(1-m)(1+\rho)^{-\frac{1}{\alpha}} + m\right]. \tag{9.1}$$

In equation (9.1), c denotes the labor costs,[9] w denotes the wage per hour, y denotes the mail volume, α is the parameter indicating economies of scale, m is the ability of the DO to adjust its labor and ρ denotes the volume shock. Note that equation (9.1) is only meaningful for negative volume shocks, as it would lead to infeasible outcomes in the case of positive volume shocks.

Equation (9.1) measures the labor costs after the negative volume shock as a function of (i) the cost frontier, $wy^{1/\alpha}$; and (ii) a cost factor (the term in brackets) expressing the labor costs relative to the efficient level of costs. This factor depends on the size of the negative volume shock, the ability to adjust labor and the returns to scale. It equals one if (a) there is no negative volume shock ($\rho = 0$); or (b) there is a negative volume shock ($\rho < 0$) and the DO can adjust its labor fully to the shock ($m = 1$). In both cases, the labor costs are at the frontier.

If there is a negative volume shock to which the DO cannot adjust its labor ($\rho < 0$ and $m < 1$) then the cost factor is larger then one. For example, it equals 1.37 if we assume, under increasing returns to scale ($\alpha = 1.25$), that the shock decreases volume by 50 percent ($\rho = -0.5$) and the DO can only adjust 50 percent of the labor required to be cost efficient ($m = 0.5$). This means that labor costs are 37 percent higher than the efficient level of costs.

Data

Using equation (9.1), we construct a dataset of 1000 DOs. This requires generating (i) the wage per hour; (ii) the volume; (iii) the volume shock; and (iv) the ability to adjust labor m. We generate our data in four steps:

1. We generate wage and volume data assuming uniformly distributed wages across DOs and log-normally distributed volumes across DOs. For each DO, the wage per hour is randomly drawn from a uniform distribution on the interval [7, 10.5]. We based this range on wage information in Internet announcements seeking to fill vacant positions for postal workers. As volumes cannot be negative, we use a log-normal distribution to draw the volume for each DO by assuming a mean of 16.56 and a standard deviation 0.75 for the corresponding normal distribution. We based these numbers on information in the public domain on the distribution of postal codes in the UK.[10]
2. We generate volume shocks for each DO under three scenarios: (i) a 'small' shock scenario in which volumes decrease by 5 percent on average; (ii) a 'medium' shock scenario in which volumes decrease by 10 percent on average; and (iii) a 'large' shock scenario in which volumes decrease by 30 percent on average. We draw the volume shocks randomly from a uniform distribution with intervals [−0.1, 0], [−0.2, 0] and [−0.6, 0] for the 'small', 'medium' and 'large' shock scenarios, respectively.[11]
3. Assuming increasing returns to scale ($\alpha = 1.25$) we calculate labor costs using the logarithmic transformation of equation (9.1).[12] For each DO, we calculate labor costs for each volume shock scenario and for each of the following labor adjustment scenarios: 0, 25, 50, 75 and 100 percent. This provides us with 15 datasets.
4. We add a randomly drawn noise term to the labor costs of step 3. This term reflects a situation in which some DOs experience cost increases or decreases in their labor costs that occur by chance. Alternatively, one can interpret this noise term such that the Cobb–Douglas function assumed here is not a completely accurate representation of minimum labor costs, with differences in fit across DOs describable through the residual noise term. We draw this noise term from a normal distribution with mean zero and a standard deviation of 0.017 which implies that, for 99 percent of the DOs, at most 5 percent of their labor costs are determined by noise.

These steps provide us with 15 datasets containing information for each DO's wage per hour, volume and labor cost. Table 9.1 shows the descriptive statistics for the dataset with 25 percent labor adjustment and volume shocks drawn according to the 'medium' shock scenario.

Table 9.1 shows that in the medium shock scenario, the mean volume shock is −10

Table 9.1 Descriptive statistics – 25% labor adjustment – medium volume shocks

Variable	Mean	Std dev.	Minimum	Maximum
Volume shock	−0.10	0.06	−0.20	0.00
Labor costs (millions)	7.54	5.49	0.83	52.60
Wage	8.76	1.02	7.00	10.49
Volume (millions)	20.18	18.59	1.73	203.19
Cost impact volume shock	1.07	0.04	1.00	1.15
Noise	0.00	0.02	−0.05	0.05

Note: The data are generated assuming increasing returns to scale with $\alpha = 1.25$.

percent and that the volume reductions in individual DOs are between 0 and 20 percent. The wage per hour lies between 7 and 10.5 and the volume distribution shows that there are small and large DOs in the data. The noise is zero on average, and at most 5 percent of the labor costs. Given increasing returns to scale and labor adjustment of 25 percent the volume shocks result in labor cost impacts between 0 and 15 percent. That is, the negative shocks result in labor costs which are between 0 and 15 percent higher than the efficient level of costs. The key question we seek to answer is whether and how SFA identifies these cost impacts as inefficiencies.

Stochastic Frontier Analysis

We use each dataset to estimate a standard stochastic cost frontier model.[13] This allows us to calculate the efficiency of DOs for different degrees of labor adjustment. A stochastic cost frontier is a cost frontier that consists of a deterministic part common to all DOs and a random part specific for each DO. A stochastic cost frontier analysis assumes that the costs observed in the data are at least as high as the stochastic cost frontier. Any difference between the labor costs and the stochastic cost frontier is due to cost inefficiencies. We estimate the following cost model:[14]

$$\ln c_i = (\beta_0 + \beta_1 \ln w_i + \beta_2 \ln y_i) + v_i + u_i. \tag{9.2}$$

The term in brackets reflects the deterministic part of the cost frontier and includes the wage per hour and volume as cost drivers. v_i denotes the stochastic part of the cost frontier, which we assume is normally distributed with mean zero. u_i denotes the cost inefficiency of DO i. The cost inefficiency is at least zero and we assume it is half-normally distributed. In other words, we estimate the 'normal–half-normal' cost frontier model using our generated data.

4 RESULTS

In this section, we show the results of estimating a stochastic cost frontier model using different datasets. These datasets vary in the assumptions on labor adjustment and the shock scenarios.

Table 9.2 Average efficiencies by volume declines – full labor adjustment (100%)

Small	Medium	Large
98.9	98.9	98.9

In the case where DOs can adjust labor hours fully following a negative volume shock, we would expect results indicating that DOs are cost efficient. In contrast, if DOs cannot adjust labor hours fully to lower volumes, we would expect results indicating that DOs are less efficient.

We first present the results assuming full labor adjustment and then the results for different scenarios of partial labor adjustment.

Efficiency – Full Labor Adjustment

If DOs are able to adjust their labor to lower volumes fully, we would expect the analysis to indicate cost efficiency. Table 9.2 presents the results assuming full labor adjustment for each of the three volume shock scenarios.

The results in Table 9.2 show average efficiencies that are close to 100, indicating cost efficiency for each of the three shock scenarios. The average efficiencies are the same for DOs with small, medium or large shocks because DOs with perfect labor adjustment are cost efficient irrespective of the size of the shock. The average efficiencies are not equal to 100 percent because the SFA confounds some cost impacts, which are due to chance, with cost inefficiencies.[15] Note that, although apparently small, a 1 percent underestimation of efficiency could lead the regulator to require significantly larger savings than would otherwise be the case.[16]

These results show that SFA already provides mildly negatively biased estimates of efficiency of DOs when they are able to adjust their labor fully. In the next subsection we present the results of estimating efficiency when DOs cannot adjust their labor fully following the volume shock.

Efficiency – Partial Labor Adjustment

If DOs cannot adjust their labor hours fully following a volume decline, they will incur unit labor costs that are higher than the unit costs of DOs on the cost frontier. Therefore, we would expect a standard efficiency analysis to identify DOs with volume declines as cost inefficient. If this were the case, it would mean that the stochastic cost frontier analysis confounded an inability to change costs to meet volume declines with cost inefficiency. We estimated the stochastic cost frontier model for each of the 12 datasets reflecting different degrees of imperfect labor adjustment (0, 25, 50 and 75 percent for each of the three volume shock scenarios). Table 9.3 presents the results (Table 9A2.3 presents the parameter estimates of equation (9.2)).[17]

Table 9.3 shows three main results. First, the average efficiencies are lower than the average efficiencies in Table 9.2, in which DOs were able to adjust labor fully to align with volumes. Second, the average efficiency increases with the ability of DOs to adjust labor hours to volume shocks. Third, DOs experiencing higher volume declines have lower

Table 9.3 Average efficiencies under declining volumes – imperfect labor adjustment

Ability to adjust labor	0%	25%	50%	75%
Magnitude of volume declines				
Small (5%)	98.2	98.4	98.6	98.7
Medium (10%)	96.0	96.8	97.7	98.5
Large (30%)	75.7	79.9	85.0	91.3

Table 9.4 Number of inefficient DOs – imperfect labor adjustment

Ability to adjust labor	0%	25%	50%	75%
Magnitude of volume declines				
Small (5%)	58	36	21	14
Medium (10%)	643	474	225	36
Large (30%)	937	915	878	800

average efficiencies. We find that these results do not change if we assume constant or decreasing returns to scale.[18]

Table 9.4 confirms these results. It presents, for each scenario, the number of DOs which appear with an efficiency level below that of the least efficient DO in the perfect labor adjustment scenario.[19]

These results are intuitive as, following a volume decline, we would expect higher unit cost increases for DOs that are more constrained in adjusting their labor. In other words, for a given volume decline, the unit costs of DOs with few constraints on labor adjustment increase by less than those of DOs that are more restrained in adjusting their labor. However, the increase in unit costs is not an increase in cost inefficiency but an increase in costs driven by the DOs' inability to adjust labor.

These results indicate that, in the presence of volume declines, SFA identifies otherwise efficiently operating DOs as cost inefficient if they cannot adjust their labor fully. The implication is that one may perceive efficiently operating DOs as cost inefficient in the context of declining volumes and imperfect labor adjustment.

In a regulatory context, this means that regulators assessing efficiencies in order to set tariffs and to provide incentives to enhance efficiency need to be prudent if they use a standard efficiency analysis. If DOs can only adjust a fraction of the required labor to lower volumes, then taking the results of standard efficiency analysis at face value may lead to the wrong conclusions.

Our results show that failure to recognize volume declines and the limited ability of DOs to adjust their labor leads to an underestimation of cost efficiency. This consequently leads to an overestimation of the scope for efficiency improvements.

5 CONCLUSION

Our analysis shows that a standard single-period SFA may find cost inefficiencies erroneously when DOs experience volume declines and their ability to adjust labor to lower volumes is limited. This implies that, in providing incentives to enhance efficiency, regulators may overestimate the scope for efficiency improvements.

Therefore, when assessing efficiency using SFA, regulators need to consider whether DOs are experiencing volume decline and whether they can adjust labor accordingly.[20] During a period of volume decline, the regulator needs to consider the impact of volume changes and obtain a view on the flexibility with which DOs can adjust their labor (for example, Bouin et al., Ch. 6, this volume). The availability of information on volumes and costs for different periods at the level of DOs allows regulators to form a view on the magnitude of volume changes and their impact on costs. Econometric panel data techniques and qualitative assessments of operational practice are tools that could potentially help regulators substantiate that view.

Panel data techniques involve the construction and use of datasets with information on labor costs and various other cost drivers. An analysis applying panel data techniques has the advantage of calculating efficiency while accounting for changes in mail volumes in each DO. There are a number of panel data stochastic frontier models that address these issues. For example, assuming that the ability to adjust labor is constant over time and modeling unobserved heterogeneity across DOs, or modeling time-varying inefficiencies as a function of volumes. Each of these models has the potential to identify inefficiencies while addressing labor adjustment under different (technical) assumptions.[21]

This does not imply that panel data models always give lower estimates of inefficiency than stochastic frontier cross-section models using the same panel data or data for one period.[22] Panel data models allow the evolution of volumes to be taken into account, but may introduce new empirical issues. The ability of a stochastic frontier panel approach to identify cost inefficiencies in delivery, and distinguish them from random noise and/or unobserved heterogeneity across DOs, depends on the data and the type of model employed. A better understanding of these empirical issues requires efficiencies to be estimated with both cross-section and panel data stochastic frontier models using DO-level data.

For a regulator, the benefit of using panel data models in an *ex ante* price control is that they allow the regulator to provide incentives for the postal operator to adjust its controllable cost drivers on the basis of cost saving calculations which do not include the effects of uncontrollable drivers, such as constraints to labor adjustment.

Postal operators can also benefit from the estimation of delivery cost inefficiencies using panel data models. A better understanding of cost inefficiencies that are manageable allows management to make informed decisions about cost savings that would meet the regulator's objectives.

NOTES

* This chapter represents the personal views of the authors and should not be taken to represent the policy of LECG Ltd or any other organization. The authors would like to thank the numerous individuals who have assisted in the preparation of this chapter by way of contributions, guidance, advice and constructive criticism. Responsibility for the content of this chapter and the views expressed therein rests with the authors alone.

1. This requirement exists irrespective of whether *ex post* or *ex ante* regulation is applied.
2. Productivity is a key component of the X-factor formula, however setting the X-factor includes other

factors such as expected growth in the market, estimates of internal inefficiency in the firm and required returns on capital. See Crew and Kleindorfer (1996).

3. In addition, Nader and Lintell (2008) report a decline in West Europe in the mail volumes of national postal operators between 2005 and 2006.
4. Crew et al. (2008) note labor conditions originating from specific collective agreements or from the special status of postal workers (of the incumbent postal operator) as one of the critical factors for the ability of management to improve efficiency.
5. For example, Ofcom commissioned a stochastic frontier analysis to assess the efficiency of British Telecom's fixed line network (see NERA, 2005). The Office of Rail Regulation (ORR) also used a stochastic frontier analysis for its periodic review of Network Rail's activities (see ORR, 2008).
6. We assume that all DOs are cost efficient to improve tractability of the results compared to an analysis in which all or some DOs are inefficient.
7. The model allows us to calculate the labor costs in period 1 for a DO (that is, point C in Figure 9.1).
8. That is, $m = (n_1 - n_{0)}/(n_1^* - n_0)$ with n_1 and n_0 denoting the labor hours in periods 1 and 0, respectively, and n_1^* denoting the cost-efficient number of labor hours in period 1. In Figure 9.1 m corresponds to the ratio of the line segments AC and AB.
9. The labor costs equal the number of labor hours times the wage per hour.
10. Using the log-normal distribution we generate a positively skewed mail volume distribution across DOs as, for example, in Cazals et al. (2001). These authors present descriptive statistics about letter volumes indicating a positively skewed letter volume distribution across post offices in France.
11. The medium shock is in line with the current (accelerating) annual volume fall prediction for the UK which is around 10 percent and the yearly fall of 14 percent for US postal services (Bradley and Burns, 2009). The largest negative shock in the large shock scenario of −60 percent reflects the disproportionate impact that volume reductions can have on some DOs, for example, due to the loss of large customers to competitors that enter the market.
12. NERA (2004) presents estimates of scale economies in the postal sector. These indicate increasing returns to scale.
13. Kumbhakar and Knox Lovell (2003) present an overview of stochastic frontier models.
14. We represent the delivery activity by a Cobb–Douglas production function (see, for example, Kumbhakar and Knox Lovell, 2003).
15. The average efficiencies would be equal to 100 if a zero cost inefficiency were estimated for each DO. Note that the standard cost frontier model assumes a variation in the cost inefficiency across DOs which is different from the variation in the cost impact of the volume shocks. Alternatively, we could use a truncated normal distribution for modeling cost inefficiencies (see, for example, Kumbhakar and Knox Lovell, 2003; LECG, 2005 and NERA, 2005). Our results were unaffected when we used a truncated normal instead of a half-normal distribution.
16. Note that with generated noise that is more concentrated around zero, we find higher average efficiencies which are closer to 100 percent.
17. Table 9A2.3 shows that the estimated coefficients of the wage and volume are very close to one and 0.8 (the reciprocal of 1.25, which is the value of α used for generating the data), respectively.
18. Table 9A2.1–2 show the results assuming constant and decreasing returns to scale, respectively.
19. The estimated efficiency of the least efficient DO in the perfect labor adjustment scenario equals 97 percent.
20. Note that the DOs' ability to adjust labor depends on the length of the period under consideration. The inability to adjust labor may be interpreted as short or long term and depends on factors like the institutional settings and the costs of adjusting labor.
21. Greene (2007) provides an overview of stochastic frontier panel data models.
22. To disentangle the effects of labor adjustments and volume shocks from other drivers of inefficiencies, our analysis uses simulated data assuming that all DOs are cost efficient in the first year.

REFERENCES

Bradley, R. and P. Burns (2009), 'Regulation in an uncertain world: who needs price protection now?', paper presented at the 17th Conference on Postal and Delivery Economics, Bordeaux, May 27–30.

Cazals, C.J., P. Florens and B. Roy (2001), 'An analysis of some specific cost drivers in the delivery activity', in M.A. Crew, and P.R. Kleindorfer (eds), *Future Directions in Postal Reform*, Boston, MA: Kluwer Academic, pp. 197–212.

Crew, Michael A. and Paul R. Kleindorfer (1996), 'Incentive regulation in the United Kingdom and the United States: some lessons', *Journal of Regulatory Economics*, **9**(3), May, 211–25.
Crew, M.A., G. d'Alcantara, P.R. Kleindorfer, P. Claeys and B. Kuypers (2008), 'Economic factors underlying postal reform in the European Union', in M.A. Crew, P.R. Kleindorfer and J. Campbell (eds), *Handbook of Worldwide Postal Reform*, Cheltenham, UK and Northampton, MA, USA: Edward Elgar, pp. 216–44.
European Commission (2008), 'Accompanying document to the Report from the Commission to the European Parliament and the Council on the application of the Postal Directive', Commission Staff Working Document.
Greene, W.H. (2007), 'The econometric approach to efficiency analysis', Chapter 2 in H.O. Fried, C.A. Knox Lovell and S.S. Schmidt (eds), *The Measurement of Productive Efficiency and Productivity Growth*, Oxford: Oxford University Press.
Hooper, R., D. Hutton and I.R. Smith (2008), 'Modernise or decline: policies to maintain the universal postal service', an independent review of the UK postal services sector, London.
Horncastle, A., D. Jevons, P. Dudley and E. Thanassoulis (2006), 'Efficiency analysis of DOs in the postal sector using stochastic frontier and data envelopment analyses', in M.A. Crew and P.R. Kleindorfer, *Liberalization of the Postal and Delivery Sector*, Cheltenham, UK and Northampton, MA, USA: Edward Elgar, pp. 149–64.
Kumbhakar, S.C. and C.A. Knox Lovell (2003), *Stochastic Frontier Analysis*, Cambridge: Cambridge University Press.
LECG (2005), 'Future Efficient Costs of Royal Mail's Regulated Mail Activities', A report for Postcomm, August.
Moriarty, R., S. Yorke, G. Harman, J. Cubbin, M. Meschi and P. Smith (2006), 'Economic analysis of the efficiency of Royal Mail units and the implications for regulatory policy' in M.A. Crew and P.R. Kleindorfer (eds), *Liberalization of the Postal and Delivery Sector*, Cheltenham, UK and Northampton, MA, USA: Edward Elgar, pp. 165–82.
Nader, F.H. and M. Lintell (2008), 'Mail Trends Update', Pitney Bowes Background Paper, No. 20081.
NERA (2004), *Economics of Postal Services: A Final Report*, A report to the European Commission.
NERA (2005), *The Comparative Efficiency of BT in 2003*, A report for Ofcom.
ORR (2008), 'Periodic Review 2008. Determination of Network Rail's Outputs and Funding for 2009–14', Office of Rail Regulation report.
Wachter M.L. and J.M. Perloff (1991), 'A comparative analysis of wage premiums and industrial relations in the British Post Office and the United States Postal Service', in M.A. Crew and P.R. Kleindorfer (eds), *Competition and Innovation in Postal Services*, Norwell, MA: Kluwer Academic, pp. 115–37.

APPENDIX 9A1 DERIVATION OF LABOR COSTS

We assume a DO delivers volume y with n hours of labor according a Cobb–Douglas production technology: $y = n^{\alpha}$. Using subscripts 0 and 1 for period 0 and period 1, respectively, the DO uses n_0 hours of labor to produce volume $y_0 = n_0^{\alpha}$ at minimum labor costs. This means that it employs just enough hours of labor to produce volume y_0 in period 0 and (at wage rate w_0) has labor cost equal to $w_0 n_0 = w_0 (y_0)^{1/\alpha}$.

Volume Shock and Labor Adjustment

Between period 0 and period 1, a volume shock ρ takes place, so that: $y_1 = (1 + \rho) y_0$. We assume that the shock is negative resulting in non-negative volumes for period 1: $-1 \leq \rho \leq 0$. We assume that the DO sets labor in period 1 according to its ability to adjust labor m:

$$n_1 = (1 - m) n_0 + (m) n_1^*. \tag{9A1.1}$$

In (9A1.1) n_1^* denotes the amount of labor that minimizes the DO's labor costs to produce volume y_1. m takes values between zero and one. If m equals zero, the DO cannot adjust labor and sets labor equal to that in period 0: $n_1 = n_0$. If m equals one, the DO adjusts its labor completely and is able to minimize costs in period 1: $n_1 = n_1^*$. That is, the DO employs an amount of labor in period 1 that lies between (i) the amount of labor it would employ if it cannot adjust labor and (ii) the amount of labor it would employ to adjust labor fully.

Labor Costs in Period 1

We can rewrite equation (9A1.1) as follows:

$$n_1 = (1 - m)\left[\frac{y_1}{(1 + \rho)}\right]^{\frac{1}{\alpha}} + m(y_1)^{\frac{1}{\alpha}}. \tag{9A1.2}$$

Rearranging the equation, we obtain the labor costs in period 1:

$$w_1 n_1 = w_1 y_1^{\frac{1}{\alpha}}\left[(1 + m)(1 + \rho)^{-\frac{1}{\alpha}} + m\right]. \tag{9A1.3}$$

Equation (9A1.3) allows for constructing datasets of DOs as explained in the main text.

APPENDIX 9A2 ADDITIONAL RESULTS

Table 9A2.1 Average efficiencies – constant returns to scale ($\alpha = 1$)

Ability to adjust labor	0%	25%	50%	75%
Magnitude of volume declines				
Small (5%)	98.0	98.2	98.5	98.7
Medium (10%)	93.6	95.5	97.0	98.2
Large (30%)	71.0	75.7	81.4	88.9

Table 9A2.2 Average efficiencies – decreasing returns to scale ($\alpha = 0.75$)

Ability to adjust labor	0%	25%	50%	75%
Magnitude of volume declines				
Small (5%)	97.7	97.9	98.2	98.6
Medium (10%)	88.6	91.8	95.3	97.7
Large (30%)	64.0	69.2	75.8	84.9

Table 9A2.3 Estimated coefficients – increasing returns to scale ($\alpha = 1.25$)

Ability to adjust labor	0%	25%	50%	75%
Magnitude of volume declines				
Small (5%)				
Constant	0.047*	0.037	0.025	0.013
Wage	0.994***	0.994***	0.995***	0.995***
Volume	0.799***	0.799***	0.800***	0.800***
Medium (10%)				
Constant	0.084*	0.066*	0.048	0.027
Wage	0.989***	0.991***	0.993***	0.994***
Volume	0.799***	0.799***	0.799***	0.800***
Large (30%)				
Constant	0.087	0.092	0.095	0.069
Wage	0.969***	0.969***	0.969***	0.974***
Volume	0.799***	0.799***	0.798***	0.799***

Note: ***, ** and * indicate statistical significance at 1%, 5% and 10%, respectively.

10. Economies of scale and scope and opening hours in post offices and agencies*

Massimo Filippini, Martin Koller and Urs Trinkner

1 INTRODUCTION

Over the last two decades, several countries around the world have been gradually liberalizing their postal sectors. The key objectives of these reforms are better efficiency within the sector, improvement of product innovation, higher quality levels, and affordable prices while maintaining the provision of a minimum universal postal service. One of the most challenging tasks for the universal service providers in this process is to improve efficiency by satisfying the request to supply a minimum universal service.

In Switzerland, the postal market is also affected by such regulatory changes. The largest and most important provider of postal services in the country is the incumbent Swiss Post, a publicly owned company. Swiss Post operates a nationwide network of postal outlets, consisting mainly of self-operated post offices and some franchised postal agencies. These postal outlets conduct mail and parcel collection, banking operations and sales activities. An important characteristic of this postal outlet network is regulated accessibility and, to some extent, politically negotiated opening hours to enhance public service and customer comfort. Consequently, the duty to operate a comprehensive postal outlet network implies minimum opening hours. Frequently, these hours exceed the time necessary to operate local demand and standby time arises. The supply of this universal service is financially unattractive, especially in rural areas, where post offices are characterized by a relatively high percentage of standby time.

To promote the reorganization of the postal market successfully, it is important to have information on economies of scale and scope, and on the impact on cost of a predefined universal postal service. From a methodological point of view, this requires the specification of a cost model that appropriately reflects the supply of the universal postal service. In this study we propose to introduce standby time as an indicator of public service in the cost model. We argue that for the estimation of optimal size of postal outlets it is important to account for the impact of the public service obligation in the empirical cost analysis.

Apart from making use of economies of scale for considerations concerning size, we calculate economies of scope to answer strategic questions such as *how* the optimal output should be produced – jointly within the same infrastructure or in separate outlets? Among others, this question arises for banking services and the sale of third-party products.

The chapter is organized as follows. Section 2 outlines the main contribution of this chapter with regard to the relevant literature available on the subject. Section 3 presents the model specifications. Section 4 introduces the data, and Section 5 provides the estimation results and measures for economies of scale and scope for different model specifications. We draw our conclusions in Section 6.

2 PREVIOUS STUDIES ON ECONOMIES OF SCALE AND SCOPE

Various studies have investigated economies of scale and scope in network industries such as the energy and transport sector, healthcare, the banking industry, or even in the sector of higher education.[1] As far as postal services are concerned, however, most empirical studies pay attention to economies of scale and scope in delivery activities (see Wada et al., 1997; Mizutani and Uranishi, 2003; Cazals et al., 2005; Bradley et al., 2006 and Farsi et al., 2006).[2] With the exception of Mizutani and Uranishi 's contribution, the results accord well with intuition and confirm the existence of economies of scale and scope. Farsi et al. (2006) have examined a subset of 327 delivery offices in Switzerland and found evidence for economies of scale, density and scope, especially for units in remote areas with low mail volume.

Apart from delivery, only a few studies are available on economies of scale and scope in postal services. Bradley and Colvin (1999) focused on mail sorting and estimated a multiproduct total cost function for 250 US sorting centers between 1988 and 1996. They found evidence for substantial economies of scale and enhanced productivity within the observed time span. The most recent investigations relevant for this study are those by Cazals et al. (2002) and Gazzei et al. (2002) on economies of scale in postal collection. Cazals et al. (2002) applied a multiproduct log–log cost function to analyze a cross-section dataset consisting of 9,168 French post offices operating in the year 1999. The results of their empirical analysis provide evidence of the existence of economies of scale, at least for small- and medium-sized post offices. No estimation of economies of scope is provided because the deployed functional form impedes straightforward computation. Gazzei et al. (2002) have modeled a translog cost function to analyze a cross-section dataset consisting of 11,415 Italian post offices operating in the year 2000. Their empirical analysis indicates the presence of economies of scale irrespective of the size of the offices.

This chapter introduces three main novelties into the discussion of economies of scale and scope in postal collection networks. We employ a quadratic functional form that allows estimation of both economies of scale and scope. Moreover, we include standby periods of opening time in the cost model specification and control for heteroskedasticity.

3 COST MODEL SPECIFICATION AND ESTIMATION METHODS

We specify a cost model that explains total costs of Swiss Post's collection network with six aggregated output variables, one input variable, and two environmental characteristics. Under the assumption of cost-minimizing behavior of postal outlets and convex production technology, we write this model as follows:

$$C = f(Q_1, Q_2, Q_3, Q_4, Q_5, Q_6, P_C, dBM, dRA), \tag{10.1}$$

where the dependent variable C represents total cost. The first five outputs ($Q_1 - Q_5$) are measured by the following parameters: letters, parcels, payment services, account management services, and sale of optional products.

The sixth output, Q_6, is the variable that represents standby periods during the opening time of these post offices. This variable allows us to control for situations in which a post office counter has to remain open even if demand is zero. In these situations, the employees at the counters are not performing any specific tasks but are waiting to serve the next customers. Gazzei et al. (2002) classify this time as 'unsaturation' and point out that its presence causes misleading efficiency estimates and biased results for economies of scale. This (upward) bias arises due to the cost of unsaturation. In a saturated process, either costs are lower or outputs higher, hence economies of scale in saturated processes are lower than in unsaturated processes. Standby time that causes this bias is not a priori a negative economic phenomenon such as inefficient organization or laziness of the employees, but might be commercially optimal or politically desired. In the latter case, it might be set indirectly as a constraint by the universal service obligation regulations that require a comprehensive postal network.[3] Consequently, the duty to operate such a network would imply a certain number of opening hours, even though the time absorbed by local demand might be lower. Our analysis has shown that the share of standby time is negatively correlated with opening hours, hence it is relatively large in post offices with short opening hours. Note that post offices with short opening hours are usually small ones located in rural areas. Hence, despite short opening hours, these post offices still exhibit relatively high standby times.

In short, standby time arises as the difference of the time absorbed by local demand and the opening time. As argued above, the provision of long opening hours is a service that is indirectly politically desired. Consequently, standby time is to a large extent a result of political obligations. We therefore interpret, unlike previous authors, this seemingly unproductive time as an output in the form of a public service.[4] A comparison might be drawn with emergency services characterized by a considerable number of standby hours. The standby time of fire brigades, for example, is widely accepted as public service.

P_C is the price of capital, measured by the cost of physical capital. The price of labor was not included in the model because it is set by a collective labor agreement and therefore does not vary significantly among units and regions.

Swiss Post's postal outlets differ considerably. Therefore, the dummy variables dBM (franchising business model, where the franchisees run a core business other than postal operations within the same infrastructure) and dRA (peripheral rural areas and alpine tourist center regions) are introduced in the model as environmental characteristics.[5] For a complete description of the variables and the corresponding data see Section 4.

The estimation of cost model (10.1) requires the specification of a functional form. We apply a quadratic functional form as it has the advantage of being able to take zero values into account.[6] As Section 4 will show, zero outputs occur in about one-third of all observations for payment and/or account management services in agencies and in small post offices. The quadratic cost function was widely used by previous studies on economies of scale and scope in network industries, for example in Baumol et al. (1982), Jara-Diaz et al. (2003) and Farsi et al. (2007). It can be written as:

$$C_i = \alpha_0 + \sum_{m}^{M}\beta_m Q_{mi} + \frac{1}{2}\sum_{m}^{M}\beta_{mm}Q_{mi}Q_{mi} + \sum_{m(m\neq n)}^{M}\sum_{n}^{M}\beta_{mn}Q_{mi}Q_{ni}$$

$$+ \gamma_{P_c}P_{Ci} + \frac{1}{2}\gamma_{P_cP_c}P_{Ci}P_{Ci} + \sum_{m}^{M}\lambda_m P_{Ci}Q_{mi} + \delta_1 dBM_i + \delta_2 dRA_i + \varepsilon_i, \qquad (10.2)$$

where subscript i denotes postal outlet $i = 1, 2, \ldots, I$. ε_i is the error term and subscripts m and n are product indices. As the quadratic function is a second-order Taylor approximation, the values of the explanatory variables have to be normalized to the approximation point. For this purpose, we choose the median value of the variables.

As expected, a preliminary econometric analysis showed that the data are affected by heteroskedasticity.[7] In order to account for this problem, two advanced econometric specifications of the error term have been considered and compared to the ordinary least squares (OLS) model. The weighted least squares (WLS) model is a version of a robust regression, where variances of the error terms are calculated in an iteratively accomplished process and assumed to be proportional to the square of the dependent variable. The process starts with the variance predicted by the OLS model and stops when changes in the variances fall below a certain limit. Finally, the variances of the error terms in the multiplicative heteroskedastic (MH) regression model are assumed to be an exponential function of the first five outputs ($Q_1 - Q_5$). The specifications of the variances of these three models can be summarized as follows:

$$\text{OLS model:} \quad \varepsilon_i \sim \text{iid}\,(0, \sigma^2)$$

$$\text{WLS model:} \quad \varepsilon_i \sim \text{iid}\,(0, \sigma_i^2), \sigma_i^2 = \sigma^2(C_i^{\text{iteratively weighted}})^2 \qquad (10.3)$$

$$\text{MH model:} \quad \varepsilon_i \sim \text{iid}\,(0, \sigma_i^2), \sigma_i^2 = \sigma^2 \exp\left(\sum_{m=1}^{5}\gamma_m Q_{mi}\right).$$

The results of the econometric estimation of the multiproduct cost function (10.2) can be used to compute economies of scale and scope.

The concept of economies of scale investigates whether or not a company operates at an economically reasonable size. Economies of scale are measured by the ratio between average and marginal costs, and the optimal size of a unit is reached if this ratio equals unity. In the presence of (dis)economies of scale, ray average costs increase (decrease) when all outputs increase proportionately. In such a situation, postal outlets would be oversized (undersized).

The concept of economies of scope examines whether or not cost complementarities across products or shared fixed costs among products are present. If (dis)economies of scope are present between the different products and services offered in postal outlets, it is advantageous to offer them jointly in the same unit (separately in different units).

Widely used definitions of economies of scale and scope of multi-output companies go back to Baumol et al. (1982). According to these definitions, the values of (global) economies of scale can be computed as follows:

$$\text{Economies of scale} \equiv \frac{C_i}{\sum_{m=1}^{M} Q_{mi}\,(\delta C_i/\delta Q_{mi})}, \qquad (10.4)$$

where δ denotes the partial derivative operator. Accordingly, the values of (global) economies of scope are given by:

$$\text{Economies of scope} \equiv \frac{\sum_{m=1}^{M} C_i(Q_{mi}, 0, 0, 0, 0, 0) - C_i(Q_{1i}, Q_{2i}, Q_{3i}, Q_{4i}, Q_{5i}, Q_{6i})}{C_i(Q_{1i}, Q_{2i}, Q_{3i}, Q_{4i}, Q_{5i}, Q_{6i})}, \quad (10.5)$$

where $C_i(Q_{mi}, 0, 0, 0, 0, 0)$ represents the cost of specialized and $C_i(Q_{1i}, Q_{2i}, Q_{3i}, Q_{4i}, Q_{5i}, Q_{6i})$ of integrated postal outlets. Unfortunately, none of the outlets in our sample is highly specialized such that it only produces one of the six outputs. However, as Pulley and Braunstein (1992) argue, measuring economies of scope requires estimating the cost function at points with some empirical support, hence simulating situations really occurring in the data. Consequently, they suggest the estimation of *quasi economies of scope*, where firm specialization is imperfect, as it stands for producing basically one output and the others to a very small extent, μ.[8] Nevertheless, we focused on economies of scope as proposed by Baumol et al. (1982) for two reasons: first, partially specialized postal outlets with at least some of the outputs being zero occur in the sample; and second, coincidental analysis has shown that the differences between the two methods are marginal.

Caves et al. (1984) propose a refinement of the analysis of economies of scale in network industries. A variable representing the density of the network is used to distinguish between economies that stem from expanding the outputs and the network size by the same factor (economies of scale) and those that stem from expanding the output in the existing network (economies of density). This differentiation is of no relevance in the case of postal collection networks, because other than in cases such as mail and parcel distribution, railways, or energy distribution, only the nodes of the network cause costs, the network itself is of a virtual nature.

4 DATA

This study is based on a cross-section dataset of 2006 with information on 2,466 postal outlets operating in Switzerland.[9] These outlets have been subdivided into two classes according to their business model. The major part of it, namely 2,348 common post offices, are run by Swiss Post, whereas 118 agencies are run by franchisees.[10] The variable for the business model (*dBM*) takes the value 1 for agencies, and 0 for common post offices. Approximately one-fifth of the post offices and one-third of the agencies are located in peripheral rural areas and alpine tourist center regions. These outlets are indicated by the value 1 of the corresponding dummy variable *dRA*. The reference region takes the value 0 and consists of urban areas and extended agglomerations.[11]

The postal outlets cover a wide range of costs and outputs. Total costs (*C*) include expenditures for infrastructure such as capital costs or rental fees, and variable costs originate from counter activities. Total costs vary by a factor of more than 1000 among the postal outlets. All of these outlets collect mail and parcels and sell further products, whereas zero outputs may occur for payment and account management services in agencies and small post offices. These first four outputs are weighted sums of different subproducts of the corresponding output. We use the internal standards of performance as the weighting factor. As all postal outlets must comply with the same internal quality guidelines and principles, we assume comparable quality levels for all units.

Mail output (Q_1) is a generic term for regular, express and registered letters including single-piece and mass mail. It is calculated as the weighted sum of thousand letter items collected. Parcel output (Q_2) is also measured in thousands, but incorporates more diverse products. Due to the similar nature of the processes involved, the weighted number of either single or bulk parcels collected is added to the weighted number of items picked up at the postal outlets by the clients. The output of payment services (Q_3) is measured in million Swiss francs transacted and can be understood analogously. The weighted volume of incoming payments is added to the weighted volume of outpayments. The fourth output, account management services (Q_4), is the weighted number of thousand account openings (closings) and the weighted number of related consulting services. The fifth output, sale of further products (Q_5), is measured by sales volumes of non-postal products such as mobile phones, prepaid cards, tickets or stationery, measured in thousand Swiss francs.

The variable representing standby time (Q_6) is an important cost driver at least for smaller post offices, measured in hours per week. This variable allows us to consider production process situations in which a post office counter has to remain open even if local demand is zero. As standby time is neither directly observable nor measurable, we calculated it in the following way:

$$\text{Standby time} \equiv OH_i - \frac{\sum_{m=1}^{M} Q_{mi} t_m}{n_i}, \qquad (10.6)$$

hence we multiplied the standard of performance value t_m necessary to operate one item or transaction m with the corresponding number of items or transactions Q_m occurring in a postal outlet and added it up. We divided this value by the number of active counters n and subtracted the result from the regulated opening hours OH. For the reasons provided in Section 3, we interpret this variable as public service and hence as output. It takes the value zero in post offices working at full capacity and in all agencies because neither is confronted with unsaturated processes. The share of standby time is negatively correlated with OH and positively with dRA.

The cost of physical capital (P_C) is measured by the rental fee per square meter (ratio of the rental fee and rented surface area). These costs are, as expected, clearly higher in urban areas and agglomerations than in rural areas.

5 RESULTS

This section shows the estimation results of the three models (OLS, WLS and MH) and the corresponding values for economies of scale and scope as described in Section 3. We first throw light on the estimation results listed in Table 10.1.

Irrespective of the model, all of the first- and most of the second-order coefficients of the output variables have the expected sign and are highly significant. In particular, the values for the standby time confirm the expectation that unsaturated processes occur and increase cost substantially. The input price of capital shows that parts of the differences among postal outlets can be explained by higher capital costs. Further, the coefficients for

Table 10.1 Regression results

Variable	Model I (OLS) Coefficient	Model II (WLS) Coefficient	Model III (MH) Coefficient
Mail output (Q_1)	2,304.5897***	2,702.1183***	2,320.7877***
0.5*(Q_1Q_1)	−0.6027***	−0.2568***	−0.5448
Parcel output (Q_2)	32,238.9200***	29,542.7860***	36,357.0830***
0.5*(Q_2Q_2)	639.8244***	792.5120***	−27.0137
Payment services (Q_3)	7,628.8800***	5,738.5846***	5,437.1513***
0.5*(Q_3Q_3)	−2.8651	6,8731***	−16.0522***
Account mgmt (Q_4)	569,494***	685,150***	875,919***
0.5*(Q_4Q_4)	333,258***	132,037	90,749
Optional products (Q_5)	783.9783***	1,053.3376***	1,193.0478***
0.5*(Q_5Q_5)	−0.09532	−0.7264*	−1.2293
Idle time (Q_6)	328.9409***	307.1991***	271.1499***
0.5*(Q_6Q_6)	−0.0953	0.0005	0.0356
(Q_1Q_2)	−16.3192	−37.0285***	−23.2299
(Q_1Q_3)	−0.6689	−2.0037***	7.6127***
(Q_1Q_4)	246.8535**	−378.8690***	−886.7600*
(Q_1Q_5)	1.6025***	5.0552***	−0.2643
(Q_1Q_6)	0.4319**	1.0561***	0.7845***
(Q_2Q_3)	−25.4011*	56.8393***	28.6351
(Q_2Q_4)	−10,112.3890***	−4,200.7490*	−5,662.0956
(Q_2Q_5)	−25.6225**	−87.8189***	−31.2114*
(Q_2Q_6)	8.3571**	−12.2944***	−7.7426*
(Q_3Q_4)	877.4381**	1,511.1075***	1,931.0032**
(Q_3Q_5)	3.4432***	−3.9179***	0.7296
(Q_3Q_6)	−0.6270	0.5495**	1.9668***
(Q_4Q_5)	−454.5662*	283.1125*	502.0613
(Q_4Q_6)	80.6345	271.5065***	−73.1837
(Q_5Q_6)	0.5016	0.2620*	−0.3344
Price capital (P_C)	2,880.7051	5,223.4350***	5,162.8234***
0.5*(P_CP_C)	−177.1466	159.9452*	179.1292*
(P_CQ_1)	8.6687*	7.7775***	0.7868
(P_CQ_2)	660.1582***	395.2747***	726.6826***
(P_CQ_3)	−55.6129***	−115.8335***	−20.8398
(P_CQ_4)	−6,441.9838	−2,882.6952	−19,915.4550***
(P_CQ_5)	11.4451	46.6424***	14.7440
(P_CQ_6)	12.8921***	5.0254***	5.1373***
Business model (*dBM*)	−202,268***	−173,005***	−167,792***
Region (*dRA*)	124,990***	62,300***	85,967***
Constant	1,504,762***	1,488,346***	1,524,107***

Note: Values normalized (not CHF); n = 2,466; *** (**, *): Significant at 1% (5%, 10%).

the business model and the region leave no doubt: first, agencies generate considerable cost reductions compared to common post offices, and second, postal outlets in sparsely populated and touristic regions drive costs.

As expected, the results of the OLS model differ from the WLS and MH models. These

Table 10.2 Economies of scale (OLS, WLS and MH models)

	1. Quartile	Median	3. Quartile	Sample mean
OLS				
Individual results	0.910	1.037	1.199	1.087
Post offices	0.996	1.062	1.261	
Post offices (rural)	1.038	1.150	1.461	
Agencies	0.974	0.965	0.981	
Agencies (rural)	1.022	1.067	1.209	
WLS				
Individual results	0.933	1.069	1.237	1.124
Post offices	1.050	1.077	1.163	
Post offices (rural)	1.072	1.122	1.259	
Agencies	1.028	0.983	0.912	
Agencies (rural)	1.053	1.033	1.024	
MH				
Individual results	1.103	1.270	1.528	1.219
Post offices	1.006	1.081	1.235	
Post offices (rural)	1.034	1.142	1.374	
Agencies	0.986	0.998	1.008	
Agencies (rural)	1.018	1.066	1.169	

differences suggest that ignoring heteroskedasticity may cause bias in the calculation of economies of scale and scope. Therefore, the WLS and the MH models are more relevant for the empirical analysis of the economies of scale and scope. Consequently, we use them to compute the economies of scale and scope at the approximation point (sample median) and at the quartiles in the sample to shed light on the impact of the magnitude and the composition of the output.[12]

The results of the economies of scale and scope are provided in Tables 10.2. and 10.3. We distinguish between post offices and agencies on the one hand and between regions on the other. In the first line of each model, we depict the values of economies of scale and scope for representative postal outlets in the sample, whereas the results of the four subsequent lines belong to hypothetical postal outlets with all outputs set at the sample median and at the first or third quartiles, respectively. Of course, a unit exhibiting exactly these values might hardly or mere coincidentally exist in the data, but representative points are suited for comparison reasons. As an exception, the values for Q_6 (standby time) are set at the sample median throughout all representative points.

These results suggest that post offices are more affected by unexploited *economies of scale* (Table 10.2) than agencies, and rural postal outlets more than the ones located in urban or suburban regions. The individual results indicate, irrespective of the model, the presence of economies of scale at the sample median, at the third quartile, and at the mean. Economies of scale increase with falling outputs, hence smaller postal outlets. Hence, albeit we classify standby time as an output, which clearly occurs more often in poorly frequented post offices, economies of scale are higher in these offices. In other words, even though we augment the output of post offices with relatively low outputs, they still face high unit costs.

Table 10.3 Economies of scope (OLS, WLS and MH models)

	1. Quartile	Median	3. Quartile	Sample mean
OLS				
Individual results	0.466	0.812	1.539	1.221
Post offices	0.209	0.502	1.191	
Post offices (rural)	0.402	0.847	1.712	
Agencies	−0.094	−0.155	−0.083	
Agencies (rural)	0.142	0.335	0.875	
WLS				
Individual results	0.351	0.576	1.013	0.753
Post offices	0.275	0.416	0.796	
Post offices (rural)	0.374	0.600	1.119	
Agencies	0.016	−0.166	−0.494	
Agencies (rural)	0.134	0.087	0.109	
MH				
Individual results	0.341	0.700	1.456	1.119
Post offices	0.178	0.489	1.091	
Post offices (rural)	0.311	0.730	1.486	
Agencies	−0.068	−0.033	0.038	
Agencies (rural)	0.088	0.287	0.723	

The results for the hypothetical postal outlets show a similar pattern. The differences between post offices and agencies between the regions are most striking, and except for agencies in the WLS model, economies of scale increase with falling outputs. Therefore, at least in rural regions, agencies exhibit lower economies of scale than common post offices.

Similar to the results for economies of scale, considerable *economies of scope* (Table 10.3) appear in almost every category of postal outlet. Hence, the models suggest that it is generally favorable to provide postal products and services jointly within the same infrastructure. Overall, rural post outlets appear to face higher economies of scope than urban or suburban outlets.[13] Similarly, and as expected, post offices exhibit higher economies of scope than agencies. Note that in agencies, economies of scope arise not mainly between postal products themselves, but mainly between postal products and all other products (groceries and so on), see Buser et al. (2008). As we analyze agencies from Swiss Post's point of view, such third party outputs are not included in the dataset and hence our measures of economies of scope are limited to postal products. However, economies of scope between groceries and postal products might be reflected indirectly by *dBM* which can be interpreted as Swiss Post's share of cost savings that are realized by the agency model by exploiting economies of scope between postal services and groceries.

6 SUMMARY AND CONCLUSIONS

The purpose of this study was to analyze the cost structure of Swiss Post's postal outlets, and in particular to assess economies of scale and scope in post offices and franchised postal agencies. Information on optimal size and production structure is of importance from a policy maker's point of view, as this hypothetical situation may be a calculation basis of reimbursements for providing the universal service. Furthermore, from a company's perspective, the question of the optimal organization of the network arises. Important questions are the optimal size of post offices, whether and where common post offices should be transformed into agencies, or whether product lines should be offered in post offices or agencies operated by partners.

An important novelty of this study is the inclusion of standby time as an indicator of public service in the cost model, as regulated accessibility and negotiated opening hours enhancing public service frequently leading to opening hours that exceed the time necessary to operate the demand.

A quadratic total cost function was estimated using a cross-section consisting of 2,468 post offices and agencies operating in the year 2006. The empirical results indicate the presence of strong economies of scale and economies of scope, especially for postal outlets with low output volumes. Moreover, the empirical analysis shows that standby time has an important effect on cost.

The results suggest that post offices are more affected by unexploited economies of scale than agencies. Similarly, rural postal outlets have higher values than the ones located in urban or suburban regions. Beyond that, economies of scale increase with falling outputs. Therefore, Swiss Post would benefit from transforming smaller post offices in rural regions into agencies. This change of the business model would also reduce standby time and, therefore, cost.[14]

The results for economies of scope follow in principle a similar pattern as economies of scale. Common post offices are more affected by unexploited economies of scope than agencies, and rural postal outlets more than the ones located in urban or suburban regions. This result supports Swiss Post's policy to offer postal and financial services as well as the sale of third-party products within the same infrastructure. The expansion of the sale of third-party products and further services might be an alternative second-best strategy for transforming common post offices into agencies in the case of political or regulatory opposition.

Such opposition against post office closures (or replacements by third-party agencies) is mainly based on two factors in Switzerland. First, agencies do not provide payment services in cash due to security and anti-money-laundering measures. Therefore, they fail to fulfill a small share of the universal service. For this case, the issue of the legitimate extent of the universal service needs to be discussed and, if necessary, properly reimbursed. Second, common post offices appear to contribute to the identity of villages, especially in remote areas. Closing down other retail businesses and small enterprises may foster resistance against post office conversions. On the other hand, joint use of infrastructure in the case of agencies could help to ensure continuing postal and other service in rural areas, which would otherwise be too costly for a dedicated post office, as well as providing more convenient opening hours.

NOTES

* The views expressed in this chapter are those of the authors and do not necessarily reflect the opinion of the institutions with which they are affiliated. Access to Swiss Post's data is gratefully acknowledged.

1. See, for example, Caves et al. (1981) (transport sector), Koshal and Koshal (1999) (higher education), Preyra and Pink (2006) (health sector) and Farsi et al. (2007) (electricity distribution).
2. See also NERA (2004) for an overview on the relevant empirical literature.
3. Some 90 percent of the population should be able to reach a post office within 20 minutes by foot or public transport.
4. Standby time as a public service is not a pure public good, as it is characterized only by nonrivalry, but not by nonexcludability. Standby time might appear to be an input to provide the other outputs, but the other outputs are provided without standby time, which is an independent service derived from the input labor.
5. We are aware that model (10.1) does not completely capture the heterogeneity that characterizes the production process in postal outlets. However, the specification of six outputs should reduce the potential unobserved heterogeneity bias. Unfortunately, panel data are not available to use econometric approaches that can solve this bias, at least partly.
6. Other functional forms such as Cobb–Douglas or translog require adjustments, for instance through a Box–Cox transformation, because logarithms are not defined for non-positive arguments. Such transformations might cause problems that lie far beyond the scope of this chapter. As a first alternative, the zero values could be replaced with small values as, for example, 0.00001 (small value transformation). But according to some authors (for example, Pulley and Braunstein, 1992), this transformation may lead to strongly biased results. Further alternatives are nonlinear econometric approaches such as, for example, the composite cost function of Pulley and Braunstein.
7. We expected heteroskedasticity due to a wide range of costs and outputs between 'small' and 'big' postal outlets, see Section 4.
8. To simulate such situations, they extended the formula for economies of scope in the following way:

$$\text{Quasi economies of scope} \equiv \frac{\sum_{m=1}^{M} C\{\mu Q_{\neq mi}, [1-(M-1)\mu]Q_{mi}\} - C(Q_{1i}, Q_{2i}, Q_{3i}, Q_{4i}, Q_{5i}, Q_{6i})}{C(Q_{1i}, Q_{2i}, Q_{3i}, Q_{4i}, Q_{5i}, Q_{6i})}.$$

   Thus, μ must be smaller than $1/M$ to achieve post office specialization.
9. This is an updated version of the data used by Jaag et al. (2009). We had to exclude four of the post offices and seven of the agencies due to missing values for total costs. Four more post offices turned out to be severe outliers with a Cook's distance exceeding the mean by a factor of more than 300. We excluded them as well.
10. 'Agency' is a generic term for different types of franchisee models; most of the franchisees run grocery stores or other retail businesses.
11. Classification implemented by the Federal Office of Spatial Development. The other data were provided by Swiss Post.
12. Taking into account the experiences from other studies, the levels of the variables listed in Table 10.2 and 10.3 should be treated with caution because of the lack of panel data.
13. For agencies, only the OLS and MH models support this result.
14. Note that standby time is not meaningful for agencies as time not spent on servicing postal customers would presumably be absorbed by complementary activities of the core business.

REFERENCES

Baumol, William J., John C. Panzar and Robert D. Willig (1982), *Contestable Markets and the Theory of Industry Structure*, New York: Harcourt Brace Jovanovich.

Bradley, Michael D. and Jeff Colvin (1999), 'Productivity and technical change in a public service enterprise', in Michael A. Crew and Paul R. Kleindorfer (eds), *Emerging Competition in Postal and Delivery Services*, Boston, MA: Kluwer Academic, pp. 75–100.

Bradley, Michael D., Jeff Colvin and Mary K. Perkins (2006), 'Measuring scale and scope economies with a structural model of postal delivery', in Michael A. Crew and Paul R. Kleindorfer (eds), *Liberalization of the Postal and Delivery Sector*, Cheltenham UK and Northampton MA, USA: Edward Elgar, pp. 103–19.

Buser, Martin, Christian Jaag and Urs Trinkner (2008), 'Economics of post office networks: strategic issues and the impact on mail demand', in Michael A. Crew, Paul R. Kleindorfer and James I. Campbell (eds), *Handbook of Worldwide Postal Reform*, Cheltenham UK and Northampton MA, USA: Edward Elgar, pp. 80–97.

Caves, Douglas W., Laurits R. Christensen and Joseph A. Swanson (1981), 'Productivity growth, scale economies, and capacity utilization in U.S. railroads, 1955–74', *American Economic Review*, **71**(5), 994–1002.

Caves, Douglas W., Laurits R. Christensen and Michael W. Tretheway (1984), 'Economies of density versus economies of scale: why trunk and local service airline cost differs', *Rand Journal of Economics*, **15**(4), 471–89.

Cazals, Catherine, Pascale Duchemin, Jean Pierre Florens, Bernard Roy and Olivier Vialaneix (2002), 'An econometric study of cost elasticity in the activities of post office strategy', in Michael A. Crew and Paul R. Kleindorfer (eds), *Postal and Delivery Services: Pricing, Productivity, Regulation and Strategy*, Boston, MA: Kluwer Academic, pp. 161–70.

Cazals, Catherine, Jean Pierre Florens and Soterios Soteri (2005), 'Delivery costs for postal services in the UK: some results on scale economies with panel data', in Michael A. Crew and Paul R. Kleindorfer (eds), *Regulatory and Economic Challenges in the Postal and Delivery Sector*, Boston, MA: Kluwer Academic, pp. 203–12.

Farsi, Mehdi, Aurelio Fetz and Massimo Filippini (2007), 'Economies of scale and scope in local public transportation', *Journal of Transport Economics and Policy*, **41**(3), 345–61.

Farsi, Mehdi, Massimo Filippini and Urs Trinkner (2006), 'Economies of scale, density and scope in Swiss post's mail delivery', in Michael A. Crew and Paul R. Kleindorfer (eds), *Liberalization of the Postal and Delivery Sector*, Cheltenham UK and Northampton MA, USA: Edward Elgar, pp. 91–101.

Gazzei, Duccio S., Carla Pace and Gennaro Scarfiglieri (2002), 'On the output elasticity of the activities of post office counters in Italy', in Michael A. Crew and Paul R. Kleindorfer (eds), *Postal and Delivery Services: Delivering on Competition*, Boston, MA: Kluwer Academic, pp. 157–67.

Jaag, Christian, Martin Koller and Urs Trinkner (2009), 'How to calculate the cost of the universal service obligation: the need for a global approach', in Michael A. Crew and Paul R. Kleindorfer (eds), *Progress in the Competitive Agenda in the Postal and Delivery Sector*, Cheltenham, UK and Northampton, MA, USA: Edward Elgar, pp. 100–112.

Jara-Diaz, Sergio, Eduardo Martinez-Budria and Francisco Javier Ramos-Real (2003), 'Adapting productivity theory to the quadratic cost function: an application to the Spanish Electric Sector', *Journal of Productivity Analysis*, **20**(2), 213–29.

Koshal, Rajindar K. and Manjulika Koshal (1999), 'Economies of scale and scope in higher education: a case of comprehensive universities', *Economics of Education Review*, **18**, 269–77.

Mizutani, Fumatoshi and Shui Uranishi (2003), 'The post office vs. parcel delivery companies: competition effects on costs and productivity', *Journal of Regulatory Economics*, **23**(3), 299–319.

NERA (2004), 'Economics of Postal Services – Final Report. A Report to the European Commission', London.

Preyra, Colin and Charles Pink (2006), 'Scale and scope efficiencies through hospital consolidations', *Journal of Health Economics*, **25**, 1049–58.

Pulley, Lawrence B. and Yale M. Braunstein (1992), *A Composite Cost Function for Multiproduct Firms with an Application to Economies of Scope in Banking*, Cambridge, MA: Vol. 74, MIT Press, pp. 221–30.

Wada, T., C. Tsunoda and J. Nemoto (1997), 'Empirical analysis of economies of scale, economies of scope, and cost subadditivity in Japanese mail service', IPTP Paper Series, 1997–08.

11. Welfare and profit implications for changes in service specification within the universal service

Philippe De Donder, Helmuth Cremer, Paul Dudley and Frank Rodriguez*

1 INTRODUCTION

In many countries in the world the mail industry is facing declining addressed mail volumes. In Europe there is also an opening of the market to competition and the prospect of mail volumes transferring from the incumbent universal service provider (USP) to alternative providers. In some countries, the increased choice has already led to some customers transferring from standard postal services to lower-priced alternatives where the customer takes on more of the mail preparation. In the presence of significant economies of scale and fixed network costs this can lead to deterioration in the financial position of the USP.

The USP is required under the Third European Postal Services Directive (2008)[1] to provide universal services of delivery for a minimum of five days per week, with collection for a minimum of five days per week, at prices that are affordable and, where required, uniform within a geographical area. In some countries the service specification exceeds this minimum requirement through national edicts.

The Directive[2] refers to an 'unfair financial burden' and envisages the prospect of a market outcome where the USP does not break even and to the calculation of a 'net cost' of the Universal Service Obligation (USO) as the change in USP profitability arising from the removal of the service constraints imposed on the USP in its provision of the USO.[3] These service constraints can include geographic uniform pricing and service specifications such as the number of collections and delivery each day of the week. The Directive provides the scope for a compensation fund or other payment mechanisms to support universal service in the event that certain conditions are met, namely the USP having an unfair financial burden and a net cost in the provision of the USO.

The unfair financial burden and the net cost of the USO are different calculations, which are related to each other. It may be the case that the unfair financial burden does not arise at all where there is a market solution in which the USP can break even. However, the case where the USP is not able to break even is of most interest given the developments in the mail market, and it is further explored in this chapter.

The previous literature has looked at approaches to the financial viability of the USPs (Crew and Kleindorfer, 2000); profitability of the USPs (Cremer et al., 2000; Rodriguez et al., 1999; Panzar, 2001); and the analysis of assessing the impact of the uniform tariff constraint of the universal service (De Donder et al., 2001, 2002). Estimates of the net cost of changes to the service specification have also been made for some countries (Bradley et al., 2009; Jaag et al., 2009); and the regulatory implications of changes in service quality have also been explored (Crew and Kleindorfer, 2009). Building on Panzar (2001), Cohen et al. (Chapter 16, this volume) develop measures of the cost of the USO and the value of the monopoly in the US for specific regulatory and market counterfactuals and apply their methodology to produce some estimates for the US.

In this chapter we consider how the net cost of changes in service specification or quality and the financial position of the USP relate to one another. Here, an unfair financial burden arises where the USP incurs a financial deficit within the market it operates, and the net cost of the USO is the change in profitability for the USP that arises from a relaxation of the USO requirements which could be put into effect if the USO were removed. The specific constraints embodied in the USO and market, and influenced by a regulator, can affect these two measures differently and even in opposite directions. Funding the unfair financial burden resulting from changes in the market (demand, competition and so on) may be achieved through various mixes of regulatory changes, including pricing constraints, USO requirements and funding mechanisms. The appropriate approach to choosing which changes achieve the highest net welfare requires at a minimum careful consideration of these factors within an appropriate framework and empirical assessment.

We consider many of these aspects, with the exception of a compensation fund, through the development of a model that introduces quality as a variable to represent the service specification in Section 2, developing the model used in De Donder et al. (2006, 2009). This development adds cross-price elasticities between the services offered by the USP and service specification or 'quality' as a variable affecting both demand and supply. Section 3 calibrates the model and Section 4 develops this into a hypothetical illustration where the USP has an unfair financial burden and is unable to break even, and the net cost of a change from the requirements of the USO is calculated from assessment of the effect on supply and demand of a relaxation for the USP in the service specification required under the USO. The focus is on the cases of the USP monopoly and competition through entrants accessing the USP's network, though the approach could also be extended to competition through entrants bypassing the USP's network (see De Donder et al., 2009). Section 5 concludes.

2 MODEL

We model two operators, the USP and a competitive fringe of identical entrants (for simplicity, we refer to 'the entrant' subsequently). There are two categories of goods: single-piece and bulk mail. We model the opening of the market to competition. Entry occurs in the bulk mail market while the USP serves the single-piece mail market de facto. We then consider a total of three postal goods, with two offered by the USP and one (bulk mail) offered by the entrant.[4]

This corresponds to the framework we have studied in De Donder et al. (2006). We enrich this model in two directions. First, we assume that the three goods are imperfect substitutes. That is, contrary to De Donder et al., there is substitution between single-piece and bulk mail as well as between the two bulk mail products offered by the operators. The second extension of De Donder et al. consists in assuming that demands depend not only on prices but also on non-price dimensions (such as speed or frequency of delivery and collection), which we label 'quality'.

The quantity of single-piece mail is denoted by x, with a unit consumer price of p_x and a quality level of q_x. Variables pertaining to the USP bulk mail are indexed by I, and by E if they relate to the entrant's bulk mail. Bulk mail USP price is denote by p_I while its quality is given by q_I. Similarly for the entrant, with p_E and q_E. The USO comprises two sets of constraints: uniform pricing constraints (imposing that USP prices be the same on both delivery areas) and non-price, or quality constraints.

Our starting point is a situation where the USP has a monopoly over both single-piece and bulk mail. The demand function for single-piece mail is given by $x^M(p_x, q_x, p_I, q_I)$ while demand for bulk mail is $y_I^M(p_x, q_x, p_I, q_I)$. See Appendix 11A for a derivation of the model and of how demand functions are obtained. The USP faces fixed costs as well as (upstream and downstream) variable costs. All these costs are assumed to be increasing in quality. More precisely, $F(q_x, q_I)$ denotes the USP fixed cost while $c_x(q_x)$ (respectively, $c_I(q_I)$) is the USP upstream variable unit cost for single-piece mail (respectively, bulk mail) and d_x (respectively, d_I) is the USP downstream variable unit cost for single-piece mail (respectively, bulk mail).

The USP's profit under monopoly is given by:

$$\Pi_I^M(p_x, q_x, p_I, q_I) = x^M(p_x, q_x, p_I, q_I)[p_x - c_x(q_x) - d_x(q_x)]$$

$$+ y_I^M(p_x, q_x, p_I, q_I)[p_I - c_I(q_I) - d_I(q_I)] - F(q_x, q_I).$$

We assume that the USP is subject to two forms of regulation. First, the USO imposes a (minimum) quality level for both single-piece and bulk mail.[5] We then have that $q_x = \bar{q}_x$ and $q_I = \bar{q}_I$. Second, USP prices are regulated. More precisely, we assume that the USP is restricted in the mark-up that its prices represent as a function of its variable costs:

$$\bar{p}_x \leq (1 + z)[c_x(\bar{q}_x) + d_x(\bar{q}_x)],$$

$$\bar{p}_I \leq (1 + z)[c_I(\bar{q}_I) + d_I(\bar{q}_I)]. \tag{11.1}$$

where the mark-up z is set exogenously by the regulator.

We now introduce competition on the bulk mail market. When consumers have access to the entrant's bulk mail product, demand functions become (see Appendix 11A):

$$x(p_x, q_x, p_I, q_I, p_E, q_E),$$

$$y_I(p_x, q_x, p_I, q_I, p_E, q_E),$$

$$y_E(p_x, q_x, p_I, q_I, p_E, q_E).$$

We assume that entry is through access only. Each unit of the entrant's bulk mail necessitates one unit of access bought from the USP at the (regulated) price a. The entrant faces no fixed costs, but has an upstream variable unit cost of $c_E(q_E)$, which is increasing in quality. With access-only entry, we assume that the entrant cannot differentiate the quality of its offering from that of the USP, so that $q_E = q_I$. As the entrant behaves competitively, its price is set at marginal cost so that $p_E = c_E(q_E) + a$ and the entrant breaks even in the absence of fixed costs. The USP's profit is given by:

$$\begin{aligned}\Pi_I(p_x, q_x, p_I, q_I, p_E, q_E, a) &= x(p_x, q_x, p_I, q_I, p_E, q_E)[p_x - c_x(q_x) - d_x(q_x)] \\ &\quad + y_I(p_x, q_x, p_I, q_I, p_E, q_E)[p_I - c_I(q_I) - d_I(q_I)] \\ &\quad + y_E(p_x, q_x, p_I, q_I, p_E, q_E)[a - d_I(q_I)] - F(q_x, q_I).\end{aligned}$$

We assume that the access charge is set according to the same regime as the end-to-end USP price, so that:

$$\bar{a} \leq (1 + z)d_I(\bar{q}_I). \tag{11.2}$$

We consider two objectives for the USP: maximizing welfare under a break-even constraint (which corresponds to the Ramsey prices and can be attained with a global price cap (GPC) (see Laffont and Tirole, 2000)) or posting the lowest prices that allow the USP to break even, with all prices exhibiting the same mark-up over marginal cost (the EPMU, or equi-proportional mark-up solution).[6] In both cases, we also apply the pricing constraints (11.1) and (11.2).[7] With the calibration assumptions we use, the pricing constraints (11.1) and (11.2) are always binding at equilibrium, both with the GPC and with the EPMU programs. Since these binding constraints determine all prices, the two programs give equivalent solutions.

The USP profit level under competition is given by $\Pi_I[\bar{p}_x, \bar{q}_x, \bar{p}_I, \bar{q}_I, c_E(\bar{q}_I) + \bar{a}, \bar{q}_I, \bar{a}]$. Since USP prices and quality are unchanged compared to the monopoly situation, it is reasonable to assume that the USP has a deficit (or would have a smaller profit if more generally monopoly profit were positive) when the bulk mail market is opened to competition. This deficit can be defined as the unfair financial burden of the USO, under a given regulatory price constraint, in a postal market opened to competition.

We assume throughout that price regulations are kept constant (relaxing these constraints would of course allow the USP to improve its financial position) and we analyze the impact of relaxing the service specification of the USO (as measured by the quality levels $\bar{q}_x$ and $\bar{q}_I$) on USP profit. In other words, the net cost of a change to the USO service specification is given as the impact of a decrease in quality on the USP profit, in the competitive situation, and for a given price regulation scheme. Observe that the impact of modifying quality on profit is not straightforward, as q_x has an impact on costs, on prices (via the price regulatory regime) and of course on demand. For instance, the impact on USP profit of varying single-piece mail quality is given by:

$$\frac{\partial \Pi_I[\bar{p}_x, \bar{q}_x, \bar{p}_I, \bar{q}_I, c_E(\bar{q}_I) + \bar{a}, \bar{q}_I, \bar{a}]}{\partial \bar{q}_x}$$

$$= \left[\frac{\partial x(\cdot)}{\partial \bar{q}_x} + \frac{\partial x(\cdot)}{\partial \bar{p}_x}\frac{\partial \bar{p}_x}{\partial \bar{q}_x}\right][\bar{p}_x - c_x(\bar{q}_x) - d_x(\bar{q}_x)]$$

$$+ x(\cdot)\left[\frac{\partial \overline{p}_x}{\partial \overline{q}_x} - \frac{\partial c_x(\overline{q}_x)}{\partial \overline{q}_x} - \frac{\partial d_x(\overline{q}_x)}{\partial \overline{q}_x}\right]$$

$$+ \left[\frac{\partial y_I(\cdot)}{\partial \overline{q}_x} + \frac{\partial y_I(\cdot)}{\partial \overline{p}_x}\frac{\partial \overline{p}_x}{\partial \overline{q}_x}\right][\overline{p}_I - c_I(\overline{q}_I) - d_I(\overline{q}_I)]$$

$$+ \left[\frac{\partial y_E(\cdot)}{\partial \overline{q}_x} + \frac{\partial y_E(\cdot)}{\partial \overline{p}_x}\frac{\partial \overline{p}_x}{\partial \overline{q}_x}\right][\overline{a} - d_I(\overline{q}_I)]$$

$$- \frac{\partial F(\overline{q}_x, \overline{q}_I)}{\partial \overline{q}_x}. \tag{11.3}$$

The second line in (11.3) measures the variation in revenues (for a given unit margin) when single-piece mail demand changes following the relaxing of the service specification of that good. Single-piece demand is affected through two channels: a quality effect (which decreases demand because of lower quality) and a price effect (which increases demand since, with a binding pricing constraint (11.1), a lower quality translates into a lower single-piece price). The sign of the net impact on single-piece demand is then ambiguous. The third line shows the impact of the modification of $\overline{q}_x$ on revenues, for a given volume, as the unit margin is affected simultaneously by changes in the regulated price $\overline{p}_x$ and in the (upstream and downstream) marginal costs. It is reasonable to assume that, whatever the price regulation studied, the single-piece mail price will not be allowed to increase following a decrease in $\overline{q}_x$. With the mark-up regulation we have assumed, we can use (11.1) to obtain:

$$\frac{\partial \overline{p}_x}{\partial \overline{q}_x} - \frac{\partial c_x(\overline{q}_x)}{\partial \overline{q}_x} - \frac{\partial d_x(\overline{q}_x)}{\partial \overline{q}_x} = z\left[\frac{\partial c_x(\overline{q}_x)}{\partial \overline{q}_x} + \frac{\partial d_x(\overline{q}_x)}{\partial \overline{q}_x}\right] > 0,$$

that is, a decrease in q_x actually decreases the unit margin made on single-piece mail, as the regulated price decreases more than the marginal costs, thereby reducing the USP's profit.

The fourth and fifth lines in (11.3) show that modifying $\overline{q}_x$ also affects the USP profit through its impact on bulk mail volumes. The net impact of decreasing $\overline{q}_x$ on both y_I and y_E is indeterminate, as the quality effect increases bulk mail volumes while the price effect decreases them. Finally, the last line is the impact of the lower fixed costs on profit when q_x is decreased, again increasing the USP's profit.

A similar equation describes the impact of decreasing $\overline{q}_I$ on the USP's profit:

$$\frac{\partial \prod_I [\overline{p}_x, \overline{q}_x, \overline{p}_I, \overline{q}_I, c_E(\overline{q}_I) + \overline{a}, \overline{q}_I, \overline{a}]}{\partial \overline{q}_I}$$

$$= \left[\frac{\partial x(\cdot)}{\partial \overline{q}_I} + \frac{\partial x(\cdot)}{\partial \overline{p}_I}\frac{\partial \overline{p}_I}{\partial \overline{q}_I} + \frac{\partial x(\cdot)}{\partial \overline{q}_E} + \frac{\partial x(\cdot)}{\partial \overline{p}_E}\frac{\partial \overline{p}_E}{\partial \overline{q}_I} + \frac{\partial x(\cdot)}{\partial \overline{a}}\frac{\partial \overline{a}}{\partial \overline{q}_I}\right][\overline{p}_x - c_x(\overline{q}_x) - d_x(\overline{q}_x)]$$

$$+ \left[\frac{\partial y_I(\cdot)}{\partial \overline{q}_I} + \frac{\partial y_I(\cdot)}{\partial \overline{p}_I}\frac{\partial \overline{p}_I}{\partial \overline{q}_I} + \frac{\partial y_I(\cdot)}{\partial \overline{q}_E} + \frac{\partial y_I(\cdot)}{\partial \overline{p}_E}\frac{\partial \overline{p}_E}{\partial \overline{q}_I} + \frac{\partial y_I(\cdot)}{\partial \overline{a}}\frac{\partial \overline{a}}{\partial \overline{q}_I}\right][\overline{p}_I - c_I(\overline{q}_I) - d_I(\overline{q}_I)]$$

$$+ y_I(\cdot)\left[\frac{\partial \bar{p}_I}{\partial \bar{q}_I} - \frac{\partial c_I(\bar{q}_I)}{\partial \bar{q}_I} - \frac{\partial d_I(\bar{q}_I)}{\partial \bar{q}_I}\right]$$

$$+ \left[\frac{\partial y_E(\cdot)}{\partial \bar{q}_I} + \frac{\partial y_E(\cdot)}{\partial \bar{p}_I}\frac{\partial \bar{p}_I}{\partial \bar{q}_I} + \frac{\partial y_E(\cdot)}{\partial \bar{q}_E} + \frac{\partial y_E(\cdot)}{\partial \bar{p}_E}\frac{\partial \bar{p}_E}{\partial \bar{q}_I} + \frac{\partial y_E(\cdot)}{\partial \bar{a}}\frac{\partial \bar{a}}{\partial \bar{q}_I}\right][\bar{a} - d_I(\bar{q}_I)]$$

$$+ y_E(\cdot)\left[\frac{\partial \bar{a}}{\partial \bar{q}_I} - \frac{\partial d_I(\bar{q}_I)}{\partial \bar{q}_I}\right] - \frac{\partial F(\bar{q}_x, \bar{q}_I)}{\partial \bar{q}_I}. \quad (11.4)$$

Equation (11.4) is even more complex than equation (11.3) because of two additional effects: (i) the entrant's quality (and thus its marginal cost and price) is also affected by variations in $\bar{q}_I$ (compare the terms within the first square brackets in the second line of both equations), and (ii) the regulated access charge is also affected (compare the last line of both equations). Note that, with the pricing constraints considered, we have that:

$$\frac{\partial \bar{p}_I}{\partial \bar{q}_I} - \frac{\partial c_I(\bar{q}_I)}{\partial \bar{q}_I} - \frac{\partial d_I(\bar{q}_I)}{\partial \bar{q}_I} = z\left[\frac{\partial c_I(\bar{q}_I)}{\partial \bar{q}_I} + \frac{\partial d_I(\bar{q}_I)}{\partial \bar{q}_I}\right] > 0,$$

$$\frac{\partial \bar{a}}{\partial \bar{q}_I} - \frac{\partial d_I(\bar{q}_I)}{\partial \bar{q}_I} = z\frac{\partial d_I(\bar{q}_I)}{\partial \bar{q}_I} > 0.$$

With all these channels through which quality affects USP profit, it is not surprising that we cannot sign this derivative in general. A similar result arises if we concentrate on the impact of modifying quality on consumer surplus and on total welfare in the economy. Moreover, we would also like to obtain information regarding the levels of these variables, such as for instance the welfare or profit levels corresponding to various degrees of relaxation of quality constraints in the USO.

To consider these questions further, we calibrate the model and resort to numerical simulations.

3 CALIBRATION

Our calibration assumptions are based on those made in De Donder et al. (2006, 2009). As in those papers, the assumptions used here do not represent the position in a particular USP or country. Indeed, the calibration is illustrative purely to give further insight and understanding of the calculations related to the unfair financial burden and net cost. We focus here on the monopoly and access-only entry cases, though the analysis could be extended to include entry through bypass of the USP's network.

We start from the hypothetical situation where the USP faces no entry and posts a price of €0.50 for the single-piece product and €0.40 for its bulk mail product. We normalize quality levels at one for both USP products ($\bar{q}_x = \bar{q}_I = 1$). Total quantities sold at those prices and quality levels are, respectively, 2 billion items of single-piece mail and 8 billion items of bulk mail. For both products, 80 percent of volumes are delivered in the urban area and the remaining 20 percent in the rural area[8]. The direct price elasticities are −0.2 for single-piece mail and −0.4 for bulk mail at these prices.

Finally, we calibrate linear demands based on these quantities, qualities, prices and elasticities.

We need further assumptions to calibrate the demand functions for bulk mail products when the market is opened to competition. We use two types of information: the extent of entry for different price configurations and the substitutability between the two bulk mail products for consumers. We assume that entrants capture 10 percent of the total market for bulk mail if both bulk mail products are priced at the same level and 50 percent of the market if entrants offer a 20 percent price discount over the USP. As for substitution between those products, we assume that the displacement ratio is initially set at 0.75, which means that three-quarters of the quantities sold by entrants are displaced from the USP, while one-quarter represents additional volumes sold in the sector.

For a quality level of one, the USP constant marginal upstream cost is c_x= €0.18 for single-piece mail and c_I= €0.12 for bulk mail. The USP urban delivery cost is the same for both kinds of mail ($d_x = d_I$), and is set at €0.11 in the urban area and €0.16 in the rural area. The fixed cost F equals €1.68 billion so that the USP breaks even in the hypothetical monopoly situation (including a normal rate of profit, F equals 40 percent of revenue of €4.2 billion). An entrant does not face any fixed cost but we assume that this results in higher variable upstream cost than the USP such that the entrant's upstream cost, c_E, is set at €0.15. The minimum pricing gap between bulk mail and single-piece mail (see note 7), k, is set at €0.06.

To this familiar set of conditions from De Donder et al. (2006, 2009), we add a regulatory constraint that no price from the USP can exceed its marginal cost plus a mark-up of 75 percent to recover fixed costs. This kind of constraint could arise from several policy requirements related to the provision of the universal service at affordable prices. In the case so defined, the 75 percent mark-up constraint is not binding and the USP in the monopoly or access-only entry cases can break even at mark-ups less than 75 percent such that all the results in De Donder et al. (2009) hold.

To illustrate the unfair financial burden and net cost, we apply a market demand reduction to the calibrated model such that the USP moves into a financial deficit – in fact we consider the impact of a 10 percent reduction in market demand (for given price and quality levels). We make the simplifying assumption that the USP's prices are geographically uniform in the single-piece and bulk mail markets. We introduce cross-price elasticities, set at 0.1, between the single-piece and bulk mail,[9] which introduces the prospect of customers transferring to lower-priced services as the customers take on more mail preparation. We also amend the displacement ratio to 0.9 to bring the ratio more in line with the consequences of entry, as observed in the UK market to date (Dudley et al., 2009).

Finally, we introduce a quality variable such that a percentage change in quality has the effect of changing demand and costs by levels that can be defined and used for illustration in the next section when deriving the net cost of a change in service specification for the USP. The illustrations focus, in the first instance, on the effect of a change in single-piece mail quality on its demand and costs, with secondary effects in the bulk mail market arising from the cross-price elasticities.[10] In these illustrations we assume that the percentage reduction in costs is greater than in demand for a reduction in service specification.[11]

Table 11.1 Prices, volumes and welfare of the base case for the USP monopoly and access-only scenarios

	Calibration	Monopoly GPC = EPMU	Access only GPC = EPMU	Access only GPC = EPMU
Price constraint mark-up		75%	75%	85%
Prices €				
USP single piece	0.500	0.525	0.525	0.555
USP bulk mail urban	0.400	0.420	0.420	0.444
USP bulk mail rural	0.400	0.420	0.420	0.444
USP access urban	–	–	0.210	0.222
USP access rural	–	–	0.210	0.222
Entrants urban	–	–	0.360	0.372
Entrants rural	–	–	0.360	0.372
Volumes, bn items				
USP single piece, urban	1.444	1.437	1.437	1.428
USP single piece, rural	0.357	0.355	0.355	0.352
USP bulk mail urban	5.701	5.592	3.457	3.055
USP bulk mail rural	1.492	1.468	0.949	0.860
Entrants urban = USP access urban	–	–	2.372	2.674
Entrants rural = USP access rural	–	–	0.577	0.644
USP, total single piece and bulk mail	8.994	8.852	6.198	5.696
Total entrants	–	–	2.949	3.317
Total market	8.994	8.852	9.147	9.013
USP profit, €bn	–0.172	–0.009	–0.221	–0.092
Consumer surplus, €bn	7.200	7.073	7.186	6.995
Welfare, €bn	7.037	7.061	6.899	6.876

4 ILLUSTRATIVE RESULTS OF THE UNFAIR FINANCIAL BURDEN AND NET COST

The Base Case

Table 11.1 shows the results of the calibrated model where the USP is a monopoly and where the USP faces access-only competition, and following a 10 percent reduction in market demand, use of uniform prices, cross-price elasticity of 0.1 and displacement ratio of 0.9. This forms the base case assuming the original service specification of the USO and for later assessment of the impact of changes to that service specification.

The first column of figures in Table 11.1 shows the prices of the original calibration for the monopoly USP with a 10 percent reduction in market demand which leads to the USP making a deficit of €0.172 billion. The second and third columns of figures show the optimized welfare outcome for the monopoly and competition through access-only cases for this market demand scenario. The optimization is subject to the price constraint of a maximum 75 percent mark-up on marginal costs (see constraints (11.1) and (11.2) in Section 2). With the 10 percent reduction in market demand, these constraints are binding in both columns, which results in the outcome of the GPC equating to the optimized EPMU.

In the monopoly case, the USP prices are higher than those in the calibration which, when combined with the inelastic demand, results in a reduction in the deficit from €0.172 billion to €0.009 billion, with a maximum 75 percent mark-up constraint. There are lower market volumes leading to a net consumer surplus falling from of €7.200 billion to €7.073 billion. We assume a cost of public funds of 0.3[12] to derive the welfare (the weighted sum of net consumer surplus and profit as defined in the appendix) in the presence of the USP making a financial deficit. The reduction in the USP's deficit contributes to an increase in the welfare from €7.037 billion to €7.061 billion.

In the access-only case, the USP single-piece and bulk mail prices are the same as those in the monopoly case, but the USP now offers an access price of €0.210 which results in an entrant price of €0.360. The entrant price is below the USP's bulk mail price of €0.420 which, under imperfect competition, leads to the transfer of 2.949 billion items to the entrant and an increase in market volumes from 8.852 billion items to 9.147 billion items. The USP has a greater deficit of €0.221 billion than in the monopoly case. The lower entrant price and increase in market volumes contribute to consumer surplus rising from €7.073 billion to €7.186 billion; the increase in the USP's deficit contributes to the fall in welfare from €7.061 billion to €6.899 billion.[13]

The figures in the last column of Table 11.1 show the corresponding results when a maximum mark-up of 85 percent applies instead of 75 percent. Under the more relaxed regulatory price constraint, the USP's prices increase, which has the effect of reducing market volumes, and lowering consumer surplus from €7.186 billion to €6.995 billion. The financial deficit reduces from €0.221 billion to €0.092 billion with the relaxation of the price constraint, but the reduction in consumer surplus dominates and welfare declines.

Hence, in this illustration with the 75 percent mark-up price constraint the transfer of the market structure from monopoly to access-only entry increases the USP's deficit and welfare declines. Relaxation of the price constraint moves the USP closer to break-even, but welfare is lower as a consequence of the impact of the higher prices on consumer surplus.

A Relaxation of the Service Specification on Single-piece Mail

In Table 11.2 we show how the net cost of change to the service specification is formed, arising from not having to fulfill part of the requirement of the USO. We consider two alternative hypothetical changes to the service quality for single-piece mail, both of which are geared to improve the financial position of the USP under the hypothesis of a change in service specification. In the first, a reduction in service specification for single-piece mail leads to a 1 percent reduction in demand and a 2 percent reduction in cost (fixed and variable) and in the second a reduction in service specification for single-piece mail leads to a 5 percent reduction in demand and a 10 percent reduction in cost. We show the results of the first change in service specification in the first, second and third columns of

Table 11.2 Prices, volumes and welfare applying to the base case two alternative changes in service specification for single-piece mail with competition through access only

	Reduction in service quality, lowers demand by 1% and costs by 2%			Reduction in service quality, lowers demand by 5% and costs by 10%		
Price constraint mark-up	Same prices GPC = EPMU 75% at original cost	75% mark-up constraint GPC = EPMU 75% at final cost	85% mark-up constraint GPC = EPMU 85% at final cost	Same prices GPC = EPMU 75% at original cost	75% mark-up constraint GPC = EPMU 75% at final cost	85% mark-up constraint GPC = EPMU 85% at final cost
Prices €						
USP single piece	0.525	0.515	0.544	0.525	0.473	0.500
USP bulk mail urban	0.420	0.416	0.440	0.420	0.399	0.422
USP bulk mail rural	0.420	0.416	0.440	0.420	0.399	0.422
USP access urban	0.210	0.206	0.218	0.210	0.189	0.200
USP access rural	0.210	0.206	0.218	0.210	0.189	0.200
Entrants urban	0.360	0.356	0.368	0.360	0.339	0.350
Entrants rural	0.360	0.356	0.368	0.360	0.339	0.350
Volumes, bn items						
USP single piece, urban	1.422	1.427	1.419	1.365	1.387	1.381
USP single piece, rural	0.351	0.352	0.350	0.337	0.343	0.341
USP bulk mail urban	3.466	3.475	3.074	3.503	3.549	3.149
USP bulk mail rural	0.951	0.953	0.864	0.959	0.969	0.881
Entrants urban = USP access urban	2.372	2.385	2.687	2.372	2.438	2.743
Entrants rural = USP access rural	0.577	0.580	0.647	0.577	0.592	0.659
USP, total single piece and bulk mail	6.190	6.207	5.707	6.164	6.248	5.751
Total entrants	2.949	2.965	3.334	2.949	3.03	3.402
Total market	9.139	9.172	9.041	9.113	9.278	9.153
USP profit, €bn	−0.161	−0.206	−0.078	0.077	−0.146	−0.026
Consumer surplus, €bn	7.142	7.192	7.003	6.969	7.216	7.038
Welfare, €bn	6.933	6.924	6.901	7.069	7.026	7.005
Difference from Table 11.1						
USP profit, €bn	0.060	0.015	0.014	0.298	0.075	0.066
Consumer surplus, €bn	−0.044	0.006	0.008	−0.217	0.030	0.043
Welfare, €bn	0.034	0.025	0.025	0.170	0.127	0.128

figures in Table 11.2 and the results of the second change in service specification in the fourth, fifth and sixth columns of figures. In these illustrations we focus on competition only through access.

The first column of figures in the table shows a scenario with access-only entry where there is a mild change in service specification and the prices are the same as those of the case shown in the second column of figures in Table 11.1. When compared to the case shown in Table 11.1 without the change in service specification, the first column of figures in Table 11.2 shows the 1 percent demand reduction to reduce consumer surplus by €0.044 billion. The 2 percent reduction in cost improves the USP's financial position by €0.060 billion – moving the deficit of €0.221 billion to a deficit of €0.161 billion – and leads to a welfare improvement of €0.034 billion.

However, the change in service specification reduces cost which would lead to lower prices being charged by the USP to meet the price constraint of the maximum 75 percent mark-up on the marginal costs; the effect of this change in prices is shown in the second column of figures in Table 11.2. When compared to the first column, all prices in the market fall, which increases total market volume and consumer surplus; the lower USP's prices increase its deficit and cause total welfare to decline. When compared to the case shown in Table 11.1 without the change in service specification, the second column of figures in Table 11.2 shows consumer surplus to increase by €0.006 billion, the USP's financial position to improve by €0.015 billion – moving from a deficit of €0.221 billion to a deficit of €0.206 billion – and welfare to improve by €0.025 billion. Hence, enforcement of the 75 percent maximum mark-up constraint dampens the impact on consumer surplus, USP's deficit and welfare.

In the third numerical column in Table 11.2 (after the change in service specification) the maximum mark-up price constraint is relaxed to 85 percent and the figures can be compared with those in the fourth column of figures in Table 11.1 under the same price constraint (prior to the change in service specification). With a more relaxed price constraint on the USP, the change in service specification increases consumer surplus by €0.008 billion, improves the USP's financial position by €0.014 billion – moving from a deficit of €0.092 billion to a deficit of €0.078 billion – and increases welfare by €0.025 billion. Hence, in this case the movements in the USP's deficit, consumer surplus and welfare, arising from mild changes in demand and costs following a change in service specification, are similar in magnitude whether a 75 or 85 percent mark-up applies to form the maximum price constraint.

The final three columns of figures in Table 11.2 show the outcome when repeating the same exercise for a scenario where the change in service specification results in substantially greater percentage changes in cost than in demand, with access-only entry. More specifically, there is assumed to be a reduction in service specification which, for single-piece mail, reduces the demand by 5 percent and costs by 10 percent. This increases the magnitude of the movements in consumer surplus, USP deficit and welfare relative to the case shown in the first three columns of figures in Table 11.2.

When compared to the case shown in Table 11.1 with the original service specification, the fourth column of figures in Table 11.2 shows the 5 percent demand reduction to reduce consumer surplus by €0.217 billion. The 10 percent reduction in cost improves the USP's financial position by €0.298 billion – moving the deficit of €0.221 billion to a surplus of €0.077 billion – and welfare improves by €0.170 billion, with the 75 percent mark-up constraint. However, when the 75 percent mark-up constraint is applied to the lower costs, these effects are again dampened as shown in the fifth column of figures in Table 11.2. When compared to the case shown in Table 11.1 without the change in service specification, the fifth column of figures in Table 11.2 shows consumer surplus to increase by €0.030 billion, the USP's financial position to improve by €0.075 billion – moving from a deficit of €0.221 billion to a deficit of €0.146 billion – and welfare to rise by €0.127 billion, with the 75 percent mark-up constraint.

Further, when an 85 percent price constraint is applied, the change in consumer surplus, USP's deficit and welfare are similar in direction but different in magnitude from the case where a 75 percent mark-up constraint applies. When compared to the case shown in Table 11.1 with the original service specification, the final column of figures in Table 11.2 shows consumer surplus to increase by €0.043 billion, the USP's financial position to improve by €0.066 billion – moving from a deficit of €0.092 billion to a deficit of €0.026 billion, and welfare to increase by €0.128 billion, with the 85 percent mark-up constraint. Hence, in this case the movement in welfare arising from major changes in demand and costs following a change in service specification is similar in magnitude whether a 75 or 85 percent mark-up applies to form the maximum price constraint, but the movements in the USP's deficit and consumer surplus differ more substantially.

For both of the hypothetical illustrations of changes to the service specification requirements of the USO, at the calibrations assumed, the consumer surplus decreases when the prices are maintained at the level prior to the change in service specification and increases when the prices are reduced to meet the maximum mark-up price constraint. In both illustrations of the hypothetical reduction in service specification, the USP's financial position and welfare improve. The improvement in welfare is of a similar magnitude whether a 75 or 85 percent mark-up applies to form the maximum price constraint, while the original deficit and improvement in deficit can differ more substantially between the two pricing constraints, when cost impacts of quality changes are larger than demand impacts.

In this set of illustrations we started with a USP that has a pricing constraint of a maximum of a 75 percent mark-up on marginal costs in the base case which included a 10 percent reduction in market demand. In the monopoly case, the USP just fails to break even and there is an unfair financial burden of €0.009 billion (see Table 11.1). With access-only competition the USP's deficit is €0.221 billion, an increase of €0.212 billion. The USP moves from a position near break-even, towards a position in which the USP incurs an unfair financial burden through increased competition and under the constraint of the 75 percent mark-up. It is fairly straightforward to envisage increases in the unfair financial burden with entry bypassing the USP's network, tighter regulatory price constraints or more adverse market demand conditions.

We have then looked at two illustrations of the consequences of a change in service specification that the USP could be assumed to undertake if it were not required to fulfill the USO. Under the constraint of a maximum 75 percent mark-up on marginal costs, the first illustration implies a net cost of €0.015 billion[14] for the change to the USO associated with the 1 percent demand and 2 percent cost scenario, and the second illustration implies a net cost of €0.075 billion for the change to the USO associated with the 5 percent demand and 10 percent cost scenario. In both instances the net cost of the change to the USO is insufficient to offset the USP's deficit. However, if, having applied the service specification changes, the USP could apply the same prices as before (for example, applying an absolute price-cap constraint rather than a 75 percent mark-up constraint), in the first illustration the deficit reduces marginally and in the second it reduces sufficiently to move the USP to a financial surplus.

When the analysis is repeated with access-only entry for a more relaxed maximum mark-up price constraint of 85 percent, we first observe that the unfair financial burden is lower at €0.092 billion. In the first illustration of a change in service specification (with a 1 percent reduction in demand and 2 percent reduction in cost) the net cost is marginally smaller at €0.014 billion, and in the second illustration (with a 5 percent reduction in demand and 10 percent reduction in cost) the net cost is noticeably smaller at €0.066 billion. Hence a relaxation of the pricing constraint has the effect of reducing the unfair financial burden and reducing the net cost, with the latter reducing less in the case of moving from a 75 to 85 percent mark-up.

A Relaxation of the Service Specification on Single-piece and Bulk Mail

In Table 11.3 we undertake a similar analysis to that used to derive Table 11.2, but instead of focusing on a change in service specification associated with a change in USO requirements for single-piece mail only, we consider a change in service specification associated with a change in USO requirements for single-piece and bulk mail. This requires an additional assumption relating to the effect of the change in service specification on delivery costs for delivery offered to bulk mail and access. We assume that for both hypothetical illustrations – namely a change in service specification reducing demand by 1 percent and cost by 2 percent and a change in service quality reducing demand by 5 percent and cost by 10 percent – the service specification of bulk mail and access reduce by the same amount, and hence the costs of delivery reduce for both with the hypothetical reduction in the USO service specification requirements.

The outcomes of the various scenarios in Table 11.3, relative to those in Table 11.2, show that the extension of the change in service specification to include bulk mail as well as single-piece mail, and with these demand and cost assumptions, results in a further improvement in the USP's financial position and increase in the net cost of the changes in service specification relating to the USO requirements. For example, with the prices constrained by a maximum 75 percent mark-up on the final marginal costs, the second column of figures in Table 11.3 relating to the change in service specification for the USO shows the net cost to increase by €0.024 billion (relative to €0.015 billion in Table 11.2). For the second illustration of a change in service specification for the USO, the fourth column of figures in Table 11.3 shows the net cost to increase to €0.113 billion (relative to €0.075 billion in Table 11.2). Marginally larger movements apply if the 75 percent maximum mark-up constraint is changed to 85 percent.

Table 11.3 also shows the extension of the change to service specification to bulk mail to increase consumer surplus substantially. The change in service specification lowers costs and leads to significant reductions in the USP's bulk mail and access prices as well as entrant prices. For example, with the prices constrained by a maximum 75 percent mark-up on the final marginal costs, the second column of figures in Table 11.3 relating to the change in service specification for the USO shows the consumer surplus to increase by €0.109 billion (relative to €0.006 billion in Table 11.2). For the second illustration

Table 11.3 Prices, volumes and welfare with 10% reduction in demand and two alternative changes in service specification for single-piece and bulk mail with access only

	Reduction in service quality, lowers demand by 1% and costs by 2%			Reduction in service quality, lowers demand by 5% and costs by 10%		
Price constraint mark-up	Same prices GPC = EPMU 75% at original cost	75% mark-up constraint GPC = EPMU 75% at final cost	85% mark-up constraint GPC = EPMU 85% at final cost	Same prices GPC = EPMU 75% at original cost	75% mark-up constraint GPC = EPMU 75% at final cost	85% mark-up constraint GPC = EPMU 85% at final cost
Prices €						
USP single piece	0.525	0.515	0.544	0.525	0.473	0.500
USP bulk mail urban	0.420	0.412	0.435	0.420	0.378	0.400
USP bulk mail rural	0.420	0.412	0.435	0.420	0.378	0.400
USP access urban	0.210	0.206	0.218	0.210	0.189	0.200
USP access rural	0.210	0.206	0.218	0.210	0.189	0.200
Entrants urban	0.357	0.353	0.365	0.345	0.324	0.335
Entrants rural	0.357	0.353	0.365	0.345	0.324	0.335
Volumes, bn items						
USP single piece, urban	1.422	1.425	1.417	1.365	1.380	1.372
USP single piece, rural	0.351	0.352	0.350	0.337	0.341	0.339
USP bulk mail urban	3.423	3.563	3.173	3.284	3.988	3.646
USP bulk mail rural	0.942	0.974	0.887	0.916	1.072	0.996
Entrants urban = USP access urban	2.476	2.371	2.667	2.894	2.366	2.643
Entrants rural = USP access rural	0.600	0.577	0.643	0.694	0.577	0.639
USP, total single piece and bulk mail	6.138	6.314	5.827	5.902	6.780	6.354
Total entrants	3.077	2.948	3.310	3.588	2.944	3.281
Total market	9.215	9.262	9.137	9.490	9.724	9.636
USP profit, €bn	−0.148	−0.197	−0.065	0.143	−0.108	0.032
Consumer surplus, €bn	7.226	7.295	7.113	7.401	7.754	7.610
Welfare, €bn	7.034	7.039	7.029	7.586	7.614	7.642
Difference from Table 11.1						
USP profit, €bn	0.073	0.024	0.027	0.364	0.113	0.124
Consumer surplus, €bn	0.040	0.109	0.117	0.215	0.568	0.615
Welfare, €bn	0.135	0.140	0.152	0.687	0.715	0.766

of a change in service specification for the USO, the fourth column of figures in Table 11.3 shows the consumer surplus to increase to €0.568 billion (relative to €0.030 billion in Table 11.2). Marginally larger movements apply if the 75 percent maximum mark-up constraint is 85 percent.

Given the magnitude of the movements in consumer surplus arising from the change in service specification with the extension of the change to the bulk mail market, there are substantive increases in welfare too. For example, with the prices constrained by a maximum 75 percent mark-up on the final marginal costs, the second column of figures in Table 11.3 relating to the change in service specification for the USO shows the welfare to increase by €0.140 billion (relative to €0.025 billion in Table 11.2). For the second illustration of a change in service specification for the USO, the fifth column of figures in Table 11.3 shows welfare to increase by €0.715 billion (relative to €0.127 billion in Table 11.2). Again marginally larger movements apply if the 75 percent maximum mark-up constraint is changed to 85 percent.

The extension of the change in service specification to include changes to the bulk mail market in addition to single-piece mail has no effect on the original unfair financial burden derived in Table 11.1. It has some effect on the net cost, increasing it further but within the illustrations the incremental change is less than that resulting from a change in service specification only on single-piece mail. However, the measures of consumer surplus and welfare rise substantially with the hypothetical change in service specification relating to the USO requirements.

5 CONCLUSIONS

The Directive refers to an 'unfair financial burden' and envisages the prospect of a market outcome where the USP does not break even and to the calculation of a 'net cost' of the USO as the change in USP profitability arising from the removal of the service constraints imposed on the USP in its provision of the USO. In this chapter we have looked at the relationship between the USP's unfair financial burden and net cost of a change to the service specification of the USO. We have shown how these may be thought of within a two-dimensional space. Along one dimension, competition can lead to the USP making a deficit and facing an unfair financial burden, when combined with a price constraint in the form of a maximum mark-up on marginal costs. Along another dimension, service specification requirements of the USO can be removed to derive a net cost contribution that can then be used to improve the USP's financial position. More generally, we can think of the unfair financial burden being offset in several ways: reductions in service specification; relaxation of price constraints; reduction in competition; increase in efficiency; or establishment of a compensation fund.

These concepts have been explored within a model that introduces service specification (or quality) and price elasticities within the demand and cost functions of the USP, and through the use of hypothetical numerical illustrations. We have shown how reductions in demand can lead to an unfair financial burden when combined with regulatory pricing constraints under a USP monopoly and USP facing competition through access only. We have also shown how relaxation of the maximum mark-up price constraint can reduce the unfair financial burden within this illustration.

In addition, we have shown how a change to service specification required under the USO can lead to changes in demand and costs to form net cost estimates of such changes. Through two illustrations where the change in service specification reduces costs more than demand, we have shown the change to lead to a positive net cost, improvement in the financial position of the USP and improvement in welfare (assuming the cost of public funds at 0.3). This is shown for a service specification change to single-piece mail, with the directional movements enhanced when extended to include service specification change to single-piece and bulk mail.

We have shown that the net cost, as well as the unfair financial burden, depend on the form and level of the regulatory price constraint. For the illustrations and calibrations used, the change in net cost associated with the change in service specification would be less than the unfair financial burden for a given price constraint mark-up. With lower levels of market demand the unfair financial burden of the base case would increase and the net cost of a given change in service specification would reduce *ceteris paribus*. Hence, though only illustrative, if the change in service specification were representative of what the USP would change in the absence of the USO requirement, and given the response of demand and cost and the other conditions assumed, the net cost in the two illustrations would provide insufficient recompense for the USP to break even and lump-sum transfers equivalent to the net cost, permitted under the Directive, would not be sufficient to ensure the provision of the universal service by the USP. The illustrations also show that relaxation of the regulatory price constraint reduces the USP's unfair financial burden more substantially than the net cost, and improves the likelihood of a break-even solution for the USP either as a direct market solution or in terms of the net cost providing sufficient recompense in lump-sum transfers to offset the USP's deficit.

We stress that the impact of a change in service specification on demand and costs is an empirical question on which there is a lack of public evidence. Our chapter includes illustrations only for how such evidence could be applied in a wider framework. As such, the chapter builds on previous work looking at welfare and the USP's finances in the presence of competition. The introduction of service specification and cross-price elasticities into the demand and cost functions brings some further insight into some of the key assumptions that need to be considered when assessing the unfair financial burden of the USP and net cost of changes to the specification of the USO. There is also further scope to extend this analysis to consider entry through bypass of the USP's network and how alternative compensation mechanisms may affect the outcome.

NOTES

* The analysis contained in this chapter reflects the views of the authors and may not necessarily be those of Royal Mail Group.

1. Reference 2008-6-EC.
2. Article 7.3 of the European Postal Services Directive 2008 states 'Where a Member State determines that the universal service obligations, as provided for in this Directive, entail a net cost, calculated taking into account Annex I, and represent an unfair financial burden on the universal service provider(s), it may introduce: (a) a mechanism to compensate the undertaking(s) concerned from public funds; or (b) a mechanism for the sharing of the net cost of the universal service obligations between providers of services and/or users'. Annex I states, 'The net cost of universal service obligations is any cost related to and necessary for the operation of the universal service provision. The net cost of universal service obligations is to be

calculated, as the difference between the net cost for a designated universal service provider of operating with the universal service obligations and the same postal service provider operating without the universal service obligations.'
3. The Directive refers to the net cost as including 'intangible and market benefits'. In this chapter we assume the intangible and market benefits to be implicit within the cost and demand functions used such that an unfair financial burden is commensurate with a financial deficit.
4. We also consider two delivery areas: urban (high density) and rural (low density). Formally, all variables pertaining to the USP should be indexed by *U* or *R*. To save on notation, we consider here a generic area and we dispense with this index *U*/*R*.
5. The second component of the USO is that prices should be the same in the urban and the rural delivery areas.
6. Due to space constraints, we refer the reader to De Donder et al. (2009) for a formal statement of these two optimization problems.
7. We further impose a minimum pricing gap between the USP's bulk mail and single-piece mail prices: $p_I \leq p_x - k$. See De Donder et al. (2009).
8. Increasing the proportion of rural mail has the effect of degrading the financial position of the USP at prices set by a given percentage mark-up on marginal costs.
9. At the initial calibration, for example, the change in demand for single-piece mail is measured by -0.2 (price change of single piece) $+ 0.1$ (price change in bulk mail).
10. The movement in demand and cost for a change in quality is an empirical issue on which there is a lack of published evidence.
11. If the percentage reduction in costs were lower than that in demand for a reduction in service specification, the impact on the USP's finances and welfare would be reversed.
12. Raising taxes generates distortions in the economy as soon as the government cannot use lump-sum taxes. Most estimates of the size of these distortions, called the 'cost of public funds', in developed countries are in the range of 0.2 to 0.3. This means that, to raise €10 (million), the government has to decrease the surplus of the agents who pay these taxes by the equivalent of €12 to 13 (million).
13. A further reduction in demand has the effect of increasing the USP's deficit of the optimized monopoly and access-only cases and further reducing the corresponding measures of consumer surplus and welfare.
14. The deficit falls in the first illustration from €0.221 billion to €0.206 billion and in the second illustration from €0.221 billion to €0.146 billion.

REFERENCES

Bradley, R., P. Burns and G. Houpis (2009), 'Costing elements of the universal service', in M.A. Crew and P.R. Kleindorfer (eds), *Progress in the Competition Agenda in the Postal and Delivery Sector*, Cheltenham, UK and Northampton, MA, USA: Edward Elgar, pp. 100–12.

Cremer, H., A. Grimaud and J.-J. Laffont (2000), 'The cost of the universal service in the postal sector', in M.A. Crew and P.R. Kleindorfer, *Current Directions in Postal Reform*, Boston, MA: Kluwer Academic, pp. 47–68.

Crew, M.A. and P.R. Kleindorfer (eds) (2000), 'Liberalization and the universal service obligation in postal service', in M.A. Crew and P.R. Kleindorfer (eds), *Current Directions in Postal Reform*, Boston, MA: Kluwer Academic, pp. 1–23.

Crew, M.A. and P.R. Kleindorfer (2009), 'Service quality, price caps and the USO under entry', in M.A. Crew and P.R. Kleindorfer (eds), *Progress in the Competition Agenda in the Postal and Delivery Sector*, Cheltenham, UK and Northampton, MA, USA: Edward Elgar, pp. 1–22.

De Donder, P., H. Cremer, J-P. Florens, A. Grimaud and F. Rodriguez (2001), 'Uniform pricing and postal market liberalization', in M.A. Crew and P.R. Kleindorfer (eds), *Future Directions in Postal Reform*, Boston, MA: Kluwer Academic, pp. 141–62.

De Donder, P., H. Cremer and F. Rodriguez (2002), 'Funding the Universal Service Obligation under liberalisation: an analysis of the postal market', in M.A. Crew and P.R. Kleindorfer (eds), *Postal and Delivery Services: Pricing, Productivity, Regulation and Strategy*, Boston, MA: Kluwer Academic, pp. 31–52.

De Donder, P., H. Cremer, P. Dudley and F. Rodriguez (2006), Pricing and welfare implications of alternative approaches to setting price controls in the postal sector', in M.A. Crew and P.R.

Kleindorfer (eds), *Progress toward Liberalization of the Postal and Delivery Sector*, New York: Springer Science + Business Media Inc., pp. 227–48.
De Donder, P., H. Cremer, P. Dudley and F. Rodriguez (2009), 'A welfare and pricing analysis of value added taxation in postal services', *Review of Network Economics*, **8**(3), 233–54.
Dudley, P., S. Agar, L. Mautino and F. Flórez Duncan (2009), 'Competition through downstream access in the UK postal sector: the first four years', in M.A. Crew and P.R. Kleindorfer (eds), *Progress in the Competition Agenda in the Postal and Delivery Sector*, Cheltenham, UK and Northampton, MA, USA: Edward Elgar, pp. 52–66.
Jaag, C., M. Koller and U. Trinkner (2009), 'Calculating the cost of the Universal Service Obligation: the need for a global approach', in M.A. Crew and P.R. Kleindorfer (eds), *Progress in the Competitive Agenda in the Postal and Delivery Sector*, Cheltenham, UK and Northampton, MA, USA: Edward Elgar, pp. 100–12.
Laffont, J.-J. and J. Tirole (2000), *Competition in Telecommunications*, Cambridge, MA: MIT Press.
Panzar, J.C. (2001), 'Funding Universal Service Obligations: the cost of liberalization', in M.A. Crew and P.R. Kleindorfer (eds), *Future Directions in Postal Reform*, Boston, MA: Kluwer Academic, pp. 101–16.
Rodriguez, F., S. Smith and D. Storer (1999), 'Estimating the cost of the Universal Service Obligation in postal service', in M.A. Crew and P.R. Kleindorfer (eds), *Emerging Competition in Postal and Delivery Services*, Boston, MA: Kluwer Academic, pp. 195–208.

APPENDIX 11A

There is a representative sender of postal goods. We denote by m the amount that the sender spends on non-postal goods (the numeraire) while R denotes his/her income. The utility function of this representative sender is:

$$u(x, q_x, y_I, q_I, y_E, q_E, m).$$

Demands for the three goods are obtained by maximizing utility subject to the budget constraint:

$$\max_{x, y_I, y_E} u(x, q_x, y_I, q_I, y_E, q_E, m)$$

$$\text{s.t. } p_x x + p_I y_I + p_E y_E + m \leq R, \qquad (11A.1)$$

from which we obtain the demand functions:

$$x(p_x, q_x, p_I, q_I, p_E, q_E),$$

$$y_I(p_x, q_x, p_I, q_I, p_E, q_E),$$

$$y_E(p_x, q_x, p_I, q_I, p_E, q_E),$$

when the three goods are available (that is, when the bulk mail market is opened to competition).

Net consumer surplus is obtained by plugging the demand functions into the utility function $u(\cdot)$ and subtracting the amount paid by the representative consumer to consume this bundle:

$$v(p_x, q_x, p_I, q_I, p_E, q_E)$$
$$= u[x(\cdot), q_x, y_I(\cdot), q_I, y_E(\cdot), q_E, m] - p_x x(\cdot) - p_I y_I(\cdot) - p_E y_E(\cdot). \qquad (11A.2)$$

Total welfare is given by:

$$W = v(p_x, q_x, p_I, q_I, p_E, q_E) + (1 + \mu)\Pi_I(p_x, q_x, p_I, q_I, p_E, q_E, a), \qquad (11A.3)$$

when $\Pi_I(\cdot) \leq 0$, where μ denotes the marginal cost of public funds.

In the case where the USP has a monopoly over bulk mail, demand functions for the two postal goods are obtained by setting y_E to zero in problem (11A.1) above, to obtain:

$$x^M(p_x, q_x, p_I, q_I), y_I^M(p_x, q_x, p_I, q_I).$$

We assume the following signs for the matrix of first-order partial derivatives:

	p_x	p_I	p_E	q_x	q_I	q_E
x	−	+	+	+	−	−
y_I	+	−	+	−	+	−
y_E	+	+	−	−	−	+

In words, we have negative own-price derivatives and positive cross-price derivatives. This illustrates the pattern of substitutions (between postal goods and other goods, between postal goods offered by the USP and between postal goods offered by the USP and by the entrant) as prices vary. We also assume positive own-quality derivatives and negative cross-quality derivatives.

12. An operational measure of the cost of universal service as cross-subsidy*

Margaret Cigno, Diane Monaco and Edward S. Pearsall

1 INTRODUCTION

The United States Postal Service (USPS) offers a diverse collection of services over a vast geographic network of processing plants, distribution centers, local delivery offices and carrier routes. The US postal service is geographically 'universal' because the same rates are charged for the same services everywhere on the network, all of the various services are mostly available for mail sent to any address, and USPS enforces common standards for qualitative aspects of its services.

USPS's rates may be geographically uniform, but its costs of delivery are not. Therefore, universal service creates geographic cross-subsidies. When USPS breaks even, the excess cost of delivering the mail on high-cost routes is just matched by the surplus generated on low-cost routes and by mail that is not delivered by carriers. If USPS runs a deficit then part of the cross-subsidy is lent to USPS by the US Treasury. The reverse occurs when USPS makes a profit.

A natural operational measure of the cost of universal service is the maximum cross-subsidy for any subset of delivery routes. This measure is supported by recent research (Pearsall, 2009) showing that when a multi-product enterprise's cost function is submodular, the smallest subset of products maximizing the aggregate cross-subsidy includes all of the enterprise's products that are responsible for cross-subsidies, and excludes all of the products that do not cause cross-subsidies. In addition it is usually possible to identify the subset of subsidized products and to calculate the maximum cross-subsidy by applying a simple myopic algorithm.

The cost function used by USPS and the US Postal Regulatory Commission (PRC) for postal cost accounting is strongly submodular[1] due almost entirely to economies of scope and scale. This makes it possible to apply the myopic algorithm to measure the cost of universal service as the maximum cross-subsidy. The amount of this cross-subsidy in FY 2007 was approximately $3 billion, and in FY 2008 $3.5 billion. These are estimates of the aggregate value exchanged geographically by US postal customers when they purchased postal services. They also include part of USPS's net losses in those years.

Our cost of universal service may be viewed as a more accurate version of the 'net avoidable cost' (NAC) definition criticized by Bradley and IBM Global Business Services (2008). NAC is usually estimated as the sum of the losses on individual routes for which avoidable costs exceed revenue. Our definition refines NAC by implicitly considering cross-subsidies for all possible combinations of postal routes and by correctly accounting for the second-order properties of the postal cost function. Our estimates are approximately 26 percent higher than estimates that use the usual definition of NAC.

The estimates are derived by applying the myopic algorithm with a cost function adapted for application to a large combined sample of daily volumes on city-carrier and rural routes. The computations of total cost are made by weighting and summing the costs for individual routes for this sample. The cost function is fit to cost accounting data found in the PRC's Annual Compliance Reports (ACR) for FY 2007 and FY 2008.

Our measurements of cross-subsidy treat the distribution of daily mail by subclasses and special services for each sampled route as a distinct composite product. Incremental costs are obtained by applying the cost function to the mail deliveries and special services for each route. Revenues are derived using average revenues per piece. When incremental cost exceeds revenue, the difference is the route's contribution to the aggregate cross-subsidy. We employ the myopic algorithm to perform a complete incremental cost (IC) test. The results are then scaled to obtain the cross-subsidy contributions of the city- and rural-carrier routes served.

The USPS samples do not include enough additional information to allow us to fully identify the properties of the routes that receive cross-subsidies. Nevertheless, we have been able to relate cross-subsidies and surpluses to several of their principal determinants. The cross-subsidies are primarily the result of variation in the volume and subclass composition of the mail delivered on the routes rather than the route's demographic or geographic characteristics.

Surprisingly, city-carrier routes are far more frequently cross-subsidized than rural routes. Among city-carrier routes, business routes are the most frequently cross-subsidized and residential routes the least. One explanation for these patterns is that the rural and city residential routes are predominantly curb routes that use vehicles more effectively than city routes which are partly done on foot. This enables the carriers to deliver larger average daily volumes. However, we cannot rule out other explanations such as differences in city/rural compensation rates, work rules, biases in our route sample or in the PRC's cost model.

Our results support a finding regarding the relative profitability of US postal routes first made by Cohen et al. (1999). USPS would not be especially vulnerable to cream-skimming by potential entrants following liberalization. Our results show that it would be difficult to identify routes that are profitable, and that the aggregate profit from cream-skimming would be small for entrants with no competitive advantage over USPS.

In Section 2 we show that universal service properties as a quasi-public good are responsible for geographic cross-subsidies. Our reasons for measuring the cost of universal service as the maximum cross-subsidy, rather than as a difference in USPS's profits, are explained in Section 3. The cost function and our methods for calibrating it are described in Section 4. The application of the complete IC test to estimate the maximum cross-subsidy and to identify the subset of cross-subsidized routes is described in Section 5. We present and interpret our findings in Section 6. Section 7 concludes.

2 UNIVERSAL SERVICE IS A QUASI-PUBLIC GOOD

Universal service is a quasi-public good because it is rivalrous (consumption by some postal customers diminishes the amount that can be supplied to others) but at the same time imperfectly excludable (senders are not limited to consuming exactly what they pay for).[2] The geographically uniform rates, availability and quality of service provided by USPS create a mismatch of benefits to rates for postal customers. Mailers sending mail to be delivered on high-cost routes benefit more than mailers sending mail to be delivered on low-cost routes, but they are charged the same for the service. Furthermore, postal service benefits the recipients of the mail as well as the senders, but only the senders pay.

Often, a good is quasi-public because it is costly to impose a tariff that accurately tracks individual consumption. This is certainly the case with US postal services. A tariff that accurately reflected the differentials in costs over postal routes would add transaction costs for USPS and non-commercial mailers that would be large in relation to the rates for the services themselves. By comparison, the uniform tariff charged to senders only is simple and cheap to collect.[3] Charges to recipients (postage due) are costly because the recipient must be offered the choice of refusing delivery before paying and USPS cannot recover its costs on refused mail.

The US postal tariff creates cross-subsidies whenever a single rate is charged for services with dissimilar costs.[4] In general, this occurs when the postal tariff fails to relate postage accurately to the cost of a hedonic property of the mail.[5] For example, Cohen and McBride (2008, p. 22) cite the 'statutory restriction that requires their rates to be uniform with respect to distance' for media and library rate mail. Mail in these subclasses, when carried long distances, is cross-subsidized because the tariff fails to account for the distance transported. In the case of the geographic scope of universal delivery service, the hedonic property that is omitted from the tariff is the relative difficulty of reaching addresses in different locations.

Not only would an accurate tariff be costly to collect, but the redistribution of expenditures from installing such a tariff would be minimal. Postage expenses are small relative to most customers' total expenditures, and individual customers send and receive mail that is a geographic mix of origins and destinations. In this respect postal customers are like customers in a restaurant dividing a common bill. When the diners finish their calculations, they are likely to discover that they are each paying about the same amount. They could have saved time and trouble by agreeing to split the bill equally in the first place. When they do this the meal becomes a quasi-public good.

The arrangement that is found, typically, to supply quasi-public goods is a state-sanctioned monopoly of a reserved area consisting of a collection of markets with restricted entry. This allows the cost of supplying the quasi-public goods to be offset, at least in part, by excess profits extracted from the reserved area. The enforced monopoly is necessary because cross-subsidies are not sustainable in a contestable market when entry and exit is costless (see Baumol et al., 1988). This is the market structure that has evolved in the US for postal services. USPS holds a statutory monopoly on the delivery of all kinds of mail except Priority mail, Express mail, Parcel Post and certain kinds of International mail.

3 DEFINING THE COST OF UNIVERSAL SERVICE

Our definition of the cost of universal service differs from the one proposed by Rodriguez et al. (1999), Bradley and Colvin (2000), Cremer et al. (2000) and Panzar (2000, 2001,

2008a and 2008b). The definition recommended by these authors, the 'profitability' definition, defines the cost of universal service as the difference in a national post's profit before and after the elimination of a Universal Service Obligation (USO).

The profitability definition has been applied in recent US studies by Bradley and IBM Global Business Services (2008), Cohen (2008) and Cohen and McBride (2008). These studies were conducted in response to a congressional directive to the PRC in the Postal Accountability and Enhancement Act (PAEA) to report annually on universal postal service and the postal monopoly. The Commission in its first report (US PRC 2008b) relied on the profitability definition for its estimates of the costs of various aspects of universal service.[6]

Panzar (2001) has emphasized that the profitability definition depends upon the 'careful specification of an unsubsidized market scenario that would prevail in the absence of the USO' (p. 101). The profitability definition is applied by defining a 'status quo benchmark' with the USO in place, and a 'relevant counterfactual' with the USO absent or modified. The cost of the USO is the increase in profit that results from replacing the status quo benchmark with the relevant counterfactual.

The relevant counterfactual and, sometimes, the status quo benchmark require assumptions about how USPS and its potential competitors respond to the changes in regulation and market conditions assumed to accompany the elimination of the USO. Panzar has proposed different formulas and measurements for a number of regulatory regimes and market conditions for counterfactuals including regulated monopoly, unregulated monopoly, competition with a reserved area, and competition without a reserved area. Each of these scenarios and others can be expected to yield a different profitability estimate of the cost of the USO.

Panzar's measurement employs comparative statics. Equilibria are determined as the outcome of thought experiments that differ with respect to the choice of exogenous controls and assumptions. The cost of the USO is measured as the difference in postal profits between experiments with and without the USO. However, to avoid extraneous effects the experiments should be done with controls that ensure that only the effect of removing the USO causes the change in profits. The only counterfactual that will yield the cost of the USO as the result of such thought experiments is the counterfactual in which cross-subsidized services are fully deleted while no other changes in predetermined conditions are allowed. None of the counterfactuals proposed by Panzar and used in recent studies is designed in this way. Consequently, none avoids introducing extraneous effects into the measurements.

All of the counterfactuals used by Bradley and IBM Global Business Services and Cohen introduce assumptions that alter prices and the demands for USPS's services in various ways. The former assume entry and price matching by USPS. Cohen makes assumptions about prices, quality of service, entrants' cost functions and market contestability. These assumptions all affect the measurements of the cost of the USO. However, the differences in the estimates are evidence of extraneous effects because the USO has been eliminated in each case.

The profitability definition makes sense as a measure of the gains and losses to USPS from specific proposals for modifying or ending the USO such as recent proposals to eliminate Saturday deliveries. In this context, estimates made using the profitability definition are necessary and reasonable for evaluating the financial consequences of the proposals. However, profitability is much less attractive as the basis for a general operational measure of the welfare consequences of the USO. A true cost–benefit analysis of the USO would address the question of whether social welfare is increased by the quasi-public good that the USO creates. For geographically uniform rates and services we would want to compare the cost savings from the simplified tariff to the economic loss that results from the redistributive effects of the cross-subsidies. The change in USPS's profit is not the correct measurement for such a welfare comparison. Instead, the appropriate way to begin is by measuring all of the geographic cross-subsidies that are caused by the uniform tariff.

Unless the counterfactual used in the profitability definition converts all cross-subsidies into profits, the profitability definition will not completely account for them. It is impossible to tell if all cross-subsidies have been included in the recent US estimates of the cost of the USO because none of the investigators makes any attempt to estimate them.

Following Panzar, the implicit status quo benchmark for our measure is the actual prices, volumes, costs and net revenue USPS earned from delivering the mail. The unsubsidized market scenario inherent in our measure is the same relevant counterfactual that is used to measure incremental and stand-alone costs. All cross-subsidized services are deleted from the enterprise's product offerings while prices and demands for the remaining services are left unchanged. Only when the status quo benchmark and the relevant counterfactual are defined in this way, does the profitability definition of the cost of the USO correspond to the aggregate transfer of value between postal customers, as a result of the USO, as they purchase postal services. When measured in this way, the cost of the USO is the maximum cross-subsidy over all subsets of services. This cost remains the same, as it should, no matter how one goes about eliminating the USO.

The relevant counterfactual for measuring the cost of the USO as a cross-subsidy is impractical and uninteresting as a plan for actually eliminating the USO. In practice USPS would reduce the frequency of delivery on unprofitable routes and/or hold the mail that it no longer delivered to be picked up at local offices. For recipients, this plan would create a transaction cost in the form of a trip to the delivery office. Many addressees would not make this trip regularly or at all. From the senders' point of view, the mail would take longer and be less certain to reach recipients.

The deterioration in the quality of service would trigger negative reactions in the demands for postal services. Modeling these reactions requires a demand model employing realistic assumptions regarding market conditions, regulation and entry. Such a model could be expected to yield forecasts of prices and volumes after elimination of the USO that differed from those of the status quo benchmark. However, none of these changes should be incorporated into the relevant counterfactual to obtain an estimate of the cost of the USO.

The purpose of the counterfactual is to provide a scenario that isolates the effects of dropping universal service from the effects of all other changes. There are many ways USPS might go about avoiding delivery on unprofitable routes by reducing delivery frequencies, modifying routes and holding mail at delivery offices. In addition, there is enough uncertainty about postal customers' demand responses to admit a variety of plausible demand models. However, the only change from the status quo benchmark that does not introduce extraneous effects is the simple deletion of mail delivered on all unprofitable routes. This is equivalent to measuring the cost of the USO as the maximum cross-subsidy.

4 THE POSTAL COST FUNCTION

Our calculations rely on cost accounting data found in the ACRs for FY 2007 and FY 2008 (US PRC 2008b and 2009). These data are employed to fit constant-elasticity single-driver versions of USPS's cost function. The cost function applies route by route to the elements of a combined weighted sample of daily subclass volumes for city-carrier and rural routes. The sample comprises 376 city-carrier business routes, 6,742 city-carrier residential routes, 67 city-carrier mixed routes and 58,327 rural routes.

The route sample provides the volumes delivered on each route on a single postal business day for 15 subclasses and categories of mail and special services.[7] The data for the city-carrier routes were obtained by sampling the mail at every tenth stop on a single day in FY 2007. The data for the rural routes are derived from the annual evaluations of the routes in FY 2007. In addition to subclass volumes, the sample provides the number of possible deliveries for each route, the Cost Ascertainment Group (CAG) of the office of the route, and the route category (RCAT) if the route is a city-carrier route. Daily revenues were estimated for FY 2007 and FY 2008 by applying average revenues per piece from the ACRs to the volumes and estimated special service transactions for the routes.

The observations in the combined sample are weighted so the sample can be scaled up to the population of USPS routes in FY 2007. USPS served 2,909 city-carrier business routes, 149,035 city-carrier residential routes, 11,501 city-carrier mixed routes and 73,191 rural routes.

The postal cost function is separated into six segments. There are segments for clerks and mailhandlers, purchased transportation, all other non-delivery costs, city-carrier in-office, city-carrier street, and rural carriers. The segments are aggregations that include all of the cost pools found in the PRC's cost accounting system. The costs for mail processing, city carriers and rural carriers also include related capital costs that are allocated proportionately following labor costs. This allocation of related capital costs is called 'piggy backing'.

The cost function resembles the single-driver cost function that USPS and the PRC both use to divide aggregate annual postal costs into attributable and institutional components. In the model, segment costs are represented by scaled constant-elasticity functions of single drivers. The drivers, in turn, are linear homogeneous functions of volumes. The single-driver model has been described by Bradley et al. (1999) and by Fenster et al. (2008) where it is shown to be submodular with respect to mail subclasses and worksharing categories.

Our adaptation of the cost function has separable system-level cost segments for mail processing (p), transportation (t) and other non-route costs (o), and separable route-level segments for city-carrier (cc) in-office (i), city-carrier (cc) street (s), and rural-carrier (rc) costs (r). Total cost is the sum of the costs of the segments.

$$C = C_p + C_t + C_o + \sum_{city} C_i^{cc} + \sum_{city} C_s^{cc} + \sum_{rural} C_r^{rc}.$$

The system-level segments are each constant-elasticity functions of an aggregate driver formed by summing drivers for all city-carrier routes (*cc*), rural-carrier routes (*rc*) and non-route mail (*nr*). Non-route mail is mail that is held to be picked up by addressees at a delivery office (PO box mail and some packages), or is delivered directly to high-volume recipients (highway contract mail):

$$C_p = K_p\left(\sum_{city} D_p^{cc} + \sum_{rural} D_p^{rc} + D_p^{nr}\right)^{E_p} \quad \text{mail processing } (p) \text{ cost}$$

$$C_t = K_t\left(\sum_{city} D_t^{cc} + \sum_{rural} D_t^{rc} + D_t^{nr}\right)^{E_t} \quad \text{transportation } (t) \text{ cost}$$

$$C_o = K_o\left(\sum_{city} D_o^{cc} + \sum_{rural} D_o^{rc} + D_o^{nr}\right)^{E_o} \quad \text{other non-delivery } (o) \text{ cost.}$$

The route-level segments are each constant-elasticity functions of a single driver for the route:

$$C_i^{cc} = K_i(D_i^{cc})^{E_i} \quad \text{city-carrier in-office } (i) \text{ cost}$$

$$C_s^{cc} = K_s(D_s^{cc})^{E_s} \quad \text{city-carrier street } (s) \text{ cost}$$

$$C_r^{rc} = K_r(D_r^{rc})^{E_r} \quad \text{rural-carrier } (r) \text{ cost.}$$

The equations for the route drivers are homogeneous linear functions of the daily volumes delivered on the city-carrier route (V_j^{cc}) or rural-carrier route (V_j^{rc}) by subclass or special service category (j):

$$D_x^{cc} = \sum_j \alpha_{xj} V_j^{cc} \quad \text{city-carrier, } j = \text{mail subclass, cost segment } x = p, t, o, i, s \text{ and } r$$

$$D_x^{rc} = \sum_j \alpha_{xj} V_j^{rc} \quad \text{rural-carrier, } j = \text{mail subclass, cost segment } x = p, t, o, i, s \text{ and } r.$$

The equations for the non-route drivers D_x^{nr} are also homogeneous linear functions of volumes by subclass and service category. However, the volumes V_j^{nr} are aggregate daily volumes of non-route mail:

$$D_x^{nr} = \sum_j \alpha_{xj} V_x^{nr} \quad \text{non-route mail, } j = \text{mail subclass, cost segment } x = p, t \text{ and } o.$$

The parameters of the postal cost functions are the constant driver elasticities (E_x) which are the average volume variabilities for the several postal cost segments, the constants (K_x) that scale the aggregate cost for each segment, and the alpha parameters of the driver equations (α_{xj}). The alpha parameters differ by cost segment (x) and by subclass (j). These parameters represent the relative per piece contributions of different kinds of mail and services for each segment. Formally, α_{xj} is the elasticity of the attributable cost driver for segment 'x' with respect to the aggregate volume for subclass 'j'. The alpha parameters are unique up to a scalar transformation. The distribution key share for cost segment 'x' and subclass 'j' is $\alpha_{xj}V_j / \sum_j \alpha_{xj}V_j$.

The notable structural features of our adaptation of the cost function are, first, that the in-office and street costs for a city carrier are a function only of the mail delivered by the city carrier on the carrier's daily route. Similarly, the delivery cost for a rural carrier is determined solely by the mail the rural carrier delivers. Costs in the system-level segments (p, t and o) are functions of aggregate daily volumes for the entire postal system. Second, the segments of the postal cost function are each strongly submodular with variabilities in the range $0 < E_x < 1$ and positive alphas, $\alpha_{xj} > 0$ for all subclasses.[8] The functionals for mail processing, transportation and other non-delivery costs are submodular with respect to total system volumes. The route-level functionals are submodular with respect to route volumes. Therefore, the aggregate cost function is submodular with respect to postal products defined as the average daily 'baskets' of mail delivered on each route.

The postal cost function was fit by calibrating it to the PRC's cost and volume data for FY 2007 and FY 2008 in the PRC's annual ACRs (US PRC 2008b and 2009). Delivery alphas were calculated separately using the aggregated route sample volumes, and by scaling the alphas derived from the total FY volumes in the ACRs. The cost function fits for FY 2007 are shown in Appendix Tables 12A.1–3. The fits for FY 2008 are similar but incorporate some FY 2008 data for competitive subclasses that remain under seal by the PRC.

The driver elasticities are estimated for each segment as the ratio of the sum of attributable costs from the annual ACR for all subclasses to total costs, including institutional costs $E_x = \Sigma_j^{xj}/C_x$.

The sample alpha parameters are estimated using annual attributable costs and aggregate daily volumes derived from the sample $\alpha_{xj} = (AC_{xj}/\Sigma_j AC_{xj})(\Sigma_j V_j/V_j)$. The formula can also be applied using annual volumes taken from the ACRs to obtain alphas, designated $\bar{\alpha}_{xj}$, that are normalized for total annual volumes of mail and services. These can be rescaled using the daily sample volumes to obtain a second set of alphas for the postal cost equation. The formula for the scaled ACR alphas is $\alpha_{xj} = \bar{\alpha}_{xj}\Sigma_j V_j/\Sigma_j \bar{\alpha}_{xj} V_j$. Both the sample and scaled ACR alpha parameters are normalized to the total daily volume of mail and service transactions, that is, $\Sigma_j \alpha_{xj} V_j = \Sigma_j V_j$.

The scale parameters K_x for the segments are found by evaluating the sum of the drivers for the segment for the daily volumes and then calculating K_x so that the cost segment expression reproduces the average daily cost of the segment for the year. For this calculation it is assumed that USPS delivers mail on 303 business days. For mail processing, transportation, non-delivery:

$$K_x = C_x\left(\sum_{city} D_x^{cc} + \sum_{rural} D_x^{rc} + D_x^{nr}\right)^{-E_x}.$$

For city-carrier in-office, city-carrier street or rural:

$$K_x = C_x^{cc/cr}\Big/\left(\sum_{city/rural} D_x^{cc/rc}\right)^{E_x}.$$

Our fit of the cost function assigns the same elasticities and the same scale parameters to all routes of a single type. Therefore, the differences in delivery costs on routes of the same type are entirely the result of differences in the values of the delivery segment drivers.

5 THE COMPLETE INCREMENTAL COST (IC) TEST

We perform complete IC tests using the myopic algorithm described in Pearsall (2009). The algorithm works by identifying product categories that either cannot be cross-subsidized (the Forward Process) or must be cross-subsidized (the Backward Process), and then resolving the differences (the Final Process). The algorithm terminates with the amount of the maximum cross-subsidy S^0 and the identity of the smallest subset of products T^0 that maximizes the cross-subsidy. T^0 includes all of the products that, in various combinations, are responsible for the cross-subsidies resulting from the stipulated prices, while it includes none of the products that are not responsible.

To apply the myopic algorithm we define an individual postal product as the 'basket' of mail delivered and services performed on a single route on a single day.[9] In this setting the algorithm identifies the subset of cross-subsidized routes by implicitly evaluating the net revenue that USPS would gain by deleting them in different combinations. When USPS breaks even, the saving S^0 is a cross-subsidy that is exactly covered by the profits made from the mail and services on unsubsidized routes, and from non-route mail held at post offices. When USPS loses money, part of the cross-subsidy is added to USPS's debt to the US Treasury and vice versa. In any case the cross-subsidy is the added cost of extending service to all of the routes in T^0.

The Backward Process is performed by deleting routes in stages. In the first stage the incremental costs of the routes are calculated using marginal costs for the system-level cost segments with none of the routes deleted. The first stage is equivalent to an IC test performed individually on the routes. Incremental cost, forgone revenue and the subsidy or surplus for each route are computed. The routes that are cross-subsidized are deleted. The volumes on the deleted routes are then subtracted from the total volumes processed, transported, and so on, and the marginal costs for the system-level components are recomputed. They will now be higher because the cost function is submodular. In the second stage incremental costs, subsidies and surpluses are recomputed for the remaining routes using the recomputed marginal costs. If any routes have been made unprofitable, they are added to the list of deleted routes, and the Backward Process continues with another round of marginal cost recalculations and evaluations. The Backward Process ends when no additional unprofitable routes are found. The routes that have been deleted at termination must be in the subset T^0.

The Forward Process is the Backward Process in reverse. At the start of the first stage all of the route mail and services are taken out and the marginal costs of the system-level segments are computed using just the totals of non-route mail and services. Incremental cost, forgone revenue, and subsidy (or surplus) are computed for each route and the mail and services on routes that are profitable are added back. These routes cannot be cross-subsidized. The first stage of the Forward Process is similar in most respects to a stand-alone cost test on individual routes. The marginal costs are recomputed for the increased volumes and the evaluation of the routes is repeated. If more routes are found to be profitable they are also added back. The Forward Process continues until no further routes are added back. At the end, the routes that have been added back cannot include any members of the subset T^0.

The Backward and Forward Processes each took 10 to 15 stages. There were few differences between the subset of deleted routes from the Backward Process and the complement of the subset of routes that were added back in the Forward Process. Where there were differences, the ambiguous routes were all very close to breaking even. Resolving the status of these few routes would cause little change in the value of the maximum cross-subsidy S^0 so the Final Process was omitted and T^0 from the Backward Process was used.

6 ESTIMATES AND ANALYSIS OF THE COST OF UNIVERSAL SERVICE

The results of the IC tests for the four cases are shown in Table 12.1. The cross-subsidy resulting from universal service in the US in FY 2007 was slightly less than $3 billion. In FY 2008 the cross-subsidy rose to around $3.5 billion. The difference between the estimates for FY 2007 and FY 2008 is mostly a reflection of USPS's greater losses in FY 2008. The two sets of alphas lead to very small differences in the estimates of the cost of the USO in both years.

NAC is calculated following the methodology used by the PRC. The method employs marginal costs for processing, transportation and non-delivery costs derived at the ACR volume totals for FY 2007 and FY 2008. A subsidy or surplus is found for each route by subtracting forgone revenue from attributable cost. NAC is the sum of net surplus over the unprofitable routes. Table 12.1 reveals that this calculation leads to values of NAC that understate of the cost of universal service by about 26 percent.

NAC falls short because the marginal costs used to compute attributable costs are calculated at the wrong point on the postal cost function. NAC misses some routes that are members of the subset T^0 and underestimates the contributions of the others to the total S^0. The correct point for the marginal cost calculation is the point with the volumes on all cross-subsidized routes deleted. The marginal costs for processing, transportation and non-delivery are all higher at this point.

The second section of Table 12.1 displays percentages of postal routes found to be cross-subsidized by the IC tests. These percentages, especially for city-carrier routes, are high because USPS lost money on the average route in both years. About 21 percent of all US mail is non-route mail. USPS makes a substantial profit on virtually all of this mail. Since USPS lost money in FY 2007 and FY 2008, the average route was cross-subsidized in both years.

The routes failing the IC test follow an unexpected pattern. A city-carrier route is far more likely to be cross-subsidized than a rural route. This happens despite the fact that USPS city-carrier routes are physically shorter and are more densely populated with delivery points than rural routes. Among city-carrier routes, business routes are more frequently cross-subsidized than mixed routes which, in turn, are more frequently cross-subsidized than residential routes. The 'Total Mail' column of the third section of the table shows that these patterns follow the average sample volumes for the routes. Low-volume routes are more likely to be cross-subsidized than high-volume routes because of economies of scale in delivery.[10]

The delivery technologies commonly employed on the routes may explain the differences in average daily volumes. City business routes are often foot routes. The carrier

Table 12.1 Results of the IC test

	ACR 2007 sample alphas ($1,000s)	ACR 2007 ACR scaled alphas ($1,000s)	ACR 2008 sample alphas ($1,000s)	ACR 2008 ACR scaled alphas ($1,000s)
Cross-subsidy cost of the USO	2,934,427	2,887,014	3,510,928	3,472,015
Net avoidable cost of the USO	2,153,544	2,130,345	2,581,385	2,571,558
NAC underestimate (%)	26.61	26.21	26.48	25.93
	Failed IC test	Failed IC test	Failed IC test	Failed IC test
City-carrier business routes (%)	86.97	78.46	88.30	81.12
City-carrier residential routes (%)	74.00	74.47	73.61	73.66
City-carrier mixed routes (%)	76.12	76.12	77.61	79.10
All rural routes (%)	24.90	24.53	32.61	32.35
	Total mail pieces per day	Route category distribution (%)		
		Foot	Motorized or park & loop	Curb
City-carrier business routes	1,515	28.97	71.03	0.00
City-carrier residential routes	2,184	5.93	70.10	23.97
City-carrier mixed routes	2,099	9.45	76.08	14.47
All rural routes	2,409	0.00	0.00	100.00

loads up with mail, walks to his/her route, delivers the mail and returns to the local delivery office for more. This is repeated until all of the day's mail is delivered. The business motorized routes and the park and loop routes employ only a minimal adaptation of the foot-route technology. Mail is transported from the office to a proximate location (or several such locations) from which it is then delivered by foot. City curb and rural routes employ a technology that is better adapted to modern roads and vehicles. On these routes the mail is delivered directly into specialized curbside receptacles without requiring the driver to dismount. The route category distributions in the third section of Table 12.1 reflect the relationship between effective vehicle usage and route volumes.

Differences in technology are only one of several possible causes of the pattern in cross-subsidies revealed by our IC tests. Among other factors are relative compensation rates, work rules and sampling biases. Average hourly compensation rates for city carriers are higher than average hourly earnings for rural carriers. The work rules for arranging mail are somewhat stricter for city carriers than for rural carriers. City carriers may not

Table 12.2 Regression analysis of results

	ACR 2007 sample alphas ANOVA	ACR 2007 ACR scaled alphas ANOVA	ACR 2008 sample alphas ANOVA	ACR 2008 ACR scaled alphas ANOVA
Possible deliveries (%)	−0.91	−1.05	−1.00	−1.08
Mail volume by subclass (%)	88.02	87.83	92.31	92.24
Office size (CAG) (%)	2.64	2.58	1.99	1.95
Route classification (RCAT) (%)	8.60	8.99	5.26	5.47
R-squared (%)	98.34	98.35	98.57	98.58

merge Delivery Point Sequenced (DPS) mail with other sorted mail before taking it to their routes. However, rural carriers are free to rearrange their DPS mail in any way that facilitates delivery. Finally, both the route sample and the ACR cost data are collected and processed separately for city and for rural carriers. This arrangement invites sampling biases due to differences in definitions and statistical methods.

USPS did not supplement the scaled route sample with enough information to allow us to fully identify the geographic or demographic properties of the routes.[11] Aside from the daily volumes by subclass, the only information that is common to all the routes in the combined sample is the number of possible deliveries, the CAG of the route's delivery office, and the RCAT. CAG is a cost-based index of the size of the delivery office that serves as a rough proxy for population density. RCAT is a two-way division of the routes, first into business, residential, mixed and rural categories, and, second, by delivery method (foot, motorized, curb, park and loop).

Table 12.2 displays analysis-of-variance (ANOVA) results derived from regressions performed to isolate the route properties causing cross-subsidies. The regressions are shown in Table 12A.4. A subsidy or surplus is computed for every route using marginal costs for the system-level cost segments evaluated with the volumes on cross-subsidized routes deleted. The subsidies and surpluses are used to fit the linear equations with possible deliveries, mail volume in each subclass, seven dummy variables for CAG, and eight dummy variables for RCAT as regressors. The ANOVA results are the percentages of the total variation in the subsidies and surpluses that are explained by each group of regressors.[12]

The subsidies and surpluses on the routes are primarily explained by the volume of mail and its distribution by subclass. The coefficient estimates in Table 12A.4 describe a relationship between cross-subsidized routes and subclasses with low or negative institutional cost coverage. Negative coefficients appear in all four of the fitted equations for Periodicals, Parcel Post, Media Mail, USPS Mail and Free Mail. All but one of the coefficients are also negative for International Mail.

A much smaller percentage of the variation is due to the route classification. Little of the variation is explained by either office size or by the number of possible deliveries on the routes. Overall, this pattern suggests that geographic and demographic characteristics are not very important determinants of cross-subsidies except for the broad distinction between city-carrier and rural routes.

7 CONCLUSION

In this chapter we present a method for estimating the cost of universal service as the maximum cross-subsidy over all USPS's city-carrier and rural routes. Universal service is a quasi-public good whose added benefits derive from the extension of service under a uniform tariff that is simple and cheap to collect, but which imperfectly matches payments by customers to the cost of the services received. The cross-subsidies that result, which we measure with complete IC tests, are the redistributed costs of extending service under such a tariff. The maximum amount of these cross-subsidies for any combination of routes is the appropriate definition of the cost of the USO for comparisons of the costs and benefits of universal service under a uniform tariff.

This cost was around $3 billion in FY 2007 and rose to around $3.5 billion in FY 2008. Our estimate for FY 2007 is somewhat lower than a recent estimate from the PRC which measured the cost of the USO using the profitability definition. The FY 2007 cost of the USO provided by the PRC in its report to Congress (US PRC 2008a) is $3.5 billion.[13] Our estimates and the PRC's profitability estimate should be compared with caution. The profitability definition does not specifically account for cross-subsidies and depends upon assumptions that introduce extraneous effects. Our measurement of the cost of universal service, which improves on NAC, includes the losses from all cross-subsidized routes and evaluates the losses at the proper point on the postal cost function.

NOTES

* The views expressed in this chapter are our own and do not necessarily represent the opinions of the United States Postal Regulatory Commission (PRC). We wish to thank John Waller, Larry Fenster, Spyros Xenakis and Kevin Harle for their encouragement and assistance.

1. The incremental cost of two or more postal services taken together is at least as large as the sum of the incremental costs of the services taken separately. The incremental cost of a subset of postal services is the cost that USPS avoids if all of the services in the subset are deleted.
2. A quasi-public good is a good that is neither rivalrous and excludable (a private good) nor non-rivalrous and non-excludable (a public good), but has some of the properties of both a private and a public good.
3. The role of transaction costs in the context of efficient pricing and entry with a reserved area is extensively analyzed in Crew and Kleindorfer (1998).
4. This occurs in many ways besides the geographic cross-subsidies we consider in this chapter. Many of these are described by Bradley and IBM Global Business Services (2008), Cohen (2008) and Cohen and McBride (2008).
5. To fit hedonic price equations to US postal tariffs, Fenster et al. (2006) devised indices for piece weight, speed of service, presort level, distance transported, automation and customer size.
6. The Commission's estimates of the cost of universal service encompass elements including nonprofit rates, small post offices, the Alaska air subsidy, the weekly frequency of delivery, as well as the geographic scope of delivery service.
7. The sample was supplemented with values for registered and certified mail derived by allocating a proportion of the total FY 2007 registered and certified mail on the basis of each route's pro-rated share of First Class single-piece letters. The sample was supplemented with values for insurance, COD and other transactions (mostly money orders) by allocating FY 2007 transactions based upon each route's proportion of parcel post volumes.
8. A cost function is strongly submodular if its cross-second derivatives with respect to volumes are negative (Pearsall, 2009). For a cost segment of the form $C_x = K_x(D_x)^{E_x}$ with $D_x = \Sigma_j \alpha_{xj} V_j$ we have

$$\frac{\partial^2 C_x}{\partial V_j \partial V_k} = E_x(E_x - 1)\alpha_{xj}\alpha_{xk}\frac{C_x}{D_x^2} < 0$$

when $0 < E_x < 1$, $\alpha_{xj} > 0$ and $\alpha_{xk} > 0$.

9. The elements of the scaled sample represent varying numbers of USPS routes in FY 2007. The average scale is 3.61. In all of the calculations described in this section, and later, the results of the calculations of incremental cost, forgone revenue, and subsidy (or surplus) for the routes in the sample are multiplied by the scales for the routes to obtain totals for the population of all routes served by USPS.
10. Evidence of sharply decreasing returns to scale in delivery is found in the low volume variabilities for the delivery cost segments displayed in Table 12A.3. For FY 2007 these variabilities are city-carrier street time 37.04 percent and rural carriers 40.62 percent. The FY 2008 variabilities are similar.
11. USPS withholds this information in order to prevent identification of the carriers.
12. A negative contribution to the total explained variation is possible because the fitted equations do not include an intercept.
13. The PRC's estimate is the cost of the delivery monopoly taken from Cohen (2008).

REFERENCES

Baumol, W.J., J.C. Panzar and R. Willig (1988), *Contestable Markets and the Theory of Industrial Structure*, New York: Harcourt, Brace, Jovanovich (rev. edn).

Bradley, M. and J. Colvin (2000), 'Measuring the cost of universal service for posts', in M.A. Crew and P.R. Kleindorfer (eds), *Current Directions in Postal Reform*, Boston, MA: Kluwer Academic, pp. 29–46.

Bradley, M., J. Colvin and J. Panzar (1999), 'On setting prices and testing cross-subsidy with accounting data', *Journal of Regulatory Economics*, **16**, 83–100.

Bradley, M. and IBM Global Business Services (2008), 'Quantitative analysis of the Universal Service Obligation', Final Report, United States Postal Service, October 8.

Cohen, R. (2008), 'Quantitative analysis of the value of the postal and mailbox monopolies', Appendix F, Section 4 of *Study on Universal Postal Service and the Postal Monopoly*, George Mason School of Public Policy, Fairfax, VA, November.

Cohen, R. and C. McBride (2008), 'Estimates of the current cost of the USO in the U.S.', Appendix F, Section 3 of *Study on Universal Postal Service and the Postal Monopoly*, George Mason School of Public Policy, November.

Cohen, R., W. Ferguson, J. Waller and S. Xenakis (1999), 'An analysis of the potential for cream skimming in the U.S. residential delivery market', in M.A. Crew and P.R. Kleindorfer (eds), *Emerging Competition in Postal and Delivery Systems*, Boston, MA: Kluwer Academic, pp 141–57.

Cremer, H., A. Grimaud and J.-J. Laffont (2000), 'The cost of universal service in the postal sector', in M.A. Crew and P.R. Kleindorfer (eds), *Current Directions in Postal Reform*, Boston, MA: Kluwer Academic, pp. 47–68.

Crew, M.A. and P.R. Kleindorfer (1998), 'Efficient entry, monopoly, and the Universal Service Obligation in postal service', *Journal of Regulatory Economics*, **14**, 103–25.

Fenster, L., D. Monaco, E.S. Pearsall, C. Robinson and S. Xenakis (2006), 'US postal services as composite goods with hedonic properties', in M.A. Crew and P.R. Kleindorfer (eds), *Liberalization of the Postal and Delivery Sector*, Cheltenham, UK and Northampton, MA, USA: Edward Elgar, pp. 369–88.

Fenster, L., D. Monaco, E.S. Pearsall, J. Waller, G. Willette and S. Xenakis (2008), 'A complete test of U.S. postal rates for cross-subsidies', presented at the 16th Conference on Postal and Delivery Economics, Center for Research in Regulated Industries (CRRI), Albufeira, Portugal, May 28–31.

Panzar, J. (2000), 'A methodology for measuring the costs of universal service', *Information Economics and Policy*, **12**, 3, 211–20.

Panzar, J. (2001), 'A methodology for measuring the costs of universal service obligations', in M.A. Crew and P.R. Kleindorfer (eds), *Future Directions in Postal Reform*, Boston, MA: Kluwer Academic, pp. 101–16.

Panzar, J. (2008a), 'Funding Universal Service Obligations', in *Handbook of Worldwide Postal Reform*, M.A. Crew, P.R. Kleindorfer and J.I. Campbell, Jr. (eds), Cheltenham, UK and Northampton, MA, USA: Edward Elgar, pp. 98–109.

Panzar, J. (2008b), 'Methodologies for costing the USO and valuating the letter and mailbox monopolies', Appendix F, Section 2 of *Study on Universal Postal Service and the Postal Monopoly*, George Mason School of Public Policy, Fairfax, VA, November.
Pearsall, E.S. (2009), 'The complete incremental cost test for cross-subsidies with a sub-modular cost function', *Journal of Regulatory Economics*, **36**, 3, December.
Rodriguez, F., S. Smith and D. Storer (1999), 'Estimating the cost of the Universal Service Obligation in postal services', in M.A. Crew and P.R. Kleindorfer (eds), *Emerging Competition in Postal and Delivery Services,* Boston, MA: Kluwer Academic, pp. 195–208.
US Postal Regulatory Commission (PRC) (2008a), *Report on Universal Postal Service and the Postal Monopoly*, December 19.
US Postal Regulatory Commission (PRC) (2008b and 2009), 'Annual Compliance Reports 2007 and 2008 Library References 1 and 2', PRC-ACR2007-LR1-2 and PRC-ACR2008-LR1-2.

APPENDIX 12A

Table 12A.1 Route sample and ACR FY 2007 volumes

Category	City carriers business rte volume per day	City carriers residential rte volume per day	City carriers mixed rte volume per day	City carriers total rte volume per day	Rural carriers total rte volume per day	All carriers total rte volume per day
First-Class Single-piece Letters	1,505,874	41,920,832	4,443,303	47,870,009	22,353,851	70,223,860
First-Class Presort Letters	1,043,459	81,570,264	6,430,317	89,044,040	41,155,031	130,199,071
First-Class Single-piece Cards	56,101	3,435,619	400,090	3,891,811	2,140,128	6,031,939
First-Class Presort Cards	50,891	5,455,408	336,823	5,843,121	2,968,461	8,811,583
Priority Mail	36,703	990,510	117,392	1,144,605	478,512	1,623,118
Express Mail	1,749	36,567	5,003	43,320	18,692	62,012
Periodicals	255,704	14,296,777	1,169,567	15,722,048	8,533,538	24,255,586
Standard Mail Extended Carrier Route	343,941	61,137,248	3,678,865	65,160,054	39,364,763	104,524,817
Standard Mail Regular Presort	1,135,053	112,542,303	7,146,458	120,823,814	57,310,385	178,134,199
Parcel Post	6,035	521,034	49,938	577,007	129,575	706,582
Bound Printed Matter	27,190	777,441	78,957	883,588	712,092	1,595,680
Media and Library Rate Mail	4,130	228,263	16,868	249,261	123,307	372,568
US Postal Service Mail	19,911	1,563,416	126,033	1,709,360	784,889	2,494,248
Free Mail	323	86,583	18,944	105,851	44,110	149,961
International Mail	24,515	478,829	66,786	570,130	214,157	784,287
Registry	162	4,515	479	5,155	2,407	7,563
Certified	10,518	292,792	31,034	334,343	156,128	490,471
Insurance	987	85,196	8,166	94,348	21,187	115,535
COD	24	2,103	202	2,329	523	2,852
Other Services	21,323	593,592	62,916	677,831	316,527	610,641
Total	4,544,594	326,019,290	24,188,140	354,752,024	17,828,265	531,196,572

Table 12A.1 (continued)

Category	ACR annual volume thousands	Annualized route volume thousands	Annual non-route volume thousands	De-annualized non-route volume per day	De-annualized total volume per day
First-Class Single-piece Letters	40,121,742	21,277,830	18,843,912	62,191,130	132,414,990
First-Class Presort Letters	49,978,441	39,450,318	10,528,123	34,746,279	164,945,350
First-Class Single-piece Cards	2,141,669	1,827,677	313,992	1,036,276	7,068,215
First-Class Presort Cards	3,656,291	2,669,910	986,381	3,255,384	12,066,967
Priority Mail	896,865	491,805	405,060	1,336,833	2,959,950
Express Mail	54,764	18,790	35,974	118,727	180,739
Periodicals	8,795,831	7,349,443	1,446,388	4,773,559	29,029,145
Standard Mail Extended Carrier Route	34,847,195	31,671,019	3,176,176	10,482,428	115,007,244
Standard Mail Regular Presort	68,668,917	53,974,662	14,694,255	48,495,890	226,630,089
Parcel Post	348,628	214,094	134,534	444,005	1,150,587
Bound Printed Matter	637,595	483,491	154,104	508,594	2,104,274
Media and Library Rate Mail	176,615	112,888	63,727	210,320	582,888
US Postal Service Mail	1,008,380	755,757	252,623	833,739	3,327,987
Free Mail	68,501	45,438	23,063	76,115	226,076
International Mail	832,587	237,639	594,948	1,963,525	2,747,812
Registry	4,321	2,292	2,029	6,698	14,261
Certified	280,226	148,613	131,613	434,367	924,838
Insurance	57,005	35,007	21,998	72,600	188,135
COD	1,407	864	543	1,792	4,644
Other Services	301,290	185,024	116,266	383,717	994,358
Total	212,878,270	160,952,561	51,925,709	171,371,977	702,568,549

Table 12A.2 ACR FY 2007 revenue and cost

Category	ACR volume	ACR rev/Pc	ACR revenue	Clerks & mailhandlers att. cost/Pc	Transportation att. cost/Pc	Other non-delivery att. cost/Pc
First-Class Single-piece Letters	40,121,742	0.493	19,773,599	0.199	0.018	0.002
First-Class Presort Letters	49,978,441	0.330	16,505,880	0.059	0.014	0.002
First-Class Single-piece Cards	2,141,669	0.260	556,962	0.136	0.004	0.001
First-Class Presort Cards	3,656,291	0.198	724,933	0.033	0.006	0.001
Priority Mail	896,865	5.836	5,233,799	1.945	1.915	0.301
Express Mail	54,764	17.358	950,578	7.024	2.329	0.312
Periodicals	8,795,831	0.249	2,187,963	0.173	0.029	0.004
Standard Mail Extended Carrier Route	34,847,195	0.174	6,073,169	0.025	0.003	0.002
Standard Mail Regular Presort	68,668,917	0.214	14,707,169	0.082	0.007	0.001
Parcel Post	348,628	3.465	1,208,149	1.538	1.059	0.283
Bound Printed Matter	637,595	1.083	690,566	0.476	0.134	0.074
Media and Library Rate Mail	176,615	2.304	406,909	1.387	0.686	0.082
US Postal Service Mail	1,008,380	0.000	0	0.361	0.040	0.003
Free Mail	68,501	0.000	0	0.618	0.081	0.005
International Mail	832,587	2.445	2,035,792	0.737	1.226	0.090
Registry	4,321	12.340	53,320	10.929	0.000	0.212
Certified	280,226	2.492	698,220	0.765	0.000	−0.006
Insurance	57,005	2.749	156,686	1.235	0.000	0.284
COD	1,407	6.799	9,566	1.786	0.000	0.498
Other Services	301,290	9.101	2,741,914	1.121	0.000	2.519
Total volume	212,878,270					
Revenue from mail & services			74,715,514 Att. costs	24,294,196	5,764,378	1,713,576
Other revenue			257,809 Other costs	4,659,448	737,651	10,678,855
Total revenue			74,973,323 Total cost	28,953,643	6,502,029	12,392,430

Table 12A.2 (continued)

Category	City carrier in-office att. cost/Pc	City carrier street att. cost/Pc	City carrier total att. cost/Pc	Rural carrier total att. cost/Pc	Delivery att. cost/Pc	Total att. cost/Pc
First-Class Single-piece Letters	0.040	0.039	0.080	0.010	0.090	0.309
First-Class Presort Letters	0.017	0.018	0.034	0.009	0.043	0.118
First-Class Single-piece Cards	0.042	0.042	0.084	0.012	0.096	0.237
First-Class Presort Cards	0.013	0.016	0.029	0.009	0.037	0.078
Priority Mail	0.093	0.191	0.284	0.081	0.365	4.526
Express Mail	0.240	0.857	1.097	0.344	1.441	11.106
Periodicals	0.048	0.019	0.067	0.026	0.093	0.300
Standard Mail Extended Carrier Route	0.021	0.019	0.039	0.022	0.061	0.091
Standard Mail Regular Presort	0.024	0.019	0.043	0.012	0.055	0.145
Parcel Post	0.084	0.259	0.343	0.129	0.473	3.353
Bound Printed Matter	0.048	0.150	0.198	0.062	0.260	0.944
Media and Library Rate Mail	0.075	0.204	0.280	0.088	0.367	2.521
US Postal Service Mail	0.051	0.016	0.066	0.009	0.076	0.480
Free Mail	0.073	0.071	0.144	0.045	0.189	0.893
International Mail	0.026	0.036	0.062	0.023	0.085	2.138
Registry	0.446	0.603	1.049	0.631	1.680	12.820
Certified	0.181	0.342	0.524	0.533	1.057	1.815
Insurance	0.068	0.259	0.326	0.424	0.750	2.269
COD	0.107	0.791	0.898	1.447	2.345	4.630
Other Services	0.089	0.235	0.323	0.185	0.508	4.148
Attributable costs	5,681,810	5,411,029	11,092,839	3,198,824	14,291,663	46,063,812
Other costs	1,143,393	9,198,238	10,341,631	4,675,389	15,017,021	31,092,974
Total cost	6,825,204	14,609,267	21,434,470	7,874,213	29,308,683	77,156,786

Table 12A.3 Derivation of cost function parameters for FY 2007

Category	ACR clerks & mailhandlers alpha	ACR transpor-tation alpha	ACR other non-delivery alpha	ACT city carriers in-office alpha	ACR city carriers street alpha	ACR rural carriers total alpha
First-Class Single-piece Letters	1.744	0.669	0.286	1.506	1.548	1.526
First-Class Presort Letters	0.520	0.514	0.259	0.622	0.695	0.657
First-Class Single-piece Cards	1.191	0.152	0.088	1.579	1.666	1.621
First-Class Presort Cards	0.293	0.212	0.133	0.470	0.631	0.548
Priority Mail	17.041	70.717	37.373	3.500	7.513	5.458
Express Mail	61.548	86.027	38.769	8.995	33.720	21.055
Periodicals	1.517	1.087	0.503	1.796	0.761	1.291
Standard Mail Extended Carrier Route	0.223	0.103	0.294	0.770	0.743	0.757
Standard Mail Regular Presort	0.717	0.252	0.167	0.892	0.743	0.819
Parcel Post	13.474	39.126	35.166	3.143	10.206	6.588
Bound Printed Matter	4.170	4.933	9.248	1.808	5.906	3.807
Media and Library Rate Mail	12.152	25.318	10.181	2.826	8.033	5.366
US Postal Service Mail	3.164	1.479	0.411	1.899	0.618	1.274
Free Mail	5.419	3.000	0.562	2.741	2.794	2.767
International Mail	6.445	45.275	11.179	0.970	1.414	1.187
Registry	95.769	0.000	26.281	16.710	23.709	20.125
Certified	6.702	0.000	−0.782	6.795	13.472	10.052
Insurance	10.823	0.000	35.229	2.545	10.171	6.265
COD	15.650	0.000	61.893	4.023	31.119	17.240
Other Services	9.824	0.000	312.877	3.319	9.232	6.203
Daily volume sum	702,568,549	702,568,549	702,568,549	702,568,549	702,568,549	702,568,549
Cost per business day	95,556,579	21,458,842	40,899,109	6,825,204	14,609,267	7,874,213
Volume variability (E)	83.91%	88.66%	13.83%	83.25%	37.04%	40.62%
Constant (K)	3.61	0.31	2445846.53	0.29	7726.14	2005.97

Table 12A.3 (continued)

Category	Sample city carriers in-office alpha	Sample city carriers street alpha	Sample rural carriers total alpha	Scaled ACR city carriers in-office alpha	Scaled ACR city carriers street alpha	Scaled ACR rural carriers total alpha
First-Class Single-piece Letters	2.013	2.162	1.041	1.571	1.647	1.623
First-Class Presort Letters	0.582	0.650	0.579	0.649	0.739	0.699
First-Class Single-piece Cards	1.448	1.528	0.662	1.647	1.772	1.723
First-Class Presort Cards	0.490	0.658	0.598	0.490	0.671	0.583
Priority Mail	4.571	9.810	8.390	3.653	7.993	5.802
Express Mail	18.950	71.036	55.663	9.386	35.872	22.382
Periodicals	1.675	0.710	1.468	1.875	0.810	1.373
Standard Mail Extended Carrier Route	0.686	0.662	1.052	0.803	0.790	0.804
Standard Mail Regular Presort	0.845	0.703	0.825	0.931	0.790	0.871
Parcel Post	3.165	10.276	19.257	3.280	10.857	7.004
Bound Printed Matter	2.174	7.102	3.070	1.887	6.283	4.047
Media and Library Rate Mail	3.337	9.486	6.929	2.949	8.546	5.704
US Postal Service Mail	1.867	0.608	0.663	1.981	0.658	1.354
Free Mail	2.956	3.013	3.824	2.860	2.972	2.941
International Mail	2.362	3.440	4.981	1.013	1.504	1.261
Registry	23.340	33.115	62.591	17.438	25.223	21.392
Certified	9.490	18.816	52.898	7.090	14.331	10.685
Insurance	2.562	10.241	63.000	2.656	10.821	6.660
COD	4.051	31.333	215.224	4.198	33.105	18.327
Other Services	2.458	6.838	9.748	3.463	9.821	6.594
Daily volume sum	354,752,024	354,752,024	176,828,265	354,752,024	354,752,024	176,828,265
Cost per business day	22,525,425	48,215,401	25,987,502	22,525,425	48,215,401	25,987,502
Number of routes	151,944	151,944	73,191	151,944	151,944	73,191
Volume variability (E)	83.25%	37.04%	40.62%	83.25%	37.04%	40.62%
Constant (K)	0.23	17.44	15.28	0.23	17.44	15.27

Table 12A.4 Regressions

	ACR 2007 coefficient	Sample alphas *t*-value	ACR 2007 coefficient	Scaled alphas *t*-value	ACR 2008 coefficient	Sample alphas *t*-value	ACR 2008 coefficient	Scaled alphas *t*-value
Intercept	−173.104	–	−170.845	–	−212.006	–	−209.872	–
Possible Deliveries	−0.008	−21.49	−0.010	−25.00	−0.010	−24.93	−0.010	−27.39
First-Class Single-piece Letters	0.091	120.43	0.137	184.29	0.117	158.31	0.155	213.00
First-Class Presort Letters	0.232	526.66	0.219	504.50	0.244	567.14	0.234	548.32
First-Class Single-piece Cards	0.015	3.68	−0.006	−1.57	0.037	9.08	0.006	1.38
First-Class Presort Cards	0.118	39.04	0.118	39.47	0.127	42.87	0.129	43.93
Priority Mail	0.602	46.43	0.798	62.45	0.629	49.62	0.831	66.06
Express Mail	3.057	39.46	5.157	67.53	3.145	41.50	4.969	66.14
Periodicals	−0.076	−51.46	−0.068	−47.03	−0.080	−55.51	−0.070	−49.18
Standard Mail ECR	0.085	281.88	0.080	271.38	0.094	320.88	0.086	296.02
Standard Mail Regular	0.066	187.00	0.053	153.61	0.065	189.99	0.057	166.32
Parcel Post	−0.419	−21.00	−0.450	−22.88	−0.536	−27.48	−0.520	−26.84
Bound Printed Matter	−0.028	−2.71	0.112	11.07	0.087	8.65	0.221	22.16
Media and Library Rate	−0.528	−20.38	−0.479	−18.73	−0.688	−27.14	−0.662	−26.31
USPS Mail	−0.557	−245.49	−0.558	−249.37	−0.859	−387.05	−0.899	−408.27
Free Mail	−1.006	−30.16	−0.959	−29.17	−0.814	−24.93	−0.742	−22.93
International Mail	−0.173	−10.20	−0.007	−0.39	−0.121	−7.29	0.056	3.38

CAG	A	−20.461	−11.37	−19.481	−10.98	−19.666	−11.17	−18.936	−10.85
	B	−21.584	−11.84	−20.338	−11.32	−20.687	−11.60	−19.730	−11.16
	C	−24.317	−13.46	−23.469	−13.18	−23.374	−13.22	−22.793	−13.01
	D	−22.442	−12.23	−21.807	−12.05	−21.536	−11.99	−21.166	−11.89
	E	−24.025	−13.10	−23.222	−12.84	−23.028	−12.83	−22.550	−12.67
	F	−16.883	−8.93	−15.960	−8.57	−16.078	−8.69	−15.478	−8.44
	G	−9.246	−4.56	−7.924	−3.97	−8.820	−4.45	−7.804	−3.97
RACT	BUS. FOOT	−32.084	−14.84	−31.223	−14.66	−36.643	−17.33	−36.205	−17.27
	BUS. MOT.	−44.522	−22.83	−45.531	−23.68	−48.589	−25.46	−49.911	−26.38
	RES. FOOT	−71.583	−38.37	−72.054	−39.18	−54.429	−29.82	−55.174	−30.49
	RES. CURB.	−69.077	−38.73	−70.466	−40.08	−52.214	−29.92	−53.799	−31.09
	RES. P&L	−77.697	−43.06	−78.968	−44.40	−60.277	−34.14	−61.831	−35.32
	MIX. FOOT	−49.054	−7.65	−48.869	−7.73	−41.853	−6.67	−42.454	−6.83
	MIX. CURB.	−68.996	−28.27	−69.699	−28.97	−60.942	−25.52	−62.036	−26.20
	MIX. P&L	−85.888	−19.35	−87.605	−20.02	−76.795	−17.69	−78.991	−18.35
Standard error		12.171		11.996		11.907		11.805	
R-squared		0.9834		0.9835		0.9857		0.9858	

13. Estimating the impact of a uniform price rule in a liberalized postal environment: the case of the United States Postal Service

Michael D. Bradley, Jeff L. Colvin, Norma B. Nieto and Daniel J. Tobias

1 INTRODUCTION

One of the ironies of research into the cost of the Universal Service Obligation (USO) is that the cost measure that can be readily calculated is of little value to policy makers and the cost measure that is extremely difficult to measure is perhaps the most important one. Universal service costs are most often discussed in the context of the viability of a USO in a liberalized environment. To make informed decisions, the policy maker must have an estimate of a given USO in that liberalized environment. Estimates of the cost of the USO under a monopoly environment are of little value to the regulator considering liberalization.

For example, in a monopoly environment, a national price uniformity restriction will not greatly disadvantage the monopolist. Under a liberalized environment, however, a uniform price restriction could be extremely costly, allowing entrants to serve the low-cost, high-profit areas and leaving the high-cost, low-profit areas for the USO operator. The estimated cost of a uniform pricing restriction under a monopoly is of almost no value in estimating its cost in a liberalized environment.

Although estimating the cost of a uniform price USO in a liberalized environment is both theoretically correct and useful for policy makers, it is difficult to do. It requires specifying and estimating the likely behavior of the incumbent, customers and competitors in the liberalized environment. In other words, it requires specifying future economic scenarios and behavior:

> A proper way to evaluate this cost is then to compare the profit levels of the operator under the alternative market equilibria: with and without the USO. *The task is for the least faint hearted* for it requires a forward looking approach . . . (Cremer et al., 2001, p. 20, emphasis added)

This chapter presents estimates of the cost and other impacts of the uniform pricing rule portion of the United States Postal Service's USO. Section 2 provides a review of the general approach. Section 3 discusses the structure of the analytical model. Section 4 presents the data requirements and the calibration of the analytical model. Section 5 presents the results, indicating the impacts of the uniform price USO in a liberalized environment. Section 6 concludes.

2 IMPLEMENTING THE PROFITABILITY APPROACH TO MEASURING USO COSTS

A consensus has emerged that the theoretically preferred approach to measuring the cost of a USO for a postal operator is the profitability approach, where the net financial position of the postal operator is calculated both with and without the USO in place. The difference in net financial position caused by the imposition of the obligation is the profitability measure of its cost.

This approach has several advantages. First, it can be applied whether or not the postal environment is liberalized. This means that the profitability approach can be used to explore the relationship between the USO and the postal monopoly or 'reserved area'. Second, the profitability approach includes both cost and demand responses to changes in the USO. Third, it is general, so it can be used to investigate different aspects of the USOs such as delivery-day requirements or uniform pricing rules.

Despite its theoretical advantages, the profitability approach has rarely been implemented, primarily because its data and computational requirements can be quite high. Not only does it require detailed data on a postal operator's costs and revenues, it also requires specifying how both the postal operator and actual and potential entrants would respond to relaxation of the USO.

A USO cost arises from the placement of a legal or policy constraint on the US Postal Service (USPS). This means that, in the ideal, the net cost of the constraint could be calculated by observing the USPS both before and after the constraint was put into place and comparing its net financial situation in the two states. The degradation in the USPS's financial position is the cost of that USO. Obviously, this ideal is unattainable because the USO restrictions are already in place. The estimation of the costs of a USO restriction thus requires estimation of the net financial position of the USPS with the restriction removed. The difference between the two net financial positions, the current actual financial position and the estimated financial position absent the constraint, is the estimate of the costs of the USO being examined. In summary, the costs of a USO can be estimated as the net improvement in the USPS's financial position arising from the removal of that obligation.

This means that implementation of the profitability approach requires taking a holistic approach to measuring the costs of a particular USO. In practical terms, this means considering both the demand response (reactions of consumers and competitors) as well as the operational response (reaction by the USPS). The computational methodology starts with identification of the USO restriction that is removed. It then pursues two tracks, one focusing on the USPS response and one focusing on the demand-side response.

On the cost side, the process starts with identification of the USPS's operational response to removal of the restriction. This response may include changes in operations, changes in product offerings, or changes in the structure of prices. Once the operational changes are identified, they must be translated into cost responses. This requires highlighting how the operational changes impact the USPS's product costs and where those changes occur geographically. The cost side of the model can then be used to calculate the resulting change in Postal Service costs.

At the same time, changes in a USO restriction may result in a reaction by the USPS's customers and/or competitors. These responses would occur on the demand side and would affect the USPS's volumes and revenue. Demand changes can arise from both market liberalization and from removing USO restrictions. For example, under liberalization, new competitors can enter the market and divert existing USPS volume and revenue.

Finally, the computational algorithm should allow for interaction between these two channels of response. It is quite likely that in some scenarios changes in postal operations could have an impact on consumer demand and competitive offerings. In addition, changes in volume and revenue may have a subsequent impact on operations and cost. The computational algorithm thus allows for interaction between the two channels. To complete the calculation, the two tracks are brought together. The final calculation combines any changes in revenue with any changes in costs to calculate the net change in the Postal Service's financial position. This net change is the profitability measure of the costs of the USO.

3 A MODEL OF THE US POSTAL MARKET

Measuring the cost of a uniform pricing USO rule in a liberalized environment requires taking into account the actions and reactions of three groups of economic agents: the incumbent monopoly postal provider, postal customers, and competitive postal providers who may enter the market under liberalization. This means that a quantitative model of the USO in a liberalized environment needs to incorporate analytical structures for each of these three groups of agents. In the model, this is accomplished with four modules, one capturing the cost structure and volume flows for the existing USPS network, one capturing the actions of entrants, one capturing actions of postal customers and one capturing the reactions of the USPS to entry in a liberalized environment.

Modeling the Existing USPS Network

Previous research, actual experience with liberalized environments, and a survey of experts on the US postal market suggest that in a liberalized environment, entry is very likely to be local. Competitors to the incumbent provider will enter in low-cost, high-density areas of the postal network and will leave the high-cost, low-density areas to the incumbent. Thus, to model the costs of a uniform service obligation under liberalization it is important to have a disaggregated model of the postal network. This was achieved by building a nationwide network model that models costs, revenues, and economic interactions at the 3-digit ZIP Code level.[1]

The model accounts for where the mail originates (for example, 3-digit ZIP Code 101) as well as where it is destined (for example, 3-digit ZIP Code 301), and allows for mail, which has its origin and destination in the same 3-digit ZIP Code and mail which is destination entered. The model relies upon regulator-approved costing models for measuring the upstream (mail processing, retail and administrative) costs as well as the transportation and delivery costs. In addition, the model explicitly allows for both city- and rural-carrier delivery within the same 3-digit ZIP Code.

Although constructing a disaggregated model is an ambitious task, it provides several advantages. First, it permits calculation of not only national USO costs but also identification of where those costs arise. Another advantage of a disaggregated model is that it permits a detailed analysis of the entry that would occur under liberalization. Because the model allows entry to occur on a 3-digit ZIP Code basis, it mirrors the likely reality that entry will occur in some 3-digit ZIP Codes across the country but not others. A disaggregated model also permits investigation of important economic issues like cream-skimming of low-cost regions.

The model captures the national volume flow among ZIP codes and calculates the cost of handling that mail. The costs are calculated for 'upstream' activities like mail processing, and for transportation and delivery. These computations are governed by a series of equations. For example, the determination of delivery costs is done separately for rural- and city-carrier delivery, each with its own equation. The equation for city-carrier delivery costs in the '*i*th' 3-digit ZIP Code is given by:

$$DC_i = ADC_i + NDC_i,$$

where ADC is attributable delivery cost and NDC is network delivery cost.[2] Attributable delivery cost is calculated as the sum of the products of delivered volume, by shape, and their associated marginal costs. The attributable delivery cost for *i*th 3-digit ZIP Code is thus given by:

$$ADC_i = \omega a_1 V_{Li} + \omega a_2 V_{Fi} + \omega a_3 V_{Si} + \omega a_4 V_{Pi},$$

where V_L is the volume of letters delivered, V_F is the volume of flats delivered, V_S is the volume of sequenced mail delivered, and V_P is the volume of parcels delivered. The '*a*' coefficients are the associated marginal times and ω is the average city-carrier wage. The time coefficients are currently embedded in the Postal Service's delivery cost models.

Network delivery cost is caused by non-volume characteristics of delivery such as the number of delivery points, the square miles of the delivery area, or the types of delivery receptacles (box, Neighborhood Delivery Collection Box Units: NDCBUs, park and loop):

$$NDC_i = b_1 DP_i + b_2 M_i^2 + b_3 \Theta_i.$$

Fortunately, the '*b*' coefficients of the network delivery costs do not have to be estimated. In other words, for each 3-digit ZIP Code, the total delivery costs DC_i are observed, and the above equation is used to compute ADC_i. The difference between these two measures is NDC_i which captures the 3-digit ZIP Code specific characteristics of delivery.

The final piece is the mapping between national destinating volumes and city-carrier delivered volumes by shape. Not all national destinating volumes are delivered by city carriers, so only that portion delivered by city carriers should be included. Separate datasets for city-carrier delivered mail, rural-carrier delivered mail and non-delivered (for example, PO Box, firm holdout) mail, by 3-digit ZIP Code are used to determine the relevant proportions. With these proportions (the δ coefficient in the following equation), city-carrier delivery cost in a given 3-digit ZIP Code can be calculated as a function of national destinating volumes:

$$DC_i = \omega a_1 \sum_{j=1}^{n} \delta_{Lij} V_{Lji} + \omega a_2 \sum_{j=1}^{n} \delta_{Fij} V_{Fji} + \omega a_3 \sum_{j=1}^{n} \delta_{Sij} V_{Sji} + \omega a_4 \sum_{j=1}^{n} \delta_{Pij} V_{Pji} + NDC_i.$$

Similar equations exist for the computation of transportation and upstream costs.

Modeling Postal Customers

One of the difficult parts of investigating universal service costs in a liberalized environment is modeling the reaction of customers to entry. Because the liberalized environment can be quite different from the existing monopoly environment, one must be cautious in using existing demand functions and parameters, like price elasticities. Consequently, a general demand model is specified and then surveys of customers were used to calibrate those models with the required parameters.

The model of postal customers has two key assumptions. First, it is assumed that the incumbent's and entrant's products are *imperfect* substitutes. Not only could the products have differences in services like address correction or frequency of delivery but they could also have differences in actual or perceived quality. For example, surveys of both large and small postal customers in the United States show that most customers are somewhat concerned about the quality of service provided by an entrant and would likely require a discount to shift their mail away from the incumbent. Second, for tractability, it is assumed that liberalization does not affect the total amount of mail being sent. This assumption eliminates the necessity of modeling the fundamentals of mail demand, keeping the focus on modeling the flows of mail to the different providers of mail service.

Demand is modeled for a competitive entrant's product in a given ZIP Code, $V_{C,i}$ as a function of the pre-liberalization volume of mail destined for that ZIP Code, V_i^*, and the competitor's relative price, $P_{C,i}/P_{I,i}^*$. Specifically, the customer's demand for the entrant's product is given by:

$$V_{C,i} = e^{\lambda(1 - P_{C,i}/P_{I,i}^*)} V_i^*.$$

Modeling Competitive Entrants

A critical aspect of the model is the determination of entry by new competitors. The cost of a uniform price USO depends upon the amount of competitive pressure faced by the USPS under liberalization. This pressure is measured by the ability of competitors to enter the market and capture volume currently handled by the USPS. Because entry is likely to be a local phenomenon, the model allows for a separate possibility of entry in each of the hundreds of 3-digit ZIP Codes. In the model, entry is required to be fair and sustainable. This means that in any 3-digit ZIP Code, the entrant's revenues must be at least sufficient to cover its costs. Entry is not sustainable if the entrant earns insufficient revenue to cover its costs. Mathematically, this condition is given by:

Entrant revenue ≥ Entrant attributable cost + Entrant network cost.

Mathematically, this condition is governed by the following equation:

$$\sum_{j=1}^{m} P_{ijC} V_{ijC} \geq \sum_{j=1}^{m} \omega_{iC} a_{jC} V_{ijC} + NDC_{iC}.$$

In this equation, P_{ijC} is the competitive entrant's price for product j in ZIP code i, V_{ijC} is the competitive entrant's volume product j in ZIP code i, a_{jC} is the entrant's delivery time per piece for product j, ω_{iC} is the wage the entrant must pay in ZIP code i, and NDC_{iC} is the competitive entrant's network delivery cost in ZIP Code i.

Modeling the Postal Service's Reaction to Entry

When entry occurs in a liberalized environment, the incumbent postal provider will lose volume, revenue and profit. If there is no uniform price USO, the incumbent is free to respond to entry by lowering price. However, such a reaction is precluded by a uniform price USO. Recall that under the profitability approach to measuring the cost of a uniform price USO, it is essential to measure the financial impact on the incumbent provider of the uniform pricing rule. The quantitative model does this by comparing the USPS's financial position when it is allowed to respond competitively to entry, to its financial position under the uniform price rule in which it must maintain a single national price.

The USPS's reaction to entry is modeled on a 3-digit ZIP Code basis as it is assumed to separately consider reacting in each ZIP Code in which entry takes place. For each ZIP with entry, the USPS considers the impact on profit of matching the competitive entrant's price. If the USPS does not match the entrant's price, then it loses $1 - \delta$ of its volume and the attendant cost and profit. In contrast, if it does match price, it wins back the volume (recall that the entry must offer a lower price to attract volume) and retains the volume but then must lower price by $(1 - \rho)$, the entrant's price discount on *all* volume destined for the ZIP Code. Thus, the Postal Service will match price and retain volume when:

$$\sum_{j=1}^{n} (P_j^* - \omega a_j)\delta V_j^* < \sum_{j=1}^{n} (\rho P_j^* - \omega a_j) V_j^*.$$

Defining Liberalization

The costs of the USO will depend upon the regulatory environment in which the USPS is operating. For example, in a regulatory environment in which the market has been fully liberalized and there is no longer a postal monopoly of any sort, entrants would be free to cream-skim and capture the profitable volumes, leaving the USPS primarily with the unprofitable ones. If so, earned revenue will fall on many carrier routes (as volume goes to competitors) despite the requirement that the carrier regularly visit each stop. This could cause USO costs to rise. Thus, the extent, nature and degree of liberalization must be considered and defined in the model.

The monopoly in the United States has two parts: the Private Express Statutes (PES) and what is known as the 'mailbox monopoly'. The PES covers the definition of the types of mail that are covered by the monopoly and the mailbox monopoly means that only items bearing postage may be placed in a mailbox. Both are important because they each impact on how entrants would behave and each is discussed in this section.

The PES are a group of laws under which the USPS generally has the exclusive right,

Table 13.1 Potential types of PES relaxation

Type	Description
Price based	Lowering the exception for letters covered by the PES from 6 times the price of single-piece letter
Weight based	Lowering the exception for letters from current 12.5 ounces to fewer ounces
Content/type based	Removing monopoly protection from all advertising mail or presorted mail sent by businesses
Shape based	Removing monopoly protection from certain shapes such as flats
Full	PES relaxed completely; all letters eligible for competition

with certain limited exceptions to carry letters for compensation.[3] Relaxing these laws is a key part of liberalization and Table 13.1 illustrates some types of relaxation of the PES that have been suggested.

In all of these scenarios, the relaxation of the PES will likely have important revenue effects on the USPS. When competition for mail volumes is introduced, the USPS is likely to find itself losing volume and revenue to entrants who can pick and choose which products, services and markets are the most profitable and in which they have the greatest competitive advantages. While these effects are anticipated to some degree in any country in which liberalization takes place, there are some characteristics unique to both the USPS and the US market which may introduce differences in the impacts of liberalization than other posts have or may have experienced. For example, substantial competitors already exist in the postal and delivery industry which increases the likelihood of successful entrants if liberalization occurs. This includes both providers of upstream sorting and transportation services and the package delivery giants.

In addition to the PES, there is the 'mailbox monopoly'. Only items bearing postage may be placed in the mailbox. In addition to impacting on classes of mail which are prohibited from delivery by the PES, it also covers types of mail not restricted by the PES. For example, a local restaurant offering delivery in a neighborhood may hang a menu on a resident's doorknob, but may not place it in the mailbox unless it has postage on it. A removal of the mailbox monopoly could take various forms that could occur with and without any relaxation of the PES. Table 13.2 presents some examples of potential degrees of relaxation of the mailbox monopoly.

Although the lifting of the PES may have a greater total impact on volume, the removal of the mailbox monopoly presents a complex set of effects on both USPS revenue and volumes as well as on operations and cost.

Opening the mailbox introduces the potential of new competition independent of any PES relaxation. If the mailbox is opened, one source of such direct competition is that of delivery of advertising materials that are not protected by the PES, which include advertising materials over 24 pages and newspapers and magazines. Consequently, the relaxation of the mailbox monopoly could lead to increases in delivery-related costs and possible reductions in service. In countries with high mail volumes, like the United States, the possibility of mailbox overcrowding is a realistic possibility. If the mailbox is full when the carrier arrives, he or she will have to make alternative arrangements to get the

Table 13.2 Examples of mailbox monopoly relaxation scenarios

Degree	PES relaxation	Description
Full	Full	Market is fully liberalized and any party providing any delivery of mail and non-mail items may place items in mailbox without restriction
Full	None	Any delivery provider delivering items not explicitly prohibited by the PES may now deliver to the mailbox without restriction
Partial	Full	Only operators licensed to deliver mail previously restricted by the PES (such as FCM letters) may deliver to the mailbox
Partial	None	Only global integrators such as FedEx, UPS and DHL may deliver items to the mailbox

mail to the customer. In addition, opening the mailbox could interfere with the collection of mail originating from the customer. With non-mail materials in the mailbox, the carrier would have to ascertain which pieces were for collection and which were not.

In sum, the model must account for the loss of additional revenue and volume to both new and existing competitors from the relaxation of the PES and/or the mailbox monopoly and for potentially higher delivery and collection costs associated with non-mail items in the mailbox.

4 CALIBRATING THE MODEL

To move from theory to measurement, the analytical model must be calibrated with numerical values that reflect actual and expected economic conditions in the postal market in the United States. This is done with a combination of official cost and volume data available from the USPS and results of surveys of current postal customers. This section presents the calibration of each of the four modules of the quantitative model.

The quantitative model uses official USPS data from the city- and rural-carrier cost systems, the transportation system, the volume measurement system, and the product cost system applied to the 3-digit ZIP Code level. Additional data for each 3-digit ZIP Code was incorporated that includes geographic and delivery characteristics such as population density, residential and business delivery points, and cost of living measures. The data for each of the 910 3-digit ZIP Codes were individually reviewed for reasonableness and consistency. In addition, the model has been calibrated such that the financial baseline data it calculates reflect the conditions in the relevant published financial reports of the USPS.

The largest effort is the calibration of the existing USPS network model. The most basic pieces of data are the national volume flows. Because the model is disaggregated, calibrating volume flows requires construction of the mail flows by shape, product and delivery profile (destination–entry and city, rural or no delivery) for each of the 910 3-digit ZIP Codes.

City delivery costs are made up of both in-office and street costs. Both in-office and street costs have an attributable cost portion which is related to the volume of mail delivered and a network (institutional) cost portion which is related to covering the network. Together these two types of cost comprise total delivery cost. The delivery cost module calculates the attributable and network costs for city-carrier delivery in each 3-digit ZIP Code. These calculations are based upon the regulator-approved methodology for calculating attributable delivery costs. For each 3-digit ZIP Code, attributable costs are calculated and network costs are found as the difference between total and attributable costs. Total rural delivery costs are also made up of attributable and network cost proportions. The attributable cost portion is based upon certain 'evaluation factors', which determine the rates at which rural carriers get paid for handing mail volume. The calculation of attributable rural delivery costs in each 3-digit ZIP Code follows regulator-approved methodology.

Calibrating the customer and entrant modules requires anticipating how each will react to liberalization scenarios. Because the United States has not had much relaxation of the PES or the mailbox monopoly, there is no readily available database that can be used for deriving parameter values. Instead, a survey of industry experts and customers was needed to gain an understanding of entrant and customer reaction to entry.

The first survey was a 'Delphi study', performed by IBM Global Business Services, which was a survey of experts with in-depth knowledge of the US postal market conducted to narrow the broad set of potential monopoly changes into a finite set of liberalization scenarios using the Delphi method. The Delphi method has been used for many studies focused on developing forecasts or future predictions for complex problems, including some in the postal economics field such as recent market entry and competition study of the European postal market.[4]

Most participants believed that liberalization would occur in a similar manner as European weight-based liberalization or with classes such as Standard mail being fully liberalized first, followed by heavier First Class mail (FCM) in incremental stages. Additional liberalization scenarios mentioned included liberalization of presorted mail before single-piece mail, FCM downstream access as the first step, and removal of the mailbox monopoly without changes in the PES.

Almost every type of potential entrant was thought to be at least somewhat likely to enter the market. Rated most likely to enter were those with a strong local delivery presence, such as local delivery companies (new or existing) or combinations of companies with upstream assets with those with delivery assets such as (i) presort bureaus/printers with local delivery companies and (ii) presort bureaus/printers with integrators such as FedEx, UPS and so on. Consortia of mailers with local delivery companies and newspaper companies were also rated likely to enter. Rated least likely to enter were printers and direct marketing companies. While participants described various entry scenarios, the overwhelming consensus was that entry would occur locally, regardless of whether entrants were national or local.

The second survey was a market research survey of the USPS's current customers. The ability of entrants to successfully capture volumes from the USPS is likely to be a key driver of USO costs in a liberalized market, so further quantitative market research was conducted to provide more robust volume diversion estimates. Opinion Research Corporation (ORC) conducted a survey of nearly 1,000 USPS customers across all of its business customer segments on behalf of the USPS.

Customers were provided with scenarios for new mail products that a reputable entrant might offer if the monopoly were relaxed. Products comparable to both FCM and Standard mail were tested. Customers were provided with detailed descriptions of the new product offerings, including specific price points relative to the USPS's and the delivery characteristics offered, such as five-day a week delivery and/or day-certain delivery. For each of the potential new product scenarios, customers were first asked to indicate how likely they would be to switch their existing mail volumes to the entrant, and then provide further detail on which subclasses they would switch. For example, one such possible new competitor was for Standard mail; the competitor would deliver three days a week to mailboxes at a price 10 percent lower than the USPS's current Standard mail prices. The likelihood to switch, existing customer volumes, and national volumes by customer segment were then used to develop a range of volume diversion percentages by class of mail for the various scenarios.

In a scenario with a new product offering similar to FCM in delivery characteristics, but priced 10 percent lower than the USPS's current price, FCM diversion was estimated to be 30 percent. Customers indicated a willingness to switch in response not just to price, but also to an offer that would include enhanced service features even at a premium price relative to the USPS's FCM.

In a scenario with a new product similar to Standard mail in delivery characteristics, but priced at 10 percent lower than the USPS's current price, total Standard mail diversion was estimated to be 40 percent. In a scenario with a new day-certain product offering that is delivered three days a week[5] to the mailbox priced at 10 percent lower than the USPS's current price, total Standard mail diversion was estimated to be 20 percent.

These results were used to calibrate the customer module. They show that customers have a propensity to switch a substantial amount of mail volume for what they perceive to be a better offer, especially in the long run. It is interesting that these levels of diversion are substantial, and are higher than conventional wisdom in the historical debates over the impacts of liberalization in the United States have indicated. This could partly be because the notion of 'new' entrants is not really accurate in the US postal market. Many large customers already have strong relationships with presorters and consolidators, who would ultimately make the choice as to the 'last-mile' provider. Thus, the risks to the end customer of switching to an unknown and untested delivery provider are greatly reduced.

Calibrating the entrant module is necessarily more open ended than calibrating either the USPS network module or the postal customer module because competitive entrants do not currently exist. Consequently, the calibration exercise for this module is necessarily forward looking. Because the USPS values for prices, wages and cost are known, calibration of the competitive entrant module begins with the USPS's values. Entrant values are then specified as deviations from those the USPS values. For example, the entrant's potential price in a given ZIP Code is modeled at a discount from the the USPS price. The discount is a parameter whose value can be chosen by the use of the model. Similarly, the entrant's physical productivity (delivery time per piece by product and shape) is specified as a percentage greater or lesser than the current USPS physical productivity. Because of its unionized workforce, the USPS pays a uniform national wage and a wage premium. The model thus reduces entrant wages by this premium but recognizes that entrant wages will vary by geographical location. Local cost of living indexes were obtained from the

Table 13.3 Examples of calibration values

Parameter	Assumptions	Calibration value
Entrant delivery network costs	Entrant may deliver only on certain days a week and will set up efficient network	32% of USPS delivery network cost
Entrant wages	Vary by metropolitan area cost of living	21% lower than USPS on average, vary by cost of living
Entrant prices	Must be lower than USPS prices	7.5% below USPS
Standard mail diversion	Only drop-shipped Standard mail of all shapes is eligible for diversion	Entrant can obtain 40% diversion in any 3-digit ZIP Code
FCM diversion	Only FCM Presort volumes are eligible for diversion	Entrant can obtain 30% diversion in any 3-digit ZIP Code
Periodicals diversion	Diverted due to PES and mailbox monopoly relaxation	Entrant can obtain 40% diversion in any 3-digit ZIP Code
Priority mail and Small Parcel diversion	Diverted due to mailbox monopoly relaxation to existing competitors	Up to 5% diverted to expeditors
Congestion effect in new entry ZIP Codes	Higher density of non-USPS volumes in mailbox	10% loss in USPS delivery productivity

US Bureau of Labor Statistics to adjust entrant wages by relative living costs. (See Table 13.3.)

The last module to be calibrated is the USPS reaction module. However, all of the parameters in this module have already been calibrated in one of the three previous modules, so no additional effort is required.

5 RESULTS

The calibrated quantitative model can now be used to calculate an estimate of the cost of the uniform price USO faced by the USPS. Two liberalization scenarios are investigated. A liberalization scenario is defined by the change in the regulatory structure and the expected response by customers to new offerings resulting from that change. For example, one such liberalization scenario would be the relaxation of the PES for Standard mail, which would result in entrants and diversion of some existing Postal Service Standard mail volumes.

Once a liberalization scenario has been defined, the model then identifies where entry will take place, calculates the amount of revenue and volume that will be captured by entrants, and measures the financial impact on the USPS. To calculate the uniform price USO, the model calculates the financial impact on the USPS when it is permitted to change the uniform price in response to entry and when it is not so permitted (the USO is in place).

Table 13.4 Standard mail PES and mailbox monopoly relaxed

Entrant delivery days	Entrant network cost (%)	Entrant price discount (%)	ZIP Codes with entry (%)	FCM Presort lost (%)	Standard mail lost (%)	Cost of the uniform price USO ($)
2	21	5.0	97	0	39	2.04
2	21	7.5	95	0	38.5	1.54
2	21	10.0	92	0	38	1.03
3	32	5.0	64	0	29	1.55
3	32	7.5	58	0	27	1.08
3	32	10.0	51	0	24	0.67

Within each liberalization scenario, a number of sensitivity analyses can be performed. The model's flexibility allows for the adjustment of many key parameters, enabling the investigation of the impact of various inputs on the calculated cost of the uniform price USO. These analyses revealed that two important parameters are the entrants' network costs and the entrants' price discount. Sensitivity analyses for these two variables are provided for each of the two liberalization scenarios presented.

Liberalization Scenario 1: Relaxation of the PES for Standard Mail and the Mailbox Monopoly

The first liberalization scenario is defined by the relaxation of the PES for Standard mail and the mailbox monopoly. With this relaxation, entrants may deliver Standard mail and the mailbox is open to all, including package delivery competitors. The quantitative market research found that 40 percent of Standard mail volume could be diverted to entrants in a similar scenario. It is initially assumed that entrants could deliver this mail, on a day-certain basis, two days a week. In order to attract existing Standard mail customers to divert volume, the entrant must provide a 7.5 percent price discount below the USPS price.

In this scenario, the competitors enter in 95 percent of ZIP Codes taking 38.5 percent of Standard mail volume. The USPS loses \$3.3 billion in profit if it cannot respond competitively. If it is allowed to match price, the USPS loss decreases to \$1.75 billion, indicating that the cost of the uniform price USO is \$1.54 billion. Sensitivity analyses are performed on this result by varying both the required price discount and the number of days required to deliver the mail. The results of the sensitivity analyses are given in Table 13.4.

This scenario's sensitivity analyses results demonstrate the impact of the entrant network costs on entry. In a scenario in which the entrant incurs 21 percent of the USPS's network costs, the entrant can successfully enter in 90 percent of 3-digit ZIP Codes, whereas a modest increase to 32 percent of the USPS's network costs can result in entry occurring in only 51 percent of 3-digit ZIP Codes. This shows the importance of entrants being able to minimize the number of delivery days. An increase of just one day a week can sharply reduce the number of ZIP Codes in which entry is successful.

Also, comparing the variations in network cost to variations in the price discount shows that the latter has less of an impact on entry. For example, when network costs are low, doubling the price discount from 5 to 10 percent has only a modest impact on entry. As one would expect, however, as network costs rise and entrants are driven to the margin, the price discount becomes more important.

Finally, note that the price discount is important for the uniform price cost of the USO. This is because this USO cost turns on the benefit to the USPS from lowering price to match competition. Removal of the USO allows the USPS to price differentially across ZIP Codes, but transaction costs continue to require it to set one price for each ZIP. This means that lowering price to match competition causes the USPS to earn less revenue on all of the volume delivered to the ZIP, not just the portion taken by the entrant. As the price discount rises, the benefit to the USPS from matching price falls and, accordingly, the cost of the uniform price USO also falls.

Liberalization Scenario 2: Relaxation of the PES for FCM Presort, Standard Mail and the Mailbox Monopoly

In this scenario, liberalization is extended to include FCM Presort mail. Entrants may deliver FCM Presort in addition to Standard mail, and the mailbox is open to all entrants and existing competitors. In similar scenarios, the ORC market research survey found that up to 30 percent of FCM Presort and 40 percent of Standard mail volume could be diverted to entrants. Because of the higher urgency of FCM, it is initially assumed that entrants need five days a week to deliver mail under this scenario. To attract volume, the entrant must provide a 7.5 percent price discount below the USPS price.

In this scenario, the competitors successfully enter in 60 percent of ZIP Codes, resulting in successful diversion of 29 percent of Standard mail volume and 22 percent of FCM Presort volume. Note that despite having more volume available for diversion, the rate of successful entry falls in this scenario compared with the first scenario. This is because of the higher network costs incurred by the entrant by the addition of an FCM product. Even with more volume in each 3-digit ZIP Code, entrants find it relatively difficult to attract enough volume to cover the network costs of delivering five days a week.

The USPS loses $4.52 billion in profit if it cannot respond competitively. If it is allowed to match the entrant's price, the USPS loss in profit decreases to $2.18 billion, indicating that the cost of the uniform price USO is $2.34 billion under this scenario. Sensitivity analyses were performed on this result by varying both the required price discount and the number of days required to deliver the mail. The results of the sensitivity analyses are given in Table 13.5.

This scenario's sensitivity analyses results demonstrate the impact of the level of the entrant's price discount on the cost of the uniform price USO. In a scenario in which an entrant delivers five days a week, a change in the entrant's price discount level from 5 to 10 percent below the USPS's price results in an increase in the cost of the uniform price USO of $1.5 billion.

Finally, because this is a disaggregated, nationwide model, it allows examination of where entry takes place. One such analysis was the examination of the 3-digit ZIP

Table 13.5 FCM Presort, Standard mail PES and mailbox monopoly relaxed

Entrant delivery days	Entrant network cost %	Entrant price discount %	ZIP Codes with entry (%)	FCM Presort lost (%)	Standard mail lost (%)	Cost of the uniform price USO ($)
5	53	5.0	66	23	31	3.16
5	53	7.5	60	22	29	2.34
5	53	10.0	56	20	27	1.61
4	43	5.0	88	38	29	3.90
4	43	7.5	85	37	28	3.02
4	43	10.0	81	36	27	2.13

Table 13.6 Characteristics of first entry ZIP Codes

3-digit ZIP Codes	3-digits ZIP Codes (%)	Total volume in group (%)	Average density (pop/sq. mi)	Average pieces per delivery point
Entry	51	57	120	2,900
Non-entry	49	43	81	2,100
All	100	100	98	2,500

Codes in which entry occurs even under relatively low starting volume diversion. This analysis is useful when modeling entry as it provides a test of the model and data against expected results. This comparison was also useful in providing some insights into where entry might occur first and whether those ZIP Codes had characteristics that might be expected, such as being located in populous urban centers.

Analysis of the baseline scenario revealed that in general 3-digit ZIP Codes that are 'first entry' tend to have more volume per delivery point and have higher population densities than those that are not. However, not all first entry ZIPs are necessarily those in the highest density urban areas nor are areas in more remote locations excluded. Suburban locations in large metropolitan areas tend to have favorable entry characteristics. A comparison of some of the characteristics of 3-digit ZIP Codes with first entry with those that do not have entry is presented in Table 13.6.

6 CONCLUSION

A classic USO is a uniform price rule in which the incumbent provider must charge the same price nationwide for a specified set of services. This chapter builds a model using the 'profitability approach' that calculates the impact of this uniform price rule in a liberalized environment. While this is difficult to calculate, the approach has the advantage of accounting for the impact of competition and diversion on the incumbent provider. In the case of the USPS, it is found that this subset of costs may be substantial, ranging from $1.5 billion to nearly $3 billion a year, under reasonable forecasts of entry.

NOTES

1. A 3-Digit ZIP Code area comprises multiple 5-digit ZIP Codes, which is the delivery address postal code; 3-Digit ZIP Codes often but not always, align with regional mail processing and distribution centers. There are 910 3-digit ZIP Codes in the United States.
2. 'Attributable costs' are defined in the United States by the postal regulator, the Postal Regulatory Commission. Attributable costs per piece for a mail product are an estimate of the product's marginal cost. For a demonstration of this point and a discussion of postal costing terminology, see Bradley et al. (1999).
3. Some of the key exceptions include letters for which the sender has paid at least six times the price currently charged for the first ounce of a single-piece First Class mail (FCM) letter weighing at least 12.5 ounces, and properly marked letters whose value or usefulness would be lost or greatly diminished if not delivered within certain time standards listed in postal regulations ('extremely urgent' letters). Additional exceptions and a full description of the PES can be found in Title 39, US Code of Federal Regulations (CFR) §§ 310 and 320.
4. This includes the 2005 ECORYS study 'Development of Competition in the European Postal Sector'.
5. Day-certain delivery would be provided if customers submit their mail at least one week in advance.

BIBLIOGRAPHY

Ambrosini, Xavier, François Boldron and Bernard Roy (2006), 'Universal Service Obligations in the postal sector: economic learnings from cross-country comparisons', in M.A. Crew and P.R. Kleindorfer (eds), *Progress Toward Liberalization of the Postal and Delivery Sector*, New York: Springer Science + Business Media, Inc., pp. 23–38.

Billette de Villemeur, E., H. Cremer, B. Roy and J. Toledano (2007), 'Worksharing, Access and bypass: the structure of prices in the postal sector', *Journal of Regulatory Economics*, **32**(1): 67–85.

Bradley, M. and J. Colvin (2000), 'Measuring the costs of universal service for posts', in M.A. Crew and P.R. Kleindorfer (eds), *Current Directions in Postal Reform*, Boston, MA: Kluwer Academic, pp. 29–46.

Bradley, M. and J. Colvin (2001), 'The role of the monopoly product in the cost of universal service', in M.A. Crew and P.R. Kleindorfer (eds), *Future Directions in Postal Reform*, Boston, MA: Kluwer Academic, pp. 163–80.

Bradley, M. and J. Colvin and J.C. Panzar (1999), 'On setting prices and testing cross-subsidy with accounting data', *Journal of Regulatory Economics*, **16**(1): 83–100.

Bradley, M., J. Colvin and M. Perkins (2002), 'Assessing liberalization in context: the importance of pre-liberalization structures', in M.A. Crew and P.R. Kleindorfer (eds), *Postal and Delivery Services: Pricing Productivity, Regulation and Strategy*, Boston, MA: Kluwer Academic, pp. 47–68.

Cremer, H., M. De Rycke and A. Grimaud (1997), 'Costs and benefits of Universal Service Obligations in the postal sector', in M.A. Crew and P.R. Kleindorfer (eds), *Managing Change in the Postal and Delivery Industries*, Boston, MA: Kluwer Academic, pp. 22–41.

Cremer, H., F. Gamsi, A. Girmaoud and J.-J. Laffont (2001), 'Universal service: an economic perspective,' *Annals of Public and Cooperative Economics*, **72**(1): 5–43.

Crew, M.A. and P.R. Kleindorfer (2000), 'Liberalization and the Universal Service Obligation in postal service', in M.A. Crew and P.R. Kleindorfer (eds), *Current Directions in Postal Reform*, Boston, MA: Kluwer Academic, pp. 3–28.

Crew, M.A. and P.R. Kleindorfer (2005), 'Competition, universal service and the graveyard spiral', in M.A. Crew and P.R. Kleindorfer (eds), *Regulatory and Economic Challenges in the Postal and Delivery Sector*, Boston, MA: Kluwer Academic, pp. 1–30.

Crew, M.A. and P.R. Kleindorfer (2006), 'The welfare effects of entry and strategies for maintaining the USO in the postal sector', in M.A. Crew and P.R. Kleindorfer (eds), *Progress toward Liberalization of the Postal and Delivery Sector*, New York: Springer Science + Business Media, Inc., pp. 3–22.

De Donder, P., H. Cremer, P. Dudley and F. Rodriguez (2006), 'Pricing and welfare implications of alternative approaches to setting price controls in the postal sector', in M.A. Crew and P.R. Kleindorfer (eds), *Progress Toward Liberalization of Postal and Delivery Sector*, New York: Springer Science + Business Media, Inc., pp. 227–47.

ECORYS (2005), 'Development of competition in the European postal sector', ECORYS Research and Consulting, July.

Panzar, J. (2001), 'Funding Universal Service Obligations: the costs of liberalization', in *Future Directions in Postal Reform*, Boston, MA: Kluwer Academic, pp. 101–16.

Rodriguez, Frank, Steven Smith and David Storer (1999), 'Estimating the cost of the Universal Service Obligation in Postal Services', in M.A. Crew and P.R. Kleindorfer (eds), *Emerging Competition in Postal and Delivery Services*, Boston: Kluwer Academic Publishers.

14. Funding the cost of universal service in a liberalized postal sector

Claire Borsenberger, Helmuth Cremer, Philippe De Donder, Denis Joram and Bernard Roy

1 INTRODUCTION

Under monopoly, the Universal Service Obligation (USO) and its financing mechanism ought to be designed in such way that efficiency losses are as small as possible. Though by no means trivial, this problem is rather standard and resembles in many respects a traditional Ramsey pricing problem.

In the presence of competition, on the other hand, additional distortions may arise. The design of the USO and of its financing mechanism may now affect the viability of existing operators as well as the entry process into the industry. To take full advantage of efficiency gains from potential or actual competition, it then becomes important to design the USO and its financing mechanism in a 'competitively neutral' manner. This is a very complex problem, as it implies that the regulatory policy must strike the right balance between two potentially conflicting objectives. On the one hand, competitive neutrality requires that no 'excessive' protection ought to be granted to the USO operator, for this might interfere with the entry process (and jeopardize the viability of potentially more efficient entrants). On the other hand, if the USO is not compensated in an appropriate way, its viability may be threatened by possibly less efficient entrants, who may find a niche in the market because of phenomena like 'cream-skimming'. This imposes a threat both to the USO itself, and to the efficiency of the competitive process in the industry.

The financing mechanism is the crucial ingredient for the reconciliation of these potentially conflicting objectives. The choice of the appropriate financing mechanism involves various tradeoffs which we propose to study in this chapter. When the market is fully liberalized (no reserved area), there are essentially two ways to finance the compensation to be paid to the universal service provider (USP). The first one is a subsidy, financed from the general budget. This is probably the most efficient solution, for it implies that the tax base is as large as possible. The efficiency cost of that transfer is then essentially equal to the overall cost of public funds in the economy. This direct transfer has also the virtue of transparency: voters and taxpayers see exactly how much the provision of USO costs and where the money comes from. More or less hidden cross-subsidies are replaced by an explicit transfer. However, this solution is often not feasible in reality.

The alternative to this transfer is to create a universal service fund, financed through implicit or explicit 'taxes' on the operators or products that are not subject to a USO. The proceeds of this fund are then used to finance a transfer to (partially) compensate the universal service operator for its obligations. Compared to the government transfer, this solution implies that the tax base is reduced to the specific sector. There are several alternative ways to levy the contributions to the universal service fund: (i) universal service taxes (or fees); for instance, specific taxes levied on the competitors' sales, (ii) access surcharges; this option is of course only available if the competing operators have to use (part of) the USO operator's network and (iii) lump-sum entry fees, which can be implemented by selling or auctioning off licenses to operate in the sector.

The design of the appropriate mechanism is a complex problem. However, (ii) is dominated by (i) when bypass is possible. The access surcharge can create inefficient bypass while the tax on the competitor does not.[1]

Consequently, if both of these options are available, taxes appear to be the better instrument. The third option amounts to a lump-sum tax on operators. It should not result in distorted prices (a sunk entry cost does not affect the pricing decisions of a profit-maximizing operator) but it may adversely affect entry. Put differently, from a purely static perspective (for a given number of active operators) it appears to be tempting to resort to this instrument. From a dynamic perspective, however, lump-sum fees may have a negative effect on welfare as they reduce the number of active operators and prevent entry of otherwise efficient firms. We shall concentrate on the universal service taxes and study how they ought to be determined. Specifically, we study the issue of the appropriate tax base. Section 2 develops the model. Section 3 presents some benchmark solutions, including the second-best optimum, while Section 4 considers the solution with a compensation fund financed by a uniform tax on all operators. Section 5 presents numerical illustrations and Section 6 concludes.

2 THE MODEL

We assume that there are two operators: the USP, indexed by I (for incumbent), and an entrant, E. We consider three goods. Single-piece mail, whose quantity is denoted by x, is supplied only by the USP. Industrial (bulk) mail is supplied by both operators and its quantity is denoted by y_I and y_E.

The utility (net surplus) of the representative sender is given by:

$$u(x) + v(y_I, y_E) - px - q_I y_I - q_E y_E, \tag{14.1}$$

where p, q_I and q_E are the consumer prices (including any tax). The demand function $x(p)$, $y_I(q_I, q_E)$ and $y_E(q_I, q_E)$ are obtained by maximizing (14.1), and the resulting indirect utility function is denoted $V(p, q_I, q_E)$.

Throughout we assume that the price of bulk mail does not exceed the single-piece rate ($p > q_I$ and $p > q_E$).[2]

The cost function of the USP is given by:

$$C_I = c_x x + k_I y_I + F_x,$$

where F_x is the fixed costs that can be linked directly to processing and delivery of single-piece mail.[3] For instance, assuming that only two deliveries per week are necessary for industrial mail, F_x reflects the network costs associated with an extra three or four deliveries per week. All other costs are assumed to be variable.[4] The entrant's cost function is:

$$C_E = k_E y_E.$$

We assume that the single-piece rate p is given and set by the regulator as part of the USO. In the analytical part, we make no assumptions about the relationship between price and marginal cost of single-piece mail. In the numerical illustration, we shall assume $p > c_2$ (Section 5). There is competition in the market for industrial mail and we assume that E sets its price at marginal cost.

We now characterize the market solution under three alternative scenarios. These solutions establish interesting benchmarks against which the outcome under a (uniform) compensation fund can be assessed.

3 BENCHMARK SOLUTIONS

Constrained First-best Solution (CFB)

Assume that p is given, but that we are otherwise in a first-best setting. In other words, we look for the best outcome (yielding the highest total surplus) that can be achieved for a given level of the single-piece rate assuming that a deficit (if any) can be covered by a lump-sum transfer (subsidy from the general budget) at no cost. This yields:[5]

$$q_I = k_I \text{ and } q_E = k_E,$$

so that all prices for industrial mail are set at marginal cost. The USP's profit at this solution is given by $(p - c_x)x(p) - F_x$. Consequently the USP realizes a deficit under 'plausible' assumptions, that is unless F_x is small while p is much larger than c_x. In the remainder of the chapter we assume that $(p - c_x)x(p) - F_x < 0$; otherwise the issue of financing the cost of USO would not arise and the solution would be trivial.

Market Equilibrium with No Explicit Financing Mechanism (NF)

In the previous scenario, a lump-sum transfer (from the general budget) was used to finance the USP's deficit. This is equivalent to assuming that the 'ideal' (free of efficiency loss) mechanism for financing of the USO is available. Let us now go to the other extreme and consider the market solution that occurs when there is *no mechanism to compensate the USP for its obligations*. In this scenario, the only customers financing the 'cost of USO' are those buying the USP's bulk mail product.

Operator I chooses its sole decision variable q_I to achieve revenues that are sufficient to cover its cost. Formally, it solves:

$$(p - c_x)x(p) + (q_I - k_I)y_I(q_I, q_E) - F_x = 0. \tag{14.2}$$

Using the property that the entrant prices at marginal cost, and rearranging, yields:

$$(q_I - k_I)y_I(q_I, k_E) = F_x - (p - c_x)x(p), \tag{14.3}$$

an equation of a single variable, namely q_I. Note that a solution may not exist. In other words, it is possible that the USP realizes a loss whatever its price (for bulk mail). For instance, when y_I and y_E are perfect substitutes, there is no solution, unless k_E is sufficiently larger than k_I. When (14.3) has no solution, we can assume for instance that the USP sets its price to minimize losses. Observe that even when the solution exists, it does not correspond to the constrained first-best efficient allocation, nor to the second-best efficient outcome, as we shall now show. In other words, it yields a lower level of welfare than these two solutions.

Second-best Solution (SB)

In this scenario, we assume that all consumers of bulk mail (including buyers of the entrant's product) contribute to the financing of the USO, and that the unit contribution may be different for the USP's and for the entrant's bulk mail. To stress the symmetry between the two operators in the setting of the optimization problem, we replace q_I by $k_I + t_I$; that is, we proceed as if the USP followed the same marginal cost pricing rule as the entrant, and was also subject to a unit tax.

Recall that p is exogenously given, so that we have to determine the welfare-maximizing values of the taxes that allow I to cover its cost. To do so, we solve:

$$\max_{t_I, t_E} \; V(p, k_I + t_I, k_E + t_E)$$

$$\text{s.t.} \; (p - c_x)x(p) + t_I y_I(k_I + t_I, k_E + t_E) + t_E y_E(k_I + t_I, k_E + t_E) - F_x = 0. \tag{14.4}$$

The solution to this problem has been extensively studied in the literature.[6] It leads to the usual Ramsey expressions:

$$\frac{t_I}{k_I + t_I} = \frac{q_I - k_I}{q_I} = \frac{\lambda}{1 + \lambda}\frac{1}{\eta_I}, \tag{14.5}$$

$$\frac{t_E}{k_E + t_E} = \frac{q_E - k_E}{q_E} = \frac{\lambda}{1 + \lambda}\frac{1}{\eta_E}, \tag{14.6}$$

where η_I and η_E are the superelasticities.[7]

Alternatively, these expressions can be written as:

$$\frac{t_I}{k_I + t_I} = \frac{q_I - k_I}{q_I} = \frac{\lambda}{1 + \lambda}\frac{1}{\varepsilon_I} - \frac{t_E}{q_I}\frac{(\partial y_E/\partial q_I)}{(\partial y_I/\partial q_I)}, \tag{14.7}$$

$$\frac{t_E}{k_E + t_E} = \frac{q_E - k_E}{q_E} = \frac{\lambda}{1 + \lambda}\frac{1}{\varepsilon_E} - \frac{t_I}{q_E}\frac{(\partial y_I/\partial q_E)}{(\partial y_E/\partial q_E)}, \tag{14.8}$$

where ε_i is the absolute value of demand elasticity for y_i $(i = I, E)$ while $(\partial y_E/\partial q_I)/(\partial y_I/\partial q_I)$ and $(\partial y_I/\partial q_E)/(\partial y_E/\partial q_E)$ are the displacement ratios (Armstrong, 2001; De Donder, 2006).

To understand the implication of these expressions, we can think about $F_x - (p - c_x)x(p)$ as the net cost of USO to finance and consider:

$$K_I = t_I y_I(k_I + t_I, k_E + t_E),$$
$$K_E = t_E y_E(k_I + t_I, k_E + t_E),$$

as the contributions of the two operators to the USO fund. Expressions (14.7) and (14.8) show that we can expect $t_E > 0$, so that it is effectively optimal to make the entrant's customers contribute to the financing of the USO cost. In other words, the special case considered in the previous subsection (where $t_E = 0$ was imposed) is effectively not optimal. Furthermore, we can expect the contributions to differ between operators both in per unit terms ($t_E \neq t_I$) and relative to their respective prices ($t_E/q_E \neq t_I/q_I$).

Observe that we have specified t_E and t_I as specific, or per unit, taxes, as opposed to *ad valorem* taxes. For the problem under investigation, this is of no relevance. As a matter of fact, the left-hand-sides of equations (14.5) and (14.6) indicate the optimal tax *rates*; therefore, imposing a per unit tax of t_I or an *ad valorem* tax of $t_I/(k_I + t_I)$ is perfectly equivalent.

Note that there is no tax on single-piece mail. To be more precise, a tax on x would increase the cost of USO; consequently, it would have to be added and deducted in (14.4) and thus would have no impact. This means that, for a given cost of USO to finance, there should be no tax on single-piece mail.[8]

While this solution is (second-best) optimal, it may not be feasible in practice in particular for political economy reasons. In practice, the compensation fund is more likely to be financed by a uniform tax on all products (x included). This is the financing scheme often used in the telecommunications sector (in particular in France) and regulators may be tempted to transpose it to the postal sector.

4 UNIFORM COMPENSATION FUND

A uniform compensation fund differs from the second-best policy in two crucial ways. First, the same tax applies to all operators. Second, it affects all products including those that are subject to a USO (namely single-piece mail in our setting). In the telecommunications sector, this tax is typically levied on an *ad valorem* basis: a uniform rate is applied to the operators' revenue. However, this is not the only conceivable design. A per unit tax could be used as an alternative. We shall now study the properties of both of these tax schemes. Interestingly, it turns out that when the tax is uniform, *ad valorem* and per unit taxes are no longer equivalent. The question that then arises is that of which of the two tax schedules is more appropriate to finance the USO fund.

Let t denote the per unit tax, while the turnover tax rate is given by τ.[9] The revenue to be collected is denoted $\overline{R}$. Since the fund is used to cover the cost of USO, we set:

$$\overline{R} = F_x - (p - c_x)x(p). \tag{14.9}$$

Equilibrium with the Per Unit Tax

To determine the equilibrium, we use the property that the entrant prices at marginal cost. The USP's price, on the other hand, is given by the break-even constraint, taking into account the fact that the USP will be paid the specified amount $\overline{R}$ from the compensation fund. Hence, for a given level of t and of $\overline{R}$, the levels of q_I and q_E (the consumer prices) are determined by

$$q_E = k_E + t, \tag{14.10}$$

$$(p - c_x - t)x(p) + (q_I - k_I - t)y_I(q_I, q_E) - F_x + \overline{R} = 0. \tag{14.11}$$

Moreover, with $\overline{R} = F_x - (p - c_x)x(p)$, equation (14.11) reduces to:

$$(q_I - k_I - t)y_I(q_I, q_E) - tx(p) = 0. \tag{14.12}$$

Equations (14.10) and (14.12) then determine the equilibrium prices q_I and q_E for a given level of t.

In order to determine the level of t, we have to impose that the amount of revenue collected, which is given by:

$$R_t = t[x(p) + y_I(q_I, q_E) + y_E(q_I, q_E)], \tag{14.13}$$

is equal to the amount that has been promised to the USP, namely that:

$$R_t = \overline{R} = F_x - (p - c_x)x(p).$$

Equilibrium with *Ad Valorem* Tax

We proceed exactly as in the previous subsection. For a given level of τ and of $\overline{R}$, the equilibrium levels of q_I and q_E are determined by:

$$q_E = \frac{k_E}{1 - \tau} \tag{14.14}$$

$$[p(1 - \tau) - c_x]x(p) + [q_I(1 - \tau) - k_I]y_I(q_I, q_E) - F_x + \overline{R} = 0, \tag{14.15}$$

and the revenue collected is:

$$R_\tau = \tau px(p) + q_I y_I(q_I, q_E) + q_E y_E(q_I, q_E). \tag{14.16}$$

Substituting for the tax revenue required from (14.9), we can once again rewrite equation (14.15) as:

$$[q_I(1 - \tau) - k_I]y_I(q_I, q_E) - \tau px(p) = 0, \tag{14.17}$$

and the implied levels of prices (q_I, q_E) and the tax rate τ are obtained by solving the system of equations (14.14), (14.17) and (14.16) after setting $\overline{R} = F_x - (p - c_x)x(p)$ in the latter equation.

Observe that, in either case (per unit or *ad valorem* tax), a solution may not exist. That is, we may be in a situation where there is no tax level for which the cost of USO can be financed and where the USP is able to break even.

Per Unit Versus *Ad Valorem* Tax

Before comparing the per unit and *ad valorem* solutions, we would like to take a step back and compare the compensation fund approach to the second-best scenario. As we have explained at the beginning of this section, a uniform compensation fund differs from the second-best approach in that the same tax is applied to both operators and to both USP's products. To compare the two allocations, it would be worthwhile to try to disentangle the impact of the two additional constraints as one moves from second-best to uniform compensation fund: on the one hand, the constraint that both UPS's products are taxed, and on the other hand, the constraint that the tax should be the same for both operators. We contend that the imposition of a compensation fund financed by taxing all postal products (that is, including single-piece mail) is not an obstacle to reaching the second-best allocation, provided that tax rates be differentiated across operators. In other words, it is the constraint that taxes be the same for both operators that explains why allocations corresponding to Section 3 ('Second-best solution') and 4 ('Equilibrium with the per unit tax' and 'Equilibrium with *ad valorem* tax') differ from one another.

To prove our point, we start with a compensation fund financed with differentiated per unit taxes for the USP and for the entrant. Let us denote by t_E the tax paid by the entrant, and t_I the tax paid by the USP (on both single-piece and bulk mail). Except that t_I may differ from t_E, the setting we consider corresponds to the one depicted in Section 3 above. We now show that the second-best allocation can be obtained in this setting. We set q_I and t_E at their second-best levels (those determined in Section 3). The tax t_E determines the entrant's bulk mail price, and the single-piece price p is by assumption set exogenously. We then obtain exactly the same allocation as in the SB scenario. We have one more variable to set (the value of t_I) and one more equation to satisfy: the amount of tax proceeds collected must equal the cost of the USO:

$$\begin{aligned}\overline{R} &= F_x - (p - c_x)x(p) \\ &= t_I[x(p) + y_I(q_I, q_E)] + t_E y_E(q_I, q_E).\end{aligned}$$

Setting t_I at the level that satisfies this budget balance equation then allows us to obtain the second-best allocation with a (non-uniform) compensation fund. The same argument can be made in the case of an *ad valorem* tax. It is thus the requirement of uniform taxation that explains the difference between a uniform compensation fund and second-best results.

In the previous subsections, we have provided a characterization of the solutions under a per unit and under an *ad valorem* tax, respectively. However, at this level of generality, we can only derive implicit expressions (and not a closed-form solution). The two relevant comparisons pertain to the existence of a solution, on the one hand, and the respective levels of welfare, on the other. Observe that existence is not merely a technical issue here, but that it tells us whether the system allows the USP to break even.

Since the uniform compensation fund implies a tax base that includes the universal service product, one can presume this mechanism to 'overtax the USP' (compared to the second-best solution) and to imply a bulk mail price for the entrant that is too low. Consequently, one can expect the level of welfare to be higher for the system which imposes the lower burden on the USP and the higher price for the entrant. A very rough intuitive argument would suggest that this is the case for the per unit tax. This is because one can expect the entrant's bulk mail prices to be below those of the USP so that the USP's share in total market turnover is larger than its share in total volume.

To shed more light on this comparison and to (in)validate these intuitive arguments, we now turn to numerical simulations.

5 NUMERICAL ILLUSTRATION

The simulations are based on a 'calibrated' version of our model. Calibrations are rather rough and merely intended to achieve a 'plausible' range of parameter values. Consequently, one should think about the simulations mainly as an illustration.

Calibration

We use the following functional forms and assumptions to calibrate the model. First, utility functions $u(x)$ and $v(y_I, y_E)$ are quadratic functions, so that demand functions $x(q)$, $y_I(q_I, q_E)$ and $y_E(q_I, q_E)$ are linear in prices. Second, the USP's (marginal) cost parameters are given by $c_x = 0.66$ and $k_I = 0.24$. The hypothetical scenario used to calibrate satisfies the following properties. We assume that the USP has a monopoly for both single-piece and bulk mail and that at current prices ($p = 0.7, q_I = p/2 = 0.35$), we have $x(p) = y_I(q_I)$. Total (variable and fixed) costs at these prices are 10 billion and the USP breaks even globally. Finally, the direct price elasticity of demand is -0.4 for single-piece and -0.8 for bulk mail.

Solving for all these constraints, we obtain the following results:

$$\begin{aligned} F_x &= 1.429 \text{ billion (that is, 14\% of total costs)}, \\ x(p) &= 13{,}333 - 5{,}442p, \\ y_I(q_I) &= 17{,}143 - 21{,}769q_I, \\ x(0.7) &= y_I(0.35) = 9.524 \text{ billion pieces.} \end{aligned}$$

Introducing the entrant, we make the following three assumptions. First, the displacement ratio is given by:

$$-\frac{(\partial y_E/\partial q_I)}{(\partial y_I/\partial q_I)} = -\frac{(\partial y_I/\partial q_E)}{(\partial y_E/\partial q_E)} = 0.75.$$

Second, the market share of the entrant is 10 per cent if it is posting the same price as the USP; it is 50 percent if the entrant's prices are 20 percent below those of the USP.

Finally, the entrant's marginal cost is given by $k_E = 0.28$. Solving for all these constraints, we obtain the demand functions under competition:

$$y_I(q_I, q_E) = 12{,}224 + 47{,}843q_E - 57{,}651q_I,$$
$$y_E(q_I, q_E) = 6{,}559 - 63{,}791q_E + 47{,}843q_I.$$

Results

Numerical results are summarized in Table 14.1. Column 1 reports results obtained under the hypothetical monopoly situation used in the first stage of the calibration detailed above. USP's prices are set exogenously at 0.7 for single-piece mail and 0.35 for bulk mail. At those prices, there are as many units of bulk mail sold as of single-piece mail (9.5 billion items of each). The net consumer surplus at those prices is given by $u(x) - px$ = €8.3 billion for single-piece mail and $v(y_I, 0) - q_I y_I$ = €2.1 billion for bulk mail. As the price of single-piece mail is set above its marginal cost (0.66), the cost of USO ($F_x - (p - c_x)x(p)$) is, at €1.05 billion, lower than the €1.4 billion of the fixed cost F_x. However, the mark-up on single-piece mail (€381 million) is insufficient to cover F_x. By assumption, the USP breaks even with those prices under monopoly. This means that the cost of USO is financed thanks to the margin generated by selling bulk mail. Total welfare is then composed exclusively of net consumer surplus and totals €10.4 billion.

The single-piece mail price is set exogenously throughout the analysis, so that single-piece mail quantities, net surplus from the consumption of this good and cost of USO are all the same under all scenarios. Column 2 reports results when the bulk mail market is opened to competition, with the USP keeping its bulk mail price at 0.35 while the entrant prices at marginal cost. In that case, the entrant's price is 20 percent lower than the USP's price, which allows the entrant to capture one-half of the bulk mail market. Total bulk mail volumes increase (compared to the monopoly situation), and so does the net consumer surplus. The entry of competitors on the bulk mail market prevents the USP from breaking even: the margin made by selling bulk mail is insufficient to cover the cost of USO generated by single-piece mail, and the USP makes a €449 million loss. Total welfare (the unweighted sum of net consumer surplus and of profits) is lower than under monopoly. The measure of welfare further deteriorates if we assume that the USP loss is financed by a transfer from the government, with a (marginal) cost of public fund of 1.3 – this result is reported in the last row of Table 14.1.

We now move to the various scenarios studied analytically above. Column 3 reports the constrained first-best (CFB) outcome, where the USP prices bulk mail at its marginal cost of 0.24. The USP then captures nearly 90 percent of the bulk mail market, and net consumer surplus increases very significantly (compared to column 2). As the USP makes no margin by selling bulk mail, its loss is equal to the cost of USO (the part of its fixed costs not covered by any margin made on selling single-piece mail). Total unweighted welfare is, of course, higher than with the calibrated prices under competition, but also higher than under monopoly. On the other hand, with a 1.3 cost of public funds, weighted welfare is lower than under monopoly.

Results with no financing mechanism are reported in column 4. With our calibration assumptions, there is no value of q_I that allows the USP to break even. Consequently, there is no way to finance the cost of USO in the absence of a supplementary financing

Table 14.1 Results with original calibration

		Calibration		CFB	NF	SB	Uniform compensation fund	
		Monopoly (1)	Competition (2)	(3)	(4)	$t_I = 0.11$, $t_E = 0.08$ (5)	Per unit $t = 0.054$ (6)	*Ad valorem* $\tau = 10.3\%$ (7)
Single-piece mail								
	p	0.7	0.7	0.7	0.7	0.7	0.7	0.7
	x	9,524	9,524	9,524	9,524	9,524	9,524	9,524
	Net consumer surplus	8,333	8,333	8,333	8,333	8,333	8,333	8,333
	Cost of USO	1,048	1,048	1,048	1,048	1,048	1,048	1,048
Bulk mail								
USP	q_I	0.35	0.35	0.24	0.34	0.35	0.37	0.36
	y_I	9,524	5,442	11,784	5,892	9,417	7,032	6,275
Entrant	q_E	–	0.28	0.28	0.28	0.36	0.33	0.31
	y_E	–	5,442	179	5,069	143	2,821	3,978
	Net consumer surplus	2,083	2,315	3,263	2,360	2,084	1,984	2,093
Contributions								
USP	K_I					1,035	895	766
Entrant	K_E					13	153	129
USP profit		0	−449	−1048	−445	0	0	−153
Welfare	Unweighted	10,417	10,200	10,549	10,248	10,417	10,318	10,273
	Weighted	10,417	10,065	10,234	10,114	10,417	10,318	10,227

Note: Prices are in euros, quantities in million items and profit, consumer surpluses and welfare in million euros.

mechanism. We report in Table 14.1 the value of q_I that minimizes the USP loss. It happens that this value is very close to the one picked to calibrate the model. Results are then close to the ones reported in column 2.

We then move to the second-best results (column 5). The (Ramsey) optimal values of the (per unit) tax rates are 0.11 for USP's bulk mail and 0.08 for the entrant's bulk mail (recall that, in this scenario, it makes no sense to tax the single-piece good). Observe that the gap between the operators' unit taxes is, at 0.03, nearly as big (in absolute value) but of opposite sign to the gap between the operators' marginal cost (0.04). Hence, the entrant's consumer price is very slightly higher than the USP's consumer price for bulk mail, with the consequence that the USP captures nearly all the bulk mail market. This scenario is, by definition, the one that generates the highest (weighted or not) welfare level when the USP breaks even under competition. This level is (by chance) very close to the welfare level obtained under monopoly with our calibration prices. Under this scenario, the contribution of the USP to the financing of the cost of the USO is $K_I = t_I y_I(k_I + t_I, k_E + t_E) =$ €1,035 million, with the entrant contributing the remaining $K_E = t_E y_E(k_I + t_I, k_E + t_E) =$ €13 million. With a very small slice of the bulk mail market, it is not surprising that the entrant contributes significantly less than the USP.

Columns 6 and 7 in Table 14.1 report results obtained with the uniform compensation fund. Column 6 focuses on the case where both operators pay the same per unit tax on all their postal products. The tax that allows the USP to break even (that is, such that the operating loss is exactly compensated by the transfer from the compensation fund) is slightly above 5 cents. The USP has to increase its (consumer) bulk mail price to 0.37 while the entrant posts a relatively low 0.33 price. Net consumer surplus is lower than under the second-best solution, and so is total welfare.

Recall that the uniform compensation fund differs from the second-best solution in two ways: first, there is a unique tax applied to the entrant and to the USP and, second, this tax is also paid on the single-piece mail product. As argued above, a non-uniform compensation fund allows to attain the second-best allocation. With our calibration assumptions, this would be the case with $t_E = 0.08$ (the same tax as in the SB column) and $t_I = 0.05$. The USP tax is lower than in the SB scenario because the tax is now paid on single-piece mail as well. Observe that it is also lower than the entrant's tax t_E (but keep in mind that the USP contribution is given by the difference between bulk mail consumer price and marginal cost, and not only by the tax rate t_I).

When we move to a uniform compensation fund, the tax rate that is imposed on both the USP and the entrant is 0.054. Compared to the second-best scenario, the entrant's tax is then lower, and so is its price. Note that we cannot infer from this that the entrant's contribution to the cost of USO is lower, since this contribution is the product of the (lower) tax by the entrant's quantity, which is larger since a lower tax translates into a lower price. Given our calibration assumptions, the entrant's contribution increases to $K_E =$ €153 million (compared to the second-best scenario) – that is, the entrant's contribution increases when the tax is restricted to be the same for both operators, although the per unit tax is lower. Finally, net consumer surplus and total welfare in the uniform compensation case are of course lower than their second-best levels.

Column 7 of Table 14.1 reports results when the uniform compensation fund is financed with a turnover tax. With our calibration assumptions, no value of the turnover tax rate allows the USP to break even (when the transfer from the compensation fund is included). As in the NF case, we have reported results corresponding to the minimization of the USP loss. The USP's contribution to the cost of USO is €766 million while the entrant's contribution is €129 million. This is not enough to cover the full cost of USO, and the shortfall materializes as a €153 million loss for the USP. In that case, total (unweighted) welfare is lower than in any other scenario with taxation.

To sum up, in this example a uniform per unit tax dominates the uniform *ad valorem* tax. Furthermore the example confirms the intuition provided at the end of Section 4. The per unit tax imposes a lower burden on the USP and yields a bulk mail price for the entrant that is higher (and thus closer to the second-best level) than under an *ad valorem* tax.

The result that there is no uniform sales tax that allows the USP to break even has proved very robust to modifications in the calibration assumptions. One way to move away from this impossibility consists in assuming that the entrant offers a bulk mail product of higher quality than the USP. To study this case, we modify our original calibration in two dimensions: we assume that the entrant's marginal cost is higher (0.325 rather than 0.28), but that this larger cost allows the entrant to propose a good of a higher quality, which translates into higher market shares for the entrant (25 percent in the case where $q_I = q_E$, rather than 10 percent originally). Results with this new calibration are reported in Table 14.2.

We shall focus only on columns 6 and 7. There is now a uniform turnover tax that allows the USP to break even. The entrant contributes more to the cost of USO with a turnover tax (K_E= €119 million) than with a per unit tax (K_E= €85 million) or than in the second-best allocation (K_E= €10 million). Observe that net consumer surplus (and hence total welfare) is larger with a per unit tax than with an *ad valorem* tax.

To sum up, the per unit tax continues to dominate. Interestingly, though, the intuition behind the result is more complex in this case. It continues to be true that the entrant's bulk mail price is lower (and further away from the second best) under the *ad valorem* tax than under the per unit tax and this explains the welfare comparison. However, the sharing of the global burden is no longer the one conjectured at the end of Section 4. The entrant does effectively have a lower price under the *ad valorem* tax. However, this now implies such a dramatic increase in demand that its overall contribution is now larger than under the per unit tax! As far as the welfare impact is concerned, the overall burden is, however, not crucial here (recall that we are in the case where the USP does break even in all cases). What determines welfare is the price structure and welfare under per unit taxes is higher because it yields prices that are closer to the second-best solution than the prices under the *ad valorem* tax.

6 CONCLUSION

In this chapter, we have studied the design of the financing mechanism associated with the USO using a model with two operators, the USP and an entrant and two postal products, single-piece and bulk mail. The single-piece product is supplied solely by the USP at a regulated rate. The bulk mail market is competitive. We have derived the optimal (second-best) solution for the financing of the USO. It implies an implicit or explicit tax on all bulk mail consumers at a rate which differs between operators; the tax can be levied

Table 14.2 Results with modified calibration

		Calibration		CFB	NF	SB	Uniform compensation fund	
		Monopoly (1)	Competition (2)	(3)	(4)	$t_I = 0.11$, $t_E = 0.08$ (5)	Per unit $t = 0.054$ (6)	*Ad valorem* $\tau = 10.2\%$ (7)
Single-piece mail								
	p	0.7	0.7	0.7	0.7	0.7	0.7	0.7
	x	9,524	9,524	9,524	9,524	9,524	9,524	9,524
	Net consumer surplus	8,333	8,333	8,333	8,333	8,333	8,333	8,333
	Cost of USO	1,048	1,048	1,048	1,048	1,048	1,048	1,048
Bulk mail								
USP	q_I	0.35	0.35	0.24	0.37	0.35	0.36	0.39
	y_I	9,524	6,842	11,802	5,900	9,431	8,191	6,300
Entrant	q_E	–	0.325	0.325	0.325	0.41	0.38	0.36
	y_E	–	3,576	155	4,225	124	1,558	3,211
	Net consumer surplus	2,083	2,238	3,263	2,105	2,084	2,041	2,004
Contributions								
USP	K_I					1,037	963	929
Entrant	K_E					11	85	119
USP profit		0	−295	−1048	−275	0	0	0
Welfare	Unweighted	10,417	10,276	10,549	10,163	10,417	10,375	10,337
	Weighted	10,417	10,187	10,234	10,080	10,417	10,375	10,337

Note: Prices are in euros, quantities in million items and profit, consumer surpluses and welfare in million euros.

on either an *ad valorem* (turnover tax) or a per unit basis. Universal service products on the other hand are not taxed. We have also shown that the market equilibrium with no explicit financing mechanism for the cost of USO is inefficient (because only the customers of the USP contribute) and may imply a deficit for the USP.

Then we have turned to the study of a uniform compensation fund. This issue is important because the second-best solution may not be feasible in practice, in particular for political economy reasons. In reality, the compensation fund is more likely to be financed by a uniform tax on all products and all operators. In the telecommunications sector, this tax is typically levied on an *ad valorem* basis: a uniform rate is applied to the operators' turnover. However, this is not the only conceivable design. A per unit tax could be used as an alternative. We have studied the properties of both of these tax schemes. Interestingly, it has turned out that when the tax is uniform, *ad valorem* and per unit taxes are no longer equivalent. We have conjectured that the per unit tax dominates under plausible assumptions in the postal sector. Our argument was based on the specific value distribution in the postal sector, which differs from those typically observed in other sectors. On the one hand the more contestable market (bulk mail) is also the one with the lower prices and the higher mark-up. On the other hand, the market with the higher prices and the higher gross revenue is also the one with the lower (and effectively negative) mark-ups. Since the uniform compensation fund implies a tax base that includes the universal service product, we can expect this mechanism to 'overtax the USP' (compared to the second-best solution) and to imply a bulk mail price for the entrant that is too low. Consequently, the level of welfare should be higher for the system that imposes the lower burden on the USP and the higher price for the entrant. Our intuitive arguments have suggested that this is the case for the per unit tax. This is because one can expect the entrant's bulk mail prices to be below those of the USP so that the USP's share in total market turnover is larger than its share in total volume. We have then proceeded to numerical illustrations which have confirmed these results. Specifically, it has turned out that both the level of welfare is higher and the likelihood that the USP is able to break even is larger under the per unit tax than under the *ad valorem* tax.[10]

NOTES

1. The determination of access charges and the issue of (in)efficient bypass in network industries have been extensively studied in the literature; see, for example, Armstrong et al. (1996) and Laffont and Tirole (2000), Armstrong (2001, 2002). Applications to the postal sector include Crew and Kleindorfer (2002), Panzar (2002, 2004), Billette de Villemeur et al. (2003, 2004, 2005), Cazalda (2006), De Donder et al. (2005). For a survey, see De Donder (2006).
2. This assumption is verified in the numerical simulations presented in Section 5. It is necessary because our specification of demand does not account for substitution between single-piece and bulk mail. In reality it is clear that $q_I > p$ would imply zero demand for the USP's bulk mail.
3. Fixed costs are understood net of any (earmarked) transfer that the USP may receive to cover specific obligations.
4. This assumption is made to ensure some symmetry in the operators' cost conditions.
5. Formally, this solution is obtained by maximizing total surplus (consumer surplus plus profits) given by:

$$V(p, q_I, q_E) + (p - c_x)x + (q_I - k_I)y_I - F_x + (q_E - k_E)y_E$$

with respect to q_I and q_E.

6. See Laffont and Tirole (2000), Armstrong (2001), Crew and Kleindorfer (2002), Billette de Villemeur et al. (2005), De Donder (2006).
7. For a formal definition, see Billette de Villemeur et al. (2005).
8. This assumes that the USP faces a single (global) budget constraint and that no *ad hoc* restrictions stating that some costs have to be financed by specific products are imposed. Observe that these kind of additional constraints are not desirable from a normative perspective and would decrease welfare.
9. We model a turnover tax at rate τ (that is, a tax on the consumer price times volume), but we could have modeled an *ad valorem* tax working as the VAT (that is, a tax on the producer price times volumes). This is just a matter of notation and has no relevance for the results.
10. It is sometimes argued that an *ad valorem* tax is easier to levy because its tax base (revenue) is part of normal accounting reporting requirements. However, this implies determining the 'relevant' part of global revenues, that is to say the part which constitutes the tax base. Moreover, the argument that items would be difficult to count should be put into perspective: in France, for example, postal operators must communicate data on volume to the regulator and invoicing procedures for bulk mail are based on volume.

REFERENCES

Armstrong, M. (2001), 'Access pricing, bypass, and universal service', *American Economic Review, AEA Papers and Proceedings*, **91** (2), 297–301.

Armstrong, M. (2002), 'The theory of access pricing and interconnection', in M.E. Cave, S.K. Majumdar and I. Vogelsang (eds), *Handbook of Telecommunication*, vol. 1, Amsterdam and New York: North-Holland, pp. 295–386.

Armstrong, M., C. Doyle and J. Vickers (1996), 'The access pricing problem: a synthesis', *Journal of Industrial Economics*, **44**, 131–50.

Billette de Villemeur, E., H. Cremer, B. Roy and J. Toledano (2003a), 'Optimal pricing and global price-cap in the postal sector', *Journal of Regulatory Economics*, **24**, 49–62.

Billette de Villemeur, E., H. Cremer, B. Roy and J. Toledano (2003b), 'Access and (non-)uniform pricing in the postal sector', in M.A. Crew and P.R. Kleindorfer (eds), *Competitive Transformation of the Postal and Delivery Sector*, Boston, MA : Kluwer Academic, pp. 43–68.

Billette de Villemeur, E., H. Cremer, B. Roy and J. Toledano (2004), 'Worksharing, pricing and competition in the postal sector', in M.A. Crew and P.R. Kleindorfer (eds), *Regulatory and Economic Challenges in the Postal and Delivery Sector*, Boston, MA : Kluwer Academic Publishers, pp. 139–62.

Cazalda, J. (2006), 'Worksharing and access discounts in the postal sector with asymmetric information', *Journal of Regulatory Economics*, **29** (1), pp. 69–102.

Crew, M.A and P.R. Kleindorfer (2002), 'Balancing access and the Universal Service Obligation', in M.A. Crew and P.R. Kleindorfer (eds), *Postal and Delivery Services: Delivering on Competition*, Boston, MA: Kluwer Academic, pp. 3–32.

De Donder, P. (2006), 'Access pricing in the postal sector: theory and simulations', *Review of Industrial Organisation*, **28**, 307–26.

De Donder P., H. Cremer and F. Rodriguez (2005), 'Access pricing in the postal sector: results from a model with bypass and customer direct access', in M.A. Crew and P.R. Kleindorfer (eds), *Regulatory and Economics Challenges in the Postal and Delivery Sector*, Boston, MA: Kluwer Academic, pp. 163–88.

Laffont, J.-J. and J. Tirole (2000), *Competition in Telecommunications*, Cambridge, MA: MIT Press.

Panzar, J. (2002), 'Reconciling competition, downstream access and universal service and universal service in postal markets', in M.A. Crew and P.R. Kleindorfer (eds), *Postal and Delivery Services: Delivering on Competition*, Boston, MA: Kluwer Academic, pp. 93–115.

Panzar, J. (2004), 'Combining liberalization and unbundling policies in postal markets', Northwestern University and University of Auckland, mimeo.

15. Cross-country comparisons of optimal mail delivery frequency

Claire Borsenberger, Denis Joram, Clément Magre and Bernard Roy*

1 INTRODUCTION

By 1 January 2011, most European countries will have fully liberalized their postal markets.[1] For the incumbents – the universal service providers (USPs) – this means the end of monopoly on letters weighing less than 50 grams. As the reserved area was the tool for financing the Universal Service Obligation (USO) until now, the full market opening (FMO) process puts high on the agenda the questions of calculating the cost of the USO and methods for financing it in a fully competitive environment.

To ensure the provision of universal services, Article 7.3 of the Third European Postal Directive (2008/6/EC) allows member states to finance the provision of universal services if it creates an unfair burden on the USP, by the following means: a public subsidy, or sharing mechanisms involving a compensation fund or a 'pay or play' mechanism.

The prerequisite to compensate the unfair burden is to estimate the net cost of USO. As explained in Boldron et al. (2009), the amount to be compensated, that is the need for financing, will depend on the net cost of USO but also on the financial situation of the USP, which depends on the competition intensity. So, the net cost of USO does not correspond exactly to the need for financing.

Currently the consensus methodology to calculate the net cost of USO in the postal sector is the profitability cost approach, defined in the postal sector by Cremer et al. (2000) and Panzar (2000), which consists of determining a counterfactual scenario in which the USP would not be subject to the USO and would maximize its profit. The net cost of USO is the difference in profits made under the USO and under the counterfactual scenario. The results make sense only if both situations (with and without USO) are considered in an FMO environment.

Inspired by economic theory, Annex 1 of the Postal Directive affirms the profitability cost approach, but has to deal with the practical impossibility of observing situations in competition for purposes of calculating USO net cost. It suggests computing the net cost for each individual element or attribute of the USO. Such an approach has already been implemented in several studies (see, for example, Copenhagen Economics, 2008; Frontier Economics, 2008; Postal Regulatory Commission, 2008). However, double-counting problems can arise (Jaag et al., 2009).

The goal of this chapter is to focus on one component of the USO – the delivery frequency constraint. It goes beyond Boldron et al. (2006), which calculates the costs the USP would save by delivering mail five times a week in urban areas and three times a week in rural areas instead of the actual process. In addition, it examines the loss of revenues due to a reduction in the delivery frequency. It extends the analysis to the 13 following countries: Belgium, Germany, Denmark, France, Italy, Spain, the United Kingdom, Finland, Sweden, the Netherlands, Ireland, Poland and the United States. Each country is broken into geographic areas, in which frequency of delivery becomes endogenous, with the possibility of choosing the delivery frequency in each area (from six to three times per week).

Section 2 presents the methodology used to determine the optimal delivery frequency zone by zone and to define what will be the counterfactual scenario. If there were no constraint on the delivery process (in terms of frequency, transit time, collection time and so on), the USP would adjust its processes in order to maximize its profit, given the demand reaction to quality and the delivery costs. Three cases of demand reaction are proposed. Section 3 presents the public data used to determine the optimal delivery frequency. The main results are presented in Section 4. Finally, Section 5 stresses the limits and drawbacks of this work and avenues for future research are drawn.

2 CALCULATING THE OPTIMAL DELIVERY FREQUENCY

Methodology to Assess the Optimal Delivery Frequency

To determine the optimal delivery frequency in each area of a country, the USP's profit earned in this area is assessed for each possible delivery frequency (down to three times a week, see below). The profit is equal to the difference between the revenues and the costs. The costs are broken down into two components: street delivery costs, and other costs.

The optimal delivery frequency in a given area is the one that maximizes the profit in this area, taking into account the costs saved and the loss of revenues. In other words, if the difference in profit resulting from the reduction of delivery frequency from six to five times per week is positive, the USP will choose not to deliver mail six times per week but five, and so on.

The change in profit in area *i* is equal to:

$$\Delta\Pi_i = p \times \Delta Volume_i - \Delta Street\ Delivery\ Cost_i - \Delta Other\ Variable\ Costs_i. \quad (15.1)$$

The following subsections describe the methodologies used to estimate, respectively, revenues and costs.

Definition of Counterfactual Scenarios Related to Mail Delivery Frequency Reduction

In the reference scenario (under the USO), the USP must deliver mail five or six times a week throughout the territory according to initial situation.[2] If there were no constraint on the delivery process (in terms of frequency, transit time, collection time and so on), the USP would adjust its processes to maximize its profit, given the demand elasticity to quality and the costs.

The extent of potential reduction of delivery frequency is restricted to three times a week. This minimal delivery frequency allows a 'priority mail' offer (D + 1/2 product) to

Table 15.1 Variability of demand scenarios (%)

Variability	Revenue loss with initially 6 deliveries per week			Revenue loss with initially 5 deliveries per week	
	6 to 5	6 to 4	6 to 3	5 to 4	5 to 3
Low	0	−1.0	−2.0	−1.0	−2.0
Medium	−1.0	−2.5	−5.0	−1.5	−4.0
High	−2.0	−5.0	−8.0	−3.0	−6.0

be maintained with a reasonable quality of service: by reducing the delivery frequency from six to three times a week, 50 percent of D + 1 items may still be delivered within a day. This is consistent with reasonable demand assumptions as described below.

It is assumed that the USP does not change the price of the postal products, and retains uniform pricing. Potential negative externalities between areas arising from a heterogeneous reduction of delivery frequency on the whole territory are ignored. Thus, mail demand in urban areas is assumed to be unaffected by the reduction in the delivery frequency in rural areas and conversely.

Depending on customers' preferences and perceptions of the usability of mail, the reduction in the frequency of mail delivery could affect primarily the priority letters or all postal products in the same way. However, a reduction in delivery frequency should have a negative impact on mail demand: if mail becomes more difficult to use or does not provide the service level required, customers might increasingly turn to non-mail alternatives (e-substitution, for example). The more drastic the reduction of frequency, the greater will be the loss of demand. This effect can be magnified as the loss of demand will be primarily the 'higher-price' items (urgent mail) as opposed to 'lower-price items' (non-urgent mail or direct mail).

In order to obtain a range of results as representative as possible, three scenarios of revenue loss (low-, medium- and high-variability scenarios) are considered – see Table 15.1.

The 'low-variability scenario' is characterized by a low sensibility of demand to the decrease in delivery frequency. In particular, in this scenario, the reduction from six to five deliveries per week has no impact on demand. Such an assumption could be justified from the case of countries where mail is currently delivered five times a week. If an additional delivery were to create additional demand and profit, operators in these countries would probably have chosen to deliver six times a week. A reduction to four deliveries per week (respectively, three) is assumed to result in a 1 percent (respectively, 2 percent) decrease of revenues. Since there is no gap in revenues between five or six deliveries per week, the same assumptions apply to countries with currently five deliveries per week.

In the 'medium-variability scenario', customers react to a decrease in delivery frequency by reducing their mail demand. In countries with currently five deliveries per week, the reduction of deliveries is lower than in countries with six deliveries. This is why the revenue losses are somewhat smaller.

Finally, the 'high-variability scenario' is based on the revenue loss assumptions made by the Postal Regulatory Commission in its 'Report on Universal Postal Service and the Postal Monopoly' (2008).

Assessment of Cost of Items

The costs are divided into two components: street delivery costs and other costs. The costs saved by a reduction in delivery frequency are primarily the fixed costs in the delivery process, but as the volumes decrease, some variable costs in all the processes can also be saved. In addition, demand transfers on the remaining delivery days create extra costs that need to be assessed. The following subsections describe how costs are modeled.

Assessment of street delivery costs

The technico-economic model (Roy, 1999) is used to compute the unit cost of street delivery for any specific geographic area,[3] using geometric models for calculating the physical length of the routes and implementing four possible modes of delivery (foot, bicycle, moped and car).[4]

To derive the cost of street delivery in a given area, some country-specific data are necessary: the quantity and weight of mail to be delivered per day of delivery; the surface area; the number of delivery points, assumed to be equal to the number of households; and the 'grouping index'. The grouping index is the ratio between the number of delivery points and the number of stop points. This index measures how 'vertical' the buildings are: the higher the grouping index, the greater the number of households per stop served. The grouping index is estimated by an econometric function of density, calibrated on French data (see Appendix 15A2).

In order to study more specifically the impact of demographic features and volumes on the cost of delivering mail five or six times a week throughout the territory, other parameters required to implement the Roy simulation tool are assumed to be the same across countries. These include: the average speeds of delivery by car, moped, bicycle or foot; the transportation mode costs; the structure of traffic by size (low-size, high-size and bulky items); the stop times; the hourly wage of postmen (assumed for consistency reason – see below – to be equal to the hourly wage in the American postal sector in 1999[5]).

In short, the street delivery process, and all costs of production factors (labor and all other costs) are assumed to be the same in all countries: differences in terms of 'home delivery' and permanent exemptions observed in some countries with difficult topography are not taken into account in this analysis. The key variables of interest in this study are only the volume to be delivered per day of delivery and the geographic and demographic characteristics of the areas in each country.

Assessment of variable costs of other processes (excluding street delivery)

Cohen et al. (2004) estimated the total cost of US Postal Service (USPS) activity in 1999 by the following function:[6]

$$\text{Total Cost} = 0.2089 \times \text{Volume} + 74.31 \times \text{Population}. \tag{15.2}$$

Cohen et al. furthermore argued that this function was a relatively good description of the costs of postal operators in many industrial countries in 1999. By knowing the total cost (Cohen et al.'s result) and the street delivery cost (Roy's model), the cost of the other processes in each country can be derived. Of course, more detailed models would

Table 15.2 Characteristics of the countries studied

Country	Number of deliveries per week	Volume (million items, 2006)	Population (2005)	Surface (km²)	Number of households (2006)	Number of NUTS areas	Average number of inhabitants per area
Belgium	5	3,000	10,478,600	30,529	4,436,000	43	243,688
Germany	6	17,600	82,435,200	357,028	39,189,000	429	192,157
Denmark	6	1,660	5,390,500	43,180	2,365,000	15	359,367
Spain	5	6,200	41,329,500	498,518	15,802,000	48	904,140
Finland	5	2,800	5,246,000	338,144	2,413,000	20	262,300
France	6	16,500	60,995,700	543,965	25,675,000	96	635,372
Ireland	5	800	4,159,200	69,797	1,400,000	8	519,900
Italy	6	6,800	58,127,000	293,953	23,567,000	106	548,368
Netherlands	6	5,400	15,680,400	40,836	7,155,000	40	392,010
Poland	5	1,800	38,204,600	314,035	12,769,000	45	848,991
Sweden	5	3,150	9,029,600	441,347	4,645,382	21	429,981
UK	6	21,000	60,228,700	243,370	25,932,000	133	452,847
USA	6	212,234	296,507,061	9,161,921	114,384,000	51	5,813,864

Sources: ECORYS for traffic, Eurostat for population, surface, number of households.

be appropriate for individual country studies, but the Cohen et al. approach will allow a rough and ready comparative assessment across countries, which is our purpose here.

To separate the variable part from the fixed one, the same reasoning as Cohen et al. is applied: the cost of the various processes of the postal activity can be estimated by a function of population and volume. To obtain the desired relationship, the cost of other processes was regressed on population and volume for each country, using ECORYS data for volume and Eurostat data for population (see Table 15.2). The following relationship is obtained from observations of the countries panel ($N = 13$):

$$\text{Other processes cost} = \underset{(0.002)}{0.153} \times \text{Volume} + \underset{(1.32)}{61.753} \times \text{Population} \qquad (15.3)$$

Standard errors appear in parentheses. Each parameter is statistically significant (the t-statistic associated with volume is equal to 75, the one associated with population to 46) and the adjusted R-squared is equal to 0.91. From (15.3), the variable unit costs of other processes (excluding street delivery) are derived.

Assessment of Revenues

Operators are assumed to break even initially, when they deliver mail five or six times a week based on the USO. Previous cost estimates provide an average 'equilibrium' price. Operators are assumed not to change their price despite the reduction in delivery frequency.

In case 1, the decrease in delivery frequency affects all items homogeneously. The change in revenue is then equal to the change in volume. In case 2, the reduction in delivery frequency affects first of all (higher-priced) 'priority items'. Therefore, for a given revenue loss, the volume decrease is proportionally less important than the one in the previous case.

According to public data on postal volumes and revenues differentiated by priority level (from French and Italian USPs), the average revenue from priority mail is about 1.3 times the average revenue from all mails.[7] This ratio is applied in simulations on priority letters to establish the case 2 results.

3 DESCRIPTION OF PUBLIC DATA USED

The relevance of this kind of approach lies in the possibility of dividing a country into relatively small areas. The US study is done at the federal state level.[8] In the European case, Eurostat established a Nomenclature of Territorial Units for Statistics (NUTS) to provide a single uniform breakdown of territorial units for the production of regional statistics for the European Union. The NUTS is a three-level hierarchical classification. Territorial units are defined in terms of the existing administrative units in the member states (see Table 15.2).

The size and the number of these NUTS differ widely between countries. They correspond to *arrondissements* in Belgium; *amtskommuner* in Denmark; *Kreise/kreisfreie Städte* in Germany; *départements* in France and so on. In Ireland, the territory is composed of seven units whereas there are 430 territorial units in Germany. Unfortunately, these public data do not make it possible to reflect correctly the topographic specificities of countries like Greece with its many islands. For these reasons, Greece was excluded from the panel of countries.

Public data on demographic (population and number of households) and geographic (surface) features of countries according to the NUTS classification come from the Eurostat website. Data are from 2005. Data on postal traffic come from ECORYS (2008). Because of missing data on distribution of mail traffic by NUTS 3, the number of mail items delivered in a territorial unit is assumed strictly proportionate to the number of inhabitants.[9]

4 PRINCIPAL RESULTS

Cost Assessments

Using the above data, unit costs of street delivery works were generated from Roy's (1999) technico-economic model and the unit costs of other processes from equation (15.3) above, obtained from Cohen et al.'s (2004) model. The results are shown in Table 15.3.

Optimal Delivery Frequency

Tables 15.4–6 present the optimal delivery frequency in terms of percentage of population impacted in each country for the three scenarios of demand loss considered crossed

Table 15.3 Cost assessment

Country	Average grouping index	Unit cost of street delivery work (Roy's model)	Unit cost of other processes (Cohen et al.'s model)	Total unit cost / average equilibrium price	Part of variable cost in other processes (%)
Belgium	1.16	0.08	0.39	0.47	41.6
Germany	1.11	0.12	0.44	0.56	34.7
Denmark	1.06	0.11	0.34	0.45	43.4
Spain	1.04	0.15	0.58	0.73	26.2
Finland	1.01	0.10	0.25	0.35	57.1
France	1.05	0.12	0.37	0.48	40.2
Ireland	1.03	0.13	0.46	0.60	32.4
Italy	1.09	0.17	0.67	0.84	22.6
Netherlands	1.18	0.08	0.35	0.42	46.2
Poland	1.06	0.28	1.51	1.79	10.5
Sweden	1.01	0.13	0.29	0.42	46.5
UK	1.12	0.07	0.35	0.42	46.5
USA	1.02	0.07	0.24	0.31	64.1

Table 15.4 Optimal delivery frequency for low demand variability scenario

	First case: all items impacted (% loss in revenue is equal to % loss in volume) % of population affected					Second case: most profitable items impacted (% loss in volume is less than % loss in revenue) % of population affected				
	6	5	4	3	(*)	6	5	4	3	(*)
France	–	6	–	94	3	–	6	–	94	3
Germany	–	–	–	100	3	–	–	–	100	3
Denmark	–	–	–	100	3	–	–	–	100	3
Italy	–	–	–	100	3	–	–	–	100	3
Netherlands	–	–	–	100	3	–	–	–	100	3
UK	–	–	–	100	3	–	–	–	100	3
USA	–	–	–	100	3	–	–	–	100	3
Belgium	na	–	–	100	3	na	–	–	100	3
Spain	na	–	–	100	3	na	–	–	100	3
Finland	na	–	–	100	3	na	–	–	100	3
Ireland	na	–	–	100	3	na	–	–	100	3
Poland	na	–	–	100	3	na	–	–	100	3
Sweden	na	–	–	100	3	na	–	–	100	3

Note: * Homogeneous optimal frequency.

Table 15.5 Optimal delivery frequency for medium demand variability scenario

	First case: all items impacted (% loss in revenue is equal to % loss in volume) % of population affected					Second case: most profitable items impacted (% loss in volume is less than % loss in revenue) % of population affected				
	6	5	4	3	(*)	6	5	4	3	(*)
France	6.0	4.5	–	89.4	3	6.0	4.5	–	89.4	3
Germany	–	5.6	15.5	78.9	3	–	5.8	19.1	75.1	3
Denmark	–	11.0	–	89.0	3	–	11.0	–	89.0	3
Italy	–	–	12.4	87.6	3	–	5.3	7.0	87.6	3
Netherlands	–	–	5.0	95.0	3	–	–	17.9	82.1	3
UK	–	7.0	23.2	69.8	3	4.9	16.4	15.2	63.5	3
USA	–	–	0.2	99.8	3	–	–	0.2	99.8	3
Belgium	na	9.7	–	90.3	3	na	9.9	–	90.1	3
Spain	na	–	–	100.0	3	na	–	–	100.0	3
Finland	na	–	–	100.0	3	na	–	–	100.0	3
Ireland	na	–	28.1	71.9	3	na	–	28.1	71.9	3
Poland	na	24.6	75.5	–	4	na	24.8	75.2	–	4
Sweden	na	–	–	100.0	3	na	–	–	100.0	3

Note: * Homogeneous optimal frequency.

Table 15.6 Optimal delivery frequency for high demand variability scenario

	First case: all items impacted (% loss in revenue is equal to % loss in volume) % of population affected					Second case: most profitable items impacted (% loss in volume is less than % loss in revenue) % of population affected				
	6	5	4	3	(*)	6	5	4	3	(*)
France	10.6	1.9	–	87.6	3	10.6	3.8	–	85.6	3
Germany	15.2	14.2	–	70.6	3	17.9	17.7	–	64.0	3
Denmark	11.0	11.5	–	77.5	3	11.0	11.5	–	77.5	3
Italy	11.9	49.9	2.7	35.4	5	12.4	62.3	3.7	21.7	5
Netherlands	5.0	13.9	–	81.1	3	5.0	40.8	–	54.3	3
UK	25.7	11.4	–	62.9	3	29.5	12.5	–	58.0	5
USA	0.2	–	–	99.8	3	0.2	10.5	–	89.3	3
Belgium	na	9.7	–	90.3	3	na	28.4	–	71.6	3
Spain	na	47.2	–	52.8	3	na	48.8	–	51.2	3
Finland	na	–	–	100.0	3	na	–	–	100.0	3
Ireland	na	28.1	–	71.9	3	na	28.1	–	71.9	3
Poland	na	100.0	–	–	5	na	100.0	–	–	5
Sweden	na	–	–	100.0	3	na	–	–	100.0	3

Note: * Homogeneous optimal frequency.

by the two cases for the ratio forgone revenue/traffic loss. Each cell gives the percentage of population for which mail is delivered six, five, four or three times a week. The homogeneous optimal frequency corresponds to the optimal uniform delivery frequency throughout the whole territory – that maximizing the profit under the constraint to maintain the same frequency everywhere for social or political reasons (such as territorial cohesion).

The first conclusion from these simulations is that the obligation to deliver mail throughout the whole territory five or six times a week is a real constraint for all countries, whatever the scenario, except Poland in the high-variability demand case. All other operators would reduce their delivery frequency on the main part of the territory if not everywhere. In particular, if, for political reasons, postal operators have to keep a uniform delivery frequency on the territory, the one that maximizes its profit is equal to three in all scenarios in France, Germany, Denmark, the Netherlands, the USA, Belgium, Spain, Finland, Ireland and Sweden; it is equal to three or five in Italy and in the UK according to the scenario considered and to three, four or five in Poland (in this last case, the legal obligation is not binding).

The second conclusion drawn from this work is that all things being equal, the potential cost savings from reducing frequency of deliveries are an increasing function of volume per capita. This explains why in Poland (47 items per inhabitant per year), the operator has fewer incentives to reduce the constrained delivery frequency. Indeed, when volumes per capita are very low, the percentage of variable costs (versus fixed costs) is much higher in the street delivery process than when the volume per capita is high. Thus, the fixed cost savings related to the suppression of one, two or three deliveries per week are counterbalanced by an increase in variable costs of street delivery costs due to the increase in mail volume in the remaining deliveries. In a low-volume economy, the increase in items to be delivered increases the number of stops. In a high-volume economy, the stops are part of the fixed costs. For a precise description of the phenomenon, see Cohen and Chu (1997) and Roy (2002).

The third salient fact of the simulations is consistent with theoretical intuition: the more sensible the demand for frequency and/or the more profitable the items lost, the less important the optimal delivery frequency reduction, since the revenue losses are too high to counterbalance the costs savings. In the low-variability scenario, all operators – except the French one – maximize their profit by delivering mail three times per week in the whole territory. In the high-variability scenario, only two operators (in Finland and Sweden) still maximize their profit with this minimalist delivery process.

The last main conclusion of this study is that all things being equal, the denser the area, the less a high delivery frequency represents an opportunity cost. This result comes from the fact that in very dense urban areas, when the traffic is important, the cost structure becomes more variable in percentage terms. The fixed costs are low (short distance between buildings, one stop for many letter boxes) and the high amount of mail creates a more variable costs economy, such that average costs and marginal costs are close to each other (see Roy, 2002). Reducing the frequency of delivery displaces mail to remaining deliveries, and the cost savings are low. A small reaction with regard to demand can easily offset these costs savings.

This result appears clearly in the high-variability scenario: operators (except in Sweden and Finland) maintain the legal delivery frequency in the densest areas (for example, Paris and surrounding departments in France; regions of Berlin, Munich and

Cologne, for example, in Germany; Naples and Milan in Italy; London, Liverpool and Southampton in the UK; Brussels in Belgium; Madrid and Barcelona in Spain). In these regions, the loss of revenue associated with a reduction of the frequency would be higher than the cost savings; in consequence, operators have incentives to deliver more frequently. In the rural areas of these countries, the optimal delivery frequency is lower (often equal to 3). In the least densely populated countries (Finland and Sweden), the optimal delivery frequency is the same (three times a week) throughout the territory.

Cross-comparison of the Net Cost of the Delivery Frequency Obligation

The obligation to deliver mail five or six times a week has a net cost summarized in Figures 15.1 and 15.2.

Expressed as a percentage of constrained revenue (the revenue earned under the legal delivery frequency constraint, equivalent to the total cost because of the break-even assumption), the (relative) net cost of this obligation varies between 0 percent in Poland in the high-variability scenario (since the legal constraint is not binding) to 7.6 percent in Sweden in the low-variability case.

The sensibility of the net cost to the assumptions of demand reaction appears clearly on the figures: the more sensitive the demand to a reduction in delivery frequency, the less important the net cost of the constraint in each country. Indeed a reduction in the delivery frequency leads to higher revenue losses, so lower net cost savings, when demand is highly elastic to frequency. Variation between cases 1 and 2 appears to be a second-order effect in simulations.

The differences observed between countries are explained by several factors: the traffic per capita, the average density and the initial frequency constraint.

Overall the relative net cost of the delivery obligation (in percentage of revenue) is higher in countries with a stronger constraint (six versus five times a week), with the notable exceptions of Sweden and Finland.

Sweden and Finland have a high relative net cost of the delivery obligation (the highest of the sample for Sweden) due to their very low density (20 inhabitants per km^2 in Sweden – there are only 278 inhabitants per km^2 in the densest populated region of Stockholm; 16 inhabitants per km^2 in Finland – there are 200 inhabitants per km^2 in the densest populated region, the Uusimaa) and their high level of volume per capita (534 items per capita in Finland, 349 in Sweden). These results should be regarded with caution for several reasons. First, the aggregation of demographic data by NUTS does not take account of the existence of empty areas, where there are few inhabitants and no postal deliveries. Second, the obligation to deliver mail five times a week is already relaxed in some areas. This is not taken into account in this model. Overall the relative net cost of the delivery obligation in Sweden and Finland should be lower than estimated.

Poland has the lowest relative net cost of the delivery obligation due to a postal activity which is not yet well developed. Overall, if the demand elasticity to frequency is relatively strong, the cost savings associated with the decrease in delivery frequency could be lower than the revenue loss in some areas. This is what happens in the densest regions in the medium-variability scenario and in the whole territory in the high-variability scenario.

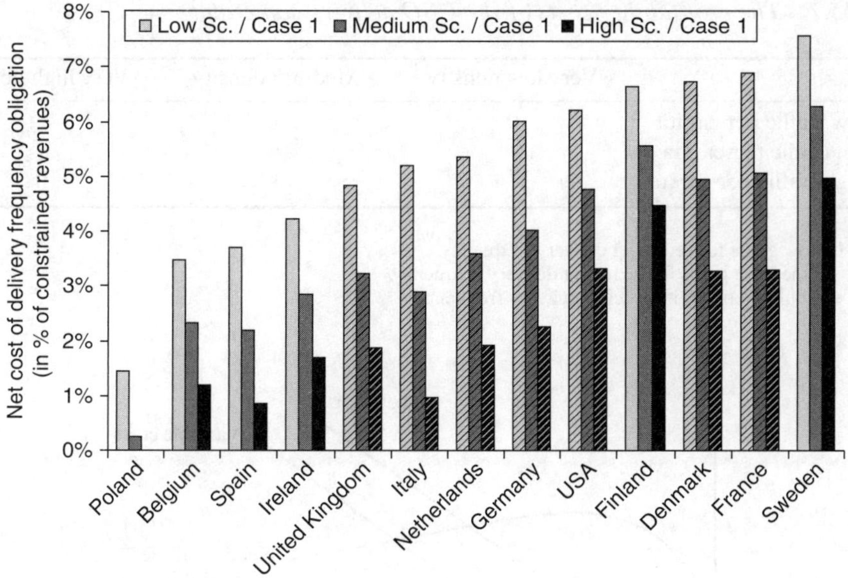

Note: Hatched columns refer to countries with six deliveries per week.

Figure 15.1 Net cost of the delivery frequency obligation in case 1

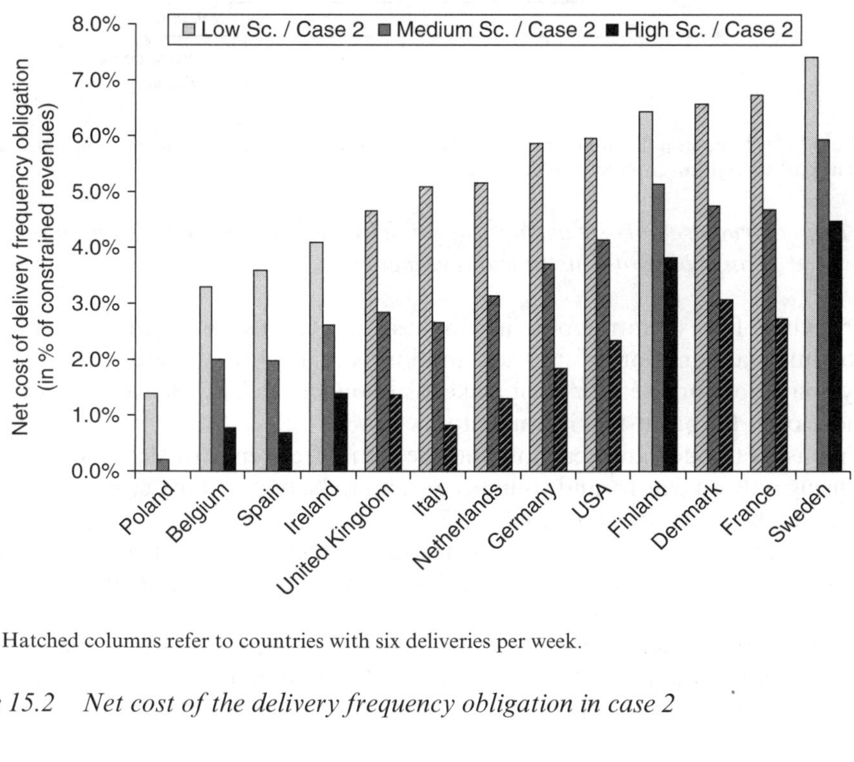

Note: Hatched columns refer to countries with six deliveries per week.

Figure 15.2 Net cost of the delivery frequency obligation in case 2

Table 15.7 The profitability costs of the USO delivery constraint

	Very low density	Medium density	Very high density
Very low traffic per capita	0	+	++
Medium traffic per capita	+	++	+
Very high traffic per capita	++	+	0

Notes: 0 : low gains for reducing delivery frequency.
+ : medium gains for reducing delivery frequency.
++: high gains for reducing delivery frequency.

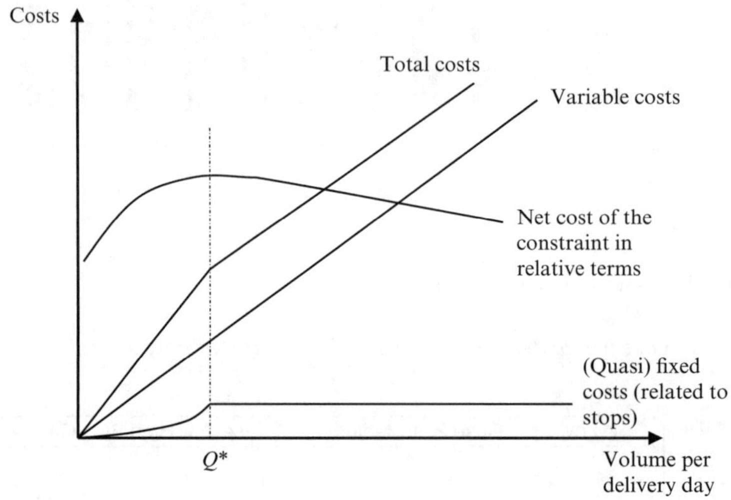

Note: For $Q > Q^*$, the stop function is saturated (no extra stop is required when mail volume increases). The part of fixed cost in total cost decreases.

Figure 15.3 Structure of costs and net cost of delivery frequency constraint in relative terms (in % of constrained revenues)

The ranking of the countries obtained in these simulations seems sensible to the break-even condition assumption. If this assumption is relaxed, the relative net cost of the delivery obligation for operators that make losses under the USO delivery constraint will be higher (lower for profit-making operators).

Putting aside the demand reaction and the initial frequency of delivery (five or six), and focusing only on density and volume per capita, the opportunity costs of the delivery frequency can be summarized in Table 15.7.

This result comes directly from the fixed/variable structure of costs of the street delivery: the gains in reducing the frequency of delivery are the highest when the cost structure of street delivery is the most fixed, and conversely the gains are lower when the cost structure is more variable (see Figure 15.3). The latter case happens with a combination of high traffic and high density (Paris, Stockholm, the Netherlands . . .), or very low traffic and low density (Italy, Poland).

5 CONCLUSIONS

As the results provided by the simulations are derived from a number of assumptions regarding how demographic and geographic drivers give rise to cost and profitability arising from changes in the delivery frequency obligation, care should be taken in interpreting them. Most importantly, this work has not relied on detailed country-specific models of PO costs, but rather on the very aggregate assessment of Cohen et al., which itself was based on 1999 data. Country specifics were accounted for in terms of delivery cost estimations, based on the Roy (1999) model. However, for this model simplifying assumptions were also made to allow cross-country comparisons, often relying on French data as a benchmark. Some general conclusions are, however, evident.

First, the obligations to deliver mail five or six times a week are a real constraint for all countries in all cases and scenarios (except Poland in the high-variability scenario): no operator maintains the initial delivery frequency throughout the whole territory. The relative net costs increase from 0.2 to 7.5 percent of the 'break-even revenue' according to the country and demand assumptions.

Gains in terms of costs come from the fact that the reduction in frequency delivery removes the fixed costs of the suppressed routes. The remaining routes absorb the remaining traffic. When the marginal costs are low compared to average costs, the gains are high, and conversely. A large difference between marginal and average costs occurs when density is low *and* traffic is sufficiently high, or when density is high *and* traffic is medium or low. Conversely, marginal cost is close to average cost when traffic per capita is so low that the structure of the route is still very variable (the stops are not saturated), or when the traffic is very high in dense areas (scale economies are exhausted).

The reaction of demand to a frequency reduction plays a crucial role: if the demand reaction is nil, any frequency reduction generates cost savings, even when marginal costs are close to average costs. If the demand reacts to a reduction in delivery frequency, the problem is to find the proper combination of the gains coming from fixed cost savings against the losses due to revenue reduction.

This work is a first attempt to understand better the USO cost drivers on the delivery frequency constraint, and allows, to some extent, country comparisons. Many imperfections and uncertainties still remain arising from the simplifying assumptions made to allow cross-country comparisons. Perhaps the most reasonable interpretation of these results is that they indicate the impact of demographic and postal density factors, which correspond to those observable in Europe and the USA, on the likely variation in profit-driven reductions in delivery frequency if uniformity of delivery frequency were not included in the USO. The variations observed, and the corresponding net cost of this element of the USO, are understandable in terms of traditional cost drivers underlying delivery costs, but the results are not obvious. In particular, the comparative exercise undertaken here provides important insights into the relative magnitude of the net cost of delivery frequency constraints on the USP under different geographic and demographic conditions. However, these results also underscore the need for further detailed analysis of this question in each country in order to assess the cost, value and demand impacts of constraints on delivery frequency. Furthermore, nothing can be deduced about the need for financing of USP: a high relative net cost does not imply an unfair burden that ought to be compensated.

NOTES

* The opinions expressed in this work are those of the authors and do not necessarily reflect the positions of Groupe La Poste.

1. Cyprus, Luxembourg, Latvia, Lithuania, Slovakia, the Czech Republic, Hungary, Romania, Malta, Poland and Greece may postpone the implementation of the Third European Directive until 31 December 2012.
2. Among the 13 countries included in our sample, only six European countries plus the United States have imposed a six-day per week delivery frequency throughout the whole territory: the USPs in France, Denmark, Italy, the United Kingdom, Germany, the Netherlands and the USA deliver mail six days a week. On the other hand, the USPs in Belgium, Spain, Poland, Finland, Ireland and Sweden deliver mail 'only' 5 days a week. The last four USPs enjoy some permanent exemption in remote areas that account for a quite large proportion of the population.
3. See D'Alcantara and Amerlynck (2006) for an application of this type of model to competitive entry and see Bernard et al. (2002) for a discussion of econometric and engineering approaches for comparing delivery costs in France and in the USA.
4. See Appendix 15A1.
5. \$18.21, equivalent to €17.42. Sources: Bureau of Labor Statistics, *Occupational Employment and Wage Estimate*, 1999; Banque de France, exchange rate of May 1999.
6. This estimate is based on the hourly wage of American postmen in 1999. This is why the wage was normalized at this level in the previous assessment of street delivery cost.
7. In Italy, in 2006, 829,217,000 priority mails generated €660 million whereas the total volume of mail (6.8 million items) generated €4 billion (source: Annual Report of Poste Italiane). In France, in 2007, a similar ratio is found using confidential data.
8. Further studies could be undertaken county by county.
9. According to Kolin and Smith (1999) and Berthelemy and Toledano (2000), mail is not distributed equally over the population. This leads to quite important variations of street delivery costs (see Bernard et al., 2002). But this simplification is mandatory in this type of cross-country comparison, as the data needed for improving mail distribution are not available.

REFERENCES

Bernard, S., R. Cohen, M. Robinson, B. Roy, J. Toledano, J. Waller and S. Xenakis (2002), 'Delivery cost heterogeneity and vulnerability to entry', in M.A. Crew and P.R. Kleindorfer (eds), *Postal and Delivery Services: Delivering on Competition*, Boston, MA: Kluwer Academic, pp. 169–84.

Berthelemy, F. and J. Toledano (2000), 'In France, mail goes where the money and businesses are', in M.A. Crew and P.R. Kleindorfer (eds), *Current Directions in Postal Reform*, Boston, MA: Kluwer Academic, pp. 133–48.

Boldron, F., C. Borsenberger, D. Joram, S. Lécou and B. Roy (2009), 'A dynamic and endogenous approach to financing the USO in a liberalized environment', in M.A. Crew and P.R. Kleindorfer (eds), *Progress in the Competitive Agenda in the Postal and Delivery Sector*, Cheltenham, UK and Northampton, MA, USA: Edward Elgar, pp. 67–82.

Boldron, F., D. Joram, L. Martin, B. Roy (2006), 'From the size of the box to the costs of universal service obligations: a cross-country comparison', in M.A. Crew and P.R Kleindorfer (eds), *Liberalization of the Postal and Delivery Sector*, Cheltenham, UK and Northampton, MA: Edward Elgar, pp. 37–52.

Cohen, R. and E. Chu (1997), 'A measure of scale economies for postal systems', in M.A. Crew and P.R. Kleindorfer (eds), *Managing Change in the Postal Delivery Industries*, Boston, MA: Kluwer Academic, pp. 115–32.

Cohen R.H., M. Robinson, G. Scarfiglieri, R. Sheehy, V. Visco Comandini, J. Waller and S. Xenakis (2004), 'The role of scale economies in the cost behavior of posts', paper presented at the 8th WIK Seminar on 'Regulating Postal Markets – Harmonised Versus Country Specific Approaches', Wissenschaftliches Institut für Infrastruktur und Kommunikationsdienste, 16–18 February, Koenigswinter, Germany.

Copenhagen Economics (2008), 'What is the cost of Post Danmark's Universal Service Obligation?', Report for the Danish Chamber of Commerce, Copenhagen, 11 March.

Cremer, H., A. Grimaud and J.-J. Laffont (2000), 'The cost of universal service in the postal sector', in M.A. Crew and P.R. Kleindorfer (eds), *Current Directions in Postal Reform*, Boston, MA: Kluwer Academic, pp. 47–68.

D'Alcantara, G. and B. Amerlynck (2006), 'Profitability of the universal service postal provider under entry with economies of scale in collection and delivery', in M.A. Crew and P.R. Kleindorfer (eds), *Progress Toward Liberalization of the Postal and Delivery Sector*, New York: Springer Science+Business Media, Inc., pp. 39–58.

Directive 2008/6/CE of 20 February 2008, amending Directive 97/67/CE with regard to the full accomplishment of the internal market of Community postal services.

ECORYS (2008), 'Main Developments in the Postal Sector (2006–2008): Countries' Sheet Summaries', Report for the European Commission, DG Internal Market and Services, 11 September.

Frontier Economics (2008), 'Net Costs of Element of the Universal Service', A report prepared for Postcomm, May.

Jaag, C., M. Koller and U. Trinkner (2009), 'Calculating the cost of the Universal Service Obligation: the need for a global approach', in M.A. Crew and P.R. Kleindorfer (eds), *Progress in the Competitive Agenda in the Postal and Delivery Sector*, Cheltenham, UK and Northampton, MA, USA: Edward Elgar, pp. 113–27.

Kolin, M. and E. Smith (1999), 'Mail goes where the money is: a study of rural mail delivery in US', in M.A. Crew and P.R. Kleindorfer (eds), *Emerging Competition in Postal and Delivery Services*, Kluwer Academic, pp. 159–80.

Panzar, J.C. (2000), 'A methodology for measuring the costs of universal service obligations', *Information Economics and Policy*, **12** (3), September, 211–20.

Postal Regulatory Commission (2008), 'Report on Universal Postal Service and the Postal Monopoly', December.

Roy, B. (1999), 'Technico-economic analysis of the costs of outside work in postal delivery', in M.A. Crew and P.R. Kleindorfer (eds), *Emerging Competition in the Postal and Delivery Services*, Boston, MA; Kluwer Academic, pp. 101–22.

Roy, B. (2002), 'The impact of postal density and structural characteristics of delivery on entry barriers', in Proceedings of the Wissenschaftliches Institut für Infrastruktur und Kommunikationsdienste (WIK), No. 10, GmbH, 7th Königswinter Seminar on '*Contestability and Barriers to Entry in Postal Markets*', November 17–19.

APPENDIX 15A1 SIMULATION MODEL FOR STREET LETTER DELIVERY

A delivery round is divided into four main components: traveling time (T), which is the time spent between the delivery office and the first delivery point; street walking time (SW), that is, the time occupied walking/driving on the streets from the first to the last visited address of the delivery round; stop time (S): the time spent getting from the street to the letter box (for example, parking the vehicle, walking up the stairs to deliver registered mail); and loading time (L), the time needed to drop the letters into the recipients' boxes.

The delivery areas (DA) are the NUTS 3 zones for European countries and the federal states for the USA. Four modes of transport are available: foot, bicycle, moped and car. In each DA, the model chooses the average mode of transport which minimizes the cost of the four above components, augmented by vehicle costs and the cost of stop-over points when necessary (if mail is too heavy to be loaded at once by the postman, a part of it is taken to stop-over boxes before delivery begins. The stop-over boxes are then unloaded during the delivery round). The number of delivery areas in the model has to be significant enough for the simulated average optimal means of transport to be representative at a national scale.

The cost function is written as:

$$CostDA = \underset{e \in E}{\text{Min}}[C_W(T_L + T_S + T_{SW} + Rt_T + Mt_s) + (SWD + Rd_T)C_{Vehic.v} + NC_{Vehic.f}],$$

where E is the set of transport modes; C_W, $C_{Vehic.v}$, $C_{Vehic.f}$, respectively, are the workforce costs, the cost per km of the transport mode and the fixed cost per vehicle per day of delivery; T_L, T_S, T_{SW}, respectively, are the loading, stop and street walking times; R is the number of delivery rounds on the area; t_T the traveling time per delivery round; Mt_s is the number of stop-over boxes and the unit time to unload such a box; SWD is the street distance walked/driven; and d_T is the traveling distance per delivery round.

The arguments of that minimization problem can be developed as follows.

- $T_L = volume \times t(GI)$, where *volume* is the volume in each delivery area per day of delivery and $t(GI)$ the loading time per item. The latter is an increasing function of the 'grouping index' (GI), that is, the average number of mail boxes per delivery point in the area. This accounts for the fact that it takes more time to drop mail in front of cluster boxes in a collective housing building rather than a single mail box at a house.
- $T_S = DP(1 - p)Stop(GI, e)$, where $Stop(GI, e)$ is the stop time per delivery point, which depends on the transport mode e and increases with GI. p is the proportion of delivery points (DP) which are not visited by the postman. It can be shown that $p = DP/(volume + DP)$.[1] The street walking distance is known for the case where all delivery points are served. In practice this is not the case. The street walking distance is obtained using a formula from Roberts (1968) showing that the shortest path joining N randomly distributed points on a disc with surface S is equivalent to $k\sqrt{NS}$ when N is large. Hence, $SWD = k\sqrt{DP(1 - p)S}$. k is estimated using observation data.

- $T_{SW} = SWD/(Speed[dist, e])$, where $Speed[dist, e]$ is the average walking/driving speed between two served delivery points, expressed as a function of their relative distance[2] in order to rank transport modes according to acceleration and deceleration.
- $R = (T_S + T_{SW} + T_L)/(t_{round} - t_T)$, where $t_T = d_T/(v_T[e])$ the traveling time (d_T is proportional to the radius of the delivery area and $v_T[e]$ is the traveling speed). t_{round} is the duration of a round.
- Finally, M is the smallest integer such that the weight of letters on the DA divided by R + M is inferior to $\gamma(e)$, namely the weight constraint of transport mode e.

Ultimately, computing the cost function for delivery involves solving a five-variables minimization problem. These variables are the surface of delivery areas, the number of delivery points, the GI, the number of letters per day of delivery in the area and the weight of mail per day of delivery. The problem is parameterized with field observations.

Notes

1. Let X be the number of items received by a letter box each day. Mail boxes are mutually independent and X is assumed to follow a Poisson distribution of parameter λ equal to the volume per delivery point per day of delivery. The share of mail boxes that receive no letter each day is hence $P(X = 0) = e^{-\lambda}$. Mail boxes are grouped in delivery points using the grouping index. It follows that the probability that the postman will not stop at a given delivery point of grouping index y is $P(X = 0)^y$. On average, $p = E[P(X = 0)^Y]$. Although it is incorrect to adjust Y with a continuous distribution, taking an exponential distribution for Y gives a very realistic fit with observed visit rates. The parameter μ of the exponential distribution is the inverse of the average GI in the delivery area. This reduces to $p = E[P(X = 0)^Y] = \int_0^\infty e^{-\lambda x}\mu e^{-\mu x}dx = \mu/(\lambda + \mu) = DP/(volume + DP)$.
2. *Speed[dist, e]* is parameterized with field observations for each transport mode and set to zero if the distance between two delivery points is inappropriate for the considered mode.

Reference

Roberts, F.D.K. (1968), ‘Random minimal trees’, *Biometrika*, **55** (1), March, 255–58.

APPENDIX 15A2 ESTIMATION OF THE GROUPING INDEX

In order to estimate the GI, a database which provides for the 36,000 French 'communes' is used: population, number of households, number of buildings, number of individual houses, number of enterprises and surface (km^2).

By aggregating these data by *départements*, to fit with the European statistical nomenclature (NUTS 3), the number of delivery points, equal to the number of households and enterprises and the number of stops, equal to the number of buildings in which postmen could enter, are defined. The ratio of these two figures corresponds to the 'real' grouping index in each *départements*.

In the absence of detailed data for all countries studied here, the GI has been estimated using an econometric model. The most relevant regression function at the French *départements* level relates the GI to demographic density:

$$GI_i = 1 + 0.00047 \times Density_i,$$

where *i* refers to the various NUTS 3 areas.

The estimated coefficient is statistically significant at the 1 percent level. The adjusted coefficient of determination of the model is greater than 94 percent.

The GI is increasing with density. Consider two areas of identical importance. A higher density in one of these areas reflects a larger population and more grouping. Similarly, a higher density due to a smaller area for the same population implies a less dispersed distribution of the population.

16. The cost of the USO in the United States

Robert Cohen, Charles McBride and John C. Panzar

1 INTRODUCTION

This analysis was undertaken as a result of a congressional mandate to quantify the cost of the Universal Service Obligation (USO) in the United States.[1] The concept of a postal USO is well established in Europe, but not in the US. Because Congress has not specifically defined the concept of the USO, we take its meaning to be contained in the statutory obligations of the US Postal Service (USPS) that directly involve services provided to senders and recipients. These have been quantified along with several potential obligations, which would arguably be included in an explicit statutory USO legislated by Congress.

The methodology for estimating the cost of the USO is based on estimating the additional profit that a profit-oriented post could make if the USO's obligations were removed. It will become clear that the counterfactual profit comparisons discussed in Section 3, below, depend upon the extent of PRC regulation that would remain if the mailbox and/or letter monopolies were removed. Judging from the experience in Sweden, the UK and New Zealand, it seems likely that some form of price-cap regulation would accompany even full liberalization. Therefore our analysis will conduct the relevant profit comparisons under the assumption that price-cap regulation of USPS remains in place, with the general structure as currently specified by the Postal Accountability and Enhancement Act of 2006 (PAEA).

This assumption plays an important role throughout our analysis. Whenever a counterfactual market outcome is specified from which to make a profit comparison, it is necessary to take into account the likely response of USPS to the changed situation. These predicted responses will typically be quite different under post-PAEA price-cap regulation than under the previous Postal Regulatory Commission (PRC) regulatory regime because of the pricing flexibility granted to USPS under PAEA. For example, USPS can respond much more quickly to the threat of entry in the post-PAEA environment. In addition, USPS's contribution losses from the required price cuts may sometimes be at least partially offset by price increases elsewhere without violating the constraint imposed by its price/revenue cap. In general, when PAEA price caps are part of the hypothetical liberalized market equilibrium, the impact on Postal Service profits will tend to be less than under the pre-PAEA regulatory regime.

The chapter proceeds as follows: Sections 2 and 3 provide the methodology; Section 4 contains the cost of the USO elements; and Section 5 contains the conclusions.

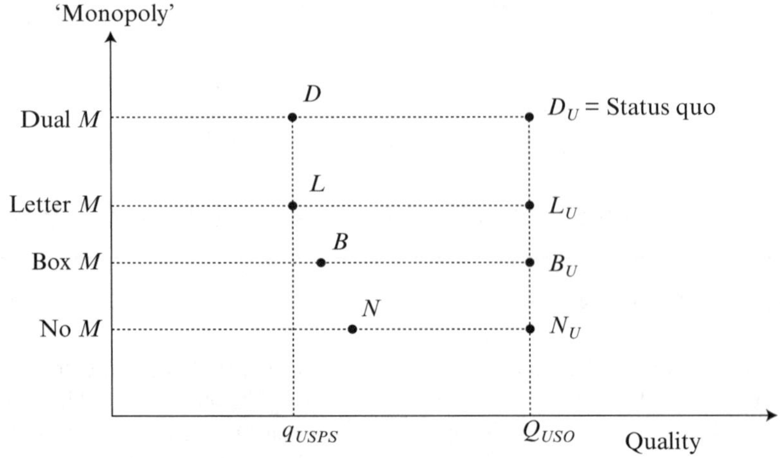

Figure 16.1 Postal policy options

2 THE PROFITABILITY APPROACH TO USO COSTING

Figure 16.1 provides a heuristic framework for visualizing the types of calculations required to obtain profitability measures of USO costs and monopoly valuations. The horizontal axis measures 'quality of service'. The vertical axis measures 'the degree of monopoly'. Of course, neither concept can be measured as a continuous variable along a single dimension. Clearly, the USO of USPS involves various dimensions of service quality and any changes might involve a quite complicated set of options. Similarly, the extent of USPS monopoly is, itself, a complicated notion, not easily quantified. Movements to the right involve a more stringent USO involving a higher quality of service. Similarly, upward movement denotes a greater degree of monopoly restrictions.

With these conventions in mind, the figure can be used to 'locate' the postal policy options of interest. We begin with the status quo situation, at the point labeled D_U. USPS is assumed to enjoy both the mailbox monopoly and the letter monopoly and to be bound by current statutory and procedural USO descriptions symbolized by the level Q_{USO}. From that starting point, removing *only* the mailbox monopoly while maintaining existing USO requirements would result in a vertical movement to L_U. Similarly, removing *only* the letter monopoly under existing USO requirements would be represented by the point B_U. Finally, the point N_U depicts the operating situation without any monopoly protection but subject to existing USO requirements.

Next, consider changes in the level of mandated service quality/USO requirements.[2] First consider a reduction in a status quo USO, for example, from six to three days per week. If monopoly protections remained the same, this would be depicted in Figure 16.1 as a horizontal movement from the status quo D_U (with quality level Q_{USO}) to the point D, which is associated with a lower quality of service level, q_{USPS}.[3] Providing the same level of service quality in the absence of the mailbox monopoly would result in hypothetical USPS operations at L.

The last two points on the figure depict hypothetical USPS operations without the letter monopoly. Point *B* reflects a situation in which USPS, with only a mailbox monopoly, is allowed to operate under a less severe USO requirement than Q_{USO}. Point *N* illustrates the analogous situation under full market liberalization.[4]

There is an important third dimension to Figure 16.1 that is not shown. Associated with each point in the {'Monopoly', 'Quality'} plane is a level of profit that can be earned by USPS under those competitive conditions and USO requirements. Diagrammatically, these profit levels would be measured as the 'height' above the page. We shall not attempt to depict profit levels on a 3D diagram, but it is important to remember that it is *profit differences* that are the quantitative magnitudes of interest.

3 COSTING THE USO

We are now in a position to illustrate how to apply this conceptual framework to the problem of measuring the quantitative impact of a policy decision such as a change in the stringency of the USO. The first step in such an analysis is to identify the relevant counterfactual. That is, we begin by specifying the situations that are to be compared. This step sounds obvious, but is often controversial and always requires a thorough understanding of the context of the policy issues involved. Once one has identified the operating scenarios relevant for comparison, it remains to carefully specify how USPS profit levels in the two situations are to be measured and compared. Of all the operational magnitudes that might differ between the two situations, the *profit* difference is the one that most accurately reflects the cost of the USO requirement at issue.

The USO is a Set of Constraints

At the most basic level, the USO consists of a *set of constraints* imposed on USPS's economic decisions relating to the products and services it provides. These may take the form of service standards and pricing constraints. Examples of service standards include the provision of six days per week delivery and rural service at 1983 levels. Pricing constraints include uniform pricing for letters and books, reduced rates for nonprofit mail, and free mail for the blind.

As we have emphasized, it is of fundamental importance to identify the qualitative type of the comparison to be made: that is, D_U to D versus N_U to N. However, substantial modeling decisions must be made even after resolving such conceptual issues. Remember, there are many dimensions of service quality that make up the USO and a complete counterfactual comparison must specify alternative standards for *all* of them. There is likely to be substantial controversy over what alternative levels are 'reasonable'. The only practicable solution would seem to be to specify particularly salient values for the important dimensions and perform the calculations for as many of the relevant combinations as possible.

The Relevant Counterfactuals for Costing the USO

Our earlier discussion identified eight different stylized operating scenarios. In principle, we could compare each of the alternatives involving the status quo level of the USO (that is, points D_U, L_U, B_U and N_U) with any of the points involving a relaxed USO requirement (that is, points D, L, B and N). However, it should be clear that most such comparisons can be ruled out on a priori grounds. For example, a comparison of the operating outcomes between D_U and L would confound two effects: the relaxation of the status quo USO standard and the elimination of the mailbox monopoly. Thus, it makes sense to consider comparing only the results of *horizontal* movements: that is, D_U to D, L_U to L, B_U to B, or N_U to N.

Depending upon circumstances, any of these horizontal comparisons might be of interest. However, we argue that the hypothetical movement from D_U to D is most relevant in the post-PAEA US postal environment. Since PAEA did not remove either the letter or mailbox monopoly, it seems most reasonable that any counterfactual analysis involving the USO should be conducted under the assumption that this monopoly protection remains in place. In contrast, in a liberalized postal environment such as that emerging in Europe, the comparison of interest would be between N_U and N. (Of course, our methodological approach is applicable to that comparison as well.)

We are now able to illustrate the calculation of USO profitability costs. We begin by identifying the service quality level associated with the status quo level of USO requirements, Q_{USO}. Next, we determine the associated level of Postal Service profitability under the current level of monopoly protection. We then compare this status quo level of Postal Service profits with the level that would be achieved if the status quo USO requirements were removed or relaxed so that the service level provided fell to q_{USPS}.[5] The difference between these two profit levels results in the profitability measure of removing the USO in the current monopoly environment (where 'Dual M' means that both mailbox and letter monopoly are maintained):

$$\begin{aligned} COST_{USO}(Q_{USO} \text{ to } q_{USPS}; \text{Dual M}) &= Profit(Q_{USO}; \text{Dual M}) - Profit(q_{USPS}; \text{Dual M}) \\ &= Profit(D_U) - Profit(D). \end{aligned}$$

This measure of the USO cost will be the primary focus of our quantitative analysis because we believe that it is the most relevant measure for the current post-PAEA regulatory environment in the US.

4 THE COST OF THE USO ELEMENTS

Tables 16.1 and 16.2 provide a summary of the quantitative results of our USO costing analysis.

The statutory USO cost of \$7.63 billion in 2007 was 10 percent of total Postal Service revenue for the year (\$74.97 billion). The potential statutory USO cost of \$0.339 billion in 2007 was 0.5 percent of revenue.

Savings from Country-wide Reductions in Frequency of Delivery

The USO cost of requiring USPS to deliver six days a week as stated in the previous section on methodology is its effect on its profits if it were a profit-maximizing institution. In order to make this calculation we must first establish a minimum frequency of

Table 16.1 Cost of the statutory elements of the USO (2007)

Elements	2007 cost ($ billion)
Six days a week delivery	5.20
Maintain small rural post offices	0.59
Nonprofit organization discounts	1.15
Losses on market dominant products	0.45
Measuring service performance	0.18
Unzoned Media Mail/Library Rate	0.06
Total	7.63

Table 16.2 Cost of the potential statutory elements of the USO (2007)

Elements	2007 cost ($ billion)
Alaska air subsidy	0.107
Uniform rate for First Class	0.130
Require delivery to all addresses	0.101
Six days a week delivery to all addresses	0.001
Total	0.339

Table 16.3 FY 2007 delivery costs ($ billion)

	Attributable costs	Fixed costs	Accrued costs	Attributable %
City delivery carriers – in office	5.70	1.15	6.84	83.2
City delivery carriers – street	5.43	9.23	14.66	37.0
Rural carriers	3.21	4.70	7.91	40.6
Total carrier delivery costs	14.34	15.07	29.41	48.8

Note: These costs include indirect costs such as supervision and administration. Total costs rounded.

delivery for a post that has a monopoly to deliver all letters to all addresses in the country. This minimum is a matter of judgment. For example, it could be five, four or three days per week. We have adopted a three days a week delivery throughout the country as the minimum frequency. This would mean that the delivery force would serve half the routes every day. However, delivery on business routes by a universal service provider would continue at five days per week since businesses are more dependent on frequent mail delivery than are households. Box section delivery would remain unchanged.

As shown in Table 16.3, rural and city delivery costs for FY 2007 were approximately $29.4 billion,[6] or about 38 percent of the total USPS accrued costs of $77.2 billion for that period. The fixed costs of delivery amount to $15.1 billion, so the fixed cost percentage of total delivery cost is about 51 percent. Fixed costs include a variety of activities that are necessary each delivery day regardless of the volume being delivered, such as the travel time required to walk or drive the route with no deviations to deliver mail. Virtually all attributable costs vary with mail volume.

In a previous study (Cohen et al., 2002) it was estimated that reducing the frequency of delivery for residential routes from six to three times a week could save as much as half the fixed costs of delivery, which in FY 1999 amounted to almost $6 billion, or 9 percent of total costs.[7] In that study, for simplicity the assumed cost function was one commonly used in postal analyses, in which total costs are assumed to equal fixed costs plus marginal costs times volume. This estimate of fixed cost savings was characterized as an upper bound, since no additional costs or loss of volume due to the reduction of delivery frequency were considered.

Effect of volume losses on delivery frequency savings

FY 2007 contribution per piece was about 13.73 cents, and total contribution was about $29.14 billion.[8] It is reasonable to expect that demand and thus USPS net revenue would decline due to decreases in delivery frequency, especially for advertising mail where the time of arrival of the mail piece often must coincide with a planned marketing event. In addition, customer dissatisfaction resulting from fewer delivery days would likely cause more rapid diversion of First Class mail to electronic alternatives and parcel volumes to competitors' services.

In this analysis, we assume a simple profile of volume losses as a function of delivery frequency, and estimate the effects on the savings as a sensitivity analysis. It was assumed that the effect of changing from six to five days per week would be modest (a 2 percent loss), but that further decreases in frequency would reduce volume by 3 percent for each additional day of frequency reduction. These results are shown are in the first three rows of Table 16.4. It can be seen by comparing Table 16.3 and the first three rows of Table 16.4 that about one-third of the savings are lost due to these assumed demand effects.

The last two rows of Table 16.4 are included to show the sensitivity of the cost savings to different assumed demand effects for the three-day delivery case: a 6 percent volume loss and a 10 percent volume loss. It should be noted that the column labeled 'Cost Savings' is the same as the net improvement in USPS profits.

At present, there is great uncertainty about how much volume would decline at the various delivery frequencies. It is therefore interesting to calculate how much volume could be lost at a given delivery frequency before the net profit from the reduction in frequency actually goes to zero. Using this same analysis, the percentage volume losses (proportional for all classes) that lead to net revenue losses equal to delivery frequency savings were calculated for 5, 4 and 3 delivery days and are shown in Table 16.5.

Savings from Closing Small Rural Post Offices

The smallest 9,200 post offices[9] in the US have counter transaction costs and post office box operation costs (per box) that are much higher than costs at larger offices. They typically have just one employee providing retail services to customers and filling post office boxes. In this analysis, we assume that rural carriers[10] will provide all retail transactions that were formerly performed at these small offices. We also assume that post office box services at these stations will be replaced by rural carrier delivery to new Neighborhood Delivery Collection Box Units (NDCBUs, cluster boxes).

For FY 2007, these offices cost $663.9 million,[11] and the annual cost per office was

Table 16.4 Cost savings from reducing delivery days with assumed volume losses (FY 2007)

Delivery days	% volume loss	Contribution loss ($ bn)	Cost savings ($ bn)	% total costs
5	2.0	0.58	1.93	2.5
4	5.0	1.46	3.56	4.6
3	8.0	2.33	5.20	6.7
3	6.0	1.75	5.78	7.5
3	10.0	2.91	4.62	6.0

Table 16.5 Volume loss necessary to negate savings from delivery frequency reduction

Delivery days	Cost savings ($bn)	% total cost	% volume loss required for zero net income
5	2.51	3.3	8.6
4	5.02	6.5	17.2
3	7.53	9.8	25.8

Note: Average contribution for all pieces = 13.7 cents; $1 billion = 7,284 million pieces or 3.43 percent of total volume.

$72,021.[12] The average retail revenue per office was $30,374, so the total FY 2007 retail revenue for these offices was about $280 million. There were about 154.5 million window transactions. In FY 2007 the total number of boxes was about 1.102 million.[13] This would be the total number of additional delivery points that would have to be served by rural carriers. The additional delivery and retail transaction costs by rural carriers is $77.7 million. The annual savings from replacing these post office operations by rural carrier operations would be the current cost of $663.9 million less $77.7 million, so the net FY 2007 annual savings would be about $586 million.

Discounts on Mail from Nonprofit Organizations[14]

In this subsection, we estimate the magnitude of increased USPS net revenue (profits) under the assumption that nonprofit rates are increased to be the same as their for-profit counterparts.[15] This increase in nonprofit rates results in an increase in contribution of about $1.20 billion in FY 2008, or about $1.15 billion in FY 2007 dollars. In FY 2007 dollars, about $940 million of this increase is due to higher nonprofit revenues, but another $210 million arises because of lower attributable costs, which in turn are caused by reduced nonprofit volume resulting from the price increases. About 98 percent of the increased contribution is from the Standard mail nonprofit categories, with the remaining two percent from the nonprofit categories in Periodicals and Package Services.

Losses on Market Dominant Products

USPS had four loss-making domestic market dominant products in 2007 (Within County and Outside County Periodicals, single-piece Parcel Post and Media Mail/ Library Rate). Had the first rate increase under the 2006 postal legislation (PAEA) gone into effect prior to the beginning of FY 2007, it would have been possible for USPS to eliminate the losses on the two parcel subclasses by using the flexibility allowed under the new price-cap rules. Under the price caps in the legislation, the 2007 losses on the two subclasses that make up the Periodical class could not have been eliminated. Thus, the loss of $448 million by Periodicals is caused by the current statutory obligations and, consequently, the negative contribution made by them is part of the cost of universal service.

Cost of Measuring Service Performance

The new postal law (PAEA) requires that USPS measure the service performance of market-dominant products on an annual basis.[16] USPS has estimated that its annual cost of measuring service for all market-dominant products is $182 million. There are 34 such products and they amount to about 95 percent of total volume.

Uniform Rate for Media Mail and Library Rate Subclasses

The Media Mail and Library Rate subclasses have a statutory restriction[17] that requires their rates to be uniform with respect to distance. Consisting largely of books, their total FY 2007 revenue is $407 million and total contribution to institutional cost is a negative $38 million.

The issue here is to estimate the additional contribution that could be earned if the two subclasses were zoned. They have a cousin subclass, Bound Printed Matter (BPM), which also consists largely of books but is zoned. The average weight of BPM is 2.2 pounds and the combined average weight of Media Mail and Library Rate is 2.1 pounds. Our approach to estimating the additional contribution from zoning uses the unit contribution of BPM as a proxy to estimate the increase in contribution from Media Mail and Library Rate.[18] For FY 2007, the combined unit contribution of Media/Library was –21.7 cents and the unit contribution from BPM was 13.9 cents, so BPM's contribution was 35.6 cents higher than Media/Library.[19] Multiplying the combined volume of Media/ Library Rate (176.6 million) by 35.6 cents results in an estimated additional $63 million contribution if Media/Library were zoned.

Cost of Potential USO Elements

The Alaska air subsidy refers to the transport by air of classes of mail that are entitled to surface transportation only. The Alaska bush has no roads, requiring mail to be airlifted at an additional cost of about $107 million. The USPS does not surcharge this mail. In a formal enumeration of the postal USO, Congress might reasonably require that surface classes be airlifted to the Alaska bush at no surcharge.

If Congress decided that First Class mail rates must be invariant with respect to distance, the USPS would no longer be free to offer dropship rates for First Class.[20] The potential additional profit from offering these discounts is estimated to be about $130 million.

The USPS currently requires 1.365 million addresses to pick up mail at their local post office. The vast majority of these addresses are located within a quarter mile of their local office. If Congress decided that these addresses should get delivery, the cost of providing rural delivery to these addresses including providing retail services for them by the carrier is estimated to be $101 million.

Currently 25,000 addresses in the US receive delivery only three days per week. If Congress decided that they should get a six days a week delivery, the additional cost is estimated to be a little less than one million dollars.

5 SUMMARY AND CONCLUSIONS

The 'cost of the USO' can be thought of as an estimate of what would happen if Congress sold the USPS without adjusting the monopoly laws to a firm intent on profiting as much as possible from ownership while being required to stay within the statutory price caps. Seeking to maximize its profit, it would eliminate all elements of the statutory USO that resulted in lower profits. We have estimated that the new owner would earn $7.6 billion more than USPS now earns.

Our calculations are highly sensitive to assumptions and the estimate for the cost of the USO would change if statutory or regulatory obligations change. In this regard, we observe that the cost of the USO is largely fixed. Most of the costs involved in maintaining current delivery frequency, maintaining the current number of small rural post offices and measuring service performance are fixed costs and they constitute 78 percent of the cost of the USO. Consequently, these costs will not decline with volume and they will become an increasingly greater burden on USPS profits if volume continues to decline. Finally, it should be noted that volume has declined by about 17 percent since fiscal year 2007 whose data we used for this chapter.

NOTES

1. This chapter is based on a study carried out by George Mason University School of Public Policy under contract to the Postal Regulatory Commission. The study was published on the PRC website as an appendix to the PRC's report to the Congress. The scope of the entire GMU study is much broader than the subjects addressed in this chapter and includes a history of the USO in the US, a history of the postal monopoly in the US, survey research on the subject of the USO, and additional topics. The website contains the entire presentation of the topics included in this chapter including the basis of the quantitative estimates, workpapers and data sources. See: http://www.prc.gov/prcpages/library/USOAppendices.aspx?AspxAutoDetectCookieSupport=1.
2. Elsewhere, we use 'quality of service' as one of seven components of universal service and universal service obligations. Here, the term 'quality' is used to encompass all such obligations.
3. As noted earlier, one may either view the USO/quality level q_{USPS} as being specified by Congress or a regulatory authority or as the unconstrained choice of USPS.
4. Again, the quality/USO standard may be a result of Postal Service decisions or regulatory constraint. However, in competitive scenarios one must also consider the possibility that market forces may dictate a higher than legally required level of service quality. This is the situation depicted in Figure 16.1 at points *B* and *N*. That is, the figure assumes that competition would force a hypothetical Postal Service protected by only a mailbox monopoly to operate at a higher level of service quality than q_{USPS}; the quality outcome in a liberalized market would be higher still.

5. As discussed earlier, this counterfactual level of service quality can have two interpretations. First, it may be viewed as the level of service quality chosen by USPS in the absence of *any* USO requirements imposed upon it. For example, if the current six days per week residential delivery obligation were eliminated and delivery frequency were left entirely to the discretion of USPS, it might freely choose to deliver three days per week. Instead, one could view a counterfactual three days per week delivery requirement as resulting from an alternative quality of service standard typically imposed upon a price-cap regulated enterprise. In Figure 16.1, q_{USPS} is one of the quality levels that maximizes profit for a monopoly Postal Service, so either interpretation would be consistent with the figure.
6. Sources: Files FY07.CRPT.xls and FY07PbackAll.xls, both in PRC-ACR2007-LR2, Docket ACR2007. These costs include 'piggyback' costs (indirect costs which are proportional to delivery costs).
7. Delivery frequencies from one to five days per week were considered.
8. See PRC Annual Compliance Report for 2007, p. 24.
9. The USPS has about 27,000 post offices and a few hundred of these have multiple retail facilities (called branches and stations) bringing the total number of retail facilities operated by postal personnel to about 37,000.
10. In the US, rural carriers perform retail transactions for customers on their routes. Frequently this is done by the customer leaving the mail piece in his/her roadside box with a note and cash, and the carrier leaves behind a receipt.
11. See PRC-ACR2007-LR2 from Docket No. ACR2007. This figure includes direct costs such as customer transactions and sorting incoming mail to boxes, as well as indirect costs such as depreciation and energy costs.
12. As a comparison, the FY 2007 cost of contract stations (agencies), which are comparable in size and functions to the smallest offices, was $79.135 million (see PRC-ACR2007-LR2, Excel workbook FY07CRpt.xls, in Docket No. ACR2007). The number of agencies (contract stations) in FY 2007 was 3,131 (see FY 2007 Annual Report, p. 56). Thus the annual cost per contract station was $25,274.
13. See Excel workbook CAGK AND CAGL POBOXES FY 2007, dated October 15, 2008.
14. The discounted categories are technically referred to as 'preferred' because not all the mailers eligible to use these discounts are nonprofit organizations. The vast majority, however, are nonprofit organizations and so we use the term 'nonprofit' here.
15. The price caps in the 2006 postal legislation (PAEA) may prevent USPS from increasing the prices of the nonprofit mail to the level charged to other mail in the subclasses. In that case, our calculation represents an upper bound on the actual amount that could be saved if the required discount were eliminated.
16. Before the current postal law, the only category measured on an end-to-end basis was single-piece First Class mail.
17. 39 U.S.C. sec. 3683.
18. This approach is supported by the high cross-elasticity of Media/Library Rate with BPM of 1.005. This is the highest cross-price elasticity between two USPS products in the set of demand equations estimated by USPS witness Thress in the R2006-1 rate proceeding.
19. FY 2007 PRC Annual Compliance Report, p. 24.
20. The USPS does not now have dropship rates for First Class, but it is the authors' opinion that if it did, they would be legal under current law.

REFERENCES

Cohen, R., M. Robinson J. Waller and S. Xenakis (2002), 'The cost of universal service in the U.S. and its impact on competition', Proceedings of the Wissenschaftliches Institut für Infrastructure und Kommunikationsdienste (WIK) GmbH, No. 10, 8th Königswinter Seminar on 'Contestability and Barriers to Entry in Postal Markets', November 17–19, available at: www.prc.gov.

Postal Regulatory Commission (PRC) (2007), 'Annual Compliance Determination', United States Postal Service Performance FY 2007.

17. Universal service auctions in liberalized postal markets*

Joan Calzada, Christian Jaag and Urs Trinkner

1 INTRODUCTION

In a liberalized market, corporations will only provide unprofitable services in exchange for some kind of compensation. Universal Service Obligations (USOs) impose several restrictions on universal service providers (USPs) such as product definitions, network size, quality levels and pricing flexibility. A USP being forced to provide uneconomic quality or suboptimal pricing structures will require fair compensation for fulfilling its public mission. Such 'subsidies' should compensate the firm for its loss in profit due to the USO (see Panzar, 2000).

Universal service auctions are an allocation mechanism with the purpose of finding the most efficient USO provider at the minimum level of compensation.[1] First, the government defines the services that must be offered, afterwards firms bid for the concessions, and finally the USO is awarded to the firm that asks for the lowest compensation to deliver a specific set of universal services. Alternatively, firms might receive a fixed subsidy and bid for other aspects, such as the price or the coverage level. Hence, auctions aim to introduce competition for the market. Potential operators are given incentives to reveal their true costs and enable the government to select the best offer.[2]

The use of auctions for allocating the right to provide public services is not new. Demsetz (1968) introduced the idea that franchising may be a good substitute for regulation in network industries. In the 1990s, USO auctions have been used recurrently in Latin America and African countries to extend the coverage of basic services such as public telephony, electricity, water, urban transport, air transport and garbage and waste collection. Wellenius (2002) shows that compared to other mechanisms for providing public services in rural areas, the countries that have used auctions have offered lower subsidies, attracted more private investment and generated more transparency in the regulatory process. This may explain why USO auctions have expanded from attractive services in low- and medium-income countries (telecommunications and electricity) to high-income countries and less attractive services for investors (water, sewerage and urban transport).

From early on, several authors such as Williamson (1976) have noted that franchising contracts can be even more problematic than regulation, especially if the initial award criteria are not clear and include a set of quality dimensions, and when there is uncertainty about the evolution of key aspects affecting the sector that make the contracts incomplete. Further obstacles to USO auctions relate to the possibility of collusion. Similarly, the size and specific cost and demand structure in concentrated industries raises a variety of issues. Further regulatory challenges arise in USO auctions in liberalized industries where USO operators do not receive substantial exclusive rights. This distinction is of special importance in postal markets in the EC where USO auctions are discussed in the context of fully liberalized markets.

The objective of this chapter is to analyze the main features of USO auctions in liberalized markets and to discuss possible applications in the postal sector.[3] We argue that although subsidy auctions could be used to expand the coverage of postal services in rural areas, especially in developing countries, its general application to determine the USO provider of an entire country may entail important disadvantages.

The chapter proceeds as follows. Section 2 provides an overview on the basic options available to governments in public procurement. Section 3 shows the main regulatory aspects that should be considered when designing a USO auction. Section 4 raises some potential problems arising from USO auctions. Section 5 assesses recent applications of USO auctions in several countries and sectors. Section 6 discusses the use of reverse auctions in the postal sector. Finally, Section 7 presents our conclusions.

2 THE ROLE OF TENDERING IN PUBLIC PROCUREMENT

In a procurement process, public authorities choose the best way to ensure the provision of a service. The decision process of the authority can be decomposed into several steps (Figure 17.1). In a first step, a package of duties and rights for the operators has to be specified. The definition of the package determines the market structure and the financial burden imposed on the operators. A key decision is whether exclusive rights are included or not.

In a second step, the public administration must decide whether it supplies the service itself or if it delegates the production to a private operator. The public provision of a service can be undertaken through two mechanisms:

1. *public production* This option is often chosen for strategic goods such as police or utilities such as water, power or postal services; and
2. *contracting for the services* The public administration can select the provider of the service through direct negotiations with selected parties, a beauty contest based on various criteria, or public tendering.

The decision of the authorities over self-production or contracting/outsourcing can be made by taking into account the following criteria:

Efficiency Who can provide a certain service more efficiently, a public or a private company? For example, public firms might face higher wages due to public servant regulations. Private companies usually incur higher capital costs and profit margins but can be expected to be more innovative and cost aware.

Risk of the activity Private firms try to avoid large and risky investments over a long time horizon. Compared to public enterprises, they have a lower risk capacity and expect a higher risk premium.

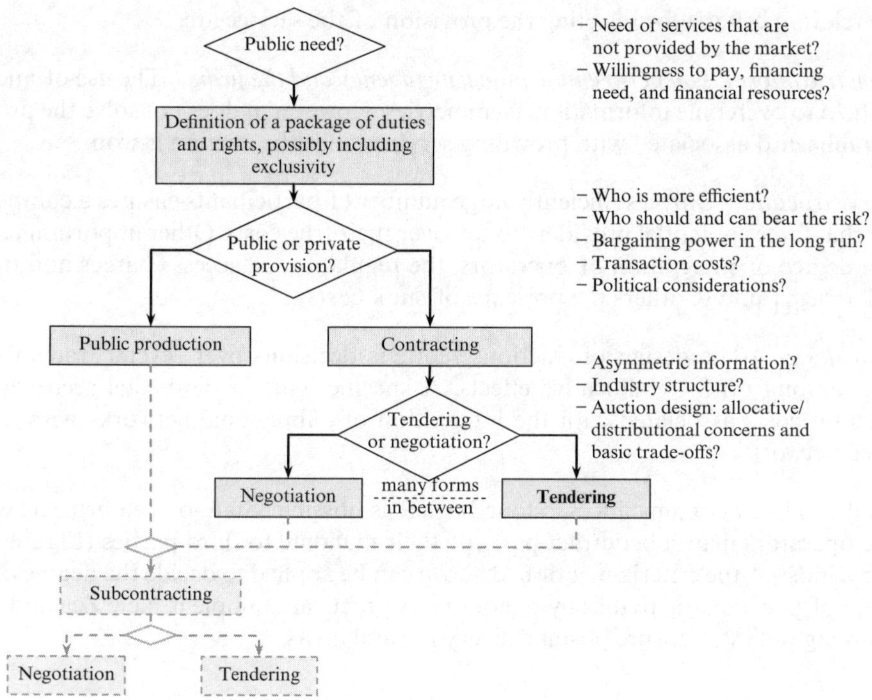

Source: Based on Jaag and Trinkner (2008).

Figure 17.1 Decision tree for public procurement

Public authorities' bargaining power Outsourcing is usually easier than insourcing. Among others, hold-up risks should be considered. If the threat of renegotiation of the contract is high, authorities might prefer self-provision of services.

Minimization of transaction costs Organizing and monitoring a tender is costly. If proper monitoring is not possible and if it is difficult to create incentives, contracting might not be appropriate.

Political considerations and national security Public authorities will take into account what is, or what should be, the role of government in the production of services and concerns related with national security.

In the case of market delegation, in a third stage public administrators can use various options to select the provider of the service:

1. *Direct negotiation* Contracts are negotiated between the authorities and third parties.
2. *Public tendering* Authorities tender a package of rights and duties, and virtually any candidate can apply for the contract.
3. *Intermediate options* In competitive dialogue (or beauty contest), a number of operators are invited to participate in the tender.

The relevant criteria for selecting the provision of the service are:

Asymmetric information between the procuring agency and the firms The use of auctions might help to overcome information asymmetries. However, it does not solve the problem of moral hazard associated with providing services once the auction is won.

Industry structure Only a sufficiently large number of participants ensures a competitive tender that forces potential providers to uncover their true costs. Other important aspects are the degree of integration of operators, the regulation of access charges and market entry barriers (among others the presence of sunk costs).

Auction design The design of auctions requires decisions over several tradeoffs that entail – among others – allocative effects. A specific issue in the postal sector is high transaction costs associated with the integration of subregional networks with a large national network.

Finally, in most circumstances, a fourth stage is possible. State-owned firms as well as private operators may subcontract parts of their mandate to third parties (Figure 17.1). Thereby, most of the criteria mentioned above can be applied to decide the degree of outsourcing of particular activities by operators. A practical example is New Zealand Post's outsourcing policy to ensure postal delivery in rural areas.

3 GENERAL FEATURES OF UNIVERSAL SERVICE AUCTIONS

In USO auctions public administrations must decide over several social, economic and financial aspects that affect the behavior of firms and influence the result of auctions.

Definition of the Projects and Selection of the Areas Auctioned

What is the general objective of the universal service policy? Who will benefit from this policy? What is the package of services offered and the funding mechanism used?

The selection of the municipalities protected by the USO policy can be made along with the needs of the population and the resources available. This implies collecting information about the local willingness to pay for the services in order to determine the interest of the program. In the presence of demand externalities between various regions such estimation may be done on a national scale.

An important aspect to be considered is the size of the regions auctioned. One must decide if the USO should be auctioned globally or divided up into various pieces and procured in smaller tenders. If the size of the regions auctioned is small, consumers are more homogeneous and firms can better estimate the profitability of supplying the service. In addition, dividing the USO into several regions enables yardstick competition. However, larger regions reduce the administrative costs of auctions and allow optimal exploitation of economies of scale and scope. Large areas also facilitate aggregating several services in the same concession. For example, the postman in charge of a geographic area might simultaneously deliver correspondence and offer financial services or insurance to the population. In order to take advantage of scale economies firms may be allowed to bid for several regions.

Contracts typically range between three and ten years. The longer the contract period is, the larger are the investment incentives for the winning operator (see Oxera, 2007). However, the longer the contract the fewer are the possibilities to adapt the USO over time to the customers' needs. Therefore, although long time horizons might be needed for dynamic efficiency considerations (investments and innovation), they might result in higher compensation needs as the bidders may require considerable risk premia. In order to moderate this problem, Engel et al. (2001) suggest using an auction design where the regulator fixes the prices of the service and firms bid for the minimum present expected value of the revenues. In this context, the duration of the concessions is adjusted according to the realization of the revenues by the operator.

Tenders may increase information asymmetries between governments and contractors compared to public provision. Hence, USO provisions must be detailed, precise and measurable. Detailed definitions on quality levels, accessibility criteria and so on increase both the operators' and regulator's legal certainty and provide a clear basis for any USO cost calculations. However, detailed contracts might unnecessarily hamper the commercial flexibility of the USO operator.

Design of Auctions

USO auctions can take various forms. Regulators must take into account the economic effects of each of these design aspects, as well as the possibility of collusion and the ability of firms to exploit scale economies:

Simultaneous and sequential auctions In sequential auctions, firms initially do not know if they will be able to win adjacent regions in subsequent auctions. As they are uncertain about the possibility of exploiting scale economies they will ask for higher subsidies.[4] This problem can be solved by auctioning all regions simultaneously. In the 1990s, Chile, Peru, Mexico, Colombia and Guatemala used simultaneous USO auctions for rural telephony, which allowed firms to acquire national conglomerates (Dymond and Oestmann, 2002).

One- or multiple-round auctions Auctions of one round only allow one bid per region. By contrast, auctions with multiple rounds finish only when no bidder offers a lower subsidy anymore. This allows firms to learn their rivals' valuations of the region. With this information, bidders can modify their own valuation of each region. The possibility of over- or underestimating the profitability of one region is one of the main justifications for using multistage USO auctions. Firms observe their rivals and understand that their own valuation for the region might be (too) high if many other bidders have already left the auction. As a result, open multiple-round auctions can reduce the firm's risk of being a victim of the 'winner's curse'. This is especially important when there is uncertainty about the cost and the demand (see Section 4). On the other hand, firms have more opportunities to collude.

Open and sealed bid auctions Open auctions do not reveal the participants' willingness to pay. The winner observes the bids of its rivals and stops bidding when the last rival leaves the auction. As a result, the winner receives the second-lowest subsidy, and nobody knows if it would have accepted a lower subsidy. However, an advantage of open auctions is that they generate more information about how other firms evaluate the region auctioned, and reduce the risk of a winner's-curse situation.[5]

Maximum subsidies Often, regulators define a maximum subsidy (reserve price) that they will be willing to grant for each region. This measure allows firms to estimate the minimum profitability that they can achieve. The effect of a maximum subsidy depends on the design of the auction and might reduce the subsidy needed.

Participants in the Auctions

Many national and international participants in the auction may increase the efficiency of the process and reduce the amount of the subsidy conceded. Hence, it is important to increase the attractiveness of the auctioned services. For example, Argentina's program of rural electrification (PAEPRA) initially failed to auction separate concessions for urban and rural areas in two provinces. Bundling rural and urban regions in the same concession then attracted several participants.

Often, firms that participate in USO auctions are not the traditional operators, but firms that have developed specific technologies adapted to the rural areas (for example, VSATS and wireless telephony in the telecommunications auctions). Dymond and Oestmann (2002) explain that these firms use auctions to promote their technology. In fact, many firms have even renounced the subsidies to enter the market.

Winner of the Auction

When considering public tendering as a means of delegating the provision of the universal service, a key issue is whether the operators will have exclusive rights in the respective market. In past USO auctions, often only one firm received the right to provide the service. However, competition in the market might lead firms to offer better services, instead of putting all their effort into winning the auction (Pitsch, 1997).

Although from a technical viewpoint it is possible to implement auctions with several firms entering the market, firms can gain fewer scale economies and as a consequence they might ask for higher subsidies. In spite of this some technologies, for example, mobile telephony, can sustain better than others the presence of more than one operator. Another example is the electricity sector, where the use of photovoltaic panels favors the presence of many competitors in the same neighborhood.[6]

Regulation of the Market

The regulation of the sector is a key element to increase the firm's interest to provide universal services. Indeed, firms favor a clear and stable regulatory regime that allows them to estimate the costs and revenues of each project and that reduces their risks.

In some Latin American (Chile, Peru, Colombia) and African (Uganda) countries, the regulator has introduced asymmetric retail and/or wholesale prices in fixed telephony to increase the attractiveness of concessions: prices in rural areas are higher than in urban regions (Dymond and Oestmann, 2002; Wallsten, 2009).

The concession's contract might also include several regulations that limit the profitability of operators. Concessions must contain the mechanism used to regulate the prices and the quality, the technology that can be used and the coverage that must be attained by operators. Contracts may also indicate who the owner of the infrastructure is and who supports all the commercial risk of their activity. For example, in Barcelona, the urban transport authority owns the vehicles and garages that are used by private operators.

4 GENERAL CONCERNS

In this section we analyze in more detail some of the concerns with auctions that have been identified in the previous section.

Allocative Concern: Selection of the Winner

The allocative objective of USO tendering is to choose the most efficient producer with the most efficient technology. However, when there is uncertainty about future market outcomes, operators may not have very precise knowledge of the net cost of the universal service. Bulow and Klemperer (2002) show that common value auctions are always won by the bidder with the highest (in reverse USO auctions by the lowest) signal. If net costs calculations are difficult and future industry prospects highly uncertain, it is likely that the auction is won by the most optimistic provider, which may not be the most efficient one.

Distributional Concern: Winner's Curse and Winner's Moral Hazard

Tendering USOs ideally guarantees that the winner is not able to earn an excessive rent at the expense of the consumers. Excessive rents may arise from the design of the auction or from the opportunistic behavior of the USP once it has won the auction.

Winner's curse Consider an auction where bidders have imprecise private information about the net cost of the USO being auctioned. To illustrate the idea, assume that the net cost of the USO is the same for all potential providers. Hence, from the point of view of productive efficiency, it does not matter who will win. However, operators can be uncertain about their costs. The auction will be won by the bidder that received the most optimistic estimate and hence requested the lowest subsidy. If the signal is symmetrically distributed around the net cost of the operators, the average winning estimate will be lower than the net costs. This is a well-known result in auction theory that is called the 'winner's curse'. A rational bidder would adjust the own bid upwards to receive a higher compensation and avoid the winner's curse. Among others, Bajari and Hortacsu (2003) present mixed empirical evidence on whether companies rationally respond to avoid a winner's curse.[7]

Winner's moral hazard At a first glance, it may seem that participants in auctions behave irrationally if they do not account for the possibility of a winner's curse (see Cox and Mark, 1984). However, if a tender leads to a systematically underfunded provision of universal services, this will likely result in renegotiations of terms in favor of the winner. Bearing in mind the possibility of renegotiation, asking initially for a low subsidy could not be so irrational after all. Once the auction is won, two scenarios are possible. If everything goes well, the winner gets a profit and keeps it. In the case of underfunding, the government will be forced to renegotiate the contract. Clearly, the bargaining position of the government and the USP will depend on the government's USO replacement costs and the USP's equity at stake. Typically, the latter will be significantly lower in size and hence the USP's liability is limited. Ultimately, the taxpayer will pay for it.[8]

A second form of moral hazard relates to the winner's incentives for short-term profit maximization. The operator that wins the auction may offer poor service, reduce investments, or find other ways to maximize short-run profits.

Cost of USO Concern: Real Options

The third concern is that tendering USOs increases its net cost compared to direct designation and public service provision.

USO tendering raises the need for detailed *ex ante* regulations on all services provided during the contract period to limit moral hazard (see above). Similarly, companies can only predict their future costs of providing the USO if they know the contract details. For example, a contract period of seven years requires detailed regulations on pricing, quality, products and coverage at the time of the auction and companies must predict market developments over the same horizon to be able to compute the net costs of the USO (see Panzar, 2000).

For the winner of the USO auction, these extensive regulations come along with important limitations in business flexibility. Such flexibility might be of special importance in times of fast technological progress (for example, 'e-substitution' in the postal sector). Jaag and Trinkner (2009) suggest that this loss of corporate flexibility can be measured by use of real options analysis. Where universal service regulations limit corporate flexibility, the winner's real options lose value. This loss will be included in any *ex ante* net cost computation of companies that plan to participate in a bid. The net costs are higher in auction mechanisms as these require – compared to direct designation – a suboptimal high level of detailed *ex ante* USO regulations.

5 SOME LESSONS OF USO AUCTIONS IN NETWORK INDUSTRIES

In the last decade, several countries have used auctions to select the USP in the telecommunications, transport, electricity and water sectors.[9] Many of the first experiences ended up with poor results. In spite of this, the accumulated experience gained worldwide with the use of this instrument has allowed the creation of a second generation of auctions that corrects many of the past mistakes. For example, some countries have substituted first-price sealed bid auctions for combinatorial or simultaneous open auctions.

In 1994, Chile was the first country to create a universal service fund and to use an auction to extend the public telephony to rural and low-income urban areas.[10] During the 1995–2000 period several auctions were successful. The first auction only considered basic telephony, but most recent projects also include access to the Internet (telecenters). Chile's success rapidly influenced other Latin American countries such as Bolivia, Brazil, Colombia, Dominican Republic, El Salvador, Guatemala, Nicaragua and Peru.[11] Later on, several African countries such as Ghana, Senegal, South Africa and Uganda also introduced universal service auctions.[12] Some of these experiences in rural telephony have offered very poor results. As anticipated in the previous section, a frequent problem in USO auctions is the winner's curse. In Peru and South Africa, for example, some operators bid too aggressively and ended up with serious financial problems.

Another problem is the absence of participants in the auctions, a situation that can increase the subsidies requested by USPs. In 2003, India launched an auction for installing public phones in 20 regions covering 520,000 municipalities (Kalra and Borgohain, 2004). Only mobile and fixed line (BSNL) operators already operating in those regions were allowed to participate in the auction. As a consequence, BSNL won the concessions in 19 regions, obtaining the maximum subsidy offered by the regulator.[13] A similar experience can be found in Australia. In 2001 the government organized an auction to increase the competition in two regions covering 80 percent of the remote areas of the country. No firm participated in these auctions to compete against the incumbent telecommunications operator.

The experiences show that the most successful auctions have been those of regions that previously were not covered by any operator, or where the installed capacity was very small. Indeed, this is usually the case in Latin American and African auctions. These are organized to attain the provision of telephony in unprofitable regions. Urban areas do not need these 'access policies', although the government might establish some USOs on already existing operators to subsidize the use of basic services.

It is also important to obtain exclusive rights to commercialize the services and to reduce market risks. In a recent telecommunications auction in Switzerland, the winner was not granted any exclusive rights. Among other things, this might explain why only the incumbent participated in the auction.

USO auctions have also been used in the electricity sector. New advances in the technology allow autonomous electric systems disconnected from the main grid to be created. These systems are used to cover the needs of residents of rural areas (light, television, radio), businesses (pumping of water, refrigerators) and public services (schools, hospitals, police stations). Rural systems use different combinations of energies, including diesel generators, mini-hydroplans, photovoltaic, wind and biomass energy.[14] Several countries in Latin America (Argentina, Bolivia, Chile, Colombia and Peru) and in Africa (Cabo Verde, Benin and Togo) have used USO auctions to select the providers of these electric systems and to determine the compensation that they should receive.

Competitive tendering is also frequent in the urban bus industry of several countries such as Denmark, Norway, Sweden, Switzerland and the UK. Several papers find that tendering reduces the average total cost per vehicle/km (Hershen and Wallis, 2005). However, the risk of using auctions is that in the long term, takeovers and increasing ownership links among firms may reduce competition and lead to an unwanted concentration of the market (Mathisen and Solvoll, 2008).

6 USO AUCTIONS IN THE POSTAL SECTOR

In this section we discuss the application of subsidy auctions in the postal sector. Thereby we try to identify the main problems and advantages relative to other mechanisms.

Table 17.1 Basic auction designs and applications in the postal sector

	Exclusive rights	No exclusive rights
One winner	Franchise bidding (Demsetz, 1968) Example: Lebanon	**USO subsidies in liberalized markets (Jaag and Trinkner, 2009)** **Example: Germany**
More than one winner	Franchise bidding and competition in the market (Milgrom, 1999; Sorana, 2000)	Multiple USO subsidies in liberalized markets (Laffont and Tirole, 2000)

Basic Auction Designs in the Postal Sector

In the postal sector, subsidy auctions are a means of allocating USOs to one or more operators as well as delegating the determination of the cost of the USO to the market. Note, however, that the cost of the USO itself (the result of the USO auction) still needs to be funded.

Table 17.1 shows the basic auction designs possible in the postal industry. The last row of the table (more than one winner) is a solution reserved to cases where there are no relevant economies of scale in the provision of the service. In the postal sector, this is certainly not the case and it will hardly ever be applied. Governments will not be prone to subsidize more than one rural delivery network or two rural post offices side by side.

'Franchise bidding' is the standard setting for auctions and the solution that has often been applied for example for spectrum auctions. To our knowledge, the only government that has granted exclusive rights in the postal sector has been Lebanon. In 1998, the postal monopoly was transferred to a private company that had won a beauty contest. Since then, LebanPost has shown a remarkable transformation process. Note that postal administrations themselves quite often procure some exclusive rights to suppliers and third parties (Step 4 in Figure 17.1). For example, New Zealand Post has for years successfully procured rural deliveries (see Oxera, 2007). The issue here is substantially simplified compared with auctioning the entire USO (and is essentially a standard and unproblematic outsourcing decision). In the European Union, exclusive rights will not be allowed under the Third Postal Directive after 2013. Therefore, the most relevant field in these postal markets is the bold area in Table 17.1.

A key decision is whether the USO should be auctioned on a national or regional scale. In the postal sector, USO requirements are usually defined nationwide and include important interdependencies between the three main dimensions price, quality and services. Postal markets are two-sided and mail demand exhibits externalities among regions. That is, demand in a given region depends on the specific offerings in all other regions (and vice versa) on both sides of the market (sender and recipient). Production exhibits substantial economies of scale and scope, which makes entry more risky than in other sectors (for example, tenders of bus lines).

Hence, in a national USO auction, one will rarely find more than two or three interested operators. In addition, one should expect the incumbent operator to be in an advantageous situation (with incremental USO costs only) whereas other operators would need to start operations first. Hence, open procedures might yield too high subsidies (even in a world without collusion).

Splitting up the USO into various regions might mitigate this problem. It reduces bidding asymmetries in favor of the incumbent and decreases the cost of market entry (WIK, 2008). This is indeed the solution that has been applied in other network industries (see Section 5). However, the application of the option to the postal sector entails several problems and conflicts: it has an impact on overall mail demand; it establishes the need for regulating access charges of regional firms; it creates problems for enforcing uniform pricing without enabling cherry picking; and finally it reduces scale and scope economies. According to Oxera (2007) it is not possible to sustain uniform prices in such a system. Note that uniform prices are often part of the USO and they are likely to foster overall mail development. A further issue relates to production externalities. Postal USO requirements include nationwide uniform products (collection days, points and times; quality; distribution days and times; price; and stamps). If the USO were split up into various regions and served by various local USPs, these local USPs might be forced to adapt their processes in other (non-USO) regions too for logistical reasons (for example, time windows). This might result in uniform processes between the various operators and thereby indirectly hamper innovation and foster collusion. More generally, from an operator's point of view, winning an auction has cross-effects on services offered in other areas both on the cost as well as on the demand side. Hence, postal markets are much more difficult to separate into regional pieces than bus lines or water and electricity distribution. Similarly, interconnection issues are harder to resolve compared to telecommunications networks where the problems are mainly technical.

Hence, in countries with integrated, well-developed postal markets, subsidy auctions will involve serious challenges both on a national as well as on a regional scale.

A different question is the use of USO auctions in unattended regions of developing countries. As we have seen in Section 5, the experience in developing countries shows that subsidy auctions have succeeded in many regions where asymmetric regional retail and wholesale prices have been established. Note that tendering previously unserved regions much more resembles franchise bidding than USO subsidies in liberalized markets.

Applications of Subsidy Auctions in the European Union

The Third European Postal Directive (2008/6/EC) envisages full market opening by 2013 and allows for competitive USO tendering: Article 7(2) of the directive states that 'Member States may ensure the provision of universal services by procuring such services in accordance with applicable public procurement rules and regulations'. According to Article 4, the Directive allows the USO to be divided into various single obligations: 'Member States may designate different undertakings to provide different elements of universal service and/or to cover different parts of the national territory'.

The meaning of Article 7(3) in relation to the tendering option is somewhat unclear. The article states that compensation or sharing mechanisms might only be implemented if a 'net cost' arises. This shall be 'verified by the national regulatory authority subject to' detailed accounting requirements. As they stand, these provisions imply that the successful bid might not be accepted *per se*. The designated USP will receive a subsidy equal to its bid only if detailed computations of the regulator lead to the same result as the auction. As a consequence, operators participating in the bid are aware that winning the auction means opening the books to the regulator. This might not be an attractive prospect. The EC provisions can be interpreted as a presumption that reverse auctions will likely not result in efficient subsidy levels in the postal sector.

So far, no subsidy auctions have been organized under the Postal Directive framework. In Germany, a tendering mechanism for universal postal services was approved in 2008, after the complete liberalization of the market. In the case that certain USO elements are not provided by the market, the law foresees auctioning the lacking USO elements. In the light of the challenges of subsidy auctions in the postal sector, the main strength of the German model is that the USO is neither tendered as a whole nor divided up into several regions. Only those parts of the USO not provided by the market will be tendered, for example, a post office, a specified quality level for basic letter service, or services in a number of remote islands. Such 'incremental subsidy auctions' might result in more bidders – and eventually in a USO provision that is less costly. However, as the subsidy auction is defined relative to Deutsche Post's service plans, it would be surprising to find another operator with smaller incremental costs.

7 SUMMARY AND CONCLUSION

Traditionally, universal services have been provided by state-owned operators with a public mission. Operators were compensated with extensive exclusive rights, which allowed them to use cross-subsidization between different regions, customers and services. In liberalized markets, such a policy cannot be used to finance the USO. Therefore, alternative mechanisms should be envisaged to guarantee the efficient provision of basic (postal) services in rural regions and to small customers. One such option is the use of subsidy auctions, a solution that has been used in other network industries for more than two decades with mixed results.

In theory, under efficient market conditions, subsidy auctions allow for finding the most efficient provider for the required service at the minimum level of compensation. In practice, the design of auctions is complex and requires the solution of several concerns and tradeoffs. The design of a tender has to consider sector-specific aspects, such as the industry structure and changing consumer needs. In order to ensure the frictionless functioning of universal services in liberalized markets, these issues would have to be thoroughly assessed and resolved before subsidy auctions or other procurement mechanisms are introduced.

Tendering postal universal services in a whole country would be fraught with large risks. Turning over the entire provision of the USO to an alternative operator other than the historic USP requires complex regulations and would cause significant social risks that render the utilization of this solution questionable. Moreover, a nationwide auction implies the participation of only a few bidders which reduces the attractiveness of this mechanism. The application of USO auctions in small regions might increase the number of participants, but this would reduce scale and scope economies and require even more complex regulatory arrangements such as regional access charges, retail prices, and quality levels combined with a harmonization of production processes and time windows of the various regional USPs. Hence, postal USO tendering does not seem to be practical for individual regions due to interdependencies among them.

The experience in developing countries shows that USO auctions for regions not serviced otherwise may succeed. However, in countries with integrated, well-developed postal markets, subsidy auctions involve serious challenges both on a national as well as on a regional scale. We conclude that tendering as an option for providing universal services is likely to be difficult to implement and would not make much sense for the provision of postal services in developed countries.

NOTES

* The views expressed are those of the authors and do not reflect the opinion of the institutions with which they are affiliated.

1. The first academic work about the use of auctions for the provision of public services is Chadwick (1859), who analyzed several English markets. The author distinguished between the competition 'for the market' and the competition 'in the market'.
2. Harstad and Crew (1999) and Sorana (2000) analyze the efficiency of USO auctions, including the issue of franchise renewal and repeated auctions over time for the USO.
3. Borrmann (2004) discusses the use of postal USO auctions in rural regions.
4. Stegeman et al. (2007) considers that sequential auctions generate higher bids when participants learn about the process. Peha (1999) explains that in the presence of scale economies simultaneous auctions generate higher subsidies than combinatorial auctions.
5. Klein (1998) shows that open auctions reduce the risk of collusion when several firms participate in the market. However, if the number of participants is small, it is preferable to use first-price sealed bid auctions to avoid the possibility of collusion.
6. Milgrom and Weber (1982) were the first to suggest more than one operator in the same USO region. See also Pirsch (1997) or Laffont and Tirole (2000).
7. See Jaag and Trinkner (2009) for a more detailed discussion.
8. Guasch et al. (2002) analyze firm-led renegotiations in Latin America using data of 307 concession projects in the sectors of transport and water in Argentina, Brazil, Chile, Colombia and Mexico between 1984 and 2000. They show that more than half of these projects were renegotiated on average 3.5 years after signing the contract.
9. Cantillon and Pesendorfer (2006) and Mathisen and Solvoll (2008) analyze the use of auctions in the bus industry of London and Norway, respectively.
10. ITU (2006) shows that 85 percent of all Latin American countries use universal service funds.
11. See Wellenius (1997), Cannock (2001) and Sepúlveda (2004).
12. In 2004, Uganda was the first African country to organize an auction (OECD, 2004).
13. Recent auctions carried out in India have solved some of these problems (Wallsten, 2009).
14. Fuente and Alvarez (2004) analyze electrification models in Latin American rural communities.

REFERENCES

Bajari, P.L. and A. Hortacsu (2003), 'The winner's curse, reserve prices, and endogenous entry: empirical insights from eBay auctions', *RAND Journal of Economics*, **34**(2), Summer.

Borrmann, J. (2004), 'Franchise bidding for postal services in rural regions', *Topics in Economic Analysis and Policy*, **4** (1), Article 10, available at http://www.bepress.com/bejeap/topics/vol4/iss1/art10.

Bulow, J. and P. Klemperer (2002), 'Prices and the winner's curse', *Rand Journal of Economics*, **33**, 1–21.

Cannock, G. (2001), 'Telecom subsides', *ViewPoint*, Note No. 234, Washington, DC: The World Bank Group.

Cantillon, E. and M. Pesendorfer (2006), 'Auctioning bus routes: the London experience', in

P. Cramton, Y. Shoham and R. Steinberg (eds), *Combinatorial Auctions*, Cambridge, MA: MIT Press, pp. 573–92.
Chadwick, E. (1859), 'Results of different principles of legislation and administration in Europe; of competition for the field, as compared with competition within the field of service', *Journal of the Statistical Society of London*, **22** (3), 381–420.
Cox, J.C. and I.R. Mark (1984), 'In search of the winner's curse', *Economic Inquiry*, **22** (4), 579–92.
Demsetz, H. (1968), 'Why regulate utilities?', *Journal of Law and Economics*, **11**, 55–66.
Dymond, A. and S. Oestmann (2002), 'Rural Telecommunications Development in a Liberalising Environment: An Update on Universal Access Funds', Intelecom Research & Consultancy Ltd.
Engel, E., R. Fisher and A. Galetovic (2001), 'Least-present-value-of-revenue auctions and highway franchising', *Journal of Political Economy*, **109**, 993–1020.
Fuente, M. and M. Alvarez (2004), 'Modelos de electrificación rural dispersa mediante energias renovables en América Latina', *Cuaderno Urbano*, **4**, 203–229.
Harstad, R.A. and M.A. Crew (1999), 'Franchise bidding without holdups: utility regulation with efficient pricing and choice of provider', *Journal of Regulatory Economics*, **15** (2), 141–63.
Guasch, J.L., J.J. Laffont and S. Straub (2002), 'Renegotiation of concession contracts in Latin America', World Bank Policy Research Working Paper 3011.
Hershen, D. and I. Wallis (2005), 'Competitive tendering as a contracting mechanism for subsidizing transport', *Journal of transport Economics and Policy*, **39**, 295–321.
ITU (2006), *Acceso Universal en Latinoamérica: situación y desafíos*, International Telecommunications Union.
Jaag, C. and U. Trinkner (2009), 'Tendering Universal Service Obligations in liberalized network industries', *Journal of Competition and Regulation in Network Industries*, **10** (4), 313–32.
Kalra, S.S. and B. Borgohain (2004), 'An enquiry into the impact of policy and regulation on rural telephony in India', *International Journal of Regulation and Governance*, **4** (2), 113–38.
Klein, M. (1998), 'Designating auctions for concessions – guessing the right value to bid and the winner's curse', *ViewPoint*, Note No. 60, Washington, DC: The World Bank.
Laffont, J.-J and J. Tirole (2000), *Competition in Telecommunications*, Cambridge, MA: MIT Press.
Mathisen, T.A. and G. Solvoll (2008), 'Competitive tendering and structural changes: an example from the bus industry', *Transport Policy*, **15** (1), 1–11.
Milgrom, P. (1999), 'Combination bidding in spectrum auctions', in S. Gillett and I. Vogelsang (eds), *Competition, Regulation and Convergence: Current Trends in Telecommunications Research*, Mahwah, NJ: Lawrence Erlbaum Associates, pp. 19–26.
Milgrom, P. and R. Weber (1982), 'A theory of auctions and competitive bidding', *Econometrica*, **50**, 1089–122.
OECD (2004), 'Leveraging telecommunications policies for pro-poor growth universal access funs with minimum-subsidy auctions', Organisation for Economic Co-operation and Development, Berlin.
Oxera (2007), 'Funding Universal Service Obligations in the Postal Sector; Report prepared for La Poste, De Post–La Poste, Hellenic Post, Poste Italiane, P&T Luxembourg, Correos, Magyar Post, Cyprus Post, Poczta Polska.
Panzar, J. (2000), 'A methodology for measuring the costs of Universal Service Obligations', *Information Economics and Policy*, **12** (3), 211–20.
Peha, J.M. (1999), 'Tradable Universal service Obligations', *Telecommunications Policy*, **23** (5), 363–74.
Pitsch, P. (1997), 'Reforming universal service: competing bidding or consumer choice', CATO Institution Briefing papers, Washington.
Sepúlveda, E. (2004), 'Minimum-subsidy auctions for public telecommunications access in rural areas', *Trends in Telecommunications Reform 2003: Promoting Universal Access to ICTs*, International Telecommunication Society.
Sorana, V. (2000), 'Auctions for Universal Service Subsidies', *Journal of Regulatory Economics*, **18** (1), 33–58.

Stegeman, J., S. Parsons, R. Frieden and M. Wilson (2007), 'Controlling universal service funding and promoting competition through reverse auctions', mimeo.
Wallsten, S. (2009), 'Reverse Auctions and Universal Telecommunications Service: Lessons from Global Experience', *Federal Communications Law Journal*, forthcoming.
Wellenius, B. (1997), 'Extending telecommunications service to rural areas – the Chilean experience: awarding subsidies through competitive bidding', Public Policy for the Private Sector, Note 105, World Bank, Washington, DC.
Wellenius, B. (2002), 'Closing the gap in access to rural communications. Chile 1995–2002', World Bank Discussion Paper 430, World Bank, Washington, DC.
WIK (2008), 'Ausschreibung von Post-Universaldiensten. Ausschreibungsgegenstände, Ausschreibungsverfahren und begleitender Regulierungsbedarf', WIK Diskussionsbeitrag 311, Wissenschaftliches Institut für Infrastructure und Kommunikationsdienste, Bad Honnef.
Williamson, O.J. (1976), 'Franchise bidding for natural monopoly: in general and with respect to CATV', *Bell Journal of Economics*, **7** (1), 73–104.

18. A team of rivals: collaboration between United States Postal Service and UPS*

Paul C. Smith and Paul E. Vogel

1 INTRODUCTION

Competing communication technologies are changing the underlying business model of the mail industry. To make matters worse, a global recession is reducing commercial mail volume, some of which is not predicted to return with better economic times. These forces are transforming the postal landscape and creating unprecedented pressure on postal operators to innovate, reduce costs and improve service.

This chapter examines the implications of one approach taken by the US Postal Service (USPS) by its outsourcing of transportation and related processing of mail to United Parcel Service (UPS) and other USPS competitors. It is common for postal operators to outsource line-haul transportation – a non-core element of mail. What is novel and noteworthy about the USPS collaboration with UPS et al. is the reliance on *competitors* to provide that transportation and processing. Such cooperation between competitors is described, as will be explained, as 'co-opetition', a term first coined in 1911, and later developed in a book on game theory in 1996.

Section 2 describes the theory of competitor collaboration ('co-opetition') and its general development. Section 3 applies that theory to USPS's vertical alignment with mailers and its role as a predicate to horizontal co-opetition with competitors. Sections 4 and 5 examine the specifics of the USPS–UPS collaboration. Section 6 discusses several public policy issues inherent in postal co-opetition. Section 7 concludes with several unaddressed questions and a look at the future of US postal co-opetition.

2 THE NOTION OF COMPETITOR COLLABORATION

The idea of one business collaborating with one or more of its competitors to satisfy its customers' needs has been antithetical to the traditional self-sufficiency that was the business norm. Enriching the competitor's shareowners, ostensibly, has been contrary to the core notions of Darwinian, eat-what-you-kill, free market capitalism. With competitor collaboration, there is a shift of the business paradigm from rivalry, in which competitors' mindsets may be characterized as engaging in a contest, to a different type of game in which resulting 'value' from different combinations and permutations is evaluated and then pursued, whether or not the combination is with a historic competitor.

The advent of game theory in the 1960s provided the metric used in *Co-opetition* (Brandenburger and Nalebuff, 1996; hereafter, Brandenburger–Nalebuff). That work

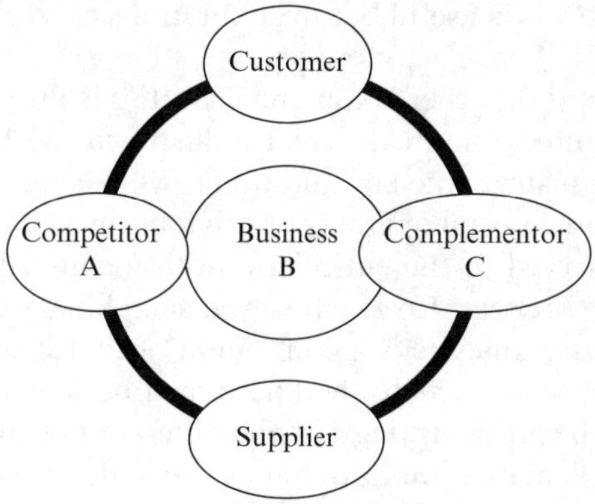

Figure 18.1 A value net

expanded on and then popularized the nascent concept of co-opetition, a term coined in 1911 by the Sealshipt Oyster Company (Cherington, 1913, p. 57, emphasis in original):

> The Sealshipt Oyster System had about 35,000 dealers who acted as agents for Sealshipt oysters [which owed its] marked success in developing its market . . . partly to its peculiarly efficient dealer work. It said to the dealer [in its sales manual]:
>
>> You are only one of several dealers selling our oysters in your city. *But you are not in competition with one another.* You are co-operating with one another to develop more business for each of you. You are in *co-opetition,* not in competition. What competition there is, is of the kind that you all can fight to common advantage. The oyster sold from the wooden tub is your only competitor. Remember – co-opetition, not competition between Sealshipt dealers.

Brandenburger–Nalebuff identify two critical components. First, co-opetition by a business is dependent on a mindset that is open to its application. The degree to which the notion of business as war is entrenched in Western commercial culture constitutes a true barrier to its serious acceptance. Second, the war mindset needs to be suspended and replaced with the idea that the conduct of business is a game, using a map of players in an industry or market that is called a 'value net' as shown in Figure 18.1. Vendors and customers are placed on the vertical dimension, and the other providers of similar goods or services are placed on the horizontal dimension, either as 'competitors' or 'complementors'.

'[A] player is your complementor if customers value your product *more* when they have the other player's product than when they have your product alone'. In contrast, 'A player is your competitor if customers value your product *less* when they have the other player's product than when they have your product alone' (Brandenburger–Nalebuff, p. 18, emphasis in orginal). For example, businesses B and C are complementors if collaborating adds more value than not. Similarly, if collaboration between businesses A and B produce less value than if they did not collaborate, then they should operate without collaboration as 'competitors'.

Brandenburger–Nalebuff's next step in applying this game theory is a set of analytic metrics to determine how the 'game' should be changed to achieve the added value. Their five-part game theory process is useful but the limitations of this chapter preclude review of it.

Postal operators' reliance on other commercial entities is far from novel. Using others has a long, well-documented role in the mail industry in the United States and other countries.[1] As in other industries, the key question is what is reserved versus what is open to sourcing from outside the postal operator or other business entity? Traditionally, 'core' functions are usually reserved to the entity and not outsourced, while 'non-core' functions can be outsourced (Meltzer, 1997). However, such binary distinctions have limited usefulness. Instead, a better analytic is a continuum of all functions of a business in an order from most to least 'core', where the line drawn between direct performance and outsourcing is based on business strategy. While different postal authorities have placed that in-house/outsource demarcation in different spots along the mail continuum, there seems to be general consensus that final 'last mile' delivery is generally retained as a core function to be performed directly by the postal operator. In contrast, line-haul transportation has a long history of being outsourced to railroads, stage coach companies, and ocean shipping companies (Baker and Leonard, 1993).

On that continuum of functions, the downstream induction of mail, presorting and other processing falls in the middle. This worksharing has been commented on in depth in the past (Elcano et al., 2000). It deserves brief mention here because the outsourced service provider – for example a mass mailer – is not external to the mail market, but instead is a direct stakeholder in the postal 'game' even in the absence of worksharing. Often that mailer is a postal operator 'friend' that is aligned with the post's interests in preserving a viable mail system. Even so, its interests are not uniformly aligned with the postal operator and, in a sense, the mailer is a 'foe' in that it is adverse to the post on matters such as the postage rates it must pay.

Co-opetition is akin to worksharing. As a business approach, worksharing shares the same motivations as co-opetition: the need to improve the value proposition to mailers by extraordinary cost reduction measures. Worksharing represents a transformational change in the mindset of what a post is, and how it functions. The 1990s' outsourcing to customers or their agents became an intermediate mindset step to the 2000s' co-opetition. The paradigm of the monolithic friend and monolithic foe gave way to a more strategic mindset that alignment and opposition can and do co-exist in relationships. In short, friends can also be foes, depending on the circumstances.

The fact that postal operators and private carriers regularly are in commercial 'combat' over bulk and single-piece customers does not necessarily preclude opportunities for collaboration that are mutually beneficial and that advance the public interest. Even so, the required *mindset change* to have it happen was substantial and a long time in coming.

3 EMERGENCE OF VERTICAL COLLABORATION UP AND DOWN THE MAIL-STREAM

Earlier in the 1970s, USPS needed a way to keep up with the growth in mail volume and population and a declining economy. New operational strategies were needed to increase service and reduce costs. USPS looked vertically along their supply chain for help. That is,

USPS looked upstream[2] to the bulk mail shippers to identify actions that those shippers could undertake to reduce its operating costs and investments.

This worksharing began in 1976 with activities that mailers could perform before the mail was inducted into the mail-stream and, in return, for which they could receive discounted rates. These activities include barcoding packages, presorting mail, and drop-shipping mail to a USPS facility close to the final destination. These arrangements contributed to mail growth in the 1970s and 1980s.

One particular aspect of the USPS worksharing is their Parcel Select product. While generally mail volume continued to increase, the Parcel Post volume in particular had begun to decline. From 1972 to 1990, annual Parcel Post volume decreased by approximately 370 million packages. In response, a new worksharing type was approved in 1991, called Parcel Select, under which Parcel Post packages could be collected, presorted, and delivered to the USPS facility closest to the final destination, thus freeing USPS of significant costs. This made Parcel Post more competitive than before, and its annual volume increased by almost 250 million pieces over the next 12 years (General Accounting Office, 2003).

Because UPS and FedEx both used it, Parcel Select was a 'bridge' to horizontal collaboration, or co-opetition, with competitors.

4 USPS AND UPS HORIZONTAL COLLABORATION

While worksharing became a bridge to horizontal collaboration, it took several independent forces to facilitate the USPS to venture across that bridge. The first was the convergence of a set of historical events.

Convergence of External Forces

From 1975 to the present, the package transportation market grew rapidly, fueled by automation, competition, and, for most of that time, a strong economy. The arrival of e-commerce impacted on the demand for shipping services; consumer expectations on performance in package delivery increased along with the demand that was stimulated by e-commerce activity. Consumers felt immediate satisfaction making a purchase, yet had to wait for the product to arrive. Transportation methods needed to work within the speed expectations of e-commerce, especially during busy holiday periods. The expansion of broadband access across the nation and the evolving consumer buying patterns increased participation in e-commerce activities.

As the new century began, package demand continued to grow, the economy was strong, and competition was stable. Then, the technology 'bubble' popped, the economy faltered and transportation providers such as USPS suffered losses. Next were the events of 9/11 that virtually shut down commerce for a week and caused a six-week interruption in transportation volumes. Shortly thereafter, the USPS mail system was buffeted by a series of anthrax attacks.

Among the many seismic changes that those three events produced were the service interruptions caused when passenger air carriers did not carry cargo while they addressed security requirements. This affected the mail movement because a segment of the transportation chain was removed as an option. Until then, in addition to the lift of a small number of dedicated aircraft, the USPS relied on passenger air carriers for much of their Priority mail volumes and during this period had to find alternative carriers.

When USPS was confronted with the confluence of these developments in the early 2000s, the organization realized that it must pursue more dramatic change and, in the context of Brandenburger–Nalebuff's value net, proceeded to explore co-opetition on the horizontal dimension.

Inadequacy of the Old System

Before co-opetition, the USPS air network had been fragmented, consisting of too many carriers, a limited number of passenger airline night-time flights, more hand-offs than necessary, which increased the risk of service failures and problems, multiple levels of overhead, redundant administrative activities, and no centralized information technology system. The networks of the passenger air carriers being relied upon were, obviously, optimized for passenger travel, not package movement. One example is the preferred time of flights: night flights are needed for time-sensitive movement of packages while people prefer day-time flights. Between 1996 and 2001, USPS had tried, as an alternative, the use of a dedicated fleet of Boeing 727 aircraft for overnight operations that were hubbed out of Indianapolis, Indiana (the Eagle Network) and out of Oakland/Sacramento, California (the Western Network, or WNET).

The Criteria in Selecting a New Basic Service Transportation Provider

Could USPS provide its own line-haul transportation? USPS is a delivery company, not an air transportation company. It had to look to others for that basic component of its service offering. The following were the most important USPS criteria for selecting a carrier:

1. *Scope: an extensive air transportation network* Economies of scope were sought from those carriers that had full geographic reach over the USPS service area. The previous approach involved integrating many different carriers into an inefficient patchwork of smaller companies. One legal hurdle to this type of efficiency gain was the US postal laws which stated the USPS 'shall make a fair and equitable distribution of mail business to carriers providing similar modes of transportation services to the Postal Service' (39 USC 101(f)). This requirement was repealed in 2008.
2. *Scale: shared network* To achieve the efficiencies that were sought, the air transportation provided to USPS would need to be on a shared, not dedicated, basis. In one of the prior USPS air networks, the USPS had acquired the entire capacity of the aircraft involved. The resulting dedicated-lift network committed the USPS for specified lift capacity despite potential future mail volume variability. Under a shared network, the USPS can have a long-term contract under which they purchase incremental space based on planned and actual mail volumes determined on short-term intervals, and thereby reduce the chance of capacity being purchased that will not be used.
3. *Reliability* The market expectations required that a high reliability of service be

achieved. The carriers were evaluated on their ability to provide consistently reliable service.

4. *Nature: 'like-kind' operations* As Postmaster General John E. Potter said in announcing the USPS–UPS collaboration, it was prudent for the Postal Service to work with suppliers that have the transportation of like commodities as a principal mission. The passenger air carriers have generally provided reliable service to the USPS although their primary mission is to move passengers. The USPS has seen that the integration of both technology and operations tends to have an easier fit when it happens with those whose core function involves moving like commodities.[3]
5. *Fleet: newer, rather than older, aircraft* As the age and the number of duty cycles of an aircraft increase, maintenance costs increase rapidly. The older the fleet, the more likely unscheduled as well as scheduled maintenance and repair could affect service performance and add to the carriers' costs. The need for reliability and efficiency resulted in a preference for carriers with the newer fleet of aircraft. In addition, the new aircraft are more fuel efficient and in better compliance with federal noise reduction standards.
6. *Resiliency: financial and operational* In the past, the carriers that were part of the air transportation patchwork were financially weaker than companies such as UPS and FedEx, and were dependent on USPS for a substantial portion of their revenue. This affected USPS's ability to modify and adapt the network to changing market needs, and also caused USPS to bear a larger percentage of the network costs. That 'static' fragility is even more pronounced in dynamic economic conditions. The ability to weather not just the weather but also recessions or other contingencies or crises is even more important to the USPS now as it is contending with reduced volumes and higher cost pressures.[4]
7. *Technology: information technology (IT) infrastructure* Sophisticated IT is needed to ensure the service performance and reliability called for by business and the general public. USPS ought to work with those who have established the IT platforms that can meet those needs. In the case of the UPS–USPS collaboration, it has allowed for these two organizations to modify their IT systems and blend the use of barcode reading technology. This technology interface provides the necessary hand-off information that is needed to comply with each company's quality standards. It also ensures that the mailer has visibility to its products, regardless of the company that has control over the package at any point in time.

In short, USPS's market-driven service requirements made UPS and other express package delivery companies a more attractive alternative.

Initial Steps

The 30-year history of worksharing, that is, vertical collaboration, was the predicate for alternative methods for mail transport. USPS began collaborating with FedEx in August 2001 to address package and mail movement. Shortly after reaching agreement with FedEx, the change in security regulations for commercial air carriers occurred in the wake of the events of 9/11. This led USPS to adjust the mail and package logistics streams. USPS had to address increasing consumer demands for volumes and service without the passenger airline component of their supply chain. The new relationship provided USPS stability and scope, but resulted in a limited variety of vendors.

Internal Changes at UPS and USPS

More important than the changed external reality was the change in mindset of both organizations that permitted joint action.

For decades, the individual mindsets of those working at USPS and UPS as well as their collective organizational culture meant that they considered each other as adversaries. As arch rivals, they not only fought for sales from similar customers but uniformly opposed anything that might benefit the other, often whether or not it might also result in mutual benefits. Within the USPS, receiving a package via UPS was unpopular and communicated as such to the sender, and the same was true at UPS. The rivalry extended beyond the marketplace to the regulatory and legislative policy-making arena. UPS was an aggressive and active adversary of the USPS in litigation before the Postal Rate Commission (now Postal Regulatory Commission) on matters involving *inter alia* rates and services, and the USPS was equally aggressive in promoting its interests in those proceedings.

Given the long history of 'commercial combat', the internal changes needed to be pervasive. So, how did it come about?

First, everyone within the industry was watching and assessing the emerging coopetition. The FedEx collaboration introduced, on a major scale, the possibilities of competitor collaboration (the 'horizontal' potential). It was itself built on the stage-setting experiences of competitor worksharing under the Parcel Select program (the 'vertical' potential). Second, achieving the internal buy-in inside USPS was itself a major accomplishment and, once done, made subsequent collaboration more likely to be acceptable. Third, UPS itself was changing, with an expanded international operation and a broader array of transportation offerings; business was *not* as usual and that resulted in a more open perspective. UPS's greater involvement in the mail industry through its ownership in Mail Boxes Etc (MBE) and its entry into mail presortation and processing, now called UPS Mail Innovations, changed the nature of its stakeholder status. Fourth, the shift in the composition of mail towards more advertising mail, and the greater sophistication of direct marketing, drove consumer purchasing decisions and resulted in a greater volume of package shipments for all the carriers in the package shipment market segment. Fifth, besides the direct impact on the size of the package delivery market, greater appreciation was given to the fact that the USPS provides an important communications infrastructure for a variety of business activities such as finance, real estate, and corporate management and employee communications. As Mike Eskew, then UPS Chairman and CEO, testified before the Presidential Commission on Postal Reform in 2004:

> Our overall corporate operations (including MBE and mail related functions) generated over $220,000,000 in postal revenues to the USPS in 2002. The Postal Service is one of our main avenues of communication with our 360,000 employees and our customers. In addition, UPS is a major benefactor of the advertising and catalogues that flow through the mail – it generates package volume for UPS and our competitors.

The Meeting of the Mindsets

The paradigm shift in mindsets started with the senior management of both USPS and UPS seeing the potential benefits of improving the relationship. In September 2002, they formed a team from each organization to begin meeting on a regular basis. These meetings resulted in accomplishments on two different planes.

First, the two teams working together resolved an array of issues and challenges that ranged from trivial operational frictions[5] to core postal legislative reforms.

One of the first tangible results of the new relationship occurred when the USPS asked the Postal Rate Commission (PRC) to approve the first ever Negotiated Service Agreement (NSA) in the fall of 2002. The USPS briefed UPS and on the merits of NSAs, since UPS opposition could have a detrimental effect. (In the past, UPS was publicly opposed to NSAs in any form.) NSAs are customized pricing arrangements for a specific customer, which can include a volume-based incentive. The proposed NSA was for Capital One bank for their First Class mail volume. UPS decided not to oppose the arrangement before the PRC. The Capital One NSA became a prime example of UPS narrowing its focus to competitive package issues, and allowing the USPS to move forward with innovative methods of enhancing their core mail products.

In 2002, the USPS provided informal advance notice and briefed UPS about a substantial pension accounting error that resulted in overfunding of their Civil Service Retirement System (CSRS). By doing so, UPS obtained answers to questions that permitted UPS to not oppose legislation (PL 108-18) to correct that $78 billion error.

Before the President signed into law Public Law 110-405 on October 13, 2008, the Department of Transportation (DOT) had regulated the rates and service of the USPS's international air transportation of mail. The USPS had long sought deregulation of this market, arguing that it restricted its choice of air carriers and made it pay above-market rates. (Passenger airlines vigorously defended the former regulated rate structure.) At USPS's request, UPS filed briefs at the DOT in support of USPS. In addition, UPS lobbied Capitol Hill and, over the three intervening years, UPS played a leadership role, which ultimately resulted in the enactment of the legislative reform (PL 110-405).

UPS has been actively participating in a broad-based coalition of the mail industry stakeholders to ensure that 'Do Not Mail' restrictions are not enacted by state legislatures that could adversely reduce mail volumes. Through that coalition, UPS engaged its state public affairs managers to help in successfully thwarting efforts in three states.

Interestingly, the outcome in each of these efforts did not compromise either organization's interests. Instead, those outcomes, in the Brandenburger–Nalebuff model, represented additional net value to each party. It has also not diminished either party's zeal in competing against each other in the package delivery market.

Second, on a more fundamental level, these joint efforts forged a working relationship between both organizations. As time went on, the relationships expanded so that direct communications occur between the right people without the need for the original relationship teams serving as intermediaries.[6]

The result has been a noteworthy shift of mindset necessary to permit co-opetition to exist. The new interactions between UPS and USPS resulted in an improved tone in public forums, a more narrow and focused opposition where legitimate differences existed, a willingness to find agreement where in fact common interests existed, and a

Table 18.1 Comparison of USPS and UPS

USPS	UPS
Founded: 1775	Founded: 1907
Annual Revenue: $75 billion	Annual Revenue: $50.5 billion
US Employees: 656,000 career employees (78,000 part-time)	Global Employees: 425,000 (355,000 US; 70,000 international), of which approximately 180,000 part-time)
Annual Deliveries: 208 billion (including 835 million pieces of international mail). Delivers 46% of world letters and cards	Annual Deliveries: 3.9 billion packages and documents
Vehicle Fleet: 221,000	Vehicle Fleet: 107,000
Aircraft: none	Aircraft: 570 operated by UPS (world's 9th largest airline)
	Global Air Hubs: 15 serving 835 airports (400 domestic and 435 international)
Service Area: Global through partners	Service Area: Every address in North America and Europe. Covers 200 countries and territories
Retail Access: 32,700 post offices plus 56,600 stores and banks that sell postage stamps and 375,000 postal drop boxes (as of 2007)	Retail Access: 23,000 retail access points (UPS customer centers, UPS stores, Mail Boxes Etc, and authorized outlets) plus 40,000 drop boxes

continuing open dialogue between both parties. The recast relationship could easily have stopped there, as just a reasonable product of the new realities of the postal and delivery marketplace ('Good fences make good neighbors', and such). However, the relationship went well beyond that, with some significant operational interaction.

5 THE USPS AND UPS ARRANGEMENTS

Comparison of Scale and Scope of USPS and UPS

Table 18.1 provides a snapshot of the two organizations. UPS has a much greater worldwide presence and employs a much greater percentage of part-time employees, while USPS has greater delivery density and retail access.

Details on the USPS–UPS Domestic Air Contract

In 2006 the USPS expanded the use of co-opetition through a new contract, this time with UPS.

When the USPS and UPS entered their agreement, the expansion of co-opetition increased over the prior, similar, arrangement and worksharing approach. Both parties had specific segments of their logistics network that they believed were efficient. UPS was very efficient in moving packages through the line-haul portion of the transportation network and had available capacity on its air network. USPS was less efficient in package movement and was dependent on a single air transportation provider to move its air packages.

The solution seemed clear, but required the leadership commitment to change the decades-old mindsets that existed within these two historic rivals. The 2006 signing of a new Air Transportation Contract between the USPS and UPS was a substantial and visible first step in creating an internal atmosphere in both organizations that would permit co-opetition. The USPS benefited in this contract by having a second, high-quality air transportation provider and the needed redundancy in its air operations. It also provided much-needed new air capacity for the very heavy volumes during the holiday mailing season. In a June 28, 2006, USPS press release on the relationship, the Postmaster General stated 'It only makes sense for the Postal Service to take advantage of the reach offered by UPS. The added advantage of the similarity of our operations will only enhance the Postal Service's ability to provide the highest levels of service for our customers'.

The 2006 Contract called for UPS to transport primarily First Class and Priority mail to and from 98 US cities. The mail would be tendered to UPS at origin airport facilities and tendered back to the USPS at destination airport facilities and would flow through the UPS air network.

Service began on July 1, 2006, with an appropriate ramp-up to ensure successful integration and execution. For that to happen, extensive internal communications were necessary. During the negotiations of the contract, the parties were subject to non-disclosure agreements, which meant that information flow and training of the field managers needed to happen over an abbreviated time of several weeks immediately after the contract was signed. In addition, it meant that both parties to the contract had to be flexible enough to accommodate the unexpected. Because under USPS personnel management practices, the USPS field managers are generally accountable for, and evaluated on, service performance, the improved performance that resulted from the contract motivated them to quickly become supporters of the new arrangement, and even sought expansion, once they saw the benefits. Investments in advanced technology by both parties allowed for systems to communicate and pass data. This integration was necessary for the co-opetition to be successful.

The USPS–UPS arrangement, in its fourth year, provides net value to both organizations in the traditional sense, and provides net value to the public in the Brandenburger–Nalebuff model. Both companies see benefits in the areas of revenue, customer service, or cost avoidance. Customers seamlessly see performance levels sustaining or increasing and more control in product costs. What consumers do not see are the details of how this arrangement works, which helps ensure the viability of competition as well as collaboration.

Other USPS–UPS Transportation-related Collaboration

Besides the 2006 Domestic Air Contract, UPS is involved in multiple other areas of transportation collaboration:

1. *Terminal handling services* UPS provides terminal handling services in support of USPS inbound and outbound mail air transportation.
2. *International mail transportation* UPS provides mail transportation between all five USPS International Service Centers to destinations in the Americas and the Pacific

Rim. UPS has also been active in the new competition for civilian, military and diplomatic mail. Contracts were awarded on April 28, 2009, and service was scheduled to begin on July 11, 2009, under the new procurement regime established by Public Law 110-405.

3. *Surface transportation of Mail Transport Equipment (MTE)* The nature of the US mail requires the USPS to consolidate specific shapes of mail into containers. Millions of mail sacks, letter trays, flat tubs and Over the Road (OTR) containers are moved every week. A disproportionate amount of the US mail moves from the east coast to the west coast, thus creating a need to periodically re-balance the MTE inventories. UPS's surface transportation network provides an efficient means for the repositioning of the MTE. UPS and USPS were able to complement each other's strengths and needs to make this process more efficient.
4. *Peak Season* During the fall Peak Season, and at other times to meet special needs, UPS has provided short-term air transportation capacity to the USPS.
5. *UPS Basic and Special cases* USPS and UPS collaborated on the introduction and implementation of UPS Basic, which offers select customers delivery by the USPS through its Parcel Select tariff offering. USPS and UPS also collaborated on the customized and synchronized delivery of Harry Potter books.
6. *UPS Package Return Service* UPS and USPS are piloting a collaborative service for returning retail merchandise. The UPS offering, Package Return Flexible Access, allows retailers to provide their customers with additional options for returning items. Customers may leave a UPS Returns® package in their mailbox or drop it off at a post office or collection box. Once a returns package arrives at the local post office, a UPS driver picks it up and transports the package back to the retailer via the UPS ground network.

Blending specific processes of two massive organizations' logistics networks can be a difficult challenge. Fortunately, technology has reached a point that allowed for these two organizations to modify their IT systems and blend the use of barcode reading technology. This technology interface provides the necessary hand-off information that is needed to ensure compliance with each company's quality standards. It also ensures that mailers have visibility to their products, regardless of the company that has control over the package at any point in time.

Responding to Challenges

The threshold challenge is recognizing that, while each organization shares many similarities, fundamental differences exist: each operates under a very different ownership system, is subject to different legal and regulatory requirements and oversight, has developed different operating procedures and systems, and has strong inward cultures, all of which make external collaboration challenging. Achieving sustained success in integrating and maintaining the collaboration required special attention. What follows are the key joint efforts established to achieve that success:

1. *Internal champions* Within each organization an internal champion and advocate was developed who 'owned' their side of the relationship. Without that,

either skeptics, or the inertia of the status quo, or both, would have thwarted the initiative.

2. *Team continuity* After an initial period, each party was able to identify those who had the capabilities necessary for the collaboration. It quickly became clear that rotating people into and out of the team only created confusion. Lack of continuity would also make other aspects difficult, such as developing trust.
3. *Mutual trust* A high level of trust between the teams was needed. While this is a standard business objective for any team effort, in the case of postal collaboration between competitors, the absence of trust turns any setback or problem into what could be perceived as a conspiracy, attempted sabotage, or worse.
4. *Multiple levels of communication* Communications occurred, and continue, between senior management of both UPS and USPS at regular intervals. Between those meetings, a communications channel exists so that problems and opportunities can be addressed early. At every level below that, both sides have established communications and meetings.
5. *Clear lines of responsibility* With a large management team and a complex set of problems to address, it became clear that each side needed to have clear leadership. Given the size and complexity of the organizations, and the multiple points of possible contact, coordination of the communications and decision making was essential.
6. *Service performance metrics and goals* Early in the relationship, performance goals and metrics were established. Both organizations have cultures under which they are prone to measure everything, so this was easier than it otherwise might have been. The challenge was to ensure that each organization synchronized its metrics.
7. *Flexibility and dispute resolution* At the beginning especially, but also throughout the contract, unforeseen situations and contingencies arose. This could involve unexpected volumes, weather, or any other human-made or natural variable. Whether the contract provided for that variable or not, both sides demonstrated an attitude of flexibility and desire to solve whatever problems arose. Where problems could not be operationally resolved, then a mutually acceptable process for fast, informal resolution was used, on an *ad hoc* basis. A contract dispute mechanism is helpful, but the will to quickly resolve disputes is more so.

6 POLICY MATTERS

Postal Policy

The primary postal policy of the United States is stated in section 101(a) of title 39, United States Code. It says that the 'basic function [of the USPS is] to provide postal services that bind the Nation together through the personal, educational, literary, and business correspondence of the people. It shall provide prompt, reliable, and efficient service to all patrons in all areas and shall render postal services to all communities'. Foremost, of course, is the public interest in having a viable mail system for personal communication and as a channel of commerce. Unlike other economic enterprises, there appears near universal political acceptance of the necessity for maintaining a postal system. What is an open political question is how that system should be structured and operated. In the US, there has been a general willingness to turn to outsourcing through advanced address processing, presortation, and downstream induction into the mail stream. In the last decade, greater focus has been on the USPS's general 'last mile' competencies and looking to other air and surface network operators as a way to improve service and reduce cost, both considered essential for the USPS to be an economically sustainable mail system. Co-opetition should be judged in the US as to the extent to which the public policy of title 39 is advanced by its use.

Competition Policy

FTC/DOJ *Guidelines for Collaboration among Competitors*

Those responsible for enforcing antitrust laws and competition policy have also undergone a mindset change. The US Federal Trade Commission (FTC) and the Antitrust Division of the Department of Justice (DOJ) formally recognized the inherent public interest in permitting such collaboration in certain cases and has issued guidelines for such arrangements. '[I]n order to compete in modern markets, competitors sometimes need to collaborate' (FTC–DOJ 2000, n. 35; hereafter FTC–DOJ Guidelines).

Under the FTC–DOJ Guidelines, the core question is whether an agreement between competitors would result in less competition than would otherwise exist without that agreement. The USPS line-haul transportation and related services being provided by the competitors[7] have resulted in service quality improvements and reduced costs. The collaboration has resulted in making the USPS more competitive, not less.

Under the FTC–DOJ Guidelines, if likelihood of competitive harm were to be indicated, then the agencies would look at six questions:

1. *Exclusivity* Will the competitors continue to compete independently in the market in which the collaboration functions?
2. *Control over assets* Do the participants in the collaboration retain or lose control over the assets needed to compete?
3. *Financial interests* What will be the nature and the extent of the participants' financial interests in the collaboration or in each other?
4. *Control of collaboration decision making* Will competitively significant decision making occur in the collaboration and who will control it?
5. *Information exchange* What is the likelihood of anticompetitive information sharing?
6. *Duration* How long will the collaboration remain in existence?

In the type of collaboration covered by this chapter, the application of these six factors provides strong assurance that the collaboration is pro-, not anticompetitive. Questions were raised in 2001 regarding the first major collaboration by USPS and a competitor, and no judicial action resulted.

Inherent safeguards in competitive unbundling

Apart from the legal criteria, cooperation with a competitor raises a fundamental business question: if improving service performance and reducing costs make each more a formidable competitor to the other, then why do it? Why go the extra step of collaborating with each other?

The answer is twofold: the nature of the network and the existence of competition. The network of each player in the postal and delivery 'game' is a complex composite of discrete service elements, each of which can be performed directly by that player or outsourced. That outsourcing only depends on the existence of multiple providers willing to compete to provide it.[8] So long as there is competition for providing a lane of transportation or other discrete service element, it behooves each competitor to seriously consider performing that service at the best terms and conditions or risk losing that particular piece of business to another competitor and the resulting network improvement would still occur. The existence of a competitive alternative ensures that a good contract from both parties' perspectives will be written and that its performance will meet those contractual terms and conditions. If the USPS is going to contract out anyway for an improved service element that will make the USPS more competitive, then there is no reason for UPS not to bid aggressively and earnestly for it.

Conversely, the same answer to that question applies to the USPS and other posts. Moreover, the operational needs of a postal operator, such as reliability, faster time in transit, and visibility, now having to function in a growing global market have become more stringent.

Security Policy

Both national security and personal privacy are even more paramount now. By increasing reliability, reducing time in transit, and providing far greater transparency by the application of information technology, the use of co-opetition has provided fewer opportunities for gaps in security and personal privacy.

7 CONCLUSION

It is significant that the world's largest postal service is partnering with the world's largest package delivery company.

The USPS commits mail, including competitive packages, to UPS and other package delivery competitors for domestic and international line-haul transportation; competitors commit their packages to the USPS for final delivery under the Parcel Select workshare program. The USPS has used the 'lowest combined cost' principle, one of the elements inherent in Brandenburger–Nalebuff's value net, in its vertical and horizontal collaboration. The other value elements have been improved reliability, reduced time in transit, and greater tracking visibility for shippers.

These bilateral offerings do not affect either party's ability or motivation to remain aggressively competitive in the package delivery market. The new approach does not impede UPS or the USPS from taking stands on public policy issues that are truly important to each organization, nor restrict vigorous competition among them in seeking business from customers. That premise has been proven true by the real-world, decade-long existence of postal co-opetition in the United States and its growing use in other countries.

The International Bureau of the Universal Postal Union (UPU) stated well the case for such partnerships (International Bureau, 2007, p. 8):

> The 3 dimensions of the postal network – physical, financial, and electronic – provide a powerful infrastructure for partnerships to exploit global commerce. In this age of 'co-opetition', partnerships with perceived competitors are opening up new and innovative ways to build stronger networks for the various actors in the postal sector.
>
> For instance, in June 2006 the United States Postal Service (USPS) awarded a 3-year contract to the specialized transportation and logistics company UPS to transport mail by plane to and from 98 U.S. cities. The agreement between two 'friendly rivals' is expected to help USPS accomplish its tasks more effectively while at the same time generating revenue of more than $100 million a year, according to estimates.
>
> What can be learnt from this example is that Posts, if they want to provide the most complete solution to their business customers, will not shy away from cooperation with other companies in the domains where these represent a valid complement to the postal network.

Posts can battle with competitors over market share, battle with suppliers over cost, and battle with customers over price, and yet also collaborate, vertically with suppliers and customers, and horizontally with traditional competitors. Under the new market conditions, as Ray Noorda of Novell said, 'you have to compete and cooperate at the same time' (Brandenburger and Nalebuff, 1996, p. 4).

The nature and extent of co-opetition is likely to change. The USPS will seek to further increase customer value through partnering (USPS, 2008). The current UPS and FedEx arrangements with USPS are one-to-one arrangements of mutual benefit. Contracting with UPS gives USPS variety and competition in their co-opetition model. Multiple worksharing options provide variety to mailers. In both these arrangements, variety controls costs, fosters consistency and mitigates risk. Where the public–private partnerships in the transportation industry may head are more toward the one-to-many relationships at a number of places within the transportation network.

The next round of co-opetition may involve complex arrangements where multiple parties carry a variety of goods regardless of the originating sale. The dissection of the transportation network to create ideal streams from any point to any point across multiple carriers may be the next iteration of co-opetition. This becomes more likely as globalization of transportation networks continues. International regulations and national prominence of specific vendors will require complex co-opetition arrangements to maximize efficiency and maintain customer service expectations.

To further the co-opetition model in the transportation market, accurate data on cost and performance for all parties are necessary at all stages of the network. Organizations need the assurance that an arrangement will be financially beneficial and meet customer expectations. For the USPS–UPS arrangement, each organization relied on its own data and interpretation of its network performance or customer needs. Each organization assumes that its data are correct. When more components of the network are added, and more organizations join the co-opetition, who will rely on what data becomes critical to promoting a winning arrangement for all parties involved and the consumers.

In conclusion, it is important to note that postal co-opetition raises other matters not discussed here because of limitations of time and space. Several, identified below, are worthy of further examination.

One is the formal, externally imposed, procurement rules that are predominantly artifacts of governmental agencies. In private industry procurement is guided by sound business practices (subject only to certain issue-specific rules, such as those to protect against age, race, gender, or religious discrimination). Do postal competitive bidding rules impede creative problem-solving and potential efficiencies that collaboration could provide?

As to energy and environmental impacts, does co-opetition that optimizes the networks of major carriers advance the national interests in emissions reduction and energy independence? What related opportunities exist for joint vehicle or fuel development, acquisition, or refueling, without affecting individual brands or firm–customer relationships?

Finally, mail and package delivery are labor-intensive industry sectors, and as such organized labor units are significant stakeholders in the success of posts and package delivery companies. What role do such stakeholders play in postal co-opetition?

NOTES

* This chapter reflects the views of the authors, and not necessarily USPS or UPS or Deloitte LLC. The authors acknowledge the contributions made by Patrick Pendergast of Deloitte LLC, and Michael Schmitz of UPS.

1. Purchasing line-haul transportation services from others has been the norm throughout the history of Royal Mail (Baker and Leonard, 1993) and the USPS; see 'A Brief History of the Package Delivery Market', available at: http://www.treas.gov/offices/domestic-finance/usps/docs/parcel_history_final1.doc, accessed 14 September 2009.
2. The USPS had also looked *downstream* to its delivery point customers. For example, the USPS encouraged mail recipients to use post office boxes, which reduced costs to the USPS and increased convenience to end users.
3. '[A] partner that has different capabilities is also likely to have different culture and operation mode. The same differentiating factors that make a partner attractive in the establishment phase may become a drag during the operational phase' (Shenkar, 2003, p. 12).
4. The topic of Supply Chain Resilience from the standpoint of mailers and shippers is gaining more attention with the market volatility (UPS and Economist Intelligence Unit, 2008).
5. For example, there was resolution of complaints over statements made by certain field representatives that otherwise would have either festered internally (perpetuating organizational hostility) or migrated into more public forums (for example, the media, the courts, or Congress).
6. See 2008 Annual Reports. USPS: http://www.usps.com/financials/_pdf/annual_report-2008.pdf. UPS: http://files.shareholder.com/downloads/UPS/632325280x0x281044/fa0304b6-7a81-457d-bf70-49179fe7b22a/UPS2008ARlores.pdf, accessed 14 September 2009.
7. UPS, FedEx, DHL and other carriers also provide similar services, and all compete aggressively to do so.
8. The plural 'providers' is used here because the post itself retains the ability to directly provide any service element to itself and thus, even if there were only one outside provider, that provider would be competing against the post itself for that offering. This is, of course, the classic 'make or buy' decision process involved in outsourcing.

REFERENCES

Baker, Rodney and Alan Leonard (1993), *Great Steamers White and Gold: A History of Royal Mail Ships and Services*, Southampton: Ensign Publications.

Brandenburger, Adam and Barry J. Nalebuff (1996), *Co-opetition: A Revolution Mindset that Combines Competition and Cooperation*, Garden City, NY: Doubleday.

Cherington, Paul Terry (1913), *Advertising as a Business Force: A Compilation of Experience Records*, Garden City, NY: Doubleday, Page & Company for the Associated Advertising Clubs of America quoting *Printers' Ink,* January 19, 1911.

Elcano, Mary S., R. Andrew German and John T. Pickett (2000), 'Hiding in plain sight: the quiet liberalization of the United States Postal System', in Michael A. Crew and Paul A. Kleindorfer (eds), *Current Directions in Postal Reform*, Boston, MA: Kluwer Academic, pp. 353–93.

Federal Trade Commission and Department of Justice (2000), *Guidelines for Collaborations Among Competitors*, available at: http://www.ftc.gov/os/2000/04/ftcdojguidelines.pdf, accessed 14 September 2009.

General Accounting Office, (2003). *U.S. Postal Service: A Primer on Postal Worksharing,* available at: http://www.gao.gov/new.items/d03927.pdf, accessed 14 September 2009.

International Bureau of the Universal Postal Union, Operations and Technology Directorate (2007), *The Postal Sector: A Key Facilitator of Global Commerce for SMEs,* available at: http://www.upu.int/news_centre/2007/en/paper_2007-05-01_the_postal_sector_a_key_facilitator_of_global_commerce_for_smes_en.pdf, accessed 14 September 2009.

Meltzer, Mark (1997), 'Outsourcing Transportation can save costs: third-party providers offer additional services to help shippers cope', *Atlanta Business Chronicle*, 28 March.

Shenkar, Oded (2003), *Public–Private Partnerships: The U.S. Postal Service–Federal Express Alliance*, IBM endowment for the Business of Government; New Ways to Management, available at: http://www.businessofgovernment.org/pdfs/ShenkarReport.pdf, accessed 14 September 2009.

UPS and Economist Intelligence Unit, (2008), 'Supply Chain Resilience: How Are Global Businesses Doing?', available at: viewswire.eiu.com/report_dl.asp?mode=fi&fi=1893834374.PDF, accessed 14 September 2009.

USPS (2008), *Vision 2013: Five-Year Strategic Plan for 2009–2013*, available at: http://www.usps.com/strategicplanning/vision2013.htm, accessed 14 September 2009.

19. Customer satisfaction models for Itella's business customers

Leeni Kiikkilä

1 INTRODUCTION

The topic of customer satisfaction (CS) evolved in management theory during the late 1980s–early 1990s, and has become one of the systematic ways of listening to customers in many organizations. This chapter aims to share the experience of Itella's long-term CS research program. It describes the current CS research system with respect to Itella business customers, how the content of the surveys are modeled and analyzed and how the results are utilized. This chapter also reviews the development of analytic methods used in CS research – from gap analysis to structural equation modeling – and presents current models measuring business CS. Furthermore, the value of customer loyalty as an ultimate consequence of CS is discussed, especially concerning the postal market and relative to our CS data. The chapter also considers the correlation between CS and position in the market relative to Itella CS and market share data. Thus, the basic approach is to combine theory and practice – conducting CS research that produces reliable, valid and relevant results that can be utilized for the improvement of business performance.

The chapter proceeds as follows. In Section 2, background on Itella is provided. Section 3 describes the underlying theory of CS models. Section 4 discusses the various levels of CS studies conducted at Itella and notes the focus of this chapter on purchase decision makers in customer organizations. Section 5 describes the structure of the general CS model underlying Itella's approach to CS studies. Section 6 explains alternative approaches to structuring CS surveys and analyzing CS data, and explains why Itella uses a correlation approach for purchase decision-maker studies. Section 7 then describes the nature of correlation studies at Itella in greater detail and reports the results of three basic CS indicators for 11 of Itella's products. Section 8 describes the use of CS results for management decision making. Section 9 concludes with challenges for the future, including being able to predict future customer satisfaction changes resulting from CS initiatives.

2 ITELLA AND BUSINESS CUSTOMERS

Itella (formerly Finland Post) is a service business whose core competency lies in managing information and material flows for its customers. Itella's services focus on three processes that are vitally important to the customers: customer relationship and sales processes, delivery and supply chain logistics processes, and invoicing and other document management processes.

Itella operates in northern and central Europe and in Russia. International activities account for 30 percent of its net sales. In Finland, Itella provides daily mail services to all citizens and organizations throughout Finland. Consumer services are delivered under the brand name Posti. The Itella Group comprises three business groups: Itella Mail Communication, Itella Information and Itella Logistics. The corporation is wholly owned by the Finnish state.

Consumers are an important customer segment as receivers of communications and parcels sent by business customers. Business customers, which are companies and organizations, generate 96 percent of Itella's revenues. The most important industries in terms of their demand for postal services include the retail and wholesale trade, the printed media, the finance and telecommunications industries and public sector organizations. Itella's business customer base is quite large – almost all businesses use at least some of Itella's services, but the number of large-volume customers is not great. The top 50 customers alone count for a significant share of volume.

3 THEORETICAL BACKGROUND TO CUSTOMER SATISFACTION

The customer as an element in management theory traditionally concerned sales and marketing. Marketing as a function was basically responsible for customer contacts, for acquiring new customers and, on the whole, responsible for creating demand for a company's products and services. In the early 1990s the development of the concept of 'service marketing' (as opposed to the marketing and production of concrete physical products) upgraded the role of the customer in management theories, because services – by definition – are produced in interaction with customers. CS became important in service management theory, and its measurement was focused on 'moments of truth' and 'critical incidents', both positive and negative, in the interaction of the customer with a service provider.

Later, within the framework of 'relationship marketing', the customer was understood as a relationship in which specific investments were made by both the customer and the service provider and which led to longer term and continuing benefits for both parties. This approach, together with 'customer relationship management', pointed to the need for managing these relationships and customer processes, as opposed to managing single purchase/sales transactions, and continuous customer relationships as a basic element in competitive business, rather than focusing only on new customers. Later developments in these theories introduced the concept of 'customer equity' or 'customer capital' in which customer relationships and the customer base are seen as part of the intangible assets of the company and are to be valued and monitored just like other material and nonmaterial assets.

However, it was not until the 'total quality management' (TQM) boom in the 1990s that customers really acquired the status of a fundamental element that all the functions of a company should be interested in – not just the marketing function. According to TQM, high quality involves more than the absence of errors or zero defects in regard to defined product standards. Quality is essentially how the customer experiences the product or service. An excellent product or service meets the needs and expectations of customers, and even exceeds them. Listening to and understanding customers (sometimes called 'customer obsession') were seen as a crucial element in business excellence. The TQM philosophy also emphasized measurement as a basic tool for management – 'what you don't measure, you can't manage'. CS measurement, including systematically collecting spontaneous customer feedback, became a fundamental tool for integrating customer experiences, needs and expectations in the continuous improvement process of both processes directly interacting with customers as well as supporting back-office processes. The resulting infrastructure of process-focused management and measurement soon became a pillar of business excellence and competitiveness in service industries everywhere.

The introduction into management theory of 'balanced scorecards' in the late 1990s emphasized the need to have other measures and criteria for success, in addition to the traditional financial criteria. Customers were one of the four critical dimensions to be measured in order to set measurable objectives. By not only setting objectives and measuring the actual performance in the four critical dimensions, but also by connecting the rewarding element in the system, the balanced scorecards have proven a powerful steering method and become a widely adopted management system, which is also in use in Itella.

In the 2000s, CS measurements have become one of the systematic ways of integrating customer needs into the improvement and development processes of companies. CS measurement has its roots in the development of management theories in the 1990s, but basically it is very pragmatic research: it aims to support successful business. Such a pragmatic approach also means that the development of CS research models and the content of the research must be carried out with a view to how CS results will actually be utilized inside the organization.

Beyond internal use of CS results, in the postal sector some regulators commission CS studies on their own initiative, in order to continuously monitor the performance of service providers from the customer's point of view. Regulators may well have CS studies carried out among consumers or businesses in general using random samples, but for the purposes of business development and improvement, business customer sampling has to be based on a customer database that includes purchase history.

4 BUSINESS CS STUDIES AT ITELLA

Itella has systematically carried out CS research since 1993. This chapter focuses on our CS research system directed at business customers. Consumer CS has also been measured, but we shall not deal with that in this chapter.

Business customers are organizations of all sizes. This means that Itella as a service provider has many customer interfaces with each customer and that there are many people in various roles in the customer organization who interact with Itella. Everybody in the customer organization has specific needs and expectations, and each one evaluates the supplier from a very different point of view, because of their different roles in the organization. For instance, the price element, whether measured as a comparative price image or as a perception of 'value for money', has a different meaning for the daily user of a service than for the purchase decision maker of a service. It may not be at all relevant to daily users in their work, but a very important element to purchase decision makers. And management may look at things from a long-term customer–supplier-relationship point

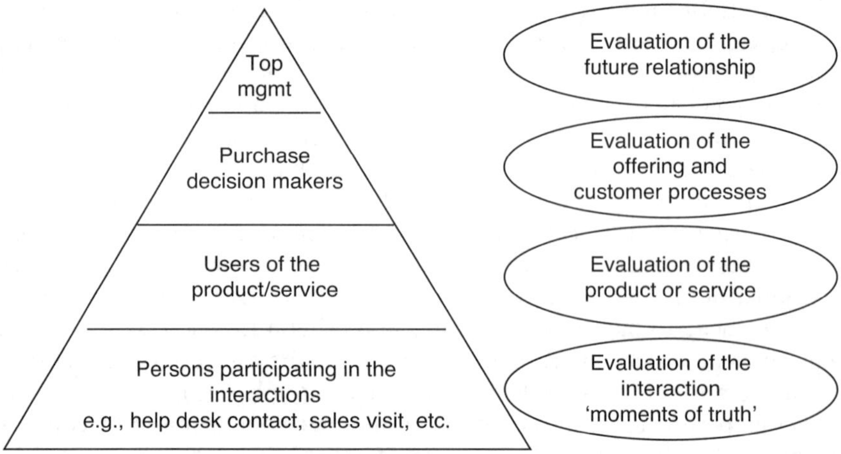

Figure 19.1 Customer organization and the relevant content of customer satisfaction

of view wherein the price is only one element of costs among all other costs incurred or saved elsewhere in the use of the service.

Thus, while a customer-driven company should listen to customers' needs in all interactions and at all organizational levels, the relevant measuring methods and content of CS may be different at each organizational level. Figure 19.1 illustrates the focus of CS content at each level of a typical customer organization.

Itella's systematic and continuous CS research is targeted at the 'purchase decision makers', that is, those in the customer organization who decide about buying and using Itella's services. So, the concept of CS in this chapter means the degree of satisfaction of the customer company's purchase decision makers and the content of CS measurement is focused on our service offering and the related interaction processes as evaluated by the customer's purchase decision maker. In addition to this, Itella also carries out other CS studies focused on the other levels of customer organization, or on particular interactions, for example, CS measurements of call centers and help desks.

5 WHAT IS CUSTOMER SATISFACTION? A GENERAL CS MODEL

Most CS models include the evaluation of operative areas (perceived performance) together with price and brand image attributes, which collectively comprise the overall CS index. Overall CS should lead to customer loyalty, which is operationalized in buying behavior or through intention, together with indicators of rational and emotional attitudes towards a service provider. Some models also incorporate competitor evaluation and measures that allow one to conclude how the focal service provider compares to the 'best in branch' or ideal supplier. The measures in the models are usually based on survey data. Figure 19.2 illustrates a typical CS model.

Most customer satisfaction models were originally developed for measuring consumer CS, or at least implicitly there is an assumption that the respondent is like a consumer

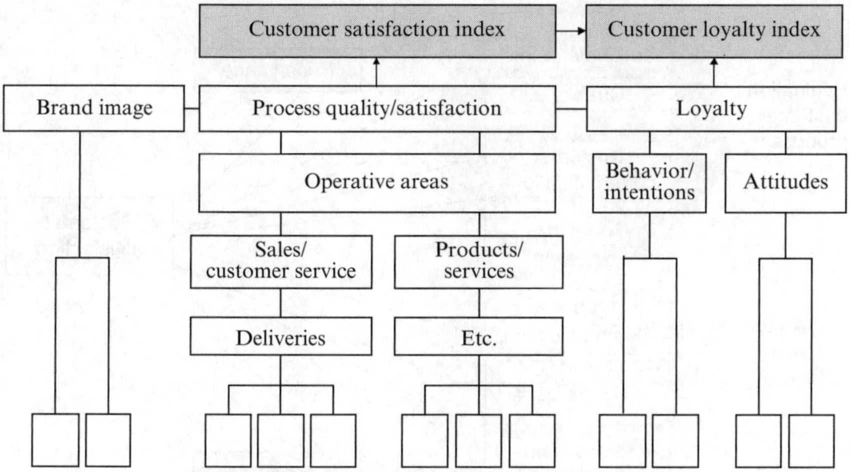

Figure 19.2 A general model of customer satisfaction

– individuals capable of deciding for themselves. Another assumption that is not usually made explicit is that the customer is assumed to have free choice among a variety of many alternative suppliers in the market and can change suppliers without incurring extra cost. Both assumptions are questionable in the case of business customers.

Conducting research on business customers also makes it more problematic to use survey data as a measure of behavior or intention, or for gauging loyalty. There is a compelling need to obtain measurements of this kind based not only on survey data but combined with data derived from the customer database and other operative systems such as sales and invoicing, by means of which actual customer behavior can be recorded. Combining such data may become problematic, because the customer's purchase data and so on in the operative systems are at the organizational level, whereas the survey data typically represent the personal opinions of decision makers who may have very different relationships to the services evaluated from those with operational interactions with the service provider. Great care must therefore be exercised in terms of the structure of the survey and the direct experience and scope of decision making of respondents to the survey.

Figure 19.3 illustrates Itella's CS model. It includes an evaluation of the main customer processes: sales and accounts management, customer service and support, communications and invoicing. The evaluations of different service offerings are grouped in the figure according to our business groups. For CS evaluation purposes, these business groups are further subdivided. Within Mail Communication there are three more detailed offers (letter communication services, direct mail and customer relationship communication services, and delivery of newspapers and magazines). Likewise, CS evaluation within Logistics service offerings is divided into four distinct types of business customer/offers and Information Logistics into five types of service offers. But to keep the picture simple, these are here shown on the business group level. Further, the model includes a price element and a brand image element. Assessments of these individual elements are combined to form the 'overall customer satisfaction'.

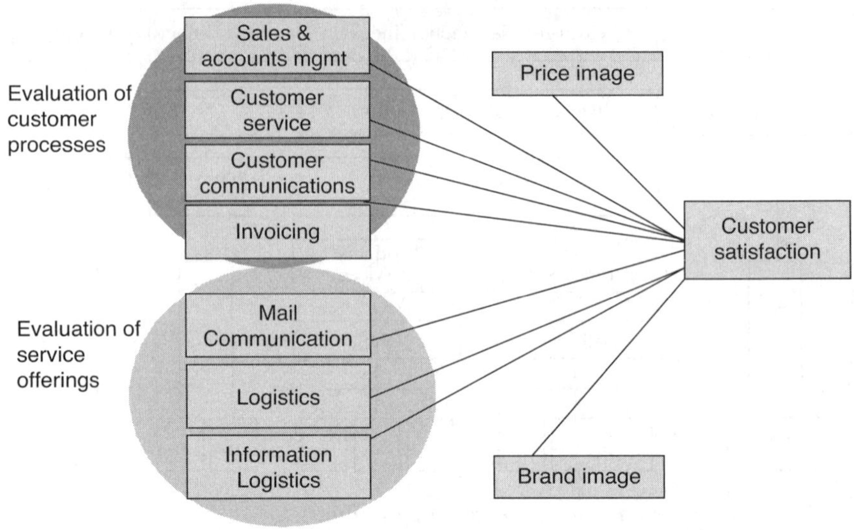

Figure 19.3 Itella's model of CS of decision makers: evaluation of service offering and customer processes

The CS model used by Itella does not include loyalty as an ultimate result – not because the importance of customer loyalty as such is rejected or denied, but mainly because we have discovered that loyalty, at least in the ways we have tried to make it operational, does not really work in the model. The loyalty measures, whether based on survey data or derived from operational systems, remain rather stable, that is, they do not appear to vary significantly with other elements in the CS model. This may be partly due to the time period considered in the CS survey: 6–12 months. The business customer's decision and purchase process may easily take longer, especially in the case of purchasing complex systems which need a separate implementation/starting-up phase before use.

Another reason for dispensing with loyalty in the model is that even though a customer may stop using one service, there may still be other services included in Itella's total offer that continue to be used by the customer, at least the traditional letter services. Therefore, loyalties at the level of the single product or at the total offering used by the customer, or at the total relationship level, are all different and require different approaches to measurement.

6 ALTERNATIVE APPROACHES TO ANALYZING CUSTOMER SATISFACTION DATA

CS research is very pragmatic in nature, so the extent to which the analysis results are understandable, utilizable and can be acted upon must be a priority. The results must be analyzed, presented and interpreted in a way that is the easiest possible for managers at all levels, and in all units, to improve their processes and offers. So the analysis could be somewhat different, were the aim to be to study the phenomenon of CS in itself from the

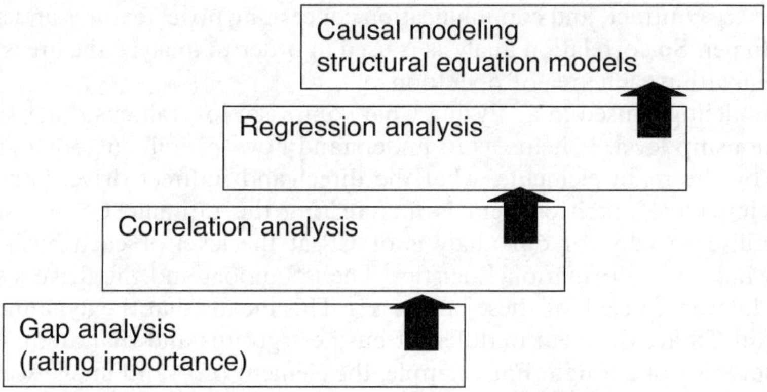

Figure 19.4 Analysis methods of CS data

point of view of pure scientific curiosity. Of course, these two aspects are not mutually exclusive: both are needed but the focus at Itella is on improving performance.

Figure 19.4 illustrates the development of analytic methods used in CS research. This development naturally reflects the general development of methods for analyzing survey data in general.

All of these methods are used in analyzing what drives CS and for charting the most important areas for improvement. They probably result in seemingly similar two-dimensional frames, wherein one dimension is performance rating and the other is importance or relevance. The difference is in how this importance is calculated. The choice of analysis method depends on the level and focus of CS content: measuring CS in the context of a particular interaction, or in the context of the whole relationship including complex offerings, will require different approaches.

In general, gap analysis is a frequently used method. This compares the performance rating and the importance rating, both solicited using the same scale. This produces easy-to-understand gaps – there will be a gap when performance is rated lower than the importance. One of the disadvantages with gap analysis is that it doubles the number of variables, because every element requires a rating both in terms of performance and in terms of importance. The data required for gap analysis is somewhat difficult to gather, at least by telephone interview – the questions sound repetitive and the interview tends to become too long. So it is best used in very focused surveys, typically CS-centered on one type of interaction such as a sales visit or help desk contact. Another disadvantage with gap analysis is that the importance asked for measures the importance at its face value, and it might leave out those unconscious, tacit things that people do not spontaneously rate as important.

In the case of complex customer relations, the content of a CS survey is usually more comprehensive than say merely the evaluation of the sales process or of a sales visit, which is why gap analysis is not used in Itella's decision-maker CS system. Instead, we use correlation and causal modeling methods. Correlation analysis is used when analyzing data concerning one main element (see Figure 19.4), in order to ascertain what sub-elements/variables are important in the overall evaluation of the main element. For example, customer communications is one of the main elements in our CS model and the two sub-elements of that are communication concerning changes of price and other terms of service contract, and communication concerning novel features and alternatives for the customer. So correlation analysis is used in order to analyze the areas in need of improvement within each area of operation.

Causal modeling is used in analyzing what comprises 'overall customer satisfaction' at the relationship level. It helps us to understand how 'overall customer satisfaction' is affected by the main elements, what the direct and indirect drivers are, and how strong the impact of each element is for creating the ultimate CS measure. It has proven useful especially for our analysis of CS at the level of each business group: Logistics, Mail and Information Logistics. The CS model and the drivers seem to be somewhat different in each of these businesses. This means that the dynamics to create and maintain CS are different in different business groups and that an analysis at the corporate level is not enough. For example, the element of brand image seems to have a strong direct impact on CS in all business groups, whereas the effect of the price element varies according to the service offered. Of course, business groups also differ from one another in the areas of business logic, and the competitors' offerings available, and these differences are further reflected in the CS model and results – but not in the way sometimes expected: customers of the more regulated services that have a Universal Service Obligation and are experiencing less competition are not the least-satisfied customers.

7 CORRELATION BETWEEN CS AND POSITION IN THE MARKET

CS research aims to support successful business, but does it really deliver what it promises? Successful business could be defined as a growing business that gains market share, but ultimately the ever-growing and market-share-gaining supplier will always end up in the dominant position in the market. Sometimes it has been implied that the customers of a dominant supplier are somehow trapped, without viable competing alternatives and thus the dominant suppliers do not need to concern themselves with customer needs and satisfaction, at least not actively as a supplier with a smaller market share. Are the customers of a dominant supplier more or less happy than the customers of a niche supplier? Or more generally, is there any correlation between market share and good CS results? This section discusses this correlation in the light of Itella's CS results concerning 11 service offerings, each located in a different market position.

Let us look at the CS indicators of these 11 service offerings: letter mail; direct mail and customer relationship marketing services; newspaper and magazine delivery services; parcel and express services; freight services; contract logistics services; iPost; printing services; eInvoice services; digitizing and scanning services; and digital transaction services. These offerings have different market shares – in Figure 19.5 they are coded with labels A–K in order of market share. In each offering three CS indicators were selected: customers' evaluation of the offering itself, of Itella as a supplier as a whole, and of the sales and accounts management process.

Looking at these three CS indicators, the sales and accounts management indicator appears to be the lowest of the three in all 11 offerings, but it tends to rise as the market share diminishes. It is interesting to note, and also quite logical, that in high/

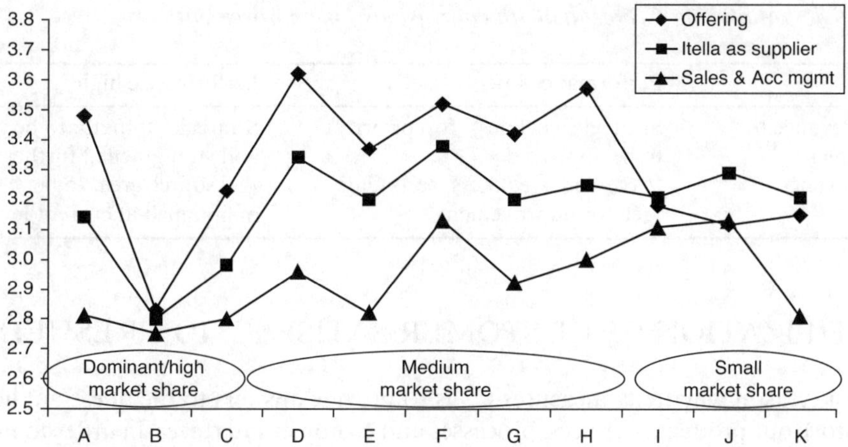

Sources: Itella Business Intelligence Team (2008) and Kiikkilä (2009).

Figure 19.5 CS indicators of 11 service offerings (coded as A–K) and their market share

dominant market share offerings, where there is less competition, the sales indicator is at its lowest, and where there is more competition the sales as evaluated by customers is also better.

The figure shows that in the smaller market share offerings (labeled I–K), the CS indicator Offering is clearly lower than in the larger market share offerings. In these cases a small market share seems to go together with low CS. On the other hand, it is interesting to note that the second CS indicator, Itella as a whole, is roughly on the same level as the other offerings. The result seems to suggest that customers believe in Itella as a supplier of such services also, but the offerings need to be improved in order to better suit customer needs and for Itella to gain a larger market share.

In the medium market share position the CS indicators, especially the Offering indicator, appear to be consistently on a good level. So here the conclusion is that good CS results are related to a good market share.

Nevertheless, there seems to be no consistent interdependence between CS indicators and market share in the dominant/high market share region. However, the figure does demonstrate that a dominant supplier can also have happy customers – as well as unhappy and somewhere-in-between customers.

Of course, the analysis of only these two variables, CS and market share, is somewhat simplistic and does not consider the underlying business dynamics, customer-base differences or degree of regulation, or other elements in the business environment that certainly have an effect on CS. Nonetheless, the results point to an interesting outcome that, in the case of Itella, CS and market share correlate in the low and medium market share regions, although not in the high/dominant area. It would appear that, to a certain degree, good CS helps businesses to grow, but having reached a certain level of market share, the benefits are likely to be less certain.

Table 19.1 Analyzing CS results with conclusions for improvement

	Performance low	Performance high
High relevance for customer	Strategic weakness: top priority to be improved	Strategic strength: to be updated and strengthened further
Low relevance	'Accepted' weakness: secondary area for improvement	A resource area: to be maintained at current level

8 UTILIZATION OF CUSTOMER SATISFACTION RESULTS

The basic reason why Itella measures CS is to provide answers to the question: how can we improve our products, services, processes and customer interfaces, in order to meet the needs and expectations of our customers, especially those with the greatest profit potential, in order to compete successfully in the marketplace?

The analytic methods used in CS typically produce a two-dimensional scatter chart calculated on the basis of priority from the customer's viewpoint and performance results. The conclusions for improving each element are obvious, and depend on how they are situated on the improvement map as set out in Table 19.1.

If they are to be used for the improvement and development of an organization, it is vital that CS results are communicated and interpreted to the 'end-users' and those who are managers and development specialists, not only to top management. One challenge in using the CS results concerns the different worlds of the customer (the decision maker in the customer organization) and the end-user of the results (the manager in the supplier organization). The utilization of CS results takes place within an organizational context, with its defined roles, responsibilities and limits. It would appear sometimes that end-users would prefer to have CS results placed in the boxes of their current organization chart, forgetting that internal organizational structures are irrelevant to the customer. CS studies must use the language of the customer – the elements that the customer is asked to evaluate must be composed in such a way that customers can observe and experience them. Thus, it seems that to some extent there is always a discrepancy and, if they are to be used, the results need to be interpreted and 'back-operationalized' in the terms of the end-users.

The implementation of balanced scorecards and an associated bonus/reward structure as a vital part of the management system have considerably increased the demand for CS results within Itella. Furthermore, CS results should be adapted to the organization structure and we have to define the right CS measures for each unit. This emphasizes the need to combine the customer database and the survey data, in order to achieve the needed organizational match.

9 CONCLUSIONS: WHAT HAVE WE LEARNED – CAN CUSTOMER SATISFACTION BE FORECAST?

The topic of forecasting CS may at first sound quite promising. Could we predict in advance that if we increased factor X by 30 percent, it would improve the final CS result by five percentage points (which would be needed to achieve the balanced scorecard bonuses)?

Unfortunately customers do not react as mechanically as this, because simultaneously changes take place in the customers' business environment – there may be new products, new competitors, new technologies in the market, price changes, new demands from the customer's customer and so on. In the eyes of the customers the relationship between Itella and the customer is not the only fact – there are many elements in the 'external' business environment that affect customers' experiences. Therefore, forecasting CS would require that the customers' business environment be defined and measured and shaped into the model, in addition to the elements in the customer–supplier relationship. This is undoubtedly too much to ask of a CS instrument.

Looking back on the CS results that we have been gathering for years, there have of course been ups and downs in the time series. There have been some rapid and dramatic drops, but improvements in CS results have been taking place somewhat slowly. This means that CS may deteriorate very quickly, in the space of half a year, but improving customer satisfaction will take much longer. It seems that there is no special magic trick for improving CS rapidly; rather there must be a long-term systematic and continuous improvement in processes and service offers. All changes and developments in respect of offerings, processes, organizational structure and so on are of course intended as improvements, but not all of these are perceived as improvements from the customer perspective, at least, not in the short term. Our CS data have shown that any major changes (not minor modifications but changes at the systems level in offers or processes), and changes in the sales organization, are often perceived negatively by customers, worsening CS results, unless the process of change systematically includes advance warning and special support to customers, so that the customer is able to cope with the change.

This brief introduction shows that CS studies, like all marketing instruments, have natural limits in their ability to map customer perceptions. At Itella, CS studies are seen not as a final answer to the question of the quality and value of services to business customers, but as an ongoing link between Itella and its customers that is an important element of Itella strategic philosophy of being customer focused.

BIBLIOGRAPHY

Arantola, Heli (2006), *Uusi väline liiketoiminnan kehittämiseen* (Customer insight) Helsinki: WS Bookwell Oy (in Finnish).

Grönroos, Christian (1990), *Service Management and Marketing: Managing the Moments of Truth in Service Competition*, Lexington, MA: Lexington Books.

Grönroos, Christian (2000), *Service Management and Marketing: A Customer Relationship Management Approach*, Chichester: John Wiley & Sons.

Itella Business Intelligence Team (2008), *Business Area Analysis Reports: Mail Communication, Logistics, and Information Logistics 2008*, Itella Research Series 37-38/2008.

Kaplan, Robert and David Norton (1996), *The Balanced Scorecard*, Boston, MA: Harvard Business School Press.

Kiikkilä, Leeni, Pekka Törrönen and Hemmi Hannu (2009), *Itella Customer Satisfaction Studies of Mail Communication, Logistics and Information Logistics 2008*, Itella Research Series 7-9/2009.

Soin, Sarv Singh (1998), *Total Quality Essentials: Using Quality Tools and Systems to Improve and Manage Your Business*, 2nd edn, New York: McGraw-Hill.

Storbacka, Kaj (2006), *Driving Growth with Customer Asset Management*, Helsinki: WSOYpro.
Storbacka, Kaj and Jarmo Lehtinen (1997), *Asiakkuuden ehdoilla vai asiakkaiden armoilla*, Helsinki: WSOY (in Finnish).
Storbacka, Kaj and Jarmo Lehtinen (2001), *Customer Relationship Management: Creating Competitive Advantage through Win–Win Relationship Strategies*, Singapore: McGraw-Hill.

20. Postal product innovation using EPPML

Leon A. Pintsov and Andrei Obrea*

The problem that is usually being visualized is how capitalism administers existing structures, whereas the relevant problem is how it creates and destroys them.

Joseph Schumpeter,
Capitalism, Socialism and Democracy, 1942

1 INTRODUCTION

The postal sector and the mailing industry are facing a daunting dilemma. The demand for the traditional postal products is in significant decline, but postal operators have momentous difficulties in innovating their product portfolios expeditiously to meet new customer demands and adapt to new economic and technological conditions. Paraphrasing Joseph Schumpeter we can say that the problem that is usually being visualized is how postal operators could effectively administer their existing products, whereas the relevant problem now is how they could create and destroy them.

Modern computing and electronic communications, while presenting a serious threat to letter mail, can be employed in the process of postal product innovation and revitalization of the postal sector. When physical mail is integrated with the Internet and web services, efficiency and effectiveness of communication can be powerfully improved. Previously (Pintsov and Obrea, 2008) we reported the basic mechanism for such integration – Extensible Postal Product Model and Language or EPPML – and its implications for postal product innovation. The description of EPPML-based technology in Section 2 below is a highly condensed and modified version of the 2008 chapter, where more details can be found. This description provides a self-contained treatment of the main enabling technology necessary for the understanding of this chapter. Section 3 briefly discusses a set of new software tools designed to facilitate the most important processes of the postal product management system. Its intent is to demonstrate how definition of postal products using EPPML can lead to automation of critical processes that are manual, slow and overall ineffective in the traditional postal environment. In Sections 4, 5 and 6 we discuss business requirements for specific communication needs of pharmaceutical, legal and government market segments that lead to new and intriguing candidate products which we call 'mutually trusted mail', 'mail with provable content' and 'vote by mail', respectively. We give a full description of each product and assess their implementation potential. The purpose of these sections is twofold. First it is to show that there is a methodology that allows us to convert a set of customer application requirements into precisely defined new mail communication products optimized to meet these requirements. The EPPML technology then can be used to enable immediate and cost-effective access by mailers to these new products. In Section 7 we conclude by summarizing the most salient characteristics and observations concerning the process of translation of business requirements into postal product descriptions.

2 POSTAL PRODUCT INNOVATION USING EPPML

Designing and delivering new products involves the following phases:

1. *Identifying useful features and attributes of a candidate new product for a given market segment (design phase)* This is usually done using traditional techniques (such as market research and focus groups) that are aimed at collection of information from customers. The collected information then must be creatively processed to identify and define with precision and clarity new and useful attributes of a candidate product. The potential customer's value of the candidate product is also assessed at this phase resulting in the range of realistic prices for the new product.
2. *Evaluating new product operational feasibility (operational analysis phase)* This is normally done in collaboration with postal operations resulting in the definition of processes, activities, workflows and equipment required for the delivery of the candidate product. The operational analysis also results in the definition of customer access requirements for the new product. These requirements include mail item design that must be followed by mailers (for example, content, format and placement of all data elements that must be visibly present on the mail item), information gathering and communication requirements, mail containerization requirements and other relevant prerequisites.
3. *Evaluating new product economic feasibility (economic analysis phase)* This is usually done first by costing the new candidate product using any of the acceptable methodologies (for example, activity-based costing or ABC). The economic viability of the candidate product depends on the spread between its value (price range) for the targeted customer segment and its cost. We addressed the cost analysis and pricing of innovative postal products in O'Brien et al. (2009).
4. *Marketing and selling new product (distribution phase)* This is normally done by alerting customers to the new product availability, its access requirements and price and promoting its features and value. It can be accomplished by direct sales force, telemarketing or advertising. This phase is the most difficult in postal product innovation since the vast majority of posts do not have an effective distribution channel for new products and normally have access to a very limited number of their customers (typically largest customers accessible by direct sales force). Marketing new products via retail facilities was proven to be ineffective.
5. *Production (delivering new product)* This phase involves design and execution of changes and modifications to postal processes and activities required for the delivery of new products.

Examination of the first four processes shows that they essentially comprise information gathering and processing activities. This suggests that they can and should be performed using modern information technology (IT). However, presently these activities to the best of our knowledge are almost entirely manual. This makes them costly, slow and overall ineffective. How can modern IT (ubiquitous computing and connectivity) be efficiently employed to speed up this process? The key is in enabling computers to create, send, receive and process information describing a broad variety of existing and future candidate products. The task is far from trivial, but fortunately a careful examination of existing postal products reveals that they have an underlying structure that is invariant to a specific postal operator's networks and processes, local market conditions and other similar considerations. This means that the structure of postal products in reality reflects the universal notion of a postal network designed for the movement of physical objects between its nodes, processes employed to facilitate such movement and its associated information and characteristics. Given that, it became possible to create a universal computer language specifically designed for the description of postal products and their associated requirements and conditions (such as product access requirements). This language, Extensible Postal Product Model and Language (EPPML) is a specialized version of the widely popular XML language that has been optimized for postal applications and recently standardized by the Universal Postal Union (UPU S54 EPPML, 2009). Use of EPPML allows for a broad improvement of efficiency and timing of postal product design and delivery processes (that is, the first four of the five product innovation phases outlined above). A brief description of the EPPML-enabled product innovation and delivery system is as follows. In the EPPML environment, the new product development process consists of multi-round exchanges of information between the postal operator and mailers and recipients.

In an interactive session with a computer the mailer is prompted to enter his/her requirements into a computer where they are automatically translated by a software tool into an EPPML document representing a candidate for postal product. Figure 20.1 is an example of a screen snapshot of the interactive software tool designed to allow mailers to specify requirements for candidate products. The mailer checks desired features from a number of product attributes categories (the three categories shown are attributes of mail item, value-added features and exception processing). The document generated by the software tool is an application for a new product by the mailer and it is communicated via the Internet directly into the postal product development environment where it is aggregated with requests from other mailers and automatically processed, resulting in the EPPML-structured description of a candidate new product.

This description of the candidate product is then forwarded to the postal operations where it is processed by another software tool in order to determine the candidate product's feasibility and its access requirements. The candidate product is modified if the original candidate is not feasible. After the operationally feasible product has been created its description is sent back to the product development environment where it will be cost estimated and priced. The feasible product candidate can also be negotiated with a regulator by using a computer assisted costing process enabled by the EPPML (O'Brien et al., 2009). If the product candidate is operationally and economically feasible and conforms with regulations it is then made available to mailers and recipients in the form of a Postal Product Definition File or PPDF. This can be done effectively via a postal website (operated by a postal IT center) or via a hosting service. In this manner new products become instantly available to all mailers that are connected to the web, which in practice is all business mailers and many casual mailers.

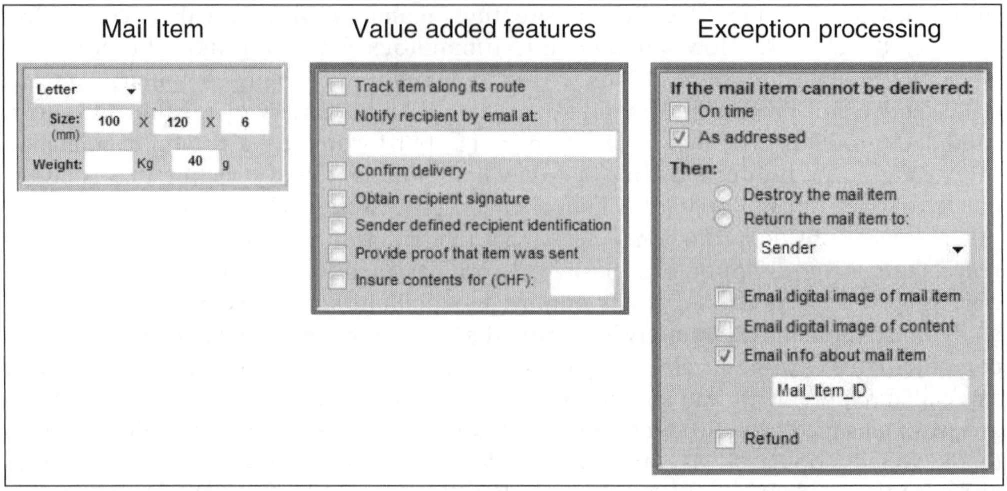

Figure 20.1 Interactive software tool designed to allow mailers to specify requirements for candidate postal products

In operational mode, mailers select available postal products by downloading their descriptions into their mail production/finishing systems. Upon selecting the best available product for their application the mail production/finishing system automatically verifies that the product access requirements can be successfully met and generates desired mail items and all the associated mailing-related and payment information. Then the mail items and the information are transferred into the postal operations for processing and delivery.

3 EPPML TOOLS

EPPML tools are created to facilitate processes in the postal and mailer domains such as the request, definition, publishing and consumption of new postal products. Postal products are formally represented using a set of conventions defined by the UPU EPPML standard (UPU S54). Each postal product is expressed by a PPDF which is an XML file whose validity can be verified according to the EPPML schema described in the standard.

Figure 20.2 shows the typical progression of a PPDF from creation by a post to consumption by the mailer. Mailers may request new features of postal products by sending PPDFs that describe such features to posts or third parties may create PPDFs for various existing postal products for the benefit of mailers that already use EPPML-enabled equipment. PPDFs are created by the post in accordance with the EPPML schema using a PPDF Editor tool. After defining a postal product and completing internal processes of verification and approval, the post launches the new product. The technical aspect of launching a product is accomplished by making the PPDF available to postal customers, for example via the web. The PPDF Publisher is a document management tool designed for this purpose. In its simplest implementation, the PPDF Publisher places copies of

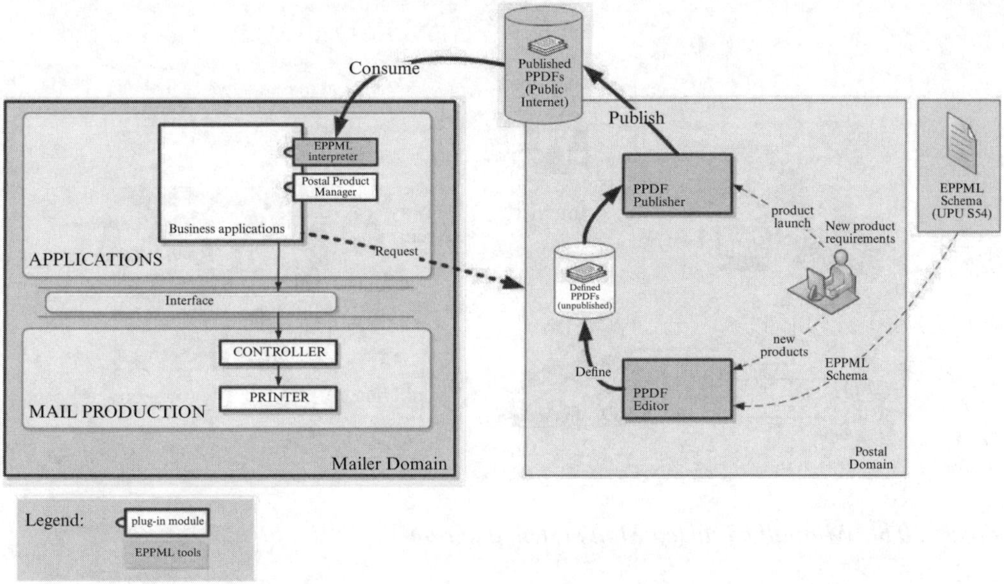

Figure 20.2 Typical progression of a PPDF from creation by the post to consumption by the mailer

PPDFs on a public website for access by all postal customers. Specialized versions of the PPDF Publisher may allow access to specific PPDFs to selected postal customers. Finally, Figure 20.2 shows PPDFs that are publicly available being accessed by the mailer's equipment and consumed by applications in the mailer domain.

4 MUTUALLY TRUSTED MAIL (MTM)

In many mailing and shipping applications there is a need to protect senders and recipients of mail items from errors, inadvertent or deliberate. Errors can be a result of incorrect computer-driven data processing or human errors as well as a result of deliberate attempts on the part of unscrupulous people to deceive or defraud a legitimate system's participants. When errors occur results can be tragic, when for example a medicine is shipped to and consequently consumed by the wrong recipient. In other instances errors result in significant and irrecoverable loss of financial resources, when for example valuable documents such as stock certificates are delivered to the wrong recipient. Yet in some other instances private and confidential documents may be sent to or received by the wrong recipient resulting in the loss and compromise of valuable information with multiple legal consequences. Thus, in a mail communication system there is increasingly a need to positively identify (mutually authenticate) senders and recipients and protect content of mail items from theft and substitution. This means that senders want to have assurances that mail items that they have sent have been received intact by their intended recipients. Likewise mail recipients want to be assured that mail items they have received or are about to receive were sent by their purported senders and that these mail items

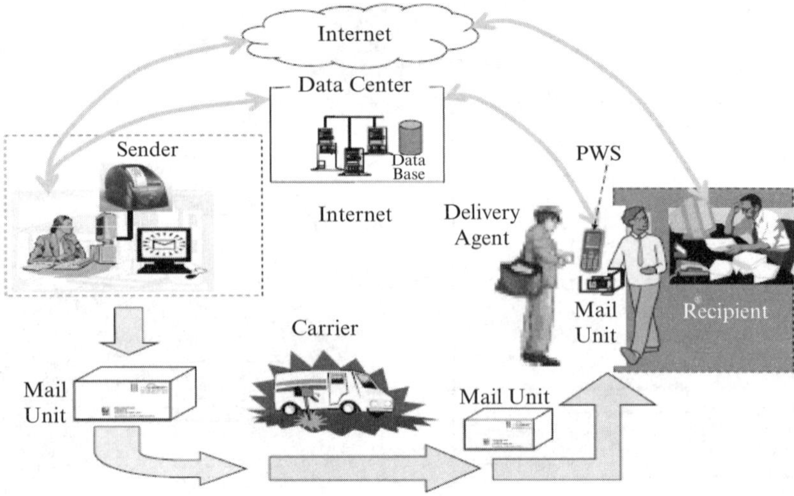

Figure 20.3 Mutually Trusted Mail system diagram

have correct content, and not some other (possibly dangerous) materials such as explosives, toxic powders or a wrong medicine. To our best knowledge, there are no products with this level of assurance on the market today.

Existing systems for authentication of recipients to senders typically require that a recipient signs for the mail item he/she has received. The signature is frequently facilitated through a portable communication device with a stylus and the signature data together with date/location information are sent for archival and dispute resolution purposes to the carrier's data center. However, there is no connection between the signature and the mail item content, and it is hard to ascertain the real identity of the recipient since any person who opens the door is typically treated as a legitimate recipient without proper verification. Besides, devices employing stylus-enabled capture of the signature are expensive and unreliable with a poor quality of data, making dispute resolution at best difficult. The data privacy is another concern since it is hard to protect the recipient's data from unauthorized intrusion, for example when the mail unit is received not by the intended recipient, but by one of the members of the household or an office co-worker. The identity of the sender is typically revealed to an outside observer without opening the mail unit via the sender's origination address. In addition, when the delivery agent makes an error and delivers mail to the wrong address it is sometimes difficult to detect because recipients may not notice small differences between addresses, especially when recipients at both addresses (correct and incorrect) are expecting mail units. This situation becomes more and more prevalent since, due to a wide proliferation of e-commerce, house and office delivery of packages and documents become an everyday occurrence with multiple carriers.

Figure 20.3 illustrates a mail communication system designed for delivery of a new postal product – Mutually Trusted Mail (or MTM). The name reflects properties of the MTM product that were specifically constructed to address these requirements. The MTM product is intended for use in many applications where there is a need for mutual

Figure 20.4 Example of mail unit with information for Mutually Trusted Mail

authentication of mailers and recipients and when the integrity of mail units and their accompanying information is also required. The MTM product is not currently offered by any carrier although its practical implementation would not seem to face serious difficulties. It has been designed to illustrate how clearly defined and understood communication requirements could lead to a definition of a new postal product. In the example shown in the Figure 20.3, the motivation was provided by pharmaceutical applications when medication is distributed using mail via postal operators or private carriers.

In Figure 20.3, the sender is represented on the left having a computer and a label printer. The sender produces a mail item containing medicaments (or other valuable and private content) that a carrier delivers via a human delivery agent to the recipient represented on the right. The delivery agent is equipped with a portable wireless scanner (PWS) with a functionality of a smart phone (for example, image capture and processing and data connectivity to a data center interfaced with the sender's computer and operated by the sender or by a carrier or by a trusted third party). The mail unit carries a label containing, for example, information presented in Figure 20.4.

The two-dimensional barcode on the left of the address block represents the *sender's definable information* whose format and placement is regulated by the carrier as a part of MTM product specification (in this case it is a data matrix code and it is in a prespecified location with respect to the destination address block). The linear barcode above the address block and on the left of postage payment data (represented by the two-dimensional barcode in the upper right-hand corner) is a tracking number for the mail unit which is normally used by the carrier. The MTM product functions as follows. When a customer (the recipient) contacts the mailer either via web or phone to order the medication (or other content), the recipient provides the mailer with verifiable and private prescription information (for example, Rx number) together with his/her address and payment information. When the mailer verifies validity of the information provided by the recipient the mail item is created and a database record stored in the data center is created. The record contains the information shown in Table 20.1.

The data in the record are indexed by the mail unit identification (tracking) number. The next three data elements (recipient name/address, mail unit content and mail unit physical attributes) represent plain text that is encrypted by the sender using one of the classic symmetric key encryption algorithms such as Digital Encryption Standard (DES)

Table 20.1 Information contained in a Mutually Trusted Mail database record

Mail item ID	Recipient name/ address	Mail unit content descrip-tion	Mail unit physical attributes	Cipher text 1	Cipher text 2	*Decryption key part 1*	*Decryption key part 2*
		Rx Num	Weight, dimensions, color of wrapping material	Sender's defined infor-mation in the barcode present on mail unit	Infor-mation stored in the database	*One time recipient ID code (OTRIC)*	*Infor-mation stored in the database*
	Plain text			Cipher text		*Encryption key*	

or Advanced Encryption Standard (AES) (Menezes et al., 1997). The encryption key (which is in this case also the decryption key) that has been used (last two columns) is divided into two parts, one of which consists of a small number (for example, 3–4 digits long) – the 'one time recipient identification code' (OTRIC). This code is communicated to the recipient via email or a telephone together with physical attributes of the mail unit prior to mail unit delivery. The remaining part of the key is stored in the database. Similarly, the cipher text resulting from the encryption of the plain text is divided into two parts. The first part (which can be made arbitrarily small for robust scanning and data interpretation by the PWS) is represented in the shipping label in the form of the sender's definable information (Figure 20.4). The remaining part is again stored in the database. When the delivery agent arrives at the recipient's location he/she scans the mail unit and captures from it the tracking number and the first portion of the cipher text. The PWS then connects to the data center and receives the second part of the cipher text and the second part of the key. After this the delivery agent asks the recipient to enter his/her OTRIC into the PWS using its key pad. When this is done the PWS contains the entire cipher text and the full decryption key, and, thus, can decrypt the cipher text into the plain text only if the OTRIC was entered correctly. In this case the recipient is authenticated to the PWS. The plain text is then displayed to the recipient and upon his/her verification of the content, address and physical attributes of the mail unit the recipient is required to confirm to the PWS his/her agreement that the mail unit is the one that is expected by the recipient. When this is completed the confirmation containing the recipient's identification code, time and location information is sent by the PWS to the data center (and thus to the sender) and the data are erased from the PWS. Examination of the features of the MTM product reveals that it meets all the requirements that were described above. The essential features of the MTM product include mail item design with the sender's *defined information* positioned left of the address block and sender's *directed information* (delivery information) containing the OTRIC that is specified by the sender and not known to any other party except the intended recipient. Note that the carrier does not have access to any private information and simply performs the mechanical action of capturing and transferring data from the mail item and the recipient without knowing the meaning of the data being captured and communicated. Note also that with the exception of the act of capturing and communication of information during delivery there are no changes required to the carrier process or work flow. The MTM product can also be modified to include dynamic re-direction of the mail unit if required by the recipient. The product can be effectively distributed by using EPPML product description language as discussed in Sections 2 and 3 above.

5 MAIL WITH PROVABLE CONTENT (MPC)

Our second example of a new postal product is concerned with the situation that is frequently encountered when there is a potential for a dispute between the sender and the recipient regarding the message that has been sent and received. This situation can be exemplified by a service cancellation notice (for instance for non-payment) that is sent by a service provider (for example, a utility or insurance company) to its customer. In this case there exists a plausible deniability on the part of the recipient that the message that has been received is in fact different than the message that has been claimed to be sent by the sender. Thus, there is a need for the sender to prove to a third party (for example, in a court of law) that a certain message has been delivered and received by a recipient at a certain time without revealing the content of the message to the carrier. Existing postal products ensure the delivery of the message (the letter) and the privacy of the content by using specialized value-added features such as delivery confirmation and registered mail. However the existing postal products have no information about the content of the message. A new postal product (mail with provable content or MPC) is designed to provide mailers with the option to demonstrate that certain information content has indeed been delivered to the recipient. Again, the MPC product is not offered by any carrier although its practical implementation would not in our opinion face serious difficulties. It has been designed to illustrate how clearly defined and understood communication requirements could lead to a definition of a new postal product. Note that achieving MPC functionality using email is extremely difficult, if not impossible. Figure 20.5 shows the fictitious cancellation message (a printed page).

The layout of the information on the page is intended for folding the page in such a way that the address block and the barcode left of it will be visible through the window in the envelope presented in Figure 20.6. The unique identification number below the address block contains the email address of the sender where information can be sent electronically by the postal operator. The bottom right-hand corner of the envelope in Figure 20.6 contains a template for physical signature of the recipient together with the date of signing.

The barcode is a standardized digital fingerprint (digest) of the message (whose optical representation is the printed page shown as Figure 20.5) with additional graphic security elements. There are several well-known computational techniques for generating such fingerprints, for example hash functions. These functions produce a standard size fingerprint (typically 128 or 160 bytes) regardless of the size of the original message and

Figure 20.5 Cancellation notice sent using mail provable content

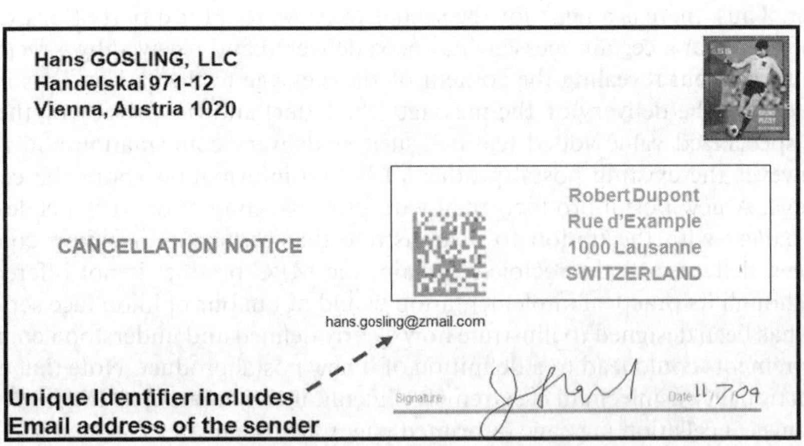

Figure 20.6 Windowed envelope for mail with provable content

are practically uniquely indicative of the message content (Menezes et al., 1997). The graphic security elements provide detection mechanism for modification or copying of the original fingerprint. During the processing of mail (for example, sorting operation) or in a separate scanning (for example, during delivery operation) the postal operator can capture the fingerprint barcode information and store it together with sender and recipient names and addresses and the time, place and proof of delivery. This information can be presented to a third party upon request and will constitute the required proof of the content delivery. The location, size and format of the barcode are specified as a part of the MPC product while its interpretation (meaning) is unknown to the postal operator.

The sender's directed information, which also forms a part of the MPC product, is a digital file containing the digest of the message together with the digital image of the mail item with the signature of the recipient and location/time of the mail item delivery event. This product can also be effectively distributed by using EPPML product description language as discussed in Sections 2 and 3, above.

6 VOTE BY MAIL (VbM)

Voting by mail is gaining acceptance as an alternative to voting in person. The process is generally well defined and includes the following steps: the voting commission creates a list of voters and prints voting ballots (there may be more than one type of ballot for each election). Ballots are mailed to voters in an outgoing envelope which contains a return envelope; voters mark their ballots, place them in the return envelope and mail them back to the voting commission where they are counted. This process was analyzed by many voting security experts. Several alternatives (for example, electronic voting) were proposed and currently there is widespread consensus that the overall security of this process is best served when at least some steps are executed using paper as a data communication and storage medium. Most current implementations of vote by mail use the postal network and First Class mail product to deliver both the outgoing package containing the blank ballot and the returned vote. The processes that take place in the voting commission are subject to intense scrutiny by security experts, civil liberties activists, politicians and many others. Most processes that could have a significant impact on the overall security of VbM are under the control of two distinct parties, the voting commission and the post. Typically the voting commission treats the post as a 'black box' which is normal for all users of the First Class mail product. Between the time when the mail ballots leave the voting commission and the time returned votes are counted, there is no additional information available to the voting commission regarding the fate of the ballots or the incoming mail items containing votes.

Our conjecture here is that the security of the voting process is its critical characteristic and that much better security can be achieved if voting commissions could have a choice of the postal product features that can be optimized for voting application. These features form a part of a new postal product – VbM – that we designed specifically for this application. This product takes advantage of the ability of the post to gather information during the normal processing of mail. The information gathered can be communicated to the voting commission to significantly enhance the overall security of VbM. Moreover, as a part of the product the information available to the voting commission can also be required to be communicated to the post enabling correlation of information for fraud and error detection.

Figure 20.7 illustrates various parties and processes that are involved in voting by mail. We simply enhanced their ability to collect and exchange information that is useful for the security and reliability of voting by mail application. To that extent all parties are connected via physical (mail item) or electronic communication channels where appropriate. The physical and electronic channels are designated by solid and dashed lines, respectively.

The new postal product resulting from our analysis of potential interactions between

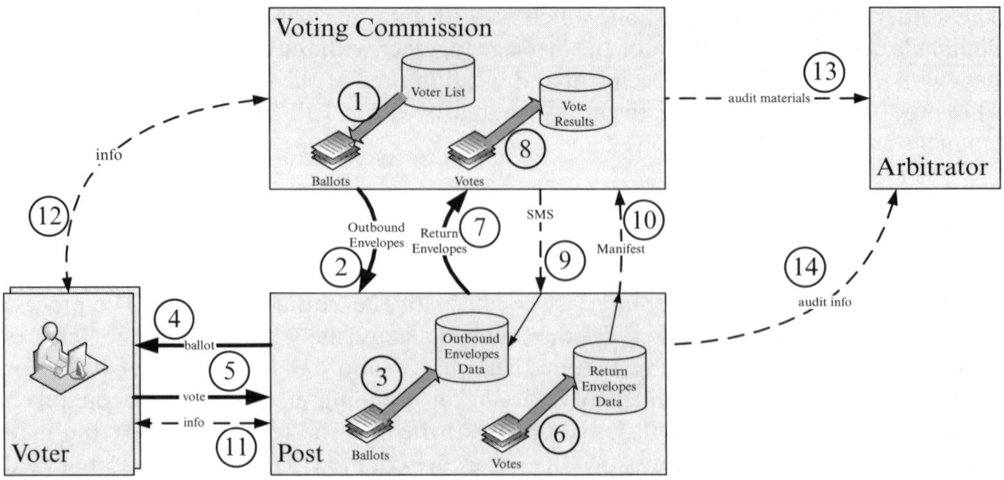

Figure 20.7 Parties and processes involved in voting by mail

Table 20.2 Processes relevant to voting by mail

Step	Process
1	Creation of ballots from voters' list by the voting commission
2	Induction of outbound envelopes containing ballots
3	Data collection from outbound envelopes within the post
4	Delivery of ballots to voter
5	Induction of mail items with votes by voter
6	Data collection from mail items with votes within post
7	Delivery of mail items with votes to the voting commission
8	Determining vote results from the mail items with votes that were delivered to the voting commission
9	Communication of the statement of mailing submission (aggregate information about the mailing) by the voting commission to the post
10	Voting commission receives the manifest of delivered mail items with votes

the post and the voting commission is characterized by a set of attributes that can be represented using the concept of EPPML. Our method requires: (i) identification of all processes between finalization of the voter list and the arrival of mail items with votes; (ii) for each process, identification of all possible opportunities for illegally influencing the outcome of the vote (these opportunities are termed 'attacks' following standard security convention) and the perpetrators of such attacks; (iii) definition of the actions that can be taken to detect (or prevent) the attack; and (iv) identification of the supporting data elements that can be effectively used for the attack detection purposes. Figure 20.7 shows the system diagram with the processes which were identified in step (i). Examples of results of our analysis following the steps (ii), (iii) and (iv) are summarized in Table 20.2 which presents a list of relevant processes.

The VbM product is designed specifically for a mailer that can implement the voting

Table 20.3 Selected features and attributes of VbM

Process	Attacks	Attack detection/ countermeasures	Supporting data attributes
Creation of ballots from voters' lists by voting commission (arrow 1)	Skipping, adding or mismatching inserts resulting in mailable but unusable mail items (missing ballot or return envelope; incorrect ballot)	The post obtains from the voting commission the acceptable range for the weight of correctly formed mail items (via SMS) and measures the weight after induction of mail items. The post compares the acceptable ranges and measured weight of mail items and communicates discrepancies together with mail item identifiers to the voting commission	1. Weight of the correctly formed outbound mail item 2. Thickness 3. SMS
Post captures and processes outbound envelope data (arrow 3)	Adding envelopes with fake ballots	The post obtains from the voting commission the count of mail items in the mailing containing ballots, together with a list of their unique identifiers. The post maintains a list of observations (sightings) updated at all processing steps for all mail items from the mailing. The post reconstructs the total number of processed mail items for the given mailing based on unique identifiers and compares it with the number of mail items inducted. The post identifies fraudulent or duplicate unique identifiers and communicates this information to the voting commission	1. SMS 2. The unique identifier on the outbound mail item

Note: SMS = Statement of mailing submission.

process defined by the voting commission. The security of this process benefits from a trusted third party (the post) that is in a position to observe and gather information about the flow of ballots and votes beyond the boundaries of the voting commission. The post could offer this service as a postal product that can be expressed and distributed using an EPPML-based system. Table 20.3 exemplifies selected features and attributes of the new contemplated postal product VbM. We have omitted several features due to their repetitive nature. The first line in the table shows the results of our analysis for Process 1, 'creation of ballots from voters' list' by the voting commission. Potential attempts to fraudulently or inadvertently change the outcome of election

Figure 20.8 Mail item containing the ballot

(attacks) are skipping, adding or mismatching inserts resulting in mailable but unusable mail items (missing ballot or return envelope; incorrect ballot). The voting commission collects information regarding the number of ballots of each type, the ballot's weight and thickness. This information in the form of aggregated data (also known as 'Statement of Mailing Submission') is then sent to the post (arrow 9 in Figure 20.7). The attack detection/countermeasures column in Table 20.3 shows how the post can detect various attacks using information obtained from several independent sources (that is, internal measurements and corresponding information from the voting commission). The last column in the table shows data attributes supporting the attack detection/countermeasures processes.

The mail item that carries the ballot (outgoing mail item) is shown in Figure 20.8. It has a unique mail item identifier (the example shows a USPS Intelligent Mail Barcode) and an additional barcode that identifies the ballot type and may include other voting commission information.

The return envelope (containing the vote) has a traditional appearance except, perhaps, a mail item identifier (for example, USPS Intelligent Mail Bar Code).

Again just as in our previous examples the ballot-type information in the outgoing mail item is defined by the voting commission (the sender), but its format, size and location are specified by the post using EPPML as a mechanism for the description of the new VbM product. The information that is to be provided by the post to the voting commission (sender-directed information) is also specified by the post as a part of the new VbM product. In this example we described a postal product that integrates the capabilities of the postal system with the voting commission applications resulting in dramatically improved security for voting by mail. This postal product is designed to respond to the specific needs of voting authorities. It defines new processes that if implemented by the post will make use of and/or generate information specific to the application (and well beyond what is normally required for delivery of First Class mail). The mailer (voting commission) has access to information that would not be available to it should it use First Class mail (which is common today). Specifically, the post provides independent, detailed information regarding the attributes of mail items and their aggregates (both outgoing and incoming) and it may implement specialized processes to help detect additions, modifications and removal of identifiable mail items (ballots and votes).

7 CONCLUSION

We (as many others) believe that the postal sector is beginning to experience a fundamental transformation. This is the transformation from the government-controlled and -owned monopolies in uncontested markets into private entities operating in highly contested (by traditional and non-traditional competitors) market segments. This transformation is a direct result of both market liberalization imposed by governments and electronic diversion that operates outside of the control of postal market regulators and participants. The inescapable outcome of these developments is that for postal operators to be successful in the new environment they must quickly re-evaluate and update their product portfolios since their traditional products have begun to experience a significant drop in demand. High volume/low-cost traditional products in the letter mail category as well as no-frill 'black-box' delivery products in the parcel category can no longer support a high fixed cost of operating extensive postal networks. In our previous work we reported the development of a new IT designed to help posts to innovate their products (Pintsov and Obrea, 2008; O'Brien et al., 2009). This technology was generally very well received by the postal community which is evidenced by the unanimous approval by the UPU Standards Board of a new worldwide technical standard that is at the core of the product innovation technology (UPU S54 Extensible Postal Product Model and Language – EPPML). However, we had no proof that there exist unmet communication needs of mailers and recipients that cannot be satisfied by traditional postal products. Moreover there was no analytical method that would allow us to uncover customer needs and to convert them into new postal products in a rigorous way. This chapter is aimed at helping to fill this gap. We developed a set of tools that work with the EPPML as well as a new methodology for examining complex business applications and isolating their communication requirements. These requirements then serve as a basis for the definition of new postal products that can be quickly and fully expressed as computerized data structures. These in turn allow for making new postal products instantly accessible to all interested mailers and mail recipients. In addition, given the willingness of the mailing industry to adapt the EPPML framework, new architectures for mail generation and finishing systems can be developed and this would allow mailers to automatically generate mail consistent with new product requirements. This means not only that posts can quickly make their new products available, but also that the mailers will be able to quickly purchase and use such products. This in principle can dramatically change the entire process of product innovation and consumption in mail communications, leading to a sustainable and profitable postal sector. In this vision of the future mail communication system the mailers would not have to adapt their business processes to existing postal products. Instead, they would be able to request postal products that adapted to their needs.

The three new postal products we have described have common features despite their entirely different motivations and purposes. This is not an accident, but a reflection of the basic design principle that business processes of the mailer and the post must be integrated and that mailers will have more freedom to request product features designed to meet their needs. All three applications require a mail item design that contains a provision for the mailer's defined information that the post must capture, process and communicate back to mailers. The post, however, specifies the format and placement for this mailer-defined information consistent with postal operational requirements as a part of the formal product specification. This arrangement allows for an important integration between a mailer's business application and postal processes. All three postal products require new processes on the part of the post designed to collect mailer-defined information in addition to the information present on the mail item. This information is also a part of the integrated business application–postal product system.

We are optimistic that soon we shall see the first practical implementations of the design methodology, technology and postal products that we have attempted to outline in this chapter.

NOTE

* The chapter expresses views and ideas of the authors that are not necessarily those of their employer, Pitney Bowes Inc.

REFERENCES

Menezes, A., P. van Oorshot and S. Vanstone (1997), *Handbook of Applied Cryptography*, Boca Raton, FL, New York, London and Tokyo: CRC Press.

O'Brien, L. Pintsov and A. Obrea (2009), 'Cost analysis and pricing of innovative postal products', in Michael A. Crew and Paul R. Kleindorfer (eds), *Progress in the Competitive Agenda in the Postal and Delivery Sector*, Cheltenham, UK and Northampton, MA, USA: Edward Elgar, pp. 128–44.

Pintsov, L. and A. Obrea (2008), 'Postal reform and product innovation', in Michael A. Crew and Paul R. Kleindorfer (eds), *Handbook of Worldwide Postal Reform*, Cheltenham, UK and Northampton, MA, USA: Edward Elgar, pp. 176–94.

UPU S54-1 Extensible Postal Product Model and Language (EPPML) (2009).

21. The environmental impacts of the US mail: initial life cycle inventory model and analysis

Lawrence G. Buc, Peter A. Soyka and Sander S. Glick

1 INTRODUCTION

This chapter describes the analytic framework and methods of this first analysis of the life cycle inventory of the major classes of the US mail. The United States Postal Service (USPS) commissioned SLS to perform this analysis as part of ongoing efforts to improve its environmental footprint and to initiate a fact-based discussion on the environmental impacts of mail. In response, we developed an analytical framework for evaluating the direct and indirect environmental aspects of mail service and the broader life cycle aspects of the mail and its components. The scope and level of precision of our analysis address the issues raised by the mailing industry, public interest organizations, and the general public. The analysis and underlying methods will inform discussions at the organizational policy level, rather than at the more detailed level of capital budgeting, pollution control engineering, program management, and so on.

We did not attempt to evaluate the potential or actual hazards posed by the mail and its subsidiary activities to human health and the environment. That would be extremely complicated, time-consuming and expensive. Instead, we focused on an initial step of characterizing the waste, pollutant emissions and energy consumption caused by four major mail products by conducting a comprehensive life cycle inventory (LCI) analysis of them. Together, the classes comprised 98.6 percent of total mail volume in government fiscal year (FY) 2006, the year of the analysis. We also conducted some limited comparisons of our initial results with a variety of data, indicators and analytical results addressing mail and closely related products.

Our analysis sheds some interesting light on the environmental footprint of the mail:

1. Total energy consumed by the four mail products accounts for 0.6 percent of national energy consumption, a figure that seems reasonable given the quantities of mail in the US economy and the energy-intensive nature of paper and board production, printing and motor vehicle transportation.
2. Mail also accounts for about 0.6 percent of US national greenhouse gas (GHG) emissions.
3. At the household level, energy and GHG emissions associated with the entire mail

life cycle are roughly comparable to those from operating any of several common home appliances over the same period of time.

4. The share of each pollutant attributable to USPS operations is variable, but is uniformly within the top five of the 17 total life cycle stages, along with the paper and board manufacturing, printing/mail production, dropshipping, and, for some parameters, landfill disposal life cycle stages.
5. On a unit basis, Periodicals and Package Services have the highest pollutant emissions and energy consumption, because of their relatively high weight and (for Periodicals) high paper and printing content.
6. On a total basis, however, Standard mail accounts for the largest share of energy consumption and pollutant emissions among the four major mail classes, because of its much higher volume relative to other classes.

The remainder of this chapter describes our methods, preliminary results and their apparent realism, and areas of uncertainty and for further development. Section 2 describes the framework that we developed to conduct the LCI analysis, the general approaches that we employed, and a number of major assumptions that underlie our preliminary estimates. Section 3 presents the basic functions of the LCI model. This section also addresses the major sources and types of data that we assembled to quantify the creation and flow of the mail, and the environmental aspects that arise from each stage in its life cycle. Section 4 presents a summary of our preliminary results and provides some comparisons to other data and analytical results. These comparisons help to put our results into context and also provide a basis for assessing the realism of our model and its outputs. Finally, Section 5 provides a discussion of important areas of uncertainty and possible further model and data development.

2 FRAMEWORK, GENERAL METHODS AND MAJOR ASSUMPTIONS

The overarching concept for an LCI is life cycle analysis (LCA), which examines the environmental impact of a product or service from the initial extraction of raw material resources used to make it through its final disposition. LCA provides the most complete perspective from which to evaluate environmental impact, and also facilitates comparisons between the mail and possible substitutes.

Today, most practitioners of LCA use a set of standard terms and conventions as defined in a series of consensus international standards.[1] These standards distinguish between two basic types of life cycle studies: LCI and LCA. The important distinction between the two is that LCA includes an additional phase, impact assessment, that links the pollutant emissions and other environmental aspects quantified by the LCI to categories and indicators of actual (or potential) human health or environmental impact. This study and model comprise an LCI, and hence include the three phases of goal and scope definition, inventory analysis and interpretation.

We applied simple screening criteria to determine which constituents and other endpoints to include in the LCI model to assist us in keeping the analysis at a tractable size, while ensuring that we have considered all potentially important materials, activities and endpoints:

- *Mass contribution* Except for particularly toxic or otherwise problematic constituents, we generally excluded from analysis constituents of a material that comprise less than one (1.0) percent of the total mass of the material.
- *Energy contribution* Similarly, we focused on the processes associated with a particular activity or life cycle stage that comprise at least 99 percent of the total energy associated with that activity or stage.
- *Environmental or human health relevance* For environmental aspects, we evaluated all available data sources for information on constituents known to be a human health and/or environmental protection concern. We did so by determining which of the candidate constituents have established US Environmental Protection Agency (EPA) reference doses, cancer slope factors, primary drinking water standards, air quality criteria (for example, NAAQS, NESHAP), or ambient water quality criteria. Generally, constituents that are present in low concentration or sporadically are eliminated from further analysis unless they possess carcinogenic potential or are acutely toxic to humans or biota. We used simple material composition and mass balance calculations to implement this screening approach.

Major Unit Processes

We analyzed the energy consumed by and waste and emissions resulting from the mail at two major levels: (i) preparation, transport, handling and delivery of the mail itself; and (ii) the major materials comprising the mail. For each mail product included, we consider the energy consumed and waste and emissions generated in producing the raw materials used, then fabricating the mail piece through a variety of cutting, printing, folding, packaging, addressing, sorting and other steps. At that point, the mailer or consolidator enters the mail piece into the USPS system, either locally or following dropshipping. USPS receives and processes the mail and transports it to another processing plant and on to the delivery unit or directly to the delivery unit, which then delivers the mail to the intended recipient. The mail recipient either discards the mail at some point following receipt, or keeps a percentage on a long-term basis. Mail that is not retained may be either recycled or discarded, at which point it enters the municipal solid waste (MSW) stream. The model apportions the weight percentage of the mail that reports to recycling, landfill disposal, and processing at a waste-to-energy facility according to user-defined assumptions.

The model also addresses the transportation required to move the mail and its components between each life cycle stage, starting with delivery of paper and other materials comprising the mail to the mail originator, ending with the final disposition of the discarded fraction of the mail in a landfill or other end-of-life management option, and covering all stages in between. Due to a paucity of data on pollutant emissions to water and land and the fact that most transport-related pollutant emissions are fossil fuel combustion emissions to air, the LCI of the transportation steps in the life cycle is limited to tracking of several major air pollutants as well as the energy (fuel) consumption involved in moving the mail from one life cycle stage to the next.

To address the environmental aspects associated with each life cycle stage and activity, we evaluated material and chemical use, consumption of liquid and other fuels (for example, natural gas, electricity), and the types of physical plant and transport vehicle equipment required. This is important because emission rates of a number of pollutants vary by equipment type, size, configuration and usage patterns.

Further documentation of model scope and processes is provided in a report issued by USPS in October 2008 (SLS Consulting, 2008).

3 LCI MODEL FUNCTIONS AND DATA

The LCI addresses all major life cycle stages for a list of indicator constituents and endpoints. It enables comparisons among mail products and provides unit and total estimates of pollutant emissions, waste generation, and fuel and energy use for each product. We describe here the initial model configuration, which examines the life cycle aspects of the four major US mail classes: First Class; Standard; Periodicals; and Package Services.

Model Functions

Wherever possible, we collected and used data representing FY 2006, so as to provide a consistent and recent time period for analysis. In keeping with broadly accepted LCI modeling practice, we employed a basic model structure focused around a common functional unit that allows 'apples-to-apples' comparisons across different mail products. The functional unit used for all major model components is *one million pieces of mail.*

For each mail product, the model takes characteristics like size, weight, density and composition, and computes the quantities of materials (principally paper, cardboard, plastics, ink and adhesives) consumed in producing it, and the waste and emissions associated with each of these materials, including the energy and emissions from transporting the materials. Our initial analysis uses the conservative assumption that all pieces are discarded by the recipient[2] within one year of receipt, yielding a steady-state condition.

Following use, post-consumer management of the mail piece is addressed by segregating the portion of the functional unit managed using each major management method (recovery, landfill disposal and combustion) according to user-specified values and assumptions, and tracking these fractions through their ultimate disposition. Again, waste and emissions for each life cycle stage and transport among them are computed and tallied by the model.

Allocation of Common Mail Processing Inputs and Outputs

USPS consumes substantial quantities of energy in operating its facilities, processing mail, and transporting mail between its facilities and the mail recipient. Using data on the aggregate quantities of energy consumed by USPS in FY 2006, it is possible to make some inferences about the total quantities of fuel that have been used in particular transport and delivery operations. However, these data do not reflect the quantities of fuel used that are attributable to individual mail products. Indeed, because most Postal transport and mail processing and all delivery operations handle multiple products simultaneously at the level of the individual vehicle, developing a 'bottom-up' inventory of fuel use by product is impossible. Instead, a means of allocating these fuels to the individual products is necessary. Note, however, that the allocation does not affect the total resource consumption and pollutant emissions but only the distribution of these environmental aspects among different mail products.

To accomplish this distribution by product, we used a relatively simple 'top-down' approach by allocating shares of resource usage and pollutant emissions to mail products based upon each product's share of the resource usage that creates these emissions. These shares for each mail product and service are published by USPS annually, and are organized by cost segment and component. The model also provides the capability to allocate the shares to mail products using three alternative methods: the weight, mail volume (number of pieces), or physical volume ('cube') of the product. None of these alternative measures is based upon principles of causality for the resource under study and thus do not comport with ISO 14044, Section 4.3.4.[3] We present the results of a sensitivity analysis of our results using these alternative distribution keys in Section 4, below.

In the base case LCI model, we applied the resource usage shares to the data on transportation and facility operation fuels to determine the full energy consumption and pollutant emissions generated during Postal Service handling, transportation and delivery of each mail product. The remaining portions of the fuel use and associated emissions not allocated to one of the four mail products considered in the analysis are distributed to all other USPS mail products, services, and finally, to institutional, or 'network', operations. Table 21.1 illustrates this process.

USPS is fundamentally a service business, not a manufacturing or utility enterprise. While there are doubtless other environmental aspects associated with USPS's stages in the mail life cycle beyond fuel consumption and related pollutant emissions, we do not believe that they are likely to be significant given the LCI parameters stated above.

Solid waste is generated at nearly all stages of the mail's life cycle. Because, however, all such waste is treated by one of a small number of management methods (primarily landfill disposal), we have aggregated the solid waste generated at each stage. We use a simplified approach in which all of the solid waste quantities reporting to landfill disposal are aggregated on a single worksheet, though in reality, solid waste generated through the life cycle is disposed of locally at each stage. The quantities of solid waste generated at each of the upstream stages can be observed on the worksheet for that stage, as desired.

Major Data Sources

The LCI model uses a variety of different types and sources of data. Some of the more important elements are briefly profiled here.

The major materials comprising the mail include various types and grades of paper and paper board, plastics, adhesives and packing materials. This implies that developing an understanding of the resources required to manufacture these materials and the associated wastes generated and pollutants emitted is important to being able to complete a life cycle inventory for the mail in any meaningful way.

Fortunately, detailed LCIs of many of these materials are available and we drew heavily on this work in assembling and analyzing the end-to-end life cycle aspects of the mail. Pertinent data for the materials and unit processes for which we have inventory data are presented in Table 21.2. These include both the environmental aspects of manufacturing various types of paper, paper board and plastics, and also the pre-combustion (upstream) waste, energy consumption and pollutant emissions associated with producing various

Table 21.1 Allocation of Postal Service inputs and environmental aspects

USPS cost segment/ component	Name	Variable applied to	Intermediate result (Mail product share of . . .)	Final result
15.2/314	Fuel & Utilities	Total facility energy consumption by fuel	USPS electricity, natural gas, and heating oil consumed	Energy (gallons, BTUs) consumed, life cycle pollutants emitted by fuel for each mail product and for the entire USPS
14.1/142, 681	Domestic Air, Domestic Air Alaska	Total aviation fuel consumption (weighted average used)	Aviation fuel consumed by USPS contract carriers	
14.1/143	Highway	Total HCR, bulk, and mobile fuel consumed	Trucking fuel (diesel, gasoline) consumed by USPS haul trucks and highway contract carriers	
14.1.3/144	Railroad	Total railroad fuel consumed	Rail fuel (diesel) consumed by USPS rail carriers	
7.2/46	Delivery activities (City)	Postal Fleet–Voyager–Retail fuel consumed	Delivery fuel (diesel, gasoline) consumed by USPS city carriers	
10/260	Rural carriers	Rural routes fuel consumed	Delivery fuel (gasoline) consumed by USPS rural carriers	

Note: HCR = Highway Contract Route.

types of transportation fuels. In some cases (for example, life cycle pollutant emissions from electricity consumption), these data have been supplemented or replaced with more recent data drawn from other sources.

Beyond this relatively rich source of relevant LCI data, information on other components of the mail life cycle is sparse. To address this limitation, we collected and adapted a series of fuel consumption and pollutant emission factors from published sources to quantify some of the important environmental aspects of life cycle stages downstream of raw material manufacturing. As a result, and to keep the model and analysis at a manageable scale, we have included only selected major air and water pollutants in the LCI model. These aspects are listed in Table 21.3.

Interestingly, hazardous waste is not among these endpoints. As counter-intuitive as this may seem, review of our major data sources showed that negligible or very small

Table 21.2 Major materials comprising the mail: published data used in the LCI model

Major category	Specific material or process	Life cycle stage(s) considered	Endpoints considered
Materials	Bleached Virgin Kraft Paper	Manufacture	Raw material consumption
	Unbleached Recycled (100%) Kraft Paper		Process energy (by type)
	Virgin Newsprint		Transportation energy (by type)
	Recycled (100%) Newsprint		Solid waste
	Virgin LDPE Film		Air emissions
	Virgin LDPE Air Packets		Water emissions
	Virgin EPS Loose Fill		
	Cornstarch Loose Fill		
	Corrugated Cardboard Boxes (38% Recycled)		
Fuels	Coal	Production	Energy use
	Natural Gas		Solid waste
	Residual Fuel Oil		Air emissions
	Distillate Fuel Oil		Water emissions
	Gasoline	Transportation	Energy
	Diesel Fuel	Use (by major type)	Total energy consumed
	Liquefied Petroleum Gas		Solid waste Air emissions
	Uranium		Water emissions
	Electricity	Generation	Fuel mix

Source: Franklin Associates (2004).

quantities of hazardous waste are expected to be generated by the activities comprising the mail life cycle and addressed by the LCI model.

In terms of the other major data types and sources employed in building the LCI model, wherever possible, we used published data from authoritative US government sources or peer-reviewed studies. In particular, we made extensive use of approaches and data developed by the US EPA. EPA has developed standardized approaches, specific methods and models, and extensive empirical data for various endpoints of interest (for example, air pollutant emission rates for different engine types and sizes). Moreover, EPA's methods and most of its data are extensively peer reviewed and revised and refined repeatedly over time.

Variability and Uncertainty of Data

As presently configured, the model calculates the life cycle emissions of an average functional unit of each of the four major classes of mail: First Class, Standard, Periodicals and Package Services. But many of the variables that drive those emissions can take on

Table 21.3 Endpoints included in the LCI model

Environmental aspects	Energy consumption
Solid waste	Transportation fuels consumed
Water pollutants	Gasoline
Total dissolved solids	Diesel
	Jet fuel
Air pollutants	Manufacturing, preparation, and facility energy consumed
Carbon dioxide	Electricity
Carbon monoxide	Natural gas
Hydrocarbons	Liquid fuels
Nitrogen oxides (NOx)	
Particulate matter	
Sulfur oxides (SOx)	

a wide range of values, which the model generally summarizes using the average. Thus, the model uses the average piece weight for each class, even though the weight of a piece of Standard mail can range up to a pound and the weight of a piece of Package Services mail can range up to 70 pounds. Similarly, some mail in each class is transported more frequently and over longer distances by USPS than other mail, goes through more facilities, and is sorted more times, all requiring more energy and producing more emissions. Again, the model finds the emissions of the average piece (or functional unit) of mail. Consequently, because results are calculated for the average functional unit, they are far less valid for mail that assumes characteristics far removed from the averages.

There is uncertainty in our results, even though we carried out the calculations to a large number of significant places.[4] At a general level, such uncertainties are very common in developing policy-relevant models, and are addressed in the same manner as in our analysis: clearly stating what they are and how the values selected influence the overall results. In the case of our LCI model, most of the uncertainties are related to factors and behavior of participants in the mail life cycle that are outside USPS. We have addressed these uncertainties by applying a series of conservative but realistic assumptions made on the basis of our extensive knowledge of the mail-stream and mail production and handling processes, solid waste management practices and related activities. In many cases, specific assumptions are based upon review of relevant literature, interviews with industry experts, and similar measures. So while the model contains a significant number of values that are uncertain, these values are unlikely to be highly inaccurate. For example, it is highly unlikely that the average distance from the mailer to USPS point of entry for mail is 50 miles rather than the five miles we have assumed, and it also is unlikely that any significant quantity of mail (or components) is transported following recycling or disposal by the recipient by any vehicle other than a large truck (collection or haul truck).[5] Accordingly, while our modeled results cannot be considered to be precise, we believe that they are accurate within a range that is typical of policy models, that is, a factor of 50 to 100 percent. If anything, our deliberately conservative estimates and overall approach are likely to overstate the overall energy consumption, waste and emissions from the mail stream, though by an unknown margin.

4 PRELIMINARY MODEL RESULTS AND INTERPRETATION

We used the model described above to perform some preliminary analysis of the four major mail classes that account for the vast majority (more than 98 percent by volume) of the mail handled by USPS. We also have attempted to better understand these results and put them into context by conducting a set of comparisons with other data and analytical results.

Results

We conducted runs of the LCI model using the data described and discussed above. Summaries of major model results are provided in Tables 21.4–7. Table 21.4 displays selected results addressing waste generation and pollutant emissions on a unit basis, using the functional unit employed in the model – one million mail pieces. Table 21.5 provides analogous results for energy consumed according to major use.

These results show that waste and emissions on a unit (piece) basis vary substantially across the four major mail classes examined here. Periodicals and, particularly, Package Services are accountable for waste generation, pollutant emissions, and energy consumption of about one order of magnitude more than First Class and Standard mail. This marked difference is primarily attributable to the relative weights (mass) of the typical mail piece within each class. Heavier mail pieces require more materials and pollutant emissions are primarily a function of mass within the context of the mail's life cycle. Another important factor in explaining the observed differences among the four mail products is the relatively large amount of printing and pages in a typical periodical in comparison with other mail products. This results in substantially higher unit facility energy consumption, solid waste generation, and hydrocarbon emissions for periodicals than one would otherwise expect, based upon product weight or density alone.

Tables 21.6 and 21.7 provide the results of Tables 21.4 and 21.5, respectively, in the aggregate, that is, for the total number of mail pieces of each major product, as of FY 2006. From this point of view, patterns evident on a unit basis change considerably, because of the relative volumes of First Class and Standard mail as compared with Periodicals and, particularly, Package Services. Standard mail now accounts for the largest share of energy consumption, waste and emissions across the board, while levels for Package Services are of one order of magnitude lower than those of the other major mail products for many of the indicators of interest.

The share of each pollutant that is attributable to Postal Service operations is highly variable, though limited. For all parameters except carbon dioxide, the share is 10 percent or less of the total. USPS's share of CO_2[6] is 14.5 percent of the total, while for several other parameters it is less than 5 percent (for example, particulate matter (2.4 percent), and solid waste (0.3 percent)). In all cases, the vast majority of the remainder is attributable to the paper and board manufacturing, printing/mail production, and, for both solid waste generation and CO_2 emissions, the landfill disposal life cycle stages. For most endpoints considered by the LCI model, the paper and board manufacturing stage of the mail life cycle dominates all subsequent stages. The relatively high contributions both for this stage and for Postal Service operations are likely due to full consideration of fuel use both in transportation and facility operation within the model for these two stages,

Table 21.4 LCI model results – major mail products: waste generation and pollutant emissions (unit basis)

Mail product	Total life cycle stage waste & emissions (kg/million pieces)				
	Solid waste	Dissolved solids	Hydro-carbons	Particulate matter	Carbon dioxide equivalent
First Class mail	20,629.56	257.88	487.40	80.62	87,106.08
Standard mail	54,124.99	614.00	620.30	198.99	162,391.23
Periodicals	212,122.34	2,267.96	5,709.66	872.40	744,465.89
Package Services	209,147.71	4,444.79	2,471.10	831.27	1,210,708.29
Other mail products*	4,957.47	1,409.94	2,313.27	127.53	913,900.50
Special Services*	1,295.36	648.54	215.29	5.41	282,299.51

Note: * Postal Service portion of life cycle only.

Table 21.5 LCI model results – major mail products: energy consumption (unit basis)

Mail product	Total life cycle stage energy consumption (MM BTU/million pieces)		
	Transportation	Facility operation	Total
First Class mail	269.08	1,292.30	1,561.39
Standard mail	381.53	2,870.28	3,251.80
Periodicals	1,245.39	12,435.85	13,681.24
Package Services	8,863.96	10,287.98	19,151.94
Other mail products*	11,901.11	2,003.04	13,904.15
Special Services*	297.43	5,507.12	5,804.55

Note: * Postal Service portion of life cycle only.

as emissions of most of the pollutants profiled here are closely and directly proportional to fossil fuel use.

This conjecture is borne out by examination of the data in Table 21.7, which show that energy used for facility operation relative to that used for transportation dominates overall and for three of the four major Postal products. Transportation energy accounts for 46 percent of the life cycle energy used in Package Services. This is likely due to the proportionately greater weight of Package Services mail pieces relative to that of other mail products. As discussed above, greater weight implies greater transportation fuel use.

Sensitivity Analysis

As discussed above, we allocated fuel used by USPS to individual mail products and to institutional, or network, uses based on causal relationships as suggested by economic theory and stipulated by the ISO Standard. We also performed a sensitivity analysis to

Table 21.6 LCI model results – major mail products: waste generation and pollutant emissions (total)

Mail product	Total life cycle stage waste & emissions (MT)				
	Solid waste	Dissolved solids	Hydro-carbons	Particulate matter	Carbon dioxide equivalent
First Class mail	2,013,752	25,173	47,577	7,870	8,502,785
Standard mail	5,545,622	62,910	63,555	20,389	16,638,534
Periodicals	1,913,887	20,463	51,516	7,871	6,716,990
Package Services	245,654	5,221	2,902	976	1,422,035
Subtotal	9,718,916	113,767	165,551	37,106	33,280,344
Postal Service product share of above	25,031	8,551	9,933	877	4,832,408
Other mail products	14,219	4,044	6,635	366	2,621,286
Special services	1,967	985	327	8	428,707
USPS Institutional	15,035	3,624	5,576	347	3,051,061
Total for USPS	56,252	17,204	22,471	1,597	10,933,462

Table 21.7 LCI model results – major mail products: energy consumption (total)

Mail product	Total life cycle stage energy consumption (MM BTUs)		
	Transportation	Facility operation	Total
First Class mail	26,266,490	126,146,878	152,413,368
Standard mail	39,091,108	294,087,259	333,178,366
Periodicals	11,236,610	112,203,273	123,439,882
Package Services	10,411,155	12,083,731	22,494,885
Subtotal	87,005,362	544,521,140	631,526,502
Postal Service share of above	46,088,274	35,532,868	81,621,142
Other mail products	34,135,233	5,745,203	39,880,435
Special Services	451,692	8,363,248	8,814,939
USPS Institutional	21,636,874	24,093,139	45,730,012
Total for USPS	102,312,073	73,734,457	176,046,529

examine the impact of using some alternative allocation mechanisms. Specifically, we calculated resource use and related emissions by mail product based on mail product pieces, weights, and three-dimensional volume, or 'cube'. The results for one endpoint of interest (CO_2-equivalent emissions) appear in Table 21.8. We selected this parameter due to the significant attention and interest being devoted to carbon emissions and climate change.

Not surprisingly, results show that the estimated fuel and pollutant emissions associated with each mail product differ markedly depending upon the distribution key chosen.

Table 21.8 LCI model results – major mail products: sensitivity of results to allocation method for USPS energy: CO2-e emissions (million MT)

	First Class	Standard mail	Period-icals	Package Services	All other mail	Special Services	Fixed	Total
Causal	2.4	1.4	0.4	0.7	2.6	0.4	3.1	10.9
Pieces	3.6	3.8	0.3	0.0	0.1	0	3.1	10.9
Weight	1.3	3.6	1.2	1.1	0.7	NA	3.1	10.9
Cube	1.0	2.0	0.7	2.2	2.0	NA	3.1	10.9

None of the three alternatives appears to have a consistent relationship to the baseline results. It should be noted, however, that regardless of which distribution key is chosen to allocate USPS fuel use and related emissions among mail products, this choice has only limited impact on the overall results of the analysis. This is because the life cycle stages involving USPS and its activities account for a relatively minor share of the total for most endpoints of interest.

It is also possible that we have not included life cycle stages, activities or phenomena that would impart substantial changes to the estimates generated by the model and this could conceivably limit the accuracy and utility of our results. To address this possibility, we performed sensitivity analysis around the issue of carbon sequestration in harvested trees. Even if one assumes, contrary to fact, that new trees are not replanted to replace harvested trees, results show that GHG emissions for all four product would change by at most about 10 percent, but it is more likely that the changes would be substantially less.

Comparisons of LCI Model Results with Other Data and LCI Studies

As one means of interpreting and validating our LCI model results, we conducted some limited comparisons of our results with nationwide statistics for industry-wide and personal energy consumption and GHG emissions. The purpose of these comparisons is not to develop or support any contention that the mail-stream does or does not have higher or lower resource consumption or pollutant emissions than other alternative means of delivering messages, information, and/or goods. It simply is a means of helping us to understand the realism of our model results. On that score, the comparisons described below suggest that our results are reasonable and realistic, that is, emissions, waste and energy use estimates are within a range that seems credible.

These comparisons, organized by model endpoint, are presented below. We begin with some data that help to put the energy consumption, waste generation and pollutant emissions estimated by the LCI model as attributable to the mail into context by assessing the scale, or overall importance of the mail's resource consumption and emissions, relative to the US as a whole. This is done by comparing the results for the four major mail classes in the aggregate to US national data for major industries and sectors of the economy. We then present some preliminary results drawn from other sources that address different types of mail products and services and compare them to our model estimates for the appropriate class(es) of mail.

Scale of mail-related emissions

Energy consumption Total energy consumed by the four mail products accounts for 0.6 percent of national energy consumption. Total estimated life cycle energy consumption for the four major mail products examined in the initial application of the LCI model is about 632 trillion BTU, about 0.6 percent of the national total. About 78 percent of this energy is consumed in the paper and paper board manufacturing process. The life cycle portions downstream of the manufacture of the mail's 'raw materials' consume about 136 trillion BTUs for the four major mail classes combined.

For comparative purposes, consider the energy consumed by other industries and economic activities, as illustrated by the following data. Total manufacturing energy use (2002 data) in the US was 22,666 trillion BTUs. Major contributors include petroleum (6,799 trillion BTUs), chemicals (6,465 trillion BTUs), paper (2,363 trillion BTUs), part of which is accounted for by the model, and primary metals (2,120 trillion BTUs) (EIA, 2007a). The 496 trillion BTUs consumed by the manufacture of paper and board used in the mail make this life cycle stage comparable to a number of other resource-intensive industries, such as the production of nitrogenous fertilizer (497 trillion BTUs), alumina and aluminum (473 trillion BTUs) and cement (409 trillion BTUs).

The total estimated life cycle energy consumed by the four major mail products downstream of paper and board production can also be compared with other commercial, rather than industrial, uses of energy. Most of this energy is used to condition (that is, heat, cool and ventilate) buildings. The 136 trillion BTUs consumed in the aggregate to make, deliver and manage the mail following use is less than the energy used in all of the major categories of building use defined and quantified by the US Department of Energy's Energy Information Administration (EIA), but is closest to the total national building energy consumption for public order and safety (209 trillion BTUs), outpatient health care (247 trillion BTUs), and religious worship (288 trillion BTUs) (EIA, 2006).

Carbon emissions Total GHG emissions attributable to the four mail products account for a fraction of 1 percent of the national total. The LCI model estimates that total life cycle carbon emissions (CO_2-equivalents) attributable to the four major mail products examined here is 33,280,344 metric tons (MT) as of FY 2006. The national US total for anthropogenic emissions of GHGs in 2006 was 7,075.6 *million* MT (EIA, 2007b). Thus, the roughly 33 million MT of CO_2-equivalent emissions emitted over the life cycle of the four mail classes comprise 0.47 percent of the US total.

By comparison, CO_2-equivalent emissions from industrial sources in the US are generally far higher, led by petroleum (304.8 million MT), chemicals (311.0 million MT) and primary metals (212.8 million MT). Total emissions from the pulp and paper industry (partially captured in the model results) amount to 102.4 million MT annually (Schipper, 2006). Note that these data address energy-related CO_2 emissions only.

Commercial sector CO_2 emissions amounted to 1,045.2 million MT in 2006, most of which was attributable to electricity use, while total industrial GHG emissions were 1,650.8 million MT; transport-related emissions were 1,990.1 million MT (EIA, 2007b). Accordingly, if end-to-end mail creation, transport and delivery, and disposition were to be included in any of these major sectors (it has elements of each), it would account for between 1.7 and 3.2 percent of the national sector total, according to our model. And if it were compared to the sum of the three, it would comprise 0.7 percent of the national total.

5 MODEL AND DATA LIMITATIONS

We believe that our LCI represents an important step forward in understanding the environmental and resource implications of the current mailing infrastructure in the US. It addresses the most environmentally important activities in the mail value chain while providing some insights into the magnitude of mail-related aspects affecting all environmental media. There are, however, limitations associated with the model and our approach more generally. This section identifies some of these and discusses some of the areas in which some further analytical and data development activity could materially improve the model.

While we are confident that we have valid data and methods for quantifying the environmental aspects of many stages in the life cycle of the mail, there are several stages and activities for which our data are old or supporting data are more limited.

Perhaps the most important limitation pertains to paper manufacturing. Paper manufacturing is the predominant source of mail-related pollutant emissions, and although we have used the most comprehensive data available, they are old. The data on paper and paper board manufacturing emissions were obtained from a study published in 2004 (Franklin Associates, 2004). Unfortunately, however, most of the underlying source data appear to have been developed in the early and mid-1990s. Because significant technological advances have since been made within the paper manufacturing industry, more recent and complete data would likely show lower unit pollutant emissions from paper production than those used in our model, at least for some pollutants. The American Paper and Forest Association is conducting new LCI analysis of various grades and types of paper and results should be forthcoming in early 2010. It will be important to compare any resulting emissions factors with those in our model and determine prospective impacts of their adoption.

The printing and mail preparation stage is one where the data, while more recent, were incomplete. For this initial version of the LCI, we adapted detailed energy consumption and air pollutant emissions data developed by EPA that characterize, across a variety of printer sizes and configurations, the flexographic printing process. Because, however, this is only one of several printing processes that are commonly used to produce products that enter the mail (MPA, 2008), it would be desirable to obtain and incorporate data with which to calculate similar environmental endpoints for the other major printing processes in use. These include offset lithography and rotogravure, among others. These processes may exhibit energy consumption and pollutant emissions patterns that are similar to those of the flexographic process, but in the absence of comparable empirical data or engineering estimates, we cannot make an assumption either way.

Similarly, we have not characterized in detail the mail preparation process itself, which may be important in evaluating the life cycle inventory for mail pieces that are mass produced (for example, most Standard mail and Periodicals). Mail preparation for these products in many cases involves adhesive application and other activities that may give rise to environmental aspects (for example, air pollutant emissions) that we have not quantified and included to this point (ibid.). Whether or not any such aspects would rise to the 1 percent threshold that we have defined as our study boundary is unclear at this point.

NOTES

1. Specifically, the ISO 14040 series of standards, guidelines and technical references on Life Cycle Assessment.
2. An exception to this general rule exists for Package Services. The user-specified weight percentage of the packages that consists of their contents is retained, and all packaging is discarded. We have assumed for our initial analysis that 85 percent of the weight of packages entering Package Services consists of content and the remaining 15 percent consists of packaging.
3. ISO 14044, Section 4.3.4.2 (Allocation procedure) states, in part, 'Where allocation cannot be avoided, the inputs and outputs of the system should be partitioned between its different products or functions in a way that reflects the underlying physical relationships between them'.
4. In fact, like many analyses, our results are displayed as they are to allow checking of computations and calculations.
5. The one exception applies to recycled and recovered materials, which may be transported by rail after they are separated and packaged at the Material Recovery Facility (MRF).
6. In this LCI model, CO_2 emissions include the CO_2-equivalent emissions of other significant global warming gases such as methane and nitrous oxide where data are available.

REFERENCES

Energy Information Administration (EIA) (2006), *2003 CBECS Detailed Tables*, Table C1A: Total Energy Consumption by Major Fuel for All Buildings.

Energy Information Administration (EIA) (2007a), *2002 Energy Consumption by Manufacturers – Data Tables*, Table 1.1: First Use of Energy for All Purposes (Fuel and Nonfuel).

Energy Information Administration (EIA) (2007b), *Emissions of Greenhouse Gases in the United States 2006*, Report #DOE/EIA-0573(2006), Washington, DC.

Magazine Publishers of America (MPA) (2008), *2008 Environment Handbook: Your Source to Understanding Magazines and the Environment*, 24 January, Washington, DC, available from: http://www.magazine.org/environment/index.aspx, accessed 20 July 2009.

Franklin Associates (2004), *Life Cycle Inventory of Packaging Options for Shipment of Retail Mail-Order Soft Goods*, April, prepared for Oregon Department of Environmental Quality.

Schipper, M. (2006), *Energy-Related Carbon Dioxide Emissions in U.S. Manufacturing*, Report #DOE/EIA-0573(2005), Energy Information Administration (EIA), Washington, D.C.

SLS Consulting, Inc. (2008), *The Environmental Impacts of the Mail: Initial Life Cycle Inventory Model and Analysis*, Submitted to Environmental Policy and Programs, US Postal Service, Washington, DC, June, available from: http://postcom.org/eco/Completed%20Internal%20Report%20on%20Initial%20LCI%20Model%207-1-08.pdf, accessed 20 July 2009.

22. Determining the impact of shape and weight of mail items on manual processing costs: an experimental approach

Stéphane Bernard, Caroline Gomez, Lise Martin and Bernard Roy*

1 INTRODUCTION

Following French regulator ARCEP's request in its decision 2008-0165 concerning cost accounting (February 2008), La Poste undertook a study on the influence of size and weight of mail items on costs of manual processes for handling mail. The results are reported here, together with a discussion of the treatment of shape and weight by other postal operators. The scope of this study involved three processes: manual sorting, in-office processes for delivery, and the loading part of the outside delivery process. This study relied on experimental methods for its analysis. Experimental methods have been used for many years in industrial process improvement, including the famous Hawthorne experiments at the Western Electric Corporation in the late 1920s (Mayo, 1949). However, this appears to be the first reported use of such an approach in support of regulatory cost accounting in the postal sector. Because of the obvious significance of human factors in manual processes for handling mail, the experimental approach developed has a number of advantages in terms of reliability of results for managerial purposes as well as credibility for regulators.

The cost accounting model is basically a top-down allocation of costs, based on ABC principles. The costs of each process are given via cost accounting information systems and, if relevant, separated by subprocesses, so-called 'economic processes'. Costs are then attributed to products via cost drivers.[1] This requires an engineering analysis of the subcategories driving costs, and a quantitative valuation of the drivers. Each product is then represented by a particular combination of the drivers. The objective of this chapter is to present the methodology including assumptions and simplifications, for evaluating cost drivers, and quantitative results.

Section 2 describes the methodology adopted and the results obtained. For confidentiality reasons, the results are presented as 'indexes', where the minimal cost is normalized to 1. The study has been carried out by creating a 'laboratory'. Some 30 postmen have been time-measured when handling 30 lots of mail, each lot being composed of a specific proportion of four categories of shape and weight patterns of the mail being processed. The assumption is made that the indexes, reflecting the relative difficulty for handling mail, should be comparable from one postman to another. About 60 000 items were handled for the experiment.

Table 22.1 Price indexes for four different items in different countries

Country	Letter 5 mm thick 20 g	Large envelope 10 mm thick 100 g	Large envelope 30 mm thick 1000 g	Packet 2000 g
Cyprus	1	1.3	3.5	5.0
Austria	1	1.8	5.0	6.8
Germany	1	2.6	4.0	7.1
France	1	2.4	7.0	9.2
Belgium	1	2.0	5.0	9.7
Ireland	1	1.7	10.9	13.7
USA	1	3.2	11.8	14.5
Spain	1	2.3	13.0	15.6
UK	1	1.6	8.3	16.8

In Section 3, we compare these methods and results with those from the United States. We study the US processes and regulatory accounting in order to identify similarities with differences and those of France. This provides the basis for a comparative study of cost distribution keys used by La Poste and the US Postal Service (USPS) for selected manual processing operations.

Section 4 concludes. Besides our positive evaluation of the experimental approach for assessing costs of manual processing operations, we also note the importance of having better estimates of weight and shape on overall attributable costs of mail services. Indeed, while weight and shape are central to pricing in the postal sector, very few papers have focused on evaluating the effects of weight and shape as cost drivers.

2 WEIGHT AND SHAPE STUDY CARRIED OUT BY LA POSTE

Pricing for Weight and Shape in Different Countries

Postal items vary in terms of weight, shape and size: from a postcard to a parcel. Given this diversity, different postal operators offer various pricing principles both in the price category definition and in the price differentiation. Table 22.1 presents the price of four different items compared to the common letter price for different countries. While the 2 kg packet is sold five times as much as the common letter in Cyprus, it is sold 16.8 times as much as the common letter in the United Kingdom. This table shows wide diversity of pricing between these two extremes.

As far as weight and shape are concerned, we can highlight three kinds of pricing for single-piece items. A first one is a cross-pricing weight and shape. Deutsche Post (Germany) applies this cross-pricing (see Appendix Figure 22A.2). From a first category for small and light items, price evolves with both weight and shape to middle-sized/middle-weight items, then large and heavy ones.

Another kind of pricing is 'false' cross-pricing. The weight remains dominant in the pricing but some shape constraints also exist. These shape constraints, often created for the extremes – small and light items or very large ones – allow a lower fare for the

Table 22.2 Mail distribution by weight and shape (%)

	≤ 20g	21–50g	51–250g	> 250g
Length ≤ 140 or height ≤ 90mm	0.3	0.0	0.0	0.0
Length ≤ 250 or height ≤ 120mm	46.9	7.8	0.5	0.0
Length ≤ 250 or height ≤ 167mm	6.8	10.1	2.5	0.0
Length ≤ 325 or height ≤ 230mm	0.7	4.2	13.2	2.5
Length ≤ 360 or height ≤ 260mm	0.1	0.5	2.3	0.8
Length ≤ 400 or height ≤ 260mm	0.0	0.0	0.2	0.0
Length ≤ 400 or height ≤ 260mm	0.0	0.0	0.2	0.1
Length > 400 or height > 300mm	0.0	0.0	0.2	0.0

regular letter size and a higher rate for very large sizes. Between these two extremes, price is related to weight only. As shown in Figures 22A.4–7, this kind of pricing can be observed, for instance, in Spain, the UK, Austria and Belgium.

The last alternative is to have a pricing based only on weight. La Poste uses this pricing for letter mail single-piece items (see Figures 22A.8–9: France and Cyprus).

Link between Weight and Shape

Mail shape and size are strongly correlated with mail weight. Table 22.2 shows the mail distribution (parcels are not considered here) by weight and size categories. It appears that items belonging to a weight category belong also, in large part, to a size category and that size increases with weight. So even if La Poste does not explicitly price by shape, the weight pricing implicitly takes shape into account.

It is then useful to carry out an analysis on the influence of weight and shape on costs. Due to the strong correlation between weight and shape, these two cost drivers will be analyzed jointly. Before considering the study conducted by La Poste, to provide the context for this study, it is important to explain briefly the use of cost distribution keys in French postal accounting and its main principles.

French Regulatory Accounting Overview

The costs from analytical accounts are first grouped by processes (sortation, transportation, delivery and so on). Process costs are then distributed to 'economic activities'. These activities correspond to distinct physical activities whose costs can be isolated by a study of analytical accounts. For instance, 'manual sorting' and 'mechanized sorting' are two distinct economic activities in the sorting process.

An economic activity can be shared by various products and the question to answer is how to allocate costs to products that share resources used in the activity. If there is no particular cost driver, the costs are allocated proportionately to the volume of each product going through this activity. For instance, this case is met for the mechanized sorting activity. Costs by sorting machine are known as well as the mail volumes sorted by one machine. As the sorting machine speed does not depend on the product handled, the costs are distributed on products according to volume.

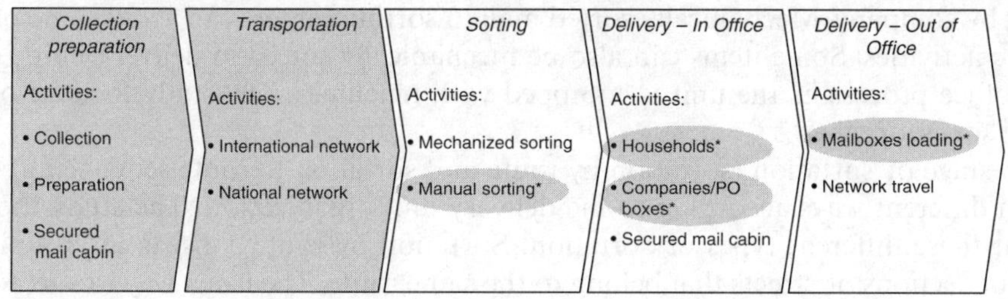

Note: *Activities studied.

Figure 22.1 Activities and subactivities studied

When the unit cost depends on the characteristics of the products handled, one must define the cost drivers that generate cost differences. An example of this situation is manual sorting activity. It has been observed that a postman takes more time to handle a mail batch with a lot of heavy items than to handle only small items. One explanation is that large items are more difficult to manipulate. This observation underlies the presumption that weight/shape is a relevant cost driver for manual sorting activity.

The next step is to allocate relevant costs according to the cost drivers defined. Going back to the manual sorting example, we have defined shape as a relevant cost driver but we still have to define which part of costs will be attributed to small format items, to large items and to packets. A distribution key is needed to allocate the correct amount of costs to each shape. The calculation of these distribution keys is the main focus of the present study.

Activities on Which the Study Focused

The study performed by La Poste focused on activities which need a distribution key. Figure 22.1 highlights the activities studied.

The first process studied is the sorting process. Sorting is a two-stage process, first by destination area (outward sorting) then by zip code (inward sorting). These sorting activities can be done on machines or manually. These two ways of sorting correspond to two distinct economic activities: mechanized and manual sorting activities. The focus here is on the latter.

Manual sorting has two divisions: sorting on rack and basket sorting. Sorting on rack is possible for all shapes except packets and parcels which are thicker than two centimeters. Basket sorting is done for these 'big' packets and parcels. The costs of these two kinds of sorting are not directly estimated in the accounting system because all weight and shape categories go through this joint manual sorting activity. Thus, cost allocations for mail items of different weight and shape must be specified via a cost distribution key.

Manual sorting activities were also studied in the delivery in-office process. There are two types of mail, households and companies/PO boxes, which correspond to two distinct economic activities. For households, the in-office activity consists in two sorting stages: separate mail by route then sort in the sequence of the route. A similar process is performed for the mail to companies and PO boxes. Sorting by code[2] is executed before sorting by company. Mechanically sorted mail in sorting centers can avoid some of these in-office activities. Some items can also be mechanically sorted in delivery units, during the in-office process, if the unit is equipped with machines. The study focused only on manual sortation phases.

Each stage of sortation (sortation by route and sortation to route sequencing) can be done in different ways according to the delivery unit organization. The study took into account these different types of sortation. Sortation by route consists in grouping the streets or sections of streets that belong to the same route. The usual way to sort to route sequence is to sort by street then to sort by street number. Two steps are required for this sorting. A new kind of rack allows postmen to sort in the route sequence directly in one step; this is the so-called 'modular hybrid rack' sortation.

Various shapes are involved in these different sortation stages. During sorting by route, shapes are processed in sequence. Mail arrives from sortation centers in separate containers according to their shape and weight. Nevertheless, identifying separately the time spent to sort each kind of shape is not possible directly in analytical accounting because all shapes are merged during the 'sorting by route' process.

The last activity where cost drivers by weight were studied was the mailbox loading in the street delivery process. Basically, street delivery can be split into three processes: the route traveling process, the stops, and the action of loading mailboxes. While route traveling and stops are considered to be fixed costs (for a sufficient volume of mail), loading the mail is the volume variable part of the street delivery process.[3]

The study focused on mailbox loading. Three types of mailboxes, giving rise to three different cases, were identified. Standard individual mailboxes are one category, where the mail bundle is ready and all shapes except packets thicker than two centimeters are dropped without difficulty. The postman needs to open the mailbox with a key to deliver the biggest packets. He/she does not need to deliver these personally to the addressee except for registered items (which require a signature acknowledging receipt). Another category is a bank of mailboxes. Such mailboxes are found in multi-unit buildings, where many people share the same address. A final sortation by recipient is needed, unlike the individual mailboxes. All shapes are dropped easily in these mailboxes, as in the individual mailbox case. The last category is 'non-standard' individual mailboxes for which the mail bundle is ready but where all packet sizes cannot be dropped easily, a delivery to the door is required when shape (or weight) is too large.

Methodology

A first question to answer is the number and definition of the weight and shape categories for which a distribution key estimate is needed. One might think that the more there are, the more precise cost accounting will become. But if too many categories are created, numerous measurements are needed and the results will be less reliable. The number of distribution keys should then be restricted.

It appears that thickness is a relevant driver discriminating between the ways items are treated in the main economic activities. For example, in manual sorting activities (sorting and in-office delivery), packets that are more than two centimeters thick are handled differently (basket sorting for instance). A thickness of two centimeters is also a relevant threshold for the ease in mailbox loading. As the slot is generally not large enough,

Table 22.3 La Poste size categories

Category	Definition
Small format	Weigh less than 50g
Large format	Weigh between 50 and 250g
Packets 1	Weigh more than 250g + thickness < 2cm
Packets 2	Weigh more than 250g + thickness > 2cm

opening standard mailboxes or delivery by hand is required for packets that are more than two centimeters thick. For all items less than two centimeters thick, a similar process for sorting and delivery can be followed so that processing time increases with size in a continuous, uninterrupted way.

Because a strong link exists between weight and shape and the French pricing is only based on weight, it is natural to construct categories solely on weight differences for mail thinner than two centimeters. Note that this driver implicitly catches the shape influence (see Table 22.2). The distinction for items thicker than two centimeters must be kept because of the specificities required for this type of mail.

The definitions of categories are given in Table 22.3.

In order not to interfere with postal service during the 'real' delivery process, and for control purposes, all measurements were made in laboratory conditions, based on reconstituted mail batches and after daily work. Six heterogeneous mail batches of 600 pieces each were assembled for the purpose of the study. Characteristics such as weight and size but also the type of packaging (plastic, paper) and addressing (typed or handwritten, position on the mail) were considered in order to match appropriately actual mail characteristics.

As in the actual process, for each activity or subactivity measured, 3–11 postmen processed one to three times the six mail batches. Nearly 1000 measurements were recorded. One measure is the time necessary for a postman to process one batch on one subactivity. Thus, each measurement corresponds to homogeneous tasks representing about one hour of manual labor.

Results

A multiple linear regression was applied to the time results obtained after removing outliers. Some of the outliers could have been explained by learning effects.

At this point, unit time by shape for each subactivity was known from the above experimental results. In order to have a distribution key by activity, each subactivity composing the activity was weighted by the mail volume processed through that subactivity. This allowed the determination of distribution keys for each activity for the year 2008. The distribution keys will change each year by updating the volume-based weight of each subactivity, while the unit time of subactivities is a valuable measurement that does not need to be updated as frequently.

For example, sorting by route, sorting in the route sequence on ordinary racks and sorting in the route sequence on 'modular hybrid racks' are three subactivities for the household activity from the delivery-in-office process. The study result is a time ratio:

Table 22.4 Distribution key for sorting process – manual sorting activity

Process	SF	LF	Packet 1	Packet 2
Sortation	1	1.46	2.28	4.47

Table 22.5 Distribution key for in-office process – households' manual sorting activity

Process	SF	LF	Packet 1	Packet 2
In-office: Households	1	1.18	2.59	3.26

Table 22.6 Distribution key for in-office process – companies/PO box manual sorting activity

Process	SF	LF	Packet
In-office: companies/ PO boxes	1	1.44	1.88

Table 22.7 Distribution key for street delivery process – mailbox loading activity

Process	SF	LF	Packet 1	Packet 2
Street delivery	1	2.15	2.86	5.64

shape studied upon small format for each subactivity. This time ratio is weighted with the mail flow processed by this subactivity to give a time ratio for the whole household activity. As the mail flow processed by each subactivity can change through time, it is important to update this data each year in order to keep distribution keys as current as possible. It is assumed that two postmen who process a mail batch at different average speeds have a similar time ratio between small and large formats.

The results of the study are shown in Tables 22.4–7. They are based on the measured times and on the weight of each subactivity composing a specific activity. The results are normalized to the unit for the lowest value. Thus, manual sorting activity, which is one part of the overall sorting process, yields a time for handling a large format (LF) item that is 1.46 times the time for handling a small format (SF) item. Similarly, a packet less than two centimeters thick takes on average 2.28 times longer to sort manually than an average SF item, and an average packet thicker than two centimeters takes 4.47 times longer to sort than an SF item. The variation of weight and shape cost drivers is higher in the process of loading the mailboxes than in the manual sortation process, because of the specificities of the mailbox slots.

Among manual sorting activities, the influence of weight and shape on costs is more important for simple sorting stages like sortation by zip code, for example. Complex judgmental activities typically give rise to lower variation in distribution keys related to weight or shape. For example, the time needed by postmen to look for the correct compartment in which to put the item is not related to the item's weight or shape. Only physical manipulation of an item is related to its weight and shape: the longer the seeking step, the smaller the effect of weight or shape on the distribution key for this sorting activity.

Cazals et al. (2001) examined marginal costs by shape for out-of-office processes. From a panel data model, they concluded that if the marginal cost of a small format item is 1, then the marginal cost of a non-standard format item is 2 and the marginal cost of a packet is 15. These figures are quite different from the study results shown in Table 22.7, especially for packets, but marginal cost computed by Cazals et al. is also quite different from the processing unit time used in the study presented here. Processing unit time does not include any stop time or any hand delivery to the door. As hand delivery is almost entirely dedicated to packets, this seems a likely explanation for the difference between the packet figures in these two studies.

3 COMPARISON WITH THE UNITED STATES

Comparison of the French results with those from USPS can be done using data published by the Postal Regulatory Commission. However, as we shall see, there are some important differences between the definitions of some activities in USPS and La Poste and these will need to be controlled for in the comparison.

First, the main principles underlying the US postal accounting system will be described. Thereafter, important differences are noted between USPS and La Poste, which give rise to some necessary adjustments in order to be able to compare the two systems. We shall see that French distribution keys need to be adapted to match USPS cost accounting boundaries. A conversion matrix between French and American shapes is also necessary to be able to compare French and US mail-streams.

US Regulatory Accounting Overview

The costs issued from the USPS accounting system are first grouped by segments, that is, groupings of accounts. For example, transportation is a segment that contains some 180 accounts related to payment of transportation by air, land or waterways. All costs from USPS are distributed over 18 cost segments.

Segment costs are then distributed to underlying components. The components are groupings of costs identified for the purpose of variability analysis. Most segments contain several components sometimes divided into subcomponents or elements. For example, 'City delivery – street activity' segment costs are split into three components: network travel, whose costs are not related to volume, delivery activities, whose costs are partly variable with volume and are allocated via econometric studies, and delivery support, variable with volume in the same proportion as the network travel and delivery activities.

Within each component, the costs are split into variable and institutional (or fixed) costs. The variability of a component is the response of the total costs of this component to a small change in volume. Institutional costs are not variable, in other words the difference between the total accrued costs and variable costs. Finally, variable costs are distributed according to cost drivers, then to products according to the distribution of each product in different cost drivers.

Table 22.8 USPS shape definition

	Max dimension	Weight
Letters	11.5 × 6.125 × 0.25 inches	3.3 oz
	292 × 156 × 6 mm	93.6 g
Flats	15 × 12 × 0.75 inches	First Class: 13 oz (368 g)
	381 × 305 × 19 mm	
Parcels	l + w + h < 108 inches	First Class: 13 oz (368 g)
	l + w + h < 274 mm	Priority mail: 70 pounds (31.8 kg)

The main principles of cost allocation are the same in both La Poste and USPS: costs are distributed on the grounds of activities that generate the costs. Since many activities are shared by several products, USPS and La Poste must define cost drivers and cost distribution keys to allocate variable costs to products.

In the United States, shape definition depends on product. Some constraints on rigidity, surface regularity, and so on exist but to keep things simple, the simplified definitions in Table 22.8 will be used.

Comparison

Sorting centers often perform mechanized sortation to the route level, and even to route sequence (DPS mail). This sorting by route at the sorting center is possible thanks to mailbox numbering. USPS owns mailboxes; they are primarily appointed by their number. This allows control of delivery maps and facilitates the sortation by route in the sorting center. For manually sorted items, sortation by route is done in the delivery unit but the associated costs are recorded in the sorting process. Different kinds of mail arrive at the delivery unit: mail sorted in the route sequence by large clients or consolidators (workshared mail), saturation mail (also conditioned by clients), mail sorted in route sequence by the sorting plant (so-called DPS mail), and finally non-automation items sorted by route in the delivery unit (including packages and registered mail). Postmen have to sort this last category into route sequence and load their vehicle. In contrast to the French process, not all mail is merged in the delivery unit. The mail remains in three separate bundles: DPS, saturation and non-DPS. Registered mail and parcels are also treated separately.

Most routes are made by car. Postmen can load individual mailboxes or stop in front of a bank of mailboxes, and take the mail corresponding to the mailboxes for several stops (park and loop process).

These are two major differences between France and the United States: shape definition and processes. Moreover, groupings of costs by segments do not fit exactly with the French processes. Two changes are therefore required to provide a basis for comparison. One is necessary to adapt French distribution keys to USPS cost categories. The other is to weight these adapted French distribution keys to USPS shapes.

First, we shall address the shape definition problem. The closest categories to American shape definitions are presented in Table 22.9.

These definitions crossed with French weight categories give the shape conversion matrix (Table 22.10).

Table 22.9 USPS shapes and corresponding French mail characteristics

USPS shape	Closest French dimensions (mm)	Closest French weight (g)
Letters	250 × 167 × 5	100
Flats	400 × 300 × 20	350
Parcels	> flats	> 350

Table 22.10 Conversion matrix: French to American shape categories (%)

	SF (< 50g)	LF (50–250g)	Packet (>250g)	Total
Letters	70.6	1.3	0.0	72
Flats	5.7	17.2	1.9	25
Parcels	0.1	0.3	3.0	3
Total	76.0	19.0	5.0	100

Table 22.11 Distribution keys comparison between USPS and La Poste – manual sorting activities

USPS shape	USPS unit time ratio	La Poste distribution key adapted to USPS costs and weighted with shape conversion matrix ratio
Letters	1.00	1.00
Flats	1.41	1.39
Parcels	1.65	2.57

The second problem we have to face is to define activities on a similar basis. The objective is to use French distribution keys but adapted to processes defined according to the activities in the associated American process. As the purpose is to compare results from its study, La Poste focused on similar activities in the United States. For each of these activities, described below, details of USPS costing and process boundaries are noted as a prelude to our comparative study of USPS and La Poste distribution keys.

Unlike in France, manual sortation of the different shape categories is done separately in the USA. This means that manual sorting activities are shape dedicated: first letters, then flats but not both at the same time. As the time spent for each of these sorting activities is known as well as the volume handled, USPS does not need a distribution key for manual sorting costs; they 'naturally' fall by shape within the accounting system. For comparison purposes, a unit time ratio has been calculated (see Table 22.11). This calculation takes into account the 'mail processing' costs.[4] It includes manual sorting activities. Sorting costs for sortation by route are recorded in the 'Mail processing' component.

In France, sortation by route is done during the in-office stage of the delivery process. In order to compare with the USPS unit time ratio, this part of the in-office process should be removed from delivery and re-aggregated with the French sorting process. The unit times from French manual sorting activities have been added to the time needed to sort mail by route in the in-office process to obtain unit times adapted to

Table 22.12 Distribution key comparison between USPS and La Poste: in-office activities

USPS shape	USPS unit cost ratio	La Poste distribution key adapted to US costs and weighted with shape conversion matrix ratio
Letters	1.00	1.00
Flats	2.74	1.22
Parcels	4.95	2.49

the USPS cost accounting structure. As a result, the adapted French distribution key is weighted with the conversion matrix ratio in order to finally compare French and American results.

Note that the distribution key calculated from French data for flats is very close to the USPS unit time ratio for this shape. The result is not close when it comes to Parcels. A first explanation could be the absence of Priority products in the USPS ratio. A second one is that the US sortation is dedicated to one single shape whereas the French study focused on mixing the shapes, since a heterogeneous mail mix is one of the major reasons why a difference exists between the times required to process the different shapes.

Cost distribution among products for USPS is available in the annual compliance report documents. Distribution of products among shapes and volume by shapes is also available. To obtain a unit cost, and to be able to construct a ratio, we divided costs by volumes. But in-office volumes are not available. The volumes that have been taken into account for the US distribution keys are the same volumes as in Cost Segment 7 'City delivery – Street activities'. This volume is unfortunately different in structure from the volume processed in in-office activities, as street delivery contains DPS mail, which is not processed in-office. This leads to an overestimation of flats and parcels ratios (as the in-office costs for small formats are divided by too large a number).

With this caveat in mind, the ratio of these values gives the unit costs per shape for the Segment 6 'City delivery – In-Office activities' which leads to the distribution key shown in Table 22.12. In order to adapt French distribution keys to this USPS cost accounting structure, only unit times for sortation in route sequence have been taken into account. Unit time for French packets more than two centimeters thick has not been taken into account as US parcels are not sorted in the route sequence. The adapted French distribution key is weighted with the conversion matrix ratio in order to finally compare French and American results.

To correct the bias described above, we made a comparison of flats and parcels only, as we suspect DPS mail to be essentially small format. Results are given in Table 22.13.

The parcel distribution key calculated from French data is quite similar to the unit cost ratios calculated from the USPS annual compliance report. The French distribution key for parcels is a bit higher than the US distribution key, but this could be explained by the fact that parcels are never sorted in the route sequence in US delivery centers, while they are sometimes merged in the delivery unit in France.

The delivery accrued costs are split between variable and institutional costs, with the variable costs then distributed to each shape based on an econometric study carried out

Table 22.13 Distribution key comparison between USPS and La Poste for flats and parcels only: in-office activities

USPS shape	USPS unit cost ratio	La Poste distribution key adapted to USPS costs and weighted with shape conversion matrix ratio
Flats	1.00	1.00
Parcels	1.81	2.04

by Michael D. Bradley for USPS (see PRC doc 2005). During a two-week period, mail volume by shape has been registered as well as the time postmen took to complete their route. These data were used to define what parts of total delivery costs were variable and within these variable costs, which are attributable to letters, flats and parcels.

In the USPS 2008 *Annual Compliance Report*, the delivery costs by shape divided by volume gives unit costs by shape which leads to the distribution keys (see Table 22.14).

In order to be as close as possible to the USPS process, the loading mailboxes times have been taken into account only for mailbox clusters. The sorting time in the route sequence for French packets more than two centimeters thick has also been taken into account. The adapted French distribution key calculated is presented in Table 22.14. The adapted French distribution key is then weighted with the conversion matrix ratio to finally compare French and American results.

Mailboxes are smaller in the United States than in France. As a result postmen may end up ringing the recipient's doorbell more often than in France or undertaking alternative actions in the event that the recipient is not at home. The time needed to interact with the recipient or undertake such alternative actions could explain the difference between the parcel distribution key calculated from French data and the USPS distribution key. Another explanation of this difference could be that American postmen have to group mail from their different bundles while their French counterparts already have all mail merged. This additional work for American postmen compared to French ones could also lead to an increase in the American cost ratio relative to that in France.

4 CONCLUSION

While pricing in the postal industry is always related to the weight (and sometimes shape) of items, very little work has been published by postal economists in this field. The study we have conducted may be of interest in promoting further research in this area.

The present study concerns only manual processes for sorting in sorting centers and delivery units, and the loading part of the street delivery process. Cost drivers were here evaluated based on weight categories. Within each weight category, current distributions by shape have been taken into account. The most efficient economic signal is to offer different prices for items which present different costs. This should lead to offering more refined price structures to account for cost differences occasioned by weight and shape. The advantage of such pricing becomes relevant when mail volumes for each of these categories of weight and shape become significant. If this is not the case, complexity

Table 22.14 Distribution key comparison between USPS and La Poste: delivery/city street activities

USPS shape	USPS unit cost ratio	La Poste distribution key adapted to USPS costs and weighted with shape conversion matrix ratio
Letters	1.0	1.0
Flats	1.1	1.45
Parcels	6.5	3.02

and transaction costs generated counterbalance the advantages of having greater price differentiation.

The analysis underlying this study is based on observations of 'batches' processed by postmen, in a laboratory context. Batches have been constituted to represent reasonable variations of actual traffic by weight and shape, allowing the results to be analyzed by standard regression analysis. The analysis shows that costs vary in a range from 1 to 4.47 in the sortation process, from 1 to 3.26 for in-office activities and 1 to 5.64 in the street delivery process, according to the weight and the shape of items.

In the second part of this study, the results of the French study were compared with the similar manual sorting processes underlying USPS cost accounting. It appears that the cost drivers calculated are very similar. Of course, these comparative results must be regarded with caution, as comparisons rely on many transformations to account for differences in both the accounting structure of La Poste and USPS as well as the structure of underlying activities reflected in the accounting structure. Nonetheless, it is instructive to compare the processes in each case. Indeed, some differences in the drivers can be explained by differences in process. In particular, the US mail sortation process includes sorting by routes (and very often the sequencing of mail for the route), processes which are part of the in-office process in France. The fact that mail is processed in three bundles before the street delivery process in the United States is probably more efficient upstream, but time is then spent by postmen in merging the bundles during the loading process. Except for parcels, this has an effect on relative cost drivers by weight in the street delivery process.

With regarded to parcels, we observe that the relative time taken in handling parcels during the in-office process is smaller in the United States than in France, but relatively much higher in the street delivery process. A plausible explanation is that the sortation of the parcels by routes is made by clerks in the USA (that is, during the sorting process) leaving very little work for the delivery unit, making the relative costs lower in the USA for this process. Then, while parcels are merged in the sequence of the route in France, making the street delivery easier, they are not sequenced in the USA, leaving more work to be done during the street delivery process.

Perhaps the most important finding from this study is the evident significance of weight and shape as fundamental drivers of postal costs. Comparison between USPS and La Poste also shows that the influence of weight and shape on costs is closely related to process, organization and available equipment, including everything from mail processing technology to the size of mailboxes. Understanding these effects and integrating them with the structure of cost accounting and tariffs remains a central challenge for both operators and regulatory authorities.

NOTES

* The opinions expressed in this chapter are those of the authors and do not necessarily reflect the positions of the Groupe La Poste. The authors would like to thank Michael Crew, Paul Kleindorfer and Jeff Colvin for their comments on an earlier draft. All errors remain the responsibility of the authors.

1. For a discussion of the theory underlying cost drivers for postal accounting purposes, and as an input for regulation and pricing decisions in the US, see Crew and Kleindorfer (2000).
2. Companies and PO boxes which receive a lot of mail have an individual code in their address. For those with less traffic, the address code is common for several companies.
3. For an extensive description of the street delivery process, see Jasinski and Steggles (1977), Cohen and Chu (1997), Roy (1999) and Bernard et al. (2002).
4. 'Mail processing' is a component belonging to Cost Segment 3 'Clerks and Mail Handlers, CAG A-J Post Office'. Most mail processing plants are equipped with a MODS (Management Operations Data System). When operators begin a sorting activity, they clock into the system, that is, that they pass their ID card over a scanning device tied to a clock and enter the MODS number associated with the operation they are currently working in. As a result, the number of hours spent on the different manual sorting activities (letter, flats, parcels and Priority) is available. Time divided by volume gives the unit time by shape, which leads to the distribution key. As Priority products are competitive products, volume data are not available. A caveat on these results is thus that a part of manual distribution costs is beyond the scope of this study.

REFERENCES

Bernard, Stéphane, Robert Cohen, Matthew Robinson, Bernard Roy, Joëlle Toledano, John Waller and Spyros Xenakis (2002), 'Delivery cost heterogeneity and vulnerability', in M.A. Crew and P.R. Kleindorfer (eds), *Postal and Delivery Services: Delivering on Competition*, Boston, MA: Kluwer Academic, pp. 169–84.

Bradley, M.D. (2005), 'Direct Testimony of Michael D. Bradley on behalf of the United States Postal Service', Postal Regulatory Commission, Docket No. R2005-1, USPS-T-14, part of the FY2002 City Carrier Street Time Survey.

Cazals, Catherine, Jean-Pierre Florens and Bernard Roy (2001), 'An analysis of some specific cost drivers in the delivery activity', in M.A. Crew and P.R. Kleindorfer (eds), *Future Directions in Postal Reform*, Boston, MA: Kluwer Academic, pp. 197–212.

Cohen, R.H. and E.H. Chu (1997), 'A measure of scale economies for postal systems', in M.A. Crew and P.R. Kleindorfer (eds), *Managing Change in the Postal and Delivery Sector*, Boston, MA: Kluwer Academic, pp. 115–32.

Crew, M.A. and P.R. Kleindorfer (2000), 'Cost estimation and economically efficient prices', in Crew and Kleindorfer (eds), *Current Directions in Postal Reform*, Boston, MA: Kluwer Academic, pp. 149–70.

Jasinski, K. and E. Steggles (1977), 'Modelling letter delivery in town areas', *Computers and Operational Research*, **4**, 287–94.

Mayo, Elton (1949), *Hawthorne and the Western Electric Company, The Social Problems of an Industrial Civilisation*, London: Routledge.

Roy, Bernard (1999), 'Technico-economic analysis of the costs of outside work in postal delivery', in M.A. Crew and P.R. Kleindorfer (eds), *Emerging Competition in Postal and Delivery Services*, Boston, MA: Kluwer Academic, pp. 101–22.

USPS (2008), *Annual Compliance Report*, US Postal Service, prc.gov.

APPENDIX 22A WEIGHT AND SHAPE IMPACTS ON PRICING OF SINGLE-PIECE PRODUCTS

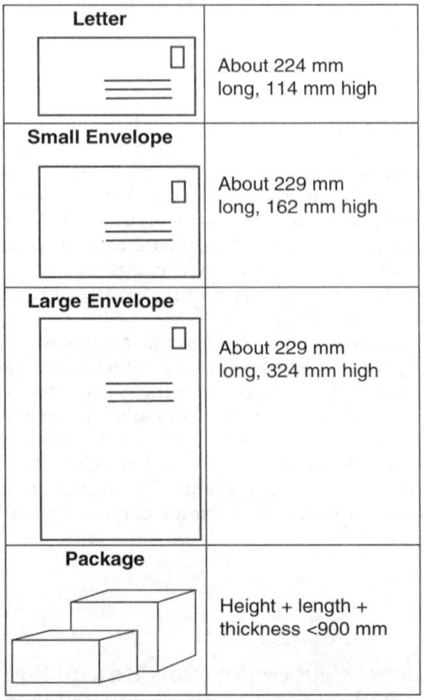

Figure 22A.1 Shape definition

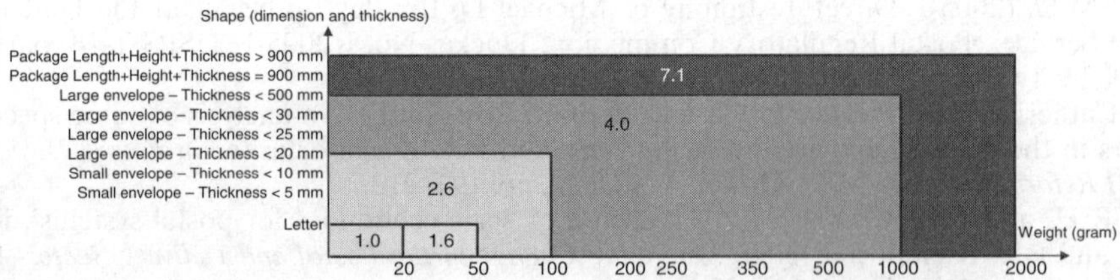

Note: The lower price in Germany is for letters about 224 mm long, 114 mm high and less than 20g. The price of a package is 7.1 times higher than this lower price.

Figure 22A.2 Germany

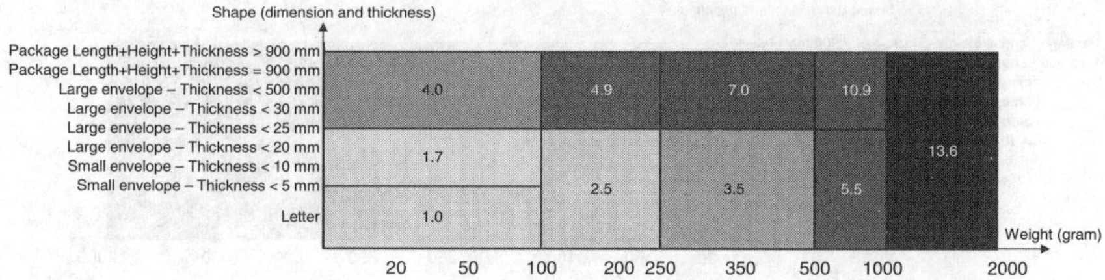

Figure 22A.3 Ireland

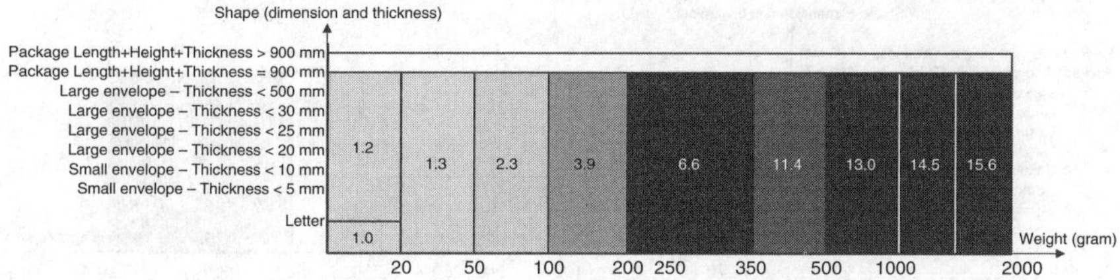

Figure 22A.4 Spain

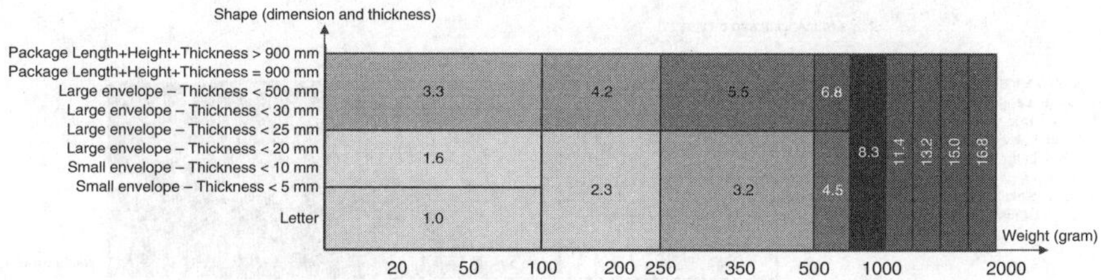

Figure 22A.5 United Kingdom

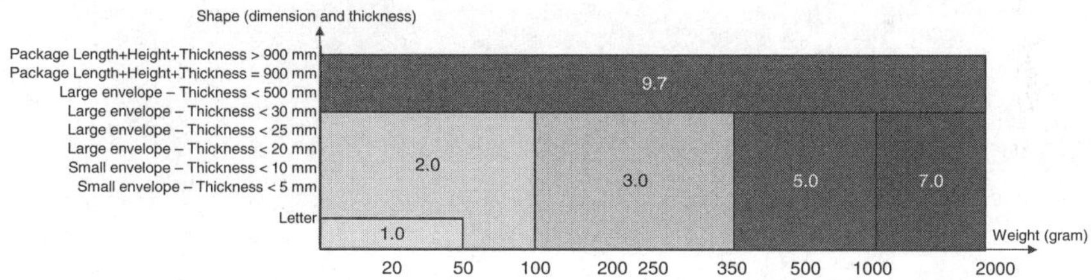

Figure 22A.6 Belgium

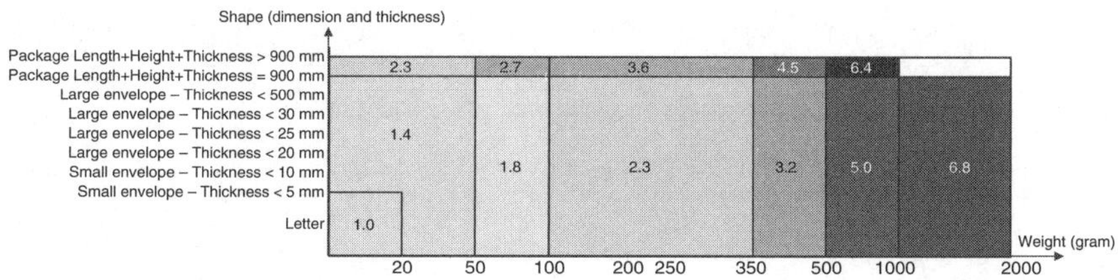

Figure 22A.7 Austria

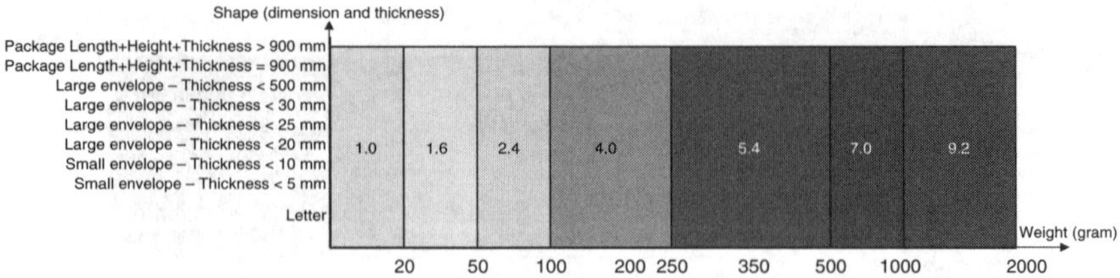

Figure 22A.8 France

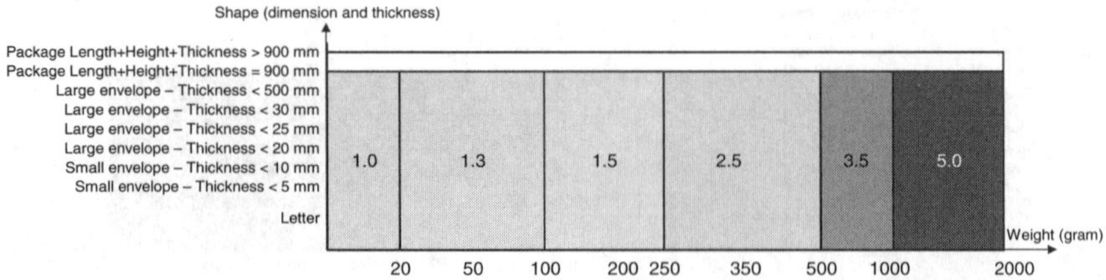

Figure 22A.9 Cyprus

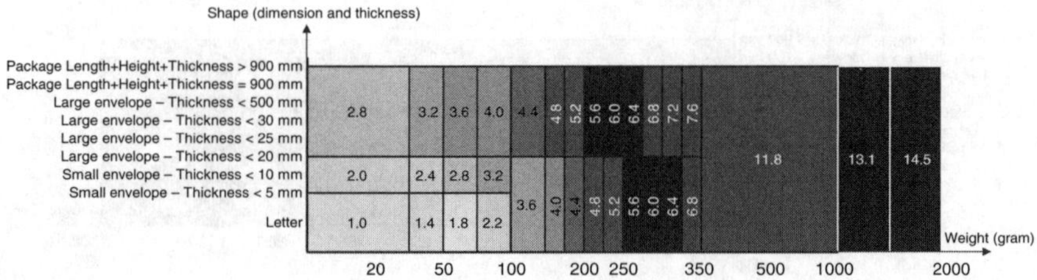

Figure 22A.10 United States

23. Assessing the cost of capital for USPs in Europe: a practical approach*

António Manuel Amaral, Paulo Louro, Carla Mota and João Cristovão

1 INTRODUCTION

The issue of cost of capital for postal incumbents and universal service providers (USPs) is the subject of an interesting debate between operators and regulators. Indeed, the viability of a USP, its operating expense (OPEX) and capital expense (CAPEX) requirements under the Universal Service Obligations, which some consider the Regulatory Asset Base (RAB) for the postal operator, requires the correct assessment of the return on capital employed by the USP, which the providers of capital should earn on their investment. Price control policy and alternative funding mechanisms must be carefully considered, taking into account the following dichotomy: return required versus return allowed by the regulator. In this chapter, we will benchmark the WACC (overall weighted average cost of capital) for the postal USPs in 12 EU member states (market peers for CTT Correios de Portugal) while also studying the cost of capital of these 12 USPs between 2003 and 2007. This will be carried out by examining the information available in the annual reports of each firm and also by using available historical market data. We shall make a number of assumptions regarding the various components of the cost of capital (in accordance with the capital asset pricing model: CAPM), with a straightforward application to all firms. This will allow us to obtain a clear idea of the sensitivity of each of the exogenous determinants of the cost of capital. Thus, the estimated values for WACC are merely indicative. We have selected a five year period, from 2003 to 2007 as it coincides with the most recent phase of solid economic growth in the global economy and stability in markets worldwide, especially financial markets. The sub-prime crisis in financial markets first appeared in 2007. However, it was in 2008 that the credit crunch, with its resulting turmoil, had a visible impact.

In Section 2 we shall present some economic and financial information on the 12 firms studied in this chapter and summarize the macroeconomic environment during the period between 2003 and 2007. In Section 3 we shall introduce and discuss the advantages and disadvantages of the CAPM and estimate each component of this model. In Section 4 we shall discuss the evolution of WACC in each country from the practical application of CAPM using the results in Section 3. In Section 5 we shall conclude with some final remarks. For a number of reasons, including data limitations and the public enterprise structure of most USPs, we conclude that the use of the CAPM/WACC approach to measuring the cost of capital of incumbents in the postal sector is not a reasonable approach.

2 ECONOMIC CONSIDERATIONS

This chapter will look at 12 postal groups across Europe: CTT (Portugal: PT), La Poste (France: FR), Correos (Spain: ES), Deutsche Post (Germany: DE), Royal Mail (UK), Austrian Post (Austria: AT), De Post–La Poste (Belgium: BE), TNT (Netherlands: NL), Poste Italiane (Italy: IT), Post Danmark (Denmark: DK), An Post (Ireland, IE) and Itella Corpotaton (Finland: FI). Although the mail business has been the core business of these companies over the years, their portfolios are becoming increasingly diverse (mail, express services, logistics, financial services) and they have evolved into multi-service economic groups.

Most of these companies are fully owned by the state: CTT, Poste Italiane, An Post, Itella Corpotaton, Correos, La Poste and Royal Mail. The remaining companies have a smaller government participation in their capital structure: in Denmark the government stake is approximately 75 per cent of the capital. In Belgium the government owns 50 percent +1 share, with the remaining capital held by the consortium of Post Danmark and CVC Capital Partners, in Austria 51 percent and in Germany the state controls 30.5 percent of shares via KfW Bankengruppe. The exception is TNT where the Dutch government recently sold its last stake in TNT capital (private investors now hold 5 percent of TNT capital and other institutional investors hold 95 percent). The public ownership issue is a very important component of cost of capital analysis, and a number of authors consider that the government cost of capital is somewhat different from other types of equity. Mehra and Prescott (1985) argued that the equity premium for public entities is, in theory, less than the average real rate of return demanded by other types of equity holders. Thus, the cost of capital to the private sector, which is equal to a weighted average of the bond rate and the rate of return to private equity, would be greater than the cost of capital to the government, which is equal to the bond rate. Hathaway (1997) claims that if the apparently lower cost of capital to government business enterprises were real, national welfare could be greatly increased by state ownership of all business enterprises if all other things were equal, that is, if government and investors were identical in all respects except for the cost of capital. On the other hand, private ownership would enhance efficiency. This is a sensitive topic, especially in the aftermath of the financial turmoil of 2008, and ideological considerations aside, it will be interesting to compare the cost of capital of a company and the level of capital held by the government.

For 2007, the economic picture of these companies can be summarized in Table 23.1. Enormous differences can be seen in the size of the companies. Although TNT presents the best economic performance of this group of companies, it did not show a clear relationship between its level of profitability and the level of government ownership. Although companies with worse performances are 100 percent state owned, we can also see that companies fully owned by the state have comparatively good results, such as is the case with CTT, Poste Italiane and La Poste. Note that the negative ROE of Royal Mail in 2007 is due to its negative equity.

The evolution between 2003 and 2007 (Table 23.2) shows that the relationship between ownership and profitability is unclear. TNT, Deutsche Post, Post Danmark and Austrian Post are still among the top performers, improving their financial ratios. However, companies such as CTT, Poste Italiane, Itella and An Post also had good results during this period. In Portugal, the CTT's revenue grew at rates well above the growth rate of the

Table 23.1 Economic activity indicators in 2007 (figures in €m)

	P	ES	DE	IT	FR	NL	BE	UK	DK	FI	IE	AT
Revenue	837	2.263	66.098	17.182	20.189	11.017	2.276	10.430	1.621	1.688	876	2.388
EBITDA*	100	191	5559	2344	1992	1541	195	436	194	163	48	293
%	*11.9*	*8.4*	*8.4*	*13.6*	*9.6*	*14.0*	*8.6*	*4.2*	*12.0*	*9.7*	*5.5*	*12.3*
Net income	73	104	1.885	844	951	986	65	150	96	79	43	123
Return on equity (ROE) (%)	29	7	17	27	28	51	8	–55	26	11	17	14
Return on assets (ROA) (%)	5	4	1	1	1	14	3	2	9	7	7	6
Capital held by state (%)	100	100	30.5	100	100	0	50 + 1	100	75	100	100	51
Labor costs on total costs (%)	56	71	29	38	65	36	68	69	62	50	71	50

Notes:
Estimate based on 2007 Annual Reports (for Royal Mail, the period ended in March 2008).
Exchange rates: €1 = 0.90; £1 = 7.45 DKK.
* EBITDA = Earnings before interest, taxes, depreciation and amortization.

Table 23.2 Evolution, 2003–2007

Annual growth (04–07)	P	ES	DE	IT	FR	NL	BE	UK	DK	FI	IE	AT
GDP (%)	1.4	3.6	1.9	1.4	2.2	2.8	2.6	2.7	2.4	3.9	5.7	3.0
Revenue (%)	5.0	4.8	12.5	19.5	3.7	−1.8	3.8	2.1	3.2	10.2	5.4	8.6
Revenue growth/ GDP growth*	4.0	1.3	7.3	17.4	1.7	−0.9	1.2	0.8	1.5	2.6	1.0	3.0
Net Income (%)	29.9	−2.8	9.5	74.8	47.3	34.6	43.6	109.6	24.5	13.8	73.8	64.1
ROE (p.p.)	−3.8	−1.1	−1.2	5.1	4.4	10.2	4.6	−13.9	2.9	0.6	9.0	2.9
ROA (p.p.)	0.8	−0.5	0.0	0.2	0.1	2.5	1.4	0.6	1.2	0.4	3.8	1.2

Notes: Estimate based on Annual Reports (2003–2007).
* Annual ratio – arithmetic mean.

Source: Eurostat, available at: http://epp.eurostat.ec.europa.eu/tgm/table.do?tab=table&init=1&plugin=1&language=en&pcode=tsieb020.

Portuguese economy. For CTT, the Courier–Express–Parcels (CEP) segment has been the main engine of growth with improvement of its market share and through acquisitions in Spain (Tourline Express). Despite the decline in importance of the core business, cost-efficiency measures have allowed the improvement of profitability ratios. It should be noted that in some countries, very significant growth in income is justified, either by the transition from losses to profit in a specific year (in 2003, De Post showed a consolidated loss of −€64 million versus a profit of €40 million in the financial year 2004; An Post in 2003 also presented a loss versus a net income of €11 million in 2004), or by the review of accounting procedures. As we have used the latest figures available, it is important to mention the most significant situations:

1. Poste Italiane – the turnover for 2004 was revised in the 2005 report to provide a better basis of comparison between these two years, in order to reflect implementation of IAS 32 and 39 and, in the case of consolidated statements, IFRS 4.
2. TNT – in the statement of income for 2005, the 2004 income has been adjusted for comparability purposes: 'In the 2005 consolidated financial statements, management has amended certain accounting and valuation methods applied in the Dutch GAAP [Generally Accepted Accounting Principles] financial statements to comply with IFRS [International Financial Reporting Standards]. The comparative figures for 2004 were adjusted to reflect these adjustments'.

The differences in economic performance can also be explained by the business portfolio and the overall cost structure (which also depends on the differences in the portfolio). Differences in portfolios are very important as regards cost of capital: the fact that these companies are multi-service platforms has wide-ranging implications, such as a more diverse asset base and capital structure with the subsequent relationships with multiple regulators with different perspectives of the cost of capital for the same company. Thus, the benchmarking of the cost of capital for these companies through a high-level analysis, based on the annual reports, should take these differences into consideration.

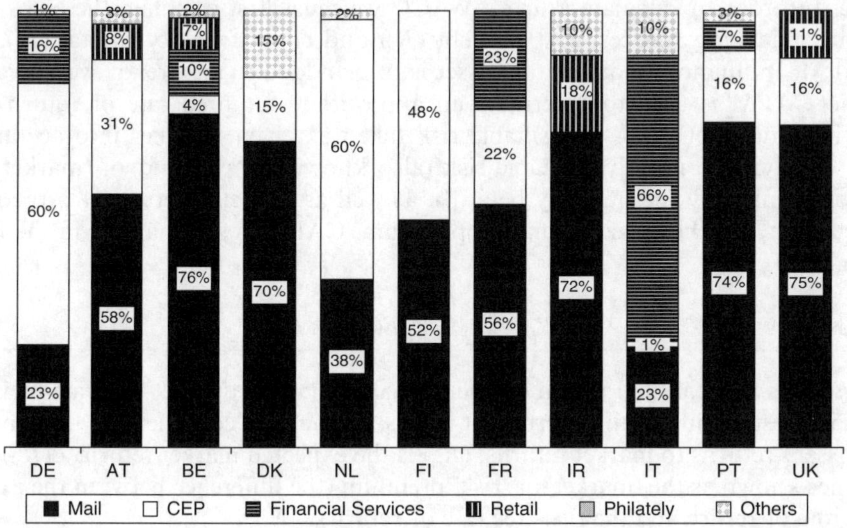

Note: Estimate based on 2007 Annual Reports (for Royal Mail, the period ended in March 2008).

Figure 23.1 Portfolio structure, 2007

Figure 23.1 shows the differences in the portfolio structure of each of the companies examined (except Spain, where the information is not available for 2007). At first glance, we can conclude that private companies or those with a lower government stake in the capital structure have portfolios oriented towards the CEP segment and are less dependent on mail. Moreover, it should also be noted that companies whose business is less dependent on the mail segment show a lower share of labor costs. This is the case for Deutsche Post and TNT, anchored mainly in the CEP business, and Poste Italiane with a significant component of financial services. These two features provide us with an insight into management objectives.

3 APPLICATION OF CAPM

The WACC is the main tool in finance to measure a firm's cost of capital. It is the appropriate discount rate to use for cash flows with risk that is similar to that of the overall firm, hence its importance in determining, in a regulated environment, the amount of revenue allowances needed to ensure that the appropriate CAPEX and OPEX expenditures are implemented.

The total capital for a firm is the value of its equity (for a firm without outstanding warrants and options, this is the same as the company's market capitalization) plus the cost of its debt (the cost of debt should be continually updated as the cost of debt changes as a result of interest rate changes). Different securities are expected to generate different returns. WACC is calculated taking into account the relative weights of each component of the capital structure.

Calculating WACC for a company with a complex capital structure is a laborious exercise. In order to calculate a firm's WACC we must first calculate the costs of the individual financing sources, cost of debt (R_d) and cost of equity capital (R_e), using the CAPM. In finance theory, if that asset is to be added to an already well-diversified portfolio CAPM is used to determine an appropriate required rate of return on an asset with that asset's non-diversifiable risk taken as given. It takes into account the asset's sensitivity to non-diversifiable risk (also known as 'systemic' or 'market' risk), often represented by the quantity beta (β), as well as expected return of a theoretical risk-free asset and the expected market premium. CAPM is summarized in the following equation:

$$E(R_i) = R_f + \beta_i[E(R_m) - R_f],$$

where $E(R_i)$ is the expected return on the capital asset; R_f is the risk-free rate of interest such as interest arising from government bonds; β_i (the beta coefficient) is the sensitivity of the asset's returns to market returns; (R_m) is the expected market return; $E(R_m) - R_f$ is sometimes known as the 'market' or 'risk' premium (the difference between the expected market rate of return and the risk-free rate of return).

Risk-free Asset R_f

The risk-free asset refers to a security that has no default risk, no maturity risk, no liquidity risk, and no risk of loss if inflation increases. This is an asset on which we know the expected return with certainty. As is noted by most academics, in practice, there is no such security, and hence there is no observable truly risk-free rate. Nevertheless, we know that Treasury bonds, securities issued by governments, are mostly risk free, and are used as a risk-free rate. Brigham and Gapenski (1991) clarify this: treasury bonds (T-bonds) which are longer-term government securities, are free of default and liquidity risks, but T-bonds are exposed to some risk due to changes in the general level of interest rates. In relation to the maturity of T-bonds, for our purposes, in a long-term analysis we must consider the long-term risk-free rates. In all peers' currencies, there is a 10-year government bond rate, which offers a realistic measure of the risk-free rate. Despite some academics choosing German government bills for investments in euros, we shall take the 10 year government bonds of each country to approximate the long-term risk-free rate. The first reason is that all the peers have overall excellent ratings (in 2009, Standard & Poor's maintained an AAA rating for most countries, except for Italy, Belgium, Spain, Ireland and Portugal. Although these five countries have a lower rating, we can assume that it is still sufficient to exclude a default scenario). Therefore, these national government bonds are generally accepted to determine the cost of capital for regulated firms. Figure 23.2 shows the evolution of the yields of government bonds in each operator's country, which we took as the risk-free assets for reference, in the period between 2003 and 2007.

We can observe a very similar performance between 2003 and 2007 for Treasury bonds in almost all countries except for the UK. Ten-year UK Gilts have higher yields than other peers in the period being studied. These bonds present a very similar yield curve within the euro area, with the same variances over time. Although Portuguese and Italian Treasury bonds performed very similarly among other euro area countries,

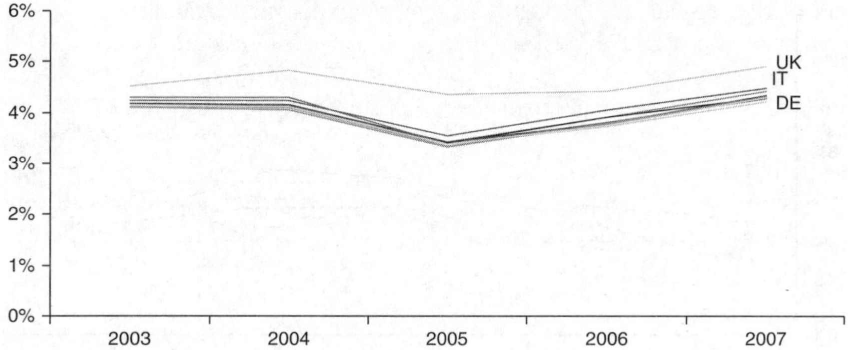

Source: Bank of England, Bank of Luxembourg and Bloomberg.

Figure 23.2 Yield curve for government bonds

they have continually resisted higher yields. On the other hand, Germany and Austria presented the lowest yields. This is not surprising, since Italy and Portugal have the poorest rating among these countries and Germany is widely regarded as a reference bond.

Market Premium $E(R_m) - R_f$

The market risk premium measures the extra return which would be demanded by investors for investing their money in a risky investment instead of investing in a risk-free asset. In order to estimate the risk premium, we used the historical premiums method which consists of the difference between the return on the market portfolio and average returns on risk-free asset over a long period of time. We took the expected returns on stocks to be the return given by the reference indexes of each country. These were the OMX Helsinki 25 for Finland, the MIB 30 for Italy, the BEL 20 for Belgium, the PSI 20 for Portugal, the DAX for Germany, the CAC 40 for France, the AEX for the Netherlands, the IBEX 35 for Spain, the Austrian ATX, the OMX Copenhagen 20 for Denmark, the FTSE 100 for the UK and the ISEQ Overall for Ireland. For the risk-free asset we took the 10-year Treasury bonds of each country as explained above. For this estimation the geometric average was used instead of the arithmetic average. This was because this average not only looks to the compound return but is also a better way of determining the return over the longest period possible for each index and it is a more accurate measure of historical performance.

Ireland showed a market premium significantly higher than other countries (around 5–10 percent higher), although this difference decreased in 2007. Austria presented a negative market premium of −0.73 percent in 2003, and then from 2004 to 2007 the market premium is in line with the other countries. The remainder have a similar market premium risk in the period under analysis even with Italy, Belgium and Germany having a slightly higher market premium. Portugal's market premium fell within the average between 2003 and 2007, and became the country with the third-highest premium in 2007 (Figure 23.3 and Table 23.3).

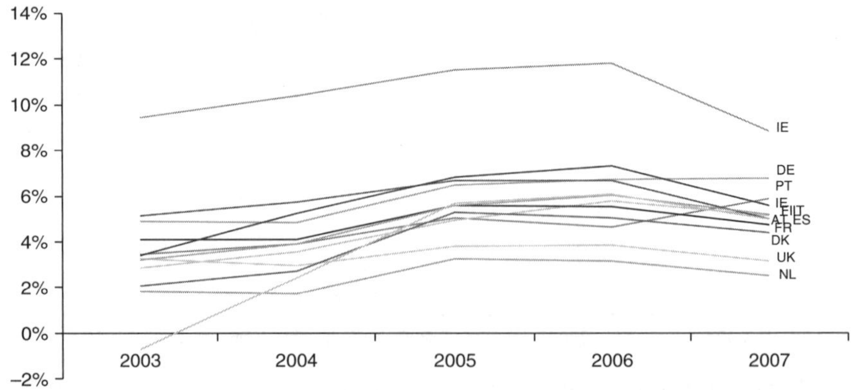

Sources: Bank of England, Bank of Luxembourg, Bloomberg and Yahoo Finance.

Figure 23.3 Market premium

Table 23.3 Market premium average

Market premium (03–07)	P	ES	DE	IT	FR	NL	BE	UK	DK	FI	IE	AT
Annual yield (average)	4.6	4.4	5.9	5.8	4.8	2.5	5.7	3.4	3.9	4.8	10.4	3.6

Sources: Bank of England, Bank of Luxembourg, Bloomberg and Yahoo Finance.

Debt and Its Expected Return: β_d and $E(R_d)$

A variety of debt instruments exist. Bank loans are debt. Bonds represent debt: these can be straight or convertible, index linked, or private placements (closely held and not widely traded). Even leases represent debt (for instance CTT long-term debt is mostly leases). Thus, when calculating the R_d, the type of debt needs to be identified.

The cost of debt (R_d) can be relatively easy to determine when the bonds of the company are widely traded. Thus, the current (market) yield on outstanding debt is the cost of debt. In practice this is not the case. Annual reports do not disclose much information, especially with regard to the types of interest paid over the year, and therefore the underlying cost of long-term debt can be difficult to determine only from a reading of such reports. In this chapter we shall focus only on long-term debt as investments are long life and we shall not consider the cost of short-term debt.

It can be assumed that debt is risk free (β_d is zero), and in practice, with these operators which are mostly held by the state and as we saw earlier with almost unblemished ratings, the risk of default is practically non-existent. Although we have assumed that β_d is zero, in general, but not always, an individual firm's cost of debt is greater than the market rate for government bonds, generally a spread indexed to its credit

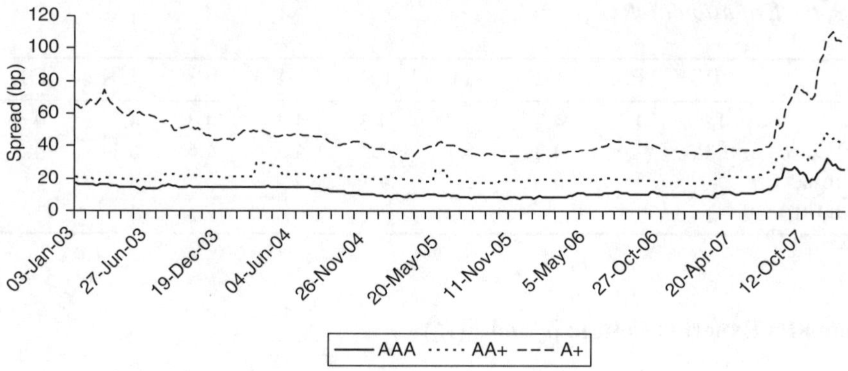

Figure 23.4 Spreads (for any maturity)

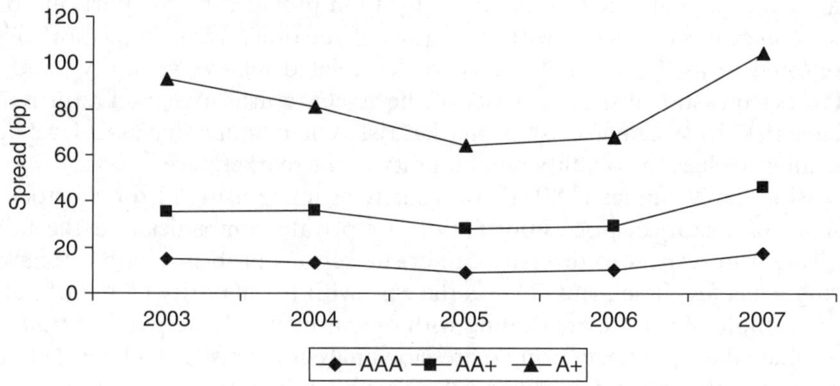

Figure 23.5 Spreads – year average (estimate)

rating. This spread includes a default risk premium, a liquidity premium (reflecting the extent to which a financial instrument is widely traded), and a maturity risk premium (associated with being locked into a particular interest rate for a long period of time). However, locking into a fixed interest rate over a long period of time can reduce the risk associated with possible increases in short-term rates. Thus, inflationary expectations affect the shape of the yield curve. For simplicity, we assumed that R_d for these firms will be established as the sum of the return of the risk-free asset plus a spread associated with the rating of its respective sovereign state. According to the latest information published by Standard & Poor's, most of these states had an AAA rating, with the exception of Spain, Belgium and Ireland which have an AA+ rating, and Portugal and Italy with A+. The evolution of the spreads (Figure 23.4) is very similar to the yield curve from the risk-free asset if we take the average for a whole year (Figure 23.5).

The evolution of R_d (Table 23.4), in this configuration, is rather obvious and is naturally similar to that of the R_f section. An important aspect to keep in mind is that the operators from the countries with the worst ratings saw a greater rise in their spread during this period.

Table 23.4 Evolution of R_d

R_d	P	ES	DE	IT	FR	NL	BE	UK	DK	FI
2003 (%)	4.7	4.3	4.2	4.8	4.3	4.3	4.4	4.7	4.5	4.3
2007 (%)	5.0	4.6	4.4	5.1	4.5	4.5	4.6	5.1	4.5	4.5
Mean annual growth (bp)	5	5	3	5	4	3	5	8	0	4

Equity and Its Expected Return: β_e and $E(R_e)$

The equity beta estimation is, in our opinion, the central issue in the analysis, especially for non-listed firms. Theoretically, the beta measures the part of the asset's statistical variance that cannot be mitigated by the diversification provided by the portfolio of many risky assets, since it is correlated with the return of the other assets in the portfolio. Beta is also referred to as 'financial elasticity' or 'correlated relative volatility', and can be referred to as a measure of the sensitivity of the asset's returns to market returns, its non-diversifiable risk, its systematic risk or market risk. On an individual asset level, measuring beta can give clues to volatility and liquidity in the marketplace.

In assessing the β_e (under CAPM), we usually estimate using historical stock prices. The absence of historical price information for private companies and the failure by many private firm owners to diversify can create serious problems with estimating and when using betas for these firms. This is the case with the majority of the postal operators in our sample. When we are dealing with operators which are publicly traded firms, we can estimate the equity beta using regression analysis against a stock market index. In the absence of such information, financial mainstream literature points to three ways in which betas can be estimated:

1. *Accounting betas* Proxy variables for the price of the equity are established, for instance, by regressing changes in a private firm's accounting earnings against changes in earnings for an equity market index. The slope of the regression is the accounting beta for the firm. Using operating earnings would yield an unlevered beta, whereas using net income would yield a levered or equity beta. There are two significant limitations with this approach. The first is that private firms usually measure earnings only once a year (some, such as CTT, publish their results twice a year, and some publish results on a quarterly basis) leading to regressions with few observations and limited statistical power. The second is that earnings are often smoothed out and subject to accounting judgments, leading to misleading accounting betas. We performed a pilot regression for CTT, but the results were not satisfactory. First, the limited time range offered only five observations. Second, the regression delivered an insignificant R^2, with a beta estimate lower than −3 with a *P*-value near 0.3.
2. *Fundamental betas* Betas of publicly traded firms are related to observable variables such as earnings growth, debt ratios and variance in earnings. Again, we face the same problem of insufficient information. Several authors have frequently presented

a low R^2, suggesting that the beta estimates which emerge from it are likely to have large standard errors.

3. *Bottom-up betas* Briefly, this method consists of considering the underlying unlevered betas of those firms which are quoted and then estimating bottom-up equity betas based upon these betas. Authors point out that low standard errors on these estimates (due to the averaging across large numbers of firms) and the forward-looking nature of the estimates (because the business mix used to weight betas can be changed) show that this can be a very useful tool.

In practice, (3) is a type of beta benchmarking, since, in our case, the beta for a postal firm can be estimated by looking at the average betas for publicly traded postal firms. Any differences in financial or even operating leverage can be adjusted for in the final estimate. In making the adjustment of unlevered betas for financial leverage, there are some extra difficulties with non-listed firms, since the debt to equity ratio that should be used is a market value ratio. While many analysts use the book value debt to equity ratio as a substitute for the market ratio for private firms, the literature suggests one of the following alternatives: first, take the assumption that the private firm market leverage will resemble the average for the industry:

$$\beta_{\text{private}} = \beta_{\text{unlevered}} [1 + (1 - \text{tax rate}) (\text{Industry Average Debt/Equity})].$$

The second is to use the firm target debt to equity ratio or its optimal debt ratio (if one can be estimated) to estimate the beta:

$$\beta_{\text{private}} = \beta_{\text{unlevered}} [1 + (1 - \text{tax rate}) (\text{Optimal Debt/Equity})].$$

The problem with this last alternative is obtaining information on the debt to equity ratios. First, the management would not be willing to specify such a target and, in the absence of this information, an optimal debt ratio is hard to estimate. The problem with this last method in the postal business is that the few firms which are listed are not really comparable in their asset structure. As we have seen before, the portfolio structure is significantly different between this set of operators. For instance, Deutsche Post and TNT in 2007 had their portfolios anchored mainly in the CEP segment, whereas the majority of the operators were largely dependent on the mail segment. Moreover, this benchmark can produce significant bias since most postal operators act in different geographical markets, with different prospects for growth, have different combinations of regulated and unregulated activities, have different activities within regulated and unregulated segments and for activities covered by rules which are not always similar in terms of incentives and guarantees of return on capital. It is argued, in some regulatory literature, that one can mitigate the problem related to differences in the portfolio structure of each firm computing the risk by segmentation (that is, risk coefficient associated with each type of asset within the asset structure of a firm). Correia Da Silva et al. (2008) stated that the risk may be expressed within a CAPM framework as an alpha risk in addition to the standard beta risk (used to estimate the expected or allowed return for the business). Despite this being one of the feasible solutions for some sectors (capital-intensive sectors such as rail, water and so on), in the postal sector, this solution is much more difficult

Table 23.5 Market equity beta

	Industry	Sector
Financial services		
Consumer financial services	1.00	1.13
Financial services – diversified	1.04	1.13
Financials – speciality	1.32	1.13
TELCOs		
Integrated telecommunication services	0.72	0.61
Wireless telecommunication services	0.47	0.61
Industrial		
Air freight & courier services	0.97	1.03
Average	0.96	1.01

Source: Reuters, May 2009.

Table 23.6 Evolution of R_e

R_e	P	ES	DE	IT	FR	NL	BE	UK	DK	FI	IE	AT
2003 (%)	7.6	7.0	9.0	9.3	8.2	6.0	7.6	7.8	6.4	7.3	13.6	3.4
2007 (%)	10.3	9.4	11.0	9.5	9.0	6.8	9.9	8.1	8.7	9.5	13.2	9.3
Mean annual growth (bp)	53	49	40	3	16	17	46	6	46	43	−8	117

to implement since the asset segmentation is not straightforward (for instance, the CTT Post Office Network and its staff work on mail business, financial services, retail, mobile communications, philately and so on).

Estimating risk parameters for non-listed firms is a major weakness in the CAPM. In these cases, with an absence of specific information on the company, it is natural to give more weight to the expectation that the risk of the company approaches the market risk, that is, beta is equal to 1. Therefore, in this chapter, we choose to adopt the market beta ($\beta_e = 1$) for all firms, even for those which are actually listed. Market data show that a $\beta = 1$ can be reasonable (Table 23.5).

Thus, the estimation for R_e and its evolution between 2003 and 2007 is similar to that of the market premium (Table 23.6).

The R_e estimate for An Post had the highest rate during this period, which reflects the dynamics of its stock market and the rate of return of its index, increasing opportunity costs for the shareholder. On the other hand, Austria presented the lowest return, reflecting the poor return of its index in 2003, but in 2007 the return demanded of it was in line with peers. CTT shareholders demanded an R_e that in 2007 was the third highest in this sample.

4 WACC ESTIMATION

The WACC is an important category as it reflects the overall costs of combined debt and equity capital used to finance business operations or acquisitions. It is the basis of determining the discount rate for the discounted cash flow business valuation method. In a regulated context, an appropriate discount rate is very important because it is the key for a fair determination of revenue allowances that enable investors to recover their investment in the CAPEX (arguably, it is less important in the postal sector because of its low capital intensity) and OPEX and, therefore, the regulator assures the requested levels of quality of service.

Leverage

Firms influence their cost of capital through a number of channels. First, the choice of capital structure affects the cost of capital. From the standpoint of investors, providing equity capital is most risky, since owners are the residual claimants on a company's net cash flows. Shareholders receive their returns through two channels: dividends and increases in the value of the firm's assets (reflected in the appreciation of the stock price). Debt holders obtain interest payments before dividends can be paid. Both require higher returns to bear the risk, though the weighted average (incremental) cost of capital can be reduced up to point as leverage is increased from zero, since the cost of debt is less than the cost of equity.

In some jurisdictions, including the firms examined in this chapter, the capital structure is regulated. This can mean that the regulator controls the company's financing method or the regulator provides incentives for the company to develop an optimal capital structure.

Table 23.7 shows the evolution of the leverage level of these firms. The values were computed using publicly available data. For debt figures, only long-term debt was considered. We observed that for the level of financial leverage, the evolution from 2003 to 2007 has been substantially different for the different operators. Operators such as Correos, Poste Italiane, La Poste and An Post presented a relatively stable structure of capital in this period, with annual variations in the financial leverage ratio of less than 1 percent Other operators, such as CTT, Austrian Post and Post Danmark have showed a decrease in their financial leverage. For CTT, the decrease is explained by the stabilization of its long-term debt and an increase in equity by incorporation of results, noting that in 2004, significant extra results were incorporated due to the review of the calculation relating to responsibilities with its health system. Moreover, there are operators such as Royal Mail and De Post/La Poste, which saw a significant increase in their level of financial leverage. In the case of Royal Mail, this increase arises mainly from the fact that its equity became negative in 2004 due to the change in accounting procedures in 2005, therefore restating 2004 values for the transition to IFRSs.

Pre- and Post-tax WACC

First, we must distinguish between the pre- and post-tax versions of WACC. A pre-tax approach includes an allowance for tax as part of the WACC. Under a post-tax approach, tax is included in expenditure cash flow rather than the WACC. Financial literature lists the advantages and disadvantages of the post- and pre-tax versions. The most important are stated in Table 23.8.

Table 23.9 shows that An Post had the highest WACC (both pre- and post-tax) in 2003

Table 23.7 Leverage

LTDebt / (LTDebt + Equity)	P	ES	DE	IT	FR	NL	BE	UK	DK	FI	IE	AT
2003 (%)	22.7	1.3	49.3	73.9	66.8	35.9	6.3	20.3	46.1	10.2	2.5	13.2
2007 (%)	4.2	0.7	44.8	72.2	67.6	41.2	48.5	107.5	33.0	4.5	1.5	8.1
Mean annual growth (p.p)	−4.6	−0.1	−1.1	−0.4	0.2	1.3	10.5	21.8	−3.3	−1.4	−0.2	−1.3

Note: Estimate based on Annual Reports (2003–2007).

Table 23.8 Pre- and post-tax WACC: advantages and disadvantages

WACC	Advantages	Disadvantages	Formula
Pre-tax	Consistent with previous regulatory decisions Light-handed incentive regulation More appropriate for government-owned entities as the taxes and dividends are paid to the same entity	Conversion to a pre-tax WACC varies with the transformation method and tax assumptions Risk of not providing sufficiently for taxes	WACC = R_e*(1 – g) /(1 – t) + R_d*g*(1 – t), where g = LTDebt/(LTDebt + Equity) and t is the corporate tax rate
Post-tax	Eliminates the complexities associated with the transformation from post- to a pre-tax Cash flow modeling of tax costs more transparent	Risk of under- or overestimating tax liabilities	WACC = R_e*(1 – g) + R_d*g*(1 – t), where g = LTDebt/(LTDebt + Equity) and t is the corporate tax rate

and 2007, despite a slight decrease from 2005 onwards. This WACC level came about due to the high market premium in this period, reflecting the significant dynamics of the Irish economy, increasing the opportunity cost of investing in postal activities. The firm with the lowest cost of capital in 2003 was Austrian Post (via low market premium), and in 2007 it was Royal Mail given the high gearing that automatically reduced the opportunity cost by decreasing the R_e component in the WACC. On the other hand, those firms that saw a rising cost of capital during this period (CTT, Correos, Deutsche Post, Post Danmark, Austria Post and Itella) was the result of the combination of two factors: increasing market premiums and decreasing leverage. The latter was particularly important in the cases of CTT, Itella and Post Danmark. Lastly, Poste Italiane, with its heavy dependence on financial services and high leverage, led to its WACC remaining stable despite increases in the market premium and its spread (R_d).

Because there are not many discrepancies in terms of tax rate in the economies studied, with the exception of Ireland, the results for the pre- and post-tax versions are equivalent, for our purposes, apart from a general reduction in the WACC (except for An Post, since

Table 23.9 Pre- and post-tax WACC

		P	ES	DE	IT	FR	NL	BE	UK	DK	FI	IE	AT	Average
Post-tax	2003 (%)	6.6	6.9	5.8	4.6	4.6	4.8	7.3	6.9	4.9	6.9	13.3	3.3	6.3
WACC	2007 (%)	10.0	9.4	7.3	4.0	4.9	5.4	6.6	3.2	6.0	9.2	13.0	8.8	7.5
	growth (bp)	67	49	29	6	7	11	−14	−73	40	46	−6	109	23
Pre-tax	2003 (%)	9.9	10.7	9.6	7.5	7.0	7.4	11.1	9.8	6.9	9.7	15.2	5.0	9.2
WACC	2007 (%)	13.3	13.0	11.8	7.9	7.4	7.2	10.0	4.6	9.5	12.4	14.9	11.7	10.4
	growth (bp)	69	64	44	7	8	−4	−22	−104	51	55	−7	134	25

Table 23.10 EBITDA margin/pre-tax WACC, 2007

2007	P	ES	DE	IT	FR	NL	BE	UK	DK	FI	IE	AT	Average
EBITDA / pre-tax WACC	0.90	0.61	0.71	1.74	1.29	1.95	0.86	0.91	1.26	0.78	0.37	1.05	1.03

Irish income tax is particularly low). However, it is not illogical to compare the WACC of these firms using the pre- or the post-tax version because of the investors' perspective, even though there are not many changes in the hierarchy of the firms displaying greater pre- or post-tax WACC.

5 FINAL REMARKS

This chapter describes the evolution of the WACC (in both pre- and post-tax versions) in the period from 2003 to 2007. This period coincided with the most recent period of solid economic growth in the global economy and stability in markets worldwide, especially financial markets. In 2003, the average pre-tax WACC was 9.2 percent and post-tax was 6.3 percent. In 2007, the figures increased to 10.4 percent and 7.5 percent respectively. It is interesting to compare the pre-tax WACC with the EBITDA margin in 2007 (Table 23.10): on average, the EBITDA is only 1.03 times greater than the pre-tax WACC. It seems to us that these WACCs are quite reasonable, considering the WACC of economic sectors which are subject to more frequent examination.

We observed a tendency of the WACC to increase during this period, largely due to the dynamism of the stock exchanges post-September 11, leading to increased opportunity costs of allocating capital to the postal business (increasing equity premiums) at a time when investing in the market brought greater return. The cost of debt was quite stable in this period with relatively low rates. For highly levered firms, such as Poste Italiane, the WACC was more stable and remained at a lower level. An Post had the highest cost of capital in this period and La Poste and Poste Italiane presented the lowest. It is interesting to note that Royal Mail, which had one of the highest WACCs in 2003, fell to the lowest in 2007 due to the rapid evolution of its leverage.

Although CAPM can provide important clues to the evolution of the cost of capital when we are dealing with private firms, we need to pay special attention to its limitations in the postal sector. These include problems of determining data on comparable firms for estimation of the company's beta, and even more fundamentally the fact that most postal operators are not private companies and have no clearly defined residual claimant. As noted in the discussion above, and also apparent in the results reported here, all of this suggests extreme caution in the use of the CAPM/WACC approach in the postal sector. The application of the CAPM, which has been used extensively in utility regulation, especially in the US, and which has an extensive literature associated with its use in the investor-owned utility sector, encounters severe difficulties in the case of the postal sector. Therefore, in view of the problems of applying standard CAPM/WACC theory to the postal sector, it is very important to look for alternative models to assess the cost of capital in the postal sector.

NOTE

* The authors would like to thank Alberto Pimenta, João Andrade e Silva, Bruno Caixeirinho and Bruno Lemos. The views expressed in this chapter are exclusively those of the authors and do not reflect the views of CTT Correios de Portugal.

BIBLIOGRAPHY

Binder, John J. and Seth W. Norton (1999), 'Regulation, profit variability and beta', *Journal of Regulatory Economics*, **15**, 249–65.

Brealey, R.A. and S.C. Myers (2003), *Principles of Corporate Finance*, 7th edn., Boston, MA: McGraw-Hill.

Brigham, Eugene F. and Louis C. Gapenski (1991), *Financial Management: Theory and Practice*, 6th edn, Chicago, IL: Dryden Press.

Copeland, T.E., T. Koller and J. Murrin (2000), *Valuation, Measuring and Managing the Value of Companies*, 3rd edn, New York: John Wiley & Sons.

Correia da Silva, L., L. Mautino, P. Dudley and E. Payling (2008), 'An incentive regime for quality of service of universal service providers in the postal sector', in M.A. Crew and P.R. Kleindorfer (eds), *Competition and Regulation in the Postal and Delivery Secto*r, Cheltenham, UK and Northampton, MA, USA: Edward Elgar, pp. 232–46.

Damodaran, Aswath (2003), *Corporate Finance: Theory and Practice*, 2nd edn, New York: John Wiley & Sons.

Damodaran, Aswath (2006), *Damodaran on Valuation: Security Analysis for Investment and Corporate Finance*, 2nd edn, New York: John Wiley & Sons.

Hathaway, N. (1997), 'Privatisation and the cost of capital', *Agenda*, Autumn, 1–10.

Jenkinson, Tim (2006), 'Regulation and the cost of capital', in Michael Crew and David Parker (eds), *International Handbook on Economic Regulation*, Cheltenham, UK and Northampton, MA, USA: Edward Elgar, pp. 146–63.

Mehra, R. and E.C. Prescott (1985), 'The equity premium: a puzzle', *Journal of Monetary Economics*, **15** (2), 145–61.

Modigliani, F. and M. Miller (1958), 'The cost of capital, corporation finance and the theory of investment', *American Economic Review*, **48**, 261–97.

Quiggin, J. (1997), 'The equity premium and the government cost of capital: a response to Neville Hathaway', *Agenda*, **4** (4), 475–85.

24. Historical development of a Universal Service Obligation in the United States

James I. Campbell Jr.

1 INTRODUCTION

In postal parlance, a 'Universal Service Obligation' or 'USO' is an obligation to provide a specific level of postal service throughout a national territory. Over the last two decades, as governments have given their post offices more commercial freedom and abolished the postal monopoly and other legal privileges, they have also found it necessary to define a USO. The USO is, in effect, a social contract between government and its citizens, defining what level of service government ensures will be maintained. In most postal reform countries, government reserves the right to contract out these obligatory services to any delivery service it chooses. As a practical matter, however, it is invariably the national postal operator – now corporatized and perhaps privatized – that is responsible for almost all of the USO. The USO thus serves as well as a contract between government and the national postal operator. Like any contract, if well drafted, the USO protects both sides of the bargain. Government's promises to the citizenry are upheld, and the national postal operator has a clear understanding of what is required and appropriately compensated for services rendered.

In the United States, there is long tradition of efficient and affordable postal service throughout the nation. The United States Postal Service (USPS) is obliged to maintain this service in the sense that if it were so foolish as to suspend any significant portion of the service Congress would force restoration very quickly. These self-evident facts of postal existence have led many observers to speak confidently of the 'USO'. In 2003, the report of the President's Commission on the United States Postal Service used the term 'universal service' or its equivalent more than 80 times. In reports on the bills that would become the Postal Accountability and Enhancement Act of 2006, congressional committees referred to 'universal service' more than 40 times.

What is the USO and where did it come from? In fact, despite near universal concern about the fate and future of the 'USO', the scope and content of this seemingly legal concept is far from clear. The postal laws of the United States – unlike those of almost all other industrialized countries – include no statutory or regulatory definition of 'universal service'.

This chapter summarizes the historical development of the laws which people have in mind (apparently) when they speak of a USO. The chapter seeks to clarify precisely which services USPS, and its predecessor the Post Office Department, have been obliged to provide and which services could be adjusted in response to shifts in public demand or financial resources. Section 2 describes the early development of the national post office as a system of post roads and post offices. Sections 3 and 4 recount the origins of postal delivery services, first in cities and then in rural areas. Section 5 summarizes the evolution of different types of postal services. Section 6 explains the development of the Postal Policy Act of 1958, the first official statement of national postal policy and the origin of many phrases considered by some to announce a national USO. Sections 7 and 8 describe the last two major postal reform acts, the Postal Reorganization Act of 1970 and the Postal Accountability and Enhancement Act of 2006, and their effects on the modern concept of a USO. Section 9 offers conclusions. Overall, the chapter argues that the legal obligations of USPS are, for the most part, the ill-defined remnants of historical happenstance. To ensure an acceptable and appropriate level of universal postal service for the future, at reasonable cost, it may be time for lawmakers and the general public to express more clearly what they really need.[1]

2 POST ROADS AND POST OFFICES

The concept of a postal service that collects from and delivers 'to everyone everywhere everyday' (a USPS slogan) is a relatively new idea in American postal law. When the United States was established in the late eighteenth century, the idea of a postal service was far different. A 'postal service' was a service for transporting a government 'mail', or pouch, containing letters between cities. The mail was transmitted by means of a series of 'posts', or relay stations, located along 'post roads'. The mail was conveyed by walking messengers (a 'foot post') or mounted riders (a 'horse post') or, as the eighteenth century progressed, by a 'stage coach'. There was no collection or delivery. Letters were posted or collected at a 'post office', commonly a tavern or general store.

Since a postal service was the only means of regular long-distance communications, it was of crucial importance to government. The Post Office was originally established by the Continental Congress on July 26, 1775, three months after the battles of Lexington and Concord and almost a year before the Declaration of Independence. In 1789, the first Congress elected under the Constitution continued the Continental Post Office while it debated how the new Post Office should be organized.

The first act of Congress specifying the format and duties of the Post Office was adopted in 1792. Although derived from English precedents, early American postal laws soon assumed a more democratic flavor. Most importantly, Congress admitted newspapers to the post for the first time. From the earliest days of the Republic, political leaders stressed the need to spread news about current events throughout the new nation to generate a sense of community. At this time, a newspaper was a single sheet of paper printed on both sides by hand press. The maximum postage rate for a newspaper was 1½ cents (¢) per sheet (rates varied by distance). By comparison, letters were discouraged by exceedingly high postage rates, varying from about 6¢–25¢ per sheet of paper. In the American democratic experiment, the Post Office was the first national broadcast network.

Congress decided that it, not the President or Postmaster General, would decide on the location of new post roads and, hence, the scope of postal service. The total length of post roads in use increased rapidly from about 1,875 miles in 1790 to 343,888 in 1880. In 1792, the list of post roads took up two pages in the *Statutes at Large*. In 1874, the list of post roads required a separate volume of 343 pages. Congress continued to designate individual post roads by statute until almost the end of the nineteenth century. After the early days, however, the Postmaster General decided which postal roads would actually be placed in service. In 1884, Congress finally declared 'all public roads and highways while kept up and maintained as such are hereby declared to be post routes'.

3 CITY DELIVERY SERVICES

At first, almost all intercity letters were collected at the post office by the addressee, who paid the postage. Although it was possible to prepay postage, it was not the custom. Some letters were delivered to recipients in the environs of a post office by messengers informally appointed by the local postmaster. Local 'letter carriers' were not salaried employees of the Post Office but paid 2¢ per letter by the addressee. A person could also drop a letter at the post office for later collection by someone residing in the same city. For each 'drop letter', the postmaster received 1¢. Custody of drop letters and delivery by letter carriers were not 'postal' services, and letters so handled were not 'in the mail'.

Local collection and delivery services were pioneered not by the Post Office, but by private companies called 'penny posts' operating in New York City and other major cities beginning in the 1840s. The Post Office's first foray into local delivery was taken in the wake of the postage reduction act of 1851. That act halved the drop letter rate to 1¢ and gave the Postmaster General authority to establish 'convenient places of deposit' and to designate 'post routes' within cities. By 1859, the Post Office had established delivery systems in 14 cities. In that year the Post Office delivered over 11 million letters, newspapers and pamphlets, but almost all were intercity items.

Not until 1863 did Congress initiate true local postal service by authorizing 'free city delivery' in major cities. 'Free' referred to delivery without a separate charge added to the prepaid charge for 'postal' services, then 3¢ per half ounce. The geographic scope of the city delivery system was left to the discretion of the Postmaster General. It could be established wherever the city carrier system was 'perfected'. The 1863 act also required prepayment of local letters – 'letters not transmitted through the mails' – at a standard rate of 2¢ per half ounce. Local delivery and intercity transportation of the mail were not viewed as a unified service. In effect, the Post Office operated two complementary businesses: the postal service and local delivery services.

City delivery was extended in stages over the next two decades. In 1865, Congress made free city delivery mandatory in every city with more than 50,000 residents. In 1879, Congress authorized, but did not require, the Postmaster General to extend the city delivery system to cities with 20,000 or more residents. In 1887, the Post Office was authorized to extend service to cities and towns with not less than 10,000 residents and from post offices with gross revenues of not less than $10,000. With such authority, the Postmaster General expanded the scope of the city delivery as demand increased and funds became available. City delivery grew linearly up to the Second World War. In 1887, there were 189 city delivery offices; in 1900, 1,440 offices; in 1920, 2,086, and in 1945, 3,884 offices.

4 RURAL AND VILLAGE DELIVERY NETWORKS

In 1890, about 19 million of the nation's 76 million inhabitants enjoyed city delivery service. Members of Congress from rural districts argued that it was inequitable to provide daily delivery to city households while requiring country residents to travel, often many miles, to retrieve their mail. The Post Office, however, resisted calls for a rural delivery service on the grounds that costs would greatly exceed revenues. Finally, in 1896, Postmaster General William Wilson agreed to experiment with 'rural free delivery' or RFD service after Congress provided enough money for a thorough test.

Rural delivery proved a success. More delivery points generated more mail. In 1902, Postmaster General Henry Payne declared that RFD should be adopted as a permanent service. He concluded, however, that RFD could feasibly serve only about one-third of the national territory (excluding Alaska) and that it was already serving one-third of that area.

Congress left the geographic scope of RFD service to the discretion of the Postmaster General. The Post Office, in turn, depended upon citizens to initiate RFD by filing a petition when three-quarters of residents were willing to receive mail by delivery and mailboxes were ready. By 1906, the number of petitions had peaked, and RFD was substantially in place. Daily service was provided on almost all routes, but the Post Office reserved the right to reduce service to three days per week if patronage lagged. As RFD expanded, the Post Office closed small 'fourth class' post offices, usually agencies in stores.

Establishment of the RFD system was heavily influenced by politics. Republicans controlled the presidency and both houses of Congress until the election of 1910. Republican areas in the North and Midwest were well supplied with rural postal routes while the Democratic South was often unable to get rural routes in operation even after they had been approved by the Post Office. Election of Democrat Woodrow Wilson as President in 1912 failed to alleviate the situation. Wilson's Postmaster General, Albert Burleson, was determined to make the Post Office more self-sufficient, and his determination set the stage for the first major confrontation over what might be called the 'USO'.

To make rural routes more efficient, Burleson decided to make greater use of automobiles. This innovation was strongly opposed by farmers and rural postmen. Consolidating and motorizing routes meant that rural carriers were displaced. Mailboxes had to be moved to different, sometimes more distant, roads. Farmers resisted motorized routes that started from a distant post office because the farmer's postal address was no longer associated with his local village. Congress was deluged with complaints.

In 1916, Congress stepped in to control the rural free delivery program and slow introduction of motorized vehicles. The House added a provision to the postal appropriations bill for 1917 that prohibited use of motor vehicles to serve rural routes unless approved by a majority of households served. The Senate added an amendment by Democratic Senator Thomas Hardwick of Georgia that required that horse-drawn routes must be between 24 and 36 miles in length and motorized routes between 50 and 75 miles. The Postmaster General was directed to reorganize the RFD system accordingly. The irrational result was that it was impossible to establish a route between 36 and 50 miles in length, a limitation that would handicap postal operations until 1925.

The Hardwick amendment included the seminal declaration, 'That rural mail delivery shall be extended so as to serve, as nearly as practicable, the entire rural population of the United States'. This the first and only time Congress specified the geographic coverage of RFD. It is the closest that Congress came to declaring a USO until 1970. A review of congressional debates suggests that Senator Hardwick's intent was to require the Postmaster General to extend the RFD program to as much of the rural population as congressional appropriations and the route length and other restrictions in the bill would allow. Hardwick stressed that this provision was a 'a mere statement of policy; it is nothing else except that', but he also noted that committee members believed that 'one of the most important things that this Government could do was to extend the Rural Delivery Service as soon as possible throughout the rural sections of this Republic, everywhere to all the people'.[2]

In its annual report for 1916, a year after the Hardwick amendment, the Post Office summed up its efforts to provide the level of service required. Postal officials estimated that mail was delivered to about 61 percent of the *rural* population, 26 percent of the national population. Other rural residents were either served only by fourth class post offices or not served at all.

About this time, postal delivery came to villages as well. 'Village delivery' referred to delivery of mail in towns too small to qualify for city delivery, that is, towns having less than 10,000 residents. Not until 1912 did Congress authorize the Post Office to experiment with postal deliveries in villages; village delivery was made permanent in 1916. Again, Congress left the scope and parameters of service up to the discretion of the Postmaster General. There was never any thought of delivering the mail to every household in a village, and to this day village residents living near a post office must collect their mail from the post office.

5 POSTAL RATES AND SERVICES

The range of rates for specific types of postal services also grew by accretion. Rates were controlled by Congress more directly than the geographic scope of service.

At first, the Post Office had only two rate classifications: a basic rate for letters and a steeply discount rate for newspapers. Magazines and pamphlets were admitted to the mails in 1794, but only if they could be transported conveniently.

In postal acts enacted in 1845 and 1851, postage rates for letters were reduced drastically. Weight-based rates (replacing rates per sheet) and less expensive paper led to introduction of envelopes (early letters were folded and sealed with wax). Prepayment of letters was encouraged by discount and then, after 1855, required. 'Cheap postage', as the movement was called, shifted the center of gravity of the postal service and precipitated a revolution in personal communications. Suddenly, ordinary Americans could correspond with one other across the country practically and inexpensively. As historian David Henkin has put it, 'The dates 1845 and 1851 thus stand at the center of a revolutionary era in nineteenth-century U.S. history, when a critical mass of Americans began reorganizing their perceptions of time, space, and community around the existence of the post' (2006, p. 3).

The preferential rates for newspapers adopted by the founding fathers gave rise to a perpetual political debate over what other types of publications deserved similar preferential treatment and which did not. A discounted rate for advertising mail originated in the inability of Postmasters General and Attorneys General to decide whether a 'price current', a list of current market prices, qualified for 'newspaper' postage or not. In 1845 Congress added a less-than-newspaper discount for 'all printed or lithographed circulars and handbills or advertisements, printed or lithographed on quarto post or single cap paper'. This was the beginning of what became third class mail, called 'Standard mail' after 1996.

The 1845 act also ended the condition that magazines and pamphlets could be transmitted by post only when there was space available and instead added a provision giving letter mail priority over other types of mail. The 1845 act further provided free postal transportation for newspapers transmitted less than thirty miles, the beginning of the 'in-county newspaper' discount. In 1852, rates for newspapers and magazines were consolidated into a single rate for periodic printed matter, the forerunner of 'Second Class' mail, called 'Periodicals' after 1996.

Postal rates were not collected into 'classes' until 1863, in the same act that introduced free city delivery. In this act, the first class included letters, and the second class periodic publications. The third class included not only non-periodic printed matter but also other mailable matter including seeds and bulbs. Third class thus replaced the letter rate category as the catch-all category. In 1879, Congress replaced the 1863 scheme with four classes of mail. First class mail was defined as 'written matter'; second class, 'periodical publications'; third class, 'miscellaneous printed matter'; and fourth class, 'merchandise'. The 1879 mail classification system lasted until 1996.

The first nationwide geographically uniform rate for letters was adopted in 1885. In that year, Congress reduced the rate for intercity letters to 2¢ per ounce and set the 'drop letter' rate at 2¢ per ounce for cities and towns where free city delivery was available. In this manner, the 2¢ letter rate became applicable to all destinations, local or national, within the free city delivery system. The 2¢ rate for letters remained in effect for almost five decades (except for a temporary increase to 3¢ during the First World War). Nonetheless, a uniform rate for letters was not seen as an inviolable principle. In 1932, in response to the budget deficits of the Great Depression, Congress added a one-cent surcharge to the first class letter rate, resulting in a 3¢ stamp. The next year, when utilities and department stores turned to private delivery services, Congress returned to the 2¢ stamp for local letters while retaining the 3¢ national letter rate. The local/national rate structure remained until June 1947, when Congress applied the 3¢ rate to all letters.

Although there were several steps to the Post Office's entry in the parcel business, the key date was 1912. By the mid-1800s, the Post Office had become a conduit for transmission of seeds, bulbs, books, and other things weighing up to three or four pounds. In 1912, Congress expanded fourth class to include parcels exceeding four pounds. Expansion of parcel post was due to several factors. Package services of private express companies, now controlled by the railroads, were widely perceived as inadequate and abusive. Rural residents, their appetites for city goods whetted by rural free delivery, wanted to be able to order goods via the Post Office. The 1912 act set an initial weight limit for parcel post of 11 pounds, but authorized the Postmaster General, with the approval of the Interstate Commerce Commission, to raise the weight limit 'in order to promote the service to the public or to insure the receipt of revenue from such service adequate to pay the cost thereof'. By 1918 the weight limit had been increased to 70 pounds for local parcels and 50 pounds nationwide.

Discounts for the mail of non-profit institutions originated in the First World War. In a bill raising taxes to pay for war-related activities, Congress introduced higher rates for the advertising content of second class publications to narrow the difference between rates for advertising in the second and third classes. At the same time, Congress established preferential rates for publications issued by educational institutions, labor unions, and professional, literary, historical and scientific societies by exempting such publications from the new rates for advertising content.

By the mid-twentieth century, American postal law was an uncodified jumble of statutory provisions mandating or authorizing a variety of services with rate preferences to answer different needs at different times. The ultimate manager of the postal system was Congress. Parties affected by the postal laws, especially those dependent on preferential rates, were well versed in how to make their cases to politicians and the general public.

6 POSTAL POLICY ACT OF 1958

After the end of the Second World War, Congress proved unable to continue management of the Post Office Department. The essential problem was that Congress repeatedly raised wages for postal employees but was unable to agree on rate increases to pay for increased wages.

By 1950, wage increases enacted by Congress in 1945, 1948 and 1949 had increased annual operating costs by approximately $800 million, about one-third of the Post Office's total budget. The deficit was about $590 million. According to the accounts of the Post Office, all categories of mail were losing money except for first class letters.

President Harry Truman's Postmaster General, Jesse Donaldson, who took office in December 1947, believed that there should be a 'proper business relationship between income and expenditures'. Donaldson annually urged Congress to raise rates, especially on classes of mail that were not covering costs, while he tried to trim costs. On April 17, 1950, Donaldson ignited a political firestorm by ending the second daily delivery of mail to about half of the nation's households. Congress failed to pass legislation overturning the Postmaster General's order by only a single vote in the Senate.

While all sides agreed that the Post Office needed more revenue, there were sharp disagreements about how rate increases should be distributed among the mail classes. The Post Office allocated costs according to a 'cost ascertainment' system initiated by Congress in 1925. This was a fully allocated costing system in which joint costs were attributed to specific products using statistical formulae. The administration's proposal to raise rates for periodicals and advertisements while leaving untouched the 3¢ stamp for first class letters was heavily influenced by the manner in which costs were allocated by the cost ascertainment system. Although the House committee broadly accepted the Post Office's approach to cost allocation, the Senate committee was skeptical of both the technicalities of the cost ascertainment methodology and the premise that rates should be based on costs.

In 1953, the Senate established an Advisory Council of prominent citizens to advise on postal policy. This was the first of several citizens' committees that have periodically helped to reshape national policy over the last four decades. The leader of the Advisory Council was Walter D. Fuller, chairman of Curtis Publishing Co., a major magazine publisher (*The Saturday Evening Post*, *Ladies' Home Journal* and so on). A majority of the other nine members were also second and third class mailers.

In January 1954, the Advisory Council issued a 364-page report. The lead recommendation was a call for adoption of a national postal policy. The report begins:

> Any proposed solution to the many problems besetting the Post Office Department must reflect some assumption as to just what Congress expects the post office to be and do. Is the post office entirely a service designed to handle mail with the greatest possible convenience to the general public regardless of cost? Or is it entirely a business whose value is to be measured by the net revenue it returns each year to the United States Treasury?

The Advisory Council answered its own question by proposing a statement of national postal policy that began, '*the Post Office Department is fundamentally a public service to the people of the United States and should be so considered*'.[3]

The Advisory Council resolved the problem of how to apportion needed rate increases by urging recognition of the – historically questionable – principle that 'the Post Office Department was established and is designed primarily for the handling of first-class mail'. Hence, the Advisory Council urged, first class rates should cover all fixed costs. Rates for other classes of mail should reflect incremental costs, except rates for certain mail categories should be discounted to stimulate their contribution to the general welfare, for example, low rates for periodicals, newspapers, books, and mail for the blind. Public funds should be used to compensate the Post Office for several types of costs such as preferential rates, subsidies for airlines, international mail services, and 'any expenditures which can be justified only on a national welfare basis' such as the costs of small post offices, rural delivery services, and 'star route' services to rural areas. The Advisory Council recommended that all postage rates should be set by Congress, divesting the Interstate Commerce Commission of authority over parcel post rates.

Meanwhile, President Dwight Eisenhower, who took office in January 1953, echoed President Truman's call for postage rates that covered costs. For five years, Congress was unable to agree on rate increases despite passing several wage bills. In general, the Senate favored the approach of its Advisory Council while the House supported an approach that distributed higher rates over several classes of mail. The result was a compromise, the postal act of 1958. In broad terms, the House got a moderate increase in the first class stamp, raised to 4¢, and the Senate got the first ever statement of national postal policy.

The postal policy title, separately named the 'Postal Policy Act of 1958', is the ultimate source for much of what is considered by many to express a USO. Stated in current terminology, the basic decisions of the 1958 act were as follows. First, postal costs deemed to be public service costs were to be paid from public funds. Second, postage rates should be set so that total postal revenues – including compensation for public service costs – would be 'approximately equal to' total postal costs. Third, first class rates were to pay a more-than-proportional share of institutional costs but not all of them. Fourth, relationships between rates for different classes of mail should reflect eight statutory factors. The 1958 act left unresolved whether rates for each category of mail should cover attributable costs, a principle strongly opposed by magazine publishers.

The Postal Policy Act of 1958 did not address all facets of postal service, only rates. It did not, for example, specify criteria for the geographic scope of postal services, access to postal services, mode or frequency of delivery, or quality of service. Nor did the act impose obligations on the Post Office. Since Congress set postage rates, the Postal Policy Act of 1958 was addressed to future Congresses, not the Post Office. That Congress would relinquish authority over postage rates in only a dozen years was wholly unforeseen. Postal policy debates of the 1950s did, however, explore in detail the scope and financing of 'public services' provided by the Post Office. The major public service was thought to be rural postal service, although the net cost of such services was unclear given the state of postal accounting. There was widespread agreement that once properly calculated, public service costs should be charged to taxpayers, not mailers. There was virtually no mention of the postal monopoly as a means of financing public service costs.

The postal act of 1958 did not eliminate the shortfall in postal finances. Although rate increases raised annual revenues by $550 million, increases in postal salaries consumed almost all of this. Moreover, some public service subsidies authorized by the 1958 act were unclaimed by the Post Office due to inadequate accounting.

In 1962, Congress not only raised postage rates but also modified the Postal Policy Act of 1958. The first class stamp price was increased to 5¢ and other rates raised, although increased revenues were again largely offset by increased wages. More significantly for postal policy, Congress revised the terms of the 1958 act to make clear that the Post Office was to calculate losses on public services by subtracting revenues earned from the fully allocated costs, not from the (far lower) revenues that would have been earned from similar postal services. Congress also explicitly added rural service to the list of public services. The bottom line was that 10 percent of the cost of the star route system and third class post offices and 20 percent of the cost of fourth class post offices and rural routes were now considered public service costs. Public service payments jumped from $63 million 1962 to $413 million 1963. Even so, the 1962 amendments failed to stop the red ink at the Post Office. Between 1962 and 1967, the Post Office ran up deficits in the range of $200 to $500 million despite public financing equal to about 11 percent of revenue.

7 POSTAL REORGANIZATION ACT, 1970

On April 5, 1967, President Lyndon Johnson asked Congress for higher postage rates. At the same time, he established the President's Commission on Postal Organization, a committee of 10 prominent citizens. The new commission was heavily laden with representatives from big business and led by Frederick Kappel, former chairman of AT&T. Its mission was to examine the need to transform the Post Office Department into 'a Government corporation, or such other form of organization as the Commission may consider desirable'. In short, the job of the Commission was to find a way to end congressional management of the Post Office.

In June 1968, the 'Kappel Commission', as it became known, recommended transformation of the Post Office into an independent, 'business-like' postal service, essentially a government-owned corporation. President Richard Nixon, who took office in January 1969, strongly supported the idea. Postal committee members in Congress, however, were highly skeptical. Postal workers were adamantly opposed. They threatened a national strike if the Nixon proposal was enacted. In the end, the postal unions were placated only by substantial pay increases and role in revising the legislation.

After an intense political free-for-all, the Postal Reorganization Act was signed by President Nixon on August 12, 1970. The Post Office Department was not transformed into a corporation as proposed by the Kappel Commission but replaced by an independent federal agency, the United States Postal Service, which was supposed to operate in a more business-like manner. A second independent federal agency, the Postal Rate Commission, was established to regulate certain features of the national postal service, primarily the allocation of costs and relationships between rates.

As part of the compromises embodied in the 1970 act, the new business-like USPS was subject to several distinctly non-business-like policy objectives and obligations. Many were taken directly from the Postal Policy Act of 1958. These became the postal policy set out in section 101 of the act and the guidelines for establishing rates and classifications found in sections 3622 and 3623. In addition, the 1970 act added policy prescriptions for which there were no clear antecedents in US postal statutes. These included statutory instructions to: (i) avoid undue or unreasonable discrimination among users; (ii) receive, transmit, and deliver mail throughout the nation; (iii) refrain from closure of small post offices solely for operating at a deficit; (iv) provide a uniform rate for letters; (v) maintain a class for letters sealed against inspection; and (vi) ensure that the rate for each class or type of mail covers its attributable costs. Echoing the 1916 postal appropriations act, the 1970 act enjoined USPS to 'serve as nearly as practicable the entire population of the United States', although the change from 'entire *rural* population' to 'entire population' eliminated the original reference to the RFD program (emphasis added).

While the Postal Reorganization Act transformed the ratemaking principles of the 1958 act into general service obligations, it failed to emulate the earlier act in providing a mechanism for compensating USPS for provision of non-commercial services. Congress rejected a permanent subsidy to pay for public services (except for a continuing annual subsidy of $460 million). Nor did Congress embrace the logical conclusion that, as public service financing was withdrawn, USPS should reduce services correspondingly. Congress simply avoided striking a balance between public services and public financing.

In the years following the debut of the USPS, results were disappointing, if not alarming. Rates and wages rose faster than inflation. The postal deficit, far from being fixed, expanded. The Senate postal committee concluded gloomily, 'If it were truly a business, the United States Postal Service would be bankrupt'. These difficulties prompted an extended congressional review of postal policy. A new commission of prominent citizens was formed, the Commission on Postal Service, but its 1977 report failed to win broad support. In the end, Congress could not agree on whether the solution was to go backwards (by subjecting USPS to more political control) or forwards (by repealing the postal monopoly and making USPS more of a business). Policy debates in the mid-1970s highlighted the ambiguities in USPS's legislative mandate, but net changes were minor.

The 1970 act divided public funding of USPS into two parts, a 'public service' subsidy and a 'revenue forgone' subsidy. In principle, the public service subsidy represented compensation for public services other than reduced rates for preferred classes of mail. The 1970 act reduced the public service subsidy in stages to a continuing annual payment of $460 million after 1984. The revenue forgone subsidy was open-ended. It compensated

USPS for the difference between reduced rates required by Congress for certain mail classes and the rates USPS would have charged otherwise.

Beginning in the 1980s, Congress retreated from both promised sources of funding. First, due to government-wide deficits arising from a recession, Congress reduced the public service subsidy more rapidly than provided in the 1970 act. The last public service subsidy was paid in 1982 (after 1984, USPS has declined the permanent annual public service appropriation of $460 million). At the same time, Congress was concerned that reduced public funding might lead USPS to reduce the level or frequency of postal services. Although the Postmaster General assured congressional committees that no such reductions were intended, Congress added provisions to postal funding acts that obliged USPS to refrain from closing small post offices and declaring that 'six day delivery and rural delivery of mail shall continue at the 1983 level'. These provisos have been included in annual appropriations acts ever since, although the precise meaning of these requirements is very unclear (for example, no one seems to know what levels of service were provided in 1983). Today (in 2009), as USPS is facing both the rise of the Internet and an even more serious economic recession, this ill-considered *ad hoc* provision from three decades earlier restricts the ability of USPS to adjust delivery schedules to reflect diminished postal revenues.[4]

Similarly, in 1986 Congress substantially reduced the revenue forgone funding by adopting a new basis for calculation. In 1993, Congress ended virtually all payments for revenue forgone. Nonetheless, Congress maintained statutory provisions requiring USPS to offer reduced rates for preferred classes of mail. In effect, Congress required USPS to collect the cost of these preferred rates from other mailers.

While Congress thus reasserted control over certain rates and practices of USPS, the 1970 act left individuals with almost no power to require USPS to meet statutory service standards. In judicial and regulatory proceedings since 1970, USPS has not been obliged by law, to any significant degree, to extend services to unserved areas, to locate a post office or collection box in a particular place, to provide delivery in a specific manner, to change the quality of a given service, or to redress a user for lapses in service. Since 1970, USPS has substantially reduced the quality of its delivery service by requiring addresses to collect their mail from curbside mailboxes or neighborhood 'cluster boxes'. Even the legal obligation to maintain rates for letters that are 'uniform throughout the United States', added in 1970, was interpreted by the Postal Rate Commission to permit geographically zoned rates.

8 POSTAL ACCOUNTABILITY AND ENHANCEMENT ACT, 2006

The Postal Accountability and Enhancement Act of 2006 (PAEA) was the first major revision of the nation's postal laws since 1970. It was 11 years in the making. The House of Representatives began work on a postal reform bill in early 1995.

During public debates over the course of this postal bill, the terms 'universal service' and 'universal service obligation' first became established in the vocabulary of postal policy. Although policy makers in other industrialized countries commonly referred to the USO, in the United States prior to 1995, there were almost no references to a USO or 'universal service' in discussions of national postal policy. USPS introduced this terminology as Congress began to consider postal reform. In its 1996 annual report, USPS referred to 'universal service' eight times. For the first USPS referred to universal service as a legal obligation or 'mandate': 'Universal service: USPS's mandate and commitment to the nation to provide mail delivery service at uniform and reasonable rates to everyone, everywhere, six days a week'. Since 1996, each annual report has liberally referred to 'universal service' and USPS's 'mandate' to provide universal service.

Terms such as 'universal service' and 'USO' are now used by all participants in postal policy discussions, including members of Congress, government agencies, postal employees, mailers and scholars. The concept of a USO has become embedded in minds of policy makers even though it is entirely missing from historical practice or the statute books ('universal service' does not appear at all in Title 39 of the United States). The PAEA left unchanged key provisions relating to the scope of national postal service, including the policy objectives from the 1970 act and the specific requirements included in annual appropriations bills. The only provisions of the PAEA that mention universal service are calls for studies by the Postal Regulatory Commission and the General Accountability Office.

9 CONCLUSIONS

What, then, is to be made of the long history of postal laws and short history of the term 'USO'?

There is no doubt that USPS, and its predecessor, the Post Office Department, were established by Congress to provide postal services to the nation. In a general sense, USPS is 'obliged' to provide a national postal service for that is its purpose. In a more specific sense, however, USPS, like the Post Office before it, has been afforded broad discretion in interpretation and implementation of general statutory objectives. For almost all of the last two and a quarter centuries, while Congress has determined the major parameters of postal policy, it has been the Postmaster General who has determined the geographic scope and specific nature of the national postal service. There have been two important exceptions to this pattern, one traditional and one extraordinary.

The traditional exception is postage rates. From the beginning of the Republic, Congress controlled every element of postage rates. In 1970, Congress delegated much of the ratemaking function to the Postal Rate Commission but retained control over rates for preferred types of mail including newspapers and magazines, the mail of non-profit institutions, and government documents. In the PAEA of 2006, Congress allowed USPS more freedom to make minor adjustments in specific rates while constraining the overall rate structure with a framework of statutory price caps. Since 1993, Congress has declined to compensate USPS for revenue lost in maintaining discounted postage rates for certain preferred mailers.

The second, less traditional exception to the general rule that the Postmaster General has been allowed to determine the specific scope and details of the national postal service is the appropriations provision that has, since the early 1980s, required USPS to maintain postal services at 1983 levels and refrain from closing small post offices. This appropriations rider does not reflect longstanding postal policy in the United States or well-considered congressional consideration. It was an *ad hoc* political reaction to an economic downturn. The appropriations 'rider' was, and remains, inconsistent with Congress's customary restraint in defining the outer limits of the national postal system in a country as vast and varied as the United States. Nonetheless the rider remains on the books and significantly hinders the flexibility of USPS to adjust to a rapidly changing postal market.

In sum, the United States has adopted broadly stated policy objectives coupled with a traditional obligation to provide discounted rates for preferred classes of mail and a less traditional requirement to maintain services at 1983 levels (together with several other lesser or less legally compelling requirements not detailed in this overview).[5] This does not add up to a 'USO' is the sense that that term is used in modern postal reform laws. US postal law does not include a social contract which defines what basic postal services all citizens may count on and clarifies the rights and obligations of those – today, the USPS – that must actually provide the services. Universal postal service is defined not by a formal obligation but by the political winds blowing through the halls of Congress on any given day.

There are, however, many examples of how to define a USO in manner that is fairer and more predictable to all concerned.[6] The most obvious is to copy the example of the Telecommunications Act of 1996. This act authorized the Federal Communications Commission (FCC) to define, and revise periodically, a regulatory definition of universal service in the light of statutory policy guidelines and changing public needs. The FCC also has the authority to ensure that the minimum level is provided, if necessary by ordering service providers to do so (and compensating them for their efforts). In the postal world, the German Post Law of 1997 adopts a similar approach. The United States has a long tradition of national postal service and a less extensive history of broadly stated postal policies. It may be time to follow the lead of other sectors and other countries and convert these ingredients into a formal 'universal service obligation'.

NOTES

1. To conserve space, legal citations and other specific references for this chapter have been kept to a minimum. Sources and additional information may be found in the references listed in the bibliography, in particular in Campbell (2008).
2. 53 Cong. Rec. 9630-31 (1916).
3. Advisory Council, *Advisory Council Report* 7 (emphasis added).
4. See, for example, Dan Eggen, 'Postal Service May Cut Deliveries; Mail Could Arrive Only 5 Days a Week', *Washington Post*, p. A2 (January 29, 2009).
5. The most important of these relates to uniformity of rates. Some would argue that USPS is legally obliged to charges rates that either (i) do not vary with distance or (ii) do not vary with destination (same charge for delivery in Montana as in New York). With the exception of a provision requiring nationally uniform rates for books and films, 39 U.S.C. §3683 (2006), it is difficult to find firm statutory support for either position. More involved legal arguments are possible, but addressing them is beyond the scope of this short history.
6. Options are summarized in the Postal Regulatory Commission (2008, pp. 178–81 and App. H, pp. 10–31).

BIBLIOGRAPHY

Advisory Council (1954), *Advisory Council Report*. Reprint, *Postal Rates and Postal Policy of the Post Office Department: Report of the Committee on Post Office and Civil Service Pursuant to S.*

Res. 49, S. Rep. No. 1086, 83d Cong., 2d Sess, Washington, DC: GPO. The Senate report is the report of the Advisory Council with a cover letter by the chairman of the committee.
Campbell, James I., Jr. (2008), 'Universal Service Obligation: History and Development of Laws Relating to the Provision of Universal Postal Services', Appendix B in Postal Regulatory Commission, 'Report on Universal Postal Service and the Postal Monopoly', December, available at: http://www.prc.gov.
Henkin, David M. (2006), *The Postal Age: The Emergence of Modern Communications in Nineteenth-Century America*, Chicago, IL: University of Chicago Press.
John, Richard R. (1995), *Spreading the News: The American Postal System from Franklin to Morse*, Cambridge, MA: Harvard University Press.
John, Richard R. (2008), 'History of Universal Service and the Postal Monopoly', Appendix D in Postal Regulatory Commission, 'Report on Universal Postal Service and the Postal Monopoly', December, available at: http://www.prc.gov.
Kielbowicz, Richard B. (1995), 'A History of Mail Classification and Its Underlying Policies and Purposes', July 17, Prepared for the Postal Rate Commission, Docket No. MC95-1, available from http://www.prc.gov.
Kielbowicz, Richard B. (2002), 'Universal Postal Service: A Policy History, 1790–1970', November 15, Prepared for the Postal Rate Commission, available from http://www.prc.gov.
Kielbowicz, Richard B. (2004), 'A Policy History of Selected Preferred Mail Categories', April 20, 1986 Prepared for the Postal Rate Commission, Docket No. C2004-1, available from http://www.prc.gov.
US Congress, House of Representatives, H.R. Rep. No. 66, 109th Cong., 1st Sess. (April 28, 2005, Part I).
US Congress, Senate, S. Rep. No. 381, 108th Cong., 2d Sess. (August 25, 2004).
US Postal Regulatory Commission (2008), 'Report on Universal Postal Service and the Postal Monopoly', December, available at: http://www.prc.gov.
US President's Commission on Postal Organization ('Kappel Commission') (1968), *Towards Postal Excellence*, Washington, DC: GPO. Reprinted as *Report of the U.S. President's Commission on Postal Organization – Entitled 'Towards Postal Excellence'*, House Comm. on Post Office and Civil Service, 94th Cong., 2d Sess. (Comm. Print 94-25, 1976), available from http://www.prc.gov.
US President's Commission on the United States Postal Service (2003), *Embracing the Future: Making Tough Choices to Preserve Universal Mail Service*, Washington, DC: GPO, available from http://www.treas.gov/offices/domestic-finance/usps/index.html.